INDEX TO PLAYS

1800-1926

AMS PRESS

NEW YORK

INDEX TO PLAYS

1800 - 1926

COMPILED BY

INA TEN EYCK FIRKINS

Reference Librarian, University of Minnesota

NEW YORK

THE H. W. WILSON COMPANY

1927

The Library of Congress cataloged this title as follows:

Firkins, Ina Ten Eyck, 1866-1937, comp.
    Index to plays, 1800–1926. New York, H. W.
  Wilson Co., 1927. [New York, AMS Press, 1971]
    307 p. 27 cm.
    ISBN 0-404-2386X
    1. Drama—19th century—Bibliography.   2.
  Drama—20th century—Bibliography.   I. Title.
  Z5781 .F57   1971   75–144606
                   016.80882

Reprinted from the edition of 1927, New York.
First AMS edition published in 1971.
Second AMS printing: 1979

Manufactured in the United States of America

AMS PRESS, INC.
NEW YORK, N.Y.

PREFACE

A need similar to that which prompted the preparation of *The Index to Short Stories* was the reason for the compilation of this bibliography. An unabating if not an increasing interest in the printed play has brought to libraries a daily call to locate the place of publication of individual plays. These are found in various places; many are published separately; many are to be found in collected works only or in volumes bearing titles other than those of the dramas desired at the moment; often they are to be found in the ever-growing lists of collections of plays; and the periodicals add their quota to the available editions. In colleges and schools the call usually is for class work; in public libraries it may be from groups of club members or from those interested in amateur theatricals. These clients desire as many copies as possible of a given play. To save the reference assistant from a repeated search through collections and magazine indexes, these references have been collected and arranged in as convenient a manner as the compiler has been able to devise.

The compiler makes no claim for completeness in her work; no one will realize more acutely than does she that there are many omissions in the index. All that has been attempted has been to supply a guide to available editions of plays by nineteenth and twentieth century authors whose work entitles them to recognition. The selection has been based on what it is believed may be the general demand, not upon the intrinsic worth of the plays themselves. People wish to see or to read plays for many reasons other than their literary or technical value; it may be because of successful production; it may be because of the subject presented; it may be because of interest in the work of a given author. The index has therefore been compiled with little idea of critical discrimination; it is an attempt merely to help readers to find what they desire. Even in this humble ambition the editor has perforce been limited to the indexing of collections readily accessible and of works listed in standard catalogs and trade-lists. There are listed in the volume 7,872 plays by 2,203 authors. Had the compiler endeavored to run down every play of an author, the work involved would have necessitated an indefinite delay in publication. She therefore asks that the work be accepted as an immediate aid to reference librarians and that it be judged not too severely on the score of incompleteness. The work has been done through the examination of collections and bibliographies in New York City, in Washington, D.C., and in the University of Minnesota.

The arrangement is in two parts, an Author Index, and a Title and Subject Index. The order of the entry in the Author Index is as follows:

Separate publication of play.
Collected works of author.
Composite collections.
Periodicals.

When a separate edition of a given play has been issued, the full bibliographical information has been given—title, publisher, place and date of publication. After this, or after the title of the play if it has appeared in collected editions or magazines only, is given, first, a word or two of description—comedy, tragedy, social, domestic—enough to suggest the character of the play and then the number of acts. Occasionally when it has been impossible to obtain a copy of a play for examination this information will be found incomplete.

In the Title and Subject Index has been given the title of the play, followed by the author's name. To locate the place of publication it is necessary to refer back to the Author Index. Subject entries are given in bold-faced type; there follows an indented list of plays upon the given subject. The subject list is not complete; it is intended merely to suggest a few titles to those seeking plays for special occasions or upon special subjects.

In Appendix A only those works of an author which contain more than one play have been entered. The separate editions of the single plays, as noted above, have been entered with full bibliographical information in the *Author Index*. Appendix B contains the composite collections indexed.

The decision to include nineteenth and twentieth century plays only was based on two reasons; first, that for the earlier important dramatists, there are many convenient collected editions in which the individual plays are readily located; the Stage Cyclopedia is a guide also to the authorship of minor plays; the second reason was that the obscurer plays are found largely in the numerous collections, and another compiler has had in progress for some years, a bibliography which will index these collections.

Perhaps the propriety of including such names as those of Friedrich Schiller, August F. von Kotzebue, or Richard Sheridan may be questioned since their dates barely turn the corner of the nineteenth century. The reason is that the plays of these authors are often called for and it is believed that their inclusion will be a convenience to reference departments.

It is a pleasure to express my appreciation of the many courtesies extended to me in the Library of Congress, the New York Public Library and Columbia University. I desire also to acknowledge my obligation to Miss Doris Reed whose careful work in verifying references for me has made the publication of my bibliography possible at this time.

INA TEN EYCK FIRKINS.

August 1, 1927.

List of Periodicals Referred to in This Index

CONTENTS

INDEX TO PLAYS
1800 - 1926

———•———

AUTHOR INDEX

Abbott, Avery
Mr. Enright entertains; a possibility in one act. Chicago. Dramatic pub. co. [1924]. 12°. 18p. Crime
Same in Poet Lore 34:127

Abbott, George, and Gleason, James
Fall guy. Comedy. 3 acts
In Mantle, B. ed. Best plays of 1924- 25 (condensed)

Abbott, George, and Weaver, John V. A.
Love 'em and leave 'em; a comedy in three acts. . . N.Y. French. c1926. 12°. 117p.

Abbott, George, joint author. *See* Dunning Philip and Abbott, George.

Abbott, George, joint author. *See* Smith, Winchell and Abbott, George.

Aber, Loureine, A.
Beggar maid. Legendary. 1 act
In Colonnade 12:79
Shadows. Poetic. 1 act
In Colonnade 13:54

Abercrombie, Lascelles, 1881-
Adder. Poetic. 1 act
In Four short plays
Poetry and drama 1:100
Deborah; a play in three acts. N.Y. Lane. 1913. 12°. 60p. Tragedy.
Deserter. Comedy. 1 act
In Four short plays
Theatre Arts M 6:237
End of the world. Poetic. 2 acts
In Four short plays
New numbers 1:61
Phoenix, tragi-comedy in three acts. London. Secker. 1923. 12°. 94p.
Staircase. Poetic. 1 act
In Four short plays
New numbers 1:170

Ackerley, Joe Randolph, 1896-
Prisoners of war; a play in three acts. London. Chatto. 1925. 108p.

Acosta, Mercedes de
Sandro Botticelli. Moffat, Yard. 1923. 12°. 49p. Tragedy. 3 acts

Adams, Arthur Henry, 1872-
Galahad Jones
In Three plays for the Australian stage
Mrs. Pretty and the Premier
In Three plays for the Australian stage
Wasters
In Three plays for the Australian stage

Adams, Oscar Fay, 1855-1919
Merchant of Venice, Act 6. Sequel. 3 scenes
In Motley jest
Cornhill booklet 3:57
Shakespearean fantasy. Parody. 8 scenes
In Motley jest

Ade, George, 1866-
College widow; a pictorial comedy in four acts. N.Y. French. c1924. 12°. 112p.
County chairman; a comedy drama. N.Y. French. c1924. 12°. 118p. 4 acts
Father and the boys; a comedy drama. N.Y. French. c1924. 12°. 120p. 4 acts
Just out of college; a light comedy in three acts. N.Y. French. c1924. 12°. 120p.
Marse Covington; a play in one act. . . Washington Commission on training camp activities. Dept. of dramatic activities among soldiers. 1918. 12°. 14p. (War Department service edition. no. 13)
Same. French. N.Y. c1923. 12°. 16p. Comedy
Mayor and the manicure, play in one act. N.Y. French. c1923. 12°. 25p. Comedy
Same in One act plays for stage and study ser 1
Nettie; a play in one act. N.Y. French. c1923. 12°. 25p. Comedy
Speaking to father; a play in one act. N.Y. French. c1923. 12°. 27p. Comedy
Sultan of Sulu; an original satire in two acts. N.Y. R. H. Russell. 1903. 12°. 127p.

Aidé, Hamilton, 1830-1906
Gleam in the darkness. Crime. 1 act
In Fortn 72:905

Aiken, Mrs. Ednah (Robinson), 1872-
Hate breeders; a drama of war and peace in one act. . . Indianapolis. Bobbs-Merrill. [1916]. 12°. 16p. Tragedy

Aiken, George L.
Uncle Tom's cabin. Slavery. 5 acts
In Moses, M. J., ed. Representative plays by American dramatists from 1765 to the present day v 2

Aitken, I. E. M.
Desperate remedy. Duologue. 1 act
In Domestic experiments and other plays

Aitken, I. E. M.—*Continued*
Other fellow. Duologue. 1 act
In Domestic experiments and other plays
Red carnations. Interlude. 1 act
In Domestic experiments and other plays
Akerman, William
Cross of sorrow. A tragedy in five acts. N.Y. Bell. 1894. 12°. 102p.
Akins, Zoe, 1886-
Daddy's gone-a-hunting. Tragedy. 3 acts
In Déclassée, etc
Déclassée. Tragedy. 3 acts
In Déclassée, etc
Greatness. Comedy. 3 acts
In Déclassée, etc
Magical city. New York. 1 act
In Forum 55:507
Papa; an amorality in three acts. N.Y. Kennerley. 1913. 12°. 95p. Comedy
Portrait of Tiero. Tragedy. 1 act
In Theatre Arts M 4:316
Such a charming young man; a comedy in one act
In One act plays for stage and study ser 1
Smart Set 48:67
Alarcon, Mariano
Sons of Adam. Tragedy of peasant life. 1 act
In Stratford J 4:75
Alcott, Louisa May, 1832-1888
Little men play. Juvenile.
In Ladies' H J 18:3 D '00
Little women play. (Arranged by. E. L. Gould). Juvenile
In Ladies' H J 18:3, 36, Ja '01
Aldis, Mrs. Mary (Reynolds) 1872-
Drama class of Tankaha, Nevada. Comedy. 1 act
In Plays for small stages
Extreme unction. Death. 1 act
In Plays for small stages
An heir at large; a play in seven scenes, from the cartoon story of John T. McCutcheon. Chicago. 12°. 115p.
Letter. Tragedy. 1 act
In Plays for small stages
Mrs. Pat and the law. Comedy. 1 act
In Plays for small stages
Mayorga, M. G. ed. Representative one-act plays
Temperament; a musical tragedy in two scenes
In Plays for small stages
Ten p.m. Problem. 1 act
In Drama 11:187
Aldrich, Thomas Bailey, 1836-1907
Judith of Bethulia, a tragedy; Boston. Houghton. 1904. 12°. 98p. 3 acts
Mercedes. Boston. Houghton. 1884. 8°. 56p. Tragedy. 2 acts
Pauline Pavlovna. A drama in one act. [In verse] Boston. Houghton. [c1890]. 12°. 11p.
Alencar, Jose de, 1829-1877
Jesuit. Brazil. 4 acts
In Poet Lore 30:475

Alexander, H. B.
Carved woman
In Cohen, H. L. ed. More one-act plays by modern authors
Alin, Hans
Poverty. The poor. 1 act
In Shay, Frank. Twenty-five short plays, international
Allan, Helen Beatrice
Place of meeting; a mystery play of to-day. N.Y. Macmillan. 1920. 16°. 64p. $1 Religious. 3 acts
Allen, Ethan, 1832-
Washington; or, The revolution; a drama founded upon the historic events of the war for American independence. Chicago. Neely. 1895. 12°. 2v. 2 pts 5 acts ea.
Allen, Carleton Kemp
Judgment of Paris; a comedy. London. Lane. [1924]. 305p.
Allotte de la Fuÿe, (Marguerite (Pichelin)
Lord of death (le maître de la mort); a play in a prologue and three acts. . . N.Y. Longmans. 1923. 12°. 95p. Jesus Christ
Alma-Tadema, Lawrence
Merciful soul. 1 act
In Anglo-Saxon R 3:107
Altair, pseud.
Chaos; a vision of eternity. . . N.Y. Mc-Murtrie. 1919. 12°. 55p. $1 The universe. 5 acts
Alvarez de Quintero, Seráfin, 1871- and Joaquin, 1873-
Bright morning (Mañana de sol) (Sunny morning). Comedy. 1 act
In Shay, F. and Loving, P. eds. Fifty contemporary one act plays
Poet Lore 27:669
Stratford J 1 no 1:39
By their words ye shall know them (Hablando se entiende la gente); comedy. 1 act
In Drama 7:26
Fountain of youth (La flor de la vida) a poetic drama in three acts; tr. by Samuel N. Baker. Cincinnati. Stewart Kidd. [c1922]. 12°. 71p.
Malvaloca, a drama in three acts. . . Tr. from the Spanish by Jacob S. Fassett, jr. . . Garden City, N.Y. Doubleday. 1916. 12°. 151p. 75c Andalusian life
Papá Juan; or, The centenarian. Comedy. 3 acts
In Poet Lore 29:253
Sunny morning. *See* Alvarez de Quintero, S. and J. Bright morning
Women's town. Comedy. 2 acts
In Turrell, C. A. tr. Contemporary Spanish dramatists
Amalie of Saxony, Princess, 1794-1870
Captain Firnewald. Romantic. 4 acts
In Six dramas
Country cousin (Der landwirth). Romantic. 4 acts
In Social life in Germany v 2
Falsehood and truth (Lüge und Wahrheit). Romantic. 4 acts
In Social life in Germany v 1

Heir of Scharfeneck (Majorats erbe);
romantic. 4 acts
In Six dramas
Princely bride (Die fürstenbraut). Court
life. 5 acts
In Social life in Germany v 2
Son's return. Romantic. 4 acts
In Six dramas
Uncle (Der oheim). Comedy. 5 acts
In Social life in Germany v 1
Uninformed girl (Die unbelesene).
Melodrama. 4 acts
In Six dramas
Young lady from the country (Das fräu-
lein vom lande). Germany. 5 acts
In Six dramas
Young ward (Der zögling). Comedy.
4 acts
In Social life in Germany v 2

Ambient, Mark
Snug little kingdom; a comedy of Bohemia in three acts. N.Y. French.
c1906. 12°. 71p.

Amend, J. G.
Pandora's box. Mythological. 1 act
In Loving, P. ed. Ten minute plays

Amherst, J. H., 1776-1851
Battle of Waterloo; a grand military
melo-drama in three acts. London.
Duncombe. [18—]. 36p.
Conflagration of Moscow. *See* Napoleon
Buonaparte's invasion of Russia or,
The conflagration of Moscow
Die Freischutz; or, The seven charmed
bullets; a melodrama in two acts.
London. [c1824?]. 18p.
Napoleon Buonaparte's invasion of Rus-
sia; or, The conflagration of Moscow.
A military and equestrian spectacle.
In three acts. London. Lacy. n.d. 32p.
(Lacy's acting edition of plays. v. 13
no. 194)
Ireland as it is; a melodrama. N.Y.
French. 185—. 3 acts
Seven charmed bullets. *See* Amherst, J.
N. Die Freischutz; or, The seven
charmed bullets
Will Watch; or, The black phantom! a
melodrama in two acts. . . London.
Duncombe. [18—]. 12°. 28p.

Ancey, George
Dupe. Comedy. 5 acts
In Clark, B. H. trans. Four plays of
the Free theatre
M. Lamblin; a comedy. 1 act
In Shay, F. and Loving, P. eds. Fifty
contemporary one act plays
Stratford J 1:34

**Anderson, Maxwell, 1888-, and Stallings,
Lawrence, 1894-**
Buccaneer. Comedy. 3 acts
In Three American plays
First flight. Andrew Jackson. 3 acts
In Three American plays
What price glory? World war. 3 acts
In Three American plays
Mantle, B., ed. Best plays of 1924-
25 (abridged)

Andreef, Leonid. *See* Andreev, Leonid N.
Andreev, Leonid Nikolaevich, 1871-1919
Anathema, a tragedy in seven scenes;
authorized translation by Herman
Bernstein. N.Y. Macmillan. 1910.
12°. 211p.
Black maskers. Symbolic. 2 acts
In Plays
He who gets slapped; a play in four acts;
tr. . . by Gregory Zilborg. N.Y.
Brentano's. [c1922]. 12°. 193p. Satire.
4 acts
Same in Mantle, B. ed. Best plays of
1921-22 (condensed)
Dial 70:247
Incident. Remorse. 1 act
In Moses, M. J. ed. Representative
one act plays of continental au-
thors
Poet Lore 27:171
Katerina (Yekaterina Ivanovna) a drama
in four acts. . . N.Y. Brentano's.
[c1923]. 12°. 181p. Comedy
King Hunger. Symbolic. 5 scenes
In Poet Lore 22:401
Life of man; a play in five acts. Tr. . .
by C. J. Hogarth. N.Y. Macmillan.
c1915. 12°. 141p. Symbolic
Same in Plays
Savva; The life of man
Moses, M. J. ed. Representa-
tive continental dramas
Love of one's neighbor, a comedy in one
act; tr. by Thomas Seltzer. N.Y.
Boni. 1914. 40p. 12°. [2nd. ed. Shay.
1917].
Same in Shay, F. and Loving, P. eds.
Fifty contemporary one-act
plays
Golden Bk 4:181
Sabine women (Pretty Sabine women).
Symbolic. 3 acts
In Plays
Drama 4 no 13:34
Samson in chains. . . N.Y. Brentano's.
1923. 12°. 207p. Biblical 5 acts
Savva. Revolutionary Russia. 4 acts
In Savva; The life of man
Sorrows of Belgium; a play in six
scenes . . . authorized translation by
Herman Bernstein. N.Y. Macmil-
lan. 1915. 132p. 12°. World war.
Steed in the senate. Satire. 1 act
In Liv Age 322:498
To the stars. Symbolic. 4 acts
In Poet Lore 18:417
Waltz of the dogs; a play in four acts. . .
N.Y. Macmillan. 1922. 12°. 141p.
Character

Andrews, Kenneth L.
America passes by. Comedy. 1 act
In Plays of the Harvard dramatic club
ser 1
Crooked man and his crooked wife. 1 act
In Plays with a punch

Andrews, Mary Raymond Shipman
Ditch. World war. 5 acts
In Scrib M 63:405

Andrews, M. R. S.—*Continued*
West Point regulation.   Comedy. 1 act
In McClure 23:385
Andrews, Matthew Page, 1879-
Birth of America; an historical drama in
three acts.   Baltimore.   Norman
Remington. 1920. 12°. 60p. $1.50
Annunzio, Gabriele d', 1864-
Daughter of Jorio (La figlia di Joria).
a pastoral tragedy. . . Boston. Little.
1907. 12°. 208p. 3 acts
Same in Moses, M. J. ed.   Representa-
tive continental dramas
Poet Lore 18:1
Dead city (La citta morta); a tragedy.
Chicago. Laird. [1902]. 12°. 282p. 5
acts
Same in Sayler, O. M. ed.   Eleanora
Duse series of plays
Dream of a spring morning (Sogno d'un
mattino di primavera).   Dementia. 5
scenes
In Poet Lore 14:6
Dream of an autumn sunset (Sogno d'un
tramonto d'autunno).   Tragedy. . 1
act
In Poet Lore 15:6
Francesca da Rimini. . . N.Y. Stokes.
[1902]. 12°. 223p.   Tragedy. 5 acts
Honeysuckle; a play in three acts. . .
London. Heinemann. 1915. 12°. 214p.
Tragedy
Giaconda (La Giaconda).   N.Y. Russell.
1902. 12°. 144p.   Tragedy. 4 acts
Same in Dickinson, T. H. ed.   Chief
contemporary   dramatists
ser 2
Pierce, J. A. and Matthews, J.
B.   eds.   Masterpieces   of
modern   drama   v   2
(abridged)
Anonymous
Ceremony of the printer's apprentice.
German morality. 1 act
In Bates, A. ed.   Drama v 4
Ansky, S., pseud.   *See* Rappoport, Solomon
Anspacher, Louis Kaufman, 1878-
Tristan & Isolde, a tragedy.   N.Y. Bren-
tano's. 1904. 8°. 123p. 5 acts
Unchastened woman, a modern comedy
in three acts.   N.Y. Stokes. [1916].
12°. 276p.
Same in Dickinson, T. H. ed.   Con-
temporary plays
Baker, G. P. ed.   Modern
American plays
Anzengruber, Ludwig, 1839-1889
Farmer forsworn; tragedy of parenthood.
3 acts
In German classics 16:112
Applegarth, Margaret Tyson, 1886-
Child in the midst. . . Missionary. 1 act
In More short missionary plays
Color blind; a missionary play in three
acts.   N.Y. Doran. [c1923]. 12°. 15p.
Same in Short missionary plays
Empty stockings.   Missionary. 1 act
In More short missionary plays

Fare, please; new Americans.   N.Y.
Doran. [c1924]. 12°. 11p. Missionary.
2 acts
Same in Short missionary plays
Galatea takes a lease on life.   Missionary.
1 scene
In More short missionary plays
Girl who fell through the earth; a Chinese
play.   N.Y. Doran. [c1923]. 12°. 17p.
Missionary. 2 scenes
Same in Short missionary plays
Gospel according to the telephone book.
Missionary. 1 scene
In Short missionary plays
Hands up.   Missionary. 1 scene
In Short missionary plays
Indelible; a shadow play.   Missionary.
10 scenes
In Short missionary plays
Jack the giant-killer; a play to secure
subscriptions for a missionary maga-
zine. 1 act
In More short missionary plays
Just suppose.   Missionary. 1 scene
In Short missionary plays
Katydid.   Missionary. 2 scenes
In More short missionary plays
Kimono.   Missionary. 5 scenes
In Short missionary plays
Latest Victor record.   Missionary. 1
scene
In Short missionary plays
Mrs. Jarley's wax-works, or things that
spoil a missionary meeting. 1 scene
In More short missionary plays
Pain street; a pageant of medical mis-
sions in five parts
In Short missionary plays
Seven keys to Mr. Bald Pate.   Mission-
ary. 1 scene
In Short missionary plays
Strictly   private;   or,   The   lady-who-
hoarded-Easter.   Missionary. 1 act
In More short missionary plays
Subscription clinic; a play to promote the
sale of missionary literature. 1 scene
In More short missionary plays
Summer Christmas tree pageant.   Mis-
sionary. 1 scene
In More short missionary plays
Wait a minute.   Missionary. 1 scene
In More short missionary plays
Yes but-ers.   Missionary. 1 act
In More short missionary plays
Applegate, Allita
Choice of Gianneta.   Florence. 1500. 1
act
In Poet Lore 36:405
Archer, William, 1856-1924
Green goddess.   N.Y. Knopf. 1921. 12°.
32°.   Melodrama. 4 acts
Same in Law, F. H. ed.   Modern
plays, short and long
Mantle, B. ed.   Best plays of
1920-21 (condensed)

Arlen, Michael, pseud. (Kuyumjian, Dikràn)
Ci-devant. Memories. 1 act
In Dial 69:125
Green hat. Sex. 4 acts .
In Mantle, B. ed. Best plays of 1925-26

Armfield, Mrs. Anne Constance
Curious herbal; telling of Mrs Elizabeth Blackwell's visit to the old Chelsea herb garden in 1732. London. Duckworth. 1922. 31p. 1 act
Fortunate shepherds; a Cotswold pastoral. London. Duckworth. 1925. 53p. 1 act
Gilded wreath. London. Duckworth. 1922. 12°. 31p. 1 act

Armfield, Maxwell
Grassblade; a Chinese fable. London. Duckworth. [1923]. 35p. 1 act
Lost silver. London. Duckworth. [1923]. 24p. 1 act
Minstrel. London. Duckworth. [1923]. 30p. 1 act

Armstrong, Alta Florence
Play of life, in seven acts. Boston. Gorham. 1917. 12°. 81p.

Armstrong, Paul, 1869-1915
Mr. Lorelei; a folk comedy. 1 act
In Smart Set 48:233

Armstrong Paul, 1869-1915, and Beach, Rex, 1877-
Going some; a play in four acts. . . N.Y. French. c1923. 12°. 127p. College.

Arnold, Sir Edwin, 1832-1904
Adzuma; or The Japanese wife; a play in four acts. N.Y. Scribner 1893. 12°. 170p. Tragedy. 4 acts
Griselda, a tragedy. . . London. Bogue. 1856. 12°. 308p.

Arnold, Matthew, 1822-1888
Empedocles on Etna. Philosophical. 1 act
In Poetical works
Merope. Oxford. Clarendon press. 1917. 12°. 175p. Tragedy. 1 act
Same in Poetical works

Arnold, Samuel James, 1774-1852
Devil's bridge. An opera, in three acts. . . London. Cumberland. [n.d.]. 12°. 52p. (In Cumberland's British Theatre. v. 42 no. 6)
Free and easy. A musical farce, in two acts. . . London. Cumberland. n.d. 12°. 50p. (In Cumberlands British theatre. v. 42 no. 3)
Man and wife; or, More secrets than one. A comedy, in five acts. . . Boston. Spencer. 1855. 12°. 75p.
My aunt: a petit comedy in two acts. . . Boston. Spencer. 1855. 12°. 29p.
Shipwreck: a comic opera, in two acts. . . N.Y. Longworth. 1805. 12°. 43p.
Same in Oxberry, W. ed. New English drama v 9 no 6

Arnstein, M.
Eternal song; a picture of labor life. 1 act
In Block, E. tr. One-act plays from the Yiddish

Artsybashev, Mikhael Petrovich, 1878-
Enemies. Marriage. 5 acts
In Jealousy, etc.
Jealousy. Marriage. 5 acts
In Jealousy, etc.
Savage. (Law of the savage). N.Y. Boni. c1924. 12°. 213p. Marriage. 5 acts
Same in Jealousy, etc.
War, a play in four acts. . . N.Y. Knopf. 1916. 12°. 73p. Survival of unfit
Same in Drama 8 no 21:12

Arundel, Lewis
Lorenzo de Medici. London. Bell. [1914]. 121p. Renaissance. 4 acts

Arundel, Mark
Don't tell Timothy; a frivolous comedy for serious acting, in three acts. London. Putnam. [1925]. 12°. 112p.

Asch, Sholom, 1880-
God of vengeance . . . authorized translation by Isaac Goldberg. . . Boston. 1918. 12°. 99p. Symbolic. 3 acts
Night. Low life. 1 act
In Shay, F. and Loving, P. eds. Fifty contemporary one-act plays
Sinner. Symbolic. 1 act
In Goldberg, I. ed. Six plays of the Yiddish theatre
Winter. Jewish life. 1 act
In Goldberg, I. ed. Six plays of the Yiddish theatre

Ash, Sholom. *See* Asch, Sholom

Ashton, Winifred. *See* Dane, Clemence, pseud.

Augier, Émile, 1820-1889
Adventuress (L'Aventurière). A comedy in four acts. N.Y. Rullman. 1888. 18°. 39p.
Equals; a comedy in three acts, freely adapted from . . . "Gendre de M. Poirier" by E. Rose. London. French. [18—?]. 12°. 34p.
False step, freely adapted from "Les lionnies pauvres" by Arthur Matthison. London. French. n.d. 12°. 48p. Comedy. 5 acts
Giboyer's son (Le fils de Giboyer). Comedy. 5 acts
In Universal anthology 27:111
Drama 1 no 4:27
Good for evil or, A wife's trial. (Adapted); a domestic lesson in two acts. London. Lacy. n.d. 12°. 24p. (Lacy's acting edition of plays. v. 43)
Green coat (L'habit vert). *See* Musset, A. de and Augier, E.
House of Fourchambault (Les Fourchambault); a comedy in 5 acts. . . N.Y. French. 1915. 12°. 89p.
Same in Four plays
Marriage of Olympe; (Olympe's marriage, Le marriage d'Olympe). Social. 3 acts
Same in Four plays
Drama 5 no 19:358

Augier, E.—*Continued*
Monsieur Poirier's son-in-law. (Le gendre de M. Poirier). Comedy. 4 acts
  Same in Four plays
          Bates, A. ed. Drama v 9
          Matthews, J. B. Chief European dramatists
          Pierce and Matthews. Masterpieces of modern drama v 2 (abridged)
Olympe's marriage. *See* Augier, E. Marriage of Olympe
Post-scriptum (Postscript); a comedy in one act. N.Y. French. 1915. 12°. 22p.
  Same in Four plays
Wife's trial. *See* Augier, E. Good for evil; or, A wife's trial
Austin, Mary (Hunter), 1868-
Arrow-maker. N.Y. Duffield. 1911. 12°. 128p. Social. 3 acts
Man who didn't believe in Christmas. Fairy. 1 act
  In St N 45:156
Azertis, Lorenzo de
Casanova, a play in three acts. . . N.Y. Brentano's. 1924. 12°. 84p. Comedy
Babcock, Mrs. Bernie, 1868-
Mammy, a drama in four acts. N.Y. Neale. 1915. 12°. 102p. Civil War
Babo, Joseph Marius, 1756-1822
Dagobert King of the Franks. Chivalry. 5 acts
  In Bates, A. ed. Drama 12:195
          Thompson, B. ed. German theatre v 4
Otto of Wittlesbach; or, The choleric court. Tragedy. 5 acts
  In Thompson, B. ed. German theatre. v 4
Bacon, Josephine Dodge Daskam, 1876-
First of October. Domestic comedy. 1 act
  In Harper 109:721
Twilight of the gods; a play in two scenes. N.Y. Kennerley. 1915. 12°. 43p. War
  Same in Forum 53:7
Wanderers. Destiny. 1 act
  In Cent o s 62:583
Bagg, Helen
Behind the lines; a war comedy in one act. Phila. Penn. co. 1908. 12°. 34p. World war
Looking for Mary Jane; a farce in three acts. Phila. Penn. co. 1915. 12°. 85p.
Bahr, Hermann, 1863-
Concert, (Das Konzert). Comedy. 3 acts
  In Dickinson, T. H. Chief contemporary dramatists ser 2
Master (Der Meister) adapted for the American stage by Benj. F. Glazer. Phila. Brown. 1918. 12°. 89p. Comedy. 3 acts
Mongrel; a play in one act.
  In Liv Age 324:70
Bailey, Helen Cheney
Demigod. Character. 1 act
  In Drama 8 no 32:505

Baillie, Joanna, 1762-1851
Alienated manor. Comedy. 5 acts
  In Dramas. v 1
          Dramatic and poetical works (Longmans)
Basil. Tragedy. 5 acts
  In Dramatic and poetical works (Longmans)
Beacon. Musical drama. 2 acts
  In Dramatic and poetical works (Longmans)
Bride. Melodrama. 3 acts
  In Dramas. v 3
          Dramatic and poetical works (Longmans)
Constantine Paleologus. Tragedy. 5 acts
  In Dramatic and political works (Longmans)
Country inn. Comedy. 5 acts
  In Dramatic and poetical works (Longmans)
De Monfort. Tragedy. 5 acts
  In Dramatic and poetical works (Longmans)
Dream. Tragedy. 3 acts
  In Dramatic and poetical works (Longmans)
Election. Comedy. 5 acts
  In Dramatic and poetical works (Longmans)
Enthusiasm. Comedy. 3 acts
  In Dramas. v 2
  In Dramatic and poetical works (Longmans)
Ethwald. Tragedy. 5 acts
  In Dramatic and poetical works (Longmans)
Family legend. Tragedy. 5 acts
  In Dramatic and poetical works (Longmans)
Henriquez. Tragedy. 5 acts
  In Dramas. v 1
          Dramatic and political works (Longmans)
Homicide. Tragedy. 3 acts
  In Dramas. v 3
          Dramatic and poetical works (Longmans)
Martyr. Religious. 3 acts
  In Dramas. v 1
          Dramatic and poetical works (Longmans)
Match. Comedy. 3 acts
  In Dramas. v 3
          Dramatic and poetical works (Longmans)
Orra. Tragedy. 5 acts
  In Dramatic and poetical works (Longmans)
Phantom. Musical drama. 2 acts
  In Dramas. v 2
          Dramatic and poetical works (Longmans)
Rayner. Tragedy. 5 acts
  In Dramatic and poetical works (Longmans)

Romiero. Tragedy. 5 acts
In Dramas. v 1
  Dramatic and poetical works (Longmans)
Second marriage. Comedy. 5 acts
In Dramatic and poetical works (Longmans)
Separation. Tragedy. 5 acts
In Dramas. v 2
  Dramatic and poetical works (Longmans)
Siege. Comedy. 5 acts
In Dramatic and poetical works (Longmans)
Stripling. Tragedy. 5 acts
In Dramas. v 2
  Dramatic and poetical works (Longmans)
Tryal. (Trial) Comedy. 5 acts
In Dramatic and poetical works (Longmans)
Witchcraft. Tragedy. 5 acts
In Dramas. v 3
  Dramatic and poetical works (Longmans)

Baird, George M. P.
Mirage. . . Cincinnati. Stewart, Kidd. 1922. 12°. 36p. Amnesia. 1 act
  Same in Shay, F. ed. Contemporary one-act plays of 1921
    Shay, F. ed. Twenty contemporary one act plays (American)
Waiting room. Cross section of life. 1 act
In Drama 15:6 O '26
Where saints have trod; a pageant-masque of missions. . . Pittsburgh. Christion endeavor union of Penn. 1924. 8°. 22p. 1 act

Baines, Frank
Tragical history of Leonardo Salviati. A noble Florentine play in four acts. London. Kegan Paul. 1908. 12°. 277p.

Baker, Elizabeth
Chains; a play in four acts. Boston. Luce. 1913. 12°. Problem.
  Same in Dickinson, T. H. ed. Contemporary plays
    Plays of today v 1
Cupid in Clapham. 1 act
In One-act plays for stage and study. Ser 3
Miss Robinson; a play in three acts. London. Sidgwick. 1920. 12°. 114p. Comedy
Miss Tassey; a play in one act. London. Sidgwick. 1913. 12°. 31p. Tragedy
  Same in Clark, B. H. ed. Representative one-act plays by British and Irish authors
Partnership; a comedy in three acts. N.Y. French. 1921. 12°. 241p.
Price of Thomas Scott; a play in three acts. London. Sidgwick. 1913. 12°. 85p. Religious

Baker, George Melville
Above the clouds. Boston. Baker. c1876. 12°.

Better than gold; a drama in four acts. Boston. Baker. c1889. 58p.
Baker, George P., 1866-
Pilgrim spirit; a pageant in celibration of the tercentenary of the landing of the Pilgrims at Plymouth, Mass. . . Boston. Jones. 1921. 12°. 136p. Historical. 4 episodes.
Baker, R. E.
Her picture. Comedy. 1 act
In Plays with a punch
Balderston, John Lloyd, 1889-
Genius of Mary; a play in three scenes. . . N.Y. Brown. 1919. 12°. 86p.
Morality play for the leisured class. N.Y. Appleton. 1 act
Baldwin, Charles Crittenden (George Gordon, pseud.), 1888-
Mary! Mary! Historical. 1 act
In Airy nothings
Baldwin, Sidney
Christmas elves. Pantomine. Juvenile
In Five plays and five pantomines
Christmas eve. Juvenile. 1 act
In Five plays and five pantomines
Christmas spirit. Juvenile. 1 act
In Five plays and five pantomines
Enchanted gate. Juvenile. 1 act
In Five plays and five pantomines
Growth of the flowers. Pantomine. Juvenile
In Five plays and five pantomines
Indian camp. Pantomine. Juvenile
In Five plays and five pantomines
Marjorie's garden. Juvenile. 1 act
In Five plays and five pantomines
Mother Nature's trumpeter. Juvenile. 1 act
In Five plays and five pantomines
Quest of the butterfly. Pantomine
In Five plays and five pantomines
Spirit of the forest. Pantomine. Juvenile
In Five plays and five pantomines
Ballard, Frederick, 1884-
Believe me, Xantippe; a comedy in four acts. N.Y. French. 1918. 12°. 140p. 50c
Dollars and chickens; a comedy in three acts. N.Y. French. c1926. 12°. 111p.
Young America; a play in three acts. . . N.Y. French. 1917. 12°. 120p. 50c Comedy
  Same in One-act plays for stage and study, Ser 2
Balzac, Honoré de, 1799-1850
Mercadet. Comedy. 3 acts
In Dramatic works v 2
  Works (Croxley ed) v 35-36
Pamela Giraud. France of Louis XVIII. 5 acts
In Dramatic works v 1
  Works (Croxley ed) v 43
Quinola's resources. (Resources of Quinola). Comedy. 5 acts
In Dramatic works v 1
  Works (Croxley ed) v 34
Resources of Quinola. *See* Balzae, H. de. Quinola's resources

Balzac, Honoré de,—*Continued*
Step-mother (Le marâtre).   Tragedy. 5
    acts.
    In Dramatic works v 2
      Works (Croxley ed) v 35-36
Vautrin.   Bourbons. 1816. 5 acts
    In Dramatic works. v 1
      Works (Croxley ed) v 34
Bangs, John Kendrick, 1862-
Barringtons' "At Home".   Farce. 1 act
    In Real thing and three other farces
Bicyclers.   Farce. 1 act
    In Bicyclers, and three other farces
      Harper 91:961
Dramatic evening.   Farce. 1 act
    In Bicyclers, and three other farces
      Harper 90:158
Fatal message.   Farce. 1 act
    In Bicyclers, and three other plays
Minister's first at home.   Farce. 1 act
    In Ladies' H J 26:16 Mr '09
Proposal under difficulties; a farce.   N.Y.
    Harper. 1913. 12°. 70p. 1 act
    Same in Bicyclers and three other
      farces
Real thing.   Farce. 1 act
    In Real thing and three other farces
      Harp B 43:134
Return of Christmas.   Farce. 1 act
    In Real thing and three other farces
Short-shrift.   Comedy. 1 act
    In Lippinc 85:337
Side-show.   Farce. 1 act
    In Real thing and three other farces
Worsted man; a musical play for ama-
    teurs.   N.Y. Harper. 1905. 12°. 85p.
Banville, Théodore F. de, 1823-1891
Charming Léandre (Le beau Léandre);
    a comedy in one act. . . N.Y. French.
    [1915]. 12°. 18p.
Goingoire.   Comedy. 9 scenes
    In Poet Lore 27:129
Socrates and his wife, a one-act comedy in
    verse. . . N.Y. Marinoni Press. [1889].
    12°. 39p.
Barbee, Lindsay, 1876-
After the game; a college comedy in two
    acts.   Chicago.   Denison. [c1907].
    12°. 31p.
All on a summer's day; a comedy in one
    act, for four men and six women.
    Chicago. Denison. [1916]. 12°. 22p.
Bluebeard.   Fairy. 1 act
    In Cinderella, and five other fairy plays
By way of the secret passage, comedy-
    drama in three acts.   Chicago. Deni-
    son. [1916]. 12°. 38p.
Call of the colors; a patriotic play in two
    acts.   Chicago. Beckley. 1918. 12°.
Christmas tree joke.   Juvenile. 1 act
    In Let's pretend
Cinderella.   Fairy. 3 acts
    In Cinderella and five other fairy plays
Comrades courageous; an eighth grade
    play in 2 acts. Chicago. Denison. 1921.
    12°. 32p.   Juvenile
Contents unknown; a comedy drama of
    mystery in three acts.   Chicago.
    Denison. c1922. 12°. 108p.

Dream that came true; a comedy-drama
    in three acts.   Chicago. Denison.
    [1913]. 12°. 76p.
Empty house; a comedy-drama in three
    acts and an epilogue.   Chicago.
    Denison. 1921. 12°. 112p.
Ever-ever land.   Fairy. 1 act
    In Let's pretend
Forest of every day.   Juvenile. 1 act
    In Let's pretend
"If Don't Believe is changed into Be-
    lieve."   Fairy. 1 act
    In Let's pretend
Jack and the beanstalk.   Fairy 3 acts
    In Cinderella and five other fairy plays
Little pink lady.   Juvenile. 1 act
    In Let's pretend
Little Red Riding Hood.   Fairy. 3 acts
    In Cinderella and five other fairy plays
Out of the stillness; a comedy drama in
    three acts.   Chicago. Denison. 1920.
    12°. 116p.
Real thing after all; an after the war
    comedy drama in three acts.   Chica-
    go. Denison. 1919. 12°. 115p.
Rescued by radio; an eighth grade play
    in two acts.   Chicago. Denison.
    [c1923]. 12°. 43p.
Ruth in a rush; a comedy in three acts.
    Chicago. Denison. 1919. 12°. 110p.
Sing a song of sixpence; a comedietta.
    Chicago. Denison. [1915]. 12°. 17p. 1
    act
Sleeping beauty.   Fairy. 3 acts
    In Cinderella and five other fairy plays
Snow White and the seven dwarfs.
    Fairy. 3 acts
    In Cinderella and five other fairy plays
Thread of destiny; a comedy-drama in
    three acts.   Chicago. Denison. 12°.
    1914. 91p.
To-morrow at ten; a comedy in one act.
    Chicago. Denison. [1916]. 12°. 12p.
Trial of hearts; a college comedy in four
    acts.   Chicago. Denison. [1915]. 12°.
    73p.
What happened at Brent's; a play for
    young people in 2 acts.   Denver,
    Col. Eldridge Entertainment house.
    1921. 12°. 31p.
When the clock strikes twelve; a comedy
    drama in three acts. . . Chicago.
    Denison. [c1921]. 12°. 102p.
When the toys awake.   Juvenile. 1 act
    In Let's pretend
Barber, Herbert Reginald
Jezebel; a tragedy in three acts.   Lon-
    don. Brenton. c1924. 151p.
Barclay, Sir Thomas, 1853-
In gremio deorum.   Super-historical
    fantasy. 1 act
    In 19 Cent 79:554
Gambetta's love story; a drama.   Lon-
    don. Chapman. 1923. 12°. 35p.   His-
    torical. 3 acts
    Same in Fortn 120:215

Sands of fate; dramatised study of an imperial conscience, a phantasy. Boston. Houghton. 1917. 12°. 253p. World war. 3 acts
Same in 19 Cent 78:444

Baring, Maurice, 1874-
After Euripides' "Electra". Dramatic criticism. 1 act
In Diminutive dramas
Ariadne in Naxos. Legendary. 1 act
In Diminutive dramas
Aulis difficulty. Historical. 1 act
In Diminutive dramas
Blue harlequin. Comedy. 1 act
In Diminutive dramas
Caligula's picnic. Historical. 1 act
In Diminutive dramas
Calpurnia's dinner-party. Historical. 1 act
In Diminutive dramas
Catherine Parr; or Alexander's horse. Historical. 1 act
In Diminutive dramas
Death of Alexander. Historical. 1 act
In Diminutive dramas
Desiderio; a drama in three acts. Oxford. Blackwell. 1906. 12°. 128p. Tragedy
Don Juan's failure. Comedy. 1 act
In Diminutive dramas
Double game . Tragedy. 3 acts
In Grey stocking and other plays
Eng R 9:252
Drawback. Comedy. 1 scene
In Diminutive dramas
Fatal rubber. Historical. 1 act
In Diminutive dramas
Greek vase. Comedy. 1 act
In Diminutive dramas
Green elephant. Comedy. 4 acts
In Diminutive dramas
Grey stocking. Social. 4 acts
In Grey stocking and other plays
His majesty's embassy. Comedy. 3 acts
In His majesty's embassy and other plays
Jason and Medea. Legendary. 1 act
In Diminutive dramas
June—and after. Comedy. 3 acts
In His majesty's embassy and other plays
King Alfred and the neat-herd. Legendary. 1 act
In Diminutive dramas
Lucullus's dinner-party. Historical. 1 act
In Diminutive dramas
Mahasena; a play in three acts. Oxford. Blackwell. 1922. 12°. 49p. Poetic
Manfroy, Duke of Athens. Melodrama. 5 acts
In His majesty's embassy and other plays
Member for literature. Farce. 1 act
In Diminutive dramas
Pious Æneas. Legendary. 1 act
In Diminutive dramas
Proserpina; a masque. Oxford. Blackwell. 1908. 12°. 67p. 3 acts

Rehearsal. Theatrical. 1 act
In Diminutive dramas
Rosamond and Eleanor. Comedy. 1 act
In Diminutive dramas
Stoic's daughter. Historical. 1 act
In Diminutive dramas
Velasquez and the "Venus". Comedy. 1 act
In Diminutive dramas
Xantippe and Socrates. Historical. 1 act
In Diminutive dramas

Barker, Harley Granville, 1877-
Farewell to the theatre. Character. 1 act
In Three short plays
Eng R 29:390
Marrying of Ann Leete: a comedy in four acts. Boston. Little. 1916. 8°. 81p.
Same in Three plays
Madras house, a play in four acts. London. Sidgwick. 1910. 8°. 144p. Comedy
Same in Dickinson, T. R. ed. Chief contemporary dramatists
Moses, M. J. ed. Representative British dramas
Rococo. Comedy. 1 act
In Three short plays
Clark, B. H. ed. Representative one-act plays by British and Irish authors
Secret life; a play in three acts. Boston. Little. 1923. 12°. 125p. Tragedy
Vote by ballot. Comedy. 1 act
In Three short plays
Voysey inheritance; a play in **five** acts. . . Boston. Little. 1916. 12°. 81p. Ethical
Same in Three plays
Dickinson, T. H. ed. Contemporary plays
Pierce and Matthews, masterpieces of modern drama v 1 (abridged)
Plays of today
Waste; a play in four acts. Boston, Little. 1916. 8°. 133p. Politics
Same in Three plays

Barker, James Nelson, 1784-1858
How to try a lover, a comedy. In three acts. . . N.Y. Longworth. 1817. 12°. 67p.
Indian princess, or La belle sauvage; an operatic melo-drame in three acts. Phila. Blake. 1808. 24°. 74p.
Marmion or, The battle of Flodden Field. A drama in five acts. N.Y. Murden. 1826. 12°. 62p.
Superstition. Colonial. 5 acts
In Quinn, A. N. ed. Representative American plays, 1763-1923 (1925 ed)
Tears and smiles. A comedy. In five acts. Phila. Palmer. 1808. 12°. 85p.

Barnard, Charles, 1838-
Joe, a comedy of child life in two acts. . . Chicago. Dramatic pub. co. [c1897]. 12°. 22p.
Pretty missionary. A comedy in two acts. Worcester, Mass. 1890. 4°. 24p.

Poor Richard. N.Y. Brentano's. 1924.
12°.
White wings, a play. . . N.Y. Boni. 1927.
12°. 204p. Comedy. 3 acts
You and I; a comedy in three acts. . .
N.Y. Brentano. c1923. 12°. 179p.
Same in Mantle, B. ed. Best plays of
1922-23 (abridged)
Youngest; a comedy in three acts. . .
N.Y. French. c1925. 12°. 126p.
Same in Mantle, B. ed. Best plays of
1924-25 (abridged)
**Barrymore, Blanche Marie Louise (Michael
Strange, pseud.)**
Clair de lune; a play in two acts and six
scenes. N.Y. Putnam. 1921. 12°.
164p. Fantasy
Barrymore, William, d. 1845
El Hyder; the chief of the Ghant Moun-
tains. A grand eastern melo-drama-
tic spectacle. In two acts. London.
Lacy. n.d. 12°. 25p. (Lacy's acting
edition of plays. v. 6 no. 82)
Gilderoy; or, The bonnie boy; a melo-
drama in two acts. . . London.
Richardson. [1829]. 12°. 54p.
Snow storm; or, Lowina of Tobolskow.
A melo-dramatic romance. . . Balti-
more. Robinson. 1818. 12°. 36p.
Wallace; the hero of Scotland. An his-
torical drama in three acts. Boston.
Spencer. [1856?]. 12°. 30p.
Bartholomew, Julia Hall
Two masques; America—The women of
Shakespeare. Boston. Gorham
press. c1916. 12°. 40p.
America. Masque. 1 scene
In Two masques
Women of Shakespeare. Masque. 1
scene
In Two masques
Bartlett, Archie Ernest, 1866-
Empire of Talinis. Tragedy. 5 acts
In Dramas of camp and cloister
Five acts of love. Poetic. 1 scene
In Dramas of camp and cloister
Last judgment. Poetic. 1 scene
In Dramas of camp and cloister
Love's enchantment. Fairy. 4 acts
In Dramas of camp and cloister
Rahna's triumph. Poetic. 1 scene
In Dramas of camp and cloister
Bartlett, Randolph
In hell with the bandits. Satire. 1 act
In Smart Set 44 no 4:195
Respective virtues of Heloise and Maggie.
Comedy. 1 act
In Smart Set 48:73 F '16
Safety first. A vivisection. 1 act
In Smart Set 49:243 My '10
Basudeb, Sree
Aunt Lasmi. Tragedy. 1 act
In Poet Lore 35:101
Bateman, Mrs. Sidney F., 1823-1881
Self; an original comedy in three acts.
N.Y. French. c1856. 12°. 46p.
Same in Moses, M. ed. Representative
plays by American dramatists for
1765 to the present day v 2

Bates, Arlo, 1850-1918
Business meeting; a parlor play in one
act. Boston. Baker. c1905. 12°. 11p.
Same in Ladies' H J 20:51 Mr '03
Gentle jury; a farce in one act. Boston.
Baker. c1897. 12°. 14p.
Mothers' meeting, an entertainment in
one scene for female characters. . .
Boston. Baker. 1909. 12°. 14p.
Bates, Esther Willard
Garafelia's husband, a play in one act.
Insanity
In Plays of the Harvard dramatic club
ser 2
Bates, William Oscar, 1852-1924
Asaph; a comedy in one act
In Drama 10:227
Dryad and the deacon; a faerie in one
scene
In Schafer, B. L. comp. Book of one
act plays
Drama 10:217
In the light of the manger; a prophetic
fantasy in one act. Biblical
In Schafer, B. L. comp. Book of one-
act plays
Drama 11:102
Jacob Leisler; a play of old New York. . .
N.Y. Kennerley. 1913. 12°. 248p.
Historical. 4 acts
Merry Mount; a comedy of New England
beginnings in three acts
In Drama 10:335
Polly of Pogue's Run, a play in one
act. . . N.Y. Shay. [c1917]. 12°. 16p.
Historical
Where do we go from here? a one-act
prevision of the impending. Satire
In Indiana prize plays 1922-23
Bax, Clifford
Apricot tree. Comedy. 1 act
In Antique pageantry
Aucassin and Nicolette. Medieval ro-
mance. 1 act
In Antique pageantry
Midsummer madness; a play for music.
London. Benn. 1923. 12°. 99p. 3 acts
Nocturne in Palermo. London. Benn.
1924. 12°. 30p. Poetic. 11 scenes
Old King Cole. London. C. W. Daniel.
1921. 12°. 89p. Mother Goose. 3 acts
Poetasters of Ispahan. Comedy. 1 act
In Antique pageantry
Square pegs Satire. 1 act
In Polite satires
Cohen, H. L. ed. Junior play book
Summit. Romantic. 1 act
In Antique pageantry
Unknown hand. Satire. 1 act
In Polite satires
Up stream; a drama in three acts. Ox-
ford. Blackwell. 1922. 12°. 85p.
South American
Volcanic island. Satire. 1 act
In Polite satires
Bax, Clifford and Rubinstein, H. F.
Shakespeare, a play in five episodes,
London. Benn. 1921. 12°. 117p. His-
torical

Bay, James
Helping the rich.   N.Y. Brentano's. 1920. 12°. 107p.   Philanthropy. 4 acts
Bayly, Thomas Haynes, 1797-1839
Barrack room.   A comedietta.   In two acts. Altered edition from a musical burletta. . . N.Y.   DeWitt. 1883. 12°. 22p.
Comfortable service.   An original farce in one act.   London.   Lacy. n.d. 12°. 21p. (Lacy's acting edition of plays. v 1 no 10)
Daughter; a drama in one act.   London. Lacy. n.d. 12°. 22p (Lacy acting edition of plays. v. 1 no. 7)
Forty and fifty a farce in one act. . . Boston. Spencer. [1857?]. 12°. 13p.
Gentleman in difficulties; an entirely original farce in one act. . . London. Strange. 1836. 12°. 24p.
How do you manage?   A farce in one act. London. Lacy. n.d. 12°. 21p. (Lacy's acting edition of plays. v. 1 no. 9)
Ladder of love: a musical drama in one act.   London. Lacy. n.d. 12°. 27p. (Lacy's acting edition of plays. v. 1 no. 6)
Lady of Munster.   See Bayly, T. H. Perfection; or, The lady of Munster
Perfection; or, The lady of Munster.   A comedy in one act. London. Lacy. n.d. 12°. 26p. (Lacy's acting edition of plays. v. 13 no. 190)
Swiss cottage; or why don't she marry? a vaudeville in one act.   London. Lacy, n.d. 12°. 22p. (Lacy's acting edition of plays. v. 1 no. 3)
Tom Noddys' secret, a farce in one act. . . Baltimore. Robinson. [1840?] 12°. 27p.
Beach, Lewis, 1891-
Ann Vroome; a play in seven scenes. N.Y. Little. 1924. 12°. 130p.   Youth and age
Brothers.   Comedy. 1 act
In Four one-act plays
    Shay F. and Loving, P. eds.   Fifty contemporary one-act plays
Clod.   Double personality. 1 act
In Four one-act plays
    Washington Square plays
Goose hangs high; a play in three acts. Boston, Little. 1924. 12°. 158p.   Comedy
Same in Mantle, B. ed.   Best plays of 1923-24 (condensed)
Guest for dinner.   Comedy. 1 act
In Four one-act plays
Let's get married; farce comedy in three acts.   Boston. Baker. 1916. 12°. 153p.
Love among the lions.   Farce. 1 act
In Four one-act plays
Square peg, a play in three acts.   Boston. Little. 1924. 12°. 140p.   Tragedy
Beach Rex Ellingwood, 1877-, and Mac-Arthur, James, 1866-1909
Spoilers; a play in four acts.   N.Y. c1906. 12°.

Becque, Henri, 1837-1899
Crows.   *See* Becque, H.   Vultures
Merry-go-round (Navette); a comedy in one act
In Vultures. . .
Quiet game.   Comedy. 1 act
In Play-book (Wis. Dram Soc) v 1 no 9
Vultures (Crows; Corbeaux).   Social. 4 acts
In Vultures. . .
    Moses, M. J. ed.   Representative continental dramas
    Pierce, J. A. and Matthews, J. B. eds. Masterpieces of modern drama v 2 (abridged)
    Drama 2 no 5:14
Woman of Paris (Parisienne); a comedy in three acts
In Vultures. . .
Beddoes, Thomas Lovell, 1803-1849
Bride's tragedy.   Tragedy. 5 acts
In Poetical works v 1
Death's jest-book; or The fool's tragedy.
Same in Poetical works
Last man.   (unfinished).   Tragedy
In Poetical works v 2
Love's arrow poisoned.   (unfinished). Tragedy
In Poetical works v 2
Second brother.   Romantic. 4 acts
In Poetical works v 2
Torrismond.   (unfinished).   Tragedy.
In Poetical works v 2
Beerbohm, Max, 1872-
Savonarola.   Tragedy. 4 acts
In Eng R 28:188
Beith, John Hay (Ian Hay, pseud.), 1876-
Crimson cocoanut.   Farce. 1 act
In Crimson cocoanut, and other plays
Late delivery.   Comedy. 3 scenes
In Crimson cocoanut, and other plays
Missing card.   Comedietta. 1 act
In Crimson cocoanut, and other plays
Queen of hearts, a comedy in one act. Phila. Penn. 1912. 12°. 17p.
Safety match; a play in four acts.   N.Y. French. c1927. 8°. 77p.
Sport of kings; a domestic comedy in three acts. . . N.Y. French. c1926. 8°. 79p.
Tilly of Bloomsbury; a comedy in three acts. . . N.Y. French. c1922. 12°. 90p. (Revised from author's novel "Happy go lucky")
Belasco, David, 1859-
Girl of the golden West, a play in four acts.   Melodrama.
In Moses, M. J. ed.   Representative American dramas, national and local
May Blossom, a comedy in four acts. N.Y. French. c1883. 12°. 69p.
Return of Peter Grimm.   Supernatural. 3 acts
In Baker, G. P. ed.   Modern American plays
    Pierce and Matthews.   Masterpieces of modern drama. v 1 (abridged)

Belasco, David, 1859-, and Long, John Luther
Madame Butterfly. Tragedy. (Japan). From story of John Luther Long. 1 act
In Quinn, A. H. ed. Representative American plays, 1767-1923 (1925 ed)

Bell, John Joy, 1871-
Courtin' Christmas; a play in one act. . . Boston. Phillips. 1924. 12°. 42p.
Pie in the oven; a comedy in one act. Boston. Phillips. 1922. 12°. 32p.
Thirst. 1 act
In Baker's anthology of one-act plays
Those class distinctions; a farce in one act
Thread o' scarlet; a play in one act. . . Boston. Phillips. 1923. 12°. 34p. Crime
Same in Marriott, J. W. ed. One-act plays of to-day
Wolves; a play in one act. London. Gowans. 1925.

Bell, John Keble (Keble Howard, pseud.), 1875-
All through Martha (Old Martha); a comedy in three acts. London. French. c1906. 16°. 66p. 1. Compromising Martha. 2. Martha the soothsayer. 3. Martha plays the fairy
Cheerful knave; a comedy in three acts. London. French. c1913. 12°. 76p.
Come Michaelmas; a play in one act. N.Y. French. c1909. 12°. 17p. Comedy
Compromising Martha (or Act 1 of "Old Martha."); a comedy in one act. London. French. c1906. 12°. 25p.
Same in All through Martha Old Martha
Dramatist at home. A dialogue in one act. N.Y. French. c1909. 16°. 15p.
Embarrassed butler; a comedy in two scenes. London. French. c1912. 12°. 16p.
Forked lightning (The green flag); a comedy. N.Y. Lane. 1916. 12°. 316p. 3 acts
Green flag; a comedy in three acts. . . N.Y. French. c1919. 12° 88p. also pub. under title Forked lightning.
Martha plays the fairy; a comedy in one act. N.Y. French. c1907. 12°. 26p. (Act 3 of Old Martha)
Same in All through Martha Old Martha
Martha the soothsayer. London. French. c1909. 16°. 19p.
Same in All through Martha
Old Martha; a comedy in two acts. London. French. c1906. 16°. 48p. 1. Compromising Martha. 2. Martha plays the fairy
Same in All through Martha
Puss in the corner; a play in one act. N.Y. French. c1923. 12°. 19p.
Smiths; a comedy without a plot. N.Y. McClure. 1907. 12°. 318p.

Sweet William; a comedy in four acts. London. Duckworth. [1922]. 12°. 136p.
Test kiss, a comedy in one act. N.Y. French. [c1922]. 12°. 15p.

Benavente y Martínez, Jacinto, 1866-
Autumnal roses. Satire. 3 acts
In Plays ser 2
Bonds of interest. Comedy. 3 acts
In Plays
Dickinson, T. H. ed. Chief contemporary dramatists ser 2
Moses, M. J. ed. Representative continental dramas
Drama. 5 no 20:568
Evil doers of good. Comedy. 2 acts
In Plays
Field of ermine. Pychological. 3 acts
In Plays ser 4
Governor's wife. Comedy. 3 acts
In Plays ser 2
Poet Lore 29:1
His widow's husband. Comedy. 1 act
In Plays
Shay, F. and Loving, P. eds. Fifty contemporary one-act plays
Golden Bk 3:342
In the clouds. Comedy. 2 acts
In Plays ser 3
Lady. Dramatic novel. 3 acts
In Plays ser 4
Magic of an hour. Dialogue. 1 act
In Plays ser 4
La Malquerida (The ill-beloved.) Tragedy. 3 acts. (Acted under title 'Passion flower')
In Plays
No smoking. (No fumadores). Comedy. 1 act
In Plays ser 2
Drama 7 no 25:78
Passion flower. *See* Benevente y Martínez, J. La Malquerida
Prince who learned everything out of books. Fairy. 3 acts
In Plays ser 3
Poet Lore 29:505
Princess Bebé. Satire. 4 acts
In Plays ser 2
Saturday night (La noche de Sábado). Symbolic. 5 Tableaux
In Plays ser 3
Poet Lore 29:129
School of princesses. Comedy. 3 acts
In Plays ser 4
Smile or Mona Lisa, a play in one act. . . Boston. Badger. [1915]. 12°. 34p. Historical
Truth. Duologue. 1 act
In Plays ser 3

Benedix, Roderich, 1811-1873
Law-suit; a comedy in one act. . . N.Y. French. [1915]. 12°. 23p.
Mabel's manoeuvre; or, a third party, (Third man). A parlor interlude in one scene. N.Y. DeWitt. 1876. 12°. 10p. Comedy
Same in Third man

Benedix, R.—*Continued*
Married bachelors; or, Pleasant surprises. A comedietta in one act. . . N.Y. De-Witt. 1876. 12°. 11p.
Obstinacy (Eigensinn). Comedy. 1 act
In Bates, A. ed. Drama. 11:284
"Table is set"! A comedy in one act. . . N.Y. Bardeen. 1888. 12°. 26p.
Third man, a comedy in one act. . . N.Y. French. [1915]. 12°. 20p. *See also* Mabel's manoeuvre
Wedding trip; a comedy in two acts. . . Chicago. Denison. c1890. 12°. 33p.
Who told the lie? A comedy in one act. . . Chicago. Denison. c1890. 12°. 17p.
Woman hater; a farce in one act. . . Chicago. Denison. c1890. 12°. 16p.

Bennett, [Enoch] Arnold, 1867-
Body and soul; a play in four acts. N.Y. Doran. [c1922]. 12°. 126p. Comedy
Bright Island. N.Y. Doran. 1924. 12°. 126p. $1.50 Comedy. 3 acts
Cupid and commonsense; a play in four acts London. New age press. 1909. 12°. 176p. Comedy
Good woman. Farce. 1 act
In Polite farces for the drawing room
Shay, F. and Loving, P. eds. Fifty contemporary one-act plays
Great adventure; a comedy in four acts. N.Y. Doran. 1913. 12°. 145p. (Dramatization of Buried alive)
Honeymoon; a comedy in three acts. N.Y. Doran. 1912. 12°. 111p.
Same in McClure 36:501
Judith. N.Y. Doran. 1919. 12°. 96p. Apocryphal. 3 acts
Love match; a play in five scenes. London. Chatto. 1922. 12°. 148p. Comedy
Question of sex. Farce. 1 act
In Polite farces for the drawing room
Sacred and profane love; a play in four acts, founded upon the novel of the same name. London. Chatto. 1919-'20. 179p. N.Y. Doran. 1920. 12° 128p. Comedy
Stepmother. Farce. 1 act
In Clark, B. H. ed. Representative one-act plays by British and Irish authors
Knickerbocker, E. Van B. ed. Twelve plays
Marriott, J. W. ed. One-act plays of to-day
Polite farces for the drawing room
Title; a comedy in three acts. N.Y. Doran. [c1918]. 12°. 111p.
What the public wants. . . N.Y. Doran. 1911. 12°. 151p. Socialism. 4 acts
Same in Liv Age 262:801; 263:32 ff. McClure 34:300 ff.

Bennett, Arnold, and Knoblock, E.
London life; a play in three acts and nine scenes. N.Y. Doran. c1924. 12°. 171p. Ambition

Milestones; a play in three acts. N.Y. Doran. 1912. 12°. 122p. Life cycle
Same in Coffman, G. R. ed. Book of modern plays
Dickinson, T. H. ed. Chief contemporary dramatists. v 2

Benson, Robert Hugh, 1871-1914
Cost of a crown. . . N.Y. Longmans. 1910. 12°. 101p. Sacred. 3 acts
Maid of Orleans. . . N.Y. Longmans. 1911. 12°. 95p. Historical. 5 scenes
Mystery play in honour of the nativity of our Lord. . . N.Y. Longmans. 1908. 12°. 101p. Sacred. 5 acts
Upper room; a drama of Christ's passion. . . N.Y. Longmans. 1925. 60p.

Benson, Stuart, and De Acosta, Mercedes
For France; a war episode in one act. *In* Outlook 116:482

Benton, Rita, 1881-
Burning fiery furnace. Biblical. 3 acts
In Bible plays
Call of Samuel. Biblical. 1 act
In Shorter Bible plays
Christmas story. Biblical. 1 act
In Bible plays
Coming down the Mount. Biblical. 4 acts
In Franklin and other plays
Daniel. Biblical. 3 acts
In Bible plays
Daughter of Jephthah. Biblical. 1 act
In Bible plays
David and Goliath. Biblical. 2 acts
In Shorter Bible plays
Esther. Biblical. 1 act
In Bible plays
Franklin. Historical. 5 acts
In Franklin and other plays
Golden calf. Biblical. 3 acts
In Bible plays
Good samaritan. Biblical. 1 act
In Shorter Bible plays
Happy man; from old Greek legend. Religious. 2 acts
In Star-child and other plays
Joseph and his brethren. Biblical. 5 acts
In Bible plays
Judgment of Solomon (Longer version). Biblical. 1 act
In Shorter Bible plays
Judgment of Solomon. (Shorter version) Biblical. 1 act
In Shorter Bible plays
King Robert of Sicily. Religious. 2 acts
In Star-child and other plays
Life beyond. Religious. 1 act
In Star-child and other plays
Manger service. Biblical. 1 act
In Shorter Bible plays
Margaret of Salem. Witchcraft. 5 acts
In Franklin and other plays
Moses in the bulrushes. Biblical. 1 act
In Shorter Bible plays
Noah's flood. Biblical. 2 acts
In Shorter Bible plays
Proving of Abraham. Biblical. 2 acts
In Shorter Bible plays

Ring of magic power. Fairy. 3 acts
In Star-child and other plays
Ruth and Boaz. Biblical. 4 acts
In Bible plays
Spark neglected burns the house. Religious. 3 acts
In Star-child and other plays
Star-child. Religious. 3 acts
In Star-child and other plays
Up, up from Egypt to the promised land. Biblical. 2 acts
In Shorter Bible plays
Where love is, there God is also. Religious. 2 acts
In Star-child and other plays
Yussouf. Religious. 2 acts
In Star-child and other plays

Bercovici, Konrad, 1882-
Costa's daughter. N.Y. Covici-McGee. 1923. 12°. 127p. Melodrama. 3 acts

Beresford, J. D., joint author. *See* Craven, A. S. and Beresford, J. D.

Bergstrøm, Hjalmar, 1868-1914
Birthday party. Old maids. 1 act
In Moses, M. J. ed. Representative one-act plays of continental authors
Karen Borneman. Social. 4 acts
In Karen Borneman, Lynggaard & co
Lynggaard & Co. Problem. 4 acts
In Karen Borneman, Lynggaard & co

Berniger, Vera, 1879-
Perfect pair; a duologue. N.Y. French. c1924. 16p.

Berkeley, Reginald Cheyne, 1890-
Eight o'clock. Tragedy. 1 act
In Lond Mercury 6:591
French leave; a light comedy in three acts. N.Y. French. 1922. 12°. 83p.

Berman, Henry
Faith of the fathers; a play in three acts. N.Y. Brown. 1922. 12°. 228p. Religious

Bernard, F. N.
Man from Denver; a comedy-drama in three acts. N.Y. French. 1913. 12°. 52p.

Bernard, Franklin
Under the flag; a romantic drama in prologue and four acts. N.Y. French. c1910. 12°. 69p.

Bernard, Tristan, 1866-
French without a master; (L'Anglais tel qu'on parle) a farce in one act. N.Y. French. [1915]. 12°. 20p.
I'm going! a comedy in one act. . . N.Y. French. c1915. 12°. 12p.
Same in Clarke, B. H. ed. World's best plays by celebrated European authors

Bernard, William Bayle, 1807-1875
Dumb belle; a farce in one act. . . Boston. Spencer. [1855?]. 12°. 22p.
Passing cloud; a romantic, drama in two acts. London. Lacy. n.d. 12°. 48p. (Lacy's acting edition of plays. v. 1 no. 11)

Practical man. An original farce in one act. London. Lacy. n.d. 12°. 24p. (Lacy's acting edition of plays. v. 1 no. 2)
Platonic attachments. An original farce. In one act. London. Lacy. n.d. 12°. 24p. (Lacy's acting edition of plays. v. 2 no. 27)
Storm in a tea cup. A comedietta in one act. London. Lacy. n.d. 12°. 20p. (Lacy's acting edition of plays. v. 14 no. 200)

Bernstein, Elsa (Porges) (Ernest Rosmer, pseud.), 1866-
John Herkner. Social. 5 acts
In Poet Lore 22:321
Twilight (Dämmerung). Blindness. 5 acts
In Poet Lore 23:363

Bernstein, Henry, 1876-
Thief (Le voleur) a play in three acts. . . Garden City. Doubleday. 1915. 12°. 149p. Melodrama

Besant, Walter, and Pollock, Walter
Charm. Comedy. 2 acts
In Charm and other drawing room plays
Glove. Historical. 1 act
In Charm and other drawing room plays
Loved I not honour more. Comedy. 1 act
In Charm and other drawing room plays
Peer and peeress. Comedy. 2 acts
In Charm and other drawing room plays
Shrinking shoe. Comedy. 2 acts
In Charm and other drawing room plays
Spy. Historical. 2 scenes
In Charm and other drawing room plays
Voice of love. Comedy. 1 act
In Charm and other drawing room plays
Wife's confession. Comedy. 1 act
In Charm and other drawing room plays

Besier, Rudolf, 1878
Don; a comedy in three acts. London. Fisher. n.d. 12°. 175p.
Lady Patricia; a comedy in three acts. London. Unwin. [1911]. 12°. 215p.

Betts, Frank
Ingiald Evilheart. Legendary. 1 act
In Saga plays
Passing of Sinfiotli. Viking age
In Saga plays
Cohen, H. L. ed. Junior play book
Sword of Sigurd. Symbolic. 3 acts
In Saga plays

Beyerlein, Franz Adam, 1871-
Lights out; a play in four acts. . . London. Heinemann. 1915. 12°. 119p. (Same as Taps)
Taps (Zapfenstreich). . . Boston. Luce. c1915. 12°. 119p. 4 acts. World war

Bierstadt, Edward Hale, 1891-
Fifth commandment.　Character. 1 act
In Drama 10:317
Sounding brass.　Cincinnati.　Stewart
Kidd. 1922. 12°. 40p.

Biez, Jacques de, 1852-
First love letter.　Farce. 1 act
In Bellevue Dramatic club: Plays for
private acting

Biggers, Earl Derr, 1884-
Inside the lines; a play in three acts.
N.Y. French. 1924. 12°. 108p.

Binns, Henry Bryan, 1873-
Adventure; a romantic variation on a
Homeric theme.　N.Y. Huebsch.
1911. 12°. 96p.　Legendary. 5 acts

Binyon, [Robert] Laurence, 1869-
Arthur; a tragedy.　Boston, Small.
[c1923]. 12°. 127p. 9 scenes
Attila, a tragedy in four acts.　London.
Murray. 1907. 12°. 134p.
Ayuli; a play in three acts.　N.Y. Apple-
ton. 1920. 12°. 152p.　Tragedy
Bombastes in the shades; a play in one
act.　Oxford Univ. press [1915]. 12°.
28p.　World war
Paris and Oenone; a tragedy in one act.
In Fortn o s 83:1137 (n s 77)

Birch, Frank
Mountebank, a play in three acts.　London. Chatto. 1925. 12°. 168p.

Bird, Charles S.
Lucky Gulch, a comedy drama in three
acts.　N.Y. French. 1916. 12°. 63p.
Petrel, the storm child; a drama in three
acts.　Boston. Baker. 1916. 12°. 58p.
Comedy

Bird, Grace Electra, and Starling, Maud
Abraham Lincoln.　Historical. 1 act
In Historical plays for children
Benjamin Franklin.　Historical. 1 act
In Historical plays for children
Christopher Columbus.　Historical. 1 act
In Historical plays for children
Ferdinand Magellan.　Historical. 1 act
In Historical plays for children
George Rogers Clark.　Historical. 1 act
In Historical plays for children
Henry Hudson.　Historical. 1 act
In Historical plays for children
James Wolfe.　Historical. 1 act
In Historical plays for children
John Smith.　Historical. 1 act
In Historical plays for children
Joliet and Marquette.　Historical. 1 act
In Historical plays for children
La Salle.　Historical. 1 act
In Historical plays for children
Lewis and Clark.　Historical. 1 act
In Historical plays for children
Sir Walter Raleigh.　Historical. 1 act
In Historical plays for children
Vaco Nunez de Balboa.　Historical. 1 act
In Historical plays for children
William Penn.　Historical. 1 act
In Historical plays for children

Bird, Robert Montgomery, 1806-1854
Broker of Bogota.　Romantic verse. 5
acts
In Quinn, A. H. ed.　Representative
American plays, 1767-1923 (1925
ed)

Biro, Lajos, 1880-
Bridegroom.　Comedy. 1 act
In Shay, Frank.　Twenty-five short
plays, international
Drama 8:154
Grandmother.　Tragi-comedy. 1 act
In Shay, F. and Loving, P. eds.　Fifty
contemporary one-act plays
Drama 8:176

Bishop, Farnham, 1886-
Scales and the sword; a social drama in
one act
In Plays of the Harvard dramatic club.
Ser 2

Bjørnson, Bjørnstjerne, 1832-1910
Bankrupt. (En fallit).　Tragi-comedy. 4
acts
In Three dramas
Beyond human power. II. (Beyond hu-
man might; Over evne: annet stykke).
Sequel to Beyond our power I.　So-
cial. 4 acts
Same in Plays ser 2
　　Dickinson, T. H. ed.　Chief
　　contemporary dramatists
Beyond human might.　*See* Bjørnson, B.
Beyond human power II.
Beyond our power. I. (Pastor Sang;
Over evne I).　Problem 2 acts
In Pastor Sang.　London. Longmans.
1893. 16°. 109p.
Plays
Pierce and Matthews, eds. Master-
pieces of modern drama v 2
(abridged)
Editor (Redaktøven).　Journalism. 4 acts
In Three dramas
Gauntlet (Glove; En Hanske).　Lon-
don.　Longmans. 1894. 12°. 151p.
Comedy. 3 acts. In some translations
Act 3, Scene 2 is called Act 4
Same in Plays
Three comedies
Bates, A.　Drama 17:225
Poet Lore 4:7
Glove.　*See* Bjørnson, B. Gauntlet
King (Kongen).　Sociological. 4 acts
In Three dramas
Leonarda.　Comedy. 4 acts
In Three comedies
Drama 1 no 3:16
Lesson in marriage.　*See* Bjørnson, B.
Newly married couple
Love and geography (Geografi og kjaer-
lighed).　Comedy. 3 acts
In Plays ser 2
Mary, Queen of Scots; a drama in five
acts. . . Chicago.　Specialty synd.
press. 1912. 12°. 232p.　Historical
New system (Det ny system).　Psy-
chological. 5 acts
In Plays

Newly married couple (A lesson in marriage; De nygifte). Comedy. 2 acts
In Lesson in marriage; a play in two acts. N.Y. Brandeis. [1910]. 16°. 66p.
Three comedies
Pastor Sang. *See* Bjørnson, B. Beyond our power. I.
Sigurd Slembe; a dramatic triology. Tr. by W. M. Payne. Chicago. Sergel. 1910. 8°. 323p. Historical. 5 acts. 1. Sigurd's first flight; 2. Sigurd's second flight, 3. Sigurd's return
When the new vine blooms (Når det ny vin blomstrer). Boston; Badger. 1911. 12°. 80p. $1.50 Comedy. 3 acts
Same in Poet Lore 22:1

Blackwood, Algernon, 1869-, and Pearn, Violet A.
Karma; a re-incarnation play in prologue, epilogue and three acts. N.Y. Dutton. [c1918]. 12°. 207p. $1.60
Through the crack; a play in five scenes. N.Y. French. c1925. 12°. 92p.

Blake, George, 1893-
Clyde-built; a play in three acts. Glasgow. Wilson. 1922 12°. 85p.
Mother, a play in two scenes. Glasgow. Wilson. 1921. 8°. 58p. Tragedy

Blanchard, Edward Leman
Harlequin Hudibras! or, Old Dame Durden and the merry droll days of the merry monarch . . . Christmas pantomine. London. Lacy. n.d. 12°. 20p. (Lacy's acting edition of plays. v. 9 no. 122)
Three temptations; a masque for moderns. 1 act
In Scott, C. ed. Drawing-room plays

Blashfield, Mrs. Evangeline (Wilbour) (Mrs. E. H. Blashfield), d. 1918
Honor of the Crequy. Comedy. 1 act
In Masques of Cupid
In Cleon's garden. Comedy. 1 act
In Masques of Cupid
Lesser evil. Comedy. 1 act
In Masques of Cupid
Surprise party. Comedy. 1 act
In Masques of Cupid

Blatt, William M., 1876-
Husbands on approval: a comedy in three acts. Boston. Baker. 1914. 12°. 197p. 50c

Bloch, Bertram
Humpty Dumpty. Fantasy. 1 act
In Poet Lore 32:76
Maiden over the wall. Fantasy. 1 act
In Drama 8 no 31:436

Block, Louis James, 1851-
At the foot of the rainbow. Comedy. 2 acts
In Capriccios
Birth and death of the prince. Legendary. 5 acts
In Capriccios
Day of days. Prothalamion. 1 act
In Capriccios

Exile, a dramatic episode. St. Louis. Jones. 1880. 12°. 120p. Poetic. 11 parts
Same in Dramatic sketches and poems
Judge; a play in four acts. Boston. Gorham. 1915. 12°. 119p. (Founded on the novel of Karl Emil Franzos) Social
Myriad-minded man—an imaginary conversation. Dialogue. 1 act
In Capriccios
On the mountain top. Legendary. 1 act
In Capriccios
World's triumph. Phila. Lippinc. 1909. 12°. 165p. Religious. 5 acts

Bloomgarden, Solomon, 1870-
Shunamite; a one-act Biblical play, by Yehoash [pseud]. Authorized translation from the Yiddish by Henry T. Schnittkind
In Shay, Frank. Twenty-five short plays, international
Stratford J 4:313

Blow, Sydney, 1878-, and Hoare, Douglas
"Oh, I say!" a farce in three acts, adapted, from the French (Une nuit de noces) of Henri Kéroul and Albert Barré. N.Y. French. c1924. 86p.

Bodenheim, Maxwell, 1893-
Unimagined Heaven. 1 act
In Seven Arts 2:193

Bodenheim, Maxwell, 1893-, and Hecht, Ben, 1893-
Gentle furniture shop. Idealism. 1 act
In Drama 10:132
Master poisoner. Poetic. 1 act
In Minna and myself
Poet's heart. Poetic. 1 act
In Minna and myself

Boker, George Henry, 1823-1890
Anne Boleyn, a tragedy. Phila. Hart. 1850. 12°. 225p. 5 acts
Same in Plays and poems v 1
Betrothal, a play in 5 acts. Comedy
In Plays and poems v 2
Calaynos: a tragedy. Phila. Butler. 1848. 12°. 218p. 5 acts
Same in Plays and poems v 1
Cumberland's British theatre v 45 no 6
Francesca da Rimini. Romantic tragedy. 5 acts
In Plays and poems v 1
Quinn, A. H. ed. Representative American plays, 1767-1923
Leonor de Guzman. Tragedy. 5 acts
In Plays and poems v 1
Podesta's daughter. Tragedy. 1 act
In Plays and poems v 2
Widow's marriage. Comedy. 5 acts
In Plays and poems v 2

Bolton, Guy Reginald
Chicken feed; or, Wages for wives; a comedy in three acts. N.Y. French. c1924. 12°. 117p.
Same in Mantle, B. ed. Best plays of 1923-24 (condensed)

Bolton, G. R.—*Continued*
"Polly preferred"; a comedy in three acts. N.Y. French. [c1923]. 12°. 98p.
Wages for wives. *See* Bolton, G. Chicken feed

Bolton, Guy Reginald, and Middleton, George, 1880-
Adam and Eva; comedy in three acts. N.Y. French. 1924. 12°. 115p.
Same in Polly with a past and Adam and Eva
Light of the world; a modern drama. . . N.Y. Holt. 1920. 12°. 205p.   Religious. 3 acts
Polly with a past.   Comedy. 3 acts
In Polly with a past and Adam and Eva

Bonnet, Theodore F.
Friend of the people; a play in four acts. . . San Fran. Pacific pub. co. 1914. 12°. 115p. $1.50

Booth, Hilliard
Doris and the dinosaur; comedy in two acts.   N.Y. French. 1924. 12°.

Bornstead, Beulah
Diabolical circle.   Historical. 1 act
In Lewis, B. R. ed.   Contemporary one-act plays

Borsock, H.
Three weddings of a hunchback.   Comedy. 1 act
In Massey, V. ed.   Canadian plays for Hart House theatre v 1

Botrel, Théodore Jean Marie, 1868-
Du Gueselin.   France. 3 acts
In Poet Lore 30:159

Bottomley, Gordon, 1874-
Britain's daughter.   Poetic. 1 act
In Gruach, and Britain's daughter
Crier by night.   London. Unicorn press. · 1902. 4°. 32p.   Tragedy. 1 act
Same in King Lear's wife, etc
Bibelot 15:297
Gruach.   Poetic. 2 scenes
In Gruach, and Britain's daughter
King Lears wife, play in one act.   N.Y. P. R. Reynolds. 1916. 12°. 96p. Tragedy. 1 act
Same in King Lear's wife, etc
Laodice and Danaë; play in one act. Boston. Four seas co. 1916. 12°. 44p. Historical
Same in King Lear's wife, etc.
Midsummer eve, a dramatic pastoral poem.   South Harting. Pear Tree press. 1905. 8°. 35p. 1 act
Same in King Lear's wife, etc
Riding to Lithend.   Portland, Me. Mosher. 1910. 12°. 61p.   Tragedy. 1 act
Same in King Lear's wife, etc
Leonard, S. A. ed.   Atlantic book of modern plays
Bibelot 16:3

Boucher, Maurice
Christmas tale in one act. . . N.Y. French. [1915]. 12°. 20p.

Boucicault, Dion, 1822-1890
Andy Blake: or, The Irish diamond, a comedy in two acts.   N.Y. French. 1856. 12°. 19p.
Arrah-na-pogue; or, the Wicklow wedding.   An Irish drama, in three acts. Chicago. Dramatic publishing co. [18—?]. 12°. 53p.
Brides of Garryowen.   *See* Boucicault, D.   Colleen Bawn; or, The brides of Garryowen
Colleen Bawn; or The brides of Garryowen.   A domestic drama in three acts. London. Lacy. [18—]. 12°. 52p.
Forbidden fruit; a comedy in three acts. N.Y. Metropolitan. 1876. 12°. 52p.
Grimaldi; or, The life of an actress.   A drama in five acts.   N.Y. 1856. 12° 36p.   Melodrama
How she loves him! a comedy in five acts.   London. Chapman and Hall. [1868] 8° 63p.
Irish diamond.   *See* Boucicault, D. Andy Blake, or, The Irish diamond
Irish heiress, a comedy in five acts. London.   Andrews. 1842. 8°. 99p.
Jessie Brown; or, The relief of Lucknow. A drama, in three acts.   N.Y. French. c1858. 12°. 32p.   Historical
Jilt.   A comedy in five acts.   N.Y. French. c1909. 12°. 64p.
Knight of Arva: a comic drama, in two acts.   N.Y. French. [1868]. 12°. 28p.
Led astray, a comedy in five acts.   N.Y. French. c1873. 12°. 57p.
Life in Louisiana.   *See* Boucicault, D. Octoroon; or, Life in Louisiana
Life of an actress.   *See* Boucicault, D. Grimaldi, or The life of an actress
London assurance.   A comedy in five acts. . . Boston. Baker. 1911. 12°. 78p.
Same in Bates, A. ed.   Drama 22:197
Matthews, J. B. and Lieder, P. R.   Chief British dramatists
Moses, M. J. ed.   Representative British dramas
Long strike.   A drama in four acts. N.Y. French. n.d. 12°. 38p.   Melodrama
Lover by proxy.   A burletta, in one act. Boston. Spencer. [1857?]. 12°. 23p.
My little girl.   Play in one act.   London. French. [18—?]. 12°. 14p.   Comedy. (Lacy's acting edition of plays. v. 129 no. 1932)
Octoroon; or Life in Louisiana.   A play in five acts.   N.Y. [1861?]. 12°. 40p.
Same in Slavery
Quinn, A. H. ed.   Representative American plays, 1767-1923
O'Dowd.   N.Y. French. 1909. 12°. 52p.
Old heads and young hearts.   A comedy in five acts.   N.Y. French. [19—?]. 12°. 73p.
Pauvrette.   A drama in five acts. N.Y. French. c1858. 12°. 36p.   Melodrama

Phantom; a drama in two acts. N.Y.
French. 1856. 12°. 28p.   Melodrama
Poor of New York. A drama in five
acts. N.Y. French. [c1857]. 12°. 45p.
Melodrama
Pope of Rome. An historical romance
in six tableaux. N.Y. French. c1858.
12°. 40p.
Prima donna. A comedy in two acts.
London. Lacy. [18—]. 12°. 20p. (Lacy's
acting edition of plays. v. 8)
Relief of Lucknow. See Boucicault, D.
Jessie Brown, or, The relief of Luck-
now
Shaughraun. An original drama in three
acts. N.Y. French. [188—?]. 12°. 63p.
Irish Comedy
Wicklow wedding. See Boucicault, D.
Arrah- na- pogue; or, the Wicklow
wedding
Willow copse. A drama. In five acts.
Boston. Spencer. [1856?]. 12°. 64p.
Melodrama

**Boucicault, Dion, 1822-1890, and Bridgeman,
John V.**
Broken vow. See Boucicault, D. and
Bridgeman, S. V. Romance in the
life of Sixtus the fifth, entitled, the
broken vow
Romance in the life of Sixtus the fifth.
entitled, the broken vow. In five
acts and seven tableaux. London.
Lacy. 1851. 12°. 52p.   Melodrama

Boulter, B. C.
Paul and Silas; a play in four scenes.
N.Y. Macmillan. 1923. 12°. 31p.   Reli-
gious

Bourchier, A.
Wedding guest. Double standard. 4 acts
In Fortn 74 sup 1

Bourdet, Edouard
Captive. N.Y. Brentano. 1927. 12°.
Tragedy. 3 acts

Bowman, James Cloyd, 1880-
Gift of white roses. . . Boston. Pilgrim
press. c1914. 12°. 79p.   Tragedy. 1
act

Bowyer, Frederick
Windmill man; a play. London. "The
Stage" play pub. bureau. 1924. 96p.

**Boyce, Neith, pseud. (Mrs. Hutchins Hap-
good), 1872-**
Two sons. 1 act
In Provincetown plays. Ser 3

Boyce, Neith, and Hapgood, Hutchins
Enemies. 1 act
In Provincetown plays.   Stewart Kidd
1921

Boyd, Jackson
Unveiling; a poetic drama in five acts.
N.Y. Putnam. 1915. 12°. 255p.   Alle-
gorical

Boyd, Thomas Stirling
Web; a play in three acts. N.Y. French.
1925. 12°. 115p.

Boyesen, Algernon
Don Juan duped.   Intrigue. 1 act
In Smart Set 33 no 4:131
Boyle, William
Building fund, a comedy in three acts.
Dublin. Gill. 1911. 12°. 36p.
Eloquent Dempsey, a comedy in three
acts. Dublin. Gill. 1911. 12°. 84p.
also Chicago. 1907
Family failing; a comedy in three acts.
Dublin. Gill. 1912. 12°. 67p.
Mineral workers, a play in four acts.
Dublin. Gill. 1910. 12°. 109p.
Bracco, Roberto, 1862-
Hidden spring.   Dementia. 4 acts
In Poet Lore 18:143
Phantasms.   Pathological. 4 acts
In Poet Lore 19:241
Snowy night.   Authorized translation
from the Italian original by Arthur
Livingston.   Tragedy. 1 act
In Shay, Frank.   Twenty-five short
plays, international
**Brace, Gladys, pseud. (Vilsack, Gladys
Brace)**
Rosamond.   Poetic. 1 act
In Rosamond, and Simonetta
Simonetta.   Poetic. 1 act
In Rosamond, and Simonetta
Bradford, Gamaliel, 1863-
Unmade in heaven, a play in four acts.
N.Y. Dodd. 1917. 12°. 138p.   Reli-
gious
Bradley, Katherine.   See Field, Michael,
pseud.
Bradley, Mary E.
That vidder; a play in five acts.   N.Y.
Hitchcock. 1926. 12°. 52p.
Brady, Jack, joint author.   See Williams,
Oscar and Brady, Jack
Brand, Alfred
Did it really happen?   Comedy. 1 act
In Infernal masculine, and other com-
edies
Infernal masculine.   Comedy. 1 act
In Infernal masculine, and other com-
edies
Three is company.   Comedy. 1 act
In Infernal masculine, and other com-
edies
Brandane, John
Change-house; a play in one act.   Bos-
ton. Phillips. 1921. 12°. 50p. (Reper-
tory plays. no. 25).   Tragedy
Same in Cohen, H. L. ed.   More one-
act plays by modern authors
Glen is mine.   Hebrides. 3 acts
In Glen is mine, and The lifting
Lifting.   Hebrides. 3 acts
In Glen is mine, and The lifting
Rory aforesaid.   1 act
In Baker's anthology of one-act plays
Brandane, John, and Yuill, A. W.
Glenforsa; a play in one act.   Boston.
Phillips. 1921. 12°. 51p. (Repertory
plays. no. 24)   Scotch comedy
Brandon, Dorothy
Outsider; a play in three acts.   N.Y.
French. c1926. 12°. 89p.

Bray, Louise Whitefield
Harbor of lost ships.   Tragedy. 1 act.
Adapted from a short story by Ellen
P. Huling
In Plays of the Harvard dramatic club
ser 2
Mis' Mercy.   Sea. 1 act
In Plays of the 47 workshop ser 3

Brereton, J. E.
Reckoning; a play in one act. . . London.
J. Williams. c1924. 20p.

Brésil, Jules, joint author. *See* D'Ennery,
A. and Brésil, J.

Bridgeman, John V.
Good run for it: a farce in one act.
London. Lacy. n.d. 12°. 18p. (Lacy's
acting edition of plays. v 14 no 198)
"Matrimonial. . . a gentleman," etc.   For
further particulars apply at an entirely original farce, in one act.
London. Lacy. n.d. 12°. 22p. (Lacy's
acting edition of plays. v. 7 no. 96)

Bridgeman, John V. joint author.   *See*
Boucicault, Dion, and Bridgeman,
John V.

Brieux, Eugene, 1858-
Americans (Les Americans chez nons)
In Cur Opinion 68:488 (excerpts)
Artists' families. (Ménages d'artistes), a
comedy in three acts. . . Garden City.
Doubleday. 1918. 12°. 98p.
Blanchette.   Comedy. 3 acts
In Blanchette, and The escape
Damaged goods, (Les avariés).   Here-
dity. 3 acts
In Three plays
Escape. (L'evasion).   Comedy. 3 acts
In Blanchette, and The escape
False gods. (La foi).   Superstition. 5 acts
In Woman on her own, etc.
Maternity.   A play in three acts. . . N.Y.
Tucker. 1907. 12°. 78p.   Problem
Same in Three plays (two versions)
Red robe (La robe rouge).   Criminal
law. 4 acts
In Woman on her own, etc.
Dickinson, T. R. ed.   Chief con-
temporary dramatists
Pierce and Matthews, ed.   Master-
pieces of modern drama v 2
(abridged)
School for mothers-in-law.   Comedy. 1
act
In International (N.Y.) 3:54
Smart Set 41 no 1:16
Three daughters of M. Dupont. Problem.
4 acts
In Three plays
Woman on her own (La femme seule).
Social. 3 acts
In Woman on her own, etc.

Brighouse, Harold, 1882-
Apple-tree; or, why misery never dies.
A play in one act. London. Gowans
& Gray. 1923. 24°. 37p. (Repertory
plays. no. 33)   Breton legend
"Bantam V. C."; a farce in three acts.
Boston. Baker. 1925. 12°. 95p.

Captain Shapely; a comedy of London
Town and the Oxford road in the
days of Queen Anne.   N.Y. Mc-
Bride. 1924. 281p.
Converts; a comedy in one act.   Boston.
Phillips. 1920. 12°. 47p.   (Repertory
plays. no. 16)
Followers.   A "Cranford" sketch.   Lon-
don. Gowans & Gray. 1922. 24°. 40p.
1 act
Same in Cohen, N. L. ed.   Junior play
book
Marriott, J. W. ed.   One-act
plays of to-day
Game.   Comedy. 3 acts
In Three Lancashire plays
Garside's career; a comedy in four acts.
Chicago. McClurg. 1915. 12°. 94p.
Happy hangman; a grotesque in one act.
London. Gowans & Gray. 1922. 24°.
39p. (Repertory plays. no. 29)   Com-
edy
Hobson's choice, a three-act comedy
Garden City. Doubleday. 1916. 12°.
134p.
How the weather is made. Comedy. 1 act
In Open-air plays
Laughing mind.   Comedy. 1 act
In Open-air plays
Little red shoes; a play in one act.   Bos-
ton. Baker. 1925. 12°. 21p.
Same in Baker's anthology of one-act
plays
Lonesome like, a play in one act.   Lon-
don. Gowans. c1914. 12°. 44p. (Reper-
tory plays. no. 12)   Social
Same in Clark, B. H.   Representative
one-act plays by British and
Irish authors
Leonard, S. A. ed.   Atlantic
book of modern plays
Marriott, J. W. ed.   One-act
plays of today ser 2
One act plays for stage and
study ser 1
Maid of France, a play in one act.   Bos-
ton. Phillips. 1917. 12°. 38p. (Reper-
tory plays. no. 14).   Joan of Arc
Same in Cohen, H. L.   One-act plays
by modern authors
Man about the place.   Comedy. 1 act
In Plays for the meadow and plays for
lawn
Mary's John; a comedy in one act. . .
N.Y. French. c1925. 12°. 65p.
Maypole morning.   Historical. 1 act
In Open-air plays
Plays for the meadow and plays for
the lawn
Night of "Mr. H."
In Cohen, H. L. ed.   More one-act
plays by modern authors
Northerners.   Lancashire. 4 acts
In Three Lancashire plays

Oak settle; a one-act comedy.   N.Y.
French. c1911. 12°. 24p. (French's
acting edition of plays.)
Odd man out; a comedy in three acts.
London. French. c1912. 12°. 87p.

Once a hero; a comedy in one act. London. Gowans & Gray. 1922. 24°. 44p. (Repertory plays. no. 30)

Paris doctor. Comedy. 1 act
In Plays for the meadow and plays for the lawn

Price of coal. London. Gowans & Gray. 1911. 12°. 41p. (Repertory plays. no. 3) Lanarkshire. 1 act

Prince who was a piper. Comedy. 1 act
In Open-air plays
Plays for the meadow and plays for the lawn

Rational princess. Comedy. 1 act
In Open-air plays

Scaring off of Teddy Dawson; a comedy in one act. N.Y. French. ᵣc1911ᵣ. 12°. 20p.

Spring in Bloomsbury; a play in one act. Boston. Phillips. c1924. 16p.

When did they meet again! 1 act
In One-act plays for stage and study Ser 3

Why misery never dies. *See* Brighouse, H. Apple-tree; or, Why misery never dies

Wrong shadow; a romantic comedy. London. Chapman. 1923. 12°. 317p.

Zach. Character comedy. 3 acts
In Three Lancashire plays

Broadhurst, George H., 1866-
Bought and paid for; a play in four acts. N.Y. French. 1916. 12°. 98p. Comedy

"Innocent;" a play in a prologue, four acts and an epilogue. . . Adapted from the Hungarian of Arpard Pasztor. N.Y. French. 1914. 12°. 98p.

Law of the land; a play in four acts. N.Y. French. c1914. 12°. 112p.

Man of the hour, a play in four acts. Revised. N.Y. French. N.Y. c1916. 12°. 132p. Comedy

What happened to Jones an original farce in three acts. N.Y. French. ᵣ1897ᵣ. 12°. 107p.

Why Smith left home. A farce in three acts. N.Y. French. c1912. 12°. 111p.

Wrong Mr. Wright; an original comedy in three acts. Rev. 1918. N.Y. French. c1918. 12°. 93p.

Broadhurst, Thomas W.
Black hand; a melodrama by Wm. B. Hurst. N.Y. ᵣ1902ᵣ. 12°. 87p.

Holy city; a drama. . . Phila. Jacobs. ᵣ1904ᵣ. 12°. 214p.

Brock, Howard
Bank account. Comedy. 1 act
In Plays of the Harvard dramatic club ser 1

Brockhurst, Joseph Sumner
Wife; or, Love and madness. A tragedy in five acts. . . Cambridge. Deighton. 1856. 8°. 213p.

Brodé, Julien Lafayette, 1881-
Within the gates of Yildiz. A play in five acts. Boston. Gorham. 1917. 8°. 149p. $1.25 Historical

Brodney, Spencer
Rebel Smith; a play in three acts. N.Y. Seibel. 1925. 12°. 120p. Labor

Brody, Alter
Rapunzel. Blindness. . . 1 act
In Theatre Arts M 9:257

Brooke, Rupert, 1887-1915
Lithuania; a drama in one act. Cincinnati. Stewart Kidd. ᵣc1915ᵣ. 12°. 39p. 50c Tragedy

Brooke, Stopford Augustus, 1832-1916
Riquet of the tuft; a love drama. London. Macmillan. 1880. 172p.

Brooker, Bertram
Efficiency. Social. 1 act
In International (N.Y.) 8:180

Brookman, Katharine Barron
Interpolated; a play.
In Poet Lore 35:78

Brooks, Charles Stephens, 1878-
At the sign of the greedy pig, a frightful comedy of beggars. 2 acts
In Frightful plays!

Luca Sarto. N.Y. Harcourt. ᵣc1924ᵣ. 12°. 186p. $2 Historical, Louis XI. 4 acts

Wappin' wharf, a frightful comedy of pirates. 3 acts
In Frightful plays!

Brooks, Shirley, 1815-1874
Anything for a change. A petite comedy in one act. London. French. n.d. 12°. 22p. (Lacy's acting edition of plays. v. 4 no. 53)

Creole; or, Love's fetters. An original drama in three acts. London. Lacy. n.d. 12°. 42p. (Lacy's acting edition of plays. v 1 no 12)

Exposition. A Scandinavian sketch . . . in one act. London. Lacy. n.d. 12°. 22p. (Lacy's acting edition of plays. v. 3 no. 44)

Guardian angel. A farce in one act. London. Lacy. n.d. 12°. 19p. (Lacy's acting edition of plays. v. 5 no. 67)

Brosius, Nancy Bancroft
Sue 'em; the first radio play printed in America. . . N.Y. Brentano's ᵣc1925ᵣ. 12°. 29p. (Awarded first; prize in the WGBS radio drama contest) 1 act

Brough, Robert Barnabas, 1828-1860
Crinoline. An original farce in one act. . . Boston. Spencer. ᵣ1856?ᵣ. 12°. 21p.

Moustache movement. An original farce in one act. London. Lacy. n.d. 12°. (Lacy's acting edition of plays. v. 14 no. 205)

Overland journey to Constantinople, as undertaken by Lord Bateman, with interesting particulars of the fair Sophia. An extravaganza. In two acts. London. Lacy. n.d. 12°. 36p. (Lacy's acting edition of plays. v. 15 no. 212)

Twelve labours of Hercules. A comedy, in two acts. London. Lacy. n.d. 12°. 35p. (Lacy's acting edition of plays. v. 6 no. 83)

Brough, William, 1826-1870

Apartments, "Visitors to the exhibition may be accommodated", etc. A piece of extravagance to "suit the times", in one-act. London. Lacy. n.d. 12°. 16p. (Lacy's acting edition of plays. v. 4 no. 48)

Comical countess. A farce in one act. . . London. Lacy. [1866?] (Lacy's acting edition of plays. no. 769)

House out of windows. A farce, in one act. London. Lacy. n.d. 12°. 16p. (Lacy's acting edition of plays. v. 8 no. 117)

How to make home happy. A comic drama. In one act. London. Lacy. 12°. n.d. 23p. (Lacy's acting edition of plays. v. 13 no. 182)

Number one, round the corner. A farce. In one act. London. Lacy. n.d. 12°. 16p. (Lacy's acting edition of plays. v. 14 no. 199)

Phenomenon in a smock frock. A comic drama in one act. London. Lacy. n.d. 12°. 23p. (Lacy's acting of plays. v. 9 no. 121)

Trying it on. A farce in one act. London. Lacy. n.d. 12°. 22p. (Lacy's acting edition of plays. v. 11 no. 5)

Brougham, John, 1810-1880

Po-ca-hon-tas; or, The gentle savage. Historical. 2 acts
    In Bates, A. ed.   Drama v 20

Brown, Alice, 1857-

Charles Lamb; a play. N.Y. Macmillan. 1924. 12°. 121p. Historical. 5 acts

Children of earth; a play of New England. N.Y. Macmillan. 1915. 12°. 212p. (Winthrop Ames prize play). Comedy. 4 acts

Crimson Lake. Tragedy. 1 act
    In One act plays

Doctor Auntie. Comedy. 1 act
    In One act plays

Hero. World war. 1 act
    In One act plays

Joint owners in Spain; a comedy in one act. Chicago Little Theatre. 1914. 12°. 20p.
    Same in One act plays

Loving cup. Comedy. 1 act
    In One act plays
        Woman's H C 40:11 My '13

March wind. Comedy. 1 act
    In One act plays

Milly dear. Marriage. 1 act
    In One act plays

Sugar house. Comedy. 1 act
    In One act plays

Web. Crime. 1 act
    In One act plays

Brown, Charles Hovey

Moses. . . Boston. 1902. 8°. 69p.

Brown, David Paul, 1795-1875

Prophet of St. Paul's, a play in five acts. Phila. Carey & Hart. 1836. 12°. 50p.

Sertorius; or, The Roman patriot. Tragedy. 5 acts
    In Moses, M. J. ed. Representative plays by American dramatists from 1765 to the present day. v 2

Brown, John Mason

Pageant of the shearmen and tailors. Miracle. 12 scenes
    In Theatre Arts M 9:824

Brown, Katharine S., and Tinnin, Glenna S.

One night in Bethlehem; a play of the nativity in a prologue and five scenes. (Washington? D.C.). c1925. 41p.

Brown, Laura Norton

Kissing goes by favor. Marital. 1 act
    In Drama 16:14

Brown, Leando

Mrs. Raford, humanist; a suffrage drama. N.Y. Landane. [c1923]. 12°. 137p. 3 acts

Browne, Porter Emerson, 1879-

Bad man; a play in three acts. N.Y. French. c1926. 12°. 97p. Melodrama
    Same in Mantle, B. ed: Best plays of 1920-21 (condensed)

Browne, Maurice

King of the Jews. Passion play. 1 act
    In Drama 6:496

Brown, Patricia

Gloria mundi; a play in one act. French. N.Y. 1925. 29p. (Winner of second Samuel French prize)

Browne, W. M.

Red or white. 1 act
    In Plays with a punch

Brownell, W. Atherton, 1866-1924

Unseen empire; a peace play in four acts. N.Y. Harper. 1914. 12°. 176p. $1.25

Browning, Robert, 1812-1889

Blot in the 'scutcheon. Tragedy. 3 acts
    In Complete poetical works
        Tatlock & Martin. eds. Representative English plays
Colombe's birthday. Romantic. 5 acts
    In Complete poetical works
Luria. Tragedy. 5 acts
    In Complete poetical works
Pippa passes. N.Y. Barse & Hopkins [1910?]. 12°. 64p. Dramatised from poem. 3 acts
Return of the druses. Tragedy. 5 acts
    In Complete poetical works
Soul's tragedy. Tragedy. 2 acts
    In Complete poetical works

Brunner, Mrs Emma Beatrice

Making a man. World war. 1 act
    In Bits of background
Over age. World war. 1 act
    In Bits of background
Spark of life. Tragedy. 1 act
    In Bits of background
Strangers. Marriage. 1 act
    In Bits of background

Brunner, Ethel H.

Elopement; or, Celia intervenes; a comedy. London. A. L. Humphreys. 1917. 87p.

Bryant, Louise Stevens, 1885-
Game. 1 act
In Provincetown plays ser 1
Bryce, Catherine Turner, 1871-
Bound or free. 1 act
In Bound or free, and The wizard of
words
Wizard of words. 1 act
In Bound or free, and The wizard of
words
Buchanan, Fannie R.
Lighting of the torch. Pilgrim masque.
1 act
In Drama 10:350
Buchanan, Fannie R., and Wilson, Clara
Who defeated Doogan? a one-act playlet
with a prolog, being a study of elec-
tion laws and a farce of election er-
rors. N.Y. Rand. c1924. 12°. 31p.
Buchanan, Thompson, 1877-
Woman's way. . . Garden City. Double-
day. 1915. 12°. 157p. Comedy. 3 acts
Buck, Gertrude, 1868-
Mother-love. Selfishness. 1 act
In Drama no 33:1
**Buckingham and Chandos, Alice Anne,
duchess of (afterward Lady Egerton)**
Everyman; a morality play. N.Y. Phil-
lips. 1922. 12°. 50c
Masque of the two strangers. London.
Gowans. 1912. 24°. 29p. Symbolic. 1
act
In Cohen, H. L. ed. One-act plays by
modern authors
Buckley, Reginald Ramsden, 1882-
Arthur of Britain; a festival drama.
London. Williams. 1914. 8°. 258p.
Glastonbury. 4 pts.
Buckstone, John Baldwin, 1802-1879
Agnes De Vere; or, The wife's revenge, a
drama in three acts. Boston. Spen-
cer. 1885. 12°. 44p.
Alarming sacrifice. A farce. In one act.
Boston. Spencer. [1885?]. 12°. 18p.
Breach of promise, or, Second thoughts
are best. A comedy, in two acts. Bos-
ton. Spencer. [1856?]. 12°. 40p.
Dream at sea. A drama. In three acts.
Boston. Spencer. [1856?]. 12°. 38p.
Duchess de la Vaubalière; a drama.
London. Strange. 1837. 32p.
Flowers of the forest; a gypsy story.
An original drama in three acts.
Boston. Spencer. [1857?]. 12°. 53p.
Green bushes; or, A hundred years ago.
An original drama in three acts. . .
Boston. [1857?]. 12°. 50p. Melo-
drama
Hundred years ago. *See* Buckstone, J.
B. The green bushes; or, A hundred
years ago.
King of the Alps. A romantic drama.
In three acts. London. Lacy. n.d.
12°. 60p. (Lacy's acting edition of
plays. v. 6 no. 87)
Kiss in the dark. A farce. In one act.
London. Lacy. n.d. 12°. 17p. (Lacy's
acting edition of plays. v. 6 no. 77)

Maid with the milking pail. A comic
drama, in one act. London. Lacy. n.d.
12°. 24p. (Lacy's acting edition of
plays. v. 10 no. 150)
Murder will out. *See* Buckstone, J. B.
Presumptive evidence; or, Murder
will out
Pet of the petticoats. An opera, in three
acts. N.Y. O. A. Roorbach. [1856?].
12°. 44p.
Presumptive evidence; or, Murder will
out. A domestic drama, in two acts.
Boston. Spencer. 1855. 12°. 34p.
Scholar. A comedy in two acts. N.Y.
O. A. Roorbach. [1856?]. 12°. 30p.
Second thoughts are best. *See* Buck-
stone, J. B. Breach of promise; or,
Second thoughts are best
Two queens. A petite comedy, in one
act. London. Lacy. n.d. 12°. 22p.
(Lacy's acting edition of plays. v. 1)
Wife's revenge. *See* Buckstone, J. B.
Agnes De Vere; or, The wife's rev-
enge
Wreck ashore. A drama in two acts.
Boston. Spencer. 1856. 12°. 39p.
Bullett, Gerald William, 1894-
Mr. Godly beside himself, a comedy in
four acts. London. Benn. 1926. 12°.
84p.
Bulwer-Lytton, Sir Edward George, 1803-
1873
Conspiracy. *See* Bulwer-Lytton, E. G.
Richelieu; or, The conspiracy
Duchesse de la Vallière. Historical. 5
acts
In Bulwer's plays
Lady of Lyons; or, Love and pride.
Romantic. 5 acts
In Bulwer's plays
Tatlock, J. S. P. and Martin, R. G.
eds. Representative English plays
Love and pride. *See* Bulwer-Lytton, E.
G. Lady of Lyons; or, Love and
pride
Many sides to a character. *See* Bulwer-
Lytton, E. G. Not so bad as we
seem, or, Many sides to a character.
Money. Comedy. 5 acts
In Bulwer's plays
Bates, A. ed. Drama 16:183
Not so bad as we seem; or, Many sides
to a character. Romantic. 5 acts
In Bulwer's plays
Richelieu; or, The conspiracy. Histori-
cal. 5 acts
In Bulwer's plays
Matthews, J. and Lieder, P. R. eds.
Chief British dramatists
Rightful heir. Melodrama. 5 acts
In Bulwer's plays
Walpole. Historical. 3 acts
In Bulwer's plays
Bunner, Henry Ayler, 1855-1896
Bobby Shaftoe. Operetta. 3 acts
In Three operettas

Bunner, H. A.—*Continued*
Courtship with variations (from Le monde renversé, by M. H. de Bornier).   Comedy. 1 act
  In Matthews, J. B.   Comedies for amateur acting
Seven old ladies of Lavender town.   Operetta. 2 acts
  In Three operettas
    Moses, M. J. ed.   Treasury of plays for children
Three little kittens of the land of pie.   Operetta. 2 acts
  In Three operettas
    Harper's Y P 7:69 D 1, '85

Bunner, Henry C., 1855-1896, and Magnus, Julian
Bad case.   Comedy. 1 act
  In Matthews, J. B.   Comedies for amateur acting

Burgess, Katharine S.
Duetto.   1 act
  In One-act plays for stage and study

Burghlie, James
Lawyer's mistake.   Domestic tragedy. 1 act
  In Smart Set 31 no 1:125

Burke, Charles
Rip Van Winkle; a legend of the Catskills; a romantic drama in two acts, adapted from Washington Irving's Sketch book.   N.Y. French. [1857?]. 12°. 27p.
  Same in Bates, A. ed.   Drama. 19:219

Burleigh, Louise, 1890-, and Bierstadt, E. H., 1891-
Punishment; a play in four acts. . . N.Y. Holt. 1916. 12°. 127p.   Social

Burnett, Dana, 1888
Impromptu.   Comedy. 1 act
  In Bookm. 57:267
It is a strange house.   1925. 188p. 12°. $2.   Individualism. 3 acts
Rain.   Suicide. 1 act
  In Drama 14:20

Burnett, Frances Hodgson, 1849-1924
Little princess.   Juvenile. 3 acts
  In Moses, M. J. ed.   Treasury of plays for children
Racketty-Packetty house
  In Moses, M. J. ed.   Another treasury of plays for children

Burr, Amelia Josephine, 1878-
By the dead waters.   Romantic. 1 scene
  In Plays in the market-place
In the mist.   Romantic. 1 scene
  In Plays in the market-place
Masque of women poets.   1 act
  In Stratford J 1:13
Pixy.   Fairy. 3 parts
  In Hearts awake; The pixy
Point of life; a play in three acts.   Englewood, N.J. Hillside press. 1907. 12°. 88p.   Historical
Shrine.   Romantic. 1 scene
  In Plays in the market-place
Throne room.   Romantic. 1 scene
  In Plays in the market-place

Walled garden.   Romantic. 1 act
  In Plays in the market-place

Burrill, Edgar White
Master Skylark; or, Will Shakespeare's ward: a dramatization of the story by John Bennett.   N.Y. Century. 1916. 12°. 177p. 5 acts
Will Shakespeare's ward.   *See* Burrill, E. W.   Master Skylark; or, Will Shakespeare's ward

Burton, Percy
Day dream in Japan.   Boston. Luce. c1916. 12°. 63p.   Poetic. 1 act

Burton, Richard, 1859
Rahab; a drama in five acts. . . N.Y. Holt. 1906. 18°. 119p.   Biblical
Tatters; a character sketch.   1 act
  In Drama 12:206

Butler, Arthur Gray
Charles I; a tragedy in five acts.   London. Frowde. 1907. 12°. 124p.
Harold; a drama in four acts.   London. Frowde. 1906. 118p.

Butler, Rachel Barton
Mamma's affair; a comedy in three acts.   N.Y. French. c1925. 12°. 103p.

Butterfield, Walton
Next step on.   N.Y. Four seas. 1924. 12°. 34p. 50c 1 act
Tea for six.   Comedy. 1 act
  In Drama 16:134

Byng, Launcelot Alfred Cranmer, 1872-
Salma; a play in three acts.   N.Y. Dutton. 1923. 12°. 110p.

Bynner, Witter, 1881-
Cake, an indulgence.   N.Y. Knopf. 1926. 12°. 169p. 4 acts.   Comedy
Cycle.   Tragedy. 1 act
  In Books of plays
Iphigenia in Tauris.   Tragedy. 1 act
  In Books of plays
Little king.   N.Y. Kennerley. 1914. 12°. 76p.   Louis XVII. 1 act
  Same in Book of plays
    Forum 51:605
Night wind.   Tragedy. 1 act
  In Books of plays
Tiger.   N.Y. Kennerley. 1913. 12°. 48p.   Comedy. 1 act
  Same in Book of plays
    Forum 49:522

Byrne, Lee
Quarry slaves, a drama.   Boston. Lee. 1904. 12°. 31p.   Social. 3 scenes

Byrne, Samuel
Silken Thomas; an Irish historical drama. . . Pittsburgh. The author. [c1918]. 12°. 104p. 5 acts

Cabell, James Branch, 1879-
Jewel merchants, a comedy in one act.   N.Y. McBride. 1921. 12°. 63p. $1.90

Caesar, Arthur
Napoleon's barber.   Comedy. 1 act
  In Shay, F. ed.   Contemporary one-act plays of 1921
    Shay, F. ed.   Twenty contemporary one-act plays (American)

Caigniez, Louis Charles, 1762-1842
Magpie or the maid? A melodrama in three acts. Tr. and altered from the French by I. Pocock. London. Miller. 1815. 8°. 52p.
Voice of nature; a drama in three acts. Tr. and altered from a French melodrama. . . by William Dunlap. . . N.Y. Longworth. 1803. 12°. 46p.

Caillevet, Gaston Armand de, 1869-
Choosing a career (La choix d'une carrière); a play in one act. Tr. by B. N. Clark. N.Y. French. [1915]. 12°. 19p. Farce

Caine, Hall, 1853-
Bondman; a drama. London. Ballantyne. 1906. 12°. 240p. Romantic. 5 acts

Caine, Hall, 1853-, **and Parker, Louis N.,** 1852
Pete; a drama in four acts. London. Collier. 1908. 12°. 164p. Marriage

Calderon, George, 1868-1915
Cinderella. Ibsen pantomine. 3 acts
In Three plays and a pantomine
Cromwell: mall o' monks. Historical. 5 acts
In Three plays and a pantomine
Derelicts. Comedy. 1 act
In Eight one-act plays
Fountain; a comedy in three acts. London. Gowans. 1911. 12°. 161p. (Repertory plays. no. 2)
Same in Three plays and a pantomine
Geminae. Farce. 1 act
In Eight one-act plays
Lamp. Religious. 1 act
In Eight one-act plays
Little stone house. A play in one act. London. Sidgwick. 1913. 12°. 32p. Russian. 1 act
Same in Eight one-act plays
        Shay, F. and Loving, P. eds. Fifty contemporary one-act plays
Longing. Tragedy. 2 scenes
In Eight one-act plays
Maharani of Arakan; a romantic comedy in one act, founded on the story of Sir Rabindranath Tagore. London. Griffiths. 1915. 12°. 64p.
Parkin bros. Comedy. 1 act
In Eight one-act plays
Peace. Farce. 1 act
In Eight one-act plays
Revolt. Labor. 4 acts
In Three plays and a pantomine
Two talismans. Comedy. 1 act
In Eight one-act plays

Calderon, George, 1868-1915, **and Hankin, St. John**
John Thompson, a comedy in three acts. London. Secker. 1913. 12°. 85p.

Caldwell, Eleanor Baird
Tobias and the angel; a play in two acts. Firenze. Succ. B. Seeber. 1925. 52p.

Calhoun, Dorothy D.
Pretties (All her life). Marital. 1 act
In Touchstone 6:26

Calthrop, Dion Clayton, 1878-
Gate of dreams; a play in one act. N.Y. French. 1914. 12°. 23p.   Civil war

Calthrop, Dion Clayton, 1878- **and Barker, Granville,** 1877-
Harlequinade; an excursion. Boston. Little. 1918. 12°. 87p. $1.25. 7 scenes

Calvert, George Henry, 1803-1889
Arnold and André. An historical drama. Boston. Little. 1864. 12°. 95p. Boston. Lee & Shepard. 1876. 12° 95p. 3 acts
Brangomar, a tragedy. Boston. Lee & Shepard. [c1883]. 12°. 110p. 5 acts
Count Julian; a tragedy. Baltimore. Hickman. 1840. 12°. 69p. 5 acts
Like unto like. Comedy. 3 acts
In Comedies
Maid of Orleans; an historical tragedy. Printed for private use. Cambridge [Mass.]. Riverside press. 1873. 12°. 134p. 5 acts
Mirabeau; an historical drama. Cambridge. Riverside press. 1873. 12°. 103p. 3 acts
Will and the way. Comedy. 5 acts
In Comedies

Cameron, George, 1868-1915
Billy; a comedy in three acts. N.Y. French. c1924. 90p.

Cameron, Margaret, 1867-
Burglar. Comedy. 1 act
In Comedies in miniature
Committee on matrimony. Comedy. 1 act
In Comedies in miniature
        McClure 21:659
Her neighbor's creed. Comedy. 1 act
In Comedies in miniature
In a street-car; monologue. 1 scene
In Comedies in miniature
Kleptomaniac. Comedy. 1 act
In Comedies in miniature
Miss Doulton's orchids. Comedy. 2 parts
In Comedies in miniature
P. A. I. L. W. R. Monologue. 1 scene
In Comedies in miniature
Patron of art. Monologue. 1 scene
In Comedies in miniature
Pipe of peace. Comedy. 1 act
In Comedics in miniature
        Knickbocker, E. Van B. ed. Twelve plays
Piper's pay; a comedy in one act. N.Y. French. c1905. 12°. 31p.
Teeth of the gift horse. N.Y. French. c1909. 12°. 31p. Comedy. 1 act
Unexpected guests. Monologue. 1 scene
In Comedies in miniature

Cameron, Margaret, and Rector, Jessie L.
White elephant. N.Y. French. 1916. 12°. 18p. 1 act

Cammaerts, Émile
Adoration of the soldiers (L'adoration des soldats). London. Longmans. [1916]. 4°. 55p. World war. 1 act

Campbell, Joseph, 1879-
Judgment; a play in two acts. Dublin. Maunsel. 1912. 12°. 35p. Irish Turn-out. Historical. 1 act
In Irish R 2:317

Candler, Martha
Faith; a miracle play (in one act). N.Y. Century. c1924. 33p.

Canfield, Mary Cass
Lackeys of the moon; a play in one act. N.Y. Hackett. 1923. 12°. 47p. Comedy

Cann, Louise Gebhard
Life is always the same. Retribution. 1 act
In Drama 9 no 34:1

Cannan, Gilbert, 1884-
Everybody's husband. N.Y. Huebsch. 1919. 12°. 35p. Social 1 act
Same in Seven plays
Fat kine and lean. Death. 1 act
In Seven plays
Gloves; a fragment of the eternal duet. Comedy. 1 act
In Theatre Arts M 4:160
In the park. Comedy. 1 act
In Seven plays
James and John; a play in one act. Boston. Phillips. [c1920]. 12°. 30p. Social
Same in Four plays
Clark, B. H. ed. Representative one-act plays by British and Irish authors
Mary's wedding; a play in one act. Boston. Phillips. [c1920]. 12°. 24p. Psychological
Same in Four plays
Shay, F. and Loving, P. eds. Fifty contemporary one-act plays
Miles Dixon; a play in two acts. Boston. Phillips. [c1920]. 12°. 43p. Social
Same in Four plays
Pierrot in hospital. Harlequinade. 1 act
In Seven plays
Polite art of conversation. *See* Cannan, G. W. B., or the Polite art of conversation
Same story. Problem. 1 act
In Seven plays
Short way with authors. A burlesque in one act. Boston. Phillips. c1920. 24°. 34p.
Same in Four plays
Someone to whisper to. Comedy. 1 act
In Seven plays
W. B., or the Polite art of conversation. Comedy. 1 act
In Seven plays

Cannon, Charles James, 1800-1860
Better late than never. Comedy. 2 acts
In Dramas
Dolores. Tragedy. 5 acts
In Dramas
Oath of office; a tragedy. N.Y. Taylor. 1854. 12°. 91p. 4 acts
Same in Dramas

Scuptor's daughter. Tragedy. 5 acts
In Dramas

Capek, Karel M., 1880-
Makropoulos secret. . . N.Y. Luce. [c1925]. 12°. 165p. $1.50. Longevity. 3 acts
Pistol of the beg. Curse. 3 acts
In Poet Lore 34:475
R. U. R. (Rossum's universal robots) a fantastic melodrama . . . Garden City. Doubleday. 1923. 12°. 187p. 4 acts
Same in Mantle, B. ed. Best plays of 1922-23 (condensed)
Solstice. Family conflict. 3 acts
In Poet Lore 35:475

Capek, Karel M., 1880-, **and Capek, Josef**
"And so ad infinitum" (The life of the insects) An entomological review in three acts, a prologue and an epilogue. The authorized translation from the Czech by Paul Selver. Freely adapated for the English stage by Nigel Playfair and Clifford Bax. London. Milford. 1923. 8°. 69p. (The play is known in the U.S. as "The world we live in")
World we live in. *See* Capek, K. and Capek, J: "And so ad infinitum."

Capus, Alfred, 1858-
Adventurer (l'aventurier). Comedy. 4 acts
In Drama 4 no 16:529
Brignol and his daughter (Brignol et sa fille); a comedy in three acts. . . Tr. by B. N. Clark. N.Y. French. [c1915]. 12°. 72p.
My tailor (Mon tailleur). Comedy. 1 act
In Shay, F. ed. Plays for strolling mummers
Smart Set 54 no 2:75

Carb, David, 1885-
Voice of the people; a play in three acts. Boston. Four Seas. 1912. 12°. 129p. Industrial

Carb, David, 1885-, **and Eaton, Walter P.,** 1878-
Queen Victoria; a play in seven episodes. N.Y. Dutton. 1922. 12°. 213p. Historical

Carey, Alice V.
New names for old; a safety first play in one act. N.Y. French. 1923. 12°. 17p. 3 acts

Carleton, John Louis, 1861-
Coom-na-Goppel. A drama in five acts for male characters only. Chicago. Dramatic pub. co. c1906. 12°. 51p. Melodrama
Medieval Hun; a five act historical drama. N.Y. Cornhill. 1921. 12°. 165p. $1.50
More sinned against than sinning. An original Irish drama in a prologue and three acts. Chicago. Dramatic pub. co. c1883. 12°. 26p. Melodrama

Carman, Bliss, 1861-, **and King, Mary Perry**
Children of the year. Masque. 1 scene
In Earth deities

Dance diurnal. Masque. 1 scene
In Earth deities
Daughter's of dawn. A lyrical pageant. . . N.Y. Kennerley. 1913. 12°.
118p. Historic women. 9 scenes

Carpenter, Edward, 1844-
Moses: a drama in five acts. London.
Moxon. ₁1875₁. 12°. 126p. (Republished
under title "Promised land", in 1910)
Promised land; a drama of a people's deliverance in five acts (in the Elizabethan style). London. Sonnenschein. 1910. 12°. 126p. Moses

Carpenter, Edward Childs, 1872-
Bab; a farcical comedy in four acts. N.Y.
French. c1925. 12°. 117p.
Cinderella-man; a comedy in four acts.
₁N.Y. Tower Bros. Stationery Co.
c1915₁. 12°. 100p.
Prairie doll. Comedy. 1 act
In One-act plays for stage and study
ser 2
Three bears; a comedy in three acts.
N.Y. French. c1926. 12°. 120p.

Carpenter, Rhys, 1889-
Tragedy of Etarre; a poem. N.Y.
Sturgis. 1912. 8°. 137p. 3 acts

Carpio, Lope Felix de Vega
King, the greatest alcade. Comedy. 3
acts
In Poet Lore 29:379

Carr, Joseph William Comyns, 1849-1916
Faust. *See* Phillips, S. and Carr, J. C.
Faust
King Arthur; a drama in prologue and
four acts. . . N.Y. Macmillan. 1895.
18°. 67p. Legendary
Tristram and Iseult; a drama in four
acts. N.Y. Knickerbocker. ₁c1906₁.
8°. 71p. Legendary

Carrión, Miguel Ramos, and Aza, Vital
Zaragueta. Comedy. 2 acts
In Poet Lore 33:1

Carroll, John S.
Looms of the gods; a drama of reincarnation. London. Constable. 1914.
12°. 88p. 5 acts

Carroll, Lewis, 1832-1898
Alice's adventures in Wonderland. *See*
Gerstenberg, Alice. Alice in wonderland

Carson, Murray, joint author. *See* Craigie, P. M. T. and Carson, M. The
bishop's move

Carson, W. G. B.
Tea. 1 act
In Baker's anthology of one-act plays.

Carton, R. C., pseud. *See* Crichett, R. C.

Carus, Paul, 1852-
Buddha; a drama in three acts and four
interludes. . . Chicago. Open Court.
1911. 12°. 68p. Religious
K'ung Fu Tze; a dramatic poem.
Chicago. Open Court. 1915. 12°. 72p.
Historical. 1 act

New moon. English diplomacy and the
triple entente. A phantasmagoria in
one act, by Barrie Americanus Neutralis. Chicago. Open Court pub. co.
1916. 8°. 36p.

Cauldwell, Samuel Milbank, d. 1916
Chocolate cake and black sand. Comedy. 1 act
In Chocolate cake and black sand
Invention of the rat trap. Comedy. 1 act
In Chocolate cake and black sand
Undoing of Giant Hotstoff. Comedy. 1
act
In Chocolate cake and black sand

Cavanah, Frances
Mr. Bunny's prize. Juvenile. 1 act
In Jagendorf, M. A. ed. One act plays
for young folks

Caverly, Robert Boodey, 1806-1887
Chocorua in the mountains. ₁N.E.₁. An
historical drama, ₁1698-1768₁. Boston.
Author. 1885. 12°. p. 251-341. Indian
Same in Battle of the bush
King Philip (N.E.); an historical drama,
₁1648-1698₁. Boston. Author. 1884. 8°.
p. 127-190. 3 acts
Same in Battle of the bush
Last night of a nation. ₁N.E.₁. an historical drama, ₁1585-1637₁. Boston. Author. 1884. 12°. 574
Same in Battle of the bush
Miantonimo ₁N.E.₁. An historical drama
₁1637-1649₁. . . Boston. Author. 1884.
12°. 124p.
Same in Battle of the bush
Regicides ₁N.E.₁. An historical drama.
₁1646-1676₁. Boston. Author. 1884.
12°. p. 193-247. 3 acts
Same in Battle of the bush

Cawein, Madison Julius, 1865-
Cabestaing. Tragedy. 3 acts
In Shadow garden and other plays
House of fear. Mystery. 3 scenes
In Shadow garden and other plays
Poet, the fool and the fairies, a lyrical
eclogue. Boston. Small, Maynard.
₁c1912₁. 12°. 259p.
Shadow garden. Fantasy. 3 scenes
In Shadow garden and other plays
Witch, a miracle. 3 scenes
In Shadow garden and other plays

Cayzer, Charles William (Whitworth Wynne, pseud.), 1869-
David and Bathshua, a drama in five acts.
N.Y. Knickerbocker. 1903. 12°. 100p.
Biblical
Same in By way of the gate v 2
Donna Marina. Historical. 4 acts
In By the way of the gate v 2
Poetry R 2:271; 3:22
Undine; a tragedy in four acts by Whitworth Wynne ₁pseud₁. N.Y. Reynolds.
1908. 12°. 74p.
Same in By way of the gate v 2

Cecil, K. N. D.
Historical tragedy of Nero. London.
Kegan Paul. 1904. 12°. 159p. Tragedy. 5 acts

Chaloner, John Armstrong, 1862-
Battle of the millionaires. *See* Chaloner,
J. A. Robbery under law; or, The
battle of the millionaires
Hazard and of the die; a drama in three
acts. Last days of Roman republic.
Roanoke Rapids, N.C. Palmetto
press. 1915. 8°. 59p. (with Serpent of
old Nile). Julius Caesar
Same in Robbery under law
Robbery under law; or, The battle of the
millionairies; a play in three acts and
three scenes., time, 1887. . . Roanoke
Rapids, N.C. Palmetto press. [c1915].
8°. 97p. Social
"Saul"; a tragedy in three acts. . .
Roanoke Rapids, N.C. Palmetto press.
1915. 8°. 66p.
Saul and David; a tragedy in two acts. . .
(with "Saul"). Roanoke Rapids, N.C.
Palmetto press. 1915. 67p. 8°. 50c
Serpent of old Nile; a drama in three
acts, time 48 B.C. . . Roanoke Rapids, N.C. Palmetto press. 1915. 8°.
66p. (with Hazard of the die). 50c
66p. Caesar and Cleopatria

Chamberlain, George Agnew, 1879-
Lost (a play in seven settings). N.Y.
Putnam. 1926. 12°. 239p.

Chambers, Charles Haddon, 1860-
Awakening; a play in four acts. Boston.
Baker. 1903. 12°. 160p. Comedy
Captain Swift; a comedy drama in 'four
acts. N.Y. French. [c1902]. 12°. 69p.
Idler; a play in four acts. . . N.Y.
French. c1902. 12°. 64p. Melodrama
Open gate. An original domestic drama
in one act. Chicago. Dramatic pub.
co. [189—?]. 12°. 19p.
Passers by; a play in four acts. London.
Duckworth. 1913. 12°. 139p. Social
Saving grace. A comedy in three acts.
N.Y. Brentano's. 1919. 12°. 104p.
Sir Anthony; a comedy of the outskirts.
N.Y. French. 1909. 12°. 118p. 3 acts
Tyranny of tears; a comedy in four acts.
Boston. Baker. 1902. 12°. 152p.

Chandler, Lilian F.
At the window. N.Y. French. 1915. 12°.
16p. 1 act
Patriot girl; a patriotic comedy in two
acts. Philadelphia. Penn. pub. co.
1914. 12°. 23p.

Cháng Kwohpin
Compared tunic. Chinese. 4 acts
In Chinese repository 18:116

Chapin, Harold, 1886-1915
Art and opportunity; a comedy in three
acts. N.Y. French. c1924. 12°. 115p.
Same in Comedies
Augustus in search of a father. London.
Gowans. 1911. 24°. 42p. (Repertory
plays. no. 4). Comedy. 1 act
Autocrat of the coffee-stall. Soldiers.
1 act
In Three one-act plays
Theatre Arts M 5:125

Dumb and the blind; a play in one-act.
London. Gowans. 1914. 24°. 40p.
(Repertory plays. no. 9) Comedy. 1
act
Elaine; a comedy in three acts. N.Y.
French. c1924. 12°. 177p.
Same in Comedies
Innocent and Annabel. Comedy. 1 act
In Three one-act plays
It's the poor that 'elps the poor. Social
1 act
In Three one-act plays
Marriott, J. W. ed. One-act plays
of to-day ser 2
Marriage of Columbine; a comedy in four
acts. N.Y. French. c1924. 12°. p. 179-
241
Same in Comedies
Muddle-Annie, a play in one act. Lon-
don. Gowans & Gray. 1921. 12°. 70p.
(Repertory plays. no. 10). Comedy
New morality; a comedy in three acts.
N.Y. French. 1924. 12°. 55p.
Same in Comedies
Philosopher of Butterbiggins; a play in
one act. Boston. Phillips. 1921. 12°.
30p. Domestic
Same in Leonard, S. A. ed. Atlantic
book of modern plays

Chapin, Harry Lorenzo, 1872-1917
Aggression won. Comedy. 1 act
In Poems and plays
Eccentric philosopher. Melodrama. 4
acts
In Poems and plays
Forsaken. Tragedy. 3 acts
In Poems and plays
Love test. Comedy. 1 act
In Poems and plays
Royal muse. Militant. 3 acts
In Poems and plays
Semeramus. Religious. 6 acts
In Poems and plays
White slave. Comedy. 2 acts
In Poems and plays

Chapman, John Jay, 1862-
Christmas in Leipsic. Juvenile. 1 act
In Four plays for children
Christmas once more. Juvenile cantata.
2 pts.
In Neptune's isle and other plays for
children
Cupid and Psyche. Mythological. 3 acts
In Cupid and Psyche
Family quarrel. Juvenile. 2 acts
In Neptune's isle and other plays for
children
Hector's farewell. Mythological. 1 act
In Homeric scenes
Hermits. Juvenile comedy. 3 acts
In Four plays for children
King Ithuriel. Juvenile. 5 acts
In Four plays for children
Lafayette. Historical. 2 scenes
In Cupid and Psyche
Lost prince. Juvenile. 3 acts
In Four plays for children

Maid's forgiveness; a play. N.Y. Moffat. 1908. 12°. 93p. Mediaeval. 3 acts

Neptune's isle. Juvenile. 3 acts
In Neptune's isle and other plays for children

Romulus and Remus. Juvenile. 2 acts
In Cupid and Psyche

Sausage from Bologna; a comedy in four acts. N.Y. Moffat. 1909. 12°. 113p.

Treason and death of Benedict Arnold; a play for a Greek theatre. N.Y. Moffat. 1910. 12°. 76p. Historical. 2 acts

Two philosophers: a quaint sad comedy. Boston. Cupples. [c1892]. 8°. 37p. 5 acts

Wilfrid the young. Juvenile. 3 acts
In Neptune's isle and other plays for children

Wrath of Achilles. Mythological. 6 acts
In Homeric scenes

Chatterji, Tapanmohan
Light-bearer. Symbolic. 1 scene
In Drama 8:383

Chatterton, Nathan G.
Cash—$2,000. Temptation. 1 act
In Drama 15:78

Chekhov, Anton P., 1860-1904
Anniversary. Comedy. 1 act
In Plays by Anton Tchekoff ser 2
Three sisters and other plays

Bear. *See* Chekhov, A. P. Boor

Boor; a comedy in one act. N.Y. French. [c1915]. 12°. 20p.
Same in Cherry orchard and other plays
Plays by Anton Tchekoff ser 2
Lewis, B. R. ed. Contemporary one-act plays
Shay, F. and Loving, P. eds. Fifty contemporary one-act plays

Cherry garden. *See* Chekhov, A. P. Cherry orchard

Cherry orchard; a comedy in four acts. . . N.Y. Brentano's. c1922. 12°. 80p. *also* New Haven. Whaples. 1908. 8°. 72p. Russian life
Same in Cherry orchard and other plays
Plays by Anton Tchekoff ser 2
Two plays
Dickinson, T. R. ed. Chief contemporary dramatists
Sayler, O. M. ed. Moscow art theatre series of Russian plays ser 1

Demon. *See* Chekhov, A. P. Uncle Vanya

Ivanhov, (Ivanhoff). Character. 4 acts
In Plays
Three sisters and other plays
Sayler, O. M. ed. Moscow art theatre series of Russian plays ser 2

Jubilee. Satire. 1 act
In Bechhofer, C. E. trans. Five Russian plays
Poet Lore 31:616

Marriage proposal. (Proposal); a comedy in one act. N.Y. French. c1914. 12°. 18p.
In Cherry orchard and other plays
Plays by Anton Tchekoff ser 2
Bates, A. ed. Drama 18:175
Knickerbocker, E. Van B. ed. Twelve plays
Thomas, C. S. ed. Atlantic book of junior plays
International. (N.Y.) 8:150

On the high road. (On the highway). Character. 1 act
In Plays by Anton Tchekoff ser 2
Three sisters and other plays
Shay, Frank. Twenty-five short plays, international
Drama 6 no 22:294

On the highway. *See* Chekhov, A. P. On the high road

Proposal. *See* Chekhov, A. Marriage proposal

Sea-gull; a play in four acts. . . London. Hendersons. 1915. 12°. 74p. Character
Same in Cherry orchard and other plays
Plays
Two plays
Moses, M. J. ed. Representative continental dramas
Pierce and Matthews, eds. Masterpieces of modern drama v 2 (abridged)
Poet Lore 24:1

Swan-song. Stage. 1 act
In Plays
Three sisters and other plays
Smith, A. M. ed. Short plays by representative authors

Three sisters; a drama in four acts. . . N.Y. Brentanos. c1922. 12°. 89p. Russian life
Same in Plays by Anton Tchekoff ser 2
Three sisters and other plays
Sayler, O. N. ed. Moscow art theatre series of Russian plays ser 1

Tragedian in spite of himself. Farce. 1 act
In Plays by Anton Tchekoff ser 2
Poet Lore 33:268

Uncle Vanya. (Demon) Russian life. 4 acts
In Cherry orchard and other plays
Plays
Sayler, O. M. ed. Moscow art theatre series of Russian plays ser 1
Poet Lore 33:317

Unwilling martyr; a jest in one act
In Three sisters, and other plays

Wedding. Comedy. 1 act
In Plays by Anton Tchekoff ser 2
Three sisters and other plays
Bechhofer, C. E. tr. Five Russian plays

Wood demon; a comedy in four acts. . . London. Chatto. 1926. 12°. 120p.

Cheltnam, Charles Smith

Christmas eve in a watchhouse. A farcical sketch in one act. London. Lacy. [18-?]. 12°. 67p. (Lacy's acting edition of play. v. 90)

Deborah; or, the Jewish maiden's wrong. A drama in three acts. London. Lacy. n.d. 12°. 38p. (Lacy's acting edition of plays. v. 63) Tragedy

Dinner for nothing: an original farce in one act. London. Lacy. [18—]. 12°. 18p. (Lacy's acting edition of plays. v. 67)

Edendale: an original drama in three acts. London. Lacy. n.d. 12°. 42p. (Lacy's acting edition of plays. v. 84) Civil war

Fairy's father: an original dramatic sketch in one act. London. Lacy. n.d. 12°. 14p. (Lacy's acting edition of plays. v. 54) Comedy

Fireside diplomacy. Comedietta. 1 act
In Scott, C. ed. Drawing-room plays

Garden party: an original dramatic sketch. London. French. n.d. 12°. 12p. Comedy. 1 act

Jewish maiden's wrong. *See* Cheltnam, C. S. Deborah; or, the Jewish maiden's wrong

Leatherlungos the great, how he storm'd, reign'd, and mizzled. An entirely new and original extravaganza. London. French. n.d. 12°. 32p. (Lacy's acting edition of plays. v. 96) 5 scenes

Lesson in love. A comedy in three acts. London. Lacy.'[18—]. 12°. 44p. (Lacy's acting edition of plays. v. 94)

Little madcap: a comic drama in one act. London. French. [18—]. 12°. 22p. (French's acting edition of plays. v. 114)

Lucky escape! a comic drama in one act (from the French). London. Lacy. [1861]. 12°. 20p.

Matchmaker. A farcical comedy. London. Lacy. [18—?]. 12°. 38p. (Lacy's acting edition of plays. v. 93)

Mrs. Green's snug little business: an original farce in one act. London. Lacy. [18—]. 12°. 18p. (Lacy's acting edition of plays. v. 65)

Railway adventure; in one act. Founded on a dramatic sketch by Eugène Verconsin, entitled, En Wagon. London. French. n.d. 12°. 12p. Comedy

Shadow of a crime: a drama in three acts. London. Lacy. n.d. 12°. 56p. (Lacy's acting edition of plays. v. 86) Melodrama

Six years after. *See* Cheltnam, C. S. Ticket-of-leave man's wife; or, Six years after

Slowtop's engagement. A farce in one act from the French. London. Lacy. [18—]. 12°. 21p. (Lacy's acting edition of plays. v. 53)

Ticket-of-leave man's wife; or, Six years after. A new and original drama in three acts. London. Lacy. n.d. 12°. 72p. (Lacy's acting edition of plays. v. 69) Melodrama

Chenevix, Richard, 1774-1830

Henry the seventh. Tragedy. 5 acts
In Two plays

Mantuan revels. Comedy. 5 acts
In Two plays

Cheney, Anne Cleveland

Nameless one (First born); a play in three acts. N.Y. Stokes. [c1916]. 12°. 131p. Tragedy

Cheng-Chin Hsiung

Marvellous romance of Wen Chun-Chin. Chinese. 1 act
In Poet Lore 35:298

Thrice promised bride. Chinese. 1 act
In Shay, Frank. Twenty-five short plays, international
Golden Bk 2:230
Theatre Arts M 7:329

Chesterton, Mrs. Frances Alice (Mrs. Gilbert K. Chesterton), 1875-

Piers Plowman's pilgrimage; a morality play. . . N.Y. French. 1925. 25p. 1 act

Chesterton, Gilbert Keith, 1873-

Magic; a fantastic comedy. N.Y. Putnam. 1913. 12°. 88p. 3 acts

Child, Francis James, 1825-1896

Il pescaballo. Comedy. 11 scenes
In Bibelot 17:373

Chin Lin Chen

Son left in the plantation of mulberry trees. Chinese. 1 act
In Poet Lore 33:595

Chirikov, Eugen

Chosen people; a drama in four acts. . . N.Y. Maccabean pub. co. [1907]. 4°. 33p. Jews

Chubb, Percival

Old year and the new. Fantasy. 1 act
In Drama 10:110

Church, Virginia

Pierrot by the light of the moon. Fantasy. 1 act
In Drama 9 no 33:139

Very social service. Satire. 1 act
In Drama 15:54

What men live by. Allegory. 2 scenes. (From story of L. N. Tolstoi)
In Law, F. H. ed. Modern plays, short and long
Drama 12:33

Churchill, Winston, 1871-

Dr. Jonathan; a play in three acts. N.Y. Macmillan. 1919. 12°. 159p. Sociological

Title-mart; a comedy in three acts. N.Y. Macmillan. 1905. 12°. 218p.

Claridge, C. J., and Soutar, Robert

Fast coach. An original farce. In one act. London. Lacy. n.d. 12°. 17p. (Lacy's acting edition of plays. v. 4 no. 51)

Clark, Hollis
Taught by mail; a play in three acts. Boseman. Montana. The author. 1917. 12°. 115p. Sociological
Clark, John
Fredegonde, Queen of the Franks; a chronical play in five acts. Capetown. Darter bros. 1913. 12°. 211p.
Hannibal; a drama in five acts. London. Simpkin. 1908. 97p.
Clarke, Amy Key
Persephone. 1 act
In Clarke, A. K. ed. Three one-act plays
Clarke, Dwight Lancelot, 1885-
Desert smoke. Allegory. 1 act
In Boston theatre guild plays. 1924
Passing of Pan; a metrical drama in a prologue and four acts. San Fran. Philopolis press. 1915. 12°. 65p. Mythological
Clarke, Henry Savile, 1841-1893
Hugger-Mugger; a farce in one act. N.Y. French. [191—]. 12°. 23p.
Lyrical lover. A new and original comedietta, in one act. London. French. [18—?]. 12°. 15p.
Claudel, Paul, 1868-
City: a play... Tr. by John Strong Newberry. New Haven. Yale press. 1920. 12°. 115p. Sociological. 3 acts
Hostage (L'Otage): a drama... New Haven Yale press. 1917. 12°. 167p. Napoleonic. 3 acts
Proteus. A satiric drama in two acts. *In* Broom 1:124-36, 268-78, 316-46
Tête-d'Or. A play in three acts. Tr. by John Strong Newberry. New Haven. Yale press. 1919. 8°. 178p. Tragedy
Tidings brought to Mary; a mystery... New Haven. Yale press. 1916. 12°. 171p. 4 acts
Clemenceau, Georges Eugene Benjamin, 1841-
Veil of happiness; a play in one act... N.Y. Priv. printed. 1920. 12°. 49p. Chinese
Clements, Claudine E.
Troubadour's dream; a play for Christmas-tide in one act and three episodes and an epilogue
In Drama 16:57
Clements, Colin Campbell, 1894-
By the Sumida river. Japan. 1 act
In Poet Lore 31:166
All on a summer's day; a charming trifle. 1 act
In Shay, F. ed. Plays for strolling mumners
Cherry-blossom river. Japan. 2 scenes
In Shay, Frank. Twenty-five short plays, international
Poet Lore 31:159
Columbine. Harlequinade. 1 act
In Plays for a folding theatre
Shay, F. ed. Treasury of plays for women
Poet Lore 31:588

Desert. Tragedy. 1 act
In Plays for a folding theatre
Father. Japan. 3 scenes
In Poet Lore 31:187
Gammer·Gurton's needle; a modern adaptation of the famous old comedy... N.Y. French. c1922. 12°. 62p.
Four who were blind. World war. 1 act
In Plays for pagans
Shay, F. ed. Treasury of plays for men
Growing old together. Japan. 1 act
In Poet Lore 31:176
Haiduc. Roumanian. 4 scenes
In Plays for pagans
Harlequin. Harlequinade. 1 act
In Plays for pagans
Poet Lore 31:579
Job; a play in one act, adapted... N.Y. French. c1923. 36p. Biblical
Life is a dream. Japan. 1 act
In Poet Lore 31:204
Stratford monthly ns 2:133
Man and his wife. Japan. 1 act
In Poet Lore 31:197
Modern harlequinade in three plays: Harlequin; Columbine; Return of Harlequin. 3 one-act plays
In Poet Lore 31:579
Moon tide. Sea. 1 act
In Plays for a folding theatre
Pierrot in Paris. Morality. 1 act
In Plays for a folding theatre
Return of Harlequin. Harlequinade. 1 act
In Plays for a folding theatre
Poet Lore 31:596
Seven plays of old Japan. Cherry-blossom river; By the Sumida river; Growing old together; Father; Man and his wife; Life is a dream
In Poet Lore 31:159
Siege. Tragedy. 1 act
In Plays for a folding theatre
Cohen, H. L. ed. More one-act plays by modern authors
Shay, F. ed. Treasury of plays for women
Spring! Comedy. 1 act
In Plays for pagans
Star dust path. Japan. 1 act
In Poet Lore 31:181
Sumida Gawa, adapted from the Japanese Noh drama by Motomasa. 1 act
In Stratford J 2:29
Three lepers of Suk-el-Gareb. Tragedy. 1 act
In Plays for a folding theatre
Yesterday: a little comedy for Victorians. 1 act
In Plays for pagans
Loving, P. ed. Ten minute plays
You; a play with a happy ending. N.Y. French. c1924. 8°. 21p. Youth. 3 acts
Same in Poet Lore 29:472

Clements, Colin Campbell, 1894-, and Saunders, J. M., 1897-
Love in a French kitchen.   Mediaeval farce. 1 act
In Poet Lore 28:722

Clements, Guy L.
Deal in ducks; a play in three acts.   Atchison, Kan. Hellener. 1921. 12°. 68p. 35c   Comedy
Spirits and spooks; a farce in one act. Chicago. Denison. 1922. 12°. 23p. 25c

Cleugh, Dennis
Pink thrift; a play in three acts.   London. Erskine Macdonald. [1918]. 12°. 112p.   Tragedy
Violet under the snow (a play for Christmastide). . . London.   Simpkin. [c1915]. 12°. 26p. 1 act
Same in Drama 13:52

Clews, Henry, Jr.
Mumbo jumbo.   N.Y. Boni. [1923]. 12°. 275p.   Satire. 4 acts

Clifford, Helen C.
Alice's blighted profession, a sketch for girls.   N.Y. Fitzgerald publishing corporation. [c1919]. 12°. 18p.   Comedy. 1 act
That parlor maid; a comedy in three acts. N.Y. Fitzgerald pub. corporation. c1922. 12°. 42p.
Wait and see; a comedy-drama in three acts.   N.Y. Fitzgerald pub. corporation. c1919. 12°. 30p.
Whose widow; a comedy in one act. N.Y. Fitzgerald pub. corporation. c1919. 12°. 18p.

Clifford, Lucy Lane (Mrs. W. K. Clifford)
Hamilton's second marriage.   Romantic. 4 acts
In Plays
Honeymoon tragedy: a comedy in one act.   London. French. 1904. 12°. 14p.
Likeness of the night; a modern play in four acts.   N.Y. Macmillan. 1900. 12°. 90p.   Social
Same in Anglo-Saxon R 4:38
Long duel; a serious comedy in four acts. N.Y. Lane. 1901. 12°. 151p.
Same in Fortn 76 sup 1
Modern way.   Comedy. 4 acts
In Plays
Searchlight; a play in one act. . . N.Y. French. c1925. 12°. 21p.   Situation
Same in 19 Cent 53:159
Thomas and the princess.   Romantic. 4 acts
In Plays
Wild proxy; a tragic-comedy of today. . . N.Y. Cassell. [c1893]. 12°. 288p.
Woman alone.   N.Y. Scribner. 1915. 12°. 77p.   Domestic. 3 acts
Same in 19 Cent 75:1144

Clinton, Inez Funk
Resurrection of Peter; a short drama for Easter. . . Boston. Pilgrim press. [c1925]. 12°. 17p. 1 act

Coakley, Thomas Francis, 1880-
Discovery of America; a pageant. . . N.Y. Frank Meaney. [c1917]. 12°. 59p. 1 act

Cobb, Lucy M.
Gaius and Gaius, Jr; a comedy of plantation days
In Koch, F. N. ed.   Carolina folk plays ser 2

Cochran, Eve Owen
Wilderness rose, a play in four acts. . . Boston. Gorham press. c1916. 12°. 72p. New England

Cohan, George Michael, 1878-
Broadway Jones; a comedy in four acts. N.Y. French. [c1923]. 12°. 122p.
"Hit-the-trail" Holliday; a comedy in four acts. . . N.Y. Cohan & Harris. c1916. 12°. 147p.
Seven keys to Baldpate; a mysterious melodramatic farce, based upon the novel Seven keys to Baldpate by Earl Derr Biggers. [n.p.] c1914. 8°. 125p.

Cohan, George Michael, 1878-, and Marcin, Max, 1879-
House of glass; a drama in four acts. [N.Y.] Cohan & Harris. c1916. 8°. 128p.   Melodrama

Coit, Henry A.
Arbitrators; a play in three acts.   Boston. Badger. [c1921]. 12°. 92p.
War's end; a play in one act.   Cyde Browne Co. Los Angeles. 1917. 50c

Coleridge, Samuel Taylor, 1772-1834
Death of Wallenstein.   Tragedy. 5 acts
In Poetical works
Fall of Robespierre.   Historical. 3 acts
In Poetical works
Osorio.   Tragedy. (Incomplete)
In Poetical works
Piccolomini.   Tragedy. 5 acts
In Poetical works
Remorse; a tragedy in 5 acts.   London. Pople. 1813. 8°. 78p.
Wallenstein.   Pt. 1. Piccolomini.   Tragedy. 5 acts.   Pt. 2. Death of Wallenstein.   Tragedy. 5 acts. Tr. from Schiller
In Poetical works
Zapolya.   Christmas. 2 Pts.
In Poetical works

Colman, George (younger), 1762-1836
Actor of all work; or, The first and second floor.   A farce. In one act. . . N.Y. Murden. 1822. 12°. 24p.
Africans; or, War, love, and duty.   Slave trade. 3 acts
In Cumberland's British Theatre v 43 no 2
Banquet gallery.   *See* Colman, G. Feudal times; or, The banquet-gallery
Battle of Hexham; a comedy in three acts.   Dublin. Longman. 1808. 12°. 55p.
Same in Cumberland's British theatre v 37 no 7
              Inchbald, Mrs. ed.   British theatre v 13
              Inchbald, Mrs. ed.   Theatre v 2

Blue Beard; or Female curiosity; a dramatick romance. London. Woodfall. 1798. 8°. 58p. 2 acts
Same in Dramatic works v 4
   Oxberry, W. New English drama v 21 no 3
   Cumberland's British theatre. v 39

Blue devils; a farce in one act. Printed by W. Burton. London. 1808. 8°. 40p.
Same in Cumberland's British theatre v 39 no 1
   Oxberry, W. ed. New English drama v 15 no 1

Englishman's fireside. *See* Colman, G. John Bull, or The Englishman's fireside

Female curiosity. *See* Colman, G. Blue Beard; or, Female curiosity

Feudal times; or, The banquet-gallery; a drama. London. Woodfall. ₁1799₁. 8°. 55p. Melodrama. 2 acts

First and second floor. *See* Colman, G. Actor of all work; or, The first and second floor

Gay deceivers; or, More laugh than love, a farce, in two acts. . . London. Cawthorn. 1808. 12°. 46p.

Giant-mountains. *See* Colman, G. Gnome-king; or, the Giant mountains

Gnome-king; or, the Giant-Mountains; a dramatick legend in two acts. London. Miller. 1819. 8°. 55p.

Heir at law; a comedy in five acts. . . Dublin. Byrne. 1800. 12°. 66p.
Same in Dramatic works v 3
   Cumberland's British theatre v 38 no 1
   Inchbald, Mrs. ed. British theatre v 14
   Inchbald, Mrs. ed. Theatre v 2

Inkle and Yarico; an opera in three acts. London. G. G. F. & J. Robinson. 1792. 8°. 72p.
Same in Dramatic works v 2
   British drama v 2:640
   Cumberland's British theatre v 16 no 6
   Inchbald, Mrs. ed. British theatre v 15
   Inchbald, Mrs. ed. Theatre v 8

Iron chest; a play in three acts. . . London. Cadell. 1796. 107p. Melodrama
Same in Cumberland's British theatre v 35 no 3
   Inchbald, Mrs. ed. British theatre v 3
   Inchbald, Mrs. ed. Theatre v 2

John Bull; or the Englishman's fireside; a comedy in five acts. London. Longman. 1805. 8°. 100p.
In Dramatic works v 1
   Cumberland's British theatre v 36 no 6

Inchbald, Mrs. ed. British theatre v 1
Inchbald, Mrs. ed. Theatre. v 5
Law of Java: a play in three acts. London. Simpkin & Marshall. 1822. 8°. 94p. Melodrama. 3 acts
Same in Dramatic works v 4

Long stories. *See* Colman, G. We fly by night; or, Long stories

Love laughs at locksmiths: a comic opera, in two acts. . . N.Y. Longworth. 1808. 12°. 47p.
Same in Cumberland's British theatre v 37 no 10
   Oxberry, W. ed. New English drama v 13 no 4

More laugh than love. *See* Colman, G. Gay deceivers; or, More laugh than love

Mountaineers; an opera in three acts. . . N.Y. Longworth, 1817. 24°. 68p. Romantic
Same in Cumberland's British theatre v 35 no 5
   Inchbald, Mrs. ed. British theatre v 1
   Inchbald, Mrs. ed. Theatre v 30

New hay at the old market. *See* Colman, G. Sylvester Daggerwood, or, New hay at the old market

Poor gentleman; a comedy in five acts. London. Longman. 1806. 8°. 77p.
Same in Cumberland's British theatre v 37 no 2
   Inchbald, Mrs. ed. British theatre v 1
   Inchbald, Mrs. ed. Theatre v 5

Review; or, The wags of Windsor; a musical farce in two acts. London. Cawthorne. 1808. 8°. 47p.
Same in Dramatic works v 3
   Cumberland's British theatre v 36 no 9
   Oxberry, W. ed. New English drama v 13 no 5

Surrender of Calais; a play in three acts. . . Dublin. Byrne. 1792. 12°. 59p. Historical
Same in Cumberland's British theatre v 40 no 2
   Inchbald, Mrs. ed. British theatre v 13
   Inchbald, Mrs. ed. Theatre v 2

Sylvester Daggerwood; or, New hay at the old market; an occasional drama. London. Cawthorne. 1808. 8°. 32p. Interlude. 1 act
Same in Dramatic works v 1
   Cumberland's British theatre v 36 no 2
   Oxberry, W. ed. New English drama v 21 no 5

Trip to Dover. *See* Colman, G. Ways and means; or, A trip to Dover

Colman, G —*Continued*
Wags of Windsor. *See* Colman, G. Review, or Wags of Windsor
War, love and duty. *See* Colman, G. Africans; or, War, love, and duty
Ways and means; or, a trip to Dover; a comedy in three acts. London. Robinson. 1788. 8°. 62p.
Same in Dramatic works v 2
    British drama v 1 :92
    Inchbald, Mrs. ed.   Collection of farces v 7
    London stage v 3 no 31
We fly by night; or, Long stories: a musical entertainment in two acts.   N.Y. Longworth. 1815. 12°. 39p.   Comedy
Who wants a guinea?   A comedy in five acts.   London. Longman. 1805. 8°. 84p.
Same in Cumberland's British theatre v 20 no 2
    Inchbald, Mrs. ed.   Modern theatre v 3
X. Y. Z.   Farce. 2 acts
In Cumberland's British theatre v 25 no 6
Colman, George, joint author.   *See* Sheridan, R. B. and Colman, G.
Colquhoun, Donald
Jean.   London. Gowans. 1914. 12°. 45p. (Repertory plays. no. 7) Scotch. 1 act
Colton, Arthur
Shanghai gesture; a play. . . N.Y. Boni. 1926. 12°. 256p.   Melodrama. 4 acts
Colton, John, 1899-, and Randolph, Clemence
Rain; a play in three acts, founded on W. Somerset Maugham's story "Miss Thompson."   N.Y. Boni. 1923. 12°. 236p.   South Seas
Same in Mantle, B. ed. Best plays of 1922-23 (condensed)
Colum, Padraic, 1881-
Betrayal.   Melodrama. 1 act
In Drama 11:3
Desert. *See* Colum, P.   Mogu, the wanderer; or, The desert
Fiddler's house.   Ireland. 3 acts
In Fiddler's house
    Three plays
Land.   A play in three acts. Dublin. Maunsel. 1905. 12°. 51p.   Comedy
Same in Fiddler's house, etc.
    Three plays
Miracle of the corn.   Famine. 1 act
In Theatre Arts M 5:323
Mogu, the wanderer; or, The desert; a fantastic comedy in three acts.   Boston. Little. 1917. 12°. 115p.
Thomas Muskerry; a play in three acts. Dublin. Maunsel. 1910. 12°. 64p.   Ireland
Same in Three plays
    Moses, M. J. ed.   Representative British drama
Comfort, Florence C.
Sing-a-song man.   Juvenile. 1 act
In Jagendorf, M. A. ed.   One-act plays for young folks

Connelly, Marc
Wisdom tooth.   Comedy. 3 acts
In Mantle, B. ed.   Best plays of 1925-26 (abridged)
Connelly, Marc, joint author.   *See* Kaufman, G. S. and Connelly, M.
Connors, Barry
Applesauce; an American comedy in three acts.   N.Y. French. c1926. 12°. 110p.
Conrad, Joseph, 1857-1924
Laughing Anne (Adapted from story "Because of the dollar").   Tropics. 3 acts
In Laughing Anne, One day more
One day more (adapted from story "To-morrow").   Character. 1 act
In Laughing Anne, One day more
    Eng R 15:16
    Smart Set 42 no 2:125
Conrad, Robert T., 1810-1858
Jack Cade.   Insurrection of 1381. 4 acts
In Moses, M. J. ed.   Representative plays by American dramatists from 1765 to the present day v 2
Converse, Florence, 1871-
Blessed birthday; a Christmas miracle play.   N.Y. Dutton. 1917. 12°. 68p. 1 act
Same in Garments of praise
Masque of sibyls.   Boston. Houghton. 1910. 12°. 78p.   Masque. 1 act
Santa conversazione; an All Saints miracle. 1 act
In Garments of praise
Soul's medicine; a Whitsuntide miracle of healing. 1 act
In Garments of praise
Three gifts.   Strike. 1 act
In Boston theatre guild plays 1924
Thy kingdom come.   Dream. 1 act
In Garments of praise
    Atlan 127:352
Conway, Olive
Becky Sharp; a play adapted from the Waterloo chapters of "Vanity Fair". 1 act
In Marriott, J. W. ed.   One-act plays of to-day
King's waistcoat.   Historical. 1 act
In Marriott, J. W.   One-act plays of to-day ser 2
Cook, Estelle
"As the twig is bent," a rural school drama.   St. Paul, Minn. Social Service Bureau. c1917. 12°. 35p.
Building the community church.   *See* Cook, Estelle. Partners, or Building the community church
Kindling the hearth fire; a rural drama. Minneapolis, Minn. 1915. 12°. 40p. (*In* Bul. of Univ. of Minnesota. Agric. Extension division. . . General Series no 36)
Partners; or, Building the community church.   St Paul, Minn. Social Service bureau. [c1917]. 12°. 32p.

Cook, George Cram, 1873-1924
Spring; a play. N.Y. Shay. 1921. 12°.
140p. Psychological. 6 scenes
Cook, George Cram, 1873-1924, joint author.
See Glaspell, Susan, and Cook, G. C.
Cook, Sherwin Lawrence
Game of comedy; a dramatic sketch in
one act, from the French. Boston.
Baker. 1902. 12°. 10p.
Same in Plays with a punch
Cook, William Percival
Carthon; a tragedy in three acts. Lon-
don. Routledge. 1909. 12°. 77p.
Cook, Winifred A.
At the last. Tragedy. 3 acts
In Plays and poems
Call from the sea. Tragedy. 3 acts
In Plays and poems
Cooke, B. B.
Gloiana. Tragedy. 1 act
In Canad M 46:403
Cooke, Britton
Translation of John Smith. Character.
2 acts and prologue
In Massey, V. ed. Canadian plays
from Hart House theatre v 1
Cooper, Edith. *See* Field, Michael, pseud
Copeau, Jacques, 1879-
House into which we were born. N.Y.
Theatre arts. 1924. 12°. 75p. $1.
Tangled lives. 3 acts
Same in Theatre Arts M 8:459
Coppée, Francois, 1842-1908
Fennel. A new romantic play. . . Lon-
don. French. [1888?]. 12°. 23p. 1 act
For the Crown (Pour la couronne).
Tragedy. 5 acts
In Pierce and Matthews, ed. Master-
pieces of modern drama v 2
(abridged)
Passer-by. *See* Coppée, F. Wanderer
Pater noster (Le pater); a play in one
act. . . N.Y. French. c1915. 12°. 29p.
Twixt eventide and dawn; a Florentine
romance. A one-act tragedy in
verse. . . N.Y. Remacly. [c1898]. 12°.
13p.
Violin maker of Cremona (La luthier de
Crèmone), a commedietta in one act.
Chicago. Drama. pub. co. 1892. 12°.
12p.
Same in Thomas, C. S. ed. Atlantic
book of junior plays
Wanderer (Le passant); (Passer-by); a
one act comedy in verse. . . N.Y.
Nesbitt. [1890]. 12°. 20p.
Same in Poet Lore 34:461
Corbett, Elizabeth F., 1887-
After glow. Supernatural. 1 act
In Poet Lore 36:311
Corbin, John, 1870-
Forbidden guests. Tragedy. 1 act
In Husband, and The forbidden guests
Husband. Comedy. 3 acts
In Husband, and The forbidden guests
Corkery, David, 1878-
Clan Falvey. Irish. 1 act
In Yellow bittern and other plays

King and hermit. Irish. 1 act
In Yellow bittern and other plays
Labour leader. A play in three acts.
Dublin. Talbot press 1920. 12°. 134p.
Trade unions
Resurrection. Ireland. 1 act
In Theatre Arts M 8:259
Yellow bittern. Irish legend. 1 act
In Yellow bittern and other plays
Cormack, Beale
Aunt Jerushy on the war-path; a rural
farce in three acts. N.Y. Fitzgerald.
1923. 12°. 61p.
Corneau, P. B.
Masks. Satire. 1 act
In Law, F. H. ed. Modern plays,
short and long
Drama 12:234
Poor boy who became a great warrior; a
play for boys. Chicago. Old Tower
press. [c1922]. 12°. 31p. Indian. 2
acts
Cornwall, Barry, pseud. *See* Proctor, Bry-
an Waller
Cournos, John, 1881-
Sport of gods; a play in three acts with
prologue and epilogue. . . London.
Benn. 1925. 12°. 99p.
Courteline, Georges, pseud. (Moinaux,
Georges), 1860-
Blank cartridge. Domestic. 1 act
In International (NY) 8:211
Peace at home; a comedy in one act.
Boston. Badger. c1918. 8°.
Same in International (NY) 7:365
Poet Lore 29:331
Pitiless policeman. Comedy. 3 scenes
In Poet Lore 28:217
Courtney, John, 1813-1865
Aged forty. An original petite comedy
in one act. London. Lacy. [18—]. 12°.
16p. (Lacy's acting edition of plays.
v. 59)
Deeds, not words; a drama in two acts.
London. French. [18—?]. 12°. 34p.
Double faced people. A comedy in three
acts. London. Lacy. [18—]. 12°. 59p.
(Lacy's acting edition of plays. v. 31)
Eustache Baudin; an original drama, in
three acts. London. Lacy. n.d. 12°.
46p. Melodrama
Horrors of war. *See* Courtney, J. Sol-
dier's progress; or, The horrors of
war
Old Joe and young Joe. A comic drama
in two acts. London. Lacy. [18—]. 12°.
32p. (Lacy's acting edition of plays.
v. 49)
Soldier's progress; or, The horrors of
war. A pictorial drama in four
parts. London. Lacy. n.d. 12°. 53p.
Melodrama
Time tries all an original drama in two
acts. London. Lacy. n.d. 12°. 24p.
Comedy
Two Polts. An original farce in one act.
London. Lacy. [18—]. 12°. 20p. (Lacy's
acting edition of plays. v. 45)

Courtney, J.—*Continued*
Wicked wife; a drama.   London. Lacy.
  ⌊18—?⌋. 12°. 22p. (Lacy's acting edition
  of plays. v. 30).   French revolution.
  1 act
Courtney, **John,** 1813-1865, **and Lacy,
  Thomas Hailes**
Clarissa Harlowe: a tragic drama in three
  acts, adapted from the French. Lon-
  don. Lacy. 18—. 12°. 46p. (Lacy's act-
  ing edition of plays. v. 77)
Courtney, **William Leonard,** 1850-
'Gaston Bonnier'; or, 'Time's revenges.'
  In two acts. 1854 and 1870.   Comedy
  In Anglo-Saxon R 8:103
Time's revenges.   *See* Courtney, W. L.
  'Gaston Bonnier'; or, 'Time's reven-
  ges'
Undine; a dream play, in three acts.
  London. W. Heinemann. 1902. 12°.
  62p.
  Same in Fortn 77:1092
Covington, **Zellah, and Simonson, Jules**
Second childhood; a farce in three acts.
  N.Y. Longmans. 1925. 12°. 92p.

Cowan, **Sada**
As I remember you.   Romantic. 1 act
  In Pomp and other plays
Ball and chain.   Social. 1 act
  In Pomp and other plays
Sintram of Skagerrak.   Tragedy. 1 act
  In Pomp and other plays
    Clements, C. C. ed.   Sea plays
    Mayorga, M. G. ed.   Representa-
    tive one-act plays
State forbids; a play in one act.   N.Y.
  Kennerley. 1915. 12°. 46p.   Heredity
  Same in Pomp and other plays
Coward, **Edward Fales,** 1862-
King Stephen; an historical drama in
  seven tableaux completed from John
  Keats' fragment. N.Y. Burrow. 1912.
  12°. 44p.

Coward, **Noel Pierce,** 1899-
Easy virtue; a play in three acts.   N.Y.
  Harper. 1926. 12°. 288p.   Sex
Fallen angels; a comedy in three acts.
  London. Benn. 1923. 12°. 87p.
  Same in Three plays
Hay fever; a light comedy in three
  acts. . . London. Benn. 1925. 107p.
  Harper. N.Y. 221p.
"I'll leave it to you"; a light comedy in
  three acts.   N.Y. French. c1920. 8°.
  71p.
Marquise; a comedy in three acts.   Lon-
  don. Benn. 1927. 12°. 96p.
Queen was in the parlour; a romance in
  three acts. London. Benn. 1926. 12°.
  89p.
Cat.   Japanese. 1 act
  In Pomp and other plays
Collaboration.   Triangle. 1 act
  In Pomp and other plays
In the morgue.   Death. 1 act
  In Pomp and other plays
    Shay, F. and Loving, P. eds.   Fifty
    contemporary one-act plays
    Forum 55:399

Pomp.   Religious. 1 act
  In Pomp and other plays
Rat trap; a play in four acts.   London.
  Benn. 1924. 12°. 86p.   Marriage
  Same in Three plays
This was a man; a comedy in three acts.
  N.Y. Harper. 1926. 12°. 244p.
Vortex, a play in three acts.   N.Y. Har-
  per. 1925. 12°. 193p.   Problem
  Same in Three plays
Young idea; a comedy in three acts.
  N.Y. French. c1924. 64p.
Cox, **Nancy Barney**
Tugging.   Character. 1 act
  In Drama 15:107
Coxe, **Arthur Cleveland,** 1818-1896
Advent; a mystery.   N.Y. Taylor. 1837.
  12°. 132p. 1 act
Saul, a mystery.   N.Y. Appleton. 1845.
  12°. 297p. 5 acts
Coyne, **Joseph Stirling,** 1803-1868
Binks the bogman; a farce in one act.
  London. Lacy. n.d. 12°. 19p.
Box and Cox, married and settled!   An
  original farce in one act. London.
  Lacy. n.d. 12°. 14p.
Buckstone at home; or, the manager and
  his friends.   An original domestic
  and dramatic apropos sketch. London.
  Lacy. ⌊18—⌋. 12°. 24p. (Lacy's acting
  edition of plays. v. 58)   Stage. 1 act
Catching a governor.   *See* Coyne, J. S.
  Pas de fascination; or, Catching a
  governor
Catching a mermaid; an amphibious piece
  of extravagance in one act.   London.
  Lacy. ⌊18—?⌋. 12°. 20p. 1 act
Cockneys in California. . . In one act.
  N.Y. Douglas. 1851. 12°. 19p.   Gold
  discoveries in California
Countess for an hour.   *See* Coyne, J. S.
  Pas de fascination; or, Catching a
  governor
Dark doings in the cupboard.   By the
  Knotting 'em brothers.   A farce, in
  one act. London. Lacy. ⌊18—⌋. 12°.
  18p. (Lacy's acting edition of plays.
  v. 64)
Did you ever send your wife to Brooklyn?
  An original farce, in one act. N.Y.
  Turner & Fisher. ⌊18—⌋. 16°. 18p.
Duck hunting.   An original farce in one
  act. London. Lacy. ⌊18—?⌋. 12°. 19p.
  (Lacy's acting edition of plays. v. 56)
Duel in the dark.   An original farce. In
  one act. London. Lacy. n.d. 12°. 17p.
Everybody's friend.   An original comedy,
  three acts.   N.Y. French. ⌊191—⌋. 12°.
  54p.
Fraud and its victims.   A drama in four
  acts.   Adapted from the French.
  "Les pauvres de Paris". Boston. Spen-
  cer. ⌊1857?⌋. 12°. 53p.
Hope of the family.   An original comedy. In three acts. London. Lacy. n.d.
  12°. 41p.
Little rebel; a farce in one act. London.
  Lacy. ⌊18—?⌋. 12°. 24p. (Lacy's acting
  edition of plays. v. 50))

Lola Montes; or, a countess for an hour. *See* Coyne, J. S. Pas de fascination; or, Catching a governor

Love in a garden. *See* Coyne, J. S. Pets of the parterre; or, Love in a garden

Love-knot. A comedy in three acts. . . Boston. Spencer. ₍1857?₎. 12°. 39p.

Man of many friends. An original comedy in three acts. . . N.Y. Roorbach. 1855. 12°. 36p.

Manager and his friends. *See* Coyne, J. S. Buckstone at home; or, the manager and his friends

My wife's daughter. A comedy in two acts. London. Lacy. n.d. 12°. 34p.

Night of peril. *See* Coyne, J. S. Old chateau; or, a night of peril

Nothing venture, nothing win. A comic drama, in two acts. London. Lacy. ₍18—?₎. 12°. 39p. (Lacy's acting edition of plays. v. 35)

Old chateau; or, A night of peril. A drama in three acts. London. Lacy. n.d. 12°. 39p. Melodrama

Pas de fascination; or, Catching a governor; a farce in one act. Originally performed under title of Lola Montes; or, A countess for an hour. Boston. Spencer. ₍1858?₎. 12°. 19p.

Pets of the parterre; or, Love in a garden: a romantic comedietta in one act. London. Lacy. ₍18-₎. 12°. 24p. (Lacy's acting edition of plays. v. 48)

Railway bubbles; an original farce in one act. London. Barth. ₍185—?₎. 12°. 22p.

Satanas and the spirit of beauty: a romantic legendary spectacle, in two acts. London. Lacy. ₍18—₎. 12°. 46p. (Lacy's acting edition of plays. v. 39)

Scene in the life of an unprotected female. A farce, in one act. Boston. Spencer. ₍1857?₎. 12°. 14p.

Secret agent. A comedy (partly from the German). London. Lacy. ₍18—?₎. 12°. 40p. (Lacy's acting edition of plays. v. 18)

Separate maintenance. A farce in one act. London. Lacy. ₍18—₎. 12°. 23p. (Lacy's acting edition of plays. v. 94)

Signal; a drama in three acts. London. French. ₍18—?₎. 12°. 40p. (French's acting edition of plays. v. 110) Melodrama

Terrible secret. A farce in one act. London. Lacy. ₍18—₎. 12°. 19p. (Lacy's acting edition of plays. v. 53)

That affair at Finchley. A comic sketch in one act. London. Lacy. ₍18—?₎. 12°. 20p. (Lacy's acting edition of plays. v. 52)

"Urgent private affairs." An original farce in one act. London. Lacy. ₍18—?₎. 12°. 23p. (Lacy's acting edition of plays. v. 24)

Vicar of Wakefield; a drama in three acts. N.Y. Taylor. ₍18—?₎. 12°. 75p. Dramatization of Goldsmith's Vicar of Wakefield. 3 acts

Wanted 1000 spirited young milliners for the gold diggings. A farce in one act. London. Lacy. n.d. 12°. 18p.

Water witches; an original farce in one act. London. Lacy. ₍18—?₎. 12°. 23p. (Lacy's acting edition of plays. v. 41)

What will they say at Brompton? A comedetta in one act. London. Lacy. ₍1857₎. 12°. 28p. (Lacy's acting edition of plays. v. 34)

Willikind and his Dinah. An original pathetic and heartrending tragedy. In three sad scenes. London. Lacy. n.d. 12°. 25p.

Woman in red; a drama in a prologue and three acts. Adapted and altered from the French piece of "La tireuse des cartes." London. Lacy. ₍18—?₎. 12°. 56p. (Lacy's acting edition of plays. v. 92) Melodrama

Woman of the world: a comedy in three acts. London. Lacy. ₍18—₎. 12°. 51p. (Lacy's acting edition of plays. v. 81)

Coyne, Joseph Sterling, 1803-1868, **and Coape, H. C.**

Samuel in search of himself. A farce in one act. London. Lacy. ₍18—₎. 12°. 21p. (Lacy's acting edition of plays. v. 36)

Coyne, Joseph Sterling, 1803-1868, **and Coyne, J. Denis**

Home wreck; a drama in three acts. Suggested by Tennyson's Poem of "Enoch Arden." London. Lacy. ₍18—?₎. 12°. 46p. (Lacy's acting edition of plays. v. 85)

Coyne, Joseph Sterling, 1803-1868, **and Hamilton, H.**

Tipperary legacy, a farce in one act. N.Y. Happy hours company. ₍n.d.₎ 12°. 18p.

Coyne, Joseph Sterling, 1803-1868, **and Talfourd, Francis**

Leo the terrible; an entirely new and original Aesopean burlesque, in one act. London. Lacy. n.d. 12°. 32p. (Lacy's acting edition of plays. v. 9 no. 126)

Craig, Anne Throop, 1869-

An Dhord Fhiam. *See* Craig, A. T. Book of the Irish historic pageant

Book of the Irish historic pageant; episodes from the Irish pageant series. "An Dhord Fhiam". N.Y. 1913. Irish history. 2 episodes

Passing of Dana's people. Irish legend. 1 act

In Poet Lore 35:605

Well of Hazels. Allegory. 1 act

In Poet Lore 34:429

Craigie, Mrs Pearl Mary Teresa (John Oliver Hobbes, pseud.), 1867-1906

Ambassador; a comedy in four acts. N.Y. Stokes. ₍1898₎. 12°. 173p.

Osbern and Ursyne; a drama in three acts. N.Y. Lane. 1900. 12°. 94p. Tragedy

Same in Anglo-Saxon R 1:124

Wisdom of the wise; a comedy in three acts. N.Y. Stokes. ₍1900₎. 12°. 136p.

Craigie, Pearl M. T., 1867-1906, and Carson, Murray
Bishop's move; a comedy in three acts. N.Y. Stokes. 1902. 12°. 57p.

Cram, Ralph Adams, 1863-
Excalibur; an Arthurian drama. Boston. Badger. 1909. 8°. 160p. 3 acts

Cranch, Christopher Pearse, 1813-1892
Satan: a libretto. Boston. Roberts Bros. 1874. 12°. 36p. 2 parts

Crandall, Irene Jean
Cabin courtship; a comedy in three acts. Chicago. Denison. [c1921]. 12°. 88p.
For freedom; a play in one act. N.Y. French. 1918. 12°. 20p.

Crane, Eleanor Maud
Little savage. A military comedy in three acts. N.Y. Dick & Fitzgerald. 1907. 12°. 50p.
Next door; a comedy of to-day. N.Y. Dick & Fitzgerald. c1906. 12°. 63p. 3 acts
Pair of idiots; a comedy in two acts. N.Y. Dick & Fitzgerald. 1902. 12°. 50p.
Rainbow kimona. A comedy in two acts for girls. N.Y. Dick & Fitzgerald. 1908. 12°. 33p.
Her victory; in one act. N.Y. Fitzgerald. 1920. 12°. 36p.

Crane, Elizabeth G.
Are you men? A drama in four acts. N.Y. Minden press. 1923. 12°. 174p. Religious
Berquin, a drama in five acts. N.Y. Scribner. 1897. 12°. 110p. Historical
Imperial republic, a drama of the day. N.Y. Grafton. [c1902]. 12°. 122p. Comedy. 5 acts
Necken; a play in two acts. N.Y. 1913. 12°. 73p. Legendary

Crane, Mabel N.
At the milliner's, N.Y. French. 1916. 12°. 20p. 25c. 1 act
Girls. N.Y. French. 1916. 12°. 18p. 25c 1 act

Cranmer-Byng, Launcelot Alfred, 1872-
Salma; a play in three acts. N.Y. Dutton. 1923. 12°. 110p. $1.50 Oriental

Craven, Arthur Scott
Fool's tragedy. London. Secker. 1913. 12°. 275p.
Last of the English; a play in four acts. London. Mathews. 1910. 12°. 159p.

Craven, Arthur Scott, and Beresford, J. D.
Perfect machine. Comedy. 1 act
In Eng R 26:393

Craven, Frank
First year; a comic tragedy of married life. N.Y. French. [1921]. 12° 107p. 75c. 3 acts
Same in Mantle, B. ed. Best plays of 1920-21. (condensed)
New brooms; a comedy in three acts. N.Y. French. c1925. 12°. 99p.

Crawford, Francis Marion, 1854-1909
Francesca da Rimini; a play in four acts. N.Y. Macmillan. 1902. 12°. 73p. Tragedy

Crawford, Jack Randall
Lovely Peggy; a play in three acts based on the love romance of Margaret Woffington and David Garrick. New Haven. Yale. 1911. 12°. 173p.
Robin of Sherwood; a comedy in three acts and four scenes. New Haven. Yale press. 1912. 12°. 150p.

Creagh-Henry, May
"Greater love hath no man", a passion play 3 scenes
In Four mystical plays
Outcasts. Miracle. 1 act
In Four mystical plays
Star; a Christmas play. 2 parts
In Four mystical plays
Four mystical plays. London Society for promoting Christian knowledge. 1924. 12°. 112p.

Creagh-Henry, May, and Marten, D.
Gate of vision; a modern mystical play. N.Y. Macmillan. 1922. 12°. 40p. 30c 3 parts
Same in Four mystical plays

Creamer, Edward S.
Orphean tragedy. N.Y. Abbey press. [c1901]. 12°. 153p. Mythological. 5 acts

Crew, Helen Coale
Password. Juvenile. 1 act
In Jagendorf, M. A. ed. One-act plays for young folks

Crigler, John Fielding
Saul of Tarsus; a religious drama. Boston. Sherman. 1914. 12°. 226p. 7 acts

Crimmins, Agnes Louise
She knows better now; a farce-comedy in three acts. Boston. Baker. 1918. 12°. 228p. 50c

Crimmins, Agnes Louise, and McFadden, Elizabeth, 1875-
Man without a country. Adapted from the story of the same name by Edward Everett Hale. N.Y. French. [c1918]. 12°. 80p. 3 acts

Critchett, R. C., (R. C. Carton, pseud.), 1853-
Bear leaders; a farce in four acts. . . N.Y. French. c1913. 12°. 182p.
Lady Huntworth's experiment; an original comedy in three acts. . . N.Y. French. 1904. 75p.
Liberty Hall; an original drama in four acts. . . N.Y. French. c1900. 12°. 76p.
Mr. Preedy and the countess; an original farce in three acts. N.Y. French. c1911. 12°. 155p.
Other people's worries; a comedy in three acts. N.Y. French. c1925. 12°. 87p.

Crocker, Bosworth, pseud. (Mary Arnold Crocker Lewisohn)
Baby carriage. Comedy. 1 act
In Humble folk
Shay, F. and Loving, P. eds. Fifty contemporary one-act plays
Cost of a hat. Character. 1 act
In Humble folk
Dog. Tragedy. 1 act
In Humble folk

First time. Character. 1 act
In Humble folk
Last straw, a play in one act. N.Y.
Shay. 1917. 12°. 30p. Tragedy
Same in Humble folk
 Lewis, B. R. ed. Contempo-
  rary one-act plays
 Mayorga, M. G. ed. Repre-
  sentative one act plays
Pawns of war; a play. . . Boston. Little.
1917. 12°. 85p. $1.25 World war. 3
acts

Cromer, James Monroe
Jeptha's daughter; a drama in five acts.
Boston. Gorham. 1916. 12°. 103p.
Biblical

Cronyn, George William, 1888-
Death in fever flat. Western. 1 act
In Shay, F. and Loving, P. eds. Fifty
 contemporary one-act plays
Sandbar queen; a play in one act as
played by the Washington Square
players. N.Y. Arena. 1918. 12°. 46p.
35c Low life

Crothers, Rachel, 1878-
Expressing Willie; a comedy in three
acts. Boston. Baker. c1925. 12°. 79p.
Same in Expressing Willie, Nice peo-
 ple, etc
He and she. Domestic. 3 acts
In Quinn, A. H. ed. Representative
 American plays, 1767-1923
Heart of Paddy Whack; a comedy in
three acts. N.Y. French. c1925. 12°.
106p.
Importance of being a woman. 1 act
In Six one-act plays
Importance of being clothed. 1 act
In Six one-act plays
Importance of being married. 1 act
In Six one-act plays
Importance of being nice. 1 act
In Six one-act plays
Katy did. Comedy. 1 act
In Smart Set 27 no 1:129
Little journey. Comedy. 3 acts
In Mary the third, etc.
Man's world; a play in four acts. Bos-
ton. Badger. ₁c1915₁. 12°. 113p.
Social
Mary the third. Comedy. 3 acts
In Mary the third, etc.
 Dickinson, T. H. ed. Contempo-
  rary plays
 Mantle, B. ed. Best plays of 1922-
  23 (condensed)
Nice people. Social. 3 acts
In Expressing Willie, etc.
 Mantle, B. ed. Best plays of 1920-
  21. (condensed)
 Moses, M. J. ed. Representative
  American dramas, national and
  local
 Quinn, A. H. ed. Contemporary
  American plays
"Old lady 31". Comedy. 3 acts
In Mary the third, etc.
Once upon a time; a comedy in four acts.
N.Y. French. c1925. 12°. 77p.

Peggy. Character. 1 act
In Six one-act plays
 Scrib M 76:175
Rector, a play in one act. N.Y. French.
c1905. 12°. 19p. Comedy
Same in One act plays for stage and
 study ser 1
39 East; a comedy in three acts. Boston.
Baker. 1925. 12°. p 191-278.
Same in Expressing Willie, etc.
Three of us; a play in four acts. N.Y.
French. c1916. 12°. 113p. Comedy
What they think. 1 act
In Six one-act plays
 Ladies' H J 46:12 F '23

Crowell, C. T.
Afternoon orator. Farce. 1 act
In New Repub 39:72

Crowley, Aleister, 1875-
Jephthah. Tragedy. 1 act
In Jephthah and other mysteries, lyri-
 cal and dramatic
Mortadello; or, The angel of Venice, a
comedy. London. Wieland. 1912. 8°.
122p.
Poem, a little drama in four scenes.
London. Privately printed. 1898. 22p.
Mystery
Same in Jephthah and other mysteries
Saviour. Religious. 1 scene
In International (NY) 12:75 Mr '18
Tannhäuser; a story of all time. Lon-
don. Trench. 1902. 4°. 141p.

Crum, John Macheod Campbell, 1872-
Play of Saint George. Farce. 1 act
In Thomas, C. S. ed. Atlantic book
 of junior plays

Culbertson, Ernest Howard
End of the trail. Tragedy. 1 act
In Nicholson, K. ed. Appleton book
 of short plays
 Theatre Arts M 8:326
Goat alley; a tragedy of negro life. Cin-
cinnati. Stewart Kidd. ₁c1922₁. 12°.
155p. 1 act
Same in Shay, F. ed. Contemporary
 one-act plays of 1921
 Shay, F. ed. Twenty con-
  temporary one-act plays
  (Later rearranged as long
  play)

Cullinan, Ralph
Loggerheads; a comedy in three acts.
N.Y. French. c1926. 12°. 90p.

Cunningham, Leon
Dralda bloom. Fantasy. 1 act
In Poet Lore 30:553
Wondership. Supernatural. 1 act
In Clements, C. C. ed. Sea plays
 Poet Lore 30:363

Curel, François, Vicomte de, 1854-
Beat of the wing. (La coup d'aile).
Comedy. 3 acts
In Poet Lore 20:321
False saint (L'enver d'une sainte); a
play in three acts. Tr. by Barrett
Clark. . . Garden City. Doubleday.
1916. 12°. 100p. Psychological

Curel, F. V. de—*Continued*
Fossils (Les fossiles).   Social. 4 acts
In Clark, B. H. tr.   Four plays of the
Free theatre

Curmieu, Georges de (Georges Ancey, pseud), 1860-
Dupe (La dupe).   Comedy. 5 acts
In Clark, B. H. tr.   Four plays of
the free theatre

Currie, Mary Montgomerie (Lamb) Singleton, Lady (Violet Fane, pseud.), d. 1905
Anthony Babington; a drama.   London.
Chapman. 1877. 12°.   Historical tragedy. 5 acts

Curry, Sarah J.
Devil's gold.   Dramatization of Chaucer's Pardoner's tale. 1 act
In Shay, F.   Treasury of plays for men

Cushing, Catherine Chisholm
Nathan Hale of '73; a drama in four acts.
New Haven. Yale. 1908. 8°. 88p.
Historical
Pollyanna; a comedy in four acts.
Adapted from the story of Eleanor H.
Porter.   N.Y. French. 12°. 110p. 75c
Prehistoric Mabel; an hysterical, evolutionary play in five ages. . . Being all
about Ding Dong, Bell. Hartford,
Conn. Meyer. 1909. 8°. 96p.

Custis, George Washington Parke, 1781-1857
Indian prophecy, a national drama in two
acts.   Founded upon a most interesting and romantic occurrence in the
life of George Washington.   Georgetown, D.C. James Thomas. 1828. 12°.
35p.
Pocahontas; or, The settlers of Virginia;
a national drama; in three acts. . .
Phila. Alexander. 1830. 12°. 47p.
Same in Quinn, A. H. ed.   Representative American plays, 1767-1923
Settlers of Virginia.   *See* Custis, G. W.
P.   Pocahontas, or The settlers of
Virginia

Dabney, Julia Parker
Children of the sunrise, a drama in two
scenes
In Poet Lore 26:565
Mademoiselle Merowsky; a play in three
acts.   Brookline, Mass.   Privately
printed. 1907. 12°. 67p.
Waters of life; a drama in four acts.
Cedar Rapids, Ia. Torch press. 1925

Dale, Irving
Friend husband, a comedy.   Chicago.
Denison. 1916. 11p. 15c 1 act
Tickets, please!   A comedy in one act.
Boston. Baker. 1916. 12°. 9p.

Dall, Ian
Noah's wife; a dramatic dialogue in
verse. . . Oxford. Blackwell. 1925.
51p.

Dalton, Test, 1877
Adam's apple, a farce-comedy in three
acts.   N.Y. French. c1926. 12°. 84p.
(Formerly published under title, "Uncle John")

Mantle of Lincoln; a play for the people.
N.Y. French. c1926. 12°. 97p.

Daly, Augustin, 1832-1899
Divorce.   A play of the period, in five
acts. . . N.Y. Printed . . . for the author, 1884. 8°. 93p.
Dollars and sense; or, The heedless ones.
A comedy of to-day in three acts. . .
N.Y. Printed . . . for the author.
1885. 8°. 71p.
Flash of lightning: a drama of life in our
day, in five acts. . . N.Y. Printed . . .
for the author. 1885. 8°. 72p.
Frou frou; a comedy of powerful human
interest in five acts. . . N.Y. French.
c1897. 12°. 59p.
Hazardous ground.   An original adaptation in four acts.   N.Y. French.
c1868. 8°. 46p.
Horizon: an original drama of contemporaneous society and of American
frontier perils. In five acts and seven
tableaux. . . N.Y.   Printed . . . for
the author. 1885. 8°. 67p.
Legend of "Norwood"; or, Village life
in New England.   An American
comedy of American life, in four
acts. . . N.Y. Printed for the author.
1807. 8°. 79p.
Love in tandem, a comedy in three
acts. . . N.Y. Printed for the author.
1892. 8°. 84p.
Nancy and company, an eccentric piece
in four acts. . . N.Y. Printed for the
author. 1886. 8°. 63p.
Needles and pins.   A comedy for the
present,   in   four   acts. . . N.Y.
Printed . . . for the author. 1884. 8°.
77p.
Our English friend.   A comedy in four
acts. . . N.Y. Printed . . . for the authors. 1884. 8°. 78p.
Pique.   A play of to-day, in five acts. . .
N.Y. Printed . . . for the author.
1884. 8°. 97p.
Under the gaslight; a totally original and
picturesque drama of life and love in
these times; in five acts. . . N.Y.
Printed . . . for the author. 1867. 4°.
48p. *Same,* in four acts. London. Lacy.
[18—?]. 60p. *also* N.Y. Wemyss. 1867.
47p.

Daly, John
Broken toys.   A drama in two acts. London. Lacy. n.d. 12°. 36p. (Lacy's acting edition of plays. v. 14 no. 203)
Times; an original drama in three acts.
London. Lacy. n.d. 12°. 52p. (Lacy's
acting edition of plays. v. 11 no. 158)

Damon, S. Foster
Persephone in Eden.   Classical. 1 act
In Dial 78:445
Sir David wears a crown.   1 act
In Ladies' H J 38:6 Je 21

Dancourt, Grenet
April shower.   Comedy. 1 act
In Beerbohm, C.   Little book of plays

Dane, Clemence, pseud. (Winifred Ashton)
Bill of divorcement; a play.   N.Y. Macmillan. 1921. 12°. 143p.   Problem
Same in Mantle, B. ed.   Best plays of 1921-22 (condensed)
Granite; a tragedy. . . London. Heinemann. 1926. 12°. 75p.
Naboth's vineyard; a stage piece.   London. Heineman. 1925. 90p.
Way things happen; a story in three acts.   N.Y. Macmillan. 1924. 12°. 242p. $2.25   Comedy
Will Shakespeare; an invention in four acts.   N.Y. Macmillan. 1922. 12°. 188p. $1.75

Dane, Essex
Cul-de-sac.   1 act
In One act plays
Fleurette & Co.   1 act
In One act plays
Happy returns.   1 act
In One act plays
On the park bench.   1 act
In Baker's anthology of one-act plays
Serpent's tooth.   India. 1 act
In One act plays
Wasp.   1 act
In One act plays
When the whirlwind blows.   1 act
In One act plays
Wooden leg.   1 act
In One act plays
Workers at the looms.   1 act
In One act plays
Wrong numbers.   1 act
In One act plays

Dangerfield, Trelawney
Old stuff.   Episode. 1 act
In Smart Set 52 no 2:77

Danner, Mrs. Paul R.   *See* Baronti, Gervé

Dargan, Olive Tilford
Carlotta.   Historical. 5 acts
In Semiramis, and other plays
Journey.   Chinese. 1 act
In Flutter of the goldleaf
Kidmir.   Historical. 4 acts
In Mortal gods
Lords and lovers.   Historical. 4 acts
In Lords and lovers, and other dramas
Mortal gods.   Comedy. 4 acts
In Mortal gods
Poet.   Poe. 5 acts
In Semiramis, and other plays
Semiramis.   Historical. 4 acts
In Semiramis, and other plays
Shepherd.   Tragedy. 3 acts
In Lords and lovers, and other dramas
Siege.   Historical. 5 acts
In Lords and lovers, and other dramas
Son of Hermes.   Comedy. 5 acts
In Mortal gods
Woods of Ida; a masque.   1 act
In Cent 74:590

Dargan, Olive Tilford, and Peterson, Frederick, 1859-
Everychild.   Fairy. 5 scenes
In Flutter of the goldleaf

Flutter of the goldleaf.   Psychological. 1 act
In Flutter of the goldleaf

Darley, George, 1795-1846
Battle of Brunanburh.   *See* Darley, G. Ethelstan; or, The battle of Brunanburh
Ethelstan, or, The battle of Brunanburh; a dramatic chronicle in five acts.   London. Moxon. 1841. 12°. 95p.   Historical
Same in Complete poetical works
May queen.   *See* Darley, G. Sylvia; or, The May Queen
Sylvia; or, The May queen.   Romantic. 5 acts
In Complete poetical works
Thomas a' Becket.   Historical. 5 acts
In Complete poetical works

Darlington, William Aubrey (Cecil), 1890-
Alf's button; an extravaganza in three acts.   London. Jenkins. 1925. 127p.

Daryl, Sidney
First brief.   Comedietta. 1 act
In Scott, C.   Drawing-room plays

Daudet, Alphonse, 1840-1897, and Belot, Adolphe
Sappho, a play in five acts. . . N.Y. Rullman. c1895. 4°. 41p.   Melodrama

Daudet, Alphonse, 1840-1897, and E. L. V. J.
Last lily ('oeillet blanc).   Comedietta. 1 act. (altered)
In Scott, C. W. ed.   Drawing-room plays

Davidson, Gustav
Mr. Pupin dreams of a stove.   A farce-satire in one act
In Stratford monthly n s 2:24

Davidson, Gustav, and Koven, Joseph
Melmoth the wanderer; a play in five acts.   Boston. Badger. 1915. 12°. 179p. $1.   Religious

Davidson, John, 1857-1909
Bruce.   A drama in five acts [and in verse].   Glasgow. Wilson & McCormick. 1886. 8°. 161p.   Chronicle play
In Plays
Godfrida; a play in four acts.   N.Y. Lane. 1899. 12°. 123p.   Legendary
Knight of the maypole, a comedy in four acts.   London. Richards. 1903. 12°. 97p.
Queen's romance; a version of Ruy Blas.   N.Y. Stokes. [c1904]. 12°. 98p. 3 acts
Romantic farce.   Comedy. 5 acts
In Plays
Scaramouch in Naxos.   Pantomine. 5 scenes
In Plays
Self's the man: a tragic-comedy.   London. Richards. 1901. 12°. 221p. 5 acts
Smith; a tragedy. . . Glasgow. Wilson. 1888. 12°. 70p. 3 acts
Same in Plays
Theatrocrat, a tragic play of church and stage.   London. Richards. 1905. 12°. 195p.
Unhistorical pastoral.   Comedy. 5 acts
In Plays

Davies, Hubert Henry, 1876-1917
Captain Drew on leave; a comedy in four
    acts.   Boston.   Baker.   1924. 12°. 170p.
    In Plays v 1
Cousin Kate; a comedy in three acts. . .
    Boston. Baker. 1910. 12°. 158p.
    Same in Plays v 1
Doormats.   A comedy in three acts.
    N.Y. French. c1920. 12°. 62p.
    Same in Plays v 2
Lady Epping's lawsuit; a satirical comedy
    in three acts. . . Boston. Baker. 1914.
    12°. 160p.
    Same in Plays v 1
Mrs. Gorringe's necklace; a play in four
    acts. . . Boston. Baker. 1910. 12°.
    176p.   Melodrama
    Same in Plays v 1
Mollusc; a new and original comedy in
    three acts.   Boston. Baker. 1914. 12°.
    157p.
    Same in Plays v 2
            Dickinson, T. H. ed.   Con-
            temporary plays
Outcast.   Marriage. 4 acts
    In Plays v 2
Single man.   Boston. Baker. 1914. 12°.
    192p.   Comedy. 4 acts
    In Plays v 2
Davies, Mary Carolyn
Slave with two faces; an allegory in one
    act. . . N.Y. Arens. 1918. 12°. 24p.
    In Shay, F. and Loving, P. eds.   Fifty
        contemporary one-act plays
Davies, William Henry, 1870-
True travellers; a tramp's opera in three
    acts.   N.Y. Harcourt. 1923. 12°. 53p.
    $2
Davis, Allan
Promised land, a drama in four acts.
    Cambridge. Harvard dram. club. 1908.
    8°. 69p.   Race prejudice
Quest for happiness; an American mor-
    ality play in three acts and eight
    scenes.   N.Y. French. c1917. 12°. 79p.
Davis Allan, and Stratton, Anna R.
Inward light; a drama in four acts. . .
    N.Y. Knopf. 1919. 12°. 135p.   Civil
    war
Davis, Allan, and Vencill, C. C.
On Vengeance Height, a play in one act.
    Baltimore.   Norman, Remington Co.
    1920. 12°. 32p.   Tennessee mountain
    Same in Knickerbocker, E. Van B. ed.
        Twelve plays
        Vagabond plays ser 1
Davis, Owen, 1874-
Detour; a play.   Boston. Little. 1922. 12°.
    122p.   Character
    Same in Moses, M. J. ed.   Representa-
        tive American dramas, na-
        tional and local
Easy come, easy go; a farce in three acts.
    N.Y. French. c1926. 12°. 113p.
Haunted house; an American comedy in
    three acts. . . N.Y. French. c1926.
    12°. 97p.

Icebound, a play.   Boston. Little, Brown.
    1923. 12°. 116p.   Comedy. 3 acts
    Same in Dickinson, T. H. ed.   Con-
        temporary plays
            Mantle, B. ed   Best plays of
            1922-23. (condensed)
Let him come and let him look; the play
    extraordinary.   N.Y. French. c1918.
    12°. 93p.   Oriental. 3 acts
Merry outlaws of Sherwood Forest.   *See*
    Davis, O. Robin Hood; or, The merry
    outlaws of Sherwood Forest
Nervous wreck; a comedy in three
    acts . . . from the novel of E. J.
    Rath. N.Y. French. c1926. 12°. 138p.
Robin Hood; or, The merry outlaws of
    Sherwood Forest; a play in three
    acts.   N.Y. French. 1923. 12°. 75p.
Davis, Richard Harding, 1864-1916
Blackmail.   Tragedy. 1 act
    In Page, Brett.   Writing for vaude-
        ville. Springfield, Mass. Home cor-
        respondence school. [c1915]. 12°.
        639p.
Dictator.   Farce. 2 acts
    In Farces
Galloper.   Farce. 3 acts
    In Farces
Miss Civilization, a comedy in one act.
    N.Y. Scribner. 1905. 12°. 47p.
    Same in Farces
Orator of Zepata city, a play in one act.
    Chicago.   Dramatic   publishing   co.
    [c1900]. 12°. 12p.
Peace manoeuvers; a play in one act. . .
    N.Y. French. c1914. 12°. 18p.   Crook
    Same in One act plays for stage and
        study ser 1
Zone police; a play in one act.   N.Y.
    French. c1914. 12°. 20p.   Army
Davis, Robert Hobart, 1869-
Room without a number; a one-act farce.
    In Smart Set 51:201
Davis, Robert Hobart, 1869-, **and Sheehan,
Perley Poore,** 1875-
Efficiency; a play in one act.   N.Y.
    Doran. 1917. 12°. 19-40p. 75c   War
Day, Frederick Lansing
Makers of light; a play in three acts.
    N.Y. Brentano's. [c1925]. 12°. 176p.
    Tragedy
Slump.   Marriage. 1 act
    In Plays of the 47 workshop ser 4
        Shay, F. and Loving, P. eds.   Fifty
        contemporary one-act plays
Day, W.
Tree of knowledge; in four acts with pro-
    logue.   London.   Gresham   Press.
    1912. 79p.
Dazey, L. H., and Dazey, C. T.
Woman's choice.   Melodrama. 1 act
    In Smart Set 30 no 4:123
Dean, A., 1893-
Just neighborly.   Satire. 1 act
    In Law, F. H. ed.   Modern plays,
        short and long
        Drama 12:10-12, 56-62
Dean, Basil, joint author.   *See* Kennedy,
    Margaret, and Dean, Basil

Deans, Harris, 1886-
Apron strings; a comedy in three acts. London. The Stage. pub. bureau. 1924. 12°. 109p.
Husbands are a problem; a comedy in three acts. N.Y. French. 1923. 12°. 77p.

Dearmer, Mrs Mabel White (Mrs Percy Dearmer), 1872-1915
Don Quixote. Romantic. 3 adventures
In Three plays
Dreamer. Poetic. 3 acts
In Three plays
Soul of the world; a mystery play of the nativity and the passion. London. Mowbray. 1911. 12°. 65p. 3 acts
Same in Three plays

De Cerkez, Florence Euphemia, 1872-
Sintram; a drama in blank verse in four acts. . . Boston. Badger. 1922. 12°. 205p. $1.50 Poetic

De La Mare, Walter John, 1873-
Crossings, a fairy play. . . N.Y. Knopf. 1923. 12°. 169p. 5 acts

Deland, Margaret. *See* Vosburgh, M. B.
Miss Maria, dramatized from Old Chester Tales

Delavigne, Jean François Casimir, 1793-1843
Louis XI; an historical drama in three acts. (adapted from Casimir Delavigne by W. R. Markwell). London. Lacy. n.d. 12°. 45p. (Lacy's acting edition of plays. v. 9 no. 134)
Monastery of St. Just. A play in three acts. Adapted by John Oxenford. London. Lacy. [1864?]. 12°. 53p. (Lacy's acting edition of plays. v. 63 no. 936). Historical

De Lesseline, Liddell
Two Cromwells; a prose tragedy in three acts. Cincinnati. Stewart Kidd. 1913. 12°. 78p.

Delf, Harry
Family upstairs; a comedy of home life. N.Y. French. c1926. 12°. 95p.

Dell, Floyd, 1887-
Angel intrudes; a play in one act. . . N.Y. Arens. 1918. 12°. 24p. Comedy
Same in King Arthur's socks, and other village plays
Provincetown plays (Stewart-Kidd 1921)
Chaste adventures of Joseph. Comedy. 1 act
In King Arthur's socks, etc.
Enigma. Domestic. 1 act
In King Arthur's socks, etc
Human nature. Morality. 1 act
In King Arthur's socks, etc
Ibsen revisited. Satire. 1 act
In King Arthur's socks, etc
King Arthur's socks. Comedy. 1 act
In King Arthur's socks, etc
Provincetown plays ser 1
Legend. Romantic. 1 act
In King Arthur's socks, etc

Long time ago. Tragic fantasy. 1 act
In King Arthur's socks, etc
Forum 51:261
Poor Harold. Comedy. 1 act
In King Arthur's socks, etc
Rim of the world. Fantasy. 1 act
In King Arthur's socks, etc
Sweet-and-twenty; a Comedy in one act. Cincinnati. Stewart Kidd. 1 act. 1921. 12°. 32p. 50c
Same in King Arthur's socks, etc
Shay, F. ed. Contemporary one-act plays of 1921
Shay, F. ed. Twenty contemporary one-act plays (American)

De Mille, Cecil Blount, 1881-
Royal mounted; a play in four acts. N.Y. French. 1920. 12°. 90p. 60c Melodrama

De Mille, Henry Churchill, 1850-1893
John Delmer's daughters. A comedy in three acts. N.Y. 1883. 8°. 66p.

De Mille, William Churchill, 1878-
Christmas spirit. Fairy. 1 act
In Christmas spirit
Deceivers; a play in one act. N.Y. French. 1914. 12°. 16p. Comedy
Same in One act plays for stage and study ser 1
"In 1999"; a problem play of the future. N.Y. French. c1914. 12°. 15p. 1 act
Man higher up. Psychological. 1 act
In Columbia monthly 8:232
Poor old Jim; a sketch in one act. N.Y. French. c1914. 12°. 16p. Comedy
Starveling; a tragedy after Maeterlinck. 1 act
In Stratford J 8 no 3:123
Strongheart, an American comedy drama in four acts. N.Y. French. [c1909]. 12°. 98p.
Same in Pierce and Matthews, eds. Masterpieces of modern drama v 1 (abridged)
Votes for fairies. Fairy. 1 act
In Christmas spirit

De Mille, William Churchill, 1878-, and **Barnard, Charles,** 1868-
Forest ring. Fairy. 3 acts
In Cohen, H. L. ed. More one-act plays by modern authors
Moses, M. J. Treasury of plays for children

Denison, Emily Herey
Dawn of music. Musical. 1 act
In Little mother of the slums, and other plays
Dolly Madison's afternoon tea. Historical. 1 act
In Little mother of the slums, and other plays
Duped. Comedy. 1 act
In Little mother of the slums, and other plays
Little mother of the slums. Social. 1 act
In Little mother of the slums, and other plays

Denison, E. H.—*Continued*
My friend's in town.   Comedy. 1 act
  In Little mother of the slums, and
    other plays
Mystery of Beacon Hill.   Comedy. 1 act
  In Little mother of the slums, and
    other plays
Yeggman.   Comedy. 2 scenes
  In Little mother of the slums, and
    other plays

Denison, Thomas Stewart, 1848-1911
Assessor.   Humorous sketch. 1 act
  In Exhibition and parlor dramas
Borrowing trouble.   Farce. 1 act
  In Exhibition and parlor dramas
    Louva, the pauper
Cobbler.   Monologue. 1 scene
  In Lively plays for live people
Country justice.   Farce. 1 act
  In Exhibition and parlor dramas
    Louva, the pauper
Danger signal; a drama.   Chicago. Deni-
    son. [1883]. 12°. 42p.
Dude in a cyclone.   Farce. 1 act
  In Lively plays for live people
Family strike.   Farce. 1 act
  In Exhibition and parlor dramas
    Odds with the enemy
First-class hotel.   Farce. 1 act
  In Lively plays for live people
Hans von Smash, a farce.   1 act
  In Louva, the pauper
Initiating a granger.   Farce. 1 act
  In Exhibition and parlor dramas
    Odds with the enemy
It's all in the pay streak.   Comedy. 3 acts
  In Lively plays for live people
Louva, the pauper.   Chicago. Denison.
    1878. 12°. 182p.   Melodrama. 5 acts
Madame Princeton's temple of beauty.
    Farce. 1 act
  In Lively plays for live people
New woman.   Comedy. 3 acts
  In Lively plays for live people
Odds with the enemy.   Melodrama. 5
    acts
  In Exhibition and parlor dramas
    Odds with the enemy
Only cold tea.   Temperance. 1 act
  In Lively plays for live people
Our country.   A historical and spectac-
    ular representation. 3 parts
  In Louva, the pauper
Patsy O'Wang.   Farce
  In Lively plays for live people
Rejected.   Farce
  In Lively plays for live people
Seth Greenback.   An amateur drama in
    four acts. . . Chicago. Denison. 1877.
    12°. p. 55-76.   Melodrama
  Same in Odds with the enemy
Sparkling cup.   Temperance. 5 acts
  In Exhibition and parlor dramas
    Odds with the enemy
Topps twins.   Farce
  In Lively plays for live people
Two ghosts in white.   Farce. 1 act
  In Exhibition and parlor dramas

Under the laurels; a drama in five acts. . .
    Chicago. Denison. c1881. 12°. 41p.
Wanted; a correspondent.   A farce. In
    two acts. Chicago. Denison. 1877. 12°.
    p. 79-95
  Same in Exhibition and parlor dramas
    Odds with the enemy

**D'Ennery, Adolph, 1811-1879, and M. J. J.
Fournier**
Belphegon; or, The mountebank and his
    wife; a romantic and domestic drama
    in three acts. Adapted. . . London.
    Lacy. n.d. 12°. 56p. (Lacy's acting
    edition of plays. v 3 no 39)

**D'Ennery, Adolphe, 1811-1879, and Jules
Bresil**
Jocrisse the juggler in three acts. . .
    Adapted. London. Lacy. [1861]. 12°.
    44p.   Melodrama

D'Ennery, Adolphe, 1811-1879, and Clement
Noémie; a drama in two acts. . .
    Adapted. London. Lacy. [1855?]. 12°.
    36p. (Lacy's acting edition of plays.
    v. 23 no. 343)   Comedy

**D'Ennery, Adolphe, 1811-1879, and Dugue
Ferdinand**
Cartouche; the French robber.   A drama
    in three acts. . . Adapted. London.
    Lacy. [18—?]. 12°. 46p. (Lacy's acting
    edition of plays. v. 76 no. 131)
Sea of ice; or, The prayer of the wrecked,
    and the Goldseeker of Mexico. Lon-
    don. Lacy. n.d. 12°. Adapted. (Lacy's
    acting edition of plays. v. 13 no. 195)
    Romantic. 5 acts

Dennis, O. M.
His honor.   Supernatural. 1 act
  In Smart Set 35 no 3:129

Dennison, Merrill
Balm.   Poverty. 1 act
  In Massey, V. ed.   Canadian plays
    from Hart House theatre v 1
Brothers in arms.   Canada. 1 act
  In Unheroic north
    Massey, V. ed.   Canadian plays
    from Hart House theatre v 1
    Shay, Frank.   Twenty-five short
    plays, international
From their own place.   Canada. 1 act
  In Unheroic north
Marsh hay.   Canadian backwoods. 4 acts
  In Unheroic north
Weather breeder.   Canadian farm life.
    1 act
  In Unheroic north
    Massey, V. ed.   Canadian plays
    from Hart House theatre v 1

Denny, Ernest, 1869-
All-of-a sudden Peggy.   N.Y. French.
    1910. 12°. 159p.   Comedy. 3 acts
Irresistible Marmaduke; an original com-
    edy in three acts. London. French.
    1920. 12°. 154p.
Just like Judy; a light comedy in three
    acts.   N.Y. French. 1922. 12°. 111p.
    75c
Vanity; a comedy in three acts.   N.Y.
    French. c1925. 12°. 119p.

Dibdin, T. J.—*Continued*

School for prejudice. Comedy. 5 acts
In Inchbald, Mrs. Modern theatre. v 4

Sixes, or, The devil's in the dice! A romantic melo-drama in two acts. . . London. Cumberland. n.d. 24°. 40p.

Suil Dhuv, the coiner: a melodramatic romance in three acts. . . London. Davidson. n.d. 12°. 47p. (Cumberland's minor theatre. v. 1 no. 6)

Twenty per cent; or, My father. A farce in two acts. . . London. Whittingham. 1816.
Same in Dibdin, T. J. London theatre v 11 no 6

Two Gregories, or, Where did the money come from? A farce, in two acts. . . London. Davidson. n.d. 12°. 28p. (Cumberland's minor theatre. v. 3 no. 6)

Two faces under a hood; a comic opera. In three acts. . . London. Printed by Brettell for Appleyards. [1807?]. 8°. 80p.

Valentine and Orson. A romantic melo-drama, in two acts. . . London. Cumberland. n.d. 12°. 28p. (Cumberland's British theatre. v. 27 no. 8)

Vicar of Wakefield. A melodramatic burletta, in three acts. . . London. John Miller. 1817. 46p.

What next? A farce in two acts. . . London. Whittingham. 1816. 24°. 35p. (Dibdin, T. J. ed. London theatre. v. 12 no. 1)
Same in London stage v 4 no 32

Zuma; or, The tree of health: an opera, in three acts. . . London. Miller. 1818. 8°. 46p.

Will for the deed, a comedy, in three acts. . . London. Longman. 1805. 8°. 64p.

Dicenta y Benedicto, Joaquin, 1863(?)-
Juan José.
In Turrell, C. A. ed. Contemporary Spanish dramatists

Dickens, Charles, 1812-1870

Is she his wife? or, Something singular, a comic burletta in one act. Boston. Osgood. 1877. 80p.
Same in Works (Nat Lib ed) v 18
Plays and poems. v 1

Lamplighter; a farce in one act as a short story. . . N.Y. Appleton. 1926. 12°. 83p.
Same in Works (Nat Lib ed) v 18
Plays and poems. v 1
Golden Bk 3:69

Mr. Nightingale's diary; a farce in one act. Boston. Osgood. 1877. 96p.
Same in Works (Nat Lib ed) v 18
Plays and poems. v 2

No thoroughfare. Melodrama. 5 acts. [with Wilkie Collins]
In Works (Nat Lib ed) v 18
Plays and poems. v 2
All the year round 18:Sup
Eve Sat 4:829

Strange gentleman. Comic burletta in two acts. . . London. Chapman. 1837. 64p.
In Works (Nat Lib ed) v 18
Plays and poems. v 1

Village coquettes, a comic opera. In two acts. . . 1837. 71p.
In Works (Nat Lib ed) v 18
Plays and poems. v 1

Dickinson, Lionel A. N.

Birds of a feather. Comedy. 1 act
In Time flies, and other plays

Fantasy. Dream. 1 act
In Time flies, and other plays

Great historical pageant of Riddington-on-Slush. Burlesque. 5 episodes
Same in Times flies, and other plays

Love potion. Farce. 1 act
In Time flies, and other plays

Mother of invention. Comedy. 1 act
In Time flies, and other plays

Time flies. Comedy. 1 act
In Time flies, and other plays

Dickinson, Thomas Herbert, 1877-

In the hospital. Illness. 1 act
In Dickinson, T. H. ed. Wisconsin plays

Dillon, Robert Arthur, 1865-

Artful old card. Comedy. 1 act
In Drawing room playlets for amateurs

"Chawlie" Sikes. Comedy. 1 act
In Drawing room playlets for amateurs

Matchmakers. Romantic. 1 act
In Drawing room playlets for amateurs

Pride. Comedy. 1 act
In Drawing room playlets for amateurs

Truthful age. Farce. 1 act
In Drawing-room playlets for amateurs

Dimond, William, 1780?-1836?

Adrian and Orrila; or, a mother's vengeance: a play in five acts. . . N.Y. Longworth. 1807. 12°. 76p.

Aethiop; or, The child of the desert; a romantic play in five acts. . . N.Y. Longworth. 1813. 12°. 76p.

Bride of Abydos; a tragick play, in three acts. . . Baltimore. Robinson. 1831. 12°. 58p.

Broken sword: a grand melo-drama in two acts. . . London. Davidson. n.d. 12°. 36p. (Cumberland's British theatre. v. 41 no. 5)

Carnival at Naples, a play in five acts. . . London. Kirby. 1831. 8°. 67p.

Child of the desert. *See* Dimond, W. Aethiop; or, The child of the desert

Conquest of Taranto; or St. Clara's eve. A play. . . N.Y. Longworth. 1817. 12°. 62p. Melodrama. 3 acts

Doubtful son, or, Secrets of a palace; a play in five acts. London. Wyatt. 1810. 82p.

Foundling of the forest: a play. Phila. Bradford. 1810. 8°. 20p. 3 acts (Cumberland's British theatre. v. 40 no. 4)

Hero of the North; an historical play. London. 1803. 87p.

Hunter of the Alps; a melodrama in two acts. London. Baker. 40p. (Cumberland's British theatre. v. 39)

Lady and the devil: a musical drama, in two acts. . . London. Davidson. n.d. 12°. 36p. (Cumberlands British theatre. v. 46 no. 2)

Mother's vengeance. *See* Dimond, W. Adrian and Orilla; or, A mother's vengeance

Peasant boy. An opera in three acts. . . London. Cumberland. [1839]. 12°. 50p. (Cumberland's British theatre. v. 40 no. 9)

Royal oak; an historical play in three acts. N.Y. Longworth. 1812. 64p. 12°.

Sea-side story; an operatic drama in two acts. London. Barker. 1801. 59p.

Secrets of a palace. *See* Dimond, W. Doubtful son; or, Secrets of a palace

Stage struck; or, The loves of Augustus Portarlington and Celestina Beverley. A farce in one act. London. Lacy. n.d. 12°. 22p. (Lacy's acting edition of plays. v. 10 no. 142)

Young hussar. An operatic drama, in two acts. . . London. Cumberland. n.d. 12°. 34p. (Cumberland's British theatre. v. 41 no. 2)

Youth, love and folly, a comic opera. . . Baltimore. Dobbin. 1807. 12°. 36p. (Cumberland's British theatre. v. 39 no. 3)

Divine, Charles, 1889-
Pirtle drums it in. . . N.Y. Appleton. 1926. 12°. 31p. Comedy. 1 act

Post mortems; a comedy of the bridge table. N.Y. Appleton. 1926. 12°. 20p.

Ditrichstein, Leon, 1865-
Are you a mason? A farcical comedy in three acts. N.Y. French. c1901. 12°. 114p.

Dix, Beulah Marie, 1876-
Across the border; a play of the present, in one act and four scenes. . . N.Y. Holt. 1915. 12°. 96p. World war

Allison's lad. Interlude. 1 act
In Allison's lad, and other martial plays
Mayorga, M. G. ed. Representative one-act plays

Captain of the gate. Supernatural. 1 act
In Allison's lad, and other martial plays
Leonard, S. A. Atlantic book of modern plays

Clemency, written for the American school peace league. Boston. [American school peace league]. 1916. 8°. 32p. War. 1 act

Dark of the dawn. Interlude. 1 act
In Allison's lad, and other martial interludes
Smith, M. M. ed. Short plays of various types

Enemy; written for the American school peace league. Boston. [American school peace league]. 1915. 8°. 24p. War. 1 act

Glorious game; written for the American school peace league. Boston. [American school peace league]. 1916. 8°. 23p. War. 1 act

Hundredth trick. Interlude. 1 act
In Allison's lad, and other martial interludes

Legend of St. Nichola. Juvenile. 1 act
In Poet Lore 25:473

Moloch; a play in a prologue, three acts and an epilogue. N.Y. Knopf. 1916. 12°. 94p. World war

Pageant of peace, written for the American School peace league. Boston. [American school peace league]. 1915. 8°. 20p. Peace. 1 act

Snare of the fowler. Interlude. 1 act
In Allison's lad, and other martial interludes

Weakest link. Interlude. 1 act
In Allison's lad, and other martial interludes

Where war comes; written for the American school peace league. Boston. [American school peace league]. 1916. 8°. 20p. War. 1 act

Dix, Beulah M., and Harper, Carrie, A.
Beau's comedy. . . N.Y. Harper. 1902. 12°. 319p.

Dix, Beulah M., and Sutherland, Evelyn G.
Road to yesterday; a comedy of fantasy. . . N.Y. French. c1925. 12°. 92p.

Rose o' Plymouth-Town; a romantic comedy in four acts. Boston. Fortune press. 1903. 8°. 111p.

Dixon, Thomas, 1864-
Man of the people; a drama of Abraham Lincoln. . . N.Y. Appleton. 1920. 12°. 155p.

Dixon, W. J.
Sir Walter Ralegh. A tragedy in five acts. . . London. Chiswick press. 1897. 93p.

Dobie, C. C.
Immortals; a Slavic fantasy. 1 act
In Overland n s 84:74

Docquois, Georges, 1863-
After the opera. Intrigue. 1 act
In Smart Set 20 no 4:103

Dodd, Lee Wilson, 1879-
Changelings; a comedy. N.Y. Dutton. [c1924]. 12°. 21p. 2 acts
Same in Mantle, B. ed. Best plays of 1923-24 (condensed)

His Majesty Bunker Bean; a comedy in four acts and five scenes, from the novel of Harry Leon Wilson. N.Y. French. c1922. 12°. 116p.

Pals first; a comedy in prologue and three acts. . . Based on novel "Pals first", by F. P. Elliott. N.Y. French. c1925. 12°. 105p.

Dondo, Mathurin Marius, 1884-
Pie and the tart. (?) Le paté et la tarte, adapted from a French farce of the fifteenth century. N.Y. Appleton. 1925. 12°. 23p. 1 act

Dondo, M. M.—*Continued*
Two blind men and a donkey, a play for
marionettes. N.Y. Appleton. 1925. 8°.
22p. 6 scenes
Same in Poet Lore 32:391

Donnay, Maurice Charles, 1859-
Free woman (L'Affranchie).   Comedy. 3
acts
In Lovers ₍and other plays₎
Gimlet.   Comedy. 1 act
In Stratford J (Boston) 3:267
Lovers (amantes).   Comedy. 5 acts
In Lovers ₍and other plays₎
Moses, M. J. ed.   Representative
continental dramas
Other danger (L'autre danger).   Com-
edy. 4 acts
In Three modern plays from the French
Drama 3 no 11:13
They (Eux!)   Interlude. 1 act
In Lovers ₍and other plays₎

Doran, Marie
Dorothy's neighbors; a comedy in four
acts.   N.Y. French. 1918. 12°. 25c
Girls over here; a new patriotic entertain-
ment in one act.   N.Y. French. 1918.
12°. 25c
Honor pupil; a comedy in four acts.
N.Y. French. c1925. 12°. 92p.
June; a comedy in four acts.   N.Y.
French. 1918. 12°. 25c
Liberty thrift girls; a patriotic play in
one act.   N.Y. French. 1918. 40p.
Molly Bawn; a comedy drama in four
acts.   N.Y. Fitzgerald. 1920. 12°. 86p.
35c
That orphan; a comedy in four acts.
N.Y. French. c1924. 12°. 96p.

Dorey, Joseph Milnor, 1876-
Under conviction.   Revival. 1 act
In Drama 9:no 33:115

Dorff, M. J.
Firefly night.   Juvenile. 1 act
In Loving, P. ed.   Ten minute plays

Dostoevskii, Fedor Mikhailovich, 1821-1881
Brothers Karamazoff.   Tragedy. 6 scenes
In Brothers Karamazoff, etc.
Sayler, O. M. ed.   Moscow art
theatre series of Russian plays
ser 2
Lady from the provinces.   Comedy. 1 act
In Brothers Karamazoff, etc.

Douglass, Vincent
Partners; a play in three periods.   N.Y.
French. c1926. 12°. 88p.

Down, Oliphant, 1885-1917
Bal masqué.   Satire. 1 act
In Three one-act plays
Dream-child.   Dream. 1 act
In Three one-act plays
Idealist.   Comedy. 1 act
In One-act plays for stage and study
ser 2
Maker of dreams, a fantasy in one act.
London. Gowans. 1914. 12°. 47p.
Same in Clark, B. H. ed.   Representa-
tive one-act plays by British
and Irish authors

Cohen, H. L. ed.   One-act
plays by modern authors
In Marriott, J. W. ed.   One-act plays
of to-day
Smith, M. M. ed.   Short plays of
various types
Tommy-by-the-way.   World war. 1 act
In Three one-act plays
Wealth and wisdom.   Comedy. 1 act
In One act plays for stage and study
ser 1

Downey, June Etta, 1875-
Study in the nude.   Tragedy. 2 scenes
In Poet Lore 31:253

Downing, Henry Francis, 1851-
Arabian lovers; or, The sacred jar, an
eastern tale in four acts. . . London.
Griffiths. ₍c1913₎. 12°. 85p.
Human nature; or, The traduced wife;
an original English domestic drama,
in four acts.   London. Griffiths.
₍c1913₎. 12°. 75p.
Lord Eldred's other daughter; an original
comedy in four acts. . . London.
Griffiths. ₍c1913₎. 12°. 85p.
Israel in Russia.   *See* Downing, H. F.
Shuttlecock; or, Israel in Russia
Placing Paul's play: a minature comedy.
London. Griffin. c1913. 12°. 24p.
Sacred jar.   *See* Downing, H. F. Ara-
bian loves; or, The sacred jar
Shuttlecock; or, Israel in Russia, an
original drama in four acts. . . Lon-
don. Griffiths. c1913. 12°. 96p.
Traduced wife.   *See* Downing, H. G.
Human nature; or, The traduced wife
Voodoo, a drama in four acts.   London.
Griffiths. ₍1914₎. 111p.   Historical

Dowson, Ernest, 1867-1900
Pierrot of the minute; a dramatic phan-
tasy in one act. . . London. Smithers.
1897. 12°. 43p.
Same in Poems
Cohen, H. L. ed.   One act
plays by modern authors
Shay, F. and Loving, P. eds.
Fifty contemporary one-act
plays

Doyle, Sir Arthur Conan, 1859-
Exile; a drama of Christmas eve.   N.Y.
Appleton. 1925. 24p. 1 act
It's time something happened; a drama.
N.Y. Appleton. 1925. 12°. 41p. 1 act
Waterloo.   1 act
In Marriott, J. W. ed.   One-act plays
of to-day ser 2

Doyle, Edward, 1854-
Cagliostro.   A dramatic poem in five
acts. N.Y. Printed for author by W.
B. Smith. ₍c1882₎. 12°. 131p.   Spirit-
ualism
Comet; a play of our times.   Boston.
Badger. 1908. 12°. 176p.   College. 6
acts
Ginevra, a play of mediaeval Florence.
N.Y. Doyle. 1912. 12°. 94p. 5 acts

Drachmann, Holger Henrik Herholdt,
1846-1908
Renaissance. Melodrama. 1 act
In Poet Lore 19:369
Dransfield, Jane, 1875-
Blood o' kings. Race prejudice. 1 act
In Shay, F. ed. Treasury of plays for
men
Joe; a Hudson Valley play. N.Y.
Rhymus. 1923. 12°. 38p. Tragedy.
1 act
Same in Shay, Frank. Twenty-five
short plays, international
Lost Pleiad; a fantasy in two acts. N.Y.
White. [c1918]. 12°. 96p.
Same in Shay, F. ed. Treasury of
plays for women
Draper, John W., 1893-
After the requiem. Poetic. 1 act
In Colonnade 13:37
Within cloister gates. 1 act
In Colonnade 11:92
Dreiser, Theodore, 1871-
Blue sphere. Idiocy. 1 act
In Plays of the natural and super-
natural
Smart Set 44:245
Dream. Dream. 1 act
In Seven Arts 2:319
Girl in the coffin. Tragedy. 1 act
In Plays of the natural and super-
natural
Smart Set 41 no 2:127
Hand of the potter, a tragedy in four
acts. N.Y. Boni. 1918. 8°. 209p.
In the dark. Supernatural. 1 act
In Plays of the natural and super-
natural
Smart Set 45:419
Laughing gas. Anaesthesia. 1 act
In Plays of the natural and super-
natural
Smart Set 45 no 2:85
Light in the window. Domestic. 1 act
In Plays of the natural and super-
natural
International (NY) 10:6
"Old Ragpicker." Dementia. 1 act
In Plays of the natural and super-
natural
Spring recital. Supernatural. 1 act
In Plays of the natural and super-
natural
Little Review 2 no 9:28
Drennan, Marie
Slippers that broke of themselves. Cin-
derella. 1 act
In Poet Lore 37:258
Valley of gloom. Allegory. 1 act
In Poet Lore 34:449
Dreyfus, Abraham, 1847-
He and she. Farce. 1 act
In Beerbohm, C. ed. Little book of
plays
On his devoted head. A domestic scene.
Tr. from "Un crâne sous une tem-
pête". . . N.Y. De Witt. [1885]. 12°.
8p. 1 act

Drinkwater, John, 1882-
Abraham Lincoln; a play, with an inter-
lude. . . Boston. Houghton. 1919.
12°. 112p. Tragedy. 6 scenes
Same in Collected plays. v 2
Dickinson, T. H. ed. Chief
contemporary dramatists ser
2
Moses, M. J. ed. Another
treasury of plays for children
Plays of today v 1
Cophetua, a play in one act. London.
Nutt. 1914. 12°. 18p. Legendary
Same in Collected plays v 1
Pawns
English medley. Masque. 3 acts
In Collected plays. v 1
God of quiet. Poetic. 1 act
In Collected plays v 1
Pawns
Little Johnny. Comedy. 1 act
In Collected plays v 2
Eng R 33:292
Mary Stuart, a play. N.Y. Houghton.
1921. 12°. 73p. Tragedy. 1 act
Same in Collected plays v 1
Oliver Cromwell; a play. Boston.
Houghton. 1921. 12°. 96p. Histori-
cal. Eight scenes
Same in Collected plays v 2
Dickinson, T. H. ed. Con-
temporary plays
Only legend, a masque of the scarlet
Pierrot. 1 act
In Collected plays v 1
Pied Piper, a tale of Hamelin City.
Masque. 1 act
In Collected plays v 1
Rebellion; a play in three acts. Lon-
don. Hutt. [1914]. 12°. 58p. Tragedy
Same in Collected plays v 1
Robert Burns. Boston. Houghton. 1925.
12°. 121p. $1.50 Biographical
Robert E. Lee; a play. Boston. Hough-
ton. 1923. 12°. 128p. Historical. 9
scenes
Same in Collected plays v 2
Robin Hood and the pedlar. Masque 1
act
In Collected plays v 1
Storm; a play in one act. Birmingham
repertory theatre. 1915. 12°. 18p.
Poetic
Same in Collected plays v 1
Pawns
Theatre Arts M 4:191
X=O: A night of the Trojan war. Poe-
tic. 1 act
In Collected plays v 1
Pawns
Marriott, J. W. ed. One-act plays
of today
Driscoll, Louise, 1875-
Child of God. Individuality. 1 act
In Seven Arts 1:34
Pageant of women. 1 act
In Drama 14:263

Driscoll, L.—*Continued*
Poor house. Self-sacrifice. 1 act
  In Cohen, H. L. ed. More one-act
    plays by modern authors
    Drama 7:448
Droz, Gustav, 1832-1895
Cardinal's illness. Comedy. 1 act
  In Bellevue dramatic club: Plays for
    private acting
Registered letter; a comedy in one act. . .
  Tr. by members of the Bellevue
  Dramatic Club of Newport. Boston.
  Baker. 1901. 12°. 23p.
  Same in Bellevue dramatic Club: Plays
    for private acting
Drum, Sidney
Six miles from a lemon; a farce in three
  acts. Boston. Baker. 1916. 12°. 163p.
Drummond, Sara King Wiley
Coming of Philibert. N.Y. Macmillan.
  1907. 12°. 163p. Poetic. 3 acts
Drury, William Price
King's hard bargain; a play in one act.
  N.Y. French. c1924. 20p.
Playwright; a heresy in one act. N.Y.
  French. c1924. 12°. 20p.
Dubourg, Augustus W., 1830?-1910
Angelica; a romantic drama in four acts.
  London. Bentley. 1892. 8°.
Art and love. Artist life. 1 act
  In Four original plays
Greencloth. Monte Carlo. 4 acts
  In Four original plays
Land and love. Romantic. 3 acts
  In Four original plays
Sympathy. A comedietta in one act.
  (Lacy's acting edition of plays. v. 96.)
  1850. 12°.
Twenty minutes under an umbrella.
  Comic interlude. [in one act]. (Lacy's
  acting edition of plays. v. 106.) 1850.
  12°.
Vittoria Contarini; or, Love the traitor.
  Romantic drama in five acts. Lon-
  don. 1875. 12°.
**Dubourg, Augustus W., 1830?-1910, and
  Taylor, Tom, 1817-1880**
New men and old acres. A comedy in
  three acts. London. Lacy. 1850. 12°.
  (Lacy's acting edition of plays. v. 90)
Sister's penance; an original drama in
  three acts. London. Lacy. 1850. 12°.
  (Lacy's acting edition of plays. v. 75)
Du Cange, Victor H. J. B., 1783-1833
All in the dark; or, The banks of the
  Elbe. A musical farce in two acts.
  Adapted . . . by J. R. Planché. . .
  N.Y. Murden. 1822. 24°. 52p.
Fate of Calas. A tragic melo-drame in
  three acts. . . Altered and adapted by
  T. Dibdin. London. Lowndes. 1820.
  8°. 42p.
Hut of the Red Mountain; or Thirty
  years of a gamester's life; a domes-
  tic melodrama. . . (Adapted from the
  French. . . "Trente ans, ou La vie
  d'un jouer"). . . London. Lowndes.
  1827. 12°. 59p.

Thérèse; or, The orphan of Geneva; a
  melodrama in three acts. . . London.
  Lowndes. [18—]. 8°. 32p.
  Same in Bates, A. ed. Drama 19:149
Duckworth, William
Cromwell. A drama. London. 1870. 8°.
  Historical. 5 acts
Duer, Caroline
Ambassador's burglar. Comedy. 1 act
  In Smart Set 5 no 3:49
Mr. Shakespeare at school. Comedy. 1
  act
  In Smart Set 7 no 2:65
Duer, Caroline King, 1865-, joint author.
  See Ford, Harriet, Where Julia rules
Duffy, Bernard
Corner, a comedy in one act. Dublin.
  Talbot press. 1921. 8°. 30p.
  Same in Four comedies
Counter-charm; a comedy in one act.
  Dublin. Talbot press. 1921. 8°. 24p.
Old lady. A comedy in one act. Dublin.
  Talbot press. 1921. 12°. 24p.
  Same in Four comedies
Special pleading, a coincidence in one act.
  Dublin. Talbot press. 1921. 8°. 23p.
Duffy, Richard, 1873-
Night of the wedding. Domestic. 1 act
  In Smart Set 25 no 1:80
Duhamel, Georges, 1884-
Combat. Struggle for existence. 5 acts
  In Poet Lore 26:409
In the shadow of statues. Coercion. 3
  acts
  In Poet Lore 25:371
Light. Symbolic. 4 acts
  In Poet Lore 25:161
Dukes, Ashley, 1885-
One more river; a modern comedy in
  three acts. London. Benn. 1927.
  12°. 80p.
Civil war; a comedy in four acts. Lon-
  . don. Swift. 1911. 133p.
Man with a load of mischief; a comedy
  in three acts. London. Benn. 1924.
  8°. 38p.
Song of drums; a heroic comedy in a
  prologue and three acts. London.
  Benn. 1926. 12°. 104p.
Dumas, Alexandre, 1802-1870
Antony. A drama in five acts. N.Y.
  Rullman. 1880. 8°. 32p.
Catherine of Cleves. A tragic drama in
  three acts. . . London. Andrews.
  1831. 8°. 116p.
Mademoiselle de Belle-Isle. A drama in
  five acts. . . N.Y. Darcy. 1855. 4°.
  71p.
Marriage of convenience; period of Louis
  XV, a comedy. . . N.Y. French.
  1899. 12°. 65p.
Paul Jones; a drama in five acts. . .
  Phila. Collins. 1839. 12°. 89p.
Dumas, Alexandre, fils, 1824-1895
Camille; a play. (Lady with the camel-
  lias). Boston. Baker. 1907. 12°. 86p.
  Emotional. 5 acts. *also* London.
  Lacy. n.d. 12°. 36p.

Demi-monde ₁Outer edge₁; a satire on society. . . Phila. Lippincott. 1850. 12°. 164p. Comedy. 5 acts

Same in Matthews, J. B. ed. Chief European dramatists

Denise. A play in four acts. N.Y. Rull-man. 1888. 8°. 55p. Problem

L'Etrangère (The foreigner). A comedy in five acts. N.Y. Rullman. 1881. 8°. 61p.

Foreigner. *See* Dumas, A., fils. L'Etrangère

Money question. Comedy. 5 acts
In Poet Lore 26:129

Monsieur Alphonse; a play in three acts. Adapted and arranged by Augustin Daly. . . N.Y. Printed for the author. 1886. 12°. 60p.

Outer edge. *See* Dumas, A. fils. Demi-monde

La princess Georges; a play in three acts. N.Y. Rullman. 1881. 8°. 28p. Melo-drama

Dumas, André
Eternal presence. Nocturne. 1 act
In Poet Lore 29:459

Dumas, William Charles, 1885-
Belshazzar. Boston. Badger. ₁1912₁. 12°. 120p. $1.25 Jewish. 5 acts

Du Maurier, Guy Louis Busson, 1865-
Englishman's home; a play in three acts. N.Y. Harper. 1909. 8°. 130p.

Dunbar, Alice (Mrs. Paul Laurence Dun-bar)
Author's evening at home. Domestic. 1 act
In Smart Set 1 no 3:105

Dunbar, N., 1845-
Ever womanly. Homily. 1 act
In Arena 31:180

Dunbar, O. H.
Blockade. Hypocrisy. 1 act
In Theatre Arts M 7:127

Duncan, G.
Proposal. Egotism. 1 act
In Harper 108:796

Duncan, William Cary, 1874-, and Matthews, Adelaide
An errand for Polly; a character comedy in three acts. N.Y. French. c1926. 12°. 93p.

Dunlap, William, 1766-1839
Aboellino, the great bandit. N.Y. D. Longworth. 1802. 12°. 82p. Melo-drama. 5 acts

André; a tragedy in five acts. . . London. Ogilvy. 1799. 12°. 110p.
Same in Dunlap Soc pub no 4
Quinn, A. H. ed. Representa-tive American plays 1767-1923

Archers; or Mountaineers of Switzerland; an opera in three acts. . . N.Y. Swords. 1796. 12°. 94p.

Darby's return. A comic sketch. 1 act. N.Y. Hodge. 1789. 8°. 14p.

Father of an only child ₁The father₁. A comedy. N.Y. Longworth. 1807. 12°. 81p. 5 acts
Same in Dunlap Soc pub no 2

Feudal baron. *See* Dunlap, W. Ribbe-mont, or, The feudal baron

Foutainville abbey; a tragedy. . . N.Y. David Longworth. 1807. 12°. p. 155-211. 5 acts

Fraternal discord: a drama in five acts. Altered from the German of A. Von Kotzebue. N.Y. D. Longworth. 1809. 12°. 69p. Comedy

Glory of Columbia; her yoemanry. A play in five acts. N.Y. Longworth. 1803. 12°. 56p. Fourth of July

Good neighbor; an interlude in one act. Altered from a scene of Iffland's. N.Y. Longworth. 1814. 12°. 12p.

Great banditti. *See* Dunlap, W. Rin-aldo Rinaldini, or, The great banditti

Huzza for the constitution! *See* Dunlap, W. Yankee chronology; or, Huzza for the constitution

Italian father; a comedy. N.Y. Long-worth. 1810. 16°. 63p. 5 acts

Leicester; a tragedy. N.Y. D. Long-worth. 1807. 12°. 150p. 5 acts

Lover's vows; a play from the German of Kotzebue. N.Y. Longworth. 1814. 12°. 74p. Melodrama. 5 acts

Mountaineers in Switzerland. *See* Dun-lap, W. Archers, or, Mountaineers in Switzerland

Peter the great; or, The Russian mother. A play altered from the German. N.Y. Longworth. 1814. 12°. 56p. Revolution. 4 acts

Ribbemont; or, The feudal baron, a tragedy in five acts. N.Y. Long-worth. 1803. 12°. 72p.

Rinaldo Rinaldini; or, The great banditti. A tragedy in five acts. . . N.Y. Au-thor. 1810. 8°. 82p.

Russian mother. *See* Dunlap, W. Peter the Great; or, The Russian mother

Tell truth and shame the devil; a comedy in two acts. . . N.Y. Swords. 1797. 12°. 45p. (Adapted from Robineau's farce "Jerome Pointu").

Travellers in America. *See* Dunlap, W. Trip to Niagara; or, Travellers in America

Trip to Niagara; or, travellers in Amer-ica. A farce in three acts. N.Y. E. B. Clayton. 1830. 12°. 54p.

Voice of nature; a drama translated and altered from the French melo-drama, called the Judgment of Solomon. N.Y. Longworth. 1807. 12°. 41p. 3 acts

Wife of two husbands, a drama. N.Y. Longworth. 1811. 12°. 55p. Melo-drama. 5 acts

Yankee chronology; or, Huzza for the constitution; a musical interlude in one act. . . N.Y. Longworth. 1812. 12°. 16p.

Dunn, Caesar
Four-flusher, he; an American comedy in
three acts.   N.Y. French. c1925. 12°.
103p.
Dunning, Phillip, and Abbott, George
Broadway, a play.   N.Y. Doran. 1927.
12°. 236p.   Melodrama. 3 acts
Dunning, Ralph Cheever
Hyllus; a drama.   N.Y. Lane. 1910. 12°.
124p.
Dunsany, Lord Edward, 1878-
Alexander. Historical. 4 acts
In Alexander and three small plays
Amusements of Khan Kharuda.   Orien-
tal mysticism. 1 act
In Alexander and three small plays
Cheeso (a story of right and wrong
where wrong triumphs).   Fantasy.
1 act
In Plays of near and far
Compromise of the king of the Golden
Isles.   Fantasy. 1 act
In Plays of near and far
Evil kettle.   Fantasy. 1 act
In Alexander and three small plays
Moses, M. J. ed.   Another treasury
of plays for children
Fame and the poet.   Comedy. 1 act
In Plays of near and far
Leonard, S. A. ed.   Atlantic book of
modern plays
Atlan 124:175
Flight of the queen (a story of the bees).
Fantasy. 4 scenes
In Plays of near and far
Glittering gate.   Symbolic. 1 act
In Five plays
Gods of the mountain.   Fantasy. 1 act
In Five plays
Moses, M. J. ed.   Representative
British dramas
Irish R 1:486
Poetry R 2:17
Golden doom.   Fantasy. 1 act
In Five plays
Clark, B. H. ed.   Representative
one-act plays by British and Irish
authors
Poetry and drama 1:431
Good bargain.   Religious. 1 act
In Plays of near and far
If, a play in four acts.   London. Put-
nam. [1921]. 12°. 160p.   Fantasia
If Shakespeare lived to-day.   Satire. 1 act
In Plays of near and far
Atlan 126:497

Jest of Hahalaba.   Alchemy. 1 act
In Atlan 139:58
King Argimenes and the unknown war-
rior.   Fantasy. 1 act
In Five plays
Dickinson, T. H. ed.   Chief con-
temporary dramatists ser 2
Irish R 1:336
Laughter of the gods.   Tragedy. 3 acts
In Plays of gods and men
Lost silk hat.   Comedy. 1 act
In **Five plays**

Night at an inn, a play in one act.   N.Y.
Sunwise Turn. 1916. 12°. 34p.   Super-
stition
Same in Plays of gods and men
Cohen, H. L. ed.   One act
plays by modern authors
Dickinson, A. D. ed. Drama
Marriott, J. W. ed.   One-act
plays of to-day
Smith, M. M. ed.   Short plays
of various types
Golden Bk 4:377
Old King's tale.   Fate. 1 act
In Alexander and three small plays
Queen's enemies.   Tragedy. 1 act
In Plays of gods and men
Tents of the Arabs.   Fantasy. 2 acts
In Plays of gods and men
Smart Set 45:229
Golden Bk 1:849
**Dunton, Edith Kellogg (Margaret Ward,
pseud.),** 1875-
Is your name Smith? a comedy in one act.
Phila. Penn. 1921. 12°. 33p. 35c
Durant, Harry, 1871-
Man within; a play of Napoleon, in four
acts. . . New York. French. c1921.
12°. 157p.
Du Souchet, Henry A., 1852-
Man from Mexico; a farcical comedy in
three acts.   N.Y. French. 1920. 12°.
107p. 75c
My friend from India; a farcical comedy
in three acts.   N.Y. French. 1912?
12°. 95p.
**Duveyrier, A. H. J. and E. A. R. de Bully
(Roger de Beauvoir)**
Chevalier de St. George a drama in three
acts.   Adapted. London. Lacy. [18—?].
12°. 35p. (Lacy's acting edition of
plays. v. 25 no. 368)
Duveyrier, Anne Honoré Joseph, 1787-1865,
and Duveyrier, Charles, 1803-1866
Mistress of the mill (La Munère de Mar-
ny); a comedietta in one act.   [adapt-
ed]. . . London. Lacy. [185—?]. 12°.
30p. (Lacy's acting edition of plays.
v. 21 no. 308)
Dyk, Victor
Ninth night.   Comedy. 1 act
In Poet Lore 29:90
Earle, E. Haworth
Griselda; a poetic drama founded on
Boccaccio's novel and Chaucer's
poem. London. Brown. [1916]. 64p.
Earle, Georgia
Before the play begins.   Chicago. Deni-
son. 1920. 12°.
Gettin' acquainted; a small town comedy
Chicago. Denison. [c1919]. 12°. 32p.
35c. 1 act
Lie that Jack built; a comedy in one act.
Chicago. Denison. 1920. 12°. 41p. 35c
Earnest, H. L.
Nocturne.   Fantasy. 1 act
In Indiana prize plays, 1922-23

Ebin, Alexander B.
John Callman; a play in three acts and a
prologue. . . N.Y. American policy-
holder. ₍c1924₎. 12°. 66p. Finance
Marriageables. A farcical comedy from
modern life in New York. n.t.p. ₍N.Y.
c1912₎. 8°. 64p.
Portia in politics, a play in three acts.
n.t.p. ₍N.Y. c1912₎. 8°. 64p. Satire
Proceed with the dance; or Louise; a
play of today. N.Y. Photoplay
classics corp. 12°. 1923. 80p.

Ebner von Eschenbach, Marie, 1830-1916
Man of the world. Boston. Badger. 1912.
12°. p. 128-133 Character. 1 act
Same in Poet Lore 22:128

Echegaray (y Eizaguirre), José, 1835-1916
Always ridiculous (Siempre en ridículo).
Comedy. 3 acts
In Poet Lore 27:233
Folly or saintliness. *See* Echegaray, J.
Madman or saint
Great Galeoto (El gran Galeoto); a drama
in three acts and a prologue. . . Bos-
ton Badger. 1914. 12°. 202p. *Also*
Doubleday. 1914. 75c. Domestic trag-
edy
Same in Great Galeoto, Folly or Saint-
liness
Clark, B. H. ed. Masterpieces
of Spanish drama
Pierce and Matthews, eds.
Masterpieces of modern
drama v 2 (abridged)
Madman divine (el loco dios); a prose
drama in four acts. . . Boston. Bad-
ger. 1912. 8°. p. 161-220 85. Also pub.
by Wessels. N.Y. Insanity
Same in Poet Lore 19:3
Madman or saint (Folly or saintliness)
(Ó locura ó santidad); a drama in
three acts. . . Boston. Badger. c1912.
8°. p. 161-220. Honor. 3 acts
Same in Great Galeoto; Folly or saint-
liness
Poet Lore 23:161
Man in black (El hombre negro).
Emotional. 3 acts
In Garnett, R. ed. Universal anthol-
ogy. v 27:346
Mariana. N.Y. Albert & Charles. Boni.
1914. 12°. 157p. Tragedy. 3 acts
Son of Don Juan (El hijo de Don Juan),
an original drama in three acts in-
spired by the reading of Ibsen's
"Gengangere". . . Boston. Roberts.
1895. 12°. 131p. Pathological
Street singer. Romantic. 1 act
In Shay, Frank. Twenty-five short
plays, international
Drama 7:62
Golden Bk 5:192
World and his wife (adaptation of Eche-
garay, J. Great Galeoto. q.v.) by C.
F. Nirdlinger. N.Y. Kennerley.
₍1908₎. 12°. 200p. Marriage. 3 acts

Eckersley, Arthur, 1875-1921
Adapted for amateurs. Farce. 1 act
In Odds and ends of a learned clerk

Art of the theatre. Farce. 1 act
In Odds and ends of a learned clerk
Boy's proposal; a little comedy in one
act. London. French. ₍1909₎. 12°.
28p.
Celtic revue. Farce. 1 act
In Odds and ends of a learned clerk
Collection will be made. Farce. 1 act
In Odds and ends of a learned clerk
Edward. Comedy. 1 act
In Odds and ends of a learned clerk
Hartleys; a play in one act. N.Y.
French. c1916. 12°. 24p. Comedy
Spoop. Farce. 1 act
In Odds and ends of a learned clerk
Susan's embellishments, a little comedy
in one act. London. French. c1918.
12°. 23p.
Tabloid. Melodrama. 1 act
In Odds and ends of a learned clerk
Smart Set 44 no 2:134

Edgeworth, M.
Dame school holiday
In Moses, M. J. ed. Another treasury
of plays for children

Egerton, Lady. *See* Buckingham and
Chandos

Ehrlich, Ida Lublenski
Changing places. 1 act
In One-act plays for stage and study
ser 3
Snaring the lion. Biblical. 1 act
In Drama 9 no 34:60

Ehrmann, Max, 1872-
Bank robbery. Farce. 1 act
In Schafer, B. L. comp. Book of one-
act plays
David and Bathsheba. Biblical. 3 acts
In Drama 7:492
Jesus; a passion play. N.Y. Baker.
₍c1915₎. 12°. 282p. 5 acts
Wife of Marobius, a play. N.Y. Ken-
nerley. 1921. 12°. 73p. Tragedy. 1
act

Einarsson, Indridi
Sword and crozier. . . Iceland. 5 acts
Same in Poet Lore 24 (i.e. 23):225

Eldridge, Paul, 1888-
Jest. Comi-tragedy. 1 act
In Stratford J 3:22
Loser. Character. 1 act
In Drama 11:166

Elkins, Felton Broomail, 1889-
Belgian baby. Farce. 1 act
In Three tremendous trifles
Figuratively speaking. Farce. 1 act
In Three tremendous trifles
Quick and the dead. Satire. 1 act
In Three tremendous trifles

Ellis, Edith
Betty's last bet; a farce comedy in three
acts. Chicago. Denison. ₍c1921₎. 12°.
149p.
Contrary Mary; a comedy in three acts.
N.Y. French. c1912. 12°. 110p.
Hiram Perkins. *See* Ellis,. E. Mary
Jane's pa
Judsons entertain; a comedy in three acts.
N.Y. French. ₍c1922₎. 12°. 119p.

Ellis, E.—*Continued*

Mary Jane's pa; a play in three acts. N.Y. Kennerley. 1914. 12°. 174p. (First produced as Hiram Perkins.ı Comedy

Whose little bride are you?   A farce-comedy in three acts.   Chicago. Denison. ₍1919₎. 12°. 152p.

Ellis, Edith M. (Mrs. Havelock), 1861-1916

Ben of Broken Bow; an original American comedy in four acts.   N.Y. French. c1925. 12°. 132p.

Mothers.   Marriage. 1 act
In Love in danger

Pixy.   Character. 1 act
In Love in danger

Subjection of Kezia: a play in one act (Adapted from story in "My Cornish neighbors") Stratford-on-Avon. Shakespeare head press. 1908. 12°. 15p.   Comedy. 1 act
Same in Love in danger
       Shay, F. and Loving, P. eds. Fifty contemporary one-act plays

Ellis, Edward, and Baker, Edith Ellis

Mrs. Clancy's car ride; a farce in one act. Washington. Commission training camp activities among the soldiers. 1918. 12°. 16p. (War Dept. Service ed. no. 11)

Ellis, Ellsworth, and Ellis, Everett

Sacrifice; a tragic drama.   Baltimore. Saulsbury. 1918. 12°. 57p. $1 3 acts

Elwes, Mary

In time of war.   Comedy. 1 act
In Temporary engagements and other plays

Stiggins entire.   *See* Elwes, M. Temporary engagements; or, Stiggins, entire

Temporary engagements; or, Stiggins entire.   Comedy. 1 act
In Temporary engagements and other plays

Two in a flat.   Comedy. 1 act
In Temporary engagements and other plays

Emerson, Edwin, 1870-

Benedict Arnold; a drama of the American revolution in three acts and a prelude.   N.Y. Printed for private distribution by the Vail-Ballou press. c1924. 142p.

Emerson, John, 1874-, **and Loos, Anita**

Whole town's talking; a farce in three acts.   N.Y. Longmans. 1925. 12°. 120p.

Emery, Gilbert

Hero.   Tragi-Comedy.   3 acts
In Mantle, B. ed.   Best plays of 1921-22 (condensed)
       Quinn, A. H. ed.   Contemporary American plays

Tarnish, a play in three acts.   N.Y. Brentano's. ₍c1924₎. 12°. 82p.   Problem
Same in Mantle, B. ed.   Best plays of 1923-24 (condensed)

Emig, Evelyn

China pig.   Frustration. 1 act
In Shay, F. ed.   Treasury of plays for women
       Poet Lore 33:439

Old order.   Youth and age. 1 act
In Poet Lore 32:586

Enander, Hilma Lewis

In the light of the stone.   Robbery. 1 act
In Three plays

Man who did not understand.   Comedy. 1 act
In Three plays

On the trail.   Crime. 1 act
In Three plays

England, George Allan, 1877-

"Under their skins".   Satire. 1 act
In Smart Set 44 no 3:107

Eno, Henry Lane

Baglioni; a play in five acts.   N.Y. Moffat. 1905. 8°. 148p.   Tragedy

Erckmann, Emile, 1822-1899, **and Chatrian, Alexandre,** 1826-1890

Bells; or, The Polish Jew.   A romantic, moral drama.   In three acts. . . N.Y. De Witt. 1872

Ernst, Alice Henson

Nightingale.   Arabian night fantasy. 1 act
In Poet Lore 37:293

Erskine, John, 1879-

Hearts enduring; a play in one scene. N.Y. Duffield. 1920. 12°. 20p.   Tragedy
Same in Cohen, H. L. ed.   More one-act plays by modern authors

Pageant of the thirteenth century for the seven hundredth anniversary of Roger Bacon., given by Columbia university. . . N.Y. Columbia univ. press. 1914. 8°. 75p.   Roger Bacon. 3 parts

Ervine, St. John Greer, 1883-

Anthony and Anna.   N.Y. Macmillan. 1925. 12°. 192p.   Comedy. 3 acts

Critics.   Satire. 1 act
In Four Irish plays

Jane Clegg: a play in three acts. . . London.   Sidgwick. 1914. 12°. 112p. Domestic tragedy
In Plays of today v 1

John Ferguson; a play in four acts. N.Y. Macmillan. c1915. 12p. 113p. Domestic tragedy

Lady of Belmont; a play in five acts. N.Y. Macmillan. 1924. 12°. 95p. (Characters those of Merchant of Venice, time, 10 yrs. after Antonio's trial).   Travesty

Magnanimous lover; a play in one act. Dublin. Maunsel & co. Ltd. 1912. 12°. 19p.   Social
Same in Four Irish plays
       Clark, B. H. ed.   Representative one act plays by British and Irish authors

Mary, Mary, quite contrary; a light comedy in four acts.   N.Y. Macmillan. c1923. 12°. 130p.

Mixed marriage; a play in four acts. Dublin. Maunsel. 1911. 12°. 55p. Catholic and Protestant
Same in Dickinson, T. H. ed.   Chief contemporary dramatists ser 2
Orangeman.   Family strife. 1 act
In Four Irish plays
Progress.   War. 1 act
In Sat Eve Post 194:10 F 11 '22
Ship; a play in three acts.   N.Y. Macmillan. 1922. 12°. 94p.   Tragedy

Esmond, Henry V., 1869-1922
Bad hats; a play in three acts.   London. Butler & Tanner. c1916. 12°. 89p.
Billy's little love affair; a comedy in three acts.   N.Y. French. c1904. 12°. 84p.
Eliza comes to stay; a farce in three acts. N.Y. French. 1913. 12°. 79p.
Her vote.   A comedy in one act. . . N.Y. French. c1910. 12°. 8p.
Law divine; a comedy in one act. . . N.Y. French. c1922. 12°. 72p.
One summer's day.   N.Y. French. c1900. 12°. 63p.   Comedy. 3 acts
When we were twenty-one, comedy in four acts. . . N.Y. French. 1903. 12°. 80p.
Same in Pierce and Matthews, eds. Masterpieces of modern drama v 1 (abridged)
Wilderness, a comedy in three acts. . . N.Y. French. c1901. 12°. 65p.

Etlinger, Karl
Altruism.   Satire. 1 act
In Shay, F. and Loving, P. eds. Fifty contemporary one-act plays

Evans, Mrs. Florence (Wilkinson)
David of Bethlehem.   Israel. 5 acts
In Two plays of Israel
Marriage of Guineth.   Poetic. 1 act
In Ride home. . . ; The marriage of Guineth
Mary Magdalen.   Israel. 4 acts
In Two plays of Israel

Evans, Gladys La Due
Little mortal child.   Fantasy. 1 act
In Poet Lore 32:409

Evans, Margaret
Faith.   Unknown soldier. 1 act
In Poet Lore 33:132

Evréinov, Nikolaï Nikolaevich, 1879-
Beautiful despot.   Comedy. 1 act
In Bechhofer, C. E. ed.   Five Russian plays
Chief thing; a comedy for some a drama for others. . . Garden City. Doubleday. 1926. 12°. 226p. 3 acts
Merry death.   Harlequinade. 1 act
In Bechhofer, C. E. ed.   Five Russian plays
Moses, M. J. ed.   Representative one-act plays by continental authors
Theatre of the soul; a mono-drama in one act. . . London. Hendersons. [1915]. 12°. 27p.

Ewers, Hanns Heinz, 1871-
Tre cento.   Passion. 1 act
In International (N.Y.) 11:135

Eyre, Archibald
Custodian. . .
In Four plays
Girl in waiting.   Boston. Luce. 1906. 12°. 325p.
Same in Four plays
Intervention of Miss Watson
In Four plays
Leading lady
In Four plays

Fagan, James Bernard, 1873-
Earth; a modern play in four acts London. Unwin. [1913]. 12°. 158p. Melodrama
Hawthorne of the U.S.A.; a play in four acts.   N.Y. French. [c1917]. 12°. 95p. Romantic farce
Wheel of life (The wheel); a play in three acts.   N.Y. Brentano's. 1923. 12°. 125p.   India

Fagin, Mary
Room 226.   Ellis Island. 1 act
In Poet Lore 36:610

Falconer, Edward
Peep o' day; or, Savourneen Deelish. A drama in four acts. N.Y. French. [18—]. 44p.

Fane, Violet, pseud.   *See* Currie, Mary Montgomerie Singleton

Farias de Issasi, Teresa
Sentence of death.   Translated from the Spanish by Lilian Saunders.   Tragedy. 1 act
Same in Shay, Frank.   Twenty-five short plays, international

Farjeon, Herbert
Friends; a play in one act.   N.Y. French. 1923. 12°. 15p.

Farjeon, Herbert, and Horsnell, H.
Advertising April; or, The girl who made the sunshine jealous; a comedy in three acts.   N.Y. French. 1923. 12°. 63p. *also* Brentano's. 1923. 12°. 95p.
Girl who made the sunshine jealous. *See* Farjeon, H. and Horsnell, H. Advertising April; or, The girl who made the sunshine jealous

Farrar, John Chipman, 1896-
Birthdays come in February.   Juvenile
In Magic sea shell, etc.
Garden at the zoo.   Juvenile. 1 act
In Jagendorf, M. A.   One-act plays for young folks
God Pan forgotten.   Juvenile
In Magic sea shell, etc
Grandmother dozes.   Juvenile
In Magic sea shell, etc
House gnomes.   Juvenile
In Magic sea shell, etc
Kingdom of the rose queens.   Juvenile
In Magic sea shell, etc
Magic sea shell.   Juvenile.   Sea. 1 act
In Magic sea shell, etc
Clements, C. C. ed.   Sea plays
Bookm 57:511
Nerves.   World war. 1 act
In Thomas, C. S. ed.   Atlantic book of junior plays
Worship the Nativity.   Juvenile
In Magic sea shell, etc

Farriss, Charles Sherwood
Robert E. Lee; a play in five acts. Boston. Badger. c1924. 131p.   Historical

Fawcett, Edgar, 1847-1904
Buntling ball; a Graeco-American play; being a poetical satire on New York society. N.Y. Funk. 1885. 12°. 154p. 1 act
New King Arthur; an opera without music. . . N.Y. Funk. 1885. 12°. 164p. Arthurian. 2 acts
When the clock struck twelve; a Christmas play in one act
In Harper's Y P 2:114

Fayder, S.
Social balance.   1 act
In Nicholson, K. ed.   Appleton book of short plays

Feldhake, Joseph A.
It can be done; a play in two acts, introducing specialties and a style show. Effingham, Ill. Feldhake. 1923. 12°. 46p.   Allegory

Fenn, Frederick, 1868-1924
Convict on the hearth: a comedy in one act.   London. French. c1908. 12°. 37p.
Nelson touch.   Adapted from "The little pale man", by Mayne Lindsay. London. French. c1908. 12°. 20p. British navy. 1 act

Fenn, Frederick, 1868-1924, and Pryce, Richard
Love child.   Motherhood. 1 act
In Eng R 4:409
'Op-o'me-thumb.   A play in one act. N.Y. French. c1904. 12°. 25p.   Comedy.
Same in Clark, B. N. tr.   Representative one-act plays by British and Irish authors
Marriott, J. W.   One-act plays of today ser 2
One act plays for stage and study ser 1

Ferber, Edna, 1887-
Eldest; a drama of American life.   N.Y. London. Appleton. 1925. 12°. 21p. Tragedy. 1 act

Ferber, Edna, 1887-, and Kaufman, George, 1889-
Old man Minick. . . A play based on the short story. . . Garden City.   N.Y. Doubleday. 1924. 12°. 271p.   Domestic problem. 4 acts
Same in Mantle, B. ed.   Best plays of 1924-25 (abridged)

Ferber, Edna, 1887-, and Levy, Newman, 1888-
$1200 a year; a comedy in three acts. Garden City. Doubleday. 1920. 12°. 173p.

Ferber, Maurice
Lord Byron; a play in eight scenes. N.Y. Appleton. 1924. 12°. 65p. 50c

Ferguson, John Alexander, 1873-
Campbell of Kilmhor; a play in one act. London. Gowans & Gray. 12°. 1915. 40p.   Scotch
Same in Leonard, S. A. ed.   Atlantic book of modern plays
Marriott, J. W. ed.   One-act plays of today

Fernald, Chester Bailey, 1869-
Cat and the cherub; a play in one act. N.Y. French. 1912. 12°. 35p.   Chinese
Married woman; a play in three acts. London. Sidgwick. 1913. 12°. 111p. Marriage
Pursuit of Pamela; a comedy.   N.Y. French. 1914. 12°. 96p. 4 acts

Ferrier, Paul, 1843-
Codicil.   Boston. Badger. 1912. 8°. p. 193-206.   Comedy. 1 act
Same in Poet Lore 19:193

Ferris, Ralph Hall
Tempted in all points; an historical play. Boston. Gorham press. 1915. 12°. 157p. 3 acts

Fetherstonhaugh, V.
Aunt Anna's foot; comedy in three acts. London. Stockwell. [1923]. 12°. 92p.
Harrison.   Comedy. 1 act
In Smart Set 33 no 3:129

Feuerlicht, E. M.
New spirit out of the dark.   France under old regime.   Historical. 1 act
In Eng J 8:627

Feuillet, Octave, 1821-1890
Fairy, a comedy in one act. . . N.Y. French. 1915. 12°. 27p. 25c
Honour before wealth; or, The romance of a poor man.   A drama, in four acts. Adapted from the French . . . by . . . Pierrepont Edwards & Lester Wallack. London. Lacy. [18—]. 12°. 54p. (Lacy's acting edition of plays v. 80)   Melodrama
Romance of a poor man.   *See* Feuillet, O.   Honour before wealth; or, The romance of a poor man
Le sphinx, a drama in four acts.   N.Y. Rullman. 1880. 8°. 28p.   Melodrama
Village; a comedy in one act. . . N.Y. French. c1915. 12°. 28p.

Ficke, Arthur Davison, 1883-
Breaking of bonds; a drama of social unrest.   Boston. Sherman, French. 1910. 12°. 79p.
Mr. Faust.   Cincinnati.   Stewart Kidd. [c1922]. 8°. 62p.   Poetic. 4 acts

Field, A. Newton
New Magdalen, a drama in a prologue and three acts.   From Wilkie Collins' story of the same name. Clyde, O. A. D. Ames. c1882. 12°. 37p.   Melodrama.

Field, Edward Salisbury, 1878-
Wedding bells; a comedy in three acts. N.Y. French. 1923. 12°. 107p.

Field, Michael, pseud. (Katherine Bradley, d. 1914, and Edith Cooper)
Accuser.
In Accuser, Tristan de Leonis and a Messiah
Anna Ruina. London. Nutt. 1899. 12°. 101p. 8°. Historical. 4 acts
Attila, my Attila! A drama. London. Matthews. 1895. Tragedy. 4 acts
Borgia. London. Poetry Bookshop. 1905. 12°. Historical
Brutus Ultor. London. Bell. 1886. 8°. Tragedy. 5 acts
Callirrhoë. Tragedy. 3 acts
In Callirrhoë, Rosamund
Dierdre. Tragedy. 5 acts
In Dierdre, Question of memory and Ras Byzance
Fair Rosamund. Tragedy. 2 acts
In Callirrhoë, Rosamund
Father's tragedy
In Father's tragedy, William Rufus and Loyalty or love?
In the name of time. London. Poetry Bookshop
Loyalty or love?
In Father's tragedy, William Rufus and Loyalty or love?
Messiah
In Accuser, Tristan de Leonis and Loyalty or love?
Noontide branches. Small sylvan drama. Oxford. Daniel. 1899. 4°. 1 act
Queen Mariamne. London. Poetry Bookshop. 1908
Question of memory. Tragedy. 3 acts
In Deirdie, Question a memory and Ras Byzance
Ras Byzance. Tragedy. 3 acts
In Deirdre, Question of memory and Ras Byzance
Race of leaves. N.Y. Lane. 1901. 8°. lxxxivp.
Stephania; a trialogue. London. Lane. 1892. 8°. 100p.
Tragic Mary. London. Bell. 1890. 8°. Tragedy. 5 acts
Tragedy of Pardon and Dian. London. Poetry Bookshop. 1911
Tristan de Leonis
In Accuser, Tristan de Leonis and Loyalty or love?
William Rufus
In Father's tragedy, William Rufus and Loyalty or love?
World at auction. . . London. Hacon. 1898. 8°.
Zander the great; a comedy in prologue and three acts. N.Y. French. 1923. 12°. 118p.

Field, Rachel Lyman, 1894-
Cinderella married. Comedy. 1 act
In Six plays
Columbine in business. Harlequinade. 1 act
In Six plays
Everygirl. Juvenile. 1 act
In St N 40:1115

Fifteenth candle. Art. 1 act
In Thomas, C. S. ed. Atlantic book of junior plays
Londonderry air. 1 act
In One-act plays for stage and study ser 3
Patchwork quilt. Fantasy. 1 act
In Six plays
Rise up, Jennie Smith: a play in one act. N.Y. French. [c1918]. 12°. 22p. Patriotic
Theories and thumbs. Fantasy. 1 act
In Six plays
Three pills in a bottle. Fantasy. 1 act
In Six plays
Plays of the 47 workshop ser 1
Wisdom teeth. Comedy. 1 act
In Six plays

Fields, Mrs. Annie Adams, 1834-1881
Orpheus, a masque. Boston. Houghton. 1900. 8°. 41p. 1 act

Fife, Evelyn Henderson
We are three; a play in one act
In Drama 16:17

Fife-Cookson, John Cookson, 1844-1911
Hannibal and Katharna, a drama in five acts. N.Y. Putnam. 1893. 12°. 190p. Historical

Fillmore, J. E.
War. Tragedy. 1 act
In Poet Lore 25:523

Finch, Lucine
At the sign of the Silver Spoon. Farce. 1 act
In Smart Set 38 no 2:75
Butterfly. Boston. Badger. Fantasy. 3 acts
In Poet Lore 21:401

Firkins, Oscar W.
After twenty-five years. Religion. 1 act
In Drama 15:99
Looking-glass. Social. 1 act
In Drama 16:171
Reference. Comedy. 1 act
In Drama 14:215
Two passengers for Chelsea; a Carlyle comedy. 1 act
In Cornhill M 60:163
Unbidden guest. Character. 1 act
In Poet Lore 35:276

Fischer, Nellie L.
Educatin' Mary; a rural play in one act. Chicago. Denison. c1924. 12°. 21p.

Fisher, H. Cecil
Great day; a play in one act. London. Labour pub. co. 1925. 12°. 28p.

Fitch, Clyde, i.e., William Clyde, 1865-1909
Barbara Frietchie, the Frederick girl. A play in four acts. N.Y. Life pub. co. 1900. 12°. 128p. Civil war
Same in Plays v 2

Beau Brummel; a play in four acts. N.Y. Lane. 1908. 12°. 142p. Historical society
Same in Plays v 1
Cohen, H. L. ed. Longer plays by modern authors

Fitch, C.—*Continued*

Captain Jinks of the Horse Marines; a fantastic comedy in three acts. N.Y. Doubleday. 1902. 12°. 166p.
Same in Plays v 2

City; a modern play of American life in three acts. Boston. Little. 1915. 12°. p. 451-636. Comedy
Same in Plays v 4
  Moses, M. J. ed. Representative American plays, national and local

Climbers; a play in four acts. N.Y. London. Macmillan. 1906. 12°. 265p. Social
Same in Plays v 2

Cowboy and the lady; a comedy in three acts. N.Y. French. c1908. 12°. 112p.

Girl with the green eyes; a play in four acts. N.Y. Macmillan. 1905. 12°. 200p. Melodrama
Same in Plays v 3

Her great match. International comedy. 4 acts
In Quinn, A. H. ed. Representative American plays, 1767-1923

Her own way; a play in four acts. N.Y. Macmillan. 1907. 12°. 235p. Romantic
Same in Plays v 3

Lovers' lane; a play in four acts. Boston. Little. 1915. 12°. p. 213-405. Romantic
Same in Plays v 1

Moth and the flame. Melodrama. 1 act
In Pierce, J. A. and Matthews, J. B. eds. Masterpieces of modern drama v 1 (abridged)

Nathan Hale; a play, in four acts. N.Y. Russell. 1899. 12°. 100p. Historical
Same in Plays v 1

Pamela's prodigy; a lively comedy. N.Y. Allen. 1893. 12°. 107p. 3 acts

Stubborness of Geraldine; a play in four acts. N.Y. Macmillan. 1906. 12°. 214p. Comedy
Same in Plays v 3

Truth; a play in four acts. N.Y. Macmillan. 1907. 12°. 237p. Comedy
Same in Plays v 4
  Dickinson, T. H. ed. Chief contemporary dramatists
  Pierce, J. A. and Matthews, J. B. eds. Masterpieces of modern drama v 1 (abridged)

Woman in the case; a play in four acts. Boston. Little. 1915. 12°. 195p. Melodrama
Same in Plays v 4

Fitzgerald, Francis Scott Key, 1896-

Porcelain and pink. Comedy. 1 act
In Smart Set 61:77

Vegetable; or, From president to postman. N.Y. Scribner. 1923. 12°. 145p. Comedy. 3 acts

Fitzgerald, Shafto Justin Adair, 1859-

Dick and the marchioness. Duologue. 1 act. (adapted from Dicken's Old Curiosity Shop).
Same in One-act plays v 2

Forgotten favorite. Melodrama. 1 act
In One-act plays v 1

Friend of the family. Comedy. 1 act
In One-act plays v 3

Jealous mistake. Domestic. 1 act
In One-act plays v 1

Last wish. Comedy. 1 act
In One-act plays v 1

Little tyrant; a comedietta for two boys and a girl. N.Y. French

Miser's revenge. Melodrama. 2 scenes
In One-act plays v 3

One goes out. Melodrama. 1 act
In One-act plays v 2

Parting. Comedy. 1 act
In Parting and waiting for the train

Time of roses. Melodrama. 1 act
In One-act plays v 2

Two hearts. Romantic. 1 act
In One-act plays v 3

Fitzgerald, S. J. A.

Waiting for the train. Comedy. 1 act
In Parting and waiting for the train

Fitzmaurice, George

Country dressmaker; a play in three acts. Dublin. Maunsel. 1914. 12°. 57p. Romantic
Same in Five plays

Dandy dolls. Superstition. 1 act
In Five plays

Linnaun Shee. Comedy. 1 act
In Dublin M 2:194

Magic glasses. Irish superstition. 1 act
In Five plays

Moonlighter. Tragedy. 4 acts
In Five plays

Pie-dish. Ireland. 1 act
In Five plays

Flagg, Isaac, 1843-

Circe; a dramatic fantasy. . . East Aurora. Roycrafters. 1915. 12°. 178p. Mythological. 2 acts

Hesperides. Mythological. 1 act
In University of California Chronicle 24:239

Persephone, a masque. San Francisco. Elder. c1916. 12°. 105p. 5 acts

Flamma, Ario

Don Luca Sperante. Sicilian. 1 act
In Dramas

Fiamme. Labor. 1 act
In Dramas

Nuvole Rosee (in Italian). 4 scenes
In Dramas

Queen's castle. Symbolic. 1 act
In Dramas

Stranger. Tragedy. 1 act
In Dramas

Flanagan, Hallie E.

Curtain. Truth. 1 act. (Prize play of Des Moines Little Theatre contest).
In Drama 13:167

Flanner, Hildegarde
Mansions, a play in one act. Cincinnati. Stewart Kidd. 1920. 12°. 38p.
Past and present generations
Same in Shay, F. and Loving, P. eds.
Fifty contemporary one-act plays

Flattery, Maurice Douglas, 1879-1925
Annie Laurie. Romantic. 4 acts
In Three plays
Conspirators. Crook. 4 acts
In Three plays
Queen of the harem; a musical comedy in two acts. . . Boston. Sparrell print. 1900. 12°. 50p.
Subterfuge. Comedy. 4 acts
In Three plays

Flavin, Martin A., 1883-
Blind man. Pantomine. 1 act
In Brains, and other one-act plays
Brains. Sea. 1 act
In Brains, and other one-act plays
Caleb Stone's death watch; a play. N.Y. French. c1925. 12°. 26p. [Prize 1924].
Comedy. 1 act
Same in Brains and other one-act plays
Drama 14:143
Casualties. Tragedy. 1 act
In Brains, and other one-act plays.
Children of the moon; a play. N.Y. Brentano's. [c1924]. 12°. 90p. Psychological. 3 acts
Emergency case. Hospital. 1 act
In Brains, and other one-act plays
Lady of the rose; a play in three acts. N.Y. French. c1925. 12°. 106p.
Question of principle. Satire. 1 act
In Brains, and other one-act plays
One-act plays for stage and study ser 2

Flecker, James Elroy, 1844-1915
Don Juan; a play in three acts. N.Y. Flecker. 1925. 12°. 122p. Tragedy
Hassan; the story of Hassan of Bagdad and how he came to make the golden journey to Samarkand. A play in five acts. London. Heinemann. 1922. 12°. 182p.

Flexner, Anne Crawford, 1874
Marriage game; a comedy in three acts. N.Y. Huebsch. 1916. 12°. 174p. $1
Mrs Wiggs of the cabbage patch; a dramatization in three acts from the novel "Mrs. Wiggs of the cabbage patch" by Alice Hegan Rice. N.Y. French. 1924. 12°. 94p. Comedy

Flexner, Hortense, 1885-
Faun. Fantasy. 1 act
In Drama 11:311
Voices. Poetic. 1 act
In Mayorga, M. G. ed. Representative one-act plays

Flowers, Priscilla
May night. Blindness. 1 act
In Poet Lore 37:551

Flynn, Edward F.
Pink deetees; an original play in three acts. Boston. Cornhill. 1919. 12°. 120p. $1.25 Comedy

Fontana, F.
House of Oedipus. Mythological. 3 periods
In Canad M 38:341, 423, 520

Forbes, James, 1871-
Chorus lady. Comedy. 4 acts
In Famous Mrs Fair and other plays
Commuters; a comedy in four acts. N.Y. French. c1916. 12°. 99p. 50c
Famous Mrs. Fair; a play in four acts. N.Y. French. c1920. 12°. 103p. Problem
Same in Famous Mrs. Fair and other plays
Moses, M. J. ed. Representative American dramas, national and local
Show shop. Farcical satire. 4 acts
In Famous Mrs. Fair and other plays
Traveling salesman; a comedy in four acts. N.Y. French. [c1908]. 12°. 125p.

Ford, Ford Madox, 1873-
Mister Bosphorus and the misers. History of poetry in Britain. 4 acts
In Poet Lore 34:532

Ford, George
Love pirate. N.Y. French. 1916. 13p. 1 act

Ford, Harriet, 1868-
Bride; a comedy in one act. N.Y. French. c1924. 12°. 21p.
Youth must be served. 1 act
In One-act plays for stage and study ser 3

Ford, Harriet, 1868-, and Duer, Caroline K., 1865-
Where Julia rules; a comedy in four acts. N.Y. French. [c1923]. 12°. 102p.

Ford, Harriet, 1868-, and O'Higgins, Harvey Jerrold, 1876-
Dickey bird. Comedy. 1 act
In One-act plays for stage and study ser 2
Dummy; a detective comedy in four acts. N.Y. French. [1925]. 12°. 113p. (Copyrighted, 1913, under title: Kidnapped)
Kidnapped. *See* Ford, H. and O'Higgins, H. J. Dummy
On the hiring line; a comedy in three acts. N.Y. French. c1923. 12°. 116p.

Forrest, Belford
Failures; an episode in a tragedy. 1 act
In Smart Set 49:223
Lost sheep. Farce. 1 act
In Smart Set 50:71

Forrest, Charles
Stolen horse; a play in four acts. London. Benn. 1925. 12°. 98p.

Forrester, Frank
Flirtation. Pantomimic comedy. 1 act
In Shay, F. ed. Plays for strolling mummers

Foster, Thomas Jefferson, joint author.
See Thanhouser, L. F. and Foster, T. J.

Forster, William
Weirwolf: a tragedy. London. Williams. 1876. 319p.

Foulke, William Dudley, 1848-
Maya; a drama. N.Y. Cosmopolitan press. 1911. 12°. 70p. Tragedy. 5 acts

Fournier, M. J. J., joint author. See D'Ennery, A. and Fournier, M. J. J.

Fowle, Frank E.
Chuzzlewits; or, Tom Pinch; a dramatization in five acts of Charles Dickens. . . "Martin Chuzzlewit." Boston. Baker. 1916. 72p. 25c

Fox, S. M.
Clodhopper. Comedy. 4 acts
In Waters of bitterness, etc
This generation; a play. N.Y. Duffield. [1913]. 12°. 158p. Social. 4 acts
Waters of bitterness. Character. 3 acts
In Waters of bitterness, etc

France, Anatole, pseud. (Jacques Anatole Thibault), 1844-1924
Bride of Corinth. Poetic. 3 parts
In Bride of Corinth and other poems and plays
Come what may. Comedy. 1 act
In Bride of Corinth and other poems and plays
Crainquebille; a comedy in three acts. . . N.Y. French. [c1915]. 12°. 43p.
Same in Bride of Corinth and other poems and plays
International (NY) 9:68
Man who married a dumb wife; a comedy in two acts. . . N.Y. Lane. 1915. 12°. 93p. 75c
Same in Bride of Corinth and other poems and plays
Golden Bk 1:41
Thaïs; a play in four acts. . . N.Y. Lane. 1909. 12°. 234p. $2. *Also* Bobbs-Merrill. 1911. $1. Melodrama

Francis, John Morgan, 1879-
Misplaced decimal; a play in three acts. N.Y. French. 1918. 12°. 25c
Unconscious burglary; a comedy in three acts. N.Y. French. [c1914]. 12°. 47p.

Francis, John Oswald, 1882-
Bakehouse; a gossips' comedy. Cardiff. Educational pub. co. 1914. 16°. 36p. 1 act
Change. Garden City. N.Y. Doubleday. 1914. 12°. 147p. Welsh. 4 acts
Poacher; a comedy in one act. Cardiff. Educational pub. co. 1914. 16°. 43p.
Same in Theatre Arts M 9:327

Francis, William Lamb
Values. Early Christian. 1 act
In International (NY) 8:319

Frank, Mrs. Florence Kiper
Cinderelline; or, The little red slipper. Chicago. Dramatic pub. co. c1913. 12°. 27p. 1 act
Garden. Fantasy. 1 act
In Drama 8:471
Jael; a poetic drama in one act. Chicago. Little Theatre. 1914. 12°. 29p. Jewish

Three spinners. Juvenile. 1 act
In Drama 16:179

Frank, Maude Morrison, 1870-
Christmas eve with Charles Dickens. 1 act
In Short plays about famous authors
Fairies' plea (adapted from Thomas Hood's "Plea of the midsummer fairies"). Interlude. 1 act
In Short plays about famous authors
In Short plays about famous authors
Miss Burney at court. Fanny Burney. 1 act
In Short plays about famous authors
Webber, J. P. and Webster, H. H. Short plays for young people
Mistake at the manor. Oliver Goldsmith. 1 act
In Short plays about famous authors
When Heine was twenty-one. Heinrich Heine. 1 act
In Short plays about famous authors

Frederick, John T., 1893-
Hunter, Symbolic. 1 act
In Stratford J 1:38 S '17

Freeman, Ethel Hale
Dramatization of Monsieur Beaucaire; made from Booth Tarkington's popular novel. Boston. Baker. 1916. 121p. 50c. Comedy. 3 acts

Freeman, Mary Wilkins
Eglantina. Romantic. 3 acts
In Ladies' H J 27:13 Jl '10
Giles Corey, yeoman; a play. N.Y. Harper. 1893. 12°. 108p. Witchcraft. 5 acts

French, Mrs. Anne (Warner), 1869-1913
Rejuvenation of Aunt Mary; a three-act comedy. N.Y. French. c1916. 12°. 87p.

Freybe, C. E.
In garrison. Suicide. 1 act
In Poet Lore 26:499

Freytag, Gustav, 1816-1895
Journalists; a comedy in four acts. . . N.Y. Hinds. 1904. 12°. 140p.
Same in German classics 12:11
Drama 3 no 9:30

Frida, Emil Bohuslav. See Vrchlicky, Jaroslav, pseud.

Froome, John Redhead, jr.
Listening. Anxiety. 1 act
In Poet Lore 28:422

Frost, Robert, 1875-
Way out. Crime. 1 act
In Cohen, H. L. ed. More one-act plays by modern authors
Seven Arts 1:347

Fruchter, M. J.
Rats. Starvation. 1 act
In Poet Lore 37:154

Fry, Horace B.
Little Italy; a tragedy in one act. N.Y. Russell. 1902. 12°. 50p.

Fuji-ko
Vampire cat of Nabeshima. Japanese. 1 act
In Smart Set 30 no 1:127

Fulda, Ludwig, 1862-
By ourselves. Boston. Badger. 1912. 8°.
p. 1-24. $1.50. Comedy. 1 act
Same in Smith, A. M. ed. Short plays
by representative authors
Poet Lore 23:1
Lost paradise; a drama in three acts. . .
N.Y. Goldmann. ｢c1897｣. 12°. 77p.
Melodrama
Tête-à-tête. Comedy. 1 act
In German classics 17:440

Fuller, Henry Blake, 1857-
After glow. Success. 1 act
In Puppet-booth
At Saint Judas's. Friendship. 1 act
In Puppet-booth
Cure of souls. Allegory. 1 act
In Puppet-booth
Dead-and-alive. Romantic. 1 act
In Puppet-booth
In such a night. Romantic. 1 act
In Puppet-booth
Light that always is. Allegory. 1 act
In Puppet-booth
Love of love. Death. 1 act
In Puppet-booth
Northern lights. Psychological. 1 act
In Puppet-booth
On the whirlwind. War. 1 act
In Puppet-booth
Ship comes in. Sea. 1 act
In Puppet-booth
Clements, C. C. ed. Sea plays
Story-spinner. Romantic. 1 act
In Puppet-booth
Stranger within the gates. Romantic. 1
act
In Puppet-booth

Fuller, Horace W.
Dear uncle. A comedy in four acts.
Adapted for the French of L'héritage
de M. Plumet. N.Y. Dram. pub. co.
c1890. 12°. 42p.
False pretensions. A comedy in two
acts. Adapted from the French "La
poudre aux yeux." N.Y. De Witt.
c1887. 12°. 35p.

Fulton, Maud
The brat; a comedy in three acts. . . N.Y.
Longmans. 1926. 12°. 99p.

Furness, Horace Howard, jr., 1865-
Gloss of youth; an imaginary episode in
the life of William Shakespeare and
John Fletcher. Phila. Lippincott.
1920. 12°. 44p. 1 act

Furniss, Grace Livingston
Box of monkeys. N.Y. Harper. ｢c1891｣.
16°. 61p. Farce-comedy. 2 acts
Same in Box of monkeys and other
farce comedies
Corner lot chorus. A farce in one act.
Boston. Baker. ｢c1891｣. 12°. 19p.
Dakota widow, a comedy in one act.
N.Y. French. 1915. 12°. 20p.
Flying wedge; a football farce in one act.
Boston. Baker. ｢c1896｣. 12°. 15p.

Jack trust. N.Y. Harper. ｢c1891｣. 16°.
63p. Farce-comedy. 3 acts
Same in Box of monkeys and other
farce comedies
Man on the box, a comedy founded on
Harold McGrath's novel. N.Y.
French. 1915. 12°. 114p. 50c. 3 acts
Perhaps, a comedy in one act. N.Y.
French. 1915. 12°. 18p.
Tulu. N.Y. Harper. ｢c1891｣. 16°. 87p.
Farce-comedy. 3 acts
Same in Box of monkeys and other
farce comedies
Veneered savage. N.Y. Harper. ｢c1891｣.
16°. 33p. Farce-comedy. 2 acts
Same in Box of monkeys and other
farce comedies

Fyfe, H. Hamilton, 1869-
Kingdom, the power and the glory, a
morality in three scenes. London.
C. W. Daniel. 1920. 12°. 111p.

Gaffney, Thomas J.
Birds of a feather; a play in four acts.
Boston. Badger. 1915. 8°. 110p. $1
Melodrama

Galbraith, Esther E.
Brink of silence. Sea. 1 act
In Clements, C. C. ed. Sea plays
Mayorga, M. G. ed. Representa-
tive one-act plays
Smith, M. M. ed. Short plays of
various types

Galdós, Benito Peréz. *See* Peréz Galdós,
Benito

Gale, Elizabeth
Just a little mistake; a comedy. Boston.
Baker. 1916. 12°. 22p. 25c. 1 act
Not quite such a goose. 1 act
In Baker's anthology of one-act plays
Romance hunters: a comedy in three acts.
N.Y. French. c1917. 12°. 66p.

Gale, Jane Winsor
Victoria. Comedy. 3 acts
In Poet Lore 26:78

Gale, Zona, 1874-
Miss Lulu Bett; an American comedy of
manners. N.Y. Appleton. 1921. 12°.
182p. 3 acts
Mister Pitt. N.Y. Appleton. 1925. 12°.
224p. $2. Domestic. 3 acts
Neighbors. Comedy. 1 act
In Dickinson, T. H. ed. Wisconsin
plays
Uncle Jimmy. Boston. Baker. 1922. 12°.
63p. Comedy. 1 act
Same in Ladies' H J 38:18 O '21

Gallarati-Scotti, Tommaso, 1878-
Thy will be done. Tragedy. 3 acts
In Sayler, O. M. ed. Eleanora Duse
series of plays

Galsworthy, John, 1867-
Bit o' love; a play in three acts. N.Y.
Scribner. 1915. 12°. 84p. Social
Same in Plays ser 4
Representative plays
Works (Manaton ed) v 20

Galsworthy, J.—*Continued*
Defeat. World war. 1 act
In Six short plays
    Works (Manaton ed) v 21
Eldest son; a domestic drama in three
    acts. N.Y. Scribner. 1912. 12°. 74p.
Same in Plays ser 2
    Works (Manaton ed) v 18
Family man, in three acts. N.Y. Scrib-
    ner. 1922. 12°. 108p. Marriage
Same in Works (Manaton ed) v 21
    Plays ser 5
Escape: an episodic play in a prologue
    and two parts. London. Duckworth.
    [1926]. 12°. 100p.
First and the last. Tragedy. 3 scenes
In Works (Manaton ed) v 21
    Six short plays
Forest; a drama in four acts. London.
    Duckworth. [1924]. 16°. 121p. Afri-
    can
Same in Plays ser 6
Foundations (an extravagant play).
    N.Y. Scribner. 1920. 12°. 90p. 3 acts
Same in Works (Manaton ed) v 20
    Plays ser 4
Fugitive; a play in four acts. London.
    Duckworth. 1913. 12°. 95p. Social
Same in Works (Manaton ed) v 19
    Plays ser 3
Hall-marked. Satire. 1 act
In Works (Manaton ed) v 21
    Little man and other satires
    Six short plays
    Atlan 113:845
Joy; a play on the letter "I" in three acts.
    London. Duckworth. 1910. 12°. 94p.
    Social. 3 acts
In Works (Manaton ed) v 18
    Plays
Justice, a tragedy in four acts. N.Y.
    Scribner. 1910. 12°. 109p. Social
Same in Works (Manaton ed) v 19
    Plays ser 2
    Representative plays
    Pierce and Matthews, ed.
    Masterpieces of modern
    drama v 1 (abridged)
    Am M 70:585, 819
    Cur Opinion 60:324 (excerpts)
Little dream; an allegory in 6 scenes.
    N.Y. Scribner. 1911. 12°. 35p.
Same in Works (Manaton ed) v 19
    — Plays ser 2
    Scrib M 49:531
Little man. Satire. 3 scenes
In Works (Manaton ed) v 21
    Little man and other satires
    Six short plays
    Cohen, H. L. ed. One act plays by
    modern authors
    Dickinson, A. D. ed. Drama
    Marriott, J. W. ed. One-act plays
    of to-day
Loyalties, a drama in three acts. Lon-
    don. Duckworth. 1922. 12°. 118p. 75c
    Race prejudice. (Jews)
Same in Works (Manaton ed) v 21
    Plays ser 5

Representative plays
    Mantle, B. ed. Best plays of
    1922-23 (condensed)
    Cur Opinion 73:750 (excerpts)
    Works (Manaton ed) v 21
Mob; a play in four acts. N.Y. Scrib-
    ner. 1914. 12°. 77p. Social
Same in Works (Manaton ed) v 20
    Plays ser 3
Old English; a play in three acts. N.Y.
    Scribner. 1925. 12°. 112p. Character
Same in Plays ser 6
Pigeon; a fantasy in three acts. N.Y.
    Scribner. 1912. 12°. 80p.
Same in Works (Manaton ed) v 19
    Representative plays
    Plays ser 3
Punch and go. Comedy. 1 act
In Works (Manaton ed) v 21
    Six short plays
Sekhet; a dream. 1 act
In Little man and other satires
    Scrib M 57:445
Show. N.Y. Scribner. 1925. 12°. 97p.
    $1. Criminals. 3 acts
Same in Plays ser 6
Silver box; a comedy in three acts. Lon-
    don. Duckworth. 1910. 12°. 89p.
Same in Works (Manaton ed) v 18
    Plays
    Representative plays
    Moses, M. J. ed. Representa-
    tive British plays
Skin game; a tragi-comedy. N.Y.
    Scribner. 1920. 12°. 115p. $1. 3 acts
Same in Works (Manaton ed) v 20
    Plays ser 4
    Mantle, B. ed. Best plays of
    1920-21 (condensed)
    Cur Opinion 69:649 (excerpts)
Strife; a drama in three acts. N.Y.
    Scribner. 1920. 12°. 239p. Strike
Same in Works (Manaton ed) v 18
    Plays
    Representative plays
    Dickinson, T. H. Chief con-
    temporary dramatists
    Cur Lit (excerpts) 48:537
Sun. Tragi-comedy. 1 act
In Works (Manaton ed) v 21
    Six short plays
    Leonard, S. A. ed. Atlantic book
    of modern plays
    Scrib M 65:513
Windows, a comedy in three acts for
    idealists and others. London. Duck-
    worth. 1922. 12°. 100p.
Same in Works (Manaton ed) v 21
    Plays ser 5

Galt, John, 1779-1839
Agamemnon. Tragedy. 3 acts
In Tragedies of Maddalen etc
Antonia. Tragedy. 3 acts
In Tragedies of Maddalen etc
Clytemnestra. Tragedy. 3 acts
In Tragedies of Maddalen, etc
Lady Macbeth. Tragedy. 3 acts
In Tragedies of Maddalen, etc

Maddalen. Tragedy. 3 acts
In Tragedies of Maddalen, etc
Watch-house; a farce in two acts. [London. 18—]. 8°. 70p.

Gamble, Hazel V.
Little fish. Comedy. 1 act
In Drama 14:185
Punch; a farce in one act. San Francisco. Banner play bureau. c1923. 12°. 8p.

Ganthony, Richard
Brace of partridges; a farcical comedy. N.Y. French. c1901. 12°. 74p.
Message from Mars; a fantastic comedy in three acts. N.Y. French. 1923. 12°. 75p.

Gardel, J. S.
Witches' mountain. Tragedy. 3 acts
In Bierstadt, E. N. ed. Three plays of the Argentine

Gardener, E.
Behind the purdah. India. 1 act
In Asia 20:273

Garland, Peter
Eternal spring; a comedy in three acts. N.Y. French. c1924. 12°. 70p.

Garland, Robert
Double miracle; a melodrama in one act. Baltimore. Norman Remington. 1921. 12°. 21p. 60c
Same in Vagabond plays ser 1
Forum 53:511
Importance of being a roughneck; a burlesque (in one-act). Baltimore. Norman Remington. 1921. 12°. 32p. 75c
Same in Vagabond plays ser 1
Love's young dream. Realistic. 1 act
In Smart Set 40 no 4:83

Garnett, Edward, 1868-
Breaking point. London. Duckworth. 1907. 12°. 115p. Tragedy. 3 acts
Feud; a play in three acts. London. Bullen. 1909. 12°. 67p. Iceland
Trial of Jeanne d'Arc, an historical play in five acts. London. Sidgwick. 1912. 12°. 79p.

Garnett, Louise Ayres
Courtship; a dramatization of Longfellow's poem "The courtship of Miles Standish"... N.Y. Rand, McNally. c1920. 12°. 62p. 3 acts
Hilltop. Juvenile. 1 act
In Three to make ready
Drama 11:277
Master Will of Stratford; a midwinter night's dream in three acts with a prologue and an epilogue. N.Y. Macmillan. 1916. 12°. 124p. Fantasy
Muffins. Juvenile. 3 scenes
In Three to make ready
Pig prince. Juvenile. 2 acts
In Three to make ready
Drama 12:240

Garnett, Richard, 1835-1906
William Shakespeare, pedagogue and poacher; a drama. . . N.Y. Lane. 1905. 12°. 111p. Comedy. 2 acts

Garrison, Theodosia, 1874-
Hour of earth. Supernatural. 1 act
In Smart Set 9 no 3:153

Gaskoin, Catherine Bellairs
Fickle Juliet. Comedy. 1 act
In Lumber room, and other plays
Fortescue's dinner party. Farce. 1 act
In Lumber room, and other plays
John Arbery's stream. Rustic idyll. 1 act
In Lumber room, and other plays
Lumber room. Comedy. 1 act
In Lumber room, and other plays
P. G.'s. Farce. 3 scenes
In Lumber room, and other plays
Them banns. Farce. 1 act
In Lumber room, and other plays
Toolip. Duologue. 2 scenes
In Lumber room, and other plays
Wrong again. Duologue. 1 scene
In Lumber room, and other plays

Gastineau, Octave
Lelia. Comedy. 1 act
In Bellevue dramatic club: Plays for private acting

Gaston, W.
Second best. Sea. 1 act
In Clements, C. C. ed. Sea plays

Gates, Eleanor (Mrs. Frederick Ferdinand Moore), 1875-
Poor little rich girl; a play in three acts. N.Y. Arrow. 1916. 12°. 236p. 75c. Fantasy
Swat the fly! a one-act fantasy. N.Y. Arrow. 1915. 12°. 31p. 25c
We are seven; a three-act musical farce. N.Y. Arrow. 1916. 12°. 236p. $1

Gautier, Judith, joint author. *See* Loti, Pierre and Gautier, Judith

Geijerstam, Gustav, 1858-1909
Criminals; an unpleasant play in tableaux. 2 tableaux
In Poet Lore 34:186

Geraldy, Paul, 1885
Nest (Noces d'argent). Social. 4 acts
In Mantle, B. ed. Best plays of 1921-22. (condensed)

Gerstenberg, Alice
Alice in Wonderland; a dramatization of Lewis Carroll's "Alice's adventures in Wonderland" and "Through the Looking glass". Chicago. McClurg. 1915. 8°. 133p. $2. 3 acts
Same in Moses, M. J. Treasury of plays for children
Attuned. Monologue. 1 act
In Ten one-act plays
Betty's degree. College. 2 acts
In Little world
Beyond. Monologue. 1 act
In Ten one-act plays
Mayorga, M. G. ed. Representative one-act plays
Buffer. Marriage. 1 act
In Ten one-act plays
Captain Joe. College. 2 acts
In Little world
Class play. College. 2 acts
In Little world

Gerstenberg, A.—*Continued*
Class president.   College. 2 acts
 In Little world
Ever young.   Comedy. 1 act
 In Four plays for four women
   Schaefer, B. L. comp.   Book of one-
     act plays
   Shay, F. ed.   Treasury of plays for
     women
   Drama 12:167
Fourteen.   Comedy. 1 act
 In Ten one-act plays
   Drama 10:180
He said and she said.   Gossip. 1 act
 In Ten one-act plays
Hearts.   Comedy. 1 act
 In Ten one-act plays
Illuminatti in drama libre.   Satire. 1 act
 In Ten one-act plays
Mah-jongg.   Comedy. 1 act
 In Four plays for four women
Overtones.   Double personality. 1 act
 In Ten one-act plays
   Dickinson, A. D. ed.   Drama
   Washington Square plays
Patroness.   Monologue. 1 act
 In Shay, F. ed.   Treasury of plays for
     women
Pot boiler.   Satire. 1 act
 In Ten one-act plays
   Knickerbocker, E. Van B.   ed.
     Twelve plays
   Shay, F. and Loving, P. eds.   Fifty
     contemporary one-act plays
Seaweed.   Comedy. 1 act
 In Four plays for four women
Their husband.   Comedy. 1 act
 In Four plays for four women
Unseen.   Comedy. 1 act
 In Ten one-act plays

Getchell, Wendell P.
Fisherman's luck; a comedy drama in
 four acts.   Boston. Baker. 1893. 12°.
 47p.

Ghose, Girish C., 1851(?)-1913
Chintamini.   Symbolic. 4 acts
 In Shay, Frank.   Twenty-five short
     plays, international
   Poet Lore 25:144

Giacosa, Giuseppe, 1847-1906
"As the leaves."   *See* Giacosa, G. Like
 falling leaves
Like falling leaves ("As the leaves";
 Come le foglie).   Character. 4 acts
 In "As the leaves' ⌊Chicago? 1908⌋ 72p.
   Stronger. . .
   Moses, M. J. ed.   Representative
     continental dramas
   Drama 1 no 1:9
Rights of the soul.   *See* Giacosa, G.
 Sacred ground
Sacred ground.   (Rights of the soul;
 Diritti dell' anima.).   Psychological.
 1 act
 In Stronger. . .
   Moses, M. J. ed. Representative one-
     act plays by continental authors
   Shay, F. and Loving, P. eds.   Fifty
   Stratford J 2:26

Stronger (Il piu forte).   Comedy. 3 acts
 In Stronger. . .
   Drama 3 no 10:32
Unhappy love (Tristi amori).   Family
 difficulties. 3 acts
 In Poet Lore 27:601
Wager; a poetic comedy in one act. . .
 (Game of chess; Una partita a scac-
 chi). N.Y. French. c1914. 12°. 16p.
 Comedy. 1 act

**Gibbes, Frances Guignard (Mrs. O. L.
 Keith)**
Face; a play in three acts.   N.Y. Brentano's. ⌊c1924⌋. 12°. 120p.   Leonardo
 da Vinci
Hilda; a play in four acts.   N.Y. Brentano's. 1923. 12°. 130p.   Poetic

Gibson, Wilfried Wilson, 1878
Agatha Steel.   Social. 1 act
 In Daily bread (Macmillan)
   Daily bread (Matthews) v 3
   Poems
Bell Haggard.   Bk. 2 of Krindlesyke. q.
 v.   Poetic. 3 parts
Betrothed.   Character. 1 act
 In Daily bread (Macmillan)
   Daily bread. (Matthews) v 1
   Poems
Blackadder.   Common life. 1 act
 In Kestrel Edge and other plays
Bloody bush edge.   Supernatural. 1 act
 In Borderlands and thoroughfares
   Poems
   New numbers 1:5
Bridal.   Poetic. 1 act
 In Stonefolds
Call.   Ethical. 1 act
 In Daily bread (Macmillan)
   Daily bread (Matthews) v 3
   Poems
Child.   Poverty. 1 act
 In Daily bread (Macmillan)
   Daily bread (Matthews) v 2
   Poems
Family's pride.   Sorrow. 1 act
 In Collected poems
   Daily bread (Macmillan)
   Daily bread (Matthews) v 1
Ferry.   Supernatural. 1 act
 In Stonefolds
   Poems
First-born.   Parenthood. 1 act
 In Daily bread (Macmillan)
   Daily bread (Matthews) v 1
   Poems
Furnace.   Labor. 1 act
 In Daily bread (Macmillan)
   Daily bread (Matthews) v 2
   Poems
Garret.   Poverty. 1 act
 In Daily bread (Macmillan)
   Daily bread (Matthews) **v 2**
   Poems

Holiday. Labor. 1 act
In Daily bread (Macmillan)
  Daily bread (Matthews) v 3
  Poems
Hoops. Psychological. 1 act
In Borderlands and thoroughfares
  Poems
House of candles. Psychological. 1 act
In Daily bread (Macmillan)
  Daily bread (Matthews) v 1
  Poems
Kestrel Edge. Tragedy. 3 scenes
In Kestrel Edge and other plays
Krindlesyke (Bk. 1. Phoebe Barrasford,
  Bk. 2. Bell Haggard.) N.Y. Mac-
  millan. 1922. 12°. 139p. $1.75. Poetic.
  2 books
Lover's leap. Tragedy. 5 scenes
In Kestrel Edge and other plays
Mates. Ethical. 1 act
In Daily bread (Macmillan)
  Daily bread (Matthews) v 3
  Poems
Mother. Psychological. 1 act
In Daily bread (Macmillan)
  Daily bread (Matthews) v 2
  Poems
Night-shift. Labor. 1 act
In Daily bread (Macmillan)
  Daily bread (Matthews) v 2
  Poems
On the road. Poverty. 1 act
In Daily bread (Macmillan)
  Daily bread (Matthews) v 1
  Poems
On the threshold. Love. 1 act
In Battle and other poems
  Poems
Operation. Character. 1 act
In Daily bread (Macmillan)
  Daily bread (Matthews) v 3
  Poems
Phoebe Barrasford. Bk. 1. of Krindle-
  syke. *q. v.* Poetic. 1 act
Queen's crags. Midsummer Eve. 1 act
In Borderlands and thoroughfares
  Poems
Red Rowan. Common life. 1 act
In Kestrel Edge and other plays
Scar. Psychological. 1 act
In Battle and other poems
  Poems
  Stonefolds
Shirt. Labor. 1 act
In Daily bread (Macmillan)
  Daily bread (Matthews) v 2
Stonefolds. Family. 1 act
In Battle and other poems
  Poems
  Stonefolds
Summer-dawn. Poverty. 1 act
In Daily bread (Macmillan)
  Daily bread (Matthews) v 3
  Poems
Winter dawn. Dementia. 1 act
In Battle and other poems
  Poems
Winter's stob. Common life. 1 act
In Kestrel Edge and other plays

Womankind; a play in one act. London.
  Nutt. [1912]. 12°. 24p. Character.
Same in Poems
Wound. Psychologic. 1 act
In Daily bread (Macmillan)
  Daily bread (Matthews) v 3
  Poems
Gifford, Franklin Kent, 1861-
All or none. Comedy. 1 act
In Drama 16:207
Gilbert, Bernard
Bonfire night; a dramatic episode.
  Rural. 1 act
In King Lear at Hordle, and other rural
  plays
Eldorado; a play in one act. Lincoln.
  Lincolnshire publishing co. [1914?].
  12°. 19p. Rural
Same in King Lear at Hordle, and
  other rural plays
Finished. Tragedy, rural
Same in King Lear at Hordle, and
  other rural plays
Gone for good. Rural. 1 act
In King Lear at Hordle, and other rural
  plays
Gone to the war. Rural. 1 act
In King Lear at Hordle, and other rural
  plays
Hordle poacher. Rural. 1 act
In King Lear at Hordle, and other rural
  plays
King Lear at Hordle. Rural. 3 acts
In King Lear at Hordle, and other rural
  plays
Old bull. Rural. 1 act
In King Lear at Hordle, and other rural
  plays
Old-times, a memory. Rural
In King Lear at Hordle, and other rural
  plays
Ruskington poacher; a play in one act.
  Lincoln. Lincolnshire publishing co.
  [1914?]. 12°. 15p. Comedy
Tanvats Nietsche. Rural. Duologue
In King Lear at Hordle, and other rural
  plays
Their father's will; a play in one act.
  Lincoln. Lincolnshire publishing co.
  [1914?]. 12°. 15p. Comedy
To arms! Rural. 1 act
In King Lear at Hordle, and other rural
  plays
Who's who? Rural.
In King Lear at Hordle, and other rural
  plays
Wicked man, a melancholy rhapsody
In King Lear at Hordle, and other rural
  plays
Gilbert, Helen
Good Sainte Anne. Healing. 1 act
In Poet Lore 35:576
Gilbert, Sir William Schwenck, 1836-1911
Brantinghame hall. Melodrama. 3 acts
In Original plays ser 4
Broken hearts. An entirely original
  fairy play, in three acts. London.
  French. [18—]. 12°. 35p.
Same in Original plays ser 2

Gilbert, W. S.—*Continued*

Bunthorne's bride. *See* Gilbert, W. S. Patience, or, Bunthorne's bride

Castle Adamant. *See* Gilbert, W. S. Princess Ida; or, Castle Adamant

Charity: an entirely original play. In four acts. London. French. [18—?]. 12°. 44p. Melodrama
Same in Original plays ser 1

Comedy and tragedy; an original drama in one act. London. French. n.d. 12°. 17p. Melodrama
Same in Original plays ser 3

Creatures of impulse. A musical fairy tale, in one act. London. Lacy. [18—]. 12°. 20p. (Lacy's acting edition of plays. v. 91)
Same in Original plays ser 4
 Shay, F. ed. Plays for strolling mummers

Dan'l Druce; a new and original drama, in three acts. London. French. [187—]. 12°. 42p. Melodrama
Same in Original plays ser 2

Dulcamara; or, the little duck and the great quack. New and original extravaganza. London. Strand printing and publishing co. 1866. 12°. 34p. 5 scenes

Engaged; an entirely original farcical comedy. [N.Y.?, 1878]. 12°. 56p. 3 acts
Same in Original plays ser 2

Fairy's dilemma. Pantomine. 2 acts
In Original plays ser 4

Fallen fairies, or, The wicked world. Fairy opera. 2 acts
In Original plays ser 4

Flowers of progress. *See* Gilbert, W. S. Utopia, limited; or, The flowers of progress

Foggerty's fairy. Fairy. 3 acts
In Original plays ser 3

Fortune-hunter. Melodrama. 3 acts
In Original plays ser 4

Fortune's toy. *See* Gilbert, W. S. Tom Cobb; or, Fortune's toy

Gentleman in black. An original musical legend. London. Lacy. [18—]. 12°. 36p. (Lacy's acting edition of plays. v. 88) 1 act
Same in Original plays ser 4

Gondoliers; or, The king of Barataria. London. Bell. 1912. 8°. 224p. Light opera. 2 acts
Same in Iolanthe and other operas
 Mikado and other plays
 Original plays ser 3

Grand duke; or, The statutory duel. Boston. Ellis. 1896. 8°. 55p. Comic opera. 2 acts
Same in Original plays ser 4

Gretchen. N.Y. Koppel. [1886?]. 8°. 48p. Melodrama. 4 acts
Same in Original plays ser 2

Haste to the wedding. Operetta. 3 acts
In Original plays ser 4

H.M.S. Pinafore; or, The lass that loved a sailor. An entirely new comic opera, in two acts. Boston. Ditson. 1878. 12°. 31p.
Same in H.M.S. Pinafore, and other plays
 Original comic operas
 Original plays ser 2
 Moses, M. J. ed. Representative British dramas

His excellency. Comic opera. 2 acts
In Original plays ser 4

Hooligan. Character study. 1 act
In Cent M 83:97

Iolanthe; or, The peer and the peri; a new and original comic opera in two acts. [Philadelphia. I. M. Stoddart]. c1882. 8°. 47p.
Same in Iolanthe and other operas
 short and long
 Mikado and other plays
 Original comic operas
 Original plays ser 1
 Law, F. H. ed. Modern plays

King of Barataria. *See* Gilbert, W. S. Gondoliers; or, The king of Barataria

Lass that loved a sailor. *See* Gilbert, W. S. H.M.S. Pinafore; or, The lass that loved a sailor

Little duck and the great quack. *See* Gilbert, W. S. Dulcamara; or, the little duck and the great quack

Medical man. Comedietta. 1 act
In Scott, C. Drawing-room plays

Merryman and his maid. *See* Gilbert, W. S. Yeoman of the guard; or, The merryman and his maid

Mikado; or, the town of Titipu. London. Bell. 1911. 8°. p. 55-106. Comic opera. 2 acts
Same in Iolanthe and other operas
 Mikado and other plays
 Original comic operas
 Original plays ser 3
 Moses, M. J. ed. Another treasury of plays for children

Mother, the maid, and the misletoe bough. *See* Gilbert, W. S. Pretty druides; or, The mother, the maid, and the misletoe bough

Mountebanks. Comic opera. 2 acts
In Original plays ser 3

Nun, the dun, and the son of a gun. *See* Gilbert, W. S. Robert the devil; or, The nun, the dun, and the son of a gun

Old score, an original comedy drama. London. French. [18—?]. 12°. 42p.

On bail. A farcical comedy, in three acts. Adapted from "Le reveillon". London. French. [18—]. 12°. 40p.

On guard. An entirely original comedy in three acts. London. French. [18—]. 12°. 47p. (Lacy's acting edition of plays. v. 98)

Palace of truth: a fairy comedy in three acts. London. Lacy. [18—]. 12°. 55p. (Lacy's acting edition of plays. v. 89)
Same in Original plays ser 1

Patience; or, Bunthorne's bride. N.Y. Doubleday. 1902. 12°. 92p. Aesthetic opera. 2 acts
Same in H.M.S. Pinafore and other plays
Original comic operas
Original plays ser 3

Peer and the peri. *See* Gilbert, W. S. Iolanthe; or, The peer and the peri

Pinafore. *See* H. M. S. Pinafore

Pirates of Penzance; or, The slave of duty. Comic opera in two acts. Philadelphia. Stoddart. c1880. 12°. 39p.
Same in Mikado and other plays
Original comic operas
Original plays ser 2

Pretty druidess; or, The mother, the maid, and the misletoe bough. An extravaganza, (founded on Bellini's opera "Norma"). London. Phillips. [1869?]. 12°. 34p. 3 scenes

Princess. A whimsical allegory. (Being a respectful perversion of Mr. Tennyson's poem). London. Lacy. [18—?]. 12°. 44p. (Lacy's acting edition of plays. v. 87) 1 act: *See also* Princess Ida
Same in Original plays ser 1

Princess Ida; or Castle Adamant. London. Chappell. [1884]. 8°. 48p. Operetta. 3 acts
Same in Original comic operas
Original plays ser 3

Pygmalion and Galatea. An entirely original mythological comedy, in three acts. N.Y. French. n.d. 12°. 36p.
Same in Original plays ser 1
Matthews, J. B. and Leider, P. R. Chief British dramatists

Randall's thumb; an original comedy in three acts. N.Y. French. [187—]. 12°. 42p.
Same in Original plays ser 4

Robert the devil; or, The nun, the dun, and the son of a gun. An operatic extravaganza. London. Phillips. [1868?]. 12°. 40p. 6 scenes

Rosencrantz and Guildenstern; a tragic episode in three tableaux, founded on an old Danish legend. London. French. [18—?]. 12°. 24p.
Same in Original plays ser 3

Ruddigore; or, The witch's curse. London. Chappell. [1887?]. 8°. 46p. Opera. 2 acts
Same in H. M. S. Pinafore, and other plays
Iolanthe and other operas
Original plays ser 3

Slave of duty. *See* Gilbert, W. S. Pirates of Penzance; or, The slave of duty

Sorcerer. Comic opera. 2 acts
In Original comic operas
Original plays ser 2

Statutory duel. *See* Gilbert, W. S. Grand duke, or, The statutory duel

Sweethearts. An original dramatic contrast in two acts. London. French. [18—?]. 12°. 20p. Comedy
Same in Original plays ser 2
Bates, A. ed. Drama 16:321
Golden Bk 4:763

Thespis. Comic opera. 2 acts
In Original plays ser 4

Tom Cobb; or, Fortune's toy. An original comedy in three acts. London. French. [18—]. 12°. 32p. (French's acting edition of plays. v. 117)
Same in Original plays ser 2

Town of Titipu. *See* Gilbert, W. S. Mikado, or, The town of Titipu

Trial by jury. Cantata. 1 act
In Original comic operas
Original plays ser 1

True to the corps! *See* Gilbert, W. S. Vivandière; or, True to the corps!

Trying a dramatist. Comedy. 1 act
In Cent 83:179

Utopia, limited; or, The flowers of progress. London. Chappell. c1893. 8°. 50p. Comic opera. 2 acts
Same in Original plays ser 3

Vivandière; or, True to the corps! An original operatic extravaganza. Liverpool. H. Montague. 1868. 12°. 31p. 5 scenes

Wedding march. *See* Michel, M. A. A. and E. M. Labiche, Wedding march

Wicked world; an original fairy comedy in three acts. N.Y. French. [187—]. 12°. 42p. [*See also* Fallen fairies; or, The wicked world]
Same in Original plays ser 1

Witch's curse. *See* Gilbert, W. S. Ruddigore; or, The witch's curse

Yeoman of the guard; or, The merryman and his maid. London. Bell. 1912. 8°. 54p. Light opera. 2 acts
Same in H. M. S. Pinafore, and other plays
Original plays ser 3

Giles, William, and Giles, Josephine
Hurricane wooing, a comedy. N.Y. Dick & Fitzgerald. 1916. 12°. 32p. 25c. 3 acts

Tickled to death; a vaudeville sketch in one act. N.Y. Dick & Fitzgerald. 1916. 12°. 6p. 15c

Gill, David
Marigold; a romantic comedy in a prologue and three acts. N.Y. French. c1924. 12°. 75p.

Gillette, William Hooker, 1855-
All the comforts of home; a comedy in four acts. . . I G. Roorbach. [c1897]. 12°. 123p.

Among thieves. Comedy. 1 act
In One-act plays for stage and study ser 2

Gillette, W. H.—*Continued*
Electricity; a comedy in three acts. . .
N.Y. French. c1924. 12°. 115p.
Same in Drama 3 no 12:12
Held by the enemy ⌐a five act war
drama⌐. . . N.Y. French. 1898? 12°.
1295. Civil war
Red owl; tabloid melodrama in one act
In One act plays for stage and study
ser 1
Secret service; an American drama ar-
ranged in four acts. . . ; a romance
of the southern confederacy. N.Y.
French. 1898? 12°. 183p.
Same in Pierce and Matthews, eds.
Masterpieces of modern
drama v 1 (abridged)
Quinn, A. H. ed. Representative
American plays
Too much Johnson. ⌐a three-act farcical
comedy. N.Y. French. c1912. 12°.
129p.
Gilliam, Edward Winslow, 1834-
Robert Burns; a drama in four acts.
Boston. Cornhill. ⌐c1914⌐. 12°. 93p.
Biographical
Gilman, Thornton
We live again. 1 act
In Wisconsin plays ser 2
Giorloff, Ruth
Jazz and minuet; a comedy in one act.
Summit. N.Y. Swartout. c1925. 25p.
Girardeau, Claude Monica, 1860-
God of the wood. Fantasy. 1 act
In Drama 10:305
Glaspell, Susan, 1882-
Bernice, a play in three acts. London.
Benn. 1924. 54p. Psychological
Same in Plays
Three plays
Theatre arts M 3:264
Close the book. Comedy. 1 act
In People, and, Close the book
Plays
Inheritors; a play in three acts. Boston.
Small. 1921. 12°. 157p. Liberty
Same in Three plays
Outside. Sea. 1 act
In Plays
Clements, C. C. ed. Sea plays
People. Journalism. 1 act
In People, and, Close the book
Plays
Suppressed desires. *See* Glaspell, Susan
and Cook, George Cram
Trifles; a play in one act. N.Y. Wash-
ington Square players. 1916. 12°. 25p.
Tragedy
Same in Plays
Shay, F. and Loving, P. eds.
Fifty contemporary one-act
plays
Verge; a play in three acts. Boston.
Small. 1921. 12°. 157p. Psychological
Same in Three plays
Woman's honor. Comedy. 1 act
In Plays

Glaspell, Susan, 1882, and Cook, George Cram, 1873-1924
Suppressed desires. French. 1 act
In Glaspell, Susan, Plays
Mayorga, M. G. ed. Representa-
tive one-act plays
Provincetown plays ser 2
Metropol 45:19, 57
Tickless time (with G. C. Cook) a com-
edy in one act. Boston. Baker. 1925.
12°. p. 275-315
Same in Glaspell, S. Plays
Shay, F. ed. Contemporary
one-act plays of 1921
Shay, F. ed. Twenty contem-
porary one-act plays (Ameri-
can)
Glass, Everett
Tumbler. Legendary. 2 scenes
In Poet Lore 37:516
Gleason, James, and Abbott, George
Fall guy. Comedy. 3 acts
In Mantle, B. ed. Best plays of 1924-
25 (abridged)
Glick, Carl
It isn't done. Comedy. 1 act
In Shay, F. ed. Treasury of plays for
men
Outclassed. Comedy. 1 act
In Shay, F. ed. Treasury of plays for
men
Prologue. Night life. 1 act
In Poet Lore 33:553
Suncold. Psychological. 1 act
In Poet Lore 36:280
Ten days later. Comedy. 1 act
In Drama 11:159
Glick, Carl, and Hight, Mary
Police matron; a melodrama in one act.
Boston. Baker. 1918. 12°. 16p.
Glick, Carl, and Sobel, Bernard
Immortal Byron. 1 act
In Poet Lore 32:441
Glover, Halcott
Hail, Caesar!
In Wat Tyler, and other plays
King's Jewry
In Wat Tyler, and other plays
Second round; a play. London. Rout-
ledge. 1923. 12°. 73p.
Wat Tyler. Historical
In Wat Tyler, and other plays
Glynn-Ward, H., pseud. (Mrs. Hilda Glynn Howard), 1887-
Aftermath. Deception. 1 act
In Poet Lore 37:501
Gnudtzmann, Albert Theodor, 1865-
Eyes that cannot see; a play in one act,
tr. from the Danish. . . Cincinnati,
Stewart Kidd. 1923. 12°. 48p.
Blindness
Same in Shay, Frank. Twenty-five
short plays, international
Gobineau, Joseph Arthur, comte de, 1816-1882
Renaissance. Savonarola. 1 act
In Smart Set 55 no 2:83
Savonarola. *See* Gobineau, J. A. Renais-
sance

Godshaw, Esther
Women in war; a patriotic entertainment in one act. Boston. Baker. 1918. 12°. 11p.
Goethe, Johan Wolfgang, von, 1749-1832
Clavidgo; a tragedy in five acts. London. Johnston. 1798. 8°. 95p.
Egmont. Historical. 5 acts
In Dramatic works (Bohn)
Faust; a tragedy. Tr. by Bayard Taylor. Boston. Osgood. 1871. 2v. 8°. [Pts. 1-2]
Same in Dramatic works (Bohn)
Bates, A. ed. Drama v 11
Goetz von Berlichingen. Historical. 5 acts
In Dramatic works (Bohn)
Iphigenia in Tauris. Tragedy. 5 acts
In Dramatic works (Bohn)
Bates, A. ed. Drama v 11
German classics 1:157
Stella. Comedy. 5 acts
In Bates, A. ed. Drama v 12:287
Torquato Tasso. Historical. 5 acts
In Dramatic works (Bohn)
Goetze, A.
Heights. Illusions. 4 acts
In Poet Lore 25:1
Gogol, Nicolay Vasilievitch, 1809-1852
Inspector-general; a comedy in five acts. . . N.Y. Knopf. 1916. 12°. 119p.
Same in Bates, A. ed. Drama 18:193
Marriage. Comedy. 2 acts
In Voynich, E. L. ed. Humour of Russia
Goldberg, Isaac, 1887-
Better son. Domestic. 1 act
In Stratford J 3:169
Golden, John, 1874-
Clock shop
In Three John Golden plays
Robe of wood
In Three John Golden plays
Vanishing princess
In Three John Golden plays
Goldring, Douglas, 1887-
Cuckoo; a comedy of adjustments. N.Y. McBride. 1926. 12°. 265p.
Fight for freedom; a play in four acts. . . N.Y. Seltzer. 1920. 12°. 98p. $1.25. Radical
Goldsmith, Oliver. *See* Dibdin, T. J. Vicar of Wakefield
Gooch, Frances Pusey
Gerry's awakening; a play in three acts. Boston. Gorham press. 1916. 12°. 100p. Romantic
Goodhue, Willis Maxwell
"Hello Bill"; a farcical comedy in three acts. N.Y. French. c1926. 12°. 75p.
Goodloe, Abbie Carter, 1867-
Antinoüs; a tragedy. Phila. Lippincott. 1891. 12°. 139p. 5 acts
Goodman, Edward
Eugenically speaking. Comedy. 1 act
In Dickinson, A. D. ed. Drama Washington Square plays
Goodman, Jules Eckert, 1876-
Chains; a play in three acts. N.Y. Brentano's. 1924. 12°. 88p. Social

Treasure Island
In Moses, M. J. ed. Another treasury of plays for children
Goodman, Kenneth Sawyer
At the edge of the wood. Masque. 1 act
In More quick curtains
Back of the yards; a play in one act. N.Y. Vaughan. 1914. 12°. 44p. Ethical
Same in Quick curtains
Barbara; a play in one act. N.Y. Vaughan. 1914. 12°. 32p. Farce
Same in Quick curtains
Behind the black cloth. Melodrama. 1 act
In More quick curtains
Dancing dolls. Chicago. Stage Guild. 1923. 12°. 31p. Comedy. 1 act
Same in More quick curtains
Quick curtains
Shay, F. ed. Plays for strolling mummers
Dust of the road; a play in one act. Chicago. Stage Guild. [c1912]. 12°. 21p. Christmas
Same in More quick curtains
Ephraim and the winged bear; a Christmas eve nightmare in one act. N.Y. Vaughan. 1914. 12°. 31p.
Same in Quick curtains
Game of chess; a play in one act. N.Y. Vaughan. 1914. 12°. 29p. Tragicomedy
Same in Quick curtains
Knickerbocker, E. van B. ed. Twelve plays
Green scarf; an artificial comedy in one act. N.Y. Shay. [c1920]. 12°. 12p.
Same in More quick curtains
Man can only do his best; a fantastic comedy in one act. Chicago Stage Guild. 1915. 12°. 52p.
Same in Quick curtains
Parting. Melodrama. 1 act
In More quick curtains
Red flag. Comedy. 1 act
In More quick curtains
Goodman, Kenneth Sawyer, and Hecht, Ben
Hand of Siva. Melodrama. 1 act
In Wonder hat, and other one-act plays
Shay, F. ed. Treasury of plays for men
Hero of Santa Maria; a ridiculous tragedy in one act. N.Y. Shay. [c1920]. 12°. 22p.
Same in Quick curtains
Wonder hat, and other one-act plays
Shay, F. ed. Contemporary one-act plays of 1921
Shay, F. ed. Twenty contemporary one-act plays of America
Idyll of the shops. Ghetto. 1 act
In Wonder hat, and other one-act plays
Two lamps. Melodrama. 1 act
In Wonder hat, and other one-act plays

Goodman, K. S.—*Continued*
Wonder hat; a harlequinade in one act. N.Y. Shay. ₁c1920₁. 12°. 24p.
Same in Wonder hat, and three one-act plays
Mayorga, M. G. ed. Representative one-act plays
Goodman, Kenneth S., and Stevens, Thomas Wood
Caesar's gods; a Byzantine masque. Chicago. Stage Guild. ₁c1913₁. 12°. 27p. 1 act
Same in Masques of East and West
Daimio's head. Masque. 5 scenes
In Daimio's head, and other masques
Masques of East and West
Holbein in Blackfriars; an improbable comedy. Chicago. Stage Guild. c1913. 12°. 32p. 1 act
Masque of Montezuma. . . Chicago. Stage guild. c1912. 8°. 32p. 1 act
Same in Daimio's head and other masques
Masques of the east and west
Masque of Quetzal's bowl. Written for the second anniversary of the house warming of the Cliff-Dwellers. ₁Chicago. Stage Guild. 1912?₁. 8°. 16p. Masque. 3 scenes
Same in Daimio's head and other masques
Masques of East and West
Montezuma. *See* Goodman, K. S. and Stevens, T. W. Masque of Montezuma
Pageant for Independence Day. Chicago. Stage Guild. ₁1912₁. 12°. 39p. 4 scenes
Same in Masques of East and West
Quetzal's bowl. *See* Goodman, K. S. and Stevens, T. W. Masque of Quetzal's bowl
Rainald and the Red Wolf; being the masque of the pilgrims and the townsfolk of Lavayne. . . Chicago. Stage Guild. c1914. 12°. 34p. 1 act
Same in Masques of East and West
Ryland, a comedy in one act. Chicago. Stage Guild. ₁c1912₁. 12°. 29p.
Same in Mayorga, M. G. ed. Representative one-act plays
Goodrich, Arthur Frederick, 1878-
So this is London; a comedy in three acts. N.Y. French. c1926. 12°. 117p.
Goodrich, Arthur Frederick, 1878-, and Palmer, Rose A.
Caponsacchi; a play in three acts, prologue and epilogue, based upon Robert Browning's poem, "The ring and the book.". . . N.Y. Appleton. 1927. 12°. 184p.
Googins, Dorothy R.
Bellman of Mons. Miracle. 3 acts
In Thomas, C. S. ed. Atlantic book of junior plays
Goold, Marshall N.
Saint Claudia; a religious drama. . . Boston. Pilgrim press. c1925. 62p.
Gordon, George, pseud. *See* Baldwin, Charles Crittenden

Gordon, Leon
As a pal. Comedy. 1 act
In Gentleman ranker, and other plays
Gentleman ranker. World war. 1 act
In Gentleman ranker, and other plays
Leave the woman out. Detective. 1 act
In Gentleman ranker, and other plays
White cargo; a play of the primitive. Boston. Four seas co. ₁c1925₁. 12°. 117p. White man in the tropics. 3
Gordon-Lennox, Cosmo Charles, 1869-
Impertinence of the creature. Duologue. 1 act
In Clark, B. H. ed. Representative one-act plays by British and Irish authors
Marriage of Kitty, adapted from the French. . . London. French. c1909. 12°. 96p.
Gore-Booth, Eva
Death of Fionavar, from The triumph of Maeve. London. Erskine Macdonald. n.d. 87p. Irish mythology. 1 act
Sorrowful princess. London. Longmans. 1907. 92p. Egyptian. 3 acts
Gorham, Herbert S.
Death of Nero; a play in one act. Historical
In Theatre Arts M 8:195
Gorky, Maxim, pseud. (Pieshkov, Aleksei Maksimorich), 1868-
At the bottom. *See* Gorky, M. Lower depths
Children of the sun. . . Boston. Badger. n.d. $1. 8°. p. 1-77. Russian life. 4 acts
Same in Poet Lore 17 no 2:1
In the depths. *See* Gorky M. Lower depths
Judge; a play in four acts. . . N.Y. McBride. 1924. 12°. 105p. Tragedy
Lower depths; a drama in four acts. . . Brentano's. ₁c1922.₁ 12°. 89p. *Also* Duffield. 1912. (At the bottom; In the depths; Night asylum; Night refuge; Night shelter; Night's lodging, Submerged) (Na Dyye); Tragedy; scenes from Russian life. 4 acts
Same in Lower depths
Night's lodging
Submerged
Bates, A. Drama. v 18:279
Dickinson, T. H. ed. Chief contemporary dramatists ser 2
Pierce and Matthews: Masterpieces of modern drama v 2 (abridged)
Sayler, O. M. ed. Moscow art theatre series of Russian plays ser 1
Drama (London) v 18:279
Poet Lore 16 no 4:3
Night asylum. *See* Gorky, M. Lower depths
Night refuge. *See* Gorky, M. Lower depths

Night shelter.   *See* Gorky, M. Lower
   depths
Night's lodging.   Scenes from Russian
   life. . . Boston.   Badger.   ₁c1906₁.   8°.
   p. 3-64.   *See* Gorky, M.   Lower
   depths
Smug citizen; a dramatic sketch in four
   acts. . . Boston.   Badger.   c1907.   8°.
   p. 1-74.   Family life
Same in Poet Lore 17 no 4:1
Submerged: scenes from Russian life.
   Boston.   Badger.   c1915.   12°.   143p.
   See Gorky, M.   Lower depths
Summer folk (Datchniki). . . Boston.
   Badger.   c1905. $1.25.   8°.   p. 1-90.
   Comedy.   4 acts
Same in Poet Lore 16 no 3:1
Gorman, H. S.
   Death of Nero.   Historical. 1 act
   In Theatre Arts M 8:195
Gosse, Edmund, 1849-
   Gods in the island.   *See* Gosse, S. Hy-
      polympia; or, The gods in the island
   Hypolympia; or, The gods in the island.
      Dodd.   N.Y.   1901.   12°.   220p.   Ironic
      fantasy.   12 pts.
   King Erik; a tragedy. . . London.   Heine-
      mann.   1893.   12°.   182p.   5 acts
Gosse, Henri de, and Forest, Louis
   Le procureur Hallers.   1 act
   In Liv Age 323:566
**Goubaux, Prosper P. (Prosper Denaux,
   pseud.), 1795-1859, and Ernest Legouve**
   Louise de Lignerolles; a tragic drama in
      five parts.   Adapted from the
      French.   London.   Lacy.   n.d.   12°.   33p.
      (Lacy's acting edition of plays. v. 14
      no. 204)
Gould, E. joint author.   *See* Mayo, Mar-
   garet and Gould, E.
Gould, Felix
   In the marshes.   Supernatural. 1 act
   In Marsh maiden and other plays
   Marsh maiden.   Supernatural. 1 act
   In Marsh maiden and other plays
   Stranger.   Supernatural. 1 act
   In Marsh maiden and other plays
Goulding, Edmund. joint author.   *See* Sel-
   wyn, Edgar and Goulding, E.
Gourmont, Remy de, 1858-1915
   Old king.   Tragedy. 1 act
   In Drama 6 no 22:206
   Theodat.   Celibacy. 1 act
   In Drama 6 no 22:184
Gozzi, Carlo, conte, 1722-1806
   Turandot, princess of China: a chinoiserie
      in three acts. . . N.Y.   Duffield.   1913.
      12°.   128p. $1
Graham, Bertha M.
   Land of the "Free".   Sociological. 1 act
   In Spoiling the broth, and other plays
   Little red box.   Romantic. 1 act
   In Spoiling the broth, and other plays
   O, the press!   Comedy. 1 act
   In Spoiling the broth, and other plays
   Pitch and toss.   Romantic. 1 act
   In Spoiling the broth, and other plays
   Rose with a thorn.   Romantic. 1 act
   In Spoiling the broth, and other plays

Spoiling the broth.   Comedy. 1 act
   In Spoiling the broth, and other plays
Taffy's wife.   Detective. 1 act
   In Spoiling the broth, and other plays
Graham, Manta S.
   Light weights.   Boston.   Cornhill.   ₁c1921₁.
      12°.   102p. $1.50
   Allied occupations.   Comedy. 1 act
   In Light weights
   By-product.   Tragedy. 1 act
   In Light weights
   Goose.   Comedy. 1 act
   In Light weights
   Trend.   Comedy. 1 act
   In Light weights
   Two's company.   Comedy. 1 act
   In Light weights
Grahn, Mary
   Idyll.   Pierrot. 1 act
   In Drama 16:255
Grant, Neil Forkes, 1882-
   Possessions; a comedy in three acts.
      N.Y.   French.   c1925.   12°.   72p.
   Valuable rival; a play in one act.   Lon-
      don.   Gowans & Gray.   1922.   24°.   29p.
      Comedy
Grant, Percy Stickney, 1860-
   Return of Odysseus; a poetic drama in
      four acts.   N.Y.   Brentano's.   1912.
      12°.   132p.   Mythological
Graves, Roberts, 1895-
   John Kemp's wager; a ballad opera.
      N.Y.   French.   1925.   12°.   75p.
Gray, Eleanor
   Eros and Psyche.   London.   Kegan Paul.
      ₁1918₁.   119p.   Mythological.   3 acts
Gray, Frances
   Beaded buckle.   Carolina. 1 act
   In Koch, F. H. ed.   Carolina folk-
      plays ser 2
Gray, Terence
   And in the tomb was found.   Egyptian.
      3 acts
   In And in the tomb was found
   Building of the Pyramid.   Egyptian. 2
      scenes
   In And in the tomb was found
   Cuchulainn: an epic drama of the Gael.
      Cambridge.   Heffer.   1925.   12°.   12s 6d.
      281p.   4 parts
   Life of the King of the South and North,
      Kamaria, Daughter of the Sun, Hat-
      shepsut.   A pageant of court life in
      old Egypt in the early XVIIIth
      dynasty, reconstructed from the mon-
      uments.   A chapter of Egyptian his-
      tory in dramatic form.   Cambridge.
      Heffer.   1920.   8°.   259p.   5 parts
   Nameless.   Egyptian. 1 act
   In And in the tomb was found
   Royal audience.   Egyptian. 1 act
   In And in the tomb was found
Green, Paul
   Blackbeard; a melodrama of pirate days
      on the Carolina coast.   1 act
   In Lord's will, and other Carolina plays
   End of the row.   Negro. 1 act
   In Lonesome road
      Poet Lore 35:58

Green, P.—*Continued*
Field god.   Negro. 3 acts
In Field god, and In Abraham's bosom
In Abraham's bosom; the biography of a
    negro in seven scenes
In Field god, and In Abraham's bosom
    Lonesome road
Granny Boling.   Negro. 1 act
In Drama 11:389
Hot iron.   Negro. 1 act
In Lonesome road
    Poet Lore 35:48
In Aunt Mahaly's cabin; a negro melo-
    drama in one act.   N.Y. French.
    1925. 12°. 35p.
Last of the Lowries.   Carolina outlaws.
    1 act
In Lord's will, and other Carolina plays
    Cohen, H. L. ed.   More one-act
        plays by modern authors
    Koch, F. H. ed.   Carolina folk-plays
        ser 1
Lord's will.   Fanaticism. 1 act
In Lord's will, and other Carolina plays
    Poet Lore 33:366
Man who died at twelve o'clock.   Negro.
    1 act
In One-act plays for stage and study
    ser 2
No 'count boy; a comedy of negro life.
    1 act
In Lord's will, and other Carolina plays
    Theatre arts M 8:773
Old man of Edenton; a melodrama of
    witchcraft times.   1 act
In Lord's will, and other Carolina plays
Old Wash Lucas, the miser.   Carolina
    folk lore.   1 act
In Lord's will, and other Carolina plays
    Poet Lore 35:254
Prayer meeting.   Folk play, N.C. 1 act.
In Lonesome road
    Poet Lore 35:232
Sam Tucker.   Negro. 1 act
In Poet Lore 34:220
Unto such glory.   1 act
In One-act plays for stage and study
    ser 3
White dresses; a tragedy of negro life. 1
    act
In Lonesome road
    Lewis, B. R. ed.   Contemporary
        one-act plays

Your fiery furnace.   Negro. 1 act
In Lonesome road

Green, Paul, and Green, Erma
Fixin's, the tragedy of a tenant-farm wo-
    man. 1 act
In Koch, F. W. ed.   Carolina folk-
    plays ser 2

Greene, B. M.
God-intoxicated man.   Spinoza. 3 acts
In Woman the masterpiece, etc
Woman the masterpiece.   Art and litera-
    ture. 4 episodes
In Woman the masterpiece, etc

Greene, Clay Meredith, 1850-1916
Awakening of Barbizon.   Comedy. 1 act
In Dispensation and other plays

Dispensation.   Religious. 1 act
In Dispensation and other plays
Star of Bethlehem.   Christmas. 1 act
In Dispensation and other plays
Through Christmas bells.   Domestic. 1
    act
In Dispensation and other plays

Greene, Henry Copley, 1871-
Father; a drama.   Nelson, N. H.   Mon-
    adnock press. 1905. 8°. 89p.   Trag-
    edy. 3 acts
Pontius Pilate.   Mystery. 3 acts
In Pontius Pilate, etc
Saint Ronan of Brittany.   Miracle. 1 act
In Pontius Pilate, etc
Théophile; a miracle play.   Boston.
    Small. 1898. 12°. 32p. 6 scenes
Same in Pontius Pilate, etc

Greene, Kathleen Conyngham
First Christmas eve.   Miracle. 1 act
In Little boy out of the wood, and
    other dream plays
Little boy out of the wood.   Dream. 1
    act
In Little boy out of the wood, and
    other dream plays
    Webber, J. B. & Webster, H. H.
        Short plays for young people
Night watch.   Dream. 1 act
In Little boy out of the wood, and
    other dream plays
Poppy seller.   Dream. 1 act
In Little boy out of the wood, and
    other dream plays
Princess on the road.   Fantasy. 1 act
In Little boy out of the wood, and
    other dream plays
    Webber, J. P. & Webster, H. H.
        Short plays for young people
Vision splendid.   Fantasy. 1 act
In Little boy out of the wood, and
    other dream plays

Greggs, Tresham D.
Queen Elizabeth; or, The origin of
    Shakespeare.   London. Macintosh.
    1872.   Shakespeare. 5 acts

Gregory, Lady Isabella Augusta, 1859-
Aristotle's bellows.   Folk-play. 3 acts
In Three wonder plays
Bogie men.   Comedy. 1 act
In New comedies
    Fortn 98:1165
    Forum 49:28
Canavans.   Tragi-comedy. 3 acts
In Irish folk-history plays ser 2
Coats.   London. Putnam. [c1913]. 12°.
    21p.   Comedy. 1 act
Same in New comedies
    Metropol 36:40
Damer's gold; a comedy in two acts.
    London. Putnam. [c1913]. 12°. 41p.
Same in New comedies
Dave.   1 act
In One-act plays for stage and study
    ser 3
Deliverer.   Tragi-comedy. 1 act
In Irish folk-history plays ser 2
Dervorgilla.   Tragedy. 1 act
In Irish folk-history, plays ser 1
    Samhain N '08 p 13

Dragon; a wonder play in three acts. N.Y. Putnam. 1920. 12°. 133p. Allegory
Same in Three wonder plays

Full moon. A comedy in one act. Dublin. Author. c1911. 12°. 49p.
Same in New comedies

Gaol gate. Tragedy. 1 act
In Seven short plays
Gaelic American D 1 '06

Golden apple; a play for Kiltartan children. . . N.Y. Putnam. 1916. 12°. 117p. Allegorical. 3 acts

Grania. Tragedy. 3 acts
In Irish folk-history plays ser 1.

Hanrahan's oath; comedy. 1 act
In Image, and other plays
Little R 4 no 7:6, 33

Hyacinth Halvey; a comedy. N.Y. Quinn. 1906. 12°. 51p. 1 act
Same in Seven short plays
Lewis, B. R. ed. Contemporary one-act plays
Samhain D '06 p 15

Image. A play in three acts. Dublin. Maunsel. 1910. 12°. 102p. Allegory
Same in Image, and other plays

Jackdaw. Comedy. 1 act
In Seven short plays

Jester. Folkplay. 3 acts
In Three wonder plays

Kincora; a play in three acts. Dublin. Maunsel. 1905. 12°. 70p. Tragedy
Same in Irish folk history plays ser 1

MacDaragh's wife. *See* Gregory, I. A. McDonough's wife

McDonough's wife (MacDaragh's wife). Irish life. 1 act
In New comedies
Outlook 99:920

On the racecourse. Comedy. 1 act
In One-act plays for stage and study ser 2

Rising of the moon. Comedy. 1 act
In Seven short plays
Dickinson, T. H. Chief contemporary dramatists
Marriott, J. W. One-act plays of to-day ser 2
Smith, M. M. ed. Short plays of various types

Shanwalla. Folk play. 4 acts
In Image, and other plays

Spreading the news. Dublin. Talbot. 1918. 12°. 35p. Comedy. 1 act
Same in Seven short plays
Clark, B. H. ed. Representative one-act plays by British and Irish authors
Cohen, H. L. ed. One-act plays by modern authors
Leonard, S. A. ed. Atlantic book of modern plays
One act plays for stage and study ser 1

Smith, A. M. ed. Short plays by representative authors
Golden Bk 2:355
Samhain N '05 p 15

Story brought by Brigit: a passion play in three acts. London. Putnam. ₁1924₁. 12°. 97p.

Travelling man. Miracle. 1 act
In Seven short plays
Moses, M. J. ed. Treasury of plays for children
Webber, J. P. and Webster, H. H. eds. Short plays for young people

White cockade. Dublin. Maunsel. 1905. 12°. 63p. Tragi-comedy. 3 acts
Same in Irish folk-history plays ser 2

Workhouse ward. Comedy. 1 act
In Seven short plays
Coffman, G. R. ed. Book of modern plays
Moses, M. J. ed. Representative British dramas
Shay, F. and Loving, P. eds. Fifty contemporary one-act plays

Wrens. Historical. 1 act
In Image, and other plays

Gregory, Odin
Caius Gracchus; a tragedy. . . N.Y. Boni. 1920. 8°. 172p. 1920. $2 5 acts
Jesus; the tragedy of man. N.Y. Colony. ₁c1923₁. 8°. 138p. 5 acts

Gregson, James R.
T'Marsdens, a comedy in three acts. London. Hodder. ₁1924₁. 12°. 156p.
Young Imeson; a play in three acts. London. Hodder & Stoughton. ₁1924₁. 16°. 176p. Comedy

Grendon, Felix, 1882-
Will he come back? a one-act comedy. N.Y. New Review pub. ass'n. 1916. 12°. 44p. 25c

Gribble, George Dunning
Masque of Venice; an entertainment in three acts. London. Benn. 1924. 130p.
Scene that was to write itself; a tragi-comedy in one act. London. Benn. 1924. 37p.

Gribble, Harry Wagstaff
All gummed up. Comedy. 1 act
In Shay, F. ed. Contemporary one-act plays of 1921
Shay, F. ed. Twenty contemporary one-act plays (American)
March hares (The temperamentalists), a fantastic satire in three acts. Cincinnati. Stewart Kidd. 1923. 12°. 180p.

Griffith, Alice Mary Matlock
Whither. Faculty wives. 1 act
In Poet Lore 35:140

Griffith, William, 1876-
Before the fairies came to America. Masque. 1 act
In International (NY) 10:316

Grillparzer, Franz, 1791-1872
Jewess of Toledo. Tragedy. 5 acts
In German classics 6:337
Sappho. A tragedy in five acts. . . Boston. Roberts. 1876. 16°. 136p.

Groff, Alice
Freedom; a play in four acts.   Boston. Badger. 1904. 58p.

Gropallo, Laura
Soul of the people; a drama tr. from the Italian by Sidney Rothschild.   N.Y. Sturgis. 1917. 12°. 137p. $3   Historical

Grover, Harry Greenwood
Thompson's luck, a tragedy in one act. Cincinnati. Stewart Kidd. c1923. 25p.
In Shay, F. ed.   Contemporary one-act plays of 1921
Shay, F. ed.   Twenty contemporary one-act plays (American)

Grundy, Sydney, 1848-1914
Arabian nights; a farce in three acts. . . London. French. [1887?]. 12°. 49p.
Bunch of violets; a play.   N.Y. French. 1901. 12°. 57p.
Fool's paradise an original play in three acts.   N.Y. French. c1898. 12°. 64p.
Glass of fashion; an original comedy in four acts.   N.Y. French. 1898. 12°. 60p.
Head of Romulus; a comedietta in one act. . . N.Y. French. 1900. 12°. 24p.
In honour bound; an original play in one act. . . London. French. [1880?]. 12°. 20p.
Late Mr. Castollo; an original farce. N.Y. French. c1901. 12°. 52p.
Little change; a farce in one scene. London. French. [18—]. 23p.
Pair of spectacles; a comedy in three acts. . . N.Y. French. c1898. 12°. 66p.
Silver shield; an original comedy in three acts.   N.Y. French. c1898. 12°. 62p.
Snowball; a farcical comedy in three acts. London. French. [1879?]. 45p.
Sowing the wind, an original play in four acts. . . N.Y. French. c1901. 12°. 56p.
Sympathetic souls; a comedietta in one act. . . N.Y. French. 1900. 12°. 19p.

Gue, Belle Willey
George Washington; a drama.   Boston. Four seas. 1924. 12°. 92p. $2   Historical. 4 scenes

Guild, Thacher Howland, 1879-1914
Class of '56.   Comedy. 1 act
In Power of a god, and other one-act plays
Higher good.   Religious. 1 act
In Power of a god, and other one-act plays
Portrait.   Fantasy. 1 act
In Power of a god, and other one-act plays
Power of a god.   Comedy. 1 act
In Power of a god, and other one-act plays

Guillemot, Jules
Unlucky star.   Farce. 1 act
In Bellevue Dramatic Club: Plays for private acting

Guimerá, Angel, 1847-
Daniela.   *See* Guimerá, A. La pecadora
Marta of the lowlands; a play in three acts. . . Garden City.   Doubleday. 1914. 12°. 111p.   Tragedy
La pecadora (Daniela); a play in three acts. . . N.Y. Putnam. 1916. 12°. 162p. Tragedy
Same in Clark, B. H. ed.   Masterpieces of Spanish drama

Guitermann, Arthur, joint author.   *See* Mendel, P. and Guitermann, A.

Guitry, Sacha, 1885-
Deburau, a comedy in an English version of H. G. Barker.   N.Y. Putnam. 1920. 12°. 226p. 4 acts
Same in Mantle, B. ed.   Best plays of 1920-21 (condensed)
Pasteur.   Historical. 1 act
In Dickinson, T. H. ed.   Chief contemporary drama

Gundelfinger, George F.
Ice lens; a four act play on college morals, (causes and consequences).   N.Y. Shakespeare Press. 1913. 212p.

Guske, Carl W.
Fata deorum.   Poetic. 1 act
In Shay, F. ed.   Contemporary one-act plays of 1921
Shay, F. ed.   Twenty contemporary one-act plays (American)

Guthrie, Arthur
Probationer, a play in four acts.   London. Gowans. 1911. 12°. 160p.
Weaver's shuttle; a comedy in three acts. London. Gowans & Gray. 1910. 12°. 125p.

Gutzkow, Karl (Ferdinand), 1811-1878
Sword and queue.   Comedy. 5 acts
In German classics 7:252
Uriel Acosta; a tragedy in five acts.   Tr. by M. M. N.Y. Ellinger. 1860. 12°. 104p.
Same in Poet Lore 7:6, 83, 140, 198, 263, 333

Gyalin, Farkas, 1866-
After the honeymoon; a comedy in one act.   N.Y. French. 1915. 12°. 15p.

Gyp, pseud.   (Martel de Janville, Sibylle Gabrielle Marie Antoinette de Riquetti de Mirabeau, Comtesse de), 1850-
Little blue guinea-hen.   Comedy. 1 act
In Poet Lore 30:60

Hafer, Engéne G.
Attorney for the defense; a play in four acts.   Chicago. Dramatic pub. co. [c1924]. 54p.
Tumult; a crashing comedy-drama in three acts.   Chicago. Dramatic pub. co. c1923. 95p.

Hagboldt, Peter
Test; a play in three acts.   Boston. Cornhill. 1918. 12°. 105p.   World war

Hagedorn, Hermann, 1882-
Heart of youth.   N.Y. Macmillan. 1915. 12°. 83p.   Religious. 4 scenes
Same in Great image, and the heart of youth
Outlook 111:744

Horse thieves; a comedy in one act. Cambridge, Mass. 1909. 12°. 48p. (Privately printed by Boston Transcript)

Keeper of the gate. Mother-love. 1 act
In Outlook 107:1056

Makers of madness; a play in one act and three scenes. N.Y. Macmillan. 1914. 12°. 95p. War

Pool of Bethesda. Faith cure. 1 act
In Outlook 108:782

Silver blade; a drama in one act. Berlin. Unger. 1907. 8°. 61p. Arthurian

Haid, Leo, 1849-
Major John André: an historical drama in five acts. Baltimore. Murphy. 1876. 12°. 68p.

Halbe, Max, 1865-
Mother Earth (1897). Marriage. 5 acts
In German classics 20:111
Rosenhagens. Character. 3 acts
In Poet Lore 21:1
Youth. . . Garden City. Doubleday. 1916. 12°. 131p. 75c. Tragedy. 3 acts

Hale, Louise Closser, 1872-
Other woman. Intrigue. 1 act
In Smart Set 34 no 2:107

Halman, Doris F., 1895-
Closet. Domestic tragedy. 1 act
In Set the stage for eight
Difficult border. Fantasy. 1 act
In Set the stage for eight
Dog. Tragedy. 1 act
In Set the stage for eight
Famine and the ghost. Fantasy. 1 act
In Set the stage for eight
It behooves us; a comedy in conservation. N.Y. French. 1918. 12°. 16p. 25c 1 act
Lady Anne. Fantasy. 1 act
In Set the stage for eight
Land where lost things go. A play in a prologue and three acts. N.Y. French. 1918. 12°. 67p. 25c. War
Playroom. Fantasy. 1 act
In Set the stage for eight
47 workshop plays ser 2
Santa claus. Christmas. 1 act
In Set the stage for eight
Voice of the snake. 1 act
In One-act plays for stage and study ser 3
Will-o'-the-wisp. Fantasy. 1 act
In Set the stage for eight
Clements, C. C. ed. Ten plays
Mayorga, M. G. ed. Representative one-act plays

Halpern, J.
Mother and son. Religious. 1 act
In Block, E. tr. One-act plays from the Yiddish

Hamilton, Alexander, 1815-1907
Cromwell; a tragedy in five acts. N.Y. Dick & Fitzgerald. [c1868]. 12°. 124p.
Same in Dramas and poems
Thomas a Becket; a tragedy in five acts. N.Y. Dick. [1863]. 12°. 106p.
Same in Dramas and poems
Canonicus. Tragedy. 5 acts
In Dramas and poems

Hamilton, Cicely Mary, 1875-
Child in Flanders; a nativity play in a prologue, five tableaux, and an epilogue. London. French. c1922. 12°. 35p.
Same in Marriott, J. W. ed. One-act plays of to-day ser 2
Diana of Dobsons; a romantic comedy in four acts. . . N.Y. French. c1925. 12°. 64p.
Jack and Jill and a friend. London. French. c1911. 12°. 20p. Comedy. 1 act

Hamilton, Cecily Mary, 1875-, and Marshall C.
How the vote was won; a play in one act. Chicago. Dramatic publishing co. [c1910]. 12°. 31p. Woman suffrage

Hamilton Clayton, 1881-, joint author. *See* Thomas, A. E. and Hamilton, Clayton

Hamilton, Clayton Meeker, 1881-, and Voigt, Bernhard
Friend indeed; a comedy-drama in three acts. . . N.Y. French. c1926. 12°. 106p.

Hamilton, Cosmo
Aubrey closes the door. A play in one act. London. French. c1904. 12°. 15p.
Blindness of virtue. N.Y. Doran. [c1913]. 12°. 127p. Social. 4 acts
Mother woman. Social. 3 acts
In Four plays
New poor. Comedy. 3 acts
In Four plays
Scandal. Comedy. 3 acts
In Four plays
Silver fox. Comedy. 3 acts
In Four plays
Wisdom of folly; a ridiculous piece in three acts (being an episode in the peaceful life of a fluffy-minded lady). N.Y. French. c1903. 12°. 73p.

Hamlen, George J.
Barbara grows up; a comedy in three acts. . . Boston. Baker. c1925. 12°. 59p.
Waldies: a play in four acts. London. Sidgwick & Jackson. 1914. 12°. 112p. Melodrama

Hamlin, Mary P.
Rock; a play in three acts showing the character development of Simon Peter. . . Boston. Pilgrim press. c1921. 8°. 37p.

Hamlin, Mary P., and Arliss, George, 1868-
Hamilton; a play in four acts. Boston. Baker. 1918. 12°. 160p. 50c. Historical

Hamsun, Knut, 1859-
In the grip of life; a play in four acts. . . N.Y. Knopf. 1924. 158p.

Haney, John Louis, 1877-
Monsieur D'Or; a dramatic fantasy. Phila. Egerton press. 1910. 12°. 145p. 4 scenes

Hankey, Donald
Passing in June 1915.   London. Long-
    mans. 1915. 12°. 27p.   World war. 4
    acts
Hankin, St John E. C., 1869-1909
Burglar who failed.   Farce. 1 act
    In Dramatic works v 3
        Plays v 2
Cassilis engagement.   Comedy. 4 acts
    In Dramatic works v 2
        Plays v 2
        Three plays with happy endings
        Dickinson, T. H. ed.   Contemporary
            plays
        Moses, M. J. ed.   Representative
            British dramas
Charity that began at home.   Comedy. 4
    acts
    In Dramatic works v 2
        Plays v 1
        Three plays with happy endings
Constant lover; a comedy of youth in one
    act.   N.Y. French. 1912. 12°. 24p.
    Same in Dramatic works v 2
        Plays v 2
        Shay, F. and Loving, P. eds.
            Fifty contemporary one-act
            plays
        Smart Set 38 no 2:133
        Theatre arts M 3:67
Last of the De Mullins.   London. Fifield.
    1909. 16°. 128p.   Sociological. 3 acts
    Same in Dramatic works v 3
        Plays v 2
Return of the prodigal.   Comedy. 4 acts
    In Dramatic works v 1
        Plays v 1
        Three plays with happy endings
Two Mr. Wetherbys.   Melodrama. 3 acts
    In Dramatic works v 1
        Plays v 1
Hankin, St. John, 1869-1909, **and Calderon,**
    G., 1868-1915
Thompson, a comedy in three acts.   Lon-
    don. Secker. [1913]. 12°. 85p.
    Same in Plays v 2
Hanna, Tacie May
House beautiful.   Comedy. 1 act
    In Drama 15:112
Hyacinths.   Saving. 1 act
    In Drama 12:338
Upon the waters.   Social. 1 act
    In Drama 14:58
Hanning, S. C.
Alchumust; a tragedy in four acts.
    Openshaw [Eng]. Buckley. 1919. 12°.
    20p.
Bruce.   Scotland. 5 scenes
    In Caledonia
Captive queen.   Scotland. 1 act
    In Caledonia
Dierdri, a play in five acts.   London.
    Stockwell. [1921]. 12°. 95p.   Irish
    historical
King of Carrick.   Scotland. 3 acts
    In Caledonia
Lord Bothwell.   Historical. 4 acts
    In Caledonia

Red Cardinal.   Scotland. 2 acts
    In Caledonia
Wails o' Glencoe.   Scotland. 2 acts
    In Caledonia
Hanshaw, T. W.
Forty-niners.   Gold mines. 5 acts
    In Bates, A. ed.   Drama v 20
Harvest.   Intrigue. 1 act
    In Smart Set 26 no 3:118
Hapgood, Mrs. Hutchins. *See* Boyce, Neith
Harcourt, Cyril
Intruder; a drama in three acts.   N.Y.
    French. 1920. 12°. 79p. 50c.   Problem
Pair of silk stockings; a comedy in three
    acts.   N.Y. French. 1920. 12°. 96p.
    75c. *Also* Burt. 1918. 60c
Place in the sun; a play in three acts.
    N.Y. French. c1914. 12°. 62p.   Com-
    edy
Hardt, Ernst, 1876-
Tristram the jester; tr. from the German
    by John Heard.   Boston. Wagner.
    1913. 12°. 185p. $1.   Legendary. 5
    acts
    Same in German classics 20:398
Hardwicke, Pelham
Bachelor of arts: A comic drama in two
    acts.   London. Lacy. n.d. 12°. 48p.
    (Lacy's acting edition of plays. v. 12
    no. 177)
Hardy, Blanche C.
Artegal, a drama; (poems and ballads).
    London.   Long.   [1914].   122p.
    Legendary. 4 acts
Hardy, E. Trueblood
Crowding the season: a comedy in three
    acts.   N.Y. French. [c1870]. 32p.
Hardy, Harold
Tragedy of Amy Robsart.   London.
    Banks. c1912. 12°. 95p.   Historical.
    4 acts
Hardy, Thomas, 1840-
Dynasts; a drama of the Napoleonic
    wars, in three parts, 19 acts and 130
    scenes. London. Macmillan. 1904. 12°.
    3v.
    Same in Works—Verse v 2, 3
Famous tragedy of the Queen of Corn-
    wall at Tintagel in Lyonnesse . . .
    arranged as a play for mummers, in
    one act. . . London. Macmillan. 1923.
    12°. 76p.
Hare, Walter Ben
Aaron Boggs, freshman; college comedy
    in three acts.   Chicago. Denison.
    [1913]. 87p.
Abbu San of old Japan; a comedy drama
    in two acts.   Chicago. Denison.
    [1916]. 54p.
Always in trouble; or, A hoodooed coon.
    Chicago. Denison. 1920. 12°. 25c
Anita's secret; or, Christmas in the steer-
    age.   Christmas. 1 act
    In White Christmas, etc
Anne what's-her-name!   A comedy of
    mystery in three acts and a pro-
    logue. . . Boston. Baker. 1922. 18°.
    134p.

Assisted by Sadie; a comedy of mystery in four acts. . . Chicago. Denison. 1919. 12°. 150p. 25c

Bashful Mr. Bobbs; a farce comedy in three acts. N.Y. Fitzgerald. 1919. 12°. 64p.

Christmas carol; or, The miser's yuletide dream. Adapted from Charles Dickens' immortal story. 3 acts
In White Christmas, etc

Christmas with the Mulligans. Christmas. 3 acts
In White Christmas, etc

Coontown millionaire, a syncopated afterpiece in one act. . . Boston. Baker. 1921. 12°. p. 196-208

Country boy scout; a comedy drama for boys in three acts. Chicago. Denison. [c1916]. 12°. 63p.

Deacon Dubbs; a rural comedy drama in three acts. Chicago. Denison. [1916]. 12°. 71p.

Dream of Queen Esther; a biblical drama in three acts. Chicago. Denison. 1920. 12°. 79p. 35c

Gimme them peanuts! a "hokum" afterpiece in three scenes. . . Boston. Baker. 1921. 12°. p. 172-188. Farce

Gold bug; a clean comedy of adventure in four acts. Chicago. Denison. 1920. 12°. 126p.

Her Christmas hat. Christmas farce. 1 act
In White Christmas, etc

Little clodhopper; an American comedy drama in three acts. Chicago. Denison. 1918. 67p.

Mrs. Tubbs does her bit; a patriotic comedy in three acts. Chicago. Beckley. 1918. 12°. 25c

Much ado about Betty; a comedy in three acts. Boston. Baker. 1916. 12°. 64p.

My Irish rose; a comedy drama of Irish life in three acts. Chicago. Denison. 1919. 12°. 91p. 35c

Over here; a drama of American patriotism in three acts. Boston. Baker. 1919. 12°. 66p.

Pageant of history, an entertainment for either in-door or out-of-door performance. . . Boston. Baker. 1914. 12°. 57p. Historical. 6 scenes

Scout master; a comedy drama in three acts, for male characters only. Boston. Baker. 1916. 12°. 51p.

Sunshine; a comedy with music; a tonic for the glooms in three acts. . . Boston. Baker. 1922. 12°. 118p.

Twelve old maids; an entertainment in one act. Boston. Baker. 1918. 30p.

White Christmas. Christmas. 1 act
In White Christmas, etc

Wishing man. Christmas. 3 acts
In White Christmas, etc

Harland, Henry, 1861-1905, **and Crackanthorpe, H.**
Light sovereign, a farcical comedy. London. Lady Henry Harland. 1917. 12°. 79p. 3 acts

Harnwell, Mrs. Anna Jane, 1872-
Sin of Ahab, a drama in one act. . . N.Y. Doran. c1922. 8°. 13-28p.
Star in the east; a Biblical drama in four acts. . . N.Y. French. c1921. 8°. 5-74p. (Prize play drama league of America)

Harnwell, Anna Jane, 1872-, **and Meeker, I.**
Sojourners. Dutch pilgrims. 1 act
In Drama 10:357

Harper, John Murdoch, 1845-
Champlain; a drama in three acts. . . Toronto. Trade pub. co. [1908]. 296p. Historical

Harrington, Helen
New fangled notions. Juvenile. 1 act
In Outwitting the weasels, and new fangled notions
Outwitting the weasels. Juvenile. 1 act
In Outwitting the weasels, and new fangled notions
Red flower; a play of Armenia to-day. N.Y. Interchurch world movement of N.A. [c1920]. 8°. 39p. 1 act

Harris, Augustus Glossip, 1825-1873
My son Diana. A farce in one act. . . Boston. Spencer. [1857?]. 12°. 17p.

Harris, Claudia L.
It's spring. Fantasy. 1 act
In Drama 11:245
Man who couldn't say "no." Character. 1 act
In Schafer, B. L. comp. Book of one-act plays
Young Mr. Santa Claus. Christmas fantasy. 1 act
In Drama 12:42

Harris, Frank, 1856-
King of the Jews. Jesus Christ. 1 act
In Eng R 8:8
Shakespeare and his love; a play in four acts and an epilogue. . . London. Palmer. [1910]. 12°. 177p.

Harris, G. Edward
Comedy of death. Death. 1 act
In Poet Lore 36:63

Harris, James Rendel, 1852-
Return of the "May flower;" an interlude. London. Longmans. 1919. 35p. 1 act

Harris, Jane Yancey
Thoroughly tested; a drama in six acts. Raleigh. N.C. Edwards & Broughton. [c1907]. 8°. 56p.

Harrison, Constance Cary (Mrs Burton Harrison), 1846-1920
Alice in Wonderland; a play for children in three acts. . . N.Y. DeWitt. [c1890]. 12°. 35p.
Behind a curtain. Comedy. 1 act
In Short comedies for amateur players
Mouse-trap. A comedietta, in one act. N.Y. DeWitt. [c1892]. 12°. 14p.
Same in Short comedies for amateur players
Russian honeymoon; a comedy in three acts. N.Y. Dramatic pub. co. [c1883]. 12°. 68p.
Tea at four o'clock. Comedy. 1 act
In Short comedies for amateur players

Harrison, C. C.—*Continued*
Two strings to her bow.   Comedy. 1 act
In Short comedies for amateur players
Weeping wives.   Comedy. 1 act
In Short comedies for amateur players

Hart, Joseph Mary Edgar, 1875-
Swords drawn; a romantic play in four acts.   Boston. Cornhill. 1919. 12°. 176p. $1.25

Harte, Bret, 1839-1902
Two men of Sandy Bar; a drama.   Boston. Houghton. 1882. 151p.   Melodrama. 4 acts

Harte, Bret, 1839-1902, and **Pemberton, T. Edgar**
Sue, a play in three acts.   Adapted from B. Harte's story The judgment of Bolinas Plain.   London.   Greening. 1902. 12°. 168p.   Justice

Hartland-Mahon, Richard
Love: the avenger; a play in four acts.   Dublin. Sealy. 1906. 144p.   Melodrama

Hartleben, Otto Erich, 1864-1905
Hanna Jagert.   Social. 3 acts
In Poet Lore 24:369
Love's carnival (Rosenmontag).   A play in five acts. . . London. Heinemann. 1904. 12°. 160p.   Oriental

Harwood, Harold Marsh, 1874-
Confederates.   1 act
In Three one-act plays
Grain of mustard seed; a play in three acts and four scenes. London. Benn. 1926. 12°. 91p.   Comedy
Mask.   (with Tennyson, J. F.). 1 act
In Three one-act plays
Honour thy father.   1 act
In Three one-act plays
Social convenience. in four acts.   London. Benn. 1926. 12°. 89p.
"Please help Emily"; a flirtation in three acts.   London. Benn. 1926. 12°. 101p.   Comedy
Supplanters; a play in four acts.   London. Benn. 1926. 12°. 116p.   Marriage

Haslett, Harriet Holmes
Dolores of the Sierra.   Mexican. 1 act
In Dolores of the Sierra, and other one-act plays
Inventor.   Domestic. 1 act
In Dolores of the Sierra, and other one-act plays
Modern menage.   Tragic farce. 1 act
In Dolores of the Sierra, and other one-act plays
Scoop.   Newspaper. 1 act
In Dolores of the Sierra, and other one-act plays
Trial marriage; a satiric comedy in three acts. . . Boston. Badger. [c1920]. 12°. 123p.
Undercurrents.   Melodrama. 1 act
In Dolores of the Sierra, and other one-act plays
When love is blind.   Comedy. 1 act
In Dolores of the Sierra, and other one-act plays

Hastings, Basil Macdonald, 1881-
Advertisement; a play in four acts.   N.Y. French. c1915. 12°. 114p.   Marriage
Fourth act; a play in one scene.   N.Y. French. c1916. 12°. 22p.   Comedy
Love—and what then?   A comedy in three acts. London. Sidgwick. 1912. 12°. 94p.
New sin; a play in three acts.   London. Sidgwick. 1912. 12°. 86p.   Tragicomedy
In Plays of today v 1
Tide; an emancipated melodrama in four acts.   London. Sidgwick. 1913. 12°. 101p.

Hastings, Basil M. joint author.   *See* Phillpotts, Eden, 1862-, and Hastings, B. M.

Hastings, Harold
Jeanne d'Arc; a play.   Morehouse, Milwaukee. 1924. 12°. 52p. 40c.   Historical. 4 acts

Hauptmann, Carl
Ephraim's breite.   Boston. Badger. 1912. $10.   Social. 5 acts
Same in Poet Lore 12:465
War—a Te deum.   4 pts.
In Drama 6:597

Hauptmann, Gerhart Johann Robert, 1862-
And Pippa dances (Und Pippa tanzt).   Legend of the glass-works. 4 acts
In Dramatic works v 5
Poet Lore 18:289
Assumption of Hannele.   *See* Hauptmann, G. Hannele
Beaver coat (Der biberpelz).   Comedy. 4 acts
In Dramatic works v 1
Before dawn (Vor sonnenaufgang), a social drama. . . Boston. Badger. c1909.
Same in Dramatic works v 1
Poet Lore 20:241
Bow of Odysseus (**Der** bogen des Odysseus).   Mythological. 5 acts
In Dramatic works v 7
Charlemagne's hostage (Kaiser Karl's geisel).   Legendary. 4 acts
In Dramatic works v 5
Colleague Crampton (Kollege Crampton).   Domestic. 5 acts
In Dramatic works v 3
Coming of peace, a family catastrophe. . . Chicago-Sergel. 1900. 12°. 119p.   *See* Hauptmann, G.   Reconciliation
Commemoration masque.   Historical. 1 act
In Dramatic works v 7
Conflagration (Der rote hahn).   Social. 4 acts
In Dramatic works v 1
Drayman Henschel (Führman Henschel).   Social. 5 acts
In Dramatic works v 2
Führman Henschel
Elga.   Dream. 6 scenes
In Dramatic works v 7
Poet Lore 17 no 1:1
Family castastrophe.   *See* Hauptmann, G. Reconciliation

Führman Henschel; a play in five acts. . .
Chicago. Dramatic pub. co. [c1910].
12°. 149p. *See* Hauptmann, G. J.
Drayman Henschel
Gabriel Schillings flight (Gabriel Schilling's flucht). Problem. 5 acts
In Dramatic works v 6
Griselda. Binghamton, N.Y. Binghamton book mfg. 1909. 12°. 54p. Psychological. 10 scenes
Same in Dramatic works v 6
Hannele, (a dream poem). N.Y. Doubleday. 1908. 12°. 103p. (Hannele's himmelfahrt; assumption of Hannele).
Symoblic. 2 acts
Same in Bates, A. ed. Drama 12:251
Poet Lore 20:161
Helios; a fragment.
In Dramatic works v 7
Henry of Aue (Der arme Heinrich).
Legendary. 5 acts
In Dramatic works v 4
Indipohdi. Poetic
In Dramatic works (Huebsch) v 8
Lonely lives. (Einsame menschen).
N.Y. DeWitt. 1898. 12°. 179p. Domestic. 5 acts
In Dramatic works v 3
Lonely lives
Maidens of the mount (Der jungfern von
Bishofsberg). Comedy. 5 acts
In Dramatic works v 6
Michael Kramer. Domestic. 4 acts
In Dramatic works v 3
German classics 18:212
Parsival. . . N.Y. Macmillan. 1915. 117p.
$1. Legendary
Pastoral. Fragment. 2 acts
In Dramatic works v 7
Pippa dances. *See* Hauptmann, G. And
Pippa dances
Rats (Die ratten). Social. 5 acts
In Dramatic works v 2
Reconciliation (Das friedensfest). Coming of peace) A play in three acts.
Boston. Badger. c1910. Domestic
Same in Dramatic works v 3
Coming of peace
Poet Lore 21:337
Rose Brand. Social. 5 acts
In Dramatic works v 2
Schluck and Jau. Masque. 5 pts.
In Dramatic works v 5
Sunken bell; (Die versunken glocke); a
fairy play in five acts. . . Garden
City. Doubleday. 1914. 12°. 143p.
Same in Dramatic works v 4
German classics 18:105
Moses, M. J. ed. Representative continental dramas
Poet Lore 10:161
Weavers (Die weber); a drama of the
forties. . . N.Y. Huebsch. 1911. 12°.
148p. Social. 5 acts
Same in Dramatic works v 1
German classics 18:16
Pierce and Matthews, eds.
Masterpieces of modern
drama v 2 (abridged)

White saviour. Poetic
In Dramatic works (Huebsch) v 8
Winter ballad. Poetic
In Dramatic works (Huebsch) 1925
Havelock, Hubert Hamlin
Sapere aude; or, Have the courage to
be wise; a drama in five acts. Boston. Stratford. 1923. 12°. 63p. $1.75
Character
Haweis, Lionel
Rose of Persia. Fairy tale. 3 acts
In Drama 11:200
Hawkins, Anthony Hope 1863-
Adventure of Lady Ursula; a comedy in
four acts. N.Y. Russell. 1898. 125p.
Also French. 1910
Pilkerton's peerage; a comedy in four
acts. N.Y. French. c1908. 112p.
Hawkridge, Winifred
Florist shop. Comedy. 1 act
In Plays of the Harvard dramatic club
ser 1
Price of orchids. Comedy. 1 act
In Smart Set 47 no 2:103
Hawthorne, Ruth, joint author. *See* Kennedy Mary, and Hawthorne, Ruth
Hay, Ian, pseud. *See* Beith, John Hay
Hayes, Alfred, 1857-
Simon de Montfort; an historical drama
in five acts. London. Methuen.
[1918]. 238p.
Hayes, Bridget T.
Winter bloom. Village love. 1 act
In Poet Lore 30:385
Hayward, Edward F. 1851-
Mothers. Boston. Badger. 1903. 27p.
Motherhood. 3 scenes
Hazelton, George Cochrane, jr., 1833-1922
Mistress Nell; a merry play in four acts.
Phila. 1900. 76p. 8°.
Raven; a play in four acts and a tableau.
N.Y. 1903. 12°. 77p. Poe
Hazelton, George C., 1833-1922, **and Benrimo, J. H.,** 1871-
Yellow Jacket, a play in the Chinese manner. . . Bobbs-Merrill. Indianapolis.
1914. $1. 3 acts
Same in Dickinson, T. H. ed. Chief
contemporary dramatists ser 2
Hazlewood, Colin Henry, 1823-1875
Going to Chobham; or, The petticoat
captains; a farce in one act. London. Lacy. n.d. 12°. 16p. (Lacy's acting edition of plays. v. 11)
Lady Audley's secret; a drama in two
acts from Miss Braddon's popular
novel. . . N.Y. Roorbach. c1889. 12°.
33p.
Waiting for the verdict; or, Falsely accused. A domestic drama, in three
acts. . . London. French. [1859?]. 12°.
48p.
Head, Cloyd, and Gavin, Mary
Curtains. Poetic. 1 act
In Poetry 16:1
Heald, Lucy, 1872-
Love in Umbria, drama of the first Franciscans. Cambridge. Riverside press.
1912. 12°. 115p.

Hearne, Isabel
Queen Herzeleid; or, Sorrow-of-Heart; an episode in the boyhood of the hero, Parzival. A poetic play in three acts. London. Nutt. 1911. 78p.

Heaton, Augustus Goodyear, 1844-
Heart of David the psalmist king. . . Washington, D.C. Neale co. 1900. 389p. Biblical. 5 pts.

Hebbel, Friedrich (Christian Friedrich), 1813-1863
Agnes Bernauer. Tragedy. 5 acts
In Poet Lore 20:1
Gyges and his ring. Tragedy. 5 acts
In Three plays
Herod and Mariamne; a tragedy in five acts. N.Y. Sergel. 1912. $1.25
Same in Three plays
    Drama 2 no 6:20
Judith, a tragedy in five acts. . . Boston. Badger. 1914. 8°.
Same in Poet Lore 25:257
Mary Magdalene. N.Y. Dodd. 1910. 12°. 179p. Biblical. 3 acts
Same in Three plays
    German classics 9:22
    Poet Lore 25:81
Siegfried's death. Tragedy, 5 acts
In German classics 9:81

Hecht, Ben, joint author. *See* Goodman, K. S. and Hecht, B.

Hedberg. Tor Harold, 1862-
Borga gard. Land holders. 4 acts
In Poet Lore 32:317
Johan Ulfstjerna. Sacrifice. 5 acts
In Poet Lore 32:1

Hedges, Bertha
Dead saint. Religion. 1 act
In Drama 12:305

Heermans, Forbes, 1856-
Between two thorns. An original scene on a staircase. N.Y. DeWitt. [1892]. 12°. 15p. Romantic. 1 act
Same in Love by induction and other plays
Down the Black cañon; or, The silent witness; a drama of the Rocky mountains. In four acts. . . N.Y. De-Witt. c1890. 12°. 40p.
In the fire-light. An original episode in one act. N.Y. DeWitt. [1892]. 12°. 14p.
Same in Love by induction and other plays
Love by induction. Comedy. 1 act
Same in Love by induction and other plays
Love's warrant. A farce in one act. N.Y. DeWitt. [1892]. 12°. 32p.
Same in Love by induction and other plays
Silent witness. *See* Heermans, F. Down the Black Cañon; or, The silent witness
Two negatives make an affirmative. A photographic comedy in one act. N.Y. DeWitt. [1892]. 12°. 28p.
Same in Love by induction and other plays

Heffner, Hubert
"Dod gast ye both!" a comedy of mountain moonshiners. 1 act
In Koch, F. N. ed. Carolina Folk-plays ser 1

Heiberg, Gunnar, 1857-
Balcony. Passion. 3 acts
In Poet Lore 33:475
Tragedy of love. Tragedy. 4 acts
In Dickinson, T. H. Chief contemporary dramatists ser 2

Heidenstam, Verner von, 1859-
Birth of God; authorized tr. from the Swedish by Karoline M. Knudsen. Boston. Four Seas. 1920. 12°. 32p. Fantasy. 1 act
Soothsayer; a play in one act. [Nobel prize 1916]. Authorized tr. from the Swedish by Karoline Knudsen. Boston. Four Seas. 1919. 12°. 48p. Allegorical

Heijermans, Herman, the younger, 1864-
Ghetto; a drama in four acts. Freely adapted by Chester Bailey Fernald. London. Heinemann. 1899. 12°. 144p. Tragedy
Good Hope. Sea. 4 acts
In Pierce and Matthews, eds. Masterpieces of modern drama v 2 (abridged)
    Drama 2 no 8:17
Jubilee. (Feest). Prison. 5 pts
In Shay, F. ed. Twenty-five short plays; international
    Drama 13:325
Saltimbank. Jealousy. 1 act
In Drama 13:363

Heinemann, William, 1863-
Finger of God, a trilogy. London. Lane. 1901. 8°.
First step, a dramatic moment. London. Lane. 1895. 8°. 71p. Social. 3 acts
Summer moths; a play in four acts. N.Y. DeWitt. 1898. 46°. 117p.
War, a play in three acts. London. Lane. 1901. 4°. 122p. [No. 2 of "The finger of God"]

Helburn, Theresa
Allison makes hay; a comedy in three acts. Boston. Baker. 1919. 12°. 146p. 50c
Enter the hero, a comedy in one act. . . N.Y. Arens. 1918. 12°. 36p. 35c
Same in Knickerbocker, E. Van B. ed. Twelve plays
    Shay, F. and Loving, P. eds. Fifty contemporary one-act plays

Hellem, Charles, Valcros, W., and Pol d'Estoc
Sabotage. Washington, D.C. Drama League. 25c. Sociological. 1 act
Same in Dramatist (Easton, Pa.). 5:425
    Smart Set 41 no 3:135

Helps, Sir Arthur, 1813-1875
Catharine Douglas, a tragedy. London. Pickering. 1843. 148p. 5 acts

King Henry the Second; an historical drama. London. Pickering. 1843. 182p. 5 acts

Hemans, Mrs. Felicia, 1793-1835
English martyrs; a scene of the days of Queen Mary. 2 scenes
In Poems

De Chatillon. Crusades. 5 acts
In Poems

Sebastian of Portugal. Historical. 4 scenes
In Poems

Siege of Valencia. Historical. 8 scenes
In Poems

Vespers of Palermo. Tragedy. 5 acts
In Poems

Hemmerde, Edward George, 1871-
Maid of honour. A play in one act. London. French. 1912. 12°. 21p.

Proud Maisie; a play in four acts. London. Richards. 1912. 77p. Tragedy

Hemmerde, Edward George, 1871-, and Neilson, Frances, 1867-
Butterfly on the wheel; a play in four acts. N.Y. French. 1922. 12°. 80p. 75c Marriage

Henderson, Sara
Bunch of keys; a comedy-drama. Lebanon. March. 1923. 12°. 44p. 35c

Cupid mixes things; a valentine comedy. Lebanon. March. 1922. 12°. 16p. 35c

Easter eggs; an Easter playlette. Lebanon. March. 1923. 12°. 12p. 25c 1 act

From frowns to smiles; a good health playlet. Lebanon. March. 1922. 12°. 16p. 25c. 1 act

Lineman; a farce in one act. Lebanon. March. 1923. 12°. 12p. 25c

Tommy and the calories; a good health comedy. Lebanon. March. 1923. 12°. 20p. 35c 1 act

Too many wives; a domestic comedy. Lebanon. March. 1922. 12°. 22p. 35c 1 act

Toothbrush fantasy; a good health playlet. Lebanon. March. 1923. 12°. 20p. 25c 1 act

Where's my toothbrush? a good health playlet. Lebanon, March. 1922. 12°. 12p. 15c 1 act

Hendrick, Frank
Wastrel hoard. N.Y. Puritan play co. 1916. 260p. $2. Social. 5 acts

Henley, William Ernest, 1849-1903, and Stevenson, Robert Louis, 1850-1894
Admiral Guinea. Historical. 5 acts
In Three plays
Works v 7

Beau Austin, a drama in four acts. . . London. Heinemann. 1897. 12°. 55p. Society
Same in Works v 7
Three plays
Plays

Deacon Brodie; or, The double life. Melodrama. 5 acts
In Works v 7
Three plays
Double life. *See* Henley, W. E. and Stevenson, R. L. Deacon Brodie; or, The double life
Macaire. Melodramatic farce. 3 acts
In Works v 7
Plays

Hennique, Leon, 1851-
Death of the Duc d'Enghien. Historical. 3 scenes
In Poet Lore 20:401

Hennequin, Alfred, 1846-
Three hats. Adapted by Arthur Shirley. Chicago. Dramatic pub. co. [18—?]. 12°. 43p. Comedy. 3 acts

Henry, Arthur, 1867-
Time; a comedy in three acts. N.Y. French. 1924. 12°. 82p. 75c

Henslowe, Leonard
Dove and the duffer. Comedy. 1 act
In Perfidious marriage, etc
Hero for a husband. Farce. 1 act
In Perfidious marriage, etc
People from the past. Farce. 1 act
In Perfidious marriage, etc
Perfidious marriage. Satire. 1 act
In Perfidious marriage, etc

Herbach, Joseph
Rehearsal; a drama in one act. Phila. Greenstone. 1911. 12°. 62p.

Herbert, Alan Patrick, 1890-
Book of Jonah as almost any modern Irishman would have written it. Farce. 1 act
In Lond Mercury 3:601
Double demon. Farce. 1 act
In Herbert, A. P. and others. Double demon and other one-act plays
Four one-act plays

Herder, Alexandra von
Jesus of Nazareth; a poetical drama in seven scenes. London. Heinemann. 1913. 249p.

Herford, Oliver, 1863-, and Schmidt, Karl
What'll you have? N.Y. Holt. 1925. 12°. 118p. $2. Comedy. 3 acts

Herrera, L. Bayon
Santos Vega. Argentine. 3 acts
In Bierstadt, E. H. ed. Three plays of the Argentine

Herrick, Gertrude
Full of the moon. Ireland. 1 act
In Poet Lore 31:379

Herts, Benjamin Russell, 1888-
Female of the species. Comedy. 1 act
In International (NY) 9:152
Son of man; a drama in four acts. N.Y. Shay. 1916. 12°. 77p. 50c Biblical

Hertz, Henrik, 1798-1870
Iolanthe. *See* Hertz, H. King René's daughter
King René's daughter; a Danish lyrical drama. . . N.Y. Holt. 1867. 12°. 100p. 7 scenes. (also published under title. Iolanthe (King René's daughter). Phila.? 1876

Hervieu, Paul, 1857-
In chains (Enchained) (Les Tenailles). . .
    Boston. Badger. [c1907]. also Wessels.
    Social. 3 acts
    Same in Dramatist 1:58
            Poet Lore 20:81
Know thyself (Connois-toi).   Problem. 3
    acts
    In Dickinson, T. R. ed.   Chief contin-
        ental dramatists
Modesty (Modestie) A comedy in one
    act. . . N.Y. French. c1913. 12°. 17p.
    Same in Lewis, B. R. ed.   Contemp-
        orary one-act plays
Labyrinth (Le dédale) a play in five
    acts . . N.Y. Huebsch. 1913. 12°.
    172p. $1
Torch race.   *See* Hervieu, P. Trail of the
    torch
Trail of the torch (La course du flam-
    beau); a play in four acts. . . Garden
    city. Doubleday. 1915. 12°. 128p. 75c
    Tragedy
    Same in Pierce and Matthews, eds.
        Masterpieces of modern
        drama v 2 (abridged)

Hervilly, Ernest d', 1839- .
Chatterbox.   Farce. 1 act
    In Beerbohm, C. ed.   Little book of
        plays
Silence in the ranks (Silence dans les
    rang).   Comedy. 1 act
    In Bellevue dramatic club plays
Soup tureen.   Comedy. 1 act
    In Bellevue dramatic club plays

Hewlett, Maurice Henry, 1861-
Agonists, a trilogy of God and man.
    (Ariadne in Naxos; Death of Hip-
    polytus; Minos, king of Crete)
    In Agonists
Argive women.   Mythological. 1 scene
    In Helen redeemed
Ariadne in Naxos.   Mythological. 1 act
    In Agonists
Death of Hippolytus.   Mythological. 1
    act
    In Agonists
Masque of dead Florentines.   Portland,
    Me. Mosher. 1911. 12°. 45p. 1 act
    Same in Bibelot 10:5
Minos, king of Crete.   Legendary. 1 act
    In Agonists
Pan and the young shepherd; a pastoral
    in two acts.   London. Lane. 1898.
    12°. 140p.

Hewlett, William
White stacks; a village comedy.   Boston.
    Houghton. 1924. 288p.

Heyse, Paul Johann Ludwig von, 1830-1914
Mary of Magdala.   An historical and
    romantic drama in five acts. . . N.Y.
    Macmillan. 1903. 12°. 135p.

Heyward, Dorothy
Love in a cupboard; comedy in one act.
    N.Y. French. c1926. 12°. 35p.

Heywood, Chester D.
Green chartreuse; a one-act play.   Wor-
    cester, Mass. c1923. 12°. 19p.

Heywood, Joseph Converse, d. 1900
Antonius; a dramatic poem.   N.Y. Hurd.
    1867. 12°. 272p.   Historical. 1 act
Herodias.   A dramatic poem.   N.Y.
    Hurd. 1867. 12°. 251p.   Biblical. 1
    act
Il nano Italiano: a most musical, most
    melancholy, most lamentably laugh-
    able very fashionably unintelligible,
    lyric tragedy, in five acts.   N.Y.
    Jones. 1862. 12°. 28p.
Salome; a dramatic poem.   N.Y. Hurd.
    1867. 12°. 222p.   Biblical. 1 act

Hibbard, George Abiah, 1858-
Matter of opinion.   Comedy. 1 act
    In Scrib M 28:233

Higgins, Aileen Cleveland, 1882-
Thekla; a drama.   Boston. Poet Lore Co.
    1907. 62p.   Early Christian. 2 scenes

Hilbert, Jaroslav, 1871-
Whom the gods destroy.   War of 1866.
    1 act
    In Poet Lore 27:361

Hill, Frederick Trevor, 1866-
Dinner's served! farce. 1 act
    In High school farces
Heathen Chinee; farce.   1 act
    In High school farces
Knotty problem; farce.   1 act
    In High school farces

Hill, Roland
Christopher Columbus; an historic drama
    in four acts.   London. Low. 1913.
    55p.
Guinevere; a tragedy in three acts. . .
    London. Matthews. 1906. 103p.
In Andalusia long ago; a poetic drama
    in four acts.   London. Low. 1914.
    47p.

Hillhouse, James Abraham, 1789-1841
Demetrius.   Tragedy. 5 acts
    In Dramas, discourse, etc v 1
Hadad; a dramatic poem.   N.Y. Bliss.
    1825. 8°. 208p.   Biblical. 5 acts
    Same in Dramas, discourses, etc v 1
Percy's masque.   Historical. 5 acts
    In Dramas, discourses, etc

Hinkley, Eleanor
Flitch of bacon.   Comedy. 1 act
    In Plays of the 47 workshop ser 2

Hinkson, Mrs Katharine Tynan, 1861-
Annunciation.   Miracle. 1 act
    In Miracle plays
Finding in the temple.   Miracle. 1 act
    In Miracle plays
Flight into Egypt.   Miracle. 1 act
    In Miracle plays
Nativity.   Miracle. 1 act
    In Miracle plays
Presentation in the temple.   Miracle. 1
    act
    In Miracle plays
Visitation.   Miracle. 1 act
    In Miracle plays

Hippius, Zinaida Nikolayevna, 1867-
Green ring; a play in four acts.   London.
    Daniels. 1920. 12°. 104p.   Marriage

Hirschbein, Perez, 1880-
Haunted inn; a drama in four acts. . .
Boston. Luce. ⟨c1921⟩. 12°. 163p.
Supernatural
In the dark (In der Finster). Symbolic.
1 act
In Goldberg, I. ed. Six plays of the
Yiddish theatre
On the threshold. Social. 1 act
In Goldberg, I. ed. Six plays of the
Yiddish theatre ser 2
Snowstorm. Wedding. 1 act
In Block, E. tr. One-act plays from
the Yiddish
Stranger. Marriage. 1 act
In Block, E. tr. One-act plays from
the Yiddish
When the dew falleth. Idyl. 1 act
In Block, E. tr. One-act plays from
the Yiddish
Hirschfeld, Georg, 1873-
Mothers. . . Garden City. Doubleday.
1916. 122p. 75c Problem. 4 acts
Hoare, Douglas, joint author. *See* Blow,
Sydney, and Hoare, Douglas
Hobart, George Vere, 1867-
Buddies; a comedy in three acts. N.Y.
French. 1924. 12°. 109p. 75c
Cure for jealousy; a comedy in one act.
Washington. Commission on training
camp activities. 1918. 12°. 20p.
Experience; a morality play of to-day.
Acting version. N.Y. H. & K. Fly Co.
⟨1915⟩. 126p. 10 episodes
Hobart, Mrs. Marie Elizabeth (Jefferys),
1860-
Athanasius; a mystery play. N.Y. Long-
mans. 1911. 12°. 121p. 3 acts
Conquering and to conquer; a mystery
play. N.Y. Domestic and foreign
missionary society. 1917. 12°. 126p.
40c 12 episodes
Great trail; an Indian mystery play.
N.Y. Domestic and foreign mission-
ary society. 1913. 12°. 62p. 2 pts.
Little pilgrims and the book beloved; a
mystery play. N.Y. Longmans. 1913.
12°. 53p. 1 act
Vision of St. Agnes' eve; a mystery play.
N.Y. Longmans. 1907. 12°. 112p. 1 act
Hobbes, John Oliver, pseud. *See* Craigie,
Pearl, M. T.
Hobbs, Mabel and Miles, Helen
David and Jonathan. Biblical. 3 scenes
In Six Bible plays
Esther. Biblical. 3 scenes
In Six Bible plays
Healing of Naaman. Biblical. 3 scenes
In Six Bible plays
Joseph and his brethren. Biblical. 3
scenes
In Six Bible plays
Moses. Biblical. 2 scenes
In Six Bible plays
Ruth and Naomi. Biblical. 3 scenes
In Six Bible plays
Hodges, Horace, and Percyval, T. Wigney
Grumpy; a play in four acts. N.Y. S.
French. c1921. 12°. 90p. Comedy

Hoffe, Monckton
Cristilinda; a play in four acts. N.Y.
French. c1926. 8°. 63p.
Hoffman, Aaron, 1880-
Nothing but lies; a farce in three acts.
N.Y. French. 1923. 12°. 85p. 75c
Two blocks away; a play in three acts.
N.Y. French. c1925. 12°. 134p.
Hoffman, Phoebe
Martha's mourning. Character. 1 act
In Mayorga, M. G. ed. Representa-
tive one-act plays
Drama 8 no 29:111
Turn of a hair; a farce for four females.
1 act
In Drama 15:85
Wedding dress. 1 act
In Nicholson, K. ed. Appleton book
of short plays
Hofmannsthal, Hugo, Edler von, 1874-
Cristina's journey home. Comedy. 3 acts
In Poet Lore 28:129
Death and the fool (Der Tor and der
Tod) a drama in one act. . . Boston.
Badger. c1914. 12°. 45p. Symbolic
Same in German classics 17:492
Moses, M. J. ed. Representa-
tive one-act plays by contin-
ental authors
Poet Lore 24:253
Death of Titian; a dramatic fragment. . .
Boston. Four Seas. 1920. 12°. 27p.
(Der Tod der Tizian). Historical. 1
act
Same in German classics 17:511
Electra; a tragedy in one act. . . N.Y.
Brentano's. 1908. 12°. 83p.
Idyll. Poetic. 1 act
In Drama 7:169
Madonna Dianora; a play in verse. . .
Boston. Badger. c1916. 12°. 44p.
Romantic tragedy. 1 act
Same in Shay, F. and Loving, P. eds.
Fifty contemporary one-act plays
Marriage of Sobeide (Die Hochzeit der
Zobeide). Oriental. 2 scenes
In German classics 20:234
Prologue for a marionette theatre.
Sketch. 1 act
In Loving, P. ed. Ten minute plays
Rose-bearer (Der Rosenkavalier); Com-
edy for music in three acts. Berlin.
Fürstner. 1912. 12°. 130p.
Venice preserved (Das gerettete Vene-
dig). Tragedy. 5 acts
In Poet Lore 26:529
White fan. Interlude. 1 act
In Mask 1:232 (incomplete)
Holbrook, Richard Thayer, 1870-
Master Pierre Patelin; a farce in three
acts; composed anonymously about.
1464. A. D. Englished by Richard T.
Holbrook. . . Boston. Baker. 1914.
12°. 121p.
Hole, W. G.
Master; a poetical play in two acts.
London. Erskine. 1913. 55p.

Hole, W. G.—*Continued*
Paris and Oenone.   Mythological. 1 act
   In Contemp 94 Sup 1 D '08
Queen Elizabeth; an historical drama in
   four acts.   London. Bell. 1904. 111p.
Holl, Henry
Grace Huntley; a domestic drama, in
   three acts. . . London. Cumberland.
   [1828?]. 44p.
Holley, Horace, 1887-
Genius.   Character. 1 act
   In Read-aloud plays
Her happiness.   Tragedy. 1 act
   In Read-aloud plays
His luck.   Psychological. 1 act
   In Read-aloud plays
Incompatibles.   Farce. 1 act
   In Read-aloud plays
Modern prodigal.   Comedy. 1 act
   In Read-aloud plays
Pictures.   Art. 1 act
   In Read-aloud plays
Rain.   Domestic. 1 act
   In Read-aloud plays
Survival.   Character. 1 act
   In Read-aloud plays
Telegram.   Sketch. 1 act
   In Read-aloud plays
Hollins, Dorothea
Quest; a drama of deliverance; in seven
   scenes and a vision.   London. Wil-
   liams. 1910. 115p.   Religious
Hollister, Gideon Hiram, 1817-1881
Thomas à Becket, a tragedy; [and other
   poems]. Boston. Spencer. 1866. 186p.
   Historical. 5 acts
Holt, Florence Taber
Comrades.   War. 1 act
   In They, the crucified, and Comrades
They the crucified.   War. 1 act
   In They, the crucified, and Comrades
Home, Ean
Mushrooms.   World war. 3 acts
   In Seven and seven
Seven and seven.   Methuen. London.
   [1918]. 16°. 188p.
Hood, Tom
Harlequin Little Red Riding Hood; or,
   The wicked wolf and the virtuous
   wood cutter.   Pantomine. 3 scenes
   In Scott, C.   ed.   Drawing room
      plays
Hooker, Brian, 1880-
Fairyland; an opera in three acts.   New
   Haven. Yale univ. press. 1915. 137p.
Mona, an opera in three acts. . . N.Y.
   Dodd. 1911. 190p.
Hope, Anthony.   *See* Hawkins, Anthony
   Hope
Hope, Ernest
Our lodger; a play in four acts.   Man-
   chester. A. Heywood. c1918. 12°. 32p.
Hopkins, Arthur
Moonshine; a one act play.   N.Y.
   French. [c1921]. 12°. 16p.   Carolina
   Same in Lewis, B. R. ed.   Contempo-
      rary plays
         One act plays for stage and
         study
      Theatre arts M 3:51

Hopp, Julius
Tears; a drama of modern life.   Boston.
   Poet Lore co. 1904. 78p.   Social. 4
   acts
Hord, Parker
Tyndale; a drama in four episodes taken
   from the life of the first translator of
   the Bible into English, the martyred
   William Tyndale.   N.Y.   Century.
   [c1925]. 12°. 97p.
Horne, Richard Henry, 1803-1884
Death of Marlowe: a tragedy in one act.
   London. Lacy. 1870. 12°. 23p. (Lacy's
   acting edition of plays. v. 89)
   Same in Bibelot 3:369
Gregory VII; a tragedy.   London. Saun-
   ders. 1840. 8°. 104p.
Judas Iscariot; a miracle play.   In two
   acts. . . London. Mitchell. 1848. 12°.
   64p.
Laura Dibalzo; or, The patriot martyrs;
   a tragedy. London. Newman. 1880.
   12°. 98p. 5 acts
Houghton, Claude
In the house of the high priest; a drama
   in one act.   London. Daniel. 1923.
   57p.
Judas; a tragedy in three acts.   Boston.
   Four Seas. 1923. 12°. 133p. $2
Houghton, Stanley, 1881-1913
Dear departed.   Comedy. 1 act
   In Five one-act plays
      Cohen, H. L. ed.   More one-act
      plays by modern authors
      Marriott, J. W. ed.   One-act plays
         of to-day ser 2
Fancy free, a fantastic comedy in one act.
   N.Y. French. c1912. 12°. 21p.
   Same in Clark, B. H. ed.   Representa-
      tive one-act plays by British and
      Irish authors
Fifth commandment.   Tragi-comedy. 1
   act
   In Five one-act plays
Hindle wakes; a play in three acts.   Lon-
   don. Sidgwick. 1912. 12°. 109p.   Lan-
   cashire.   Social
   Same in Works v 2
      Dickinson, T. H. ed.   Con-
         temporary plays
Independent means; a comedy in four
   acts.   N.Y. French. c1911. 12°. 87p.
   Same in Works v 1
Marriages in the making.   Comedy. 3
   acts
   In Works v 1
Master of the house.   Domestic quarrels.
   1 act
   In Five one-act plays
Old testament and the new.   Fana-
   ticism. 1 act
   In Works v 3
Partners.   Comedy. 3 acts
   In Works v 2
Perfect cure.   Comedy. 3 acts
   In Works v 2
Phipps.   Comedy. 1 act
   In Five one-act plays
      One act plays for stage and study
      ser 1

Younger generation; a comedy for parents in three acts. N.Y. French. c1910. 12°. 70p.
Same in Works v 1

Housman, Laurence, 1867-
Apollo in Hades. Classic. 1 act
In The wheel
As good as gold; a play in one act. N.Y. French. c1916. 12°. 27p. St. Francis of Assisi
Bethlehem, a nativity play. . . N.Y. Macmillan. 1902. 16°. 70p. 2 acts
Bird in hand, a play in one act. N.Y. French. c1916. 12°. 29p. Comedy
Blind eyes. St. Francis. 1 act
In Little plays of St. Francis
Bride feast. St. Francis. 1 act
In Little plays of St. Francis
Brief life. St. Francis. 1 act
In Little plays of St. Francis
Brother Elias. St. Francis. 1 act
In Little plays of St. Francis
Brother Juniper. St. Francis. 1 act
In Little plays of St. Francis
Brother Sun. St. Francis of Assisi. 1 act
In Little plays of St. Francis
Cohen, H. L. ed. Junior play book
Brother Wolf. St. Francis of Assisi. 1 act
In Little plays of St. Francis
19 Cent 88:813
Builders. St. Francis. 1 act
In Little plays of St. Francis
Chapter. St. Francis. 1 act
In Little plays of St. Francis
Chinese lantern, a play. London. Sidgwick. 1908. 8°. 89p. China. 3 acts
Christmas tree. Christmas. 1 act
In False premises
Drama 11:75
Comforter, a political finale. 1 act
In Angels and ministers
Cure of souls. St. Francis. 1 act
In Followers of St. Francis
Death of Alcestis. Greek. 1 act
In The wheel
Death of Orpheus. London. Sidgwick. 1921. 12°. 68p. Mythological. 3 acts
Death of Socrates; a dramatic scene, founded upon two of Plato's dialogues, the "Crito" and the "Phaedo". London. Sidgwick & Jackson. 1925. 12°. 53p. 1 act
Doom of Admetus. Greek. 1 act
In The wheel
Fellow-prisoners. St. Francis. 1 act
In Little plays of St. Francis
Fool and his money. Comedy. 1 act
In False premises
Fool's errand. Franciscan. 1 act
In Followers of St. Francis
His favorite flower. Political myth. 1 act
In Angels and ministers
House fairy. Fairy. 1 act
In False premises
Instrument. Woodrow Wilson. 1 act
In Dethronements

King-maker. Charles Stewart Parnell. 1 act
In Dethronements
Last disciple. Franciscan. 1 act
In Followers of St. Francis
Lepers. St. Francis. 1 act
In Little plays of St. Francis
Likely story; a roadside comedy in one act. N.Y. French. c1916. 12°. 25p.
Lord of the harvest, a morality in one act. N.Y. French. [1916]. 12°. 13p.
Lovers meeting. Franciscan. 1 act
In Followers of St. Francis
Lysistrata; a modern paraphrase from the Greek of Aristophanes. London. Woman's press. 1911. 12°. 77p. 2 scenes
Man of business. Joseph Chamberlain. 1 act
In Dethronements
Moonshine. Christmas. 1 act
In False premises
Nazareth; a morality in one act. N.Y. French. c1916. 12°. 17p.
Order of release. St. Francis. 1 act
In Fortn 126:289
Our lady of poverty. St. Francis. 1 act
In Little plays of St. Francis
Pains and penalties; an historical tragedy in four acts. London. Sidgwick. c1911. 12°. 80p.
Possession; a peep-show of Paradise. London. Caper. 1921. 12°. 61p. 1 act
Same in Angels and ministers
Queen: God bless her! Victorian. 1 act
In Angels and ministers
Return of Alcestis a play in one act. N.Y. French. c1916. 12°. 22p. Classical
Revellers. St. Francis. 1 act
In Little plays of St. Francis
19 Cent 90:616
Seraphic vision. Franciscan. 1 act
In Little plays of St. Francis
Marriott, J. W. ed. One-act plays of to-day
Sister Clare. St. Francis. 1 act
In Little plays of St. Francis
Sister Death. St. Francis. 2 scenes
In Little plays of St. Francis
Sister Gold. St. Francis. 1 act
In Little plays of St. Francis
Snow man; a morality in one act. N.Y. French. c1916. 12°. 20p.
Same in Clark, B. H. ed. Representative one-act plays by British and Irish authors
Torch of time. Social. 1 act
In False premises
Unknown star. *See* Paull, H. M. and Housman, L. Unknown star

Housman, Lawrence, 1867-, and Barker, H. G.
Love in a Dutch garden. *See* Housman, L. and Barker, H. G. Prunella; or, Love in a Dutch garden
Prunella; or, Love in a Dutch garden. Boston. Little. 1916. 88p. $1. Youth's awakening. 3 acts

Housum, Robert
Corsican lieutenant.   1 act
In One-act plays for stage and study
    ser 2
Eligible Mr. Bangs.   1 act
In One-act plays for stage and study
    ser 3
Silvia runs away; a farce in three acts. . .
    N.Y. French. c1920. 12°. 109p.

Hovey, Richard, 1864-1900
Birth of Galahad.   Arthurian. 5 acts
In Launcelot and Guenevere v 3
Holy Graal.   Arthurian. 3 acts
In Launcelot and Guenevere v 5
King Arthur.   Arthurian. 1 act
In Launcelot and Guenevere v 5
Launcelot and Guenevere; a poem in
    dramas.   Boston. Small. 1898-1907.
    5v.   Legendary
Marriage of Guenevere.   Arthurian. 5
    acts
In Launcelot and Guenevere v 2
Quest of Merlin.   Masque. 1 act
In Launcelot and Guenevere v 1
Taliesin.   Masque. 1 act
In Launcelot and Guenevere v 4
    Poet Lore 8:1

Howard, Bronson, 1842-1908
Aristocracy.   A comedy in four acts.
    Privately printed. 1898. 12°. 74p.
Banker's daughter.   Privately printed.
    c1878. 12°. 57p.   Melodrama. 5 acts
Henrietta, a comedy in four acts.   N.Y.
    French. 1901. 12°. 82p.
Kate; a comedy in four acts.   N.Y. Har-
    per. 1906. 12°. 210p.
Old love-letters; a comedy in one act.
    London. French. 1897. 12°. 24p.
One of our girls.   A comedy in four
    acts. Privately printed. 1897. 12°. 56p.
Pistols for seven.   *See* Howard, B.
    Saratoga; or, Pistols for seven
Saratoga; or, "Pistols for seven.   A
    comic drama in five acts.   N.Y.
    French. [1874?]. 12°. 68p.
Shenandoah; a military comedy in four
    acts.   N.Y. French. 1897. 8°. 71p.
    Civil war
    Same in Pierce and Matthews, eds.
        Masterpieces of modern
        drama v 1 (abridged)
        Quinn, A. H. ed.   Repre-
        sentative American plays
Young Mrs. Winthrop; a play in four
    acts. N.Y. French. c1899. 12°. 56p.
    Comedy

Howard, Henry Newman, 1861-
Constantine the great.   A tragedy. Lon-
    don. Dent. 1906. 12°. 123p. 4 acts
Guanches.   Idyll. 1 act
In Collected poems
Kiartan the Icelander.   London. Dent.
    1902. 12°. 107p.   Tragedy. 5 acts
    Same in Collected poems

Savonarola.   London. Dent. 1904. 12°.
    138p.   Tragedy. 5 acts
    Same in Collected poems

Howard, Homer Hildreth
Child in the house.   Inebriety. 1 act
In Poet Lore 24:433

Howard, Katharine, 1858-
Candle flame; a play (for reading only).
    Boston. Sherman. 1914. 12°. 32p.
    Allegory. 3 acts
Eve.   Boston. Sherman. 1913. 12°. 49p.
    Woman's rights. 1 act
House of future.   Allegory. 13 scenes
In Two plays, and a rhapsody
House of life.   Allegory. 1 act
In Two plays, and a rhapsody

Howard, Sidney Coe, 1891-
Lexington, a pageant drama of the
    American freedom, founded upon
    great sayings, to be acted in dumb
    show compiled for the celebration of
    the one hundred and fiftieth anniver-
    sary of the battle of Lexington,
    April 19th, 1775. [Lexington, Lexing-
    ton historical society. c1924]. 12°. 84p.
    4 pts.
Lucky Sam McCarver; four episodes in
    the rise of a New Yorker.   N.Y.
    Scribner. 1926. 12°. 232p.   Dramatic
    biography. 4 acts
Ned McCobb's daughter; a comedy.
    N.Y. Scribner. 1926. 12°. 198p. 3 acts
Silver cord; a comedy in three acts.
    N.Y. Scribner. 1927. 12°. 204p.
Swords.   N.Y. Doran. 1921. 12°. 171p.
    $1.50   Mediaeval. 4 acts
They knew what they wanted; a comedy
    in three acts.   Garden City, N.Y.
    Doubleday. 1925. 12°. 179p.
    Same in Mantle, B. ed.   Best plays of
        1924-25 (condensed)

Howard de Walden, Thomas Evelyn Ellis,
    1880-
Bronwen.   Legendary.
In Cauldron of Annion
Children of Don.   London. Edward Ar-
    nold. 1912. 12°. 95p.   Legendary. 3
    acts
    Same in Cauldron of Annion
Dylan, son of the wave.   London. Simp-
    kin. 1918. 12°. 73p.   Legendary. 3
    acts
    Same in Cauldron of Annion

Howe, Julia Ward, 1819-1910
Leonora; or, The world's own.   *See*
    Howe, J. W.   World's own
World's own (a dramatic poem).   Bos-
    ton. Ticknor. 1857. 12°. 141p.   Trag-
    edy. 5 acts
    Same in Quinn, A. H. ed.   Representa-
        tive American plays (Leonora)

Howell, Corrie Crandall
Forfeit.   Lynching. 1 act
In Poet Lore 36:136

Howell-Carter, Josephine
Hilarion.   Episode. 1 act
In Poet Lore 26:374

Howells, William Dean, 1837-1920
Albany depot. N.Y. Harper. 1892. 16°.
68p. 5 scenes. Farce
Same in Minor dramas v 1
Bride roses; a scene. Boston. Hough-
ton. 1900. 12°. 48p. Chance. 1 act
Same in Minor dramas v 2
Harper 87:424
Counterfeit presentment. Comedy. Bos-
ton. Houghton. [c1905]. 12°. 199p. 4
acts
Elevator; farce. Boston. Osgood. 1885.
12°. 84p. 1 act
Same in Minor dramas v 1
Sleeping-car and other farces
Harper 70:111
Evening dress; farce. N.Y. Harper.
1893. 24°. 59p. 1 act
In Minor dramas v 2
Cosmopol 13:116
Father and mother. *See* Howells, W. D.
Mother and father
Five o'clock tea; farce. New York.
Harper. 1894. 24°. 46p. 1 act
Same in Minor dramas v 1
Mouse-trap and other farces
Harper 76:86
Garroters; farce. N.Y. Harper. 1894.
24°. 90p. 1 act
Same in Minor dramas v 1
Mouse-trap and other farces
Harper 72:146
Her opinion of his story. Comedy. 1 act
Same in Minor dramas v 2
Harp B 41:429
Impossible. Mystery. 1 act
In Harper 122:116
Indian giver; a comedy. Boston.
Houghton. 1900. 24°. 99p. 1 act
Same in Minor dramas v 2
Harper 94:235
Letter of introduction; farce. N.Y.
Harper. 1892. 24°. 61p. 1 act
Same in Minor dramas v 2
Harper 84:243
Likely story; farce. N.Y. Harper. 1894.
24°. 54p. 1 act
Same in Minor dramas v 1
Love's stowaway. *See* Howells, W. D.
Sea-change; or, Love's stowaway
Masterpiece of diplomacy
In Minor dramas v 2
Mother. Motherhood. 1 act
In Harper 106:21
Mother and father. Dramatic passages.
N.Y. Harper. 1909. 12°. 54p. Mys-
tery. 1 act
Same in Harper 100:869
Mouse-trap. Farce. 1 act
In Minor dramas v 1
Mouse-trap and other farces
Harper 74:64
Night before Christmas. Morality. 1 act
In Daughter of the storage
Harper 190:207
Out of the question; a comedy. Bos-
ton. Houghton. [1905]. 24°. 183p. 6
acts

Parlor-car; a farce. Boston. Houghton.
[1904]. 24°. 74p. 1 act
Same in Minor dramas v 1
Sleeping-car and other farces
Atlan 38:290
Parting friends; a farce. N.Y. Harper.
24°. 1911. 57p. 1 act
Same in Harper 121:670
Previous engagement; comedy. N.Y.
Harper. 1897. 24°. 65p. 1 act
Same in Minor dramas v 2
Harper 92:28
Register; a farce. Boston. Houghton.
1884. 91p. 1 act
Same in Minor dramas v 1
Sleeping-car and other farces
Harper 68:70
Room forty-five; a farce. Boston.
Houghton. 1900. 24°. 61p. 1 act
Same in Minor dramas v 2
Saved. Emotional. 1 act
In Harp W 52:22 D 26 '08
Sea-change; or, Love's stowaway; a lyr-
icated farce in two acts and an
epilogue. Boston. Ticknor. 1888.
24°. 151p.
Self-sacrifice. Farce-tragedy. 1 act
Same in Daughter of the storage
Harper 122:748
Sleeping-car; a farce. Boston. Osgood.
1883. 74p. 1 act
Same in Minor dramas v 1
Sleeping-car and other farces
Smoking-car. Farce. 1 act
Same in Minor dramas v 2
Smoking-car and other farces
True hero. Melodrama. 1 act
In Harper 119:866
Unexpected guests; a farce. N.Y. Har-
per. 1893. 24°. 54p. 1 act
Same in Minor dramas v 2
Harper 86:211

Hoyt, Charles H.
Texas steer; or, "Money makes the mare
go." Comedy. 3 acts
In Moses, M. J. ed. Representative
American dramas, national and
local

Hsiung, C. C. *See* Cheng Ching Hsiung

Hudson, Holland
Action! a melodramatic farce in one act.
N.Y. Appleton. 1924. 12°. 26p.
Same in Shay, F. ed. Treasury of
plays for men
Kite. 1 act
In One-act plays for stage and study
ser 3
Pearl of dawn. Fantasy. 1 act
In Shay, F. ed. Contemporary one-
act plays of 1921
Shay, F. ed. Twenty contempo-
rary one-act plays (American)
Shepherd in the distance; a pantomine in
three scenes. Cincinnati. Stewart
Kidd. c1921. 12°. 28p.
Same in Shay, F. and Loving. P. eds.
Fifty contemporary one-act plays

Hueffer, Oliver Madox, 1877-
Fountain of honour.   Psychological. 1 act
In Love's disguises
Good example.   Pastoral. 1 act
In Love's disguises
Love and death.   Allegorical. 1 act
In Love's disguises
Love-match.   Romantic. 1 act
In Love's disguises
Master of art.   François Villon. 1 act
In Love's disguises

Hughes, Babette
Bound for Mexico; a melodrama in one act.   N.Y. French. c1926. 12°. 20p.
One egg.   1 act
In Nicholson, K. ed.   Appleton book of short plays

Hughes, E. L.
Recoil.   Character. 1 act
In Canad M 54:125

Hughes, Elizabeth
Women for votes. . . N.Y. Dutton. 1912. 97p. 3 acts

Hughes, Glenn
Bottled in bond; a tragic farce in one act.   N.Y. Appleton. 1925. 12°. 21p.
Same in Drama 13:170
Red carnations
In One-act plays for stage and study ser 2
Pierrot's mother; a fantastic play in one act.   Cincinnati. Stewart Kidd. c1923. 12°. 31p.
Same in Nicholson, K. ed.   Appleton's book of short plays

Hughes, Hatcher
Hell-bent for heaven; a play in three acts.   N.Y. Harper. 1924. 12°. 187p. $1.50
Blue Ridge Mts.
Same in Mantle, B. ed.   Best plays of 1923-24 (condensed)
Ruint; a folk comedy in four acts.   N.Y. Harper. 1925. 12°. 214p.

Hughes, Richard Arthur Warren
Comedy of good and evil.   Religious. 3 acts
In Rabbit and a leg
Danger.   Melodrama. 1 act
In Rabbit and a leg
Man born to be hanged.   Tragedy. 1 act
In Rabbit and a leg
Sisters' tragedy.   Oxford, Blackwell. 1922. 12°. 32p.   Tragedy. 1 act
Same in Rabbit and a leg

Hughes, Rupert, 1872-
Cat-bird; a comedy in three acts.   [N.Y.?]. c1920. 12°. 89p.
For she's a jolly good fellow; a farce in one act. . . Washington. . . Dept. of dramatic activities among the soldiers. 1918. 12°. 19p.
On the razor edge.   Tragi-comedy. 1 act
In Lippinc 85:73 Ja '10
She borrowed her own husband.   Comedy. 1 act
In Lippinc 77:541

Hugo, Victor, 1802-1885
Amy Robsart.   Historical. 5 acts
In Dramas (Estes) v 1
Dramas (Sterling) v 1
Dramatic works (Athenaeum Society) v 2
Angelo.   Tragedy. 2 pts.
In Dramas (Estes) v 1
Dramas (Sterling) v 1
Dramatic works (Athenaeum Society) v 2
Burgraves.   Tragedy. 3 pts.
In Dramas (Estes) v 3
Dramas (Sterling) v 3
Dramatic works (Athenaeum Society) v 2
Cromwell.   Historical. 5 acts
In Dramas (Estes) v 3
Dramas (Sterling) v 3
Dramatic works (Athenaeum Society) v 3
Esmeralda.   Romantic. 4 acts
In Dramas (Estes) v 2
Dramas (Sterling) v 2
Dramatic works (Athenaeum Society) v 3
Fool's revenge (The king's diversion, King's amusement). (Le roi s'amuse). Tragedy. 5 acts
In Dramas (Estes) v 4
Dramas (Sterling) v 4
Dramatic works (Bohn)
Dramatic works (Athenaeum Society) v 1
Bates, A. ed.   Drama v 9:24
Hernani.   Oxford. Clarenden. 1906. 12°. 106p.   Tragedy. 5 acts
Same in Dramas (Estes) v 1
Dramas (Sterling) v 1
Dramatic works (Athenaeum
Dramatic works (Bohn)
Society) v 1
Matthews, J. B. ed.   Chief European dramatists
King's amusement.   *See* Hugo, V. Fool's revenge
King's diversion.   *See* Hugo, V. Fool's revenge
Lucretia Borgia.   Tragedy. 3 acts
In Dramas (Estes) v 4
Dramas (Sterling) v 4
Dramatic works (Athenaeum Society) v 1
Marion de Lorme.   Tragedy. 5 acts
In Dramas (Estes) v 4
Dramas (Sterling) v 4
Dramatic works (Athenaeum Society) v 1
Mary Tudor.   Historical. 3 pts.
In Dramas (Estes) v 2
Dramas (Sterling) v 2
Dramatic works (Athenaeum Society) v 3
Ruy Blas.   A drama in five acts.   N.Y. Rullman. c1894. 8°. 68p.   Romantic
In Dramas (Estes) v 2
Dramas (Sterling) v 2
Dramatic works (Bohn)
Ruy Blas

Torquemada. Historical. 3 acts
In Dramas (Estes) v 2
    Dramas (Sterling) v 2
Twin brothers (Twins). Historical. 3 acts
In Dramas (Estes) v 1
    Dramas (Sterling) v 1
    Dramatic works (Athenaeum Society) v 1

Huie, James L.
Quentin Durward: a drama founded on the celebrated novel of the same name. . . London. Black. 1823. 78p. Historical. 3 acts

Hull, H. R.
Idealists. Disillusion. 1 act
In Touchstone 1:457
Release. Domestic tyranny. 1 act
In Touchstone 6:122

Humphrey, Maud, 1868-
Why girls stay home; a satiric comedy in one act. Cincinnati. Stewart Kidd. c1923. 39p.

Hunter, Rex
Hands and the man. Comedy. 1 act
In Stuff o'dreams, and other plays
Romany road. Gypsy. 1 act
In Stuff o'dreams, and other plays
Stuff o'dreams. Character. 1 act
In Stuff o'dreams, and other plays
Wild goose. Adventure. 1 act
In Stuff o'dreams, and other plays

Hurlbut, William
Bride of the lamb. Religious revival. 3 acts
In Mantle, B. ed. Best plays of 1925-26

Hurwitz, Bertha
Adopted son; a play in four acts. Boston. Stratford. 1920. 12°. 90p. $1.50 Allegory

Hutchins, Mrs Hapgood. *See* Boyce, Neith, pseud.

Hymer, John B. joint author. *See* Shipman, Samuel and Hymer, J. B.

Hutchins, Will, 1878-
Jeanne d'Arc at Vaucouleurs. Historical. 3 scenes
In Poet Lore 21:97

Hutchison, Isobel, W.
How joy was found; a fantasy. N.Y. Stokes. [1917]. 128p. Scottish folk tale. 5 acts

Hutton, Joseph
Fashionable follies.
In Moses, M. J. ed. Representative plays by American dramatists from 1765 to the present day v 2
Orphan of Prague. A new drama. In five acts. Phila. Palmer. 1808. 12°. 58p.
School for prodigals; a comedy. In five acts. . . Phila. Stiles. 1809. 16°. 62p.

Hyde, Douglas
Bursting the bubble (Pleusgadh na bulgóide). Dublin. Baile-Atha-Cliath. 1903. 12°. 32p. Comedy. 1 act
Lost saint. Irish folk-lore. 1 act
In Gregory, Lady I. A. Plays and dreames
    Samhain O '02 p 19
Marriage. Irish folk-lore. 1 act
In Gregory, I. A. Poets and dreamers
    Shay, F. Twenty-five short plays, international
    Poet Lore 20:135
Nativity. Religious. 1 act
In Gregory, I. A. Poets and dreamers
Poorhouse. Comedy. 1 act
In Gregory, I. A. Spreading the news
    Samhain. S '03 p 19
Righ Seumas. Tr. by Lady Gregory. Dublin. Baile Atha Cliath. [190?]. 12°. 27p. Comedy. 1 act
Twisting of the rope. Comedy. 1 act
In Cohen, H. L. Junior play book
    Gregory, I. A. Poets and dreamers
    Poet Lore 16:12
    Samhain O '01 p 30

Hyde, Florence E.
Captain of the host. Melodrama. 3 acts
In Captain of the host; The supreme test
Supreme test. Melodrama. 4 acts
In Captain of the host; The supreme test

Ibsen, Henrik, 1828-1906
Brand; a dramatic poem. . . N.Y. Dutton. [1915?]. 12°. 223p. Social. 5 acts
Same in Collected works (Archer) v 3
    Works (Viking ed) v 3
Caesar's apostasy. *See* Ibsen, H. Emperor and Galilean. Pt. 2
Cataline. Historical. 3 acts
In Early plays (Orbeck)
Comedy of love. *See* Ibsen, H. Love's comedy
Doll's house. (Et dukkehjem). Social. 3 acts
In Collected works (Archer) v 7
    Works (Viking ed) v 7
    Doll's house and two other plays
    Ibsen's prose dramas (Archer) v 1
    Classic drama v 2
    Matthews, J. B. ed. Chief European dramatists
Emperor and Galilean (Kejser og Galilaeer). Pt. 1. Caesar's apostasy. 5 acts; Pt. 2. Emperor Julian. 5 acts. Historical
Same in Collected works (Archer) v 5
    Ibsen's prose dramas (Archer) v 4
    Works (Viking ed) v 5
Emperor Julian. *See* Ibsen, H. Emperor and Galilean. Pt. 1
Enemy of the people (En folke fiende). Social 5 acts
In Collected works (Archer) v 8
    Works (Viking A.) v 8
    Ibsen's prose dramas (Archer) v 2

Ibsen, H.—*Continued*
   Ghosts (Everyman's)
   Pillars of Society, and other plays
   Coffman, G. R. ed.   Book of modern
     plays
  Feast at Solhoug (Gildet paa Solhoug).
    Historical. 3 acts
   In Collected work (Archer) v 1
     Works (Viking ed) v 1
  Ghosts. (Gengangere). Social. 3 acts
   In Collected work (Archer) v 7
     Works (Viking ed) v 7
     Ghosts (Everyman's)
     Ibsen's prose dramas (Archer) v 2
     Pillars of Society and other plays
     Bates, A. ed.   Drama 17:281
     Sayler, O. M. ed.   Eleanora Duse
      series of plays
  Hedda Gabler; a drama in four acts. . .
    N.Y. U.S. Book co. [c1891]. 12°. 272p.
    Social
   Same in Collected works (Archer) v 10
     Works (Viking ed) v 10
     Hedda Gabler (Everyman)
     Ibsen's prose dramas (Archer)
      v 5
     Master builder (Boni)
  John Gabriel Borkman.   N.Y. Stone.
    1897. 12°. 198p. (Green tree library).
    Social. 4 acts
   Same in Works (Viking ed) v 11
  Lady from the sea (Fruen fra havet).
    Social. 5 acts
   In Collected works (Archer) v 9
     Works (Viking ed) v 9
     Doll's house (Everyman's)
     Ibsen's prose dramas (Archer) v 5
     Sayler, O. M. ed.   Eleanora Duse
      series of plays
  Lady Inger of Östråt.   (Fru Inger til
    Östråt).   Historical. 5 acts
   In Collected works (Archer) v 1
     Works (Viking ed) v 1
     Ibsen's prose dramas (Archer) v 3
     Lady Inger of Ostraat (Everyman's)
  League of youth (De unges forbund).
    Social. 5 acts
   In Collected works (Archer) v 6
     Works (Viking ed) v 6
     Ibsen's prose dramas (Archer) v 1
     Lady Inger of Ostraat. (Every-
      man's)
     Wild duck, etc (Boni)
  Little Eyolf (Lille Eyolf); tr. by Wm.
    Archer.   Chicago. Stone. 1894. 12°.
    164p. (Green tree library).   Social.
    3 acts
   Same in Collected works (Archer) v 11
     Works (Viking ed) v 11
  Love's comedy (Comedy of love) (Kjaer-
    lighedens komedie).   Tr. by C. H.
    Herford. London. Duckworth. 1900.
    167p.   Social. 3 acts
   Same in Collected works (Archer) v 1
     Works (Viking ed) v 1
     Lady Inger of Ostraat (Every-
      man's)

  Master builder (Bygmester Solness).
    Social. 3 acts
   In Collected works (Archer) v 10
     Works (Viking ed) v 10
     Master builder (Boni)
  Olaf Liljekrans.   Romantic. 3 acts
   In Early plays (Orbeck)
  Peer Gynt; a dramatic poem.   N.Y.
    Dutton. [1922?]. 12°. 242p. (Every-
    man's library).   Symbolic. 5 acts
   Same in Collected works (Archer) v 4
     Works (Viking ed) v 4
     Ibsen's prose dramas v 6
  Pillars of society (Samfundets støtter)).
    Social. 4 acts
   In Collected works (Archer) v 6
     Works (Viking) v 6
     Ibsen's prose dramas (Archer) v 1
     Master builder, etc (Boni)
     Pillars of society and other plays
      (Camelot series)
     Pretenders (Everyman's)
  Pretenders (Kongs-Emnerne).   Histor-
    ian. 5 acts
   In Collected works (Archer) v 2
     Works (Viking) v 2
     Ibsen's prose dramas (Archer) v 3
     Pretenders (Everyman's)
  Rosmersholm.   Social. 4 acts
   In Collected works (Archer) v 9
     Works (Viking) v 9
     Ibsen's prose dramas (Archer) v 5
     Pretenders (Everyman's)
     Wild duck, etc (Boni)
  Vikings of Helgeland (Warriors of Hel-
    geland) (Haermaendene paa Helge-
    land).   Historical. 4 acts
   In Collected works (Archer) v 2
     Works (Viking) v 2
     Ghosts (Everyman's)
     Ibsen's prose dramas (Archer) v 3
  Warrior's barrow (Kaempehöjen).   Vik-
    ings. 1 act
   In Early plays (Orbeck)
  Warriors of Helgeland.   *See* Ibsen, H.
    Vikings of Helgeland
  When we dead awaken; (Når vi døde
    rågner) a dramatic epilogue in 3 acts.
    tr. by Wm. Archer. Chicago. Stone.
    1900. 12°. 157p.   Social. 3 acts
   Same in Collected works (Archer) v 11
     Works (Viking ed) v 11
  Wild duck (Vildanden).   Social. 5 acts
     Works (Viking) v 8
     Doll's house (Everyman's)
     Ibsen's prose dramas (Archer) v 2
     Wild duck etc (Boni)
     Moses, M. J. ed.   Representative
      continental dramas

Idzumo, Takeda
Bushido.   Tragedy. 1 act
  In Law, F. H. ed.   Modern plays,
    short and long
Pine-tree (Matsu); a drama adapted from
    the Japanese.   London. Iris publish-
    ing company. [1916]. 12°. 125p.   **Jap-
    anese. 1 act**

Ilsley, S. Marshall
Feast of the holy innocents. 1 act
In Wisconsin plays ser 2

Inchbald, Mrs. Elizabeth Simpson, 1753-1821
Animal magnetism. Farce. 3 acts
In Cumberland's British theatre v 14 no 6
London stage v 4 no 39
Appearance is against them; a farce. London. Robinson. 1785. 48p.
Same in London stage v 4 no 12
Child of nature. Farce. 2 acts
In Cumberland's British theatre v 11
Inchbald's, E. S. ed. Collection of farces v 1
Everyone has his fault. Comedy. 5 acts
In Cumberland's British theatre. v 7 no 7
Inchbald, E. S. ed. British theatre v 20
Inchbald, E. S. ed. Theatre v 2
London stage v 2
Oxberry, W. New English drama v 16
I'll tell you what. A comedy in five acts. . . London. Robinson. 1786. 8°. 88p.
Same in Inchbald, E. S. ed. Modern theatre v 7
Lover's vows. Romantic. 5 acts
In Cumberland's British theatre v 17
Married man. A comedy in three acts. . . London. Robinson. 1789. 8°. 63p.
Midnight hour. Comedy. 3 acts
In Cumberland's British theatre v 15
Inchbald, E. S. ed. Collection of farces v 1
Oxberry, W. New English drama v 13
Mogul tale. A farce in two acts. . . London. Cumberland. n.d. 12°. 25p. (Cumberland's British theatre. v. 42 no. 9)
Same in London stage v 4 no 1
Next door neighbors. Comedy. 3 acts
In Inchbald, E. S. ed. Modern theatre v 7
Such things are; a play in five acts. . . London. Robinson. 1788. 8°. 74p.
Same in Inchbald, E. S. ed. British theatre v 3
Inchbald, E. S. ed. Theatre v 9
London stage v 3
To marry or not to marry . . . a comedy in five acts. . . Baltimore. Warner. 1805. 12°. 69p.
Same in Inchbald, E. S. ed. British theatre v 9
Inchbald, E. S. ed. Theatre v 21
Wedding day. A drama in two acts. . . London. Cumberland. n.d. 12°. 26p. (Cumberland's British theatre. v. 39 no. 10) Farce
Same in Inchbald, E. S. ed. Collection of farces v 1
London stage v2 no 14

Oxberry, W. ed. New English drama v 21
Widow's vow. A farce in two acts. . . London. Robinson. 1786. 8°. 35p.
Wise man of the east. Comedy. 5 acts
In Inchbald, E. S. ed. Modern theatre v 7
Wives as they were, and maids as they are: a comedy in five acts. . . London. Davidson. n.d. 12°. 63p. (Cumberland's British theatre. v. 10)
Same in Inchbald, E. S. ed. British theatre v 8
Inchbald, E. S. ed. Theatre v 22
London stage v 3 no 47

Irving, Washington, 1783-1859
Rip Van Winkle (as played by Joe Jefferson. Dramatized from W. I's story). Comedy. 4 acts
In Law, F. H. ed. Modern plays short and long
Quinn, A. H. ed. Representative American plays, 1763-1923 (1925 ed)

Irwin, Grace Luce
Art for art's sake. Farce. 1 act
In Drawing room plays
Domestic dilemma. Farce. 1 act
In Drawing room plays
Heroes. Farce. 1 act
In Drawing room plays
Innocent villain. Farce. 1 act
In Drawing room plays
Intimate acquaintance. Farce. 1 act
In Drawing room plays
Music hath charms. Farce. 1 act
In Drawing room plays
Wedding of Mah Foy. Farce. 1 act
In Drawing room plays

Issassi, Teresa Farias de
Sentence of death. 1 act
In Shay, F. ed. Twenty-five short plays, international

Isham, Frederic Stewart, 1866-1922, and Marcin, Max, 1879-
Three live ghosts; a comedy in three acts. . . N.Y. French. [c1922]. 8°. 86p.

Iwasaki, Yozan T.
Nari-kin. Japanese. 1 act
In Iwasaki, J. T. tr. Three modern Japanese plays

Izzet-Melyh
Disenchanted. 1 act
In Shay, F. ed. Twenty-five short plays, international

J. S. of Dale, pseud. *See* Stimson, Frederic Jessup

Jack, Adolphus Alfred, 1868-
Mathilde; a play. London. Constable. 1908. 91p. Historical. 5 acts

Jackson, Fred, 1886-
Full house; a farce in three acts. N.Y. French. c1922. 12°. 122p.
Naughty wife; a comedy in three acts. . . N.Y. French. c1925. 12°. 91p.

Jackson, Myrtle, B. S.
Congratulations.   School honors. 1 act
In Merry-thought plays
Domestic dilemma.   Duologue. 1 scene
In Merry-thought plays
Dream.   Academic nightmare. 1 act
In Merry-thought plays
Meg, the match-girl.   Christmas. 2 acts
In Merry-thought plays
Princess and the pea.   Fairy. 3 acts
In Merry-thought plays
Things she would rather have left un-
said.   Triologue. 1 act
In Merry-thought plays

Jacob, Fred, 1882-
And they met again.   Comedy. 1 act
In One third of a bill
Autumn blooming.   Domestic comedy. 1
act
In One third of a bill
Basket.   Canadian. 1 act
In One third of a bill
Clever one.   Satire. 1 act
In One third of a bill
Man's world.   Comedy. 1 act
In One third of a bill

Jacobi, Paula
Chinese lily.   Underworld. 1 act
In Forum 54:551

Jacobs, William Wymark, 1863-
Establishing relations; a comedy in one
act.   N.Y. French. [1925]. 12°. 19p.
Keeping up appearances; a farce in one
act.   N.Y. French. c1919. 12°. 18p.

**Jacobs, William Wymark, 1863-, and Hub-
bard, Philip E.**
Love passage; a comedy in one act.   N.Y.
French. 1913. 12°. 27p.

**Jacobs, William Wymark, 1863-, and Mills,
Horace**
Admiral Peters, a comedy in one act.
London. French. 1909. 12°. 13p.

**Jacobs, William Wymark, 1863-, and Park-
er, Louis Napoleon, 1852-**
Beauty and the barge; a farce in three
acts.   N.Y. French. c1910. 12°. 148p.
Monkey's paw; a story in three scenes.
N.Y. French. c1910. 12°. 35p.   Magic
Same in Marriott, J. W.   One act
plays of to-day ser 2

**Jacobs, William Wymark, 1863-, and Rock,
Charles**
Ghost of Jerry Bundler.   London.
French. c1908. 16°. 19p.   Super-
natural. 1 act
Same in One act plays for stage and
study
Grey parrot.   N.Y. French. c1908. 16°.
19p. 1 act

**Jacobs, William Wymark, 1863-, and Sar-
gent, Herbert C.**
Boatswain's mate, a play in one act.
London. French. c1907. 12°. 26p.   Sea
Castaway; a farce in one act.   N.Y.
French. c1924. 20p.

Changeling.   A play in one act.   London. French. c1908. 16°. 24p.   Comedy
In the library.   N.Y. French. 1912. 12°.
20p.   Crime. 1 act

Jaffa, Minnie Zuckerberg, 1886-
In walked Jimmy; an American comedy
of optimism in four acts.   N.Y.
French. 1920. 114p. 60c

Jagendorf, Moritz Adolf, 1888-
Bumbo and Scrumbo and Blinko.   Juv-
enile. 1 act
In Jagendorf, M. A. ed.   One-act plays
for young people
Farce of the worthy Master Pierre Pate-
lin. tr. from the mediaeval French.
N.Y. Appleton. 1925. 55p. 1 act
Same in Shay, F. ed.   Twenty-five
short plays, international
Firefly night.   Juvenile. 1 act
In Fairyland and footlights
In King Lugdub's forest.   Juvenile. 1
act
In Fairyland and footlights
King Groog and his grouch.   Juvenile. 1
act
In Fairyland and footlights
Mee-Mee and But-Zee.   Juvenile. 1 act
In Fairyland and footlights
One in a hundred years.   Juvenile. 1 act
In Jagendorf, M. A. ed.   One-act plays
for young people
Pierre Patelin.   *See* Jagendorf, M. A.
Farce of the worthy Master Pierre
Patelin
Sad tale of the tarts of the terrible queen
of hearts.   Juvenile. 1 act
In Fairyland and footlights

James, Henry, 1843-1916
Album.   Comedy. 3 acts
In Theatricals ser 2
Daisy Miller; a comedy in three acts.
Boston. Osgood. 1883. 12°. 189p.
Same in Atlan 51:433, 577, 721
Disengaged.   Comedy. 3 acts
In Theatricals ser 1
Reprobate.   Comedy. 3 acts
In Theatricals ser 2
Tenants.   Comedy. 3 acts
In Theatricals ser 1

James, May F.
Weighed in the balance: a drama in four
acts.   Boston. Badger. 1916. 12°. 50p.
$1.   War

Jameson, Robert Francis
Touch at the times; a comedy in five
acts. . . London. Chapple. 1812. 80p.

Janney, S.
East Wind's revenge.   Juvenile. 1 act
In Jagendorf, M. A. ed.   One-act plays
for young folks

Jarosy, Rudolf
Warm reception.   A comedietta in one
act. Tr. from the German "Im
Schneegestöber". . . N.Y.   DeWitt.
c1890. 12°. 11p.

Jarrell, Myra Williams
Case of Mrs. Kantsey Know. Comedy.
1 act
In Drama 12:210

Jasper, Walter
Susanna; a drama in five acts. Boston.
Mayhew. 1908. 12°. 100p. Poetic

Jast, Louis Stanley, 1858-
Call of the ninth wave. Poetic. 1 act
In Lover and the dead woman, etc
Geisha's wedding. Melodrama. 1 act
In Lover and the dead woman, etc
Harbour. Mystic. 1 act
In Lover and the dead woman, etc
Lover and the dead woman. Poetic. 1
act
In Lover and the dead woman, etc
Loves of the elements. Ballet. 1 act
In Lover and the dead woman, etc
Venus and the shepherdess. Poetic. 1
act
In Lover and the dead woman, etc

Jenkins, Floyd, McGraw, Donald, and Darrow, Richard Putnam
Dolls and toy-balloons a musical comedy
up to date. . . N.Y. Baltimore. Broadway pub. co. 1910. 12°. 108p. 2 acts
Wilderness; an American play. N.Y.
Broadway pub. co. 1912. 12°. 95p.
Romantic. 5 acts

Jennings, Gertrude E.
Acid drops. Comedy. 1 act
In Four one-act plays
Allotments; a play in one act. N.Y.
French. 1918. 16p.
At the ribbon counter; a play in one act.
N.Y. French. 1920. 12°. 20p. 30c
Bathroom door. N.Y. French
Between the soup and the savoury.
Comedy. 1 act
In Four one-act plays
Bobbie settles down; a comedy. N.Y.
French. c1920. 8°. 24p.
Calais to Dover; a farce in one act.
N.Y. French. c1922. 12°. 20p.
Cat's claws; a comedy in one act. N.Y.
French. 1923. 12°. 19p.
Five birds in a cage. N.Y. French
Have you anything to declare? A
farce. . . N.Y. French. c1926. 12°.
24p. 1 act
Hearts to sell. N.Y. French. c1922. 12°.
10p. Juvenile. 1 act
"I'm sorry—it's out!". A comedy in one
act. N.Y. French. c1920. 12°. 25p.
In the cellar; a play in one act. N.Y.
French. 1920. 12°. 29p.
Isabel, Edward and Anne; a comedy in
three acts. N.Y. French. c1923. 12°.
74p.
Love among the paint pots; a comedy in
three acts. N.Y. French. c1922. 8°.
63p.
"Me and my diary"; a comedy in one act.
N.Y. French. c1921. 12°. 32p.
New poor; a farce in one act. N.Y.
French. c1920. 12°. 35p.
No servants; a comedy in one act. N.Y.
French. c1919. 12°. 27p.

Poached eggs and pearls; a canteen comedy in two scenes. N.Y. French.
[c1917]. 12°. 46p.
Pros and cons. Comedy. 1 act
In Four one-act plays
Rest cure. Comedy. 1 act
In Four one-act plays
Secret of the castle. N.Y. French.
c1922. 12°. 15p. Juvenile. 1 act
Waiting for the bus; a play in one act.
N.Y. French. c1919. 12°. 16p.
Woman's influence; a play in one act.
(London. Actresses franchise league.
1912?) 32°. 24p. Woman suffrage
Young person in pink; a comedy in three
acts. N.Y. French. 1921. 12°. 73p.
75c

Jennings, Gertrude E., and Boulton, E.
Elegant Edward; a comedy in one act.
N.Y. French. 1919. 12°. 22p.

Jerome, Jerome Klapka, 1859-
Celebrity; a play in three acts. London. Hodder. 1926. 12°. 93p.
Master of Mrs. Chilvers; an improbable
comedy. London. Unwin. 1911. 12°.
167p.
Miss Hobbs; a comedy in four acts.
N.Y. French. c1902. 12°. 66p.
Passing of the third floor back; an idle
fancy in a prologue, a play, (1 scene)
and an epilogue. N.Y. Dodd. 1921.
12°. 197p. Allegory
Robina in search of a husband; a farce
in four acts. N.Y. French. [1913].
12°. 90p.
Woodbarrow farm; a play in three acts.
N.Y. French. 1904. 12°. 69p. Comedy

Jerrold, Douglas William, 1803-1857
All in the Downs. *See* Jerrold, D. W.
Black-ey'ed Susan; or, All in the
Downs
Black-ey'ed Susan; or, All in the Downs.
A nautical and domestic drama in
two acts. Boston. Spencer. [1857?].
12°. 28p.
Same in Comedies and dramas
Moses, M. J. ed. Representative British dramas
Bride of Ludgate. Comedy. 2 acts
In Cumberland's British theatre v 30
no 1
Bubbles of the day. A comedy in five acts.
London. How. 1842. 12°. 126p.
Same in [Works] comedies
Catspaw. Comedy. 5 acts
In [Works] comedies
Dorothy's fortune. *See* Jerrold, D. W.
St. Cupid, or, Dorothy's fortune
Doves in a cage. Comedy. 2 acts
In [Works] Comedies and dramas
Golden calf; a comedy. In three acts. . .
London. Richards. [1832.] 12°. 66p.
Housekeeper. Comedy. 2 acts
In [Works]. Comedies and dramas
Nell Gwynne; or, The prologue. Historical. 2 acts
In [Works]. Comedies and dramas

Jerrold, D. W.—*Continued*
Painter of Ghent.   Melodrama. 1 act
  In [Works].   Comedies and dramas
Prisoner of war.   War 1803. 2 acts
  In [Works] Comedies
Prologue.   *See* Jerrold, D. W. Nell
  Gwynne; or, The prologue
Rent day.   A domestic drama in two
  acts. London. Lacy. n.d. 12°. 47p.
  Same in [Works] Comedies and dramas
Retired from business.   Comedy. 3 acts
  In [Works] Comedies
St. Cupid; or, Dorothy's fortune.   Com-
  edy. 3 acts
  In [Works] Comedies
Schoolfellows.   Comedy. 2 acts
  In [Works].   Comedies and dramas
Time works wonders.   Comedy. 5 acts
  In [Works] Comedies
Wedding gown.   Comedy. 2 acts
  In [Works].   Comedies and dramas
Wives by advertisement; or, Courting in
  the newspapers a dramatic satire, in
  one act. . . London.   Duncombe.
  [18—]. 16°. 22p.
Jerrold, William Blanchard, 1826-1884
Cool as a cucumber; a farce in one act.
  London. Lacy. n.d. 12°. 26p. (Lacy's
  acting edition of plays. v. 5 no. 62)
Jesse, F. Tennyson, joint author.   *See*
  Harwood, Harold Marsh
Jex, John
Mr. Willoughby calls.   Social. 1 act
  In Passion playlets
Nest.   Sex. 1 act
  In Passion playlets
Unnecessary atom.   Social. 1 act
  In Passion playlets
Violet souls.   Satire. 1 act
  In Passion playlets
Jiménez Rueda, Julio
Unforeseen.   Old Mexico. 3 acts
  In Poet Lore 35:1
Jirásek, Alois, 1851-
Dobromila Rettig.   Comedy. 3 acts
  In Poet Lore 31:475
Lantern.   Bohemia. 4 acts
  In Poet Lore 36:317
John, Gwen
Ambrosia.   Comedy. 1 act
  In Dublin M 2:7
Case of Teresa.   Domestic. 1 act
  In Plays
Corinna; or, The strenuous life.   Society.
  1 act
  In Plays
Edge o'dark.   Social. 1 act
  In Plays
    Eng R 12:592
In the rector's study.   Ethical. 3 scenes
  In Plays
Luck of war; a play in one act.   Boston.
  Phillips. 1922. 12°. 47p.   Enoch
  Arden
  Same in Plays of innocence
Mr. Jardyne.   Mystery. 1 act
  In Dublin M 2:246
On the road.   Sketch. 1 act
  In Plays of innocence

Outlaws.   Common life. 1 act
  In Plays
    Manchester playgoer
Peakland wakes.   Morris dance. 1 act
  In Plays of innocence
Prince. Oxford. Blackwell. 1923. 12°. 88p.
  (British drama league library of
  modern British drama. no. 6)   Queen
  Elizabeth. 8 scenes
Sealing the compact.   Sociological. 1 act
  In Plays
Strenuous life.   *See* John, G. Corinna;
  or, The strenuous life
Tale that is told.   Justice. 1 act
  In Plays of innocence
Johnson, Frederick Green, 1890-
Am I intruding?   A mystery comedy in
  three acts. . . Chicago.   Denison.
  [c1922]. 12°. 134p.
Johnson, Larry E.
Brother Elks; a comedy in three acts.
  Chicago. Denison. 1923. 12°. 220p.
Shake-up; a one-act comedy.   Chicago.
  Denison. c1925. 12°. 23p.
Johnson, Martyn
Mr. and Mrs. Roe.   Comedy. 1 act
  In Drama 13:92
Johnston, Mary, 1870-
Goddess of reason.   Boston. N.Y.
  Houghton. 1907. 12°. 234p.   French
  republic. 5 acts
Johnston, T. P.
Patrick Hamilton; a tragedy of the Re-
  formation in Scotland, 1528.   Edin-
  burgh. Blackwood. 1882. 133p.   His-
  torical. 3 acts
Johnstone, John Beer, 1803-1891
Ben Bolt.   An original drama. In two
  acts. London. Lacy. [185—?]. 12°. 24p.
  (Lacy's acting edition of plays. v. 16
  no. 228)
Drunkard's children; a drama in two acts.
  N.Y. French. n.d. 12°. 27p.   Melo-
  drama
Gale Breezely; or, the tale of a tar.   A
  drama in two acts. London. Lacy.
  n.d. 12°. 24p.   Melodrama
Gipsy farmer; or, Jack and Jack's brother.
  An original drama in two acts. Lon-
  don. Lacy. n.d. 12°. 30p.   Melodrama
Jack and Jack's brother.   *See* Johnstone,
  J. B. Gipsy farmer; or, Jack and
  Jack's brother
Lawyer's legend.   *See* Johnstone, J. B.
  Tufelhausen; or, The lawyer's legend
Pedrillo; or, A search for two fathers.
  A drama in two acts. London. Lacy.
  n.d. 12°. 28p.   Comedy
Republicans of Brest.   *See* Johnstone, J.
  B. Sailor of France; or, The republi-
  cans of Brest
Sailor of France; or, The republicans of
  Brest.   An original drama in two
  acts. London. Lacy. n.d. 12°. 22p.
  Historical
Search for two fathers.   *See* Johnstone,
  J. B. Pedrillo; or, A search for two
  fathers

Tale of a tar. *See* Johnstone, J. B. Gale Breezely; or, The tale of a tar

Tufelhausen; or, The lawyer's legend an original romantic drama in two acts. London. Lacy. ₁18—?₁. 12°. 20p.

Jones, Grace Latimer, 1879-
What makes Christmas Christmas; a morality play in one act. Columbus, O. Spain and Glenn. 1917. 12°. 44p.

Jones, Henry Arthur, 1851-
Carnac Sahib; an original play in four acts. N.Y. Macmillan. 1899. 12°. 142p. Social

Case of rebellious Susan; a comedy in three acts. N.Y. Macmillan. 1894. 12°. 118p.
Same in Representative plays

Clerical error; a comedy in one act. N.Y. French. c1906. 12°. 21p.

Crusaders; an original comedy of modern London life. . . N.Y. Macmillan. 1893. 12°. 115p. 3 acts
Same in Representative plays v 2

Dancing girl; a drama in four acts. N.Y. French. c1907. 12°. 119p. Comedy
Same in Representative plays v 1

Deacon, a comedy sketch in two acts. N.Y. French. ₁189—₁. 12°. 23p.

Divine gift; a play in three acts. N.Y. Doran. 1913. 12°. 178p. Social
Same in Representative plays v 4

Dolly reforming herself; a comedy in four acts. N.Y. French. c1910. 12°. 95p.
Same in Representative plays v 4

Dolly's little bills
In One-act plays for stage and study ser 1

Elopement; a comedy in two acts. Ilfracombe. Tait. ₁1879?₁. 12°. 45p.

Galilean's victory; a tragi-comedy of religious life in England in four acts. London. Chiswick press. 1907. 100p.

Goal. Tragi-comedy. Death. 1 act
In Representative plays v 4
Theatre of ideas
Clark, B. H. ed. Representative one-act play by British and Irish authors
Am M 63:451

Grace Mary. Supernatural. 1 act
In Representative plays v 4
Theatre of ideas

Her tongue. Comedy. 1 act
In Theatre of ideas

Hypocrites, a play in four acts. N.Y. French. c1908. 12°. 169p. Social
Same in Representative plays v 3

Joseph entangled; a comedy in three acts. N.Y. French. c1906. 12°. 141p.

Knife
In One-act plays for stage and study ser 2

Judah; an original comedy in three acts. N.Y. Macmillan. 1894. 12°. 104p.
Same in Representative plays v 1

Liars, an original comedy in four acts. N.Y. French. c1909. 12°. 153p.
Same in Representative plays v 3
Pierce and Matthews, eds. Masterpieces of modern drama v 1 (abridged)

Lie; a play in four acts. N.Y. Doran. c1915. 12°. 110p. Social

Manoeuvres of Jane; an original comedy in four acts. N.Y. Macmillan. 1905. 12°. 124p.

Mary goes first; a comedy in three acts and an epilogue. . . Garden City. Doubleday. 1914. 12°. 163p.
Same in Representative plays v 4

Masqueraders; a play in four acts. N.Y. French. c1909. 12°. 135p. Social
Same in Representative plays v 2
Moses, M. J. ed. Representative British dramas

Michael and his lost angel; a play in five acts. N.Y. Macmillan. 1895. 12°. 107p. Social
Same in Representative plays v 3
Pierce and Matthews, eds. Masterpieces of modern drama v 1 (abridged)

Middleman, a play in four acts. N.Y. French. c1907. 12°. 122p. Social
Same in Representative plays v 1

Mrs. Dane's defense; a play in four acts. N.Y. Macmillan. 1905. 12°. 127p. Social
Same in Representative plays v 3

Physician; an original play in four acts. N.Y. Macmillan. 1899. 12°. 114p. Social

Rogue's comedy; a play in three acts. N.Y. Macmillan. 1898. 12°. 131p. Comedy

Saints and sinners, a new and original drama of modern English middle-class life, in five acts. N.Y. Macmillan. 1891. 12°. 142p. Social

Sweet Will. A comedy in one act. London. French. 1887. 12°. 24p.

Tempter; a tragedy in verse in four acts. . . N.Y. Macmillan. 1893. 12°. 108p.
Same in Representative plays v 2

Triumph of the Philistines and how Mr. Jorgan preserved the morals of Market Pewberry under very trying circumstances a comedy in three acts. . . N.Y. Macmillan. 1899. 12°. 122p.

We can't be as bad as all that! a play of English society in three acts. N.Y. Priv. pr. 1910. 12°. 121p.

White washing Julia; an original comedy in three acts and an epilogue. N.Y. Macmillan. 1905. 12°. 136p.

Jones, Henry Arthur, 1851-, **and Herman, Henry,** 1832-1894
Silver king; a drama in five acts. N.Y. French. c1907. 12°. 169p. Social
Same in Representative plays v 1

Jones, Howard Mumford, 1892-
Fascinating Mr. Denby. *See* Sage, S. and Jones, H. M.

Jones, H. M.—*Continued*
Shadows.   Arabesque. 1 act
In Wisconsin plays ser 2
Sundial.   Symbolic. 1 act
In Texas Review 5:92. O '19

Jones, Joseph Stevens, 1811-1877
Captain Kyd; or, The wizard of the sea.
A drama in four acts.   Boston.
Spencer. [1856]. 12°. 44p.   Melodrama
Carpenter of Rouen; or, A revenge for
the massacre of St. Bartholomew; a
romantic drama in three acts.   Lon-
don. Lacy. n.d. 12°. 33p. (Lacy's act-
ing edition of plays. v. 4. no. 60)
Fortune teller of Lynn.   *See* Jones, J.
S. Moll Pitcher, or, The fortune teller
of Lynn
Green Mountain boy.   A comedy in two
acts. N.Y. French. 1860. 12°. 29p.
Moll Pitcher; or, The fortune teller of
Lynn. . . Boston. Spencer. 1855. 12°.
64p.   Melodrama. 4 acts
People's lawyer, a comedy in two acts.
Boston. Spencer. 1856. 12°. 36p. (Also
pub. Boston. Baker. c1890. under title
Solon Shingle; or, The people's law-
yer)
Same in Bates, A. ed.   Drama v 20
Moses, M. J. ed.   Representa-
tive plays by American
dramatists from 1765 to the
present day v 2
Solon Shingle; or, The people's lawyer.
See Jones, J. S.   People's lawyer
Surgeon of Paris; a historical drama in
four acts.   Boston. Spencer. 1856.
12°. 41p.
Wizard of the sea.   *See* Jones, J. S.
Captain Kyd; or, The wizard of the
sea

Jones, Willis K.
Spiced wine.   Old Peru. 1 act
In Poet Lore 36:84

Jordan, Elizabeth Garver, 1867-
Lady from Oklahoma; a comedy in four
acts. N.Y. Harper. 1911. 256p.

Joseph, Mrs Helen Haiman
Princesses; a symbolic drama for marionettes.   Cincinnati. Stewart Kidd.
c1923. 34p. 1 act

Joseph, Leon Edward
Wistful waiting; a play in one act.   N.Y.
French. c1926. 12°. 23p.

Joyce, James, 1882-
Exiles; a play in three acts.   N.Y.
Huebsch. 1918. 194p.   Social

Judge, James P.
Love test; a rural comedy-drama in three
acts. N.Y. French. c1925. 12°. 118p.

Jullien, Jean, 1854-1897
Serenade.   Bourgeois study. 3 acts
In Clark, B. H. tr.   Four plays of the
Free theatre

Justema, William, jr.
Chi-Fu.   China. 1 act
In Drama 13:356

Kahane, J.
Black magic.   Tragedy. 3 acts
In Two plays
Master.   Psychological. 1 act
In Two plays

Kahn, Alfred, 1882-, joint author. *See*
Shapleigh, Mabelle

Kaiser, Georg, 1878-
From morn to midnight; a play in seven
scenes. . . N.Y.   Brentano's. [c1922].
12°. 154p.   Mystery
Same in Poet Lore 31:317
Gas, a play in five acts, tr. from the Ger-
man by Herman Scheffauer. Boston.
Small. 1924. 12°. 96p.   Eternal forces

Kamban, Gudmundur, 1888-
Hadda Padda; a drama in four acts.   Tr.
by Luise Peller from the Icelandic.
N.Y. Knopf. 1917. 13-80p.   Tragedy

Kaplan, Ysabel De Witte, 1877-
Madonna and the scarecrow.   Fantasy.
3 acts
In Poet Lore 34:254
Princess Weaver of the skies.   Japanese.
1 act
In Poet Lore 32:267

Kaspar, Robert A., 1884-
Man you love; a play in four acts.   Bos-
ton. Badger. [1914]. 149p.   Sociologi-
cal
Some people marry; a play in three acts.
Boston. Badger. [1914]. 122p.   Social

Kaucher, Dorothy
Bos'n.   River. 1 act
In Poet Lore 36:583

Kaufman, George S., 1899-
Butter and egg man; a comedy in three
acts.   N.Y. Boni. [c1926]. 12°. 223p.
Same in Mantle, B. ed.   Best plays of
1925-26 (abridged)
If men played cards as women do.   N.Y.
French. c1926. 12°. 14p. 1 act

**Kaufman, George S., 1889-, and Connelly,
Marc, 1890-**
Beggar on horseback, a play in two
parts. . . N.Y. Boni. c1924. 12°. 237p.
Same in Mantle, B. ed.   Best plays of
1923-34 (abridged)
Dulcy; a comedy in three acts. . . N.Y.
Putnam. 1921. 12°. 207p. 12°.
Same in Cohen, H. L. ed.   Longer
plays by modern authors
Mantle, B. ed.   Best plays of
1921-22 (condensed)
Moses, M. J. ed.   Representa-
tive American dramas, na-
tional and local
Merton of the movies, in four acts, a
dramatization of Harry Leon Wil-
son's story of the same name.   N.Y.
French. c1925. 12°. 112p.   Comedy
Same in Mantle, B. ed.   Best plays of
1922-23 (condensed)
To the ladies; a comedy in three acts. . .
N.Y. French. 1923. 12°. 100p.
Same in Cohen, H. L. ed.   Longer
plays by modern authors
Quinn, A. H.   Contemporary
American plays

Kaufman, George S., joint author. *See* Ferber, Edna, 1887-, and Kaufman, G. S.

Kaufman, S. Jay
Kisses. Comedy. 1 act
In Smart Set 47 no 2:259

Kavanaugh, Katharine
Ambition; a play in one act. Chicago. Dramatic pub. co. 1923. 12°. 17p. 50c Justice
Betty; the girl o' my heart; a play in three acts. Chicago. Dramatic pub. co. ₁c1923₁. 12°. 63p. 50c Romantic
Converted suffragist; a play in one act for female characters. N.Y. Dick & Fitzgerald. 1912. 12°. 8p. Comedy
Diamond chip; a ranch play in four acts. Chicago. Dramatic pub. co. 1924. 12°. 54p. 50c
Easy terms; a domestic comedy in one act. Chicago. Denison. 1922. 12°. 18p. 25c
Four adventurers; a comedy for girls. N.Y. Fitzgerald. 1922. 12°. 15p. 25c. 1 act
Friendly tip; a playlet in one act. N.Y. Fitzgerald. 1922. 12°. 16p. 25c. Comedy
Gentle touch; vaudeville sketch in one act. N.Y. Dick & Fitzgerald. 1912. 12°. 10p.
It ain't my fault; a comedy in one act. N.Y. Fitzgerald. 1922. 12°. 20p. 25c
Oh! Susan! a four-act comedy-drama. Chicago. Dramatic publishing company. ₁c1924₁. 12°. 57p.
Second-story Peggy; a four-act comedy-drama. Chicago. Dramatic publishing co. ₁c1924₁. 12°. 55p.
Settled out of court; a domestic comedy in one act. Chicago. Denison. 1923. 12°. 225p. 25c
Stormy night; a comedy in one act. N.Y. Dick & Fitzgerald. 1912. 12°. 12p.
Watch my smoke! a three act comedy-drama. Chicago. Dramatic publishing co. ₁c1924₁. 12°. 59p.
When Jane takes a hand; a play in four acts. Chicago. Dramatic pub. co. 1923. 12°. 64p. 50c. Comedy
Will o' the wisp; a romantic Irish comedy drama in three acts. Chicago. Dramatic pub. co. 1923. 12°. 66p. 50c
Woman's stratagem; a play in one act. Chicago. Dramatic pub. co. 1924. 12°. 18p. 50c. Comedy
Woman's way; a play in one act. Chicago. Dramatic pub. co. 1923. 12°. 50c

Kearney, Patrick
Great noontide. Satire. 1 act
In Drama 11:109
Man's man; a comedy of life under the "L". N.Y. Brentano's. 1925. 3 acts
Tongues of fire. Married life. 1 act
In Drama 11:397

Kearns, John
Enchanted thorn. Fairy Tale. 1 act
In Drama 11:324

Keats, John, 1795-1821
King Stephen, a fragment. *See* Coward, E. F. King Stephen

Keble Howard, pseud. *See* Beel, John Keble

Keeler, Charles
Pagoda slave. Burmese. 1 act
In Drama 12:163

Kelly, George Edward, 1887-
Craig's wife; a drama. Boston. Little. 1926. 12°. 174p. Marriage. 3 acts
Same in Mantle, B. ed. Best plays of 1925-26 (abridged)
Daisy Mayme; a comedy. Boston. Little. 1927. 12°. 193p. 3 acts
Finders-keepers; a play in one act. Cincinnati. Stewart Kidd. 1923. 12°. 50p. Psychological
Same in Nicholson, K. ed. Appleton's book of short plays
Shay, F. ed. Contemporary one-act plays of 1921
Shay, F. ed. Twenty contemporary one-act plays (American)
Flattering word. Vaudeville. 1 act
In Flattering word, and other one-act plays
One of those things. 1 act
In One-act plays for stage and study ser 3
Poor Aubrey. Vaudeville. 1 act
In Flattering word, and other one-act plays
Show-off; a transcript of life in three acts. Boston. Little. 1924. 12°. 129p. $1.75 Comedy
In Mantle, B. ed. Best plays of 1923-24 (condensed)
Moses, M. J. ed. Representative American dramas, national and local
Smarty's party. Vaudeville. 1 act
In Flattering word, and other one-act plays
Torch-bearers; a satirical comedy in three acts. . . N.Y. French. 1924. 12°. 189p. 75c
Weak spot. Vaudeville. 1 act
In Flattering word, and other one-act plays

Kemble, Charles, 1775-1854
Budget of blunders. A farce. In two acts. . . Phila. T. H. Palmer. 1823. 36p. 12°.
Plot and counterplot; or, The portrait of Cervantes: a farce in two acts
In Cumberland's British theatre v 41 no 7
Point of honour. Comedy. 3 acts
In Cumberland's British theatre v 28 no 4
Sketch of The wanderer; or, The rights of hospitality. An historical drama. . . London. Scales. ₁1808?₁. 12°. 28p. 1 act

Kemble, Frances Anne, 1809-1893
English tragedy.   Tragedy. 5 acts
In Plays
Mademoiselle de Belle Isle (tr. and
adapted from Dumas) *q.v.*
Mary Stuart (adapted from Schiller).
Tragedy. 5 acts
In Plays
Star of Seville.   London.   Saunders.
1837. 8°. 146p. 5 acts

Kemp, Harry, 1883-
Boccaccio's untold tale.   Plague. 1 act
In Boccaccio's untold tale, and other
one-act plays
Shay, F. and Loving, P. eds.   Fifty
contemporary one-act plays
Calypso.   1 act
In Boccaccio's untold tale, and other
one-act plays
Don Juan's Christmas eve.   1 act
In Boccaccio's untold tale, and other
one-act plays
Game called kiss.   1 act
In Boccaccio's untold tale, and other
one-act plays
Judith.   1 act
In Boccaccio's untold tale, and other
one-act plays
Peril of the moon.   1 act
In Boccaccio's untold tale, and other
one-act plays
Prodigal son; a comedy in one act. . .
New York. E. Arens. 1919. 12°. 28p.
(The flying stag plays for little thea-
tre. no. 8)
Solomon's song.   Tragi-comedy. 1 act
In Boccaccio's untold tale, and other
one-act plays
Shay, F. ed.   Contemporary one-act
plays of 1921
Shay, F. ed.   Twenty contemporary
one-act plays (American)
Their day.   1 act
In Boccaccio's untold tale, and other
one-act plays
White hawk.   1 act
In Boccaccio's untold tale, and other
one-act plays

Kemper, Sallie
Old Chester secret.   Motherhood. 1 act
In Boston theatre guild plays

Kennard, M. C.
Flight of the herons.   Sacrifice. 1 act
In Drama 14:97

Kennedy, Charles O'Brien
And there was light
In One act plays for stage and study
ser 2

Boys will be boys; a comedy of the soul
of man under prosperity, in three
acts (founded on Irvin S. Cobb's
short story). . . N.Y. French. c1925.
12°. 91p.

Kennedy, Charles Rann, 1871-
Army with banners; a divine comedy of
this very day in five acts. . . N.Y.
Huebsch. 1919. 12°. 149p.   Millenium

Idol breaker; a play of the present day
in five acts. . . N.Y. Harper. 1914.
12°. 177p.   Symbolic
Necessary evil; a one-act stage play for
four persons. . . N.Y. Harper. 1913.
12°. 110p.   Social
Rib of the man; a play of the new world,
in five acts.   N.Y. Harper. c1917.
12°. 187p.   Allegory
Servant in the house. . . N.Y. Harper.
1908. 12°. 151p.   Symbolic. 5 acts
In Golden Bk 2:795
Terrible meek; a one-act stage play for
three voices. . . N.Y. Harper. 1912.
12°. 43p.   Christ
Winterfeast. . . N.Y. Harper. 1908. 12°.
159p.   Tragedy. 5 acts

Kennedy, Charles William, 1882-, **and Wil-
son, James Southall,** 1880-
Pausanias; a dramatic poem.   N.Y.
Neale. 1907. 60p.   Historical. 3 acts

Kennedy, Harriet L.
Lion's mouth; adapted from the story
"The sleeping sickness" by George
Madden Martin.   N.Y. London.
Appleton. 1924. 31p.

Kennedy, Margaret, and Dean, Basil
Constant nymph; a play in three acts,
from the novel of Margaret Kennedy. . . Garden City. Doubleday.
1926. 12°. 271p.   Character

Kennedy, Mary, and Hawthorne, Ruth
Mrs. Partridge presents; a comedy in
three acts.   N.Y. French. c1925. 12°.
100p.
Same in Mantle, B. ed.   Best plays of
1924-25 (abridged)

Kenyon, Bernice Lesbia, 1897-
Alchemist.   Mediaeval. 1 act
In Shay, F. ed.   Treasury of plays for
men

Kenyon, Charles, 1880-
Kindling, a comedy drama in three
acts. . . Garden City. Doubleday.
1914. 12°. 147p.
Same in Dickinson, T. H. ed.   Contemporary plays

Kerley, Rosialee
Wedding guest.   Historical. 1 act
In Poet Lore 33:232

Kester, Katharine
Penny a flower.   Fantasy. 1 act
In Drama 15:59 D '24
Rondo capriccio.   Youth. 1 act
In Poet Lore 37:458

Ketchum, Arthur
Other one.   Interlude. 1 act
In Plays of the 47 workshop ser 3

Kidder, Augusta Raymond
His and hers; a one-act play.   N.Y.
French. c1926. 12°. 20p.

Kidder, Edward E.
Easy Dawson; a three act comedy.   N.Y.
French. c1926. 12°. 91p.
Lively legacy; a fantastic farce-comedy in
three acts and six scenes. . . N.Y.
(?). 1900. 8°. 82p.

Kielland, Alexander Lange. 1849-1906
Three couples. Comedy. 3 acts
In Drama 7 no 26:240
Kiesing, Maurice R.
Abu Bakar. Comic opera. 2 acts
In Dramas and poems ser 2
Queen Adelaide. Romantic. 3 acts
In Dramas and poems ser 1
Vagrant king. Romantic. 3 acts
In Dramas and poems ser 2
Kikuchi, Kan
Madman on the roof. Japanese. 1 act
In Iwasaki, Y. T. tr. Three modern
Japanese plays
Kimball, Rosamond
Call to the youth of America. Patriotic.
1 act
In Patriotic pageants of today
Wooing of Rebekah. Biblical
In Wooing of Rebekah, and other Bible
plays
You and I and Joan; a play for girls in
six scenes. N.Y. French. c1924. 47p.
Kimball, Rosamond, joint author. *See*
Thorpe, Josephine, and Kimball, Rosa-
mond
King, Beulah
Gorgeous Cecile; in three acts. N.Y.
Fitzgerald. 1920. 12°. 54p. 25c Com-
edy
His sisters; a farce in one act. N.Y.
Fitzgerald. 1920. 12°. 18p. 25c
Poor dear Uncle James; a farce-comedy
in three acts. N.Y. Fitzgerald. 1920.
12°. 63p. 25c
King, Beulah, and Shute, James L.
Happiness at last; a comedy in three
acts. N.Y. Fitzgerald. c1922. 12°.
47p.
King, D. G.
Brothers. Justice. 1 act
In Indiana prize plays 1922-23
King, Georgiana Goddard
Way of perfect love. N.Y. Macmillan.
1908. 108p. Mystery. 4 acts
King, Grace Elizabeth, 1852-
Splendid offer. Comedy. 1 act
In Dramas 16:213
King, Pendleton
Cocaine; a play in one act. Shay. N.Y.
1917. 12°. 14p. Suicide
Same in Provincetown plays (Stewart
Kidd 1921)
Kingdom, John M.
Fountain of beauty; or The king, the prin-
cess, and the geni. A fairy extrava-
ganza in two acts. London. Lacy. n.d.
12°. 34p. (Lacy's acting edition of
plays. v. 12. no. 168)
Marcoretti; or, The brigand's sacrifice.
A romantic drama, in three acts. . .
N.Y. DeWitt. c1874. 12°. 34p.
Kingsbury, Sara
Christmas guest. Forgiveness. 1 act
In Drama 8:455
Rich young man; a play in three acts.
N.Y. Abingdon press. c1924. 42p.

Kinkead, Cleves, 1882-
Common clay. N.Y. French. c1917. 12°.
99p. Social. 4 acts
Four-flushers. Satirical farce. 1 act
In Plays of the Harvard dramatic club
ser 2
Kinross, Martha
Tristram and Isoult; a poetic drama.
London. Macmillan. 1913. 87p. Le-
gendary. 3 pts.
Kirker, Katherine
Lady compassionate. Dante. 1 act
In Poet Lore 33:239
Kister, Mark Alexis
Hard heart. Tragedy. 1 act
In Plays of the 47 workshop ser 3
Kitching, H. St. A.
Fate of Ivan. Tragedy. 5 acts
In Moral plays
Johnnies in Spain. *See* Kitching H. St.
A. Miss Betsy Bull; or, The Johnnies
in Spain
Keep your temper! or, Know whom you
marry. Comedy. 5 acts
In Moral plays
Miss Betsy Bull; or, The Johnnies in
Spain. Melodrama. 3 acts
In Moral plays
Klauber, A. J.
Exile. Dante. 1 act
In Poet Lore 33:246
Green-eyed monster. Farce. 1 act
In Smart Set 43 no 1:133
Kleene, Alice Cole
Kirsten; a play in four acts. Boston.
Sherman. 1913. 93p. Fairy
Klein, Charles, 1867-1915
Daughters of men, a play in three acts.
N.Y. French. c1917. 12°. 90p.
Gamblers; a play in three acts. N.Y.
French. n.d. 12°. 79p. Melodrama
Lion and the mouse; a play in four acts.
N.Y. French. [19—?]. 12°. 110p. So-
cial
Maggie Pepper, a play in three acts.
N.Y. French. c1916. 12°. 106p. Social
Next of kin; a comedy in three acts.
N.Y. French. c1917. 12°. 85p.
Third degree; a play in four acts. N.Y.
French. [c1908]. 12°. 117p. Melo-
drama
Klein, Charles, 1867-1915, and Clarke, J. I.
C.
Heartsease, a play in four acts. . . N.Y.
French. c1916. 12°. 70p. Romantic
Kleist, Heinrich von, 1777-1811
Feud of the Schroffensteins. Historical.
5 acts
In Poet Lore 27:457
Knevels, Gertrude
Dragon's glory; a Chinese comedy in four
scenes. N.Y. Appleton. 1924. 12°.
53p. 50c
Knoblauch, Edward. *See* Knoblock, Ed-
ward
Knoblock, Edward, 1874-
Kismet; an Arabian night in three acts.
N.Y. Doran. c1911. 12°. 128p.

Knoblock, E.—*Continued*
Little silver ring
In War committee
Lullaby. Social. 4 acts
In Lullaby, and other plays
Marie-Odile; a play in three acts.   N.Y.
Tower bros. c1910. 12°. 77p.   Social
Same in Lullaby, and other plays
My lady's dress; a play in three acts. . .
Garden City. Doubleday. 1916. 12°.
165p. 75c.   Social
Paganini; a play in three acts.   [New
York. Tower bros. c1915]. 12°. 230p.
50c
Tiger! tiger!   Social. 4 acts
In Lullaby, and other plays
War committee
In War committee
Knowles, James Sheridan, 1784-1862
Alfred the Great, or The patriot King.
Historical. 5 acts
In Dramatic works
Beggar of Bethnal Green.   Comedy. 3
acts
In Dramatic works
Bridals of Messina.   *See* Knowles, J. S.
John of Procida; or, The bridals of
Messina
Caius Gracchus.   Tragedy. 5 acts
In Dramatic works
Cumberland British theatre v 6 no 4
Daughter.   Tragedy. 5 acts
In Dramatic works
Hunchback; a play in five acts.   N.Y.
DeWitt. c1876. 69p.   Romantic
Same in Dramatic works
John of Procida; or The bridals of Mes-
sina.   Tragedy. 5 acts
In Dramatic works
Love.   Romantic. 5 acts
In Dramatic works
Cumberland's British theatre v 40
no 1
Love chase; a comedy in five acts.   Lon-
don. Moxon. 1837. 111p.
Same in Dramatic works
Love's disguises.   *See* Knowles, J. S.
Woman's wit, or, Love's disguises
Maid of Mariendorpt.   Romantic. 5 acts
In Dramatic works
Old maids.   Comedy. 5 acts
In Dramatic works
Patriot king.   *See* Knowles, J. S. Alfred
the Great, or The patriot king
Rose of Arragon.   Historical. 5 acts
In Dramatic works
Secretary.   Comedy. 5 acts
In Dramatic works
Virginius.   Tragedy. 5 acts
In Dramatic works
Cumberland's British theatre v 6
Dolby's British theatre v 12 no 3
Moses, M. J. ed.   Representative
British dramas
no 3
Wife; a tale of Mantua; a play in five
acts.   London. Moxon. 1833.   Trag-
edy
Same in Dramatic works

William Tell; a play in five acts.   Lon-
don. Dolby. [1825?]. 83p.   Tragedy
Same in Dramatic works
Cumberland's British theatre
v 22 no 7
Woman's wit; or Love's disguises; a play
in five acts.   Boston. Nichols. [1838].
63p.   Romantic
Same in Dramatic works
Knowlton, A. R.
Why Jessica! a comedy in one act.   Bos-
ton. Baker. 1918. 24p.
Knowlton, Don, and Knowlton, Beatrice
Way the noise began.   Comedy. 1 act
In Drama 12:20
Knox, Florence C.
For distinguished service.   Comedy. 1
act
In Shay, F. ed.   Treasury of plays for
women
Kobun, Leon, 1872-
Black sheep.   Social. 1 act
In Goldberg, I. ed.   Six plays of the
Yiddish theatre ser 2
Secret of life.   Philosophical. 1 act
In Goldberg, I. ed.   Six plays of the
Yiddish theatre ser 2
Koch, Frederick Henry, 1877-
Raleigh, the shepherd of the ocean.
Raleigh. N.C. Edwards & Broughton.
1920. 8°. 95p.   Pageant. 3 episodes
Koerner, Theodor, 1791-1813
Rosamunda; a tragedy in four acts. . .
Folkestone.   J. J. Goulden. 1878. 12°.
26p.
Same in Koerner.   Life of Carl Theo-
dor Koerner v 2
Zring.   Tragedy. 5 acts
In Koerner. Life of Carl Theodor Kör-
ner v 2
Koning, Marie Metz
White lie.   Marriage. 1 act
In Loving, P. ed.   Ten minute plays
**Konstantin Konstantinovich, grand duke
of Russia ("K.P."), 1858-**
King of the Jews; a sacred drama from
the Russian of "K.P." . . . by Vic-
tor E. Marsden. London. Cassell.
1914. 12°. 159p. 4 acts
Kori, Torahiko
Kanawa: the incantation; a play for
marionettes.   London. Gowans. 1918.
24°. 22p. 1 act
Kosor, Josip
Invincible ship.   Serbo-Croatian. 5 acts
In People of the universe
Passions furnace.   Serbo-Croatian.   4
acts
In People of the universe
Reconcilation.   Serbo-Croatian. 3 acts
In People of the universe
Woman.   Serbo-Croatian. 3 acts
In People of the universe
Kotzebue, August, F. F. von, 1761-1819
Abbé de l'Epée
In Dramatic works v 3

Adelaide of Wulfingen; a tragedy in four acts. . . London. Vernor & Hood. 1798. 8°. 108p.
Same in Dramatic works v 1
Thompson, B. German theatre v 2
Birthday; a comedy in three acts. . . altered by T. Dibdin. London. Longman. 1800. 8°. 79p.
Corsicans. A drama in four acts. . . London. Beel. 1799. 8°. 91p. Patriotic
Count Benyowsky; or, The conspiracy of Kamschatka. A tragi-comedy in five acts. London. Richardson. 1798. 8°. 205p.
Same in Dramatic works v 3
Thompson, B. German theatre v 2
Count of Burgundy; a comedy. In four acts. Tr. from the German by Charles Smith. N.Y. C. Smith. 1800. 8°. 69p.
Same in Dramatic works v 1
Daughter. *See* Kotzebue, A. F. F. von. Sighs; or, The daughter
Deaf and dumb; or, The orphan. Historical. 5 acts
In Thompson, B. German theatre v 3
Death of Rolla. *See* Kotzebue, A. F. F. von. Pizarro in Peru, or, The death of Rollo (continuation of The Virgin of the Sun)
East Indian; a comedy in three acts. N.Y. Smith. 1800. 12°. 80p.
Same in Dramatic works v 2
Egotist and pseudo-critic. (Herr Gottlieb Merks; der egoist und kritikus). Comedy. 2 acts
In Bates, A. ed. Drama 11:303
False delicacy. Romantic. 5 acts
In Thompson, B. German theatre v 3
False shame. A comedy in four acts. London. Vernor & Hood. 1799. 8°. 74p.
In Dramatic works v 3
Family distress; or, Self-immolation. A play in three acts. . . London. Phillips. 1799. 8°. 49p. Boston. Blake. 1799. 77p. Comedy
Same in Dramatic works v 1
Force of calumny; a play in five acts. . . London. Phillips. 1799. 8°. 108p. Melodrama
In Dramatic works v 2
Fraternal discord: a drama in five acts. Altered from the German by W. Dunlap. N.Y. Longworth. 1809. 12°. 69p. Comedy
Happy family. A drama in five acts. London. Vernor & Hood. 1799. 8°. 102p. Domestic
In Dramatic works v 2
Thompson, B. German theatre v 3
Horse and the widow; a farce . . . altered and adapted by T. Dibdin. London. J. Baker. 1799. 8°. 31p. 1 act

How to die for love; or, The rival captains. A farce in two acts. Adapted from a sketch in one act called "Blind Geladen". Phila. Turner. 1833. 12°. 30p.
Same in Cumberland's British theatre v 40 no 6
Indian exiles, a comedy in 3 acts. Tr. by B. Thompson. London. Vernor & Hood. 1800. 8°. 84p.
Same in Thompson, B. German theatre v 3
Indigence, and nobleness of mind (Armuth and Edelsinn). A comedy in five acts. . . N.Y. C. Smith. 1800. 8°. 64p.
Same in Dramatic works v 1
Joanna of Montfaucon. A dramatic romance of the fourteenth century . . . adapted by R. Cumberland. London. Lackington. 1800. 8°. 88p. 5 acts
La Peyrouse: a comedy in two acts. Tr. by Charles Smith. N.Y. C. Smith. 1800. 8°. 40p.
Same in Dramatic works v 1
Lover's vows; a play in five acts. Altered from tr. of Mrs. Inchbald and B. Thompson, by J. N. Payne. Baltimore. Dobbin. 1809. 12°. 90p. (Adaptation of Das kind der liebe). Romantic
Same in Dramatic works v 3
Bates, A. ed. Drama 21:143
Cumberland's British theatre v 17 no 7
London stage v 3 no 28
Thompson, B. ed. German theatre v 2
Library ser 3 v 8:1 (condensed)
Man of forty. A comedietta in one act. Adapated . . . by Wm. Poel. London. French. [1880]. 12°. 20p.
Natural son. *See* Kotzebue, A. F. von. Lovers' vows; or, The natural son
Negro slaves, a dramatic historical piece in three acts. London. Cadell. 1796. 8°. 142p.
Noble lie: a comedy in one act . . . being the conclusion of. . . The stranger, or, Misanthropy and repentance. London. Pitkeathley. 1799. 8°. 39p.
Orphan. *See* Kotzebue, A. F. F. von. Deaf and dumb; or, The orphan
Pagenstreiche; or, A page's frolics: a comedy. . . London. Clauke. 1853. 12°. 166p. 5 scenes
Page's frolics. *See* Kotzebue, A. F. F. von. Pagenstreiche; or, A page's frolics
Patriot father; an historical play in five acts. . . London. Printed for private circulation. 1850. 12°. 66p. Hussites
Pizarro; or, The death of Rolla (Pizarro in Peru, or The death of Rolla; Piz-

Kotzebue, A. F. F. von—*Continued*
arro; or, The Spaniards in Peru; Spaniards in Peru; or The death of Rolla). Romantic tragedy. 5 acts
In Dramatic works v 2
British drama v 2:17
Cumberland's British theatre v 1 no 4
London stage v 1 no 1
Oxberry, W. ed. New English drama v 20 no 1
Thompson, B. ed. German theatre v 1
Quaker. Historical. 1 act
In Pennsylvania M of Hist 29:439
Reconciliation; or, The birthday. A comedy in five acts. . . Tr. by C. Ludger. London. Ridgway. 1799. 8°. 114p.
Rival captains. *See* Kotzebue, A. F. F. von. How to die for love; or, The rival captains
Sighs; or, The daughter. A comedy in five acts. . . London. Rickaby. 1799. 8°. 87p.
Spaniards in Peru. *See* Kotzebue, A. F. F. von. Pizarro; or, The Spaniards in Peru
Stranger: a comedy. N.Y. Printed for Naphtali Judah. 1799. 8°. 56p. 5 acts
In Cumberland's British theatre v 14 no 2
London stage v 3 no 26
Oxberry, W. ed. New English drama v 21 no 1
Thompson, B. ed. German theatre v 1
Virgin of the sun, a play in five acts. . . N.Y. Hopkins for Dunlap. 1800. 12°. 80p. Incas. For continuation see 'Death of Rolla'
Same in Dramatic works v 2
Thompson, B. ed. German theatre v 1
Wanderer; or, The rights of hospitality. (Eduard in Schottland, oder, Die nacht eines Flüchtlings); a drama in three acts. . . London. Brettell. 1808. 8°. 64p Historical
Widow and the riding horse. A dramatic trifle in one act. London. Phillips. 1799. 12°. 20p. Interlude
Wild-goose chase: a play in four acts. . . N.Y. Hopkins for Dunlap. 1800. 8°. 104p. Romantic
Wild youth: a comedy for digestion. N.Y. Smith. 1800. 8°. 74p. 3 acts
Same in Dramatic works v 1
Wise man of the east. An alteration of the "Writing desk". A play in five acts. . . from the German by Mrs. Inchbald. London. G. G. & J. Robinson. 1799. 8°. 80p. Comedy
Same in Inchbald, E. S. ed. Modern theatre v 17:117
Writing-desk; or, Youth in danger. A play in four acts. London. G. G. and J. Robinson. 1799. 8°. 114p. Comedy
Same in Dramatic works v 3

Youth in danger. *See* Kotzebue, A. F. F. von. Writing desk; or, Youth in danger
Koven, Joseph
By the beard of the prophet. Comedy. 2 scenes
In Miracle of Saint Masha, and other plays
God save the heir. Death. 1 act
In Miracle of Saint Masha, and other plays
In the desert. Biblical. 4 scenes
In Miracle of Saint Masha, and other plays
Miracle of Saint Masha. Religious. 1 act
In Miracle of Saint Masha, and other plays
Kraemer, O. J., and Humphreys, L. W.
Dollars and sense. Boston. Gorham press. 1915. 109p. Pacifist. 4 acts
Kraft, Irma
Ambition in Whitechapel. Jewish. 1 act
In Power of Purim and other plays
Because he loved David so. Jewish. 1 act
In Power of Purim and other plays
Maccabean cure. Jewish. 1 act
In Power of Purim and other plays
Power of Purim. Jewish. 1 act
In Power of Purim and other plays
To save his country. Jewish. 1 act
In Power of Purim and other plays
Kreymborg, Alfred, 1883-
Adverbs; a tête-a-tête in nine movements. Comedy. 1 act
In Rocking chairs and other comedies
At the sign of the thumb and nose. Unmorality play. 1 act
In Plays for merry Andrews
Blue and green. Shadow play 1 act
In Plays for poem-mimes
Puppet plays
Helpless Herberts. Comedy. 1 act
In Rocking chairs and other comedies
Theatre Arts M 8:119
Jack's house. Cubic play. 1 act
In Plays for poem-mimes
Puppet plays
Jane, Jean, and John. 1 act
In One-act plays for stage and study ser 3
Lima beans. Scherzo-play. 1 act
In Plays for poem-mimes
Puppet plays
Mayorga, M. G. ed. Representative one-act plays
Provincetown plays ser 3
Manikin and Minikin. Bisque play. 1 act
In Plays for poem-mimes
Puppet plays
Lewis, B. R. ed. Contemporary one-act plays
Shay, F. ed. Treasury of plays for women
Monday, a lame minuet. 1 act
In Plays for merry Andrews
Drama 10:264
Not too far from the angels. Comedy. 1 act
In Rocking chairs and other comedies

People who die. Dream. 1 act
In Plays for poem-mimes
Puppet plays
Pianissimo. Nodding play. 1 act
In Puppet plays
Rocking chairs. Comedy. 1 act
In Rocking chairs and other comedies
Shay, F. ed. Treasury of plays for
women
Silent waiter. Tragi-comedy. 1 act
In Plays for merry Andrews
Shay, F. ed. Treasury of plays for
men
There's a moon tonight; a romantic com-
edy in three acts. . . N.Y. French.
1926. 12°. 133p.
Trap doors. Travesty. 1 act
In Rocking chairs and other comedies
Theatre Arts M 9:742
Uneasy street. Folk play. 1 act
In Plays for merry Andrews
Vote the new moon. Toy play. 1 act
In Plays for merry Andrews
Shay, F. ed. Treasury of plays for
men
When the willow nods. Dance. 1 act
In Plays for poem-mimes
Puppet plays

**Kravchinskiĭ, Sergïeĭ M. (Sergei Stepniak,
pseud), 1852-1893**
New convert; a drama in four acts. . .
Tr. from the Russian by Thomas B.
Eyges. Boston. Stratford. [c1917].
121p. $1.50 Political. 4 acts

Krohn, Josephine Elliott
Old King Cole. Juvenile. 2 acts
In Old King Cole and other mediaeval
plays
Queen of hearts. Juvenile. 2 acts
In Old King Cole and other mediaeval
plays
Simple Simon. Juvenile. 2 acts
In Old King Cole and other mediaeval
plays
Sing a song of sixpence. Juvenile. 3
scenes
In Old King Cole and other mediaeval
plays

Kummer, Mrs. Clare (Beecher)
"Be calm, Camilla!" a comedy in two acts.
N.Y. French. c1922. 12°. 89p.
Bridges. . . N.Y. French. c1922 12°. 18p.
Comedy. 1 act
Chinese love; a play in one act. N.Y.
French. c1922. 12°. 19p. Chinese
Choir rehearsal; a play in one act. N.Y.
French. c1922. 12°. 19p. Comedy
"Good gracious, Annabelle!," a romantic
farce comedy in three acts. N.Y.
French. c1922. 12°. 106p.
Papers. 1 act
In One-act plays for stage and study
ser 3
Rescuing angel; a comedy in three acts.
N.Y. French. c1923. 12°. 100p.
Robbery, a comedy in one act. N.Y.
French. [1921]. 12°. 20p.
Same in One act plays for stage and
study ser 1

Rollo's wild oat; a comedy in three acts.
N.Y. French. c1922. 12°. 117p.
Successful calamity; a comedy in two
acts. N.Y. French. c1922. 12°. 96p.
Pomeroy's past; a comedy in three acts.
N.Y. French. c1926. 12°. 103p.

Kummer, Frederick Arnold, 1873-
Finer clay. Character. 5 scenes
In Phryne, etc
Phryne. Classical. 1 act
In Phryne, etc
Temptation. Biblical. 1 act
In Phryne, etc

Kussy, Nathan, 1872-
Crooks; a playlet. Washington com-
mission on training camp activities.
Dept. of dramatic activities among
the soldiers. 1918. 13p. (War dept.
Service ed. no. 5) 1 act

Kvapil, Jaroslav, 1868-
Clouds. Psychological. 3 acts
In Poet Lore 21:417
Will o' the wisp. Social. 4 acts
In Poet Lore 27:1

Levin, Zebullon, 1874-
Poetry and prose. 1 act
In Goldberg, I. ed. Six plays of the
Yiddish theatre ser 2

Labiche, Eugène Marin, 1815-1888
Grammar, a comedy in one act. N.Y.
French. [c1915]. 12°. 25p.
Two cowards (Les deux timides). a com-
edy in one act. . . N.Y. French. c1915.
12°. 24p.

**Labiche, Eugène Marin, 1815-1888, and
Jolly, Alphonse**
Under a spell; a comedy in one act. . .
Boston. Baker. 1888. 12°. 24p.

**Labiche, Eugène Marin, 1815-1888, and Mar-
tin, Edouard, 1815-1866**
Bluffers, or, Dust in the eyes. A comedy
in two acts. Adapted. N.Y. French
c1912. 12°. 82p.
Papa Pettingill: a comedy. . . Baker
1904. 25c. 1 act
Perrichon's journey (Le voyage de Monsieur Perrichon). Comedy. 4 acts
In Pierce and Matthews, ed. Masterpieces of modern drama v 2
(abridged)

**Labiche, Eugène Marin, 1815-1888, and
Michel, Marc Antoine Amédie, 1812-
1868**
Leghorn hat. Comedy. 5 acts
Same in Poet Lore 28:1
Wedding march (Le chapeau de paille
d'Italie.) [Adapted] by W. S. Gilbert.
London. French. [1874?]. 12°. 34p.
(Lacy's acting of plays v. 114. no.
1703) *See also* Leghorn hat

Lacy, Ernest, 1863-1916
Bard of Mary Redcliffe. Phila. Brown.
1916. 205p. Romantic. 5 acts
Same in Plays and sonnets v 1
Chatterton. Tragedy. 1 act
In Plays and sonnets v 2
Rinaldo, the doctor of Florence. Trag-
edy. 5 acts
In Plays and sonnets v 2

Laferrière, Adolphe, joint author. *See*
Pierron, Eugene, and Laferrière, Adolphe

Laffan, Bertha Jane (Mrs. De Courcy), d. 1912
On the right road. Domestic. 1 act
In Book of short plays
One Christmas eve. Christmas. 1 act
In Book of short plays
Our John. Romantic. 1 act
In Book of short plays
Salvation of Teddie. Melodrama. 1 act
In Book of short plays
Shakespearean interlude. 1 act
In Book of short plays
Their experiment. Comedy. 1 act
In Book of short plays

Lamb, Osborn Rennie
Iberian. Anglo-Greek play... [N.Y. Ames & Rollinson. [c1903]. 119p. 3 scenes
Parting of the ways; a drama in four acts. N.Y. The author. [1910]. 12°. 186p.
Plea of love; a comedy in verse; founded on the life of Catullus... N.Y. Ames & Rollinson. [c1907]. 12°. 55p.
Sailor's sweetheart; a comedy in one act. N.Y. Ames & Rollinson. [1907]. 67p.
String; a drama in one act, being a dramatization... founded on Guy de Maupassant's... "La ficelle". N.Y. A. & R. press. c1907. 12°. 42p. Circumstantial evidence

Lambe, John Lawrence
Beethoven deaf. Historical. 1 act
In Experiments in play-writing
Covered fire. Romantic. 3 acts
In Experiments in play-writing
English gentleman. Romantic. 3 acts
In Experiments in play-writing
House of winds. Tragedy. 1 act
In Experiments in play-writing
King Roderick. Tragedy. 5 acts
In Experiments in play-writing
Rousseau's disciple. Historical. 4 acts
In Experiments in play-writing

Lamkin, Nina B.
America yesterday and to-day. Chicago. Denison. [1917]. 48p.
Gifts we bring; a Christmas pageant for boys and girls, or for grown-ups... Chicago. Denison. [c1917]. 12°. 37p.
Passing of the kings; a pageant... Chicago. Denison. c1920. 8°. 86p.

Landes, Leonard
His partner's wife. Melodrama. 3 acts
In Playwright
Playwright. Comedy. 4 acts
In Playwright

Landor, Walter Savage, 1775-1864
Andrea of Hungary. Historical. 5 acts
In Andrea of Hungary and Giovanna of Naples
Giovanna of Naples. Historical. 5 acts
In Andrea of Hungary and Giovanna of Naples

Lang, Louisa Lockhart
On the hire system. Drawing-room comedy. 1 act
In Blackw 170:591

Langner, Lawrence
Another way out; a play in one act. N.Y. Shay. Washington Square players. 1916. 36p. Comedy
Same in Five one-act comedies
Shay, F. and Loving, P. eds. Fifty contemporary one-act plays
Broken image; a comedy in one act. Washington. Arens. 1918. 32p. 35c
Family exit. Comedy. 1 act
In Five one-act comedies
Licensed. Comedy. 1 act
In Five one-act comedies
Matinata. Comedy. 1 act
In Five one-act comedies
Shay, F. ed. Contemporary one-act plays of 1921
Shay, F. ed. Twenty contemporary one-act plays (American)
Moses; a play of protest and a proposal. N.Y. Boni. 1924. 12°. 187p. $2
Patent applied for; a farcical comedy in one act. Washington. Arens. 1918. 24p. 35c
Pie. Comedy. 1 act
In Five one-act comedies

Larkin, Margaret
El Cristo; a drama in one act. N.Y. French. c1926. 12°. 17p.

Larra, Mariano Jose de, 1809-1837
Quitting business. Comedy. 5 acts
In Poet Lore 35:159

Larric, Jack
Easy mark; a comedy drama in three acts. N.Y. French. c1926. 8°. 112p.

Larrimer, Mary
Attainment. 1 act
In Plays
Cabin call. 1 act
In Plays
Days of Thanksgiving. 1 act
In Plays
Gull of unrest. 1 act
In Plays
In search of the ideal. 1 act
In Plays
Lies. 1 act
In Plays
Mercurial youth. 1 act
In Plays
Motherhood. 1 act
In Plays
Official bondage. 1 act
In Plays
Sacrifice. 1 act
In Plays
Symphony that lives. 1 act
In Plays

Laska, Edward
We've got to have money; comedy in three acts. N.Y. French. c1926. 12°. 161p.

Lathrop, William Addison
Parson of Pure mountain. N.Y. French.
1923. 12°. 28p. 50c
Lavedan, Henri [Leon Émile], 1859-
Afternoon walk. Bourgoisie. 1 act
In Five little dramas
Moses, M. J. ed. Representative
one-act plays by continental au-
thors
Poet Lore 28:403
Age of folly. Comedy. 1 act
In Poet Lore 30:1
Along the quays. Bourgoisie. 1 act
In Five little dramas
Moses, M. J. ed. Representative
one-act plays by continental au-
thors
Poet Lore 28:385
Bad news. Social. 1 act
In Poet Lore 30:19
Distress. Comedy. 1 act
In Poet Lore 30:24
For ever and ever. Romantic. 1 act
In Five little dramas
Moses, M. J. ed. Representative
one-act plays by continental au-
thors
Poet Lore 28:391
Friend. Comedy. 1 act
In Poet Lore 30:15
In wedlock. Comedy. 1 act
In Poet Lore 30:7
Not at home. Bourgoisie. 1 act
In Five little dramas
Moses, M. J. ed. Representative
one-act plays by continental au-
thors
Poet Lore 28:407
Prince d'Aurec. Comedy. 3 acts
In Three modern plays from the
French
Pierce and Matthews, eds. Master-
pieces of modern drama v 2
(abridged)
Sunday on Sunday goes by. War. 1
scene
In Poet Lore 27:185
Their heart. . . Boston. Badger. 1920.
8°. 34p. $1.50. Comedy. 6 pts. Con-
tents. Age of Folly, In wedlock, a
friend, Bad news, Distress, Epilogue
Same in Poet Lore 30:1
Two husbands. Comedy. 1 act
In Poet Lore 19:207
Where shall we go? Domestic. 1 act
In Moses, M. J. ed. Representative
one-act plays by continental au-
thors
Poet Lore 28:397
Lavelle, Alice Elizabeth
Puppets of fate; a drama in four acts and
a prologue. Boston. Gorham. [1914].
63p. Napoleon
Lawler, Lillian Beatrice, 1898
In the kitchen of the king. Juvenile. 1
act
In Jagendorf, M. A. ed. One-act plays
for young folks

Lawrence, Charles Edward, 1870-
Hour of Prospero; a play in one act.
London. Gowans. 1927. 24°. 36p.
Shakespeare. 1 act
Same in 19 Cent 92:685
Message of Lazarus. Biblical. 1 act
In 19 Cent 91:170
Spikenard. Religious. 1 act
In Cornhill magazine 50:413
Lawrence, David Herbert, 1885-
David, a play. N.Y. Knopf. 1926. 12°.
130p. $2. Biblical. 16 scenes
Touch and go; a play in three acts. N.Y.
Seltzer. 1920. 12°. 103p. $1.25. La-
bor
Widowing of Mrs. Holroyd; a drama in
three acts. Boston. Little. 1914. 12°.
93p. $1 Tragedy
Laws, Anna Cantrell
Twice-told tale. Social. 1 act
In Drama 8:400
Lawson, James, 1799-1880
Liddesdale; or The border chief; a trag-
edy. [with other dramas]. Yonkers.
1874. 312p. 5 acts
Same in Liddesdale [with other dramas]
Giordano; a tragedy. N.Y. Clayton.
1832. 102p. 5 acts
Maiden's oath. Domestic. 5 acts
In Liddesdale. . . [with other dramas]
Lawson, John Howard
Processional; a jazz symphony of Ameri-
can life, in four acts. . . N.Y. Seltzer.
1925. 12°. 218p.
Roger Bloomer; a play in three acts. . .
N.Y. Seltzer. 1923. 12°. 225p.
Character
Lay, Elizabeth A.
Trista. Folk-superstition. 1 act
In Koch, F. H. ed. Carolina folk-plays
ser 2
When witches ride. Carolina Folk su-
perstition. 1 act
In Koch, F. H. ed. Carolina folk-plays
ser 1
Layton, Frank George (Stephen Andrew,
pseud.), 1872-
Philip's wife. A play in three acts.
London. A. C. Fifield. 1914. 12°. 64p.
Problem
Politicians; a comedy in four acts. Lon-
don. Sidgwick. 1913. 12°. 102p. 4 acts
Prophet; a play. London. Daniel. 1922.
12°. 91p. Religious. 6 scenes
Lea, Gordon
Reconstruction; a play in three acts
(November-December, 1918). . .
Cambridge. Heffer. 1919. 84p. 12°.
Social
Leacock, Stephen Butler, 1869-, and Hast-
ings, Basil Macdonald, 1881-
"Q"; a farce. N.Y. French. 1915. 23p.
1 act
Learsi, Rufus
Triumph of instinct. Comedy. 1 act
In Drama 14:26 O '23

Leavitt, John McDowell, 1824-
Afranius.   Tragedy. 5 acts
In Afranius, and Idumean
Idumean.   Tragedy. 5 acts
In Afranius, and Idumean

Le Brun, Pierre Antoine, 1785-1873
Marie Stuart; a tragedy in five acts. . .
N.Y. Darcie and Corbyn. 1855. 4°.
47p.

Ledoux, Louis Vernon, 1880-
Story of Eleusis; a lyrical drama.   N.Y.
Macmillan. 1916. 96p. 5 acts
Yzdra; a tragedy in three acts.   N.Y.
Putnam. 1909. 174p.

Lee, Francis
Historic drama; The glorious revolution,
5th November, 1688. . . London. The
author. [181—?]. 8°. 68p. 5 acts

Lee, H. Fletcher
Robert Burns; a play in three acts.
London. Sands. 1926. 12°. 144p.

Lee, Harry Sheridan, 1874-
Little poor man (Il poverello); the life
drama of St. Francis of Assisi; play
in four acts.   N.Y. Dutton. 1920. 12°.
169p. $2

Lee, Henry Washington, 1815-1874
El Cid Campeador; an opera in three acts
and eight scenes. Chicago. Ritzmann.
[c1917]. 34p.

Lee, Jennette Barbour, 1860-
Symphony play; a play in four acts.
N.Y. Scribner. 1916. 12°. 192p. $1.
Symphony

Lee, Mary Elizabeth
Black death; or, Ta-ün.   Plague. 1 act
In Poet Lore 28:691
Honor cross.   War. 1 act
In Poet Lore 27:702

Lee, Vernon, pseud.   *See* Paget, Violet

Leeman, Jean
Martyr, a tragedy of Belgium. . . San
Francisco. Belgian women's war re-
lief committee. 1916. 12°. 80p. 5 acts

Le Gallienne, Richard, 1866-
Orestes; a tragedy.   N.Y. Kennerley.
1910. 50p. 1 act

Legouvé, Ernest, 1807-1903
By the cradle.   Monologue
In Bellevue Dramatic Club: Plays for
private acting
Foresight; or, My daughter's dowry.   A
comedy in two acts. . . Adapted. N.Y.
Happy Hours. [1879]. 12°. 28p.
Medea.   A tragedy in three acts. . .
London. Lacy. [1861?]. 12°. 27p.

Legouvé, Ernest, joint author.   *See* Scribe,
A. E. and Legouvé, E. *also* Goubaux,
P. P. and Legouvé, E.

Legouvé; Ernest and Merimeé, P.
Love flower. [Flower of Tlencen].   A
comedietta in one act. N.Y.   Happy
hours. [1879].
Same in Bellevue Dramatic Club: Plays
for private acting

Leighton, William, jr., 1833-1911
At the court of King Ediom; a drama.
Phila. Lippincott. 1878. 158p.   North-
umbria. 5 acts
Sons of Godwin; a tragedy.   Phila. Lip-
pincott. 1877. 188p.   Historical. 5 acts

**Leinster, Murray, and Jenkins, George B.
jr.**
Beautiful thing.   Romantic. 1 act
In Smart Set 59 no 3:89

Leisher, Frank H.
Blue bird (realistic comedy in five acts).
Los Angeles. Calif. Press of Gem
pub. co. [c1926]. 12°. 75p.

Leland, Robert De Camp
Purple youth; a play in one act.   Boston.
Four Seas. 1918. 37p.   Farce

Lemaître, Jules, 1853-1914
Pardon (Forgiveness).   Comedy. 3 acts
In Three modern plays from the French
Poet Lore 24:209

Lemon, Mark, 1809-1870
Ancestress! or, The doom of Barostein;
a melodrama in two acts.   London.
Duncombe. n.d. 16°. 30p.
Demon gift, or, Visions of the future; a
melodrama in two acts. . . London.
Pattie. n.d. 12°. 24p.
Domestic economy.   A farce in one act.
London. Lacy. n.d. 12°. 17p. (Lacy's
acting edition of plays v. 2. no. 21)
Doom of Barostein!   *See* Lemon, M.
Ancestress! or, The doom of Baro-
stein!
Familiar friend.   A farce in one act. . .
London. Pattie. [1840]. 12°. 23p.
Gentleman in black, a burletta in one
act. . . London. Pattie. [1840?]. 12°.
20p.
Gwynneth Vaughan.   A drama . . . in
two acts. . . Boston. Spencer. [1857?].
12°. 28p.
Honesty the best policy: a drama in two
acts. . . London. Davidson. n.d. 12°.
40p.
Same in Cumberland's   British   theatre
v 45 no 5
House of ladies; a burletta in one act. . .
London. Pattie. n.d. 12°. 22p.
Ins and outs; a burletta, in two acts. . .
London. Pattie. n.d. 12°. 30p.
Jack in the Green; or, Hints on etiquette.
An original farce, in the vulgar
tongue.   London. Lacy. n.d. 12°.
19p. 1 act (Lacy's acting edition of
plays. v. 2 no. 24)
Ladies' club, a comic drama in two acts.
London. Lacy, n.d. 12°. 32p. (Lacy's
acting edition of plays. v. 13. no. 189)
Mind your own business.   An original
drama . . . in three acts. . . London.
A comedy. [184—?]. 12°. 59p.
Pupil of Da Vinci! au operatic burletta, in
one act. . . London. Pattie. n.d. 12°.
24p.
Three secrets, a drama in two acts (partly taken from the French). . . London. Pattie. n.d. 12°. 24p.

Lennep, Jakob van, 1802-1868
Village on the frontier.   Farce. 1 act
In Werner, A. tr.   Humour of Holland

Lengyel, Menyhért
Typhoon; a play in four acts. . . N.Y.
Siegel. 1913. 12°. 120p. 75c.   Japanese

Lenormand, Henri René, 1882-
Failures. (Les ratés.)   Life's controlling
forces. 14 scenes
In Failures
Time is a dream.   Psychological. 6
scenes
In Failures

Leonard, William Ellery Channing, 1876
Glory of the morning; a play in one act.
Madison, Wis. Wisconsin dram. soc.
1912. 12°. 53p.   Indian
Same in Dickinson, T. H. ed.   Wisconsin plays
Red Bird; a drama of Wisconsin history
in four acts.   N.Y. Huebsch. 1923.
12°. 149p.

Lent, Evangeline M.
Rag doll.   Episode. 1 act
In Smart Set 28 no 1:100

Le Sar.   *See* Péladan, J.

Leslie, Noel
Cult of content.   Boston. Four seas.
1921. 12°. 31p.   Allegory. 1 act
For king and country.   World war. 1 act
In Three plays
War fly.   World war. 1 act
In Three plays
Waste.   Tragedy. 1 act
In Three plays

Levick, Milnes
Wings of the mesh.   Colloquy. 1 act
In Smart Set 59 no 3:95

Levinger, Elma Ehrlich
Child of the frontier; a one-act play about
Abraham Lincoln. N.Y. Appleton.
1925. 12°. 19p.
Jephthah's daughter; a biblical drama in
one act.   Prize play; Drama League
of America. N.Y. French. c1921. 8°.
36p.
Same in Cohen, H. L. ed.   Junior
play book
Thomas, C. S. ed.   Atlantic
book of junior plays

Levy, Ben W.
This woman business, a play in three
acts.   London. Benn. 1925. 12°. 118p.

**Lewes, George Henry (Slingsby Lawrence,
pseud.), 1817-1878**
Game of speculation.   A comedy in three
acts. London. Lacy. n.d. 12°. 45p.
(Lacy's acting edition of plays. v. 5.
no. 61).   Adaptation of Balzac's
Mercadet
Lawyers.   A comedy. In three acts. . .
London. Lacy. [1853?]. 12°. 28p.
(Lacy's acting edition of plays. v. 11.
no. 154)
Noble heart.   A play. In three acts.
Boston. Spencer. [1858?]. 12°. 39p.
Tragedy

Sunshine through the clouds.   A drama
in one act. Adapted from "La joie
fait peur" by Madame de Girardin.
London. Lacy. n.d. 12°. 29p. (Lacy's
acting edition of plays. v. 15. no. 218)

**Lewes, George Henry, 1817-1878, and
Mathews, Charles**
Strange history.   A dramatic tale, in
eight chapters. London. Lacy. n.d.
12°. 64p. (Lacy's acting edition of
plays. v. 10. no. 139)

Lewis, Mrs. Estelle A. B., 1824-1880
King's stratagem; or, The pearl of Po-
land; a tragedy in five acts. London.
Trübner. 1874. 12°. 94p.
Sappho; a tragedy in five acts.   London.
Trüber. 1875. 12°. 132p.

Lewis, Leopold
Bells.   Adapted from Erckmann-Chatrian.   The Polish Jew.   *See* Erckmann-Chatrian

Lewisohn, Ludwig, 1882-
Garden.   Modern morality. 1 act
In International (NY) 10:44
Lie.   Ideas. 1 act
In Smart Set 41 no 4:137
New England fable.   Allegory. 1 act
In International (NY) 11:117

**Lewisohn, Mrs. Mary Arnold (Mrs. Ludwig
Lewisohn).**   *See* Crocker, Bosworth,
pseud.

Lewinson, Minna
Every student.   Allegory. 1 act
In English J 3:109

Leycester, Laura, joint author.   *See* Weaver, Wyn, and Leycester, Laura

Lille, Herbert
As like as two peas.   A farce in one act.
London. Lacy. n.d. 12°. 28p. (Lacy's
acting edition of plays v. 15. no. 225)

Linares Rivas, Manuel, 1866-
Claws
In Turrell, C. A. ed.   Contemporary
Spanish dramatists

Lincoln, J. W., and Montgomery, J.
Rather rough on Robert; a farce.   Phila.
Penn. pub. co. 1915. 17p. 1 act

Lincoln, Joseph Crosby, 1870
Managers; a comedy of Cape Cod.   N.Y.
Appleton. 12°. 1925. 34p.
Same in Nicholson, K. ed.   Appleton
book of short plays

Lindau, Norman C.
Cooks and cardinals.   Comedy. 1 act
In Plays of the 47 workshop ser 2

Lindau, Paul, 1839-
Maria and Magdalena, a play in four acts.
Adapted . . . by L. J. Holleinus. N.Y.
DeWitt. [1874]. 44p.

Lindsey, William, 1858-
Red wine of Roussillon; a play in four
acts. Boston. Houghton. 1915. 174p.
Tragedy

Linsky, Fannie Barnell
Hut, a comedy in three acts.   Boston.
Baker. 1922. 12°. 54p.

Lipkind, Goodwin
What happened on Chamika; a play for adults in one act. N.Y. Bloch. 1924. 40p.

Lippmann, Julie Mathilde, 1864-
Martha-by-the-day; a comedy in three acts. N.Y. French. 1919. 118p. 60c

Litchfield, Grace Denio, 1849-
Nun of Kent; a drama in five acts. N.Y. Putnams. 1911. 12°. 125p. Historical
Same in Collected poems
Vita; a drama. Boston. Badger. 1904. 12°. 56p. Allegory
Same in Collected poems
Women as advocates. Comedy. 1 act
In Ind 55:1627

Locke, Edward, 1869-
Case of Becky. Dual personality. 1 act
In Hearst's 22:113

Lodge, George Cabot, 1873-1909
Cain; a drama. Boston. Houghton. 1904. 12°. 155p. Biblical. 3 acts
Same in Poems and dramas v 1
Herakles. Boston. Houghton. 1908. 12°. 272p. Mythological. 12 scenes
Same in Poems and dramas v 2

Lodovici, Cesare
Idiot. Problem. 3 acts
In Poet Lore 30:317
L'Eroica. Death. 1 act
In Poet Lore 34:159
Woman, of no one. Emotional. 3 acts
In Poet Lore 32:159

Loevins, Frederick (F. Thaumazo, pseud)., 1870-
Warrant; a play in five acts. Brooklyn. 1909. 64p. Melodrama

Logan, Algernon Sydney
Messalina; a tragedy in five act. Phila. Lippincott. 1890. 147p.
Saul; a dramatic poem. Phila. Lippincott. 1883. 80p. Biblical. 3 acts

Lomas, B. A.
Crown for a song. Comedy. 4 acts
In Romantic dramas
Miriam. Tragedy. 5 acts
In Romantic dramas

London, Jack, 1876-1916
Acorn-planter; a California forest play. . . N.Y. Macmillan. 1916. 84p. 12°. 2 acts
Scorn of women; in three acts. N.Y. Macmillan. 1906. 12°. 256p. Comedy
Theft; a play in four acts. N.Y. Macmillan. 1910. 12°. 272p. Melodrama

Long, Lily Augusta
Radisson the voyageur; a verse drama in four acts. N.Y. Holt. 1914. 114p. Historical

Longfellow, Henry Wadsworth, 1807-1882
Dramatized scenes from Longfellow's "Hiawatha" by Valerie Wyngate. London. Kegan Paul. French. 1916. 95p.
Spanish student. 3 acts
In Poetical works
　　Bates, A. ed. Drama 19:195

Lonsdale, Frederick, 1881-
Aren't we all? a comedy. N.Y. Brentano's. 1924. 90p. $1 4 acts
Last of Mrs. Cheyney. Comedy. 3 acts
In Mantle, B. ed. Best plays of 1925-26 (abridged)

Loos, Anita, joint author. *See* Emerson, John and Loos, Anita

Lopez, Sabatino, 1867-
Sparrow. War. 1 act
In Goldberg, I. tr. Plays of the Italian theatre

Lord, Alice E.
Vision's quest. A drama in five acts. . . Baltimore. Cushing. 1899. 123p. Christopher Columbus

Lord, Daniel A.
Dreamer awakes. A mission crusade masque. As produced at St. Louis and at Cincinnati with the title: "God wills it!" Revised by the author and John J. Fehring. ⌊Cincinnati, Ohio⌋. Catholic Students' Mission Crusade. ⌊c1923.⌋ 8°. 35p. 4 episodes
Flame leaps up. Religious. 1 act
In Six one-act plays
God wills it! *See* Lord, D. A. Dreamer awakes
Mistress Castlemaine's Christmas dinner. Christmas. 1 act
In Six one-act plays
Pageant of peace; a Christmas masque. . . Chicago. Loyola Univ. press. c1924. 8°. 46p.
Rainbow gold. Fantasy. 1 act
In Six one-act plays
Road to Connaught. Catholic and Protestant. 1 act
In Six one-act plays
　　Cath W 110:382
Sight of the blind. Religious. 1 act
In Six one-act plays
Sir Folly. Religious. 1 act
In Six one-act plays

Lord, Katharine
Buried treasure. Pirate. 1 act
In Plays for school and camp
Day Will Shakespeare went to Kenilworth. Pageant. N.Y. 1916. 18p. $1
Same in Little playbook
Greatest gift. Christmas. 1 act
In Little playbook
Honorable miss. Japanese. 1 act
In Plays for school and camp
June magic. Garden. 1 act
In Little playbook
Katjen's garden. Juvenile. 1 act
In Little playbook
Kris Kringle makes a flight. Christmas. 3 acts
In Plays for school and camp
Minister's dream. Thanksgiving fantasy. 1 act
In Little playbook
　　Delin 80:358 N '12
Pied piper. Juvenile. 7 scenes
In Plays for school and camp
Raven man. Indian. 1 act
In Plays for school and camp

Three bears. Juvenile. 2 scenes
In Plays for school and camp
Yuletide rose. Christmas miracle. 1 act
In Little playbook

Lord, William Wilberforce, 1819-1907
André: a tragedy in five acts. N.Y.
Scribner. 1856. 8°. 138p.

Lorde, Andre de, 1870-
At the telephone
In One-act plays for stage and study
ser 2
Woman who was acquitted. Melodrama
In Moses, M. J. ed. Representative
one-act plays by continental au-
thors

**Loti, Pierre, pseud. (Louis Marie Julien
Viaud), 1850-1923, and Gautier, Judith**
Daughter of heaven... N.Y. Duffield.
1912. 12°. 192p. China. 4 acts

**Louden, Thomas, and Thomas, Albert Ells-
worth, 1872-**
Champion; a comedy in three acts. N.Y.
French. 1922. 12°. 75c

Lounsbery, Grace Constant
Delilah; a drama in three acts. N.Y.
Lane. 1904. 16°. 128p. Biblical

Louys, Pierre, 1870-
At the setting of the sun. 1 act
In Loving, P. ed. Ten minute plays
Crepuscule. Romantic. 1 act
In International (NY) 6:102

Lovell, Caroline
War woman. American revolution. 1 act
In Drama 13:23

Lovett, Robert Morss, 1870-
Cowards. Unmarried mother. 4 acts
In Drama 7:330

Loving, Pierre, 1893-
Autumn. Growing old. 1 act
In Drama 13:61
Drift-flake; a Christmas fairy play for
grown-ups and children. Chicago.
Bookfellows. 1921. 16°. 25p. 1 act
Indian summer. Marriage. 1 act
In Loving, P. ed. Ten minute plays
Stick-up; a rough-neck fantasy. Cincin-
nati, Stewart Kidd. 1922. 12°. 24p. 50c
1 act
Same in Shay, F. ed. Treasury of
plays for men

Lowe, Lucy
Bitterly reviled. World war. 1 act
In Poet Lore 33:300

Loy, M.
Pamperers. Satire. 1 act
In Dial 69:65

Loyson, Paul Hyacynthe, 1873-
Apostle, (L'apôtre). a modern tragedy in
three acts. Garden City. Doubleday.
1916. 120p. 75c

Lucas, Daniel Bedinger, 1836-1909
Blockade runner. *See* Lucas, D. B.
Maid of Northumberland; or, The
blockade runner
Hildebrand. Civil war. 3 acts
In Dramatic works
Kate McDonald. Civil war. 5 acts
In Dramatic works

Maid of Northumberland; or, The block-
ade runner. Civil war. 5 acts
In Dramatic works
Maid of Northumberland

Lucas, Edward Verrall, 1868-
Same star, a comedy in three acts. Lon-
din. Methuen. ₁1924₁. 12°. 113p.

Ludwig, Otto, 1813-1865
Forest warden (Hereditary forestry.)
(Erb förster); a tragedy. in five acts
In German classics 9:280
Poet Lore 24:129

Lummis, Eliza O'Brien
Dear Saint Elizabeth; a tragic romance
of true history, in four acts and eight
scenes with musical accompaniment.
Boston. Badger. 1912. 12°. 68p.

Lunarcharski, Anotoli Vasilievich, 1876-
Faust and the city. Government. 11
scenes
In Three plays
Magi. Fantasy. 13 scenes
In Three plays
Vasila the wise. Fairy. 14 scenes
In Three plays

Lunn, Joseph, 1784-1863
Family jars. A farce. In one act. London. Lacy. n.d. 12°. 24p. (Lacy's acting edition of plays. v. 14 no. 210)
Hide and seek: a petite opera, in two
acts. . London. Cumberland. n.d.
12°. 36p.
Same in Cumberland's British theatre
v 12 no 2
Lofty projects; or, Arts in an attic: a
farce, in two acts. . London. Cumberland. n.d. 12°. 29p.
Same in Cumberland's British theatre
v 10 no 5
Dolby's British theatre v 11 no
4
Management; or, The prompter puzzled.
A comic interlude, in one act. . London. Cumberland. n.d. 12°. 32p.
Same in Cumberland's British theatre
v 38 no 5
Roses and thorns; or, Two houses under
one roof. . London. Cumberland.
n.d. 12°. 57p. Comedy. 3 acts
Same in Cumberland's British theatre
v 12 no 5
Shepherd of Derwent Vale; a drama, in
two acts. . London. Cumberland.
n.d. 12°. 42p.
Same in Cumberland's British theatre
v 10 no 2

Lyall, Eric
Dream gate. Pierrot. 1 act
In Two Pierrot plays
Dream stone. Pierrot. 1 act
In Two Pierrot plays
Poetry R 6:217

Lydston, George Frank, 1858-
Blood of the fathers; a play in four acts.
Chicago. Riverton. 1912. 241p. Here-
dity

Lynch, Thomas J.
Rose of Ettrick Vale; or, The bridal of the borders. A drama, in two acts. London. Lacy. n.d. 12°. 32p. (Lacy's acting edition of plays. v. 7 no. 92)

Lyttelton, Edith Sophy, 1865-
Christmas morality play. London. Methuen. 1908. 29p. 1 act
Dame Julian's window. Morality. 1 act
In 19 Cent 73:435
Peter's chance, a play in three acts. London. Duckworth. 1912. 74p. Melodrama
Thumbscrew. Sweatshop. 1 act
In 19 Cent 69:938

Macauley, Elizabeth Wright
Marmion, a melo-drama founded upon Walter Scott's celebrated poem of Marmion. . . Cork. O'Connor. 1811. 45p. 8°. 3 acts

McBride, H. Elliott
On the brink; or, The reclaimed husband. A temperance drama in two acts. Chicago. Denison. 1878. 34p.
Two drams of brandy. A temperance play in one act. N.Y. Roorbach. [1881]. 12p.
Under the curse. A temperance drama in one act. N.Y. Roorbach. [1881]. 8p.

McCauley, Clarice Vallette
Conflict; a drama in one act. Baltimore. Norman-Remington. 1921. 12°. 48p. 75c. Social
Same in Shay, F. ed. Contemporary one-act plays of 1921
Shay, F, ed. Treasury of plays for women
Shay, F. ed. Twenty contemporary one-act plays (American)
Vagabond plays ser 1
Dinah, queen of the Berbers; a religious drama in three acts. . . N.Y. Abington. c1920. 8°. 39p.
Queen's hour. A springtime morality play in one act
In Drama 10:295
Seeker; a pageant drama. . . N.Y. Abingdon. c1920. 8°. 78p.
Sons of strangers; a masque for friendly souls. . . N.Y. Council for home missions. c1924. 8°. 23p.

McChesney, Dora Greenwell, 1871-1912
Outside the gate. Christmas. 1 act
In Fortn 80:1035

McClellan, Walter
Delta wife; a play. N.Y. Appleton. 1924. 22p. 1 act

McClure, T.
End of Pierrot. Fantasy. 1 act
In Smart Set 50:76 D '16

McClure, Victor, joint author. *See* Woodhouse, V. H. and McClure, Victor

McCourt, Edna Wahlert
Jill's way. Comedy. 3 scenes
In Seven Arts 1:328
Truth. Maternity. 1 act
In Seven Arts 1:475

McCracken, J. L. N.
Earning a living; a comedy in five acts. . . Pudney & Russell. 1849. 8°. 63p.

McDermott, John Francis
Queen comes to pray. Vengeance. 1 act
In Poet Lore 36:450

MacDonald, George, 1824-1905
Within and without. New York. Scribner. 1872. 12°. 292p. Religious. 5 acts

MacDonald, Malcolm
Guatemozin. A drama. Phila. Lippincott. 1878. 12°. 1911. Mexico. 5 acts

MacDonald, Zillah K.
Circumventin' Saandy. Comedy. 1 act
In Drama 16:29
Feather fisher. War. 1 act
In Touchstone 4:120
Light along the rails. Subway. 1 act
In Touchstone 3:229
Long box. Death. 1 act
In Drama 14:180
Markheim; a dramatization from the story of R. L. Stevenson. 1 act
In Morningside plays

McEvoy, Charles, 1879-
All that matters; a play in four acts. London. St. Martin's press. [1911]. 16°. 241p. Romantic
David Ballard; a play in three acts. Boston. Baker. c1925. 12°. 103p. Romantic
Gentlemen of the road; a play in one act. London. Bullen. 1907. 12°. 20p. Comedy
His helpmate; a play in one act. London. Bullen. 1907. 12°. 27p. Tragedy
Likes of her; a play in three acts. N.Y. French. 1923. 12°. 49p. Comedy
Lucifer. A play in one act. London. Bullen. 1907. 12°. 15p. Tragedy
Three Barrows; a play in four acts. London. Benn. 1924. 12°. 107p. Character
When the devil was ill; a play in four acts. London. Bullen. 1908. 12°. 101p. Comedy

McEvoy, Joseph Patrick, 1895-
Potters; an American comedy. . . Chicago. Reilly. 1924. 12°. 258p. $1.50 3 acts

McFadden, Elizabeth Apthorp, 1875-
Why the chimes rang; a play in one act. . . N.Y. French. c1915. 12°. 56p. Christmas

McFadden, Elizabeth Apthorp, 1875-, and Crimmins, Agnes Louise
Man without a country; a play in a prologue, three acts and an epilogue. . . N.Y. French. 1918. 80p. 25c. Patriotism

MacFarlane, Anne
Slippers. Fantasy. 1 act
In Poet Lore 32:425

Macfie, Ronald Campbell, 1867-
Valdimar; a poetic drama. London. Macdonald. 1912. 12°. 119p. Tragedy. 5 acts

McGee, Thomas D'Arcy, 1825-1868
Roman martyr. *See* McGee, T. G. Sebastian, or The Roman martyr
Sebastian; or, The Roman martyr. A drama founded on Cardinal Wiseman's celebrated tale of "Fabiola". N.Y. Sadlier. 1801. 12°. 52p. Tragedy. 4 acts

Macgowan, J., tr.
Beauty; a Chinese drama. Tr. from the original. . . London. Morrice. 1911. 81p. 12°.

McGuire, W. A.
Six cylinder love. Comedy. 3 acts
In Mantle, B. ed. Best plays of 1921-22 (condensed)

McHugh, Augustin
Officer 666; a melodramatic farce in three acts. N.Y. French. c1917. 12°. 105p. 50c

MacInnis, Charles Pattison
Immortality. Fantasy. 1 act
In Drama 16:258

Macintire, Elizabeth, and Clements, Colin
Ivory tower. Fantasy. 1 act
In Poet Lore 35:127

Mack, Willard
Kick in; a play in four acts. N.Y. French. c1925. 12°. 93p. Melodrama

Mackall, Lawton, 1888-, and Bellamy, Francis Rufus, 1886-
Scrambled eggs; a barnyard fantasy. Cincinnati. Stewart Kidd. c1922. 12°. 29p. 1 act

Mackay, Constance D'Arcy
Abraham Lincoln. Patriotic pageant. 1 act
In Patriotic plays and pageants for young people
Ashes of roses. 18th century. 1 act
In Beau of Bath and other one-act plays
Beau of Bath. 18th century. 1 act
In Beau of Bath and other one-act plays
Benjamin Franklin episode. Patriotic pageant. 2 scenes
In Patriotic plays and pageants for young people
Law, F. H. ed. Modern plays, short and long
Boston tea party. Patriotic pageant. 1 act
In Patriotic plays and pageants for young people
Woman's H C 38:13 Je '11
Brewing of brains. Lincolnshire folk play. 1 act
In Silver thread and other folk plays
Christmas guest. Juvenile. 1 act
In House of the heart and other plays for children
Thomas, C. S. ed. Atlantic book of junior plays
Counsel retained. 18th cenutry. 1 act
In Beau of Bath and other one-act plays
Dame Greel o'Portland town. Historical. 1 act
In Plays of the pioneers

Daniel Boone, patriot. Pageant. 1 act
In Patriotic plays and pageants for young people
Elf child. Fairy. 1 act
In House of the heart and other plays for children
Enchanted garden. Fairy. 1 act
In House of the heart and other plays for children
Ferry farm episode. Pageant. 1 act
In Patriotic plays and pageants for young people
Festival of Pomona. (Masque of Pomona) Spring. 1 act
In Forest princess and other masques Drama 5:161
Foam maiden. Celtic folk-play. 1 act
In Silver thread and other folk plays
Forest princess. Masque. 1 act
In Forest princess and other masques
Forest spring. Italian folk play. 1 act
In Silver thread and other folk plays
Fountain of youth. Fantasy. 1 act
In Plays of the pioneers
Franklin. N.Y. Holt. 1922. 197p. 12°. Historical. 4 acts
George Washington's fortune. Historical. 1 act
In Patriotic plays and pageants for young people
Gift of time. Christmas masque. 1 act
In Forest princess and other masques
Gooseherd and the goblin. Fairy. 1 act
In House of the heart and other plays for children
Gretna Green. 18th century. 1 act
In Beau of Bath and other one-act plays
Hawthorne pageant. (In witchcraft days. 1 act Merrymount. 1 act)
In Patriotic plays and pageants for young people
House of the heart. Symbolic. 1 act
In House of the heart and other plays for children
In witchcraft days. Hawthorne pageant. 1 act
In Patriotic plays and pageants for young people
Little pilgrim's progress. Allegory. 1 act
In House of the heart and other plays for children
St N 37:60
Masque of Christmas. 1 act
In Forest princess and other masques
Masque of conservation. 1 act
In Forest princess and other masques
Masque of Pomona. *See* Mackay, C. D'A. Festival of Pomona
May-day. Fantasy. 1 act
In Plays of the pioneers
Memorial day pageant, arranged for communities and schools. N.Y. Harper. c1916. 12°. 29p. 1 act
Merrymount. (Hawthorne pageant). 1 act
In Patriotic plays and pageants for young people
Nimble-Wit and Fingerkins. Fairy. 1 act
In House of the heart and other plays for children

Mackay, C. D'A.—*Continued.*

On Christmas eve.   Juvenile. 1 act
  In House of the heart and other plays
      for children
Pageant of hours.   Allegory. 1 act
  In House of the heart and other plays
      for children
Pageant of patriots.   Series of one-act
    plays
  In Patriotic plays and pageants for
      young people
Pageant of Schenectady in celebration of
    the two hundredth and fiftieth anni-
    versary of the founding of Schenec-
    tady. . . Schenectady Gazette press.
    1912. 12°. 64p.
Passing of Hiawatha.   Indian. 1 act
  In Plays of the pioneers
Pilgrim interlude.   Pageant of patriots.
    1 act
  In Patriotic plays and pageants for
      young people
Pioneers.   Interlude. 1 act
  In Plays of the pioneers
Prince of court painters.   18th century. 1
    act
  In Beau of Bath and other one-act plays
Princess and the pixies.   Fairy. 1 act
  In House of the heart and other plays
      for children
Princess Pocahontas.   Indian. 1 act
  In Patriotic plays and pageants for
      young people
Siegfried.   German folk-play. 1 act
  In Silver thread and other folk plays
Silver lining.   18th century. 1 act
  In Beau of Bath and other one-act plays
      Smith, A. M. ed.   Short plays by
        representative authors
      Smith, M. M. ed.   Short plays of
        various types
Silver thread.   Cornish folk play. 3 acts
  In Silver thread and other folk plays
      for young people
      Moses, M. J. ed.   Treasury of plays
        for children
Snow witch.   Russian folk play. 1 act
  In Silver thread and other folk plays
      for young people
Sun goddess.   Masque of old Japan. 1
    act
  In Forest princess and other masques
Three wishes. (Trois souhaits).   French
    folk play.   1 act
  In Silver thread and other folk plays
      for young people
Troll magic.   Norwegian folk play. 1 act
  In Silver thread and other folk plays
      for young people
Vanishing race.   Indian. 1 act
  In Plays of the pioneers

Mackay, Isabel E.

Last cache.   1 act
  In One-act plays for stage and study
      ser 3
Second lie.   Malice. 1 act
  In Massey, V. ed.   Canadian plays
      from Hart House theatre v 1

Weak-end.   Farce. 3 act
  In Third book of short plays
When two's not company.   Farce. 1 act
  In Third book of short plays
Woman's a woman for a' that.   Com-
    edy. 1 act
  In Short plays

Mackaye, Mrs. Mary Kieth

Pride and prejudice; a play founded on
    Jane Austen's novel.   N.Y. Duffield.
    1905. 168p. 4 acts

Mackaye, Percy Wallace, 1875-

Anti-matrimony; a satirical comedy.
    N.Y. Stokes. [1910]. 12°. 160p. 4 acts
Antick.   Wayside sketch. 1 act
  In Yankee fantasies
Caliban by the yellow sands.   Garden
    City, N.Y. Doubleday. 1916. 12°. 223p.
    $1.25.   Shakespeare centenary. 3 acts
Canterbury pilgrims, a comedy.   N.Y.
    Macmillan. 1903. 8°. 210p. 3 acts
Cat-boat.   Fantasy for music. 1 act
  In Yankee fantasies
Chuck.   Orchard fantasy. 1 act
  In Yankee fantasies
Evergreen tree.   N.Y. Appleton. 1917.
    8°. 81p. $2.   Christmas masque. 12
    actions
Fenris the wolf; a tragedy.   N.Y. Mac-
    millan. 1905. 12°. 150p. 4 acts
Garland to Sylvia; a dramatic reverie with
    a prologue.   N.Y. Macmillan. 1910.
    12°. 177p. 4 acts
George Washington a dramatic action
    with a prologue. . . N.Y. Knopf.
    [1920]. 8°. 191p.   Historical. 3 acts
  Same in Nicholson, K. ed.   Appleton
      book of short plays
Gettysburg.   Historical. 1 act
  In Yankee fantasies
      Cohen, H. L. ed.   One-act plays
        by modern authors
      Leonard, S. E. ed.   Atlantic book
        of modern plays
Glass of truth.   *See* Mackay, P. W.
    Scarecrow; or The glass of truth
Immigrants; a lyric drama. . . N.Y.
    Huebsch. 1915. 8°. 138p. $1.   Sociolo-
    gical. 4 acts
Kinfolk of Robin Hood.   Legendary. 4
    acts
  In Thomas, C. S. ed.   Atlantic book
      of junior plays
Mater; an American study in comedy.
    N.Y. Macmillan. 1908. 8°. 163p. 3 acts
  Same in Poems and plays v 2
Napoleon crossing the Rockies.   Ken-
    tucky mountains. 1 act
  In One-act plays for stage and study
      ser 3
      Cent 107:867
Pilgrim and the Book. N.Y. Amer. Bible
    Soc. [c1920]. 8°. 23p.   Religious. 1 act
Rip Van Winkle; folk-opera in three
    acts. . . N.Y. Knopf. 1919. 8°. 86p.
Roll call; a masque of the Red Cross.
    Washington.   Nat.   headquarters,
    Amer. Red Cross. 1918. 8°. 65p. 10 ac-
    tions

Saint Louis; a civic masque.   Garden
City, N.Y. Doubleday. 1914. 12°. 99p.
$1. 2 pts.
Sam Average.   Silhouette. 1 act
In Yankee fantasies
Lewis, B. R. ed.   Contemporary
one-act plays
Mayorga, M. G. ed. Representative
one-act plays
Sanctuary;   a   bird   masque. . . N.Y.
Stokes. [1914]. 12°. 71p. $1. 10 actions
Sappho and Phaon; a tragedy. . . N.Y.
Macmillan. 1907. 12°. 225p. 3 acts
Same in Poems and plays v 2
Scarecrow; or, The glass of truth, a trag-
edy of the ludicrous.   N.Y. Macmil-
lan. 1908. 8°. 179p. 4 acts
Same in Poems and plays v 2
Moses, M. J. ed.   Representa-
tive American dramas—na-
tional and local
Pierce and Matthews, eds.
Masterpieces   of   modern
drama v 1 (abridged)
Quinn, A. H. ed. Representa-
tive American plays 1767-
1923
Sinbad, the sailor . . . Boston. Houghton.
[c1917]. 12°. 146p. $1.25.   Fantasy. 3
acts
This fine pretty world; a comedy of the
Kentucky mountains. N.Y. Macmillan.
1924. 12°. 194p. $1.50. 3 acts
Thousand years ago; a romance of the
Orient. . . Garden City, N.Y. Doubleday. 1914. 12°. 130p.   Comedy. 4 acts
To-morrow; a play in three acts.   N.Y.
Stokes. 1912. 12°. 176p.   Social. 3
acts
Washington, the man who made us; a
ballad play. . . N.Y. Knopf. 1919. 12°.
313p.   Historical. 3 acts
Will of song; a dramatic service of community singing. . . N.Y. Boni. 1919.
12°. 60p.
**Mackaye, Percy, and Stevens, Thomas
Wood**
Book of words of the pageant and
masque of Saint Louis. The words of
the pageant by T. W. Stevens; the
words of the masque by Percy Mackaye. 2nd ed. Pub. by authority of the
Book committee. Saint Louis Pageant
and Drama Association. 1914. 8°. 103p.
MacKaye, Steele, 1842-
Hazel Kirke; a domestic drama in four
acts.   N.Y. c1908. 95p.   Comedy
Same in Quinn, A. H. ed.   Representative American plays, 1767-1923
Mackenzie, Agnes Mure
Half-loaf; a comedy of chance and error
in three acts.   London. Heinemann.
[1925]. 12°. 159p.
Mackenzie, J. B.
Thayendanegea;   an   historico-military
drama.   Toronto. Briggs. 1898. 12°.
179p. 5 acts

Mackereth, James Allan
Death of Cleopatra; a dramatic poem. . .
N.Y. Longmans. 1920. 12°. 95p.
McKinney, Isabel, 1879-
Mud.   Love. 1 act
In Poet Lore 30:417
McKnight, Robert Wilson
Pigeon.   World war. 3 acts
In Poet Lore 30:579
McLaren, James Henry, 1864-
Joan of Arc, a drama recital.   San Fran-
cisco. Elder. 1917. 12°. 74p.   His-
torical. 2 pts.
McLaughlin, Robert H.
Eternal Magdalene; a modern play in
three acts.   N.Y. French. 1918. 100p.
50c
MacLean, Arthur
Knight of the piney woods; a one-act
play.   N.Y. Appleton. 1925. 12°. 20p.
McLellan, C. M. S., 1865-
Leah Kleschna; a play in five acts. . .
N.Y. French. c1920. 12°. 93p.   Prob-
lem
**Macleod, Fiona, pseud.   *See* Sharp, Wil-
liam**
MacManus, Seumas
Woman of seven sorrows.   Dublin. Gill.
1905. 12°. 45p.   Allegory. 1 act
**MacManus, Seumas, and O'Concannon,
Thomas**
Hard-hearted man; in English and Irish.
Mount Charles, Co. Donegal. O'Mol-
loy. 1906. 93p.   Comedy. 3 scenes
MacMillan, Dougald, 1897-
Off Nags Head; or, The bell buoy; a
tragedy of the North Carolina coast.
1 act
In Koch, F. H. ed.   Carolina folk-plays
ser 1
Law, F. H. ed.   Modern plays, short
and long
MacMillan, Mary Louise
Apocryphal episode.   Homeric. 1 act
In Third book of short plays
At the church door.   Fantasy. 1 act
In More short plays
Dress rehearsal of Hamlet.   Comedy. 1
act
In More short plays
Dryad.   Fantasy. 1 act
In More short plays
Entr'acte.   Comedy. 1 act
In Short plays
Fan and two candlesticks.   Cincinnati.
Stewart Kidd. c1922. 12°. 23p.   Val-
entine. 1 act
Same in Short plays
Futurists.   Farce. 1 act
In Short plays
Gate of wishes.   Hallowe'en. 1 act
In Short plays
Poet Lore 22:469
His second girl.   Comedy. 1 act
In More short plays
Honey.   Childhood. 4 acts
In More short plays
In heaven.   Farce. 1 act
In Third book of short plays

MacMillan, M. L.—*Continued.*
In Mendelesia.   Comedy. 2 pts.
In More short plays
Luck?   Farce. 4 acts
In Short plays
Modern masque.   Burlesque. 1 act
In Short plays
Pan or Pierrot; a masque.   N.Y. Apple-
ton. 1924. 12°. 47p. 1 act
Peter Donnelly.   Comedy. 1 act
In Third book of short plays
Pioneers.   Indian. 5 acts
In More short plays
      Law, F. H. ed.   Modern plays,
      short and long
Ring.   Comedy. 1 act
In Short plays
Rose.   Romantic. 1 act
In Short plays
Shadowed star. . . Cincinnati.   Consum-
er's League. 1908. 12°. 24p.   Christ-
mas. 1 act
Same in Short plays
      Dickinson, A. D. ed.   Drama
      Shay, F. and Loving, P. eds.
      Fifty contemporary one-act
      plays
      Smith, A. M. ed.   Short plays
      by representative authors
Standing moving.   Comedy. 1 act
In Third book of short plays
Storm.   Farce. 1 act
In Third book of short plays

McMullen, Joseph Carl, 1882-
Good evening, Clarice!   A farce comedy
of domestic life in three acts. Boston.
Baker. 12°. 1922. 148p.

Mary made some marmalade; a play in
three acts.   Boston. Baker. 1925.
83p.

Macnaghten, T. C.
Old maid's birthday; a retrospect.   Episode of a morning. London. Matthews. 1911. 16°. 50p. 1 act

Macnamara, Margaret
Light gray or dark?   A play in one act.
London. C. W. Daniel. 1920. 12°. 26p.
Social
Love-fibs; a rustic comedy in one act.
London. Daniel. 1920. 12°. 32p.
Mrs. Hodges; a comedy of rural politics
in two scenes. London. C. W. Daniel.
1920. 12°. 45p.
Mrs. Jupp obliges; a small domestic com-
edy in one act.   London. Labour
pub. co. [1925]. p. 7-21
Witch; a drama in one act, for five wom-
en-players and a lightning-expert.
London. Daniel. 1920. 12°. 25p.
Yesterday; an historical comedy in four
acts. . . London. Benn. 1926. 12°.
128p.

McNeile, Herman Cyril (Sapper, pseud.),
1888-, and Du Maurier, Sir Gerald, 1873-
Bulldog Drummond; a play in four acts
from the novel by "Sapper".   N.Y.
French. c1925. 12°. 83p.

McNulty, Edward
Lord mayor.   A Dublin comedy in three
acts. London. Maunsel. 1917. 50p.
Mrs. Mulligan's millions; a comedy in
three acts. . . Dublin. Maunsel. 1918.
12°. 58p.

MacNutt, Francis A.
Balboa.   Historical
In Three plays
Victorious duchess
In Three plays
Xilona
In Three plays

McNutt, Patterson, joint author. *See* Morrison, Anne, and McNutt, P.

MacQueen, Lawrence I.
Sacrifice.   Religion. 1 act
In Drama 11:216

Macready, William, d. 1829
Irishman in London: a farce, in two
acts. . . London.   Cumberland. [c
1821]. 12°. 31p. (Cumberland's British
theatre. no. 148)

MacSwiney, Terence Joseph, 1879-1920
Revolutionist; a play in five acts.   Dublin. 1914. 136p.   Ireland

Madách, Imre, 1823-1864
Tragedy of man; dramatic poem. . . N.Y.
Arcadia press. [1908]. 8°. 224p. 14
scenes

Maddox, John Medex, 1789-1861
A. S. S.   A farce. In one act. London.
Lacy. n.d. 12°. 20p. (Lacy's acting
edition of plays. v. 10 no. 148)
Chesterfield Thinskin, a farce in one
act. . . London. Lacy. n.d. 12°. 24p.
(Lacy's acting edition of plays. v. 12
no. 167)
Curious case.   A comic drama in two
acts. London. Lacy. n.d. 12°. 34p.
(Lacy's acting edition of plays. v. 12
no. 171)
Fast train!   High pressure!! Express!!!
A short trip. London. Lacy. n.d. 12°.
20p. (Lacy's acting edition of plays.
v. 10 no. 149). 1 act
First night.   A comic drama in one act.
London. Lacy. n.d. 12°. 30p. (Lacy's
acting edition of plays. v. 13 no. 188)
King and deserter.   A drama . . . In two
acts. Boston. Spencer. [1857?]. 12°.
22p.

Maeterlinck, Maurice, 1862-
Aglaivaine and Selysette, a drama in five
acts.   N.Y. Dodd. 1911. 12°. 165p.
$1.25.   Tragedy. 5 acts
Same in Intruder, etc
      Poet Lore 14:11
Alladine and Palomides.   Tragedy. 5 acts
In Miracle of Saint Antony, etc
      Pélléas & Mélisande (Dodd)
      Plays (Green tree library) ser 2
      Three little dramas
      Three plays
      Poet Lore 7:280
Ardiane and Barbe Blene.   Comedy. 3
acts
In Plays (Dodd)
      Sister Beatrice

Betrothal; a sequel to the Blue Bird; a fairy play in five acts. . . N.Y. Dodd. 1918. 222p.

Blind (Sightless) (Les aveugles). Symbolic. 1 act
In Blind, the intruder
  Plays (Green tree library) ser 1
  Sightless
  Moses, M. J. ed. Representative one-act plays by continental authors
  Poet Lore 5:159, 218, 273

Blue bird (L'Oiseau bleu); a fairy play in five acts. . . N.Y. Dodd. 1910. 12°. 241p. $2. (A later edition contains alterations and additions. 6 acts)

Burgomaster of Stilemonde; a play in three acts. . . N.Y. Dodd. 1918. 12°. 148p. World war

Cloud that lifted. Emotional. 3 acts
In Cloud that lifted, and The power of the dead

Death of Tintagiles (La morte de Tintagiles). London: Gowans. Tragedy. 5 acts
In Death of Tintagiles
  Intruder, etc
  Plays (Green tree library) ser 1
  Three little dramas
  Three plays
  Bates, A. ed. Drama 21:253
  Shay, F. ed. Treasury of plays for women

Home. *See* Maeterlinck, M. Interior

Interior (Home; Interior). N.Y. Stokes. Death. 1 act
In Miracle of Saint Antony, etc
  Three little dramas
  Three plays
  Shay, F. ed. Twenty-five short plays, international
  New Rev 11:543

Intruder (L'Intruse). Death. 1 act
In Blind
  Intruder, etc
  Miracle of Saint Antony etc
  Plays (Green tree lib.) ser 1
  Princess Maleine (2)
  Cohen, H. L. ed. One-act plays by modern authors
  Shay, F. and Loving, P. eds. Fifty contemporary one act plays

Joyzelle. . . Symbolic. 5 acts
In Joyzelle. . . Monna Vanna
  Poet Lore 16:1

Mary Magdalene; a play in three acts. . . N.Y. Dodd. 1910. 12°. 179p. $1.20. Biblical

Miracle of Saint Antony. 1 act
In Miracle of Saint Antony, etc

Monna Vanna; a play in three acts. . . N.Y. Harper. 1903. 12°. 143p. Love
In Joyzelle, etc
  Moses, M. J. ed. Representative continental dramas
  Pierce and Matthews, eds. Masterpieces of modern drama v 2 (abridged)
  Poet Lore 15 no 3:1

Pélleas and Mélisande; a drama in five acts. . . N.Y. Crowell. [1894]. 12°. 135p. Tragedy
Same in Miracle of Saint Antony, etc
  Pelleas and Mélisande, etc
  Plays (Green tree lib.) ser 2
  Dickinson, ed. Chief contemporary dramatists
  Pierce and Matthews, ed. Masterpieces of modern drama v 2 (abridged)
  Poet Lore 6:413

Power of the dead. Dream. 4 acts
In Cloud that lifted, and The power of the dead

Princess Maleine: New York. Dodd. 1913. 12°. 208p. $1.25. Tragedy. 5 acts
In Plays (Dodd)
  Princess Maleine, and The intruder

Seven princesses. Symbolic. 1 act
In Intruder
  Plays (Green tree lib.) ser 1
  Poet Lore 6:29

Sightless. . . London. Scott. *See* Maeterlinck, M. Blind

Sister Beatrice. Miracle. 3 acts
In Plays (Dodd)
  Sister Beatrice, etc
  Anglo-Saxon R 6:90

Magnus, Julian
Alfred the Great. Historical
In Woloski, a tragedy, and poems
Trumped suit. (from Les deux timides by M. E. Labiche). Comedy. 1 act
In Matthews, B. ed. Comedies for amateur acting
Woloski. Tragedy
In Woloski, a tragedy, and poems

Magnus, Julian, and Bunner, Henry Cuyler
Bad case. Comedy. 1 act
In Matthews, J. B. ed. Comedies for amateur acting

Mahoney, James
Mourner. Fantasy. 1 act
In Plays of the 47 workshops ser 4

Mair, Charles, 1838-
Tecumseh, a drama, and Canadian poems. . . . Toronto. Radisson Society of Canada. 1926. 8°. 470p.

Major, Montgomery
Spadassin! a comically fantastic tragedy. 1 act
In Poet Lore 36:265

Makee, Walt
Scratch race; a comedy in one act. Boston. Baker. 1900. 13p.
Same in Plays with a punch

Makazawa, Ken
Persimmon thief. Comedy. 1 act
In Drama 16:97

Malleson, Miles, 1888-
Artist (from Chekhov). Social. 1 act
In Young heaven, & three other plays
Black 'ell—a war play in one act. N.Y. Shay. 1917. 12°. 22p.
Same in 'D' Company, and Black 'ell
Conflict, a comedy in three acts. London. Benn. 1925. 12°. 121p.

Malleson, M.—*Continued.*

'D' Company. World war. 1 act
In 'D' Company, and Black 'ell

Fanatics, a comedy in three acts. . . London. Benn. 1924. 12°. 123p.

Little white thought; a fantastic scrap. London. Hendersons. [1916]. 12°. 24p. 1 act

Man of ideas. Farce. 1 act
In Young heaven, & three other plays

Maurice's own idea; a little dream play. Boston. Baker internat. play bureau. c1924. 12°. 29p. 1 act

Merrileon Wise, a play in three acts. London. Benn. 1926. 12°. 102p.

Michael (Tolstoi's What men live by adapted for the stage). Allegory. 1 act
In Young heaven, & three other plays

Paddy pools. Fairy. 3 scenes
In Cohen, H. L. ed. Junior play book

Young heaven. Dream. 1 act
In Young heaven, & three other plays

Youth; a play in three acts. London. Henderson. 1916. 12°. 81p. Romantic

Mallock, George Reston

Arabella. [London]. Swift. 1912. 127p. Romantic. 3 acts

Maloney, William Brown

Knave's move; a play in one act. Washington. Commission on training camp activities. Dept. of dramatic activities among the soldiers. 1918. War Dept. service. no. 9

Maltby, Henry Francis, 1880-

Three birds; a comedy in three acts. London. "The Stage" play pub. bureau. 1924. 127p.

Rotters; a tale of a respectable family in three acts. London. "Stage" play pub. bureau. 1922. 118p.

Manco, Silverio

Juan Moreira. Argentine. 2 acts
In Bierstadt, E. H. ed. Three plays of the Argentine

Manley, William F.

Crowsnest. Sea. 1 act
In Plays of the 47 workshops ser 3

Mann, Arthur Sitgreaves

Prince Ivo of Bohemia; a romantic tragedy in five acts. N.Y. Grafton press. c1906. 84p.

Mann, H. A.

His chance. 1 act
In Plays with a punch

Mann, Hugh

Bound. Social. 3 acts
In Bound and Free

Free. Social. 4 acts
In Bound and Free

New lights; a drama in four acts. Boston. Badger. 1904. 51p. New Memnists. 4 acts

Manners, John Hartley, 1870-

All clear. Zeppelins. 1 act
In Three plays

Day of dupes. Allegory. 1 act
In Happiness and other plays

Girl in waiting; a comedy in four acts. Boston. Baker. 1922. 12°. 112p. 75c

God my faith. Pacifism. 1 act
In Three plays

God's outcast. World war. 1 act
In Three plays

Hanging and wiving. 1 act
In One act plays for stage and study ser 2

Happiness. Psychological. 1 act
In Happiness and other plays

Harp of life; a play. N.Y. Doran. 1921. 12°. 206p. $1.25. Problem. 3 acts

House next door; a comedy in three acts . . . suggested by "Die von Hochsattel." by Stein and Heller. Boston. Baker. 1912. 12°. 157p.

Just as well; a modern romance. Comedy in one act. London. French. 1912. 12°. 18p.
Same in Happiness and other plays

Ministers of grace. Domestic. 1 act
In Smart Set no 1:129

National anthem; a drama. N.Y. Doran. 1922. 12°. 203p. $1.25 Younger generation. 4 acts

Out there; a dramatic composition in three parts. . . N.Y. Dodd. 1918. 12°. 182p. World war

Peg o' my heart, a comedy. N.Y. French. c1918. 12°. 140p. 3 acts

Queen's messenger. N.Y. French. 1900. 12°. 26p. Comedy. 1 act

Woman intervenes; a play in one act. N.Y. French. c1913. 12°. 22p. Comedy
Same in Smart Set 36 no 4:113

Wooing of Eve; an entirely artificial and sentimental comedy in three acts. N.Y. French. 1920. 12°. 108p. 60c

Wreckage; a drama in three acts. N.Y. Dodd. 1916. 12°. 224p. $1. Drug habit

Mansfield, Beatrice Cameron, 1868-

Quality of mercy; a play in one act. N.Y. French. c1925. 12°. 16p.

Manzaburo

Suma Genji. Japanese. 1 act
In Drama 5 no 18:219

Mapes, Victor, 1870-

Amethyst; a comedy in four acts. N.Y. French. c1925. 12°. 140p.

Captive, a play in four acts. N.Y. French. c1918

Flower of Yeddo; a Japanese comedy, in one act, in verse. N.Y. French. c1906. 12°. 27p.
Same in One act plays for stage and study ser 1

Hottentot; a comedy in three acts. N.Y. French. 1923. 12°. 78p. Horse

Lassoo; a comedy in four acts. N.Y. French. c1918. 12°. 139p.

Maquairie, Arthur, 1874-

Days of the Magnificent; a drama of old Florence in blank verse and prose. London. Bickers. 1911. 155p. Historical. 3 acts

Fioralisa; a romantic drama in three acts and a pageant. London. Bickers. 1910. 102p.

Happy kingdom; a comedy in three acts, written in blank verse and prose. 1913. 150p.

Marble, Annie Russell, 1864-
Standish of Standish, by Jane G. Austin. Dramatized by Annie Russell Marble. Boston. Houghton. 1919. 86p. 12°. Colonial America. 3 acts

Marcin, Max, 1879-, and Atwell, Roy
Here comes the bride; comedy in three acts. N.Y. French. 1921. 12°. 132p. 60c

Marcin, Max, and Cohan, M.
House of glass; a drama in four acts. . . N.Y. Cohan & Harris. 1916. 12°. 128p. Melodrama

Marcy, Mrs Edna (Tobias), 1877-
Free union; a one-act play of "free love". Chicago. Kerr. 12°. 64p.

Marenco, Carlo
Pia dei Tolomei; a tragedy in five acts. Tr. by T. Williams. London. Francis. 1856. 12°. 97p.

Markievicz, Casimir Dunin, 1874-
Memory of the dead; a romantic drama of 1898, in three acts. Dublin. Tower Press. 1910. 12°. 80p. 3 acts

Markey, J.
Black sheep. War. 2 scenes
In Canad M 48:345

Marks, Jeannette Augustus, 1875-
Deacon's hat. Comedy. 1 act
In Three Welsh plays
Cohen, H. L. ed. One-act plays by modern authors
Lewis, B. R. ed. Contemporary one-act plays
Schafer, B. L. ed. Book of one-act plays
Happy thought. Farce. 1 act
In International (NY) 6:36
Merry, merry cuckoo. Character. 1 act
In Three Welsh plays
Cohen, H. L. ed. One-act plays by modern authors
Mayorga, M. ed. Representative one-act plays
Smith, A. M. ed. Short plays by representative authors
Dramatist (Easton Pa) 4:291
Sun chaser; a play in four acts. Cincinnati. Stewart Kidd. 1922. 12°. 119p.
Wasted lives
Welsh honeymoon. Comedy. 1 act
In Three Welsh plays
Cohen, H. L. ed. One-act plays by modern authors
Smart Set 38:135 no 3

Marks, Mrs. Lionel. *See* Peabody, Josephine Preston

Marquis, Don, 1878-
Dark hours; five scenes from a history. Garden City, N.Y. Doubleday. 1924. 12°. 155p. Biblical

Old soak; a comedy in three acts. N.Y. French. c1926. 12°. 94p.
Same in Mantle, B. ed. Best plays of 1922-23 (condensed)

Out of the sea; a play in four acts. Garden City. Doubleday. 1927. 12°. 133p. Cornwall.

Words and thoughts; a play in one act. N.Y. Appleton. 1924. 12°. 27p. Psychological
Same in Carter and other people

Marquina, Eduardo, 1879-
When the roses bloom again
In Turrell, C. A. tr. Contemporary Spanish dramatists

Marsh, Arnold
Ulstermen; a play in three acts. London. Maunsel. 1921. 12°. 56p. Ireland

Marsh, Elizabeth N.
Body and soul. Boston. Cornhill. 1920. 12°. 88p. $1.25. Supernatural. 8 scenes

Kaiser's reasons; a drama in three acts with interludes. N.Y. Duffield. 1918. 8°. 172p. $1.50. World war

Marshall, Abigail
Accomplice. Psychological. 1 act
In Shay, F. ed. Treasury of plays for men
Shay, F. ed. Twenty-five short plays, international

Marshall, Robert
His excellency the governor; a farcical romance, in three acts. London. Heinemann. 1904. 12°. 151p.

Marston, John Westland, 1819-1890
Anne Blake. A play in five acts. Boston. Spencer. [1856?]. 12°. 35p.
Same in Dramatic and poetical works v 1

Borough politics. Comedy. 2 acts
In Dramatic and poetical works v 2
Donna Diana. Comedy. 3 acts
In Dramatic and poetical works v 2
Hard struggle; a domestic drama in one act. . . Boston. Spencer. [1857?]. 12°. 21p.
Same in Dramatic and poetical works v 2
Life for life. Romantic. 4 acts
In Dramatic and poetical works v 1
Life's ransom; a play in five acts. Boston. Spencer. [1856?]. 12°. 44p.
Same in Dramatic and poetical works v 1
Marie de Méranie. Tragedy. 5 acts
In Dramatic and poetical works v 1
Patrician's daughter, a tragedy in five acts. . . Boston. Spencer. 1856. 12°. 39p.
Same in Dramatic and poetical works v 1
Pure gold. Romantic. 4 acts
In Dramatic and poetical works v 2

Marston, J. W.—*Continued.*
Strathmore.   Tragedy. 4 acts
    In Dramatic and poetical works v 1
Wife's portrait.   Domestic. 2 acts
    In Dramatic and poetical works v 2

Martel de Janville, Sibylle (Gyp. pseud)
Little blue guinea-hen.   Comedy. 13
    scenes
    In Poet Lore 30:60

Marthold, Jules de, 1847-
On the eve of the wedding.   Monologue.
    1 act
    In Bellevue Dramatic Club: plays for
    private acting

Martin, Allan Langdon
"Smilin' through"; a romantic comedy in
    three acts.   N.Y. French. c1924. 100p.

**Martin, George Madden, and Kennedy,
Harriet L.**
Lion's mouth.   N.Y. Appleton. 1 act

Martin, Helen, 1868-, and Howe, Frank
Mennonite maid; a character study in
    three acts. . . N.Y. Longmans. 1924.
    12°. 75c

Martin, John Joseph, 1893-
Charlie Barringer.   Poor farm. 1 act
    In Theatre Arts M 5:242
Wife of Usher's Well.   Supernatural. 1
    act
    In Poet Lore 30:94
Yniard; a tragedy of the fantastic.   Cin-
    cinnati. Stewart Kidd. 1923. 12°. 54p.

Martin, William Frank
Sir Harry Vane; a drama in five acts.
    Boston. Roxburgh Pub. Co. [1907].
    8°. 263p.   Historical

Martinez Sierra, Gregorio, 1881-
Cradle song,   Comedy. 2 acts
    In Plays v 1
        Poet Lore 28:625
Kingdom of God.   Social. 3 acts
    In Plays v 2
Love magic.   Comedy. 1 act
    In Plays v 1
        Drama 7:40
Lover.   Comedy. 1 act
    In Plays v 1
        Moses, M. J. ed.   Representative
        one-act plays by continental au-
        thors
        Stratford J 5:33
Madame Pepita.   Comedy. 3 acts
    In Plays v 1
Poor John.   Comedy. 1 act
    In Plays v 1
        Drama 10:172
Romantic young lady.   Comedy. 3 acts
    In Plays v 2
Two shepherds.   Comedy. 2 acts
    In Plays v 2
Wife to a famous man.   Comedy. 2 acts
    In Plays v 2

Martyn, Edward, 1859-
Dream physician; a play in five acts.
    N.Y. Brentano's. 1918. 87p. $1.
Grangecolman, a domestic drama in three
    acts.   Dublin. Maunsel

Heather field, play in three acts.   Lon-
    don. Duckworth. 1917. 12°. 92p.
    Same in Heatherfield and Maeve
Maeve; a psychological drama in two
    acts.   Dublin. Talbot. [1917]. 12°. 51p.
    Same in Heatherfield and Maeve

Masefield, John, 1878-
Berenice. (tr. from Racine).   Tragedy. 5
    acts
    In Esther and Berenice
        Verse plays
Campden wonder.   Tragedy. 3 scenes
    In Poems and plays v 2
        Prose plays
        Tragedy of Nan, and other plays
Esther.   Tragedy. 4 acts
    In Esther and Berenice
        Verse plays
Faithful; a tragedy in three acts.   Lon-
    don. Heinemann. 1915. 12°. 131p.
    Same in Poems and plays v 2
        Prose plays
Good Friday, a dramatic poem.   N.Y.
    Macmillan. 1915. 64p.   Crucifixion. 1
    act
    In Poems and plays v 2
        Philip the king; and other poems. . .
        Verse plays
        Fortn 104:993 D '15
King's daughter; a tragedy in verse.
    N.Y. Macmillan. 1923. 12°. 170p. 5 acts
    Same in Verse plays
Locked chest.   Legendary. 1 act
    In Locked chest, etc
        Poem and two plays
        Poems and plays v 2
        Prose plays
        Smith, A. M. ed.   Short plays by
        representative authors
Melloney Holtspur; or The pangs of
    love. . . Macmillan. N.Y. 1922. 8°.
    151p. $2.50.   Love. 4 acts
    Same in Prose plays
Mrs. Harrison.   Tragedy. 1 act
    In Poems and plays v 2
        Prose plays
        Tragedy of Nan, and other plays
Pangs of love.   *See* Masefield, J. Melloney
    Holtspur; or, The pangs of love
Philip the king.   Historical. 1 act
    In Philip the king, and other poems
        Poems and plays v 2
        Verse plays
Pompey.   *See* Masefield, J.   Tragedy of
    Pompey
Sweeps of ninety-eight.   Comedy. 1 act
    In Locked chest, etc
        Poem, and two plays
        Poems and plays v 2
        Prose plays
Tragedy of Nan.   N.Y. Macmillan. 1921.
    12°. 127p. 1 act
    Same in Poems and plays v 2
        Prose plays
        Tragedy of Nan, and other
        plays

Tragedy of Pompey the Great.   Boston.
    Little. 1910. 12°. 95p. 3 acts
    In Poems and plays v 2
        Prose plays
        Tragedy of Pompey
    Moses, M. J. ed.   Representative
        British dramas
        Plays of today v2

Mason, Alfred Edward Woodley, 1865-
    Green stockings; a comedy in three acts.
        N.Y. French. c1914. 12°. 117p.
    Witness for the defense; a play in four
        acts.   N.Y. French. c1913. 12°. 103p.

**Mason, Mrs. Caroline Atherton (Caroline
    Briggs)**
    One a day.   1 act
    In Morningside plays

Massey, Edward
    Plots and playwrights, a comedy.   Bos-
        ton. Little. 1917. 12°. 99p. $1. 2 pts.
    Same in Baker, G. P. ed.   Modern
        American plays

Masters, Edgar Lee, 1869-
    Bread of idleness; a play in four acts.
        Chicago. Rooks. 1911. 12°. 173p.   So-
        cial
    Locket; a play in three acts. . . Chicago.
        Rooks press. 1910. 12°. 110p.   Social
    Maximilian; a play in five acts.   Boston.
        Badger. 1902. 12°. 154p.   Historical
    Trifler; a play. . . Chicago. Rooks press.
        1908. 12°. 131p.

Mather, Frank Jewett, 1868-
    Ulysses in Ithaca; a drama in four acts.
        N.Y. Holt. c1926. 12°. 133p.

Mathews, Charles James, 1803-1878
    Bachelor's bedroom; or, Two in the morn-
        ing.   A comic scene. . . Boston.
        Spencer. [1856?]. 12°. 15p. 1 act
    Dowager.   A comedy in one act. . . Bos-
        ton. Spencer. [1857?]. 12°. 28p.
    Little Toddlekins.   A comic drama. In
        one act. . . Boston. Spencer. [1857?].
        12°. 26p.

Mathews, Cornelius, 1817-1889
    False pretenses; or, Both sides of good
        society.   A comedy in five acts. New
        York. 1856. 12°. 88p.
    Politicians; a comedy in five acts.   N.Y.
        B. G. Trevett. 1840. 12°. 118p.
    Witchcraft: a tragedy in five acts.   N.Y.
        French. 1852. 99p. 24°.

Mathews, Frances Aymer
    Lady Jane's highwayman.   Comedy. 1
        act
    In Harp W 47:1979

Matthews, Adelaide, joint author.   *See*
    Duncan, William Cary and Matthews,
    Adelaide

Matthews, E. V. B.
    At the eleventh hour.   Melodrama. 1 act
    In Harp B 38:232

Matthews, James Brander, 1852-
    Decision of the court; a comedy.   N.Y.
        Harper. 1893. 12°. 60p. 5 acts
    Edged tools.   A play in four acts.   N.Y.
        French. c1873. 12°. 47p.   Melodrama

Frank Wylde [from Le serment d'Horace,
    by M. H. Mürger].   Comedy. 1 act
    In Matthews, J. B. ed.   Comedies for
        amateur acting
Heredity.   *See* Matthews, J. B. Too
    much Smith; or, Heredity
This picture and that; a comedy.   N.Y.
    Harper. 1894. 12°. 76p. 13 scenes
Too much Smith; or, Heredity.   A phy-
    siological and psychological absurdity
    in one act, by Arthur Penn (pseud).
    Boston. Baker. 1902. 12°. 50p.
    Same in Matthews, J. B.   Comedies
    for amateur acting, under title
    Heredity

Maturin, Edward, 1812-1881
    Viola; a play in four acts.   N.Y. French.
        c1858. 32p. 12°.   Melodrama

Maugham, William Somerset, 1874-
    Caesar's wife, a comedy in three acts.
        London. Heinemann. 1922. 12°. 156p.
    Circle; a comedy in three acts.   N.Y.
        Doran. 1921. 12°. 92p. $1.25
    Same in Dickinson, T. H. ed.   Con-
        temporary plays
            Mantle, B. ed.   Best plays of
            1921-22 (condensed)
    Constant wife; a comedy in three acts.
        N.Y. Doran. [c1926]. 12°. 216p.
    East of Suez; a play in seven scenes
        N.Y. Doran. 1922. 12°. 138p. $1.25.
        Melodrama. 4 acts
    Explorer; a melodrama in four acts.
        Chicago. Dramatic pub. co. [1907]. 12°.
        152p.
    Home and beauty; a farce in three acts.
        London. Heinemann. 1923. 12°. 182p.
    Jack Straw; a farce in three acts.   Lon-
        don. Heinemann. 1912. 12°. 156p.
    Lady Frederick; a comedy in three acts.
        London. Heinemann. 1912. 12°. 163p.
    Land of promise; a comedy in four acts.
        London. Bickers. 1913. 78p.
    Landed gentry; a comedy in four acts.
        Heinemann. 1913. 168p. 4 acts
    Loaves and fishes; a comedy in four acts.
        London. Heinemann. 1924. 12°. 191p.
    Man of honour; a play in four acts.
        London. Chapman. 1903. 8°. 50p.
        Tragedy
    Mrs. Dott; a farce in three acts.   Lon-
        don. Heinemann. 1912. 173p. 3 acts
    Our betters; a comedy in three acts.
        London. Heinemann. 1923. 12°. 210p.
    Same in Dickinson, T. H. ed.   Chief
        contemporary dramatists ser 2
    Penelope; a comedy.   London. Heine-
        mann. 1912. 213p. 3 acts
    Rain.   *See* Colton, J. and Randolph, C.
        Rain
    Smith; a comedy in four acts.   London.
        Heinemann. 1913. 200p. 4 acts
    Tenth man; a tragic comedy.   London.
        Heinemann. 1913. 214p. 3 acts
    Unattainable; a farce in three acts.   Lon-
        don. Heinemann. 1923. 12°. 197p.
    Unknown; a play in three acts.   Lon-
        don. Heinemann. 1920. 12°. 168p.

Maupassant, Guy de, 1850-1893
Comedy of marriage (Household peace) (La paix du mariage).   Comedy. 2 acts
In Life and works of Guy de Maupassant v 14
   Bates, A. ed.   Drama 9:243
Household peace.   *See* Maupassant, G. de.   Comedy
Musotte; or, A critical situation.   Comedy. 3 acts
In Life and works of Guy de Maupassant v 14
Tale of old times.   Romantic. 1 act
In Life and works of Guy de Maupassant v 13

Maury, Anne Fontaine
May day in Canterbury; a Chaucerian festival; celebrated at Wheaton college May 23rd, 1925. Boston. Baker. 1925. 69p.

Maxwell, G.
Morning's work.   Comedy. 1 act
In 19 Cent 52:167

Maxwell, William Babington
Last man in.   London. Gowan's and Gray. 1910. 24°. 37p.
Six men, one woman.   Gowans. London. 1910.

Mayer, Edwin Justus
Firebrand; a comedy in the romantic spirit.   N.Y. Boni. 1925. 12°. 223p. $2.   Cellini. 3 acts
Same in Mantle, B. ed.   Best plays of 1924-25 (abridged)

Mayhew, Henry, 1812-1887
Wandering minstrel: a farce in one act.   Boston. Spencer. [185—?]. 12°. 19p.

Mayhew, Henry, 1812-1887, **and Mayhew, Athol**
Mont Blanc.   A comedy, in three acts.   London. Printed for private circulation. 1874. 8°. 63p. (From Labiche, E. Le voyage de M. Perrichon)

Mayne, Rutherford, pseud.   *See* Waddell, Samuel

Mayo, Margaret (Lillian Clatten). (Mrs. Edgar Selwyn), 1882-
Baby mine; a farce in three acts.   N.Y. French. 1924. 12°. 118p.

Mayo, Paul
Beatrice Eden; a play in three acts.   Boston. Stratford. 1921. 12°. 79p. $2.   Psychological

Mayor, Beatrice
Pleasure garden: a play in four acts.   London. Sidgwick & Jackson. 1925. 12°. 128p.   Comedy
Thirty minutes in a street.   Comedy. 1 act
In Four one-act plays
   Herbert, A. P. and others.   Double demon and other one-act plays

Mazaud, Emile
Holiday.   Friendship. 1 act
In Theatre Arts M 6:33

Mears, Stannard, joint author.   *See* Stange, Hugh Stanislaus, and Mears, Stannard

Meeker, Arthur
Hardy perennials.   Comedy. 1 act
In Drama 13:292

Megrue, Roi Cooper, 1883-
Honors are even; a play in three acts.   Boston. Baker. 1924. 12°. 104p. 75c.   Comedy
Interviewed.   Detective. 1 act
In Smart Set 32 no3:121
Same old thing.   Comedy. 1 act
In One-act plays for stage and study ser 2
Seven chances; a comedy in three acts.   N.Y. French. 1924. 12°. 116p. 75c
Tea for three; an angle on a triangle. . .   Boston. Baker. 1924. 12°. 100p. 75c.   Comedy. 3 acts
Under cover; a melodrama in four acts.   N.Y. French. 1918. 12°. 140p.
Under fire; a play of yesterday, to-day and to-morrow, in three acts.   N.Y. French. c1918. 12°. 165p.   World war

Megrue, Roi Cooper, and Hackett, W. I.
It pays to advertise; a farcical fact in three acts.   N.Y. French. 1917. 12°. 118p.
Same in Moses, M. J. ed.   Representative American dramas, national and local

Meigs, Cornelia, 1884-
Helga and the white peacock, a play in three acts for young people. . . N.Y. Macmillan. 1922. 12°. 81p.   Juvenile
Steadfast princess.   N.Y. Macmillan. 1916. 12°. 87p.   Fairy. 2 acts

Meilhac, Henri, 1831-1897, **and Halévy, Ludovic,** 1834-1908
Bachelor's box (Le petit hôtel).   A comedietta in one act. . . N.Y. Pub. for the trade. 1880. 12°. 18p. (De Witt"s acting plays)
La cigale.   A comedy in three acts. . . Adapted. . . N.Y. Happy hours co. 1879. 12°. 72p.
Frou-Frou.   A play in five acts. . . London. Lacy. n.d. 12°. 36p.   Melodrama
In Pierce and Matthews, eds.   Masterpieces of modern drama v 2 (abridged)
Indian summer (L'été de la Saint Martin); a comedy in one act.   N.Y. French. c1913. 12°. 30p.
Panurge's sheep (Les brebis de Panurge); a comedy in one act. . . N.Y. French. c1915. 12°. 32p.
Widow (La veuve); a comedy in three acts. . . N.Y. DeWitt. 1877. 12°. 29p.

Meilhac, Henri, and Narrey
Cigarette from Java.   Comedy in one act. . . Boston. 1879. 21p.

Meiby, Gustav
King Saint Olaf; a drama in five acts.
Boston. Badger. [c1916]. 12°. 143p. $1.
Historical

Mencken, Harry Louis, 1880-, and Nathan, George Jean, 1882-
Heliogabalus, a buffoonery in three acts.
N.Y. Knopf. 1920. 12°. 183p. $2

Mendel, P., and Guitermann, A.
Journeys end in lovers' meeting. Romantic. 1 act
In Ladies' H J 19:9 F '02

Merimée, Prosper, 1803-1870
African love. Comedy. 1 scene
In Plays of Clara Gazul
Conspirators (Les mécontents). Comedy. 14 scenes
In Novels, tales and letters v 3.
Golden Bk 1:537
Heaven and Hell. Comedy. 1 act
In Plays of Clara Gazul
Ines Mendo; or, Prejudice vanquished.
Comedy. 2 pts.
In Plays of Clara Gazul
Bates, A. ed. Drama 21:105
Prejudice vanguished. *See* Merimée, P.
Ines Mendo; or, Prejudice vanquished
Spaniards in Denmark. Comedy. 3 acts
In Plays of Clara Gazul
Temptation of Saint Antony. *See* Merimée, P. Woman is a devil; or, The temptation of Saint Antony
Woman is a devil; or, The temptation of Saint Antony. Comedy. 3 scenes
In Plays of Clara Gazul

Merimée, Prosper, joint author. *See* Legouvé, E. and Merimée, P.

Merington, Marguerite
Abe Lincoln and little A. D. 1 act
In Holiday plays
Artist mother and child. Mme. Vigée Lebrun and daughter. 1 act
In Picture plays
Bluebeard. Fairy. 1 act
In Fairy tale plays
Captain Letterblair; a comedy in three acts. . . Indianapolis. Bobbs-Merrill. [1906]. 12°. 212p.
Christmas party. 1 act
In Festival plays
Cinderella. Fairy. 1 act
In Fairy tale plays
Cranford; a play in three acts, made from Mrs. Gaskell's famous story. N.Y.
Fox. 1905. 12°. 99p. Comedy
Same in Ladies' H J 18:5, 40, F '01
Daphne; or, The pipes of Arcadia. Three acts of singing nonsense. N.Y.
Century. 1896. 12°. 166p. Fantasy
Dulce et decorum club. Memorial Day.
1 act
In Holiday plays
Father Time and his children. New Year. 1 act
In Festival plays
First flag. Fourth of July. 1 act
In Holiday plays

Gainsborough lady. Duchess of Devonshire. 1 act
In Picture plays
Scrib M 31:65
Gibson play; a two-act comedy based on Mr. Charles Dana Gibson's series of cartoons, "A widow and her friends" originally printed in "Life." N.Y.
Life. [c1901]. 12°. 108p.
In Ladies' H J 18:70, Mr '01
Grouse out of season. Comedy. 1 act
In Harp B 37:1018
Hansel and Gretel. Fairy. 1 act
In More fairy tale plays
Hearts of gold; or, Lovely Mytlie.
Fairy. 1 act
In More fairy tale plays
His mother's face. Une fête champêtre.
1 act
In Picture plays
Last sitting. Mona Lisa. 1 act
In Picture plays
Lovely Mytlie. *See* Merington, M.
Hearts of gold; or, Lovely Mytlie
Lover's knot. Romantic. 1 act
In Harp B 44:384
Millet group. Angelus. 1 act
In Picture plays
Miracle of good St. Valentine. *See* Merington. Tertulla's garden, or, The miracle of good St. Valentine
Pipes of Arcadia. *See* Merington, M.
Daphne; or The pipes of Arcadia
Princess Moss Rose. For every child's birthday. 1 act
In Festival plays
Priscilla, Myles and John. Thanksgiving day. 1 act
In Holiday plays
Puss in boots. Fairy. 2 acts
In More fairy tale plays
Queen and emperor. Queen Louisa. 1 act
In Picture plays
Red Riding Hood. Fairy. 1 act
In Fairy tale plays
Salon Carré fantasy. Young man with a glove. 1 act
In Picture plays
Setness of Abijah. Comedy. 1 act
In Harp B 37:204
Seven sleepers of Ephesus. Easter. 1 act
In Festival plays
Tertulla's garden; or, The Miracle of good St. Valentine. 1 act
In Festival plays
Moses, M. J. Treasury of plays for children
Three bears. Fairy. 1 act
In More fairy tale plays
Vicar of Wakefield; a play founded on Oliver Goldsmith's novel. N.Y.
Duffield. 1909. 12°. 146p. $1.25. Comedy. 5 acts
Washington's birthday pageant. 1 act
In Holiday plays

Merivale, Philip
 Knut at Roeskilde, a tragedy.   Boston.
    Four seas. 1922. 12°. 72p. 2 scenes
 Wind over the water.   Boston.   Four
    Seas. 1920. 12°. 50p. $1.   Poetic. 1
    act
**Merz, Charles Andrew, 1893, and Tuttle,
 Frank Wright**
 Quentin Durward; a dramatic adaptation
    of Sir Walter Scott's novel.   New
    Haven.   University Dramatic Assn.
    1914. 8°. 92p. 3 acts
Metcalfe, John
 Bunderly boggard.   Yorkshire. 3 acts
    In Bunderley boggard and other plays
 Rum an' tea doo.   Yorkshire. 1 act
    In Bunderley boggard and other plays
 T'kal oil.   Yorkshire. 1 act
    In Bunderley boggard and other plays
 T'roadmen.   Yorkshire. 2 acts
    In Bunderley boggard and other plays
Meurice, Paul, 1820-1905
 Fan Fan, the tulip; or, A Soldier's for-
    tune.   A drama (melodrama) in two
    acts.   Adapted. . . London.   Lacy.
    [1864?]. 12°. 38p. (Lacy's acting edi-
    tion of plays. v. 65 no. 974)
Meyer, Adolph E.
 Little fool.   Comedy. 1 act
    In Drama 17:13
Meyer, Mrs. Annie Nathan, 1867-
 Dominant   sex.   N.Y. Brander.   1911.
    112p.   Social. 3 acts
 Dreamer.   N.Y. Broadway pub. co. 1912.
    112p.   Social. 3 acts
 New way; a comedy in three acts.   N.Y.
    French. c1925. 12°. 95p.
Mick, Hettie, L.
 Maid who wouldn't be proper.   Puppet.
    3 acts
    In Law, F. H. ed.   Modern plays,
    short and long
Michelson, Miriam, 1870-
 Bygones.   Comi-tragedy. 1 act
    In Smart Set 51 no 3:81
Mickiewicz, Adam, 1798-1855
 Forefather's eve (prologue and scenes i-
    v).   Translated from the Polish by
    Dorothea   Prall   Radin. . . London.
    School of Slavonic studies in the Uni-
    versity of London. King's College.
    1925. 45p.
Middleton, George, 1880-1916
 Among the lions.   Satire. 1 act
    In Masks
       Smart Set 51 no 2:327
 Back of the ballot; a woman suffrage
    farce in one act.   N.Y. French.
    [c1915]. 12°. 28p.
 Black tie.   Race prejudice. 1 act
    In Possession
 Cheat of pity.   Social. 1 act
    In Tradition
 Circles.   Social. 1 act
    In Possession
 Criminals; a one-act play about marriage.
    N.Y. Huebsch. 1915. 12°. 43p. 50c
 Embers.   Social. 1 act
    In Embers

Failures.   Social. 1 act
    In Embers
 Gargoyle.   Character. 1 act
    In Embers
 Good woman.   Character. 1 act
    In Possession
       Mayorga, M. G. ed.   Representa-
       tive one-act plays
 Groove.   Character. 1 act
    In Possession
 House.   Domestic. 1 act
    In Masks
 In his house.   Social. 1 act
    In Embers
 Jim's beast.   Character. 1 act
    In Masks
 Madonna.   Character. 1 act
    In Embers
 Man masterful.   Character. 1 act
    In Embers
       Forum 42:362
 Masks.   Character. 1 act
    In Masks
 Mothers.   Psychological. 1 act
    In Tradition, etc
 Nowadays; a contemporaneous comedy.
    N.Y. Holt. 1914. 12°. 218p. 8°. $1. 3
    acts
 On bail.   Character. 1 act
    In Tradition
       Smart Set 39 no 3:135
 Possession.   Character. 1 act
    In Possession
 Reason.   Comedy. 1 act
    In Masks
 Road together; a contemporaneous drama
    in four acts.   N.Y. Holt. 1916. 12°.
    204p.   Social
 Their wife.   Social. 1 act
    In Tradition
 Tides.   War. 1 act
    In Masks and other one-act plays
       Leonard, S. A. ed.   Atlantic book
       of modern plays
 Tradition.   Independence of women. 1
    act
    In Tradition
       Lewis, B. R. ed.   Contemporary
       one-act plays
 Unborn.   Social. 1 act
    In Possession
 Waiting.   Social. 1 act
    In Tradition
Middleton, George, and Bolton, Guy
 Adam and Eva.   Comedy. 3 acts
    In Polly with a past, and Adam and
       Eva
 Cave girl; a new American comedy in
    three acts.   N.Y. French. c1925. 121p.
 Polly with a past.   Comedy. 3 acts
    In Polly with a past, and Adam and
       Eva
Middleton, Richard Barham, 1882-1911
 District visitor; with a short sketch of his
    life.   Baltimore. Norman-Remington.
    1924. 12°. 28p.   Death. 1 act
    Same in Eng R 15:497

Millay, Edna St. Vincent, 1892-
Aria da capo; a play in one act. N.Y. Harper. 1920. 12°. 51p. 50c. Pierrot
Same in Provincetown plays (Stewart Kidd 1921)
Three plays
Shay, F. and Loving, P. eds. Fifty contemporary one-act plays
Chapbook 3 no 14
King's henchman. N.Y. Harper. 1927. 12°. 132p. A. S. legendary history. 3 acts
Lamp and the bell; a drama in five acts. N.Y. Harper. 1923. 12°. 38p. $1.50 Poetic
Same in Three plays
Shay, F. ed. Treasury of plays for women
Two slatterns and a king; a moral interlude. Cincinnati. Stewart Kidd. 1921. 12°. 18p. 50c. 1 act
Same in Three plays
Shay, F. ed. Contemporary one-act plays of 1921
Shay, F. ed. Twenty contemporary one-act plays (American)

Miller, Alice Duer, 1874-
What are they fighting for? War. 1 act
In Sat Eve Post 192:10 F 21 '20

Miller, Alice Duer, 1874-, and Milton, Robert
Charm school; a comedy in three acts. N.Y. French. 1922. 12°. 146p. 75c. Girls' school

Miller, Alice Duer, joint author. *See* Thomas, Albert Ellsworth and Duer, Alice Duer

Miller, Chester Gore
Chichuahua. A new and original social drama in four acts. Chicago. Kehm, Fietsch & Wilson. 1891. 16°. 95p.
Father Junipero Serra. A new and original historical drama, in four acts. . . Chicago. Skeen, Baker. 1894. 16°. 160p.

Miller, Joaquin, 1841-1913
Danites in the Sierras. San Fran. Whitaker. 1910. 12°. 62p. 4 acts. Western
Same in '49 and the Danites
Poems v 6
Forty-nine; an idyl drama of the Sierras. San Fran. Whitaker. 1910. 12°. 120p. Western. 4 acts
Same in '49 and the Danites
Poems v 6
Oregon idyl. Western. 4 acts
In Poems v 6
Silent man: a comedy-drama in four acts. N.Y. c1883. 8°. 61p.
Tally-ho. Western. 3 acts
In Poems v 6

Miller, Marion Mills, 1864-
Return of Odysseus; a Greek choric play in two continuous acts, separated by an interlude of visions. Boston. Stratford. 1917. 12°. 119p. $1

Millingen, John Gideon, 1782-1862
Bee-hive; a musical farce, in two acts. . . London. Cumberland. n.d. 12°. 40p.
Same in Cumberland's British theatre v 30 no 4
Ladies at home; or, Gentlemen, we can do without you. A female interlude in one act. London. Lacy. n.d. 12°. 15p. (Lacy's acting edition of plays. v. 10 no. 146)

Millward, Florence M.
Alternative. Tragedy. 1 act
In Four short plays
Henry wakes up. Comedy. 1 act
In Four short plays
Her chance. 1 act
In Three more plays
Irene obliges. Farce. 1 act
In Four short plays
Re-enter Mrs. Roylance. 1 act
In Three more plays
This room is engaged. Farce. 1 act
In Four short plays
When the post has been. 1 act
In Three more plays

Milman, Henry Hart, 1791-1868
Fall of Jerusalem; a dramatic poem. London. Murray. 1820. 167p. 8°. Religious. 1 act
Martyr of Antioch: a dramatic poem. N.Y. Grattan. 1822. 12°. 108p.

Miln, Mrs. Louise Jordan, 1864-
Purple mask; adapted from the play "Le chevalier au masque", of M. M. Paul Armont and Jean Manoussi. . . N.Y. Stokes. [1921]. 12°. 307p.

Milne, Alan Alexander, 1882-
Acting edition of Ariadne; or, Business first; a comedy in three acts. N.Y. French. c1926. 12°. 55p.
Ariadne; or Business first. Satire. 2 acts
In Four plays
Liv Age 324:562 (excerpts)
Artist; a duologue. . . N.Y. French. c1923. 12°. 16p.
In Cohen, H. L. ed. More one-act plays by modern authors
Belinda; an April folly in three acts. N.Y. French. 1922. 12°. 57p. 50c (Acting edition) Comedy
Same in First plays
Boy comes home; a comedy in one act. N.Y. French. c1926. 12°. 22p.
Same in First plays
Marriott, J. W. ed. One-act plays of to-day
Camberley triangle; a comedy in one act. N.Y. French. c1925. 12°. 20p.
Same in Second plays
Dover road; an absurd comedy in three acts. N.Y. French. c1923. 8°. 72p.
Same in Three plays
Mantle, B. ed. Best plays of 1921-22 (condensed)
Great Broxopp. Comedy. 4 acts
In Three plays
Lucky one. Romantic. 3 acts
In First plays

Milne, A. A.—*Continued.*
Make-believe; a children's play in a pro-
logue and three acts. . . N.Y. French.
c1925. 12°. 54p.
Same in Second plays
          Moses, M. J. ed.   Another
          treasury of plays for children
Man in the bowler hat; a terribly exciting
affair.   N.Y. French. c1923. 12°. 21p.
Comedy. 1 act
Same in Ladies' Home Journal one-act
          plays
          One act plays for stage and
          study ser 1
Ladies' H J 40:5 Ap '23
Mr. Pim passes by; a comedy in three
acts.   N.Y. French. 1921. 12°. 67p.
75c (Acting edition).   *Also* Doran.
1922. 12°. 315p. $1.75
Same in Second plays
Portrait of a gentleman in slippers, a
fairy tale in one act.   N.Y. French.
c1926. 12°. 20p.
In Four plays
Red feathers.   Operetta. 1 act
In First plays
Romantic age.   Comedy. 3 acts
In Second plays
Stepmother; a play in one act.   N.Y.
S. French. c1921. 12°. 20p.   Comedy
Same in Second plays
Success; a play in three acts. . . N.Y. &
London. Putnam. 1926. 12°. 219p.
Same in Four plays
To have the honour; a comedy in three
acts. . . N.Y. French. c1925. 12°.
65p.
Same in Four plays
Truth about Blayds.   Comedy. 3 acts
In Three plays
Wurzel-Flummery.   A comedy in one
act. N.Y. French. 1922. 12°. 29p. 50c.
also 2 acts. N.Y. French. 1922
Same in First plays
          Cohen, H. L.   One-act plays
          by modern authors

Milner, Henry M.
Massaniello; or, The dumb girl of Por-
tici; a musical drama in three acts. . .
London. Davidson. n.d. 12°. 40p.
Same in Cumberland's minor theatre v
1 no 9
Mazeppa; or, The wild horse of Tartary;
a romantic drama in three acts.
Dramatized from Lord Byron's poem.
N.Y. French. [18—?]. 52p.
Same in Cumberland's minor theatre v
5 no 2

Milosz, O. W., 1877-
Mephiboseth; mystery in three scenes and
epilogue
In Stratford J 1 Winter 1917:40
Miguel Manara.   Mystery. 6 scenes
In Poet Lore 30:224

Milton, Ernest, 1892-
Christopher Marlowe; a play in five acts
with a prologue by Walter de la
Mare. London. Constable. 1924. 226p.

Mirbeau, O.
Scruples.   Comedy. 1 act
In Loving, P. ed.   Ten minute plays

Mitchell, Langdon Elwyn, 1862-
In the season.   A one act comedy. Lon-
don. French. [18—]. 12°. 17p.
Kreutzer sonata; a play in four acts;
adapted from the Yiddish of Jacob
Gordin.   N.Y. H. G. Fiske. 1907.
12°. 78p.
New York idea; a comedy in four acts.
Boston. Baker. 1908. 12°. 175p.
In Pierce and Matthews, eds.   Mas-
          terpieces of modern drama v 1
          (abridged)
          Quinn, A. H. ed.   Representative
          American plays 1767-1923
Picture book of Becky Sharpe; a play in
four acts; founded on Thackeray's
'Vanity Fair'. . . N.Y. Stone. [1899].
fol. 30p.

Mitchell, Silas Weir, 1829-1914
Barabbas.   Biblical. 1 act
In Complete poems
          Book news monthly 32:361
Cup of youth.   Poetic. 3 scenes
In Complete poems
Francis Drake; a tragedy of the sea. . .
Boston. Houghton. 1893. 8°. 60p.
Historical. 1 act
Same in Complete poems
Francis Villon.   Historical. 1 act
In Complete poems
Masque.   Poetic. 1 act
In Masque and other poems
Medal.   Poetic. 1 act
In Complete poems
Miser, a masque.   1 act
In Complete poems
Philip Vernon; a tale in prose and verse.
N.Y. Century. 1895. 12°. 55p.   His-
torical. 5 pts.
Same in Complete poems
Violin.   Poetic. 1 act
In Complete poems
Wager.   Poetic. 1 act
In Complete poems
          Wager and other poems
Wind and sea.   Poetic. 2 scenes
In Complete poems

Mitford, Mary Russell, 1786-1855
Alice.   Romantic. 1 scene
In Dramatic works v 2
Captive.   Romantic. 1 scene
In Dramatic works v 2
Charles I.   An historical tragedy in five
acts. London. Duncombe. 1834. 8°.
80p.
Same in Dramatic works v 1
          Works
Cunigunda's vow.   Romantic. 1 scene
In Dramatic works v 2
Emily.   Romantic. 1 scene
In Dramatic works v 2
Fair Rosamond.   Tragedy. 1 scene
In Dramatic works v 2
Fawn.   Romantic. 1 scene
In Dramatic works v 2

Foscaria; a tragedy in five acts. .
London. Cumberland. n.d. 12°. 559p.
(Cumberland's British theatre. v. 38
no. 4)
Same in Dramatic works v 1
    Works
    Foscari and Julian
Gaston de Blonderville. Romantic. 3
acts
In Dramatic works v 2
Henry Talbot. Tragedy. 1 scene
In Dramatic works v 2
Inez de Castro. Tragedy. 5 acts
In Dramatic works v 2
Julian; a tragedy in five acts. N.Y.
Gilley. 1823. 93p. 12°.
Same in Dramatic works v 1
    Works
    Foscari and Julian
Masque of the seasons. Tragedy. 1
scene
In Dramatic works v 2
Otto of Wittelsbach. Tragedy. 5 acts
In Dramatic works v 2
Painter's daughter. Romantic. 1 scene
In Dramatic works v 2
Rienzi; a tragedy in five acts. . . London.
Davidson. n.d. 12°. 66p.
Same in Dramatic works v 1
    Works
Sadak and Kalasrade. Romantic opera. 2
acts
In Dramatic works v 2
Siege. Romantic. 1 scene
In Dramatic works v 2
Wedding ring. Romantic. 1 scene
In Dramatic works v 2

Mixon, Ada
Peace on earth. Fantasy for children. 1
act
In Poet Lore 28:65

Mobert, Helen L.
Singing pool. East Indian life. 1 act
In Poet Lore 30:275

Moeller, Philip, 1880-
Helena's husband. Historical comedy. 1
act
In Five somewhat historical plays
    Shay, F. and Loving, P. eds. Fifty
    contemporary one-act plays
    Washington Square plays
Little supper. Comedy of 'La Grande
Maitresse'. 1 act
In Five somewhat historical plays
Madame Sand. Comedy. N.Y. Knopf.
1917. 12°. 167p. 3 acts
Molière; a romantic play in three acts.
N.Y. Knopf. 1919. 12°. 237p.
Pokey; or The beautiful legend of the
amorous Indian. Comedy. 1 act
In Five somewhat historical plays
Roadhouse in Arden. Whimsicality. 1 act
In Five somewhat historical plays
Sisters of Susannah. Biblical farce. 1
act
In Five somewhat historical plays

Sophie; a comedy with a prologue for
the reader by Carl Van Vechten.
N.Y. Knopf. 1919. 12°. 246p. $1.75.
3 acts
Two blind beggars; and one less blind;
a tragic-comedy in one act, as played
by the Washington Square players,
N.Y. Arens. 1918. 21p. 1 act

**Moinaux, Georges (Georges Courtelline,
pseud),** 1860-
Peace at home. Comedy. 1 act
In Poet Lore 29:331

Molnár, Ferenz, 1878-
Devil; adapted by Oliver Herford. . .
N.Y. Kennerley. c1908. 12°. 224p.
Comedy. 3 acts
Dinner. Comedy. 1 act
In Smart Set 67:73 F '22
Fashions for men. Comedy. 3 acts
In Fashions for men, and The swan
Guardsman; a comedy in three acts. . .
Boni. 1925. 12°. 189p. $2
Host. Comedy. 1 act
In One-act plays for stage and study
ser 2
Liliom; a legend in seven scenes and a
prologue. N.Y. Boni. 1921. 12°.
185p. $1.75 Symbolic
In Mantle, B. ed. Best plays of 1920-
21 (condensed)
Matter of husbands. Comedy. 1 act
In Loving, P. ed. Ten minute plays
Putty club. Comedy. 1 act
In Theatre Arts M 7:251
Swan. Comedy. 3 acts
In Fashions for men, and The swan
    Mantle, B. ed. Best plays of 1923-
    24 (condensed)
Two slaps in the face. 1 act
In Golden Bk 2:65

Molnár, Ferenc (Franz), and Teleki, Joseph,
1878-
Actress. Comedy. 1 act
In Smart Set 33:119 Mr '11

Moncrieff, William Thomas, 1794-1857
All at Coventry; or, Love and laugh: a
musical farce, in two acts. . . Lon-
don. Davidson. n.d. 12°. 44p.
Bashful man. Comedy. 2 acts
In London stage 4 no 21
Birthday dinner. *See* Moncrieff, W. T.
Parson's nose! or, The birthday din-
ner
Borrowing a husband; or, Sleeping out;
a petit comedy in one act. . . London.
Lacy. 1821. 8°. 38p.
Cataract of the Ganges; or, The Rajah's
daughter; a grand romantic drama, in
two acts. . . London. Cumberland.
n.d. 12°. 41p.
Same in Cumberland's British theatre
v 33 no 8
Checque on my banker. *See* Moncrieff,
W. T. Wanted a wife; or, A checque
on my banker
Council of Trent. *See* Moncrieff, W. T.
Jewess; or, The council of Trent

Moncrief, W. T.—*Continued.*
Eugene Aram; or, Saint Robert's cave; a drama in three acts... London. Davidson. ɪn.d.ɪ 12°. 68p.
Same in Cumberland's minor theatre v 10 no 4
Giovanni in London; or, The libertime reclaimed; an operatic extravaganza, in two acts. . . London. Cumberland. n.d. 12°. 47p.
Same in Cumberland's British theatre v 17 no 5
London stage 3 no 38
How to take up a bill; or, The village Vauxhall. A vaudeville in one act. (from L'amie Bontemps, de M. M. Théaubon et Mélesville). . . London. Lunbird. 1837. 36p. 8°.
Jewess; or, The council of Trent. An historical drama, in three acts. N.Y. Phelan. ɪc1840ɪ. 12°. 62p.
Joconde; or, The festival of the Rosiere: a musical comedy, in three acts. . . London. Cumberland. ɪn.d.ɪ. 12°. 48p.
Same in Cumberland's minor theatre v 12 no 4
King Charles the Second"s merry days, *See* Moncrieff, W. T. Rochester, or King Charles the Second's merry days
Libertine reclaimed. *See* Moncrieff, W. T. Giovanni in London; or, The libertine reclaimed
Life in London. *See* Moncrieff, W. T. Tom and Jerry; or, Life in London
Monsieur Tonson; a farce in two acts. . . N.Y. Murden. 1822. 12°. 34p.
In Cumberland's British theatre v 16 no 1
London stage 3:no 3
Parson's nose! or, The birthday dinner. A comedy in one act. . . London. Pub. for the author. 1837. 8°. 30p.
Party wall; or, In and out! A comic interlude, in one act; altered from . . . Kotzebue's "Gefahrliche nachbarschaft". . . N.Y. Clayton. 12°. 24p. 1 act
Pickwickians. *See* Moncrieff, W. T. Sam Weller; or, The Pickwickians
Rochester; or, King Charles the second's merry days; a burletta in three acts. . . London. Lowndes. 1819. 8°. 63p.
Sam Weller; or, The Pickwickians. A drama in three acts. . . London. (T. Stagg). 1837. 8°. 153p. Comedy
Sleeping out. *See* Moncrieff, W. T. Borrowing a husband, or, Sleeping out
Somnambulist; or, The phantom of the village. A dramatic entertainment in two acts. . . London. Cumberland. ɪn.d.ɪ 12°. 40p.
Same in Cumberland's British theatre v 18 no 6

Spectre bridegroom; or, A ghost in spite of himself. A farce. In two acts, Founded on a story . . . in the sketch book. N.Y. Murden. 1821. 12°. 36p.
Same in Cumberland's British theatre v 16 no 3
Tom and Jerry; or, Life in London. An operatic extravaganza, in three acts. . . London. Moncrieff. 1826. 12°. 142p. (Founded on "Life in London" by Pierce Egan)
Same in Cumberland's British theatre v 33 no 5
Village Vauxhall. *See* Moncrieff, W. T. How to take up a bill, or, The village Vauxhall
Wanted a wife; or, A checque on my banker. A comedy in five acts. . . London. Lownes. 1819. 8°. 68p.
Winterbottoms! or, My aunt, the dowager. A farce in one act. . . London. Pub. for the author. 1837. 8°. 36p.

Monkhouse, Allan Noble, 1858-
Choice. War. 1 act
In War plays
Conquering hero; a play in four acts. N.Y. Stokes. 1924. 12°. 96p. $1.50 War
Education of Mr. Surrage; a comedy in four acts. London. Sidgwick. 1913. 12°. 93p.
First blood, a play in four acts. London. Benn. 1924. 12°. 101p. Labor
Grand cham's diamond. Theft. 1 act
In Marriott, J. W. ed. One-act plays of to-day
Hayling family. Tragedy. 3 acts
In Four tragedies
Mary Broome, a comedy in four acts. London. Sidgwick. 1912. 12°. 84p.
Night watches. War. 1 act
In War plays
Marriott, J. W. One-act plays of to-day ser 2
Reaping the whirlwind. Tragedy. 1 act
In Four tragedies
Resentment. Tragedy. 1 act
In Four tragedies
Shamed life. War. 1 act
In War plays
Sons & fathers; a play in four acts. London. Benn. 1925. 12°. 98p. Family
Stricklands. Tragedy. 3 acts
In Four tragedies

Monroe, Harriet, 1860-
After all. Hell. 1 act
In Passing show
Poet Lore 12:321
At the goal. Poetic. 1 act
In Passing show
It passes by. Poetic. 1 act
In Passing show
Modern minuet. Poetic. 1 act
In Passing show
Thunderstorm. Poetic. 2 acts
In Passing show
Valeria. Tragedy. 5 acts
In Valeria, and other poems

Monroe, J. R.
Argo and Irene. Comedy. 3 acts
In Dramas and miscellaneous poems
Malachi and Miranda. Melodrama. 4 acts
In Dramas and miscellaneous poems

Montanelli, Guiseppe
Camma; a tragedy in three acts. . . London. Francis. 1857. 12°. 89p.

Montenegro, Carlota
Alcestis; a drama. Boston. Poet Lore Co. 1909. 12°. 110p. Mythological. 3 acts

Montgomery, James
Nothing but the truth; a comedy in three acts. N.Y. French. c1920. 12°. 109p.
"Ready money"; a comedy in three acts. Rev. 1920. N.Y. French. c1920. 12°. 113p.

Moody, William Vaughn, 1869-1910
Death of Eve. Biblical. 1 act
In Poems and plays v 1
Faith healer; a play in four acts. Boston. Houghton. 1909. 12°. 160p. Faith cure.
Same in Poems and plays v 2
Quinn, A. H. ed. Representative American plays 1767-1923
Fire-bringer. Boston. Houghton. c1904. 12°. Promethean. 3 acts
Same in Poems and plays v 1
Great divide; a play in three acts. N.Y. Macmillan. 1909. 167p. Cave man. Melodrama
Same in Poems and plays v 2
Dickinson, T. H. ed. Chief contemporary dramatists
Pierce and Matthews, eds. Masterpieces of modern drama v 1 (abridged)
Masque of judgment. . . Boston. Houghton. c1900. 12°. 127p. Paradise lost. 5 acts
In Poems and plays v 1

Moon, Lorna
Corp'
In Doorways in Drumorty
Courtin' of Sally Ann
In Doorways in Drumorty
Silk both sides
In Doorways in Drumorty
Sinning of Jessie MacLean
In Doorways in Drumorty
Tattie-doolies
In Doorways in Drumorty
Wanting a hand
In Doorways in Drumorty

Moore, Bernard Francis
Captain Jack; or, The Irish outlaw. Original Irish drama in three acts. Boston. Baker. [c1889]. 12°. 40p.
Faugh-a-Ballagh; or, The wearing of the green. A romantic Irish play in three acts. Boston. Baker. 1899. 12°. 39p.
Ferguson of Troy; a farce comedy in three acts. . . Boston. Baker. 1900. 12°. 50p.

Irish agent. A play of Irish life in four acts. Boston. Baker. [c1889]. 12°. 41p.
Irish outlaw. *See* Moore, B. F. Captain Jack; or, The Irish outlaw
Irish rebel. A romantic play of the days of '98, in three acts. Boston. Baker. 1903. 12°. 38p.
King of the Philippines. A farce-comedy in three acts. Boston. Baker. 1901. 12°. 47p.
Poverty flats. A play of western life in three acts. Boston. Baker. 1899. 12°. 35p.
Rough rider; a play in four acts. . . Boston. Baker. 1898. 12°. 35p.
Suzette. A farce-comedy in three acts. Boston. Baker. 1903. 12°. 47p.
Wearing of the green. *See* Moore, B. F. Faugh-a-Ballagh; or, The wearing of the green
Weeping willows. A romantic play in three acts. Boston. Baker. 1903. 12°. 53p.
Wrecker's daughter; a drama in three acts. . . Boston. Baker. 1896. 12°. 32p.

Moore, Bessie Collins
On Bayou la Batre. Superstition. 1 act
In Poet Lore 37:576

Moore, Carlyle, 1875-
Stop thief; a farcical fact in three acts. N.Y. French. 1917. 104p.

Moore, Charles Leonard, 1854-
Banquet of Palacios. A comedy. Phila. C. L. Moore. 1889. 16°. 196p. 6 scenes
Ghost of Rosalys; a play. Phila. For the author. 1900. 12°. 174p. Supernatural. 4 acts

Moore, E. Hamilton
Thrytho; a drama. London. Sherratt. 1904. 8°. 155p. Norse mythology. 5 acts

Moore, Frank Frankfurt, 1855-
Discoverer. Columbus. 5 acts
In Discoverer
In the Queen's room. Mary Queen of Scots. 1 act
In Discoverer

Moore, George, 1853-
Apostle. Dublin, Maunsel. 1911. 12°. 100p. Biblical. 3 acts
Same in Dial 74:537; 75:43
Bending of the bough; a comedy in five acts. Chicago. Stone. 1900. 12°. 192p.
Coming of Gabrielle. N.Y. Boni. 1921. 12°. 132p. $4. Comedy. 3 acts
Same in Eng R 30:202-16, 296-310, 392-403
Elizabeth Cooper; a comedy in three acts. Boston. Luce. 1913. 80p. 75c
Same in International (NY) 7:215, 252, 284
Esther Waters; a play in five acts. Boston. Luce. 1913. 152p. 8°. Problem
Strike at Arlington; a play in three acts. London. Scott. 1893. 12°. 175p. Sociological

Moore, Horatio Newton, 1814-1859
Orlando; or, A woman's virtue.   A tragedy in five acts. Phila. Turner. 1835.
12°. 60p.

Moore, Raymond
Great moments.   Juvenile comedy. 1 act
In Shay, F. ed.   Plays for strolling
mummers

Moore, Thomas
M. P.; or, The blue stocking; a comic
opera in three acts. . . London. J.
Power. 1811. 8°. 94p.

Moore, Thomas Sturge, 1870-
Orpheus and Eurydice.   Poetic. 3 acts
In Fortn 92 sup 1

Moorman, Frederic William, 1872-1919
All souls' night's dream.   Dream. 1 act
In Plays of the Ridings
Ewe lamb.   Rustic farce. 2 acts
In Plays of the Ridings
May king; a play in three acts.   London.
Constable. 1914. 12°. 56p.   Legendary history
Potter Thompson.   Legendary. 3 scenes
In Plays of the Ridings

More, Federico, 1889-
Interlude.   Poet. 1 act
In Shay, F. and Loving, P. eds.   Fifty
contemporary one-act plays

Moreau, Eugène, 1866-1876, **Siraudin, Paul,
and Delacour, A. (pseud.)**
Courier of Lyons; or, The attack upon
the mail.   A drama in four acts.
Translated from the French. London.
Lacy. n.d. 12°. 44p. (Lacy's acting
edition of play. v. 15 no. 220).   Melodrama

Moreton, A. H.
Commandment pro tem; a farce in one
act. N.Y. French. 1918. 11p.

Morette, Edgar
In the swath.   World war. 1 act
In Six one-act plays
Nine o'clock express.   Farce. 1 act
In Six one-act plays
Scherzo in two flats.   Farce. 1 act
In Six one-act plays
Short cut.   Suicide. 1 act
In Six one-act plays
Waif.   Reign of Terror. 1 act
In Six one-act plays
Woman's verdict.   Melodrama. 1 act
In Six one-act plays

Morgan, Edward J.
Return.   Psychological. 1 act
In Drama 11:119

Morgan, Geoffrey F., 1882
In hot tamale land; a topical musical comedy in two acts.   Chicago. Denison.
1921. 12°. 41p. 35c
Royal cut-up; a musical comedy in two
acts.   Chicago. Denison. 1921. 12°.
38p. 35c

Morgan, Jacques
At the club.   Satire. 1 act
In Smart Set 47 no 1:251

Morgan, Lady Sydney Owenson, 1783?-1859
Easter recess.   Sociological. 4 scenes
In Dramatic scenes from real life v 1
Temper.   Comedy. 1 scene
In Dramatic scenes from real life v 1

Morland, Henry
Restoration of Cain; a mystery in three
acts.   London. Potter-Sarvent. 1916.
60p. 12°.

Morley, Christopher Darlington, 1890-
Bedroom suite.   Comedy. 1 act
In One-act plays
Outlook 133:79
East of Eden.   Genesis up to-date. 1 act
In One act plays
New Repub 39:318
Good   theatre.   Shakespeare   revisits
theatre. 1 act
In Sat R Lit 2:695
On the shelf.   Comedy. 1 act
In One act plays
Lit R 4:385 D 22 1923
Rehearsal.   Comedy. 1 act
In One act plays
Shay, F. ed.   Contemporary one-act
plays of 1921
Shay, F. ed.   Treasury of plays for
women
Thursday evening.   Cincinnati. Stewart
Kidd. c1922. 12°. 35p.   Comedy. 1 act
Same in One act plays
Shay, F. ed.   Twenty contemporary   one-act   plays
(American)
Walt.   Whitman. 1 act
In One act plays
Bookm 59:646

Morley, Malcolm
Beauty versus the beast.   Comedy. 1 act
In Told by the gate
Cosher!   Tragedy. 1 act
In Told by the gate
Masterpiece.   Psychological. 1 act
In Told by the gate
Motor mishap.   Social. 1 act
In Told by the gate
Recollections.   Matrimonial duologue. 1
act
In Told by the gate
Told by the gate.   Love cycle. 1 act
In Told by the gate

Morris, Angela
Dorinda dares.   Comedy. 1 act
In Boston theatre guild plays 1924

Morris, Edwin Bateman
Freshman.   Comedy. 3 acts
In College comedies
Junior.   Comedy. 3 acts
In College comedies
Senior.   Comedy. 3 acts
In College comedies
Sophomore.   Comedy. 3 acts
In College comedies

Morris, Mrs Elizabeth Woodbridge, 1870
Crusade of the children.   N.Y. Century.
1923. 12°. 94p.   Religious. 5 acts

Morris, William
Defence of Guenevere. Legendary
In Defence of Guenevere and other
poems
Love is enough; or, The freeing of Phar-
amond. A morality. London. Ellis.
1873. 12°. 134p. 1 act
Same in Collected works v 9
Sir Peter Harpdon's end. Tragedy. 5
scenes
In Collected works v 1
Defence of Guenevere
Bibelot 20:247

Morrison, Anne
Wild Westcott; a comedy in three acts.
N.Y. French. c1926. 12°. 109p.

Morrison, Anne, and McNutt, Patterson
Pigs; a comedy in three acts. N.Y.
French. c1924. 87p.

Morrison, George Austin, jr., 1864-
Lafayette; or, The maid and the Marquis;
an original burlesque in three acts. . .
N.Y. (A. E. Chaseman & Co.). 1890.
8°. 86p.

Morse, Northrop
Peach bloom; an original play in four
acts. N.Y. Medical Review of Re-
views. 1913. 184p. 12°. Social

Morselli, Ercole Luigi, 1882-1921
Gastone, the animal trainer. Farce. 1 act
In Goldberg, I. tr. Plays of the Ital-
ian theatre
Water upon fire. Symbolic. 1 act
In Goldberg, I. tr. Plays of the Ital-
ian theatre

Morton, John Maddison, 1811-1891
After a storm comes a calm. Comedietta in one act. London. French.
[18—]. 12°. p. 49-68. (French's acting
edition of plays. v. 134)
Same in Comediettas and farces
"Alabama" (altered from H. M. sloop
"Spitfire"). A transatlantic nautical
extravanganza. London. T. H.
Lacy. [18—?]. 12°. 22p. (Lacy's acting
edition of plays. v. 62) 3 scenes
At sixes and sevens. An original com-
edietta. London. French. [18—]. 12°.
18p. (French's acting edition of plays.
v. 124) 1 act
Atchi! a comedietta in one act. London.
Lacy. [18—?]. 12°. 21p.
Aunt Charlotte's maid; a farce in one act.
London. Lacy. [18—]. 12°. 30p. (Lacy's
acting edition of plays. v. 38)
Away with melancholy; a farce in one
act. London. Lacy. n.d. 12°. 19p.
(Lacy's acting edition of plays. v. 14
no. 196)
Betsy Baker! or, Too attentive by half.
A farce. In one act. London. Lacy.
n.d. 12°. 19p. (Lacy's acting edition
of plays. v. 8 no. 118) also Boston.
Spencer. 1856
Box and Cox. A romance of real life,
in one act. London. Lacy. n.d. 12°.
24p. (Lacy's acting edition of plays.
v. 5 no. 73)
Same in Comediettas and farces

Brother Ben. A farce in one act. London. Lacy. [1850?]. 12°. 24p. (Lacy's
acting edition of plays. v. 34)
Capital match! A farce. In one act. London. Lacy. n.d. 12°. 20p. (Lacy's acting edition of plays. v. 8 no. 116)
Catch a weazel; a farce in one act. London. Lacy. [18—]. 12°. 28p. (Lacy's
acting edition of plays. v. 54)
Corporal's wedding! or, a kiss from the
bride. A farce in one act. London.
French. [18—]. 12°. 27p.
Day's fishing. A farce in one act. London. Lacy. [18—]. 12°. 22p. (Lacy's
acting edition of plays. v. 83)
Declined—with thanks. Original farce
in one act. London. French. [18—].
12°. p. 107-130
Same in Comediettas and farces
Dinner for six. *See* Morton, J. M. Who
stole the pocket book? or, A dinner
for six
Done on both sides. A farce in one act.
London. French. [18—?]. 12°. 36p.
Don't judge by appearances. A farce.
London. Lacy. [18—]. 12°. 23p. (Lacy's
acting edition of plays. v. 24) 1 act
Double-bedded room: a farce in one act.
London. Lacy. [18—]. 12°. 21p. (Lacy's
acting edition of plays. v. 60)
Drawing rooms, second floor, and attics.
A farce. . . London. Lacy. [18—?].
12°. 30p. (Lacy's acting edition of
plays. v. 62) 1 act
Dying for love. A comedy in one act. . .
Boston. Spencer. [1858?]. 12°. 18p.
Eight hours at the sea-side. A farce, in
one act. London. French. [18—]. 12°.
16p.
Englishmen's house is his castle. Lon-
don. Lacy. [18—]. 12°. 20p. (Lacy's
acting edition of plays. v. 31) Farce.
1 act
Express! A railway romance, in one com-
partment (Adapted from the French).
London. French. [18—]. 12°. p. 69-86.
Same in Comediettas and farces
First come, first served. Comedietta in
one act. London. French. [18—]. 12°.
24p.
Same in Comediettas and farces
Fitzsmythe of Fitzsmythe Hall, a farce.
London. Lacy. [18—?]. 12°. 30p.
(Lacy's acting edition of plays. v. 46)
1 act
Friend Waggles: a farce in one act. London. Lacy. [1850]. 12°. 32p. (Lacy's
acting edition of plays. v. 33)
From village to court. A comic drama.
In two acts. London. Lacy. n.d. 12°.
28p. (Lacy's acting edition of plays.
v. 15 no. 217)
Game of romps. A farce. London. Lacy.
[18—]. 12°. 18p. (Lacy's acting edition
of plays. v. 18) 1 act
Going to the Derby: an original farce in
one act. London. Lacy. [18—]. 12°.
28p. (Lacy's acting edition of plays.
v. 37)

Morton, T. M.—*Continued*

Grimshaw, Bagshaw and Bradshaw. A farce in one act. London. Lacy. n.d. 12°. 26p. (Lacy's acting edition of plays. v. 4 no. 54)

Highwayman: an original farce, in one act. London. French. ₁18—₁. 12°. 24p.

Hopeless passion: a petite comedy in one act. London. Lacy. n.d. 12°. 24p. (Lacy's acting edition of plays. v. 5 no. 63)

How stout you're getting! A farce. London. Lacy. ₁18—₁. 12°. 23p. (Lacy's acting edition of plays. v. 22) 1 act

Husband to order. A serio-comic drama in two acts. London. Lacy. ₁18—₁. 12°. 43p. (Lacy's acting edition of plays. v. 43)

If I had a thousand a year. A farce in one act. London. Lacy. ₁18—₁. 12°. 32p. (Lacy's acting edition of plays. v. 79)

In the pigskin. *See* Morton, J. M. Steeple-Chase; or, In the pigskin

Irish tiger. A farce in one act. London. Lacy. ₁1846₁. 12°. 24p. (Lacy's acting edition of plays. v. 34)

John Dobbs. A farce in one act. London. Lacy. n.d. 12°. 22p. (Lacy's acting edition of plays. v. 7 no. 100)

"The king and I." A farce in one act. London. Lacy. ₁18—₁. 12°. 26p. (Lacy's acting edition of plays. v. 40)

King, queen and knave. *See* Morton, J. M. Muleteer of Toledo; or, King, queen and knave

Kiss and be friends. A new farce, in one act. London. French. ₁18—₁. 12°. 16p.

Kiss from the bride. *See* Morton, J. M. Corporal's wedding! or, A kiss from the bride

Lad from the country. A farce in one act. London. French. ₁18—₁. 12°. 20p.

Lend me five shillings. A farce in one act. N.Y. French. ₁18—₁. 12°. 31p.

Little mother. A comic piece, in two acts. London. Lacy. ₁18—₁. 12°. 33p. (Lacy's acting edition of plays. v. 91)

Little savage: a farce in one act. London. Lacy. ₁18—₁. 12°. 30p. (Lacy's acting edition of plays. v. 38)

Love and hunger. A farce in one act. London. Lacy. ₁18—₁. 12°. 30p. (Lacy's acting edition of plays. v. 42)

Maggie's situation. An original comedietta in one act. London. French. ₁18—₁. 12°. 19p. (French's acting edition of plays. v. 120)

Margery Daw; or, The two bumpkins: a farce. London. Lacy. ₁18—₁. 12°. 24p. (Lacy's acting edition of plays. v. 54) 1 act

Master Jones's birthday: a farce in one act. London. Lacy. ₁18—₁. 12°. 22p. (Lacy's acting edition of plays. v. 81)

Midnight watch! an original drama, in one act. . . London. Duncombe & Moon. ₁1848?₁. 12°. 29p. Comedy

Milliner's holiday: a farce in one act. London. Lacy. ₁18—₁. 12°. 26p. (Lacy's acting edition of plays. v. 38)

Most unwarrantable intrusion. A comic-interlude in one act. London. Lacy. n.d. 12°. 15p. (Lacy's acting edition of plays. v. 7 no. 93)

Muleteer of Toledo; or, King, Queen and Knave. A comic drama in two acts. . . London. Lacy. ₁185—₁. 12°. 28p.

My bachelor days. A farce in one act. London. French. ₁18—?₁. 12°. 16p.

My first fit of the gout. An original farce in one act. London. Lacy. n.d. 12°. 16p. (Lacy's acting edition of plays. v. 11)

My husband's ghost! A comic interlude in one act. Boston. Spencer. ₁1857?₁. 12°. 14p.

My precious Betzy! A farce. In one act. London. Lacy. n.d. 12°. 18p. (Lacy's acting edition of plays. v. 8 no. 115)

My wife's bonnet. A farce in one act. . . London. Lacy. ₁1864?₁. 12°. 27p. (Lacy's acting edition no. 94)

My wife's second floor. An original farce in one act. London. Lacy. ₁18—₁. 12°. 24p. (Lacy's acting edition of plays. v. 44)

Narrow squeak. An original farce, in one act. London. French. ₁18—?₁. 12°. 15p.

Newington Butts! A farce. In two scenes. London. Lacy. ₁18—₁. 12°. 20p. (Lacy's acting edition of plays. v. 73)

Old honesty. A comic drama in two acts. Boston. Spencer. ₁1868?₁. 12°. 42p.

On the sly! A farce in one act. London. Lacy. ₁18—₁. 12°. 30p. (Lacy's acting edition of plays. v. 63)

Our wife; or, The rose of Amiens. A comic drama, in two acts. Boston. Spencer. ₁1856?₁. 12°. 28p.

Pepperpot's little pets! In one act. London. French. ₁18—₁. 12°. p. 25-48. Comedietta
Same in Comediettas and farces

Poor Pillicoldy. A farce in one act. . . Boston. Spencer. ₁1856?₁. 12°. 22p.

Pouter's wedding. A farce in one act. London. Lacy. ₁18—₁. 12°. 24p. (Lacy's acting edition of plays. v. 67)

Prince for an hour: a comic drama in one act. London. Lacy. ₁18—₁. 12°. 26p. (Lacy's acting edition of plays. v. 25)

Regular fix: a farce in one act. London. Lacy. ₁18—₁. 12°. 26p. (Lacy's acting edition of plays. v. 48)

Rights and wrongs of women. A farce. London. Lacy. ₁18—₁. 12°. 26p. (Lacy's acting edition of plays. v. 26) 1 act

Rose of Amiens. *See* Morton, J. M. Our wife; or, The rose of Amiens

Sent to the tower. A farce in one act. . . Boston. Spencer. ₁1856?₁. 12°. 16p.

She would and he wouldn't; a comedy. London. Lacy. ₁18—₁. 12°. 40p. (Lacy's acting edition of plays. v. 56) 2 acts

Slice of luck. A farce. London. Lacy. ₁18—?₁. 12°. 24p. (Lacy's acting edition of plays. v. 76) 1 act

Slight mistakes! An original farce in one act. London. French. ₁18—₁. 12°. 20p.

Something to do. A farce. London. French. ₁18—?₁. 12°. 15p. 1 act

Steeple-chase; or, In the pigskin. An original farce in one act. London. Lacy. ₁18—₁. 12°. 24p. (Lacy's acting edition of plays. v. 66)

Take care of Dowb—. A farce in one act. London. Lacy. ₁1857₁. 12°. 26p. (Lacy's acting edition of plays. v. 34)

Taken from the French. An original comedietta in one act. London. French. ₁18—₁. 12°. p. 87-106 *In* Comediettas and farces

Thirty-three next birthday: a farce in one act. London. Lacy. ₁18—₁. 12°. 24p. (Lacy's acting edition of plays. v. 38)

Three cuckoos. A farce in one act. London. Lacy. ₁18—₁. 12°. 30p. (Lacy's acting edition of plays. v. 40)

Ticklish times. A farce in one act. . . Boston. Spencer. ₁1857?₁. 12°. 23p.

Too attentive by half. *See* Morton, J. M. Betsy Baker! or, Two attentive by half

Trumpeter's wedding. A musical farce in one act. London. Duncomb & Moon. ₁18—₁. 24°. 28p.

Two bumpkins. *See* Morton, J. M. Margery Daw; or, The two bumpkins

Two buzzards; or, Whitebait at Greenwich. A farce in one act. . . Boston. Spencer. ₁1856?₁. 12°. 24p.

Two Puddifoots. A farce. London. Lacy. ₁18—?₁. 12°. 23p. (Lacy's acting edition of plays. v. 78) 1 act

Which of the two? a comedietta in one act. London. Lacy. ₁18—₁. 12°. 30p. (Lacy's acting edition of plays. v. 40)

Who do they take me for. An original farce in one act. London. French. ₁18—₁. 12°. 26p.

Who's my husband. A farce in one act. London. Lacy. ₁18—₁. 12°. 26p. (Lacy's acting edition of plays. v. 80)

Who stole the pocket-book? or, a dinner for six, a farce. In one act. London. Lacy. n.d. 12°. 19p. (Lacy's acting edition of plays. v. 6 no. 84)

Who's the composer? A comic drama. In two acts. London. French. ₁18—?₁. 12°. 32p.

Woodcock's little game. A comedy-farce in two acts. London. Lacy. ₁18—₁. 12°. 40p. (Lacy's acting edition of plays. v. 63)

Wedding breakfast: a farce in one act. London. J. Duncombe. ₁184—?₁. 24°. 24p.

Wooing one's wife. A farce. London. Lacy. ₁18—₁. 12°. 28p. (Lacy's acting edition of plays. v. 52) 1 act

Morton, John Maddison, joint author. *See* Morton, Thomas, and Morton, John Maddison

Morton, John Maddison, 1811-1891, and Morton, Edward
My wife's come! A farce in one act. London. Duncombe. ₁184—₁. 24°. 22p.

Morton, John Maddison, 1811-1891, and Vicars, W. A.
Going it! Another lesson of fathers. A farcical comedy in three acts. London. French. ₁18—₁. 12°. 55p.

Morton, John Maddison, 1811-1891, and Williams, T. J.
Change partners; an original comedietta in one act. N.Y. Roorbach. ₁c1891₁. 12°. 17p.

Morton, Martha, 1865-
Bachelor's romance: an original play in four acts. N.Y. French. 1916. 12°. 84p. 50c

Her lord and master; a comedy in four acts. N.Y. French. c1912. 97p.

Morton, Michael, and Traill, Peter
After the theatre; a play in one act. London. "The Stage" play pub. bureau. 1924. 32p.

Morton, Thomas, 1764?-1838
Children in the wood: a musical piece in two acts. . . London. Cumberland. n.d. 12°. 28p. (Cumberland's British theatre. v. 17 no. 1)

Columbus; or, A world discovered. An historical play. . . London. Miller. 1792. 12°. 66p.

Cure for the heartache: a comedy in five acts. . . London. Davidson. n.d. 12°. 68p.
Same in Cumberland's British theatre. v 16 no 4

Education; a comedy in five acts. . . London. Longman. 1813. 76p.
Same in Cumberland's British theatre v 16 no 7

Gotobed Tom! A farce in one act. London. Lacy. n.d. 12°. 18p. (Lacy's acting edition of plays. v. 8 no. 119)

Invincibles: a musical farce in two acts. . . London. Cumberland. n.d. 12°. 38p.
Same in Cumberland's British theatre v 36 no 7

'Methinks I see my father!' or, 'Who's my father?'. A farce in two acts. . . London. Davidson. n.d. 12°. 29p.
Same in Cumberland's British theatre. v 45 no 7

Pretty piece of business. A comedy. In one act. London. Lacy. n.d. 12°. 22p. (Lacy's acting edition of plays. v. 12 no. 176)

Roland for an Oliver: a farce, in two acts. . . . Boston. Spencer. 1855. 12°. 39p.
Same in Cumberland's British theatre v 44 no 5

Morton, T.—*Continued*

School of reform; or, How to rule a wife, a comedy, in five acts. . . London. Davidson. [n.d.]. 12°. 65p.

Same in Cumberland's British theatre v 17 no 6

Inchbald, Mrs. ed. British British theatre v 8

Inchbald, Mrs. ed. Theatre v 21

Secrets worth knowing: a comedy in five acts. . . London. Cumberland. n.d. 12°. 57p. (Cumberland's British theatre. v. 18 no. 4)

Same in Inchbald, Mrs. ed. Modern theatre v 3

Sink or swim! a comedy. In two acts. London. Lacy. n.d. 12°. 26p. (Lacy's acting edition of plays. v. 7 no. 98)

Slave: an opera, in three acts. . . London. Davidson. n.d. 12°. 60p. (Cumberland's British theatre. v. 22 no. 3)

Speed the plough: a comedy in five acts. . . London. Davidson. n.d. 12°. 69p. (Cumberland's British theatre. v. 15 no 6)

Same in Inchbald, Mrs. ed. British theatre v 1

Inchbald, Mrs. ed. Theatre v 30

Town and country; a comedy in five acts. . . N.Y. Douglas. 1848. 12°. 68p.

Same in Cumberland's British theatre v 23 no 9

Way to get married. A comedy. n.p. 18—? 12°. 78p.

Same in Cumberland's British theatre v 20 no 5

World discovered. *See* Morton, T. Columbus; or, A world discovered

Zorinski. Poland. 3 acts
In Inchbald; Mrs. ed. Modern theatre v 3

Morton, Thomas, 1764?-1838, and Morton, John Maddison

All that glitters is not gold; or, The poor girl's diary. A comic drama in two acts. . . N.Y. Roorbach. c1889. 12°. 46p.

Poor girl's diary. *See* Morton, T. and J. M. All that glitters is not gold; or, The poor girl's diary

Slasher and crasher! An original farce. In one act. London. Lacy. n.d. 12°. 21p. (Lacy's acting edition of plays. v. 8 no. 110). *Same* French. N.Y. [187—?]. 12°. 30p.

Same in Drama (N.Y.) 1:17-25

Thumping legacy. A farce. In one act. London. Lacy. n.d. 12°. 18p. (Lacy's acting edition of plays. v. 5 no. 65). Same. French. N.Y. [18—]. 12°. 19p.

To Paris and back for five pounds. An original farce. In one act. London. Lacy. n.d. 12°. 21p. (Lacy's acting of edition of plays. v. 9 no. 135)

Two Bonycastles. A farce in one act. London. Lacy. n.d. 12°. 21p. (Lacy's acting edition of plays. v. 5 no. 68). Same. French. London. [18—]. 12°. 32p.

Waiting for an omnibus in the Lowther Arcade on a rainy day. A farce, in one act. London. Lacy. n.d. 12°. 18p. (Lacy's acting edition of plays. v. 15 no. 219)

Where there's a will there's a way. A comic drama in one act. London. Lacy. n.d. 12°. 24p. (Lacy's acting edition of plays. v. 9 no. 129)

Woman I adore! a farce. In one act. London. Lacy. n.d. 12°. 22p. (Lacy's acting edition of plays. v. 8 no. 12)

Writing on the wall! a melodrama. In three acts. London. Lacy. n.d. 12°. 48p. (Lacy's acting edition of plays. v. 7 no. 99)

Your life's in danger. A farce in one act. London. Lacy. n.d. 12°. 19p. (Lacy's acting edition of plays. v. 9 no. 131)

Moser, Gustav von, 1825-1903

Arabian nights. A farce in three acts. Founded on the German of von Moser. By Sidney Grundy. London. French. [1887?]. 12°. 49p.

"I shall invite the major", a petite comedy in one act. . . N.Y. DeWitt. c1875. 12°. 16p.

Lot 49; farce in one act. [adapted] by W. J. Fisher. London. French. [1888?]. 16°. 20p.

Marble arch. Comedietta in one act. [Adapted] by Edward Rose and A. J. Garraway. N.Y. French. [18882?]. 12°. 15p.

On change. A farce in three acts. . . Arranged for the English stage by Miss Everetta Lawrence. N.Y. French. [1885?]. 12°. 53p.

Our regiment. A farcical comedy, in three acts. Adapted . . . by Henry Hamilton. . . N.Y. French. [1883?]. 12°. 55p.

Private secretary: a farcical comedy in three acts. By Charles Hawtry. N.Y. French. c1907. 12°. 90p.

White horse [Der Schimmel]. Comedy in one act, literally translated from the German of G. von Moser. Cambridge, Mass., W. H. Wheeler, printer. 1887. 12°. 18p.

Mosher, John Chapin

Fee Fo Fum. Fairy. 1 act
In Seven Arts 1:602

Quay of magic things. Comedy. 1 act
In Drama 10:188

Sauce for the emperor; a comedy in one act. N.Y. Shay. 1916. 12°. 330p.
Same in Smart Set 51:199 no 1

Motomasa
Sumida Gawa (Sumida river). Adapted from the Noh drama. 1 act
In Royal Society of Literature. London. Tr. ser 2 v 29:169
Stopes, M. C. C. Plays of old Japan
Stratford J (Boston) 2:29 Ja '18

Mountford, George F.
Friday for luck; a comedy in one act. Chicago. Denison. c1924. 12°. 30p.
Rats! one-act farce. Chicago. Denison. ₍c1924₎. 12°. 30p.

Mowatt, Mrs Anna Cora. *See* Ritchie, Mrs. Annie Cora Mowatt

Mowery, William Byron
Election of the roulette. Russian life (1850). 1 act
In Poet Lore 33:525

Moylan, Thomas King
Curse of the country; a play in three acts. Dublin. Duffy. 1917. 12°. 96p. Ireland
Naboclish. Comedy. 2 acts
In Naboclish . . . and Uncle Pat
Paid in his own coin. Comedy. 3 acts
In Paid in his own coin . . . , and Tactics
Tactics. Farce. 1 act
In Paid in his own coin . . . , and Tactics
Uncle Pat. Comedy. 1 act
In Naboclish . . . and Uncle Pat

Muellner, Amand Gottfried Adolph, 1774-1829
Guilt; or, The gipsey's prophecy. A tragedy. . . ₍5 acts₎. from the German by W. E. Frye. London. For the author. 1819. 8°. 88p.

Münch-Bellinghausen, Eligius Franz J. Freiherr von (Frederick Hahn, pseud.), 1806-1871
Gladiator of Ravenna; a tragedy in five acts. Trans. . . by W. H. Charlton. London. Lacy. ₍1861₎. 8°. 103p.
Griselda; a dramatic poem in five acts. . . N.Y. Young Women's Christian Assn. c1876. 12°. 152p. Arthurian
Ingomar, the barbarian. A play in five acts. . . London. Lacy. ₍185—?₎. 12°. 62p. (Lacy's acting edition of plays. v. 75 no. 1111)
Son of the wilderness. A play in five acts. Translated in to English verse by Wm. H. Charlton. London. Lacy. n.d. 12°. 59p. (Lacy's acting edition of plays. v. 7 no. 101). *Also* N.Y. Ludwig. 1848. 12°. 166p.

Mukerji, Dhan Gopal, 1890-
Judgment of India. India. 1 act
In Dickinson, A. D. ed. Drama
Shay, F. and Loving, P. eds. Fifty contemporary one-act plays
Shay, F. Treasury of plays for men
Layla-Majnu; a musical play in three acts. . . San Francisco. Elder. ₍1916₎. 8°. 61p. East India

Muldoon, John, and Muldoon, Joseph M.
For Ireland's sake; or, under the green flag; a romantic Irish drama. Dublin. Ponsonby. 1910. 104p. 3 acts

Mullins, Helene
Truth about liars. Comedy. 1 act
In Poet Lore 34:145

Munro, C. K.
At Mrs. Beam's, a comedy. N.Y. Knopf. 1926. 12°. 183p. 3 acts
Battle of Tinderley Down. *See* Munro, C. K. Storm; or, The battle of Tinderley Down
Progress. A play in two parts. London. Collins. ₍c1924₎. 12°. 232p. Farce
Rumour; a play in two parts. N.Y. Knopf. 1924. 12°. 228p. $2. War. Symbolic. 2 acts each part
Storm; or, The battle of Tinderley Down; a comedy. London. Collins. ₍1924₎. 12°. 233p. 3 acts

Murray, Douglas
Man from Toronto; a comedy in three acts. N.Y. French. c1919. 12°. 106p.
Uncle Ned; a comedy in four acts. N.Y. French. c1920. 12°. 111p.

Murray, Douglas
Artistic touch. 1 act
In Sentimental cuss, and three other plays
Gingerbread's partner. 1 act
In Sentimental cuss, and three other plays
Sentimental cuss. 1 act
In Sentimental cuss, and three other plays
Squaring the circle. 1 act
In Sentimental cuss, and three other plays

Murray, Gilbert, 1866-
Andromache; a play in three acts. Portland, Me. Mosher. 1913. 12°. 88p. Mythological
Carlyon Sahib; a drama in four acts. London. Heinemann. 1900. 156p. Tragedy

Murray, Thomas C.
Autumn fire; a play in three acts. London. Allen & Unwin. ₍1925₎. 12°. 85p. Marriage
Birthright; a play in two acts. Dublin. Maunsel. 1911. 12°. 43p. Ireland
Briery gap. Tragedy. 1 act
In Spring and other plays
Maurice Harte; a play in two acts. Dublin. Maunsel. 1912. 12°. 60p. Psychological
Sovereign love. Comedy. 1 act
In Spring and other plays
Spring. Old age. 1 act
In Spring and other plays

Murray, William Henry Wood, 1790-1852
Cramond brig: a drama in two acts. . . London. Davidson. n.d. 12°. 22p. Comedy
Same in Cumberland's British theatre v 47 no 1

Murray, W. H. W.—*Continued*
Diamond cut diamond. An interlude in one act. Altered from "How to die for love". London. Lacy. n.d. 12°. 15p. (Lacy's acting edition of plays. v. 7 no. 103)
Gilderoy. A drama in two acts. London. Lacy. n.d. 12°. 24p. (Lacy's acting edition of plays. v. 9 no. 130)
Mary, Queen of Scots; or, The escape from Loch Leven. An historical drama, in two acts. London. Lacy. n.d. 12°. 26p. (Lacy's acting edition of plays. v. 4 no. 58)

Musset, Alfred de, 1810-1857
All is fair in love and war. A drawing-room comedy in one act. York. Sampson. 1868. 12°. 58p. (Adaptation of L'ane et le ruisseau)
Andre del Sarto. Comedy. 3 acts
 In Complete writings v 3
Barberine. Comedy. 3 acts
 In Comedies
 Complete writings v 3
Bettine. Comedy. 1 act
 In Complete writings v 5
[Caprice]. Good little wife; a comedy in one act. . . London. Lacy. [18—?]. 12°. 22p. (Adapted from "Un caprice")
 Same in Poet Lore 33:395
 Complete writings v 5
Carmosine. Comedy. 3 acts
 In Complete writings v 5
Chandelier. *See* Musset, A. de. Chandler
Chandler. Comedy. 3 acts
 In Complete writings v 4
 Bates, A. ed. Drama 9:173 (under title Chandelier)
Door must be either open or shut (Il faut qu 'une porte soit ouverte ou fermée). Comedy. 1 act
 In Comedies
 Complete writings v 5
Fantasio. Comedy. 2 acts
 In Comedies
 Complete writings v 3
Follies of Marianne. Comedy. 3 acts
 In Complete writings v 3
Laurette's wedding. *See* Musset, A. de. Venetian night; or, Laurette's wedding
Lorenzaccio. Comedy. 5 acts
 In Complete writings v 4
Louison. Comedy. 2 acts
 In Complete writings v 5
No trifling with love (Ou ne badine pas avec l'amour). Comedy. 3 acts
 In Comedies
 Complete writings v 3
One can not think of everything. Comedy. 1 act
 In Complete writings v 5
Prudence spurns a wager. Comedy. 3 acts
 In Complete writings v 4

Venetian night; or, Laurette's wedding. Comedy. 1 act
 In Complete writings v 3
Musset, Alfred de, 1810-1857, and Augier, Emile
Green coat; a comedy in one act. N.Y. French. [c1915]. 12°. 21p.
Musset, Alphonse de. *See* Musset, Alfred de

Myall, Charles A.
Ships on the sand. Peasant. 1 act
 In Drama 12:153

Mygatt, Tracy Dickinson
Aino puku. Finnish. 1 act
 In World Outl 4:20 Je '18
Children of Israel, a play in three acts. . . N.Y. Doran. 1922. 12°. 92p. Biblical
Good Friday; a passion play of now. . . N.Y. Privately printed. [c1919]. 12°. 52p. Conscientious objector. 1 act
Seventy-three voted yes. Women's rights. 1 act
 In World Outl 4:18 S '18
Watchfires; a play in four acts. . . N.Y. Privately printed. 1917. 12°. 50p. War

Najac, Émile de, 1828-1889, and Hennequin, Alfred 1842-1887
Babie; a comedy in three acts. . . Translated from the French by F. E. Chase. Boston. Baker. 1886. 61p.

Nakamura, Kichizo, 1877-
Razor, Psychological. 1 act
 In Iwasaki, Y. T. tr. Three modern Japanese plays

Nakazawa, Ken
Persimmon thief. Comedy. 1 act
 In Drama 16:97

Narodmy, Ivan
Fortune favors fools. Musical comedy. 1 act
 In Poet Lore 23:305
Skygirl, a mimodrama, in three acts, on a star, prologue and epilogue on the earth; dramatic episodes of a life fifty thousand years ahead of ours. . . N.Y. Britons pub. co. [c1925]. 8°. 103p.

Narrey, Charles, 1825-1892
Sophronisba. . . Oh! Comedy. 1 act
 In Bellevue Dramatic Club: plays for private acting

Nathan, George Jean, 1882-
Fanny's second play. Satire. 1 act
 In Bottoms up
Letters. Satire. 1 act
 In Bottoms up
Queen of the veronal ring. Melodrama. 1 act
 In Bottoms up

Neän, (pseud.)
Oïné; or, The aureole and the wondrous gem; a play in four acts. London. Dent. 1911. 12°. 88. Romantic

Neave, Adam
Woman and superwoman; a comedy of 1923 in three acts. London. Griffiths. [1914]. 12°. 88p.

Neihardt, John Gneisenau, 1881-
Eight hundred rubles. Retribution. 1 act
In Forum 53:393

Neilson, Francis, 1867-
Bath road. Comedy. 3 acts
In Drama 13:175
Day before commencement; a comedy in
four acts. N.Y. Huebsch. 1925. 12°.
155p. $1.50
Desire for change; a comedy in three
acts. N.Y. Huebsch. 1920. 12°. 124p.
$1.50
Impossible philanthropist; a comedy in
four acts. N.Y. Huebsch. 1924. 12°.
115p. $1.50
Mixed foursome; a comedy in three acts.
N.Y. Huebsch. 1924. 12°. 106p. $1.50
Sin-eater's Hallowe'en; a fantasy in one
act and two scenes. N.Y. Huebsch.
1924. 12°. 89p. $1.50

Nesbitt, Catherine May, 1884-
Demshur man; or, The devil looks after
his own; a rural comedy. N.Y.
French. c1924. 26p. 1 act

Nessesson, Elsa Behaim
In the secret places. Loyalty. 1 act
In Drama 17:43

Nethercot, Arthur H.
Funeral march of a marionette
In Poet Lore 31:232
Grecian urn. Art. 1 act
In Poet Lore 33:142
Peter Gink. Radicalism. 1 act
In Poet Lore 35:118

Neumann, Sara
Old order. Domestic. 1 act
In Drama 11:147

Newman, Benjamin W.
Salt water. Sea. 1 act
In Poet Lore 36:232

Newmarch, E.
Cynthia. Suffragette comedietta. 1 act
In Cynthia; a suffragette, and, In the
muffled moonlight
In the muffled moonlight. Comedietta.
1 act
In Cynthia; a suffragette, and, In the
muffled moonlight

Newton, Alfred Edward, 1863-
Doctor Johnson; a play. Boston. Atlan-
tic monthly press. 1923. 12°. 120p.
Biographical. 4 acts

Newton, Harry L., 1872-
Mr. and Mrs. Fido; a vaudeville sketch.
Chicago. Denison. [1907]. 12°. 10p.
1 act

Nichol, John
Hannibal; a historical drama. . . Glasgow. J. Maclehose. 1873. 12°. 284p.
5 acts

Nichols, Adelaide
Devil's field. Outdoor. 1 act
In Haunted circle, and other outdoor
plays
Gardener's cap. Outdoor. 1 act
In Haunted circle, and other outdoor
plays

Haunted circle. Outdoor. 1 act
In Haunted circle, and other outdoor
plays
Shepherd's pipe. Christmas miracle. 1
act
In Haunted circle, and other outdoor
plays

Nichols, Anne
Abie's Irish rose; a comedy in three acts.
N.Y. c1924. 43p.

Nichols, Edward Percy, and Nichols, W. B.
Coloman. N.Y. Gomme. 1916. 12°. 136p.
$1. 5 acts

Nichols, Robert Malise Bowyer, 1893-
Guilty souls; a drama in four acts. N.Y.
Harcourt. 1922. 12°. 181p. $1.75 Psy-
chological

Nicholson, Kenyon, 1894-
Anonymous letter. Comedy. 1 act
In Garden varieties
Bug man. Comedy. 1 act
In Garden varieties
Smart Set 62:83-89 Je '20 (under
title: Gentle assassin)
Casino gardens. Tragedy. 1 act
In Garden varieties
Smart Set 64:77-86
Confession. Tragedy. 1 act
In Garden varieties
Gentle assassin. *See* Nicholson, K.
Bug man
Marriage of little Eva. Comedy. 1 act
In Garden varieties
Meal ticket; a farce-comedy in three acts.
N.Y. French. c1926. 12°. 96p.
Meet the missus! Comedy. 1 act
In One act plays for stage and study
ser 2
Smart Set 68:85 Ag '22 (under title:
Meet the wife)
Meet the wife. *See* Nicholson, K. Meet
the missus?
Sally and company; a comedy in three
acts. N.Y. French. c1925. 12°. 101p.
So this is paris green. Burlesque. 1 act
In Garden varieties
White elephants. Comedy. 1 act
In Garden varieties

Nicholson, Kenyon, and Behrman, Samuel
Night's work; a comedy in one act. N.Y.
French. c1926. 12°. 21p.

Nicholson, Kenyon, and Pendray, Edward
Organ; a play in one act. N.Y. French.
c1926. 12°. 25p.

Nicholson, Kenyon, and Reed, Dena
Three graces; a comedy in three acts. . .
N.Y. French. c1925. 12°. 86p.

Nicholson, Meredith, 1866-, **and Nicholson,
Kenyon**
Honor bright; a comedy in three acts.
N.Y. French. 105p. 12°.

Nil Durpan
Indigo planter's mirror; a drama. . .
Edinburgh. Macphail. 1862. 8°. 61p.
4 acts

Nirdlinger, Charles Frederic
Aren't they wonders?   A holiday trag-
edy. 1 act
In Four short plays
Big Kate, a diplomatic tragedy.   1 act
In Four short plays
First lady of the land; a play in four acts.
Boston. Baker. 1914. 209p. 50c. Dolly
Madison
Just off the avenue; a play in three acts.
N.Y. Kennerley. 1917. 12°. 157p. Ro-
mantic
Look after Louise, an everyday tragedy.
1 act
In Four short plays
Real people, a sawdust tragedy.   1 act
In Four short plays
World and his wife . . after the verse of
José Echegaray's El gran Galeoto.
N.Y. Kennerley. c1908. 12°. 215p.
Social. 3 acts
Same in Moses, M. G. ed.   Representa-
tive continental dramas
Nishikigi. *See* Japanese plays
Noel, Joseph
House of rest.   Morgue. 1 act
In Three plays
Terms of peace
In Three plays
Wasters
In Three plays
Wild oats
In Three plays
Noguchi, Yone, 1875-
"Bussu".   Comedy. 1 act
In Yokyokukai 6 no 4:5
Cormorant fisher.   Religious. 1 act
In Yokyokukai 5 no 4:1
Delusion of a human cup.   Poetic. 1 act
In Yokyokukai 5 no 5:6
Demon's mallet (Demon's shell).   Folk-
farce. 1 act
In Poet Lore 17 no 3:44
Yokyokukai 5 no 4:6
Everlasting sorrow.   Supernatural. 1 act
In Yokyokukai 6 no 5:11
Melon thief.   Folk-farce. 1 act
In Poet Lore 15:40
Moon night-bell.   Comedy. 2 scenes
In Yokyokukai 6 no 6:1
Mountain she-devil.   Noh play. 1 act
In Poet Lore 29:447
Perfect jewel maiden.   Japanese. 1 act
In Poet Lore 28:334
Shower; the moon.   Noh play. 1 act
In Poet Lore 29:455
Poetry Review (Lond) 8:189
Tears of the birds.   Noh play. 1 act
In Poet Lore 29:451
Two blind men.   Comedy. 1 act
In Yokyokukai 6 no 1:4
Nooshich, Branislav
Prince of Semberia.   Ransom. 1 act
In Poet Lore 33:85
Nordau, Max Simon, 1849-1923
Question of honor.   A tragedy of the
present day. In four acts. . . Boston.
Luce. 1907. 12°. 169p.

Norrevang, A.
Woman and the fiddler. . . Phila. Brown.
1911. 12°. 105p.   Norwegian folklore.
3 acts
Norris, Mrs. Kathleen, 1880-, **and Totheroh,
Dan W.**
Kelly kid; a comedy in one act.   Boston.
Baker. c1926. 12°. 24p.
Norton, Allen
Convolvulus; a comedy in three acts.
N.Y. Claire Marie. 1914. 72p.
Norton, Franklin Pierce, 1852-
Abraham Lincoln; or, The rebellion.
Historical. 5 acts
In Six dramas of American romance
and history
Dora Dimple's beau.   Sketch. 2 scenes
In Foibles
Financier of New York.   Romantic. 4
acts
In Six dramas of American romance
and history
Foibles.   Farcical comedy. 3 acts
In Foibles
King of Wall Street.   Romantic. 5 acts
In Six dramas of American romance
and history
Kingdom of mind, a drama beginning in
a library.   N.Y. Schulte. c1918. 4°.
40p.   Romantic. 4 acts
Lady of the swamp; a drama consisting
of a prologue, five scenes, epilogue. . .
N.Y. Schulte. c1916. 4°. 46p.   Ro-
mantic
Machiavelli; a drama. . . N.Y. Schulte.
c1915. 4°. 44p.   Historical. 4 acts
Otornis, the Indian of Mexico.   Histori-
cal. 4 acts
In Six dramas of American romance
and history
Rebellion.   *See* Norton, F. P.   Abra-
ham Lincoln; or, The rebellion
Secretary of state.   Thomas Jefferson. 4
acts
In Six dramas of American romance
and history
Third term.   Prophetic. 5 acts
In Six dramas of American romance
and history
Whose wife?. . . a drama.   N.Y.
Schulte. c1917. 4°. 40p.   Romantic.
4 acts
Norton, Louise
Little wax candle.   A farce in one act.
N.Y. Claire Marie. 1914. 12°. 38p.
Norwood, Robert W., 1874-
Man of Kerioth. . . N.Y. Doran. c1919.
12°. 138p.   Biblical. 5 acts
Witch of Endor; a tragedy.   N.Y. Dor-
an. c1916. 12°. 121p. $1.25. 5 acts
Novak, Arne
Advent of spring in the South; an imag-
inary conversation.   Charles IV and
Petrarch. 1 scene
In Selver, P. ed.   Anthology of mod-
ern Slavonic literature
Novak, David
City; a grotesque adventure.   Life. 1 act
In Poet Lore 36:208

Noyes, Alfred, 1880-
Belgian Christmas Eve, being "Rada" re-written and enlarged as an episode of the Great War. N.Y. Stokes. [c1915]. 71p.
Rada, a drama of war in one act. N.Y. Stokes. [1914]. 31p.
Robin Hood and the three kings. *See* Noyes, A. Sherwood; or, Robin Hood and the three kings
Sherwood; or Robin Hood and the three kings; a play in five acts. . . N.Y. Stokes. 1911. 12°. 224p.
Same in Collected poems v 2

Nugent, Eliott and Lindsey, H.
Apartments to let. Farce. 1 act
In Nicholson, K. ed. Appleton book of short plays

Nugent, J. C., and Nugent, Elliott
Kempy; a comedy of American life in three acts. N.Y. French. 1924. 12°. 106p. 75c
Poor nut; a comedy in three acts. . . N.Y. French. 1925. 12°. 140p.

Oakes, A. H.
Teacher taught (from Le roman d'une pupille, by M. P. Ferrier). Comedy. 1 act
In Matthews, J. B. ed. Comedies for amateur acting

O'Brien, Edward Joseph Harrington, 1890-
At the flowing of the tide. Christmas. 1 act
In Forum 52:375

O'Brien, Seumas, 1880-
Black bottle
In One-act plays for stage and study ser 2
Blind; a comedy in one act. . . N.Y. Arens. 1918. 12°. 24p.
Cobbler's den. 1 act
In One-act plays for stage and study ser 3
Duty. Comedy. 1 act
In Duty, and other Irish comedies
Jurisprudence. Comedy. 1 act
In Duty, and other Irish comedies
Magnanimity. Comedy. 1 act
In Duty, and other Irish comedies
Matchmakers. Comedy. 1 act
In Duty, and other Irish comedies
Retribution. Comedy. 1 act
In Duty, and other Irish comedies

O'Casey, Sean
Juno and the paycock
In Two plays
Plough and the stars; a tragedy in four acts. N.Y. Macmillan. 1926. 12°. 136p.
Shadow of the gunman
In Two plays

O'Conor, Norreys Jephson, 1885-
Fairy bride. . . N.Y. Lane. 1916. 12°. 99p. $1. Fairy. 3 acts

O'Connor, Patricia
My dear! Comedy. 1 act
In Drama 14:188

O'Dea, Mark
Miss Myrtle says yes. Episode. 1 act
In Red bud women
Not in the lessons. Episode. 1 act
In Red bud women
Shivaree. Episode. 1 act
In Red bud women
Drama 11:11
Song of Solomon. Episode. 1 act
In Red bud women
Drama 11:154

O'Donnell, T. C.
Sandman's brother. Juvenile. 1 act
In Jagendorf, M. A. ed. One-act plays for young folks

Oehlenschläger, Adam Gottlob, 1779-1850
Aladdin; or, The wonderful lamp. A dramatic poem in two parts. . . Edinburgh. Blackwood. 1863. 16°. 298p.
Axel and Valborg, an historical tragedy in five acts. . . N.Y. Grafton. 1906. 12°. 120p.
Hakon Jail; a tragedy in five acts. . . London. Hookham. 1840. 12°. 221p.
Same in Nebraska Univ Studies 5:39
Palnatoke; a tragedy. In five parts. . . London. Priv. printed. 1855. 12°. 65p.
Out of the frying pan; a one act comedy. . . London. French. n.d. 24°. 12°
Three brothers of Damascus. Comedy (abstract)
In Blackwood 39:717

Oglesbee, Delle Houghton
Ten fingers of Francois. Christmas play of old Provence. 1 act
In Drama 14:65

O'Higgins, Harvey Jerrold, 1876-, and Ford, Harriet, 1868-
Dummy; a detective comedy in four acts. N.Y. French. c1925. 113p. (copyrighted under title Kidnapped.)
Mr. Lazarus; a comedy in four acts. N.Y. French. c1926. 12°. 134p.
On the hiring line; a comedy in three acts. N.Y. French. 1923. 12°. 116p.
"When a feller needs a friend"; a play in three acts. . . [N.Y.] [c1920]. 12°. 108p. Comedy

Ohnet, Georges, 1848-
Forge master (Le maître de forges). (Iron manufacturer). A drama in four acts and five tableaux. . . N.Y. Rullman. [1888?]. 8°. 48p. *Also* Chicago. Rand. 1890. Social
Same in Bates, A. ed. Drama v 9:285

Okamoto, Kido, 1872-
Battle of Samurai and Christian spirits. Japanese. 1 act
In Liv Age 314:532
Lady Hosokawa. Historical. 2 acts
In Poet Lore 37:1

O'Keeffe, John, 1747-1833
Agreeable surprise: a comic opera in two acts. . . London. Cumberland. [1832?]. 24°. 39p. (Cumberland's British theatre. v. 31)

O'Keeffe, J.—*Continued*
Castle of Andalusia.   Comic opera. 3 acts
  In Cumberland's British theatre v 32
    Inchbald, Mrs. ed.   British theatre
    v 10
    Inchbald, Mrs. ed.   Theatre v 19
Dead alive; or, The double funeral.   A
  comic opera. In two acts. . . N.Y.
  Hodge. 1789. 12°. 46p.
Double funeral.   *See* O'Keeffe, J. Dead
  alive; or, The double funeral
Farmer.   Farce. 2 acts
  In Cumberland's British theatre v 27
    Inchbald, Mrs. ed.   Collection · of
    farces v 2
Fontainebleau.   Comic opera. 3 acts
  In Cumberland's British theatre v 32
    Inchbald, Mrs. ed.   Theatre v 7
Highland reel.   Farce. 3 acts
  In Cumberland's British theatre v 18
    Inchbald, Mrs. ed.   Collection of
    farces v 2
Lie of a day.   Comedy. 3 acts
  In Inchbald, Mrs. ed.   Modern theatre
    v 10
Merry mourners.   *See* O'Keeffe, J.
  Modern antiques; or, The merry
  mourners
Modern antiques; or, The merry mourn-
  ers.   Farce. 2 acts
  In Cumberland's British theatre v 29
Peeping Tom of Coventry.   Musical
  farce. 2 acts
  In Cumberland's British theatre v 31
Poor soldier; a comic opera in two
  acts. . . N.Y. Longworth. 1808. 24°.
  36p.
  Same in Cumberland's British theatre v
    20
    Inchbald, Mrs. ed.   Collection
    of farces v 2
Prisoner at large.   Comedy. 2 acts
  In Cumberland's British theatre v 26
    Inchbald, Mrs. ed.   Collection of
    farces v 2
Son-in-law.   Comic opera. 2 acts
  In Cumberland's British theatre v 31
Sprigs of laurel.   Musical farce. 2 acts
  In Cumberland's British theatre v 39
Wild oats; or, The strolling gentleman.
  Comedy. 5 acts
  In Cumberland's British theatre v 34
    Inchbald, Mrs. ed.   British theatre
    v 2
    Inchbald, Mrs. ed.   Theatre v 8
    Oxberry, W. ed. New English drama
    v 22
Young Quaker.   Comedy. 5 acts
  In Cumberland's British theatre v 37

Olcott, Virginia
April fool.   Juvenile. 1 act
  In Holiday plays for home, school and
    settlement
Cave of the fates.   New Year's day. 2
  acts
  In Holiday plays for home, school and
    settlement

Day before Thanksgiving.   Juvenile. 1
  act
  In Holiday plays for home, school and
    settlement
Dora, her flag.   Patriotic. 1 act
  In Patriotic plays for young people
Every-girl's friends.   Patriotic. 2 acts
  In Patriotic plays for young people
Flower of the ages.   Easter. 2 acts
  In Holiday plays for home, school and
    settlement
Flowers in the palace garden.   Fairy. 1
  act
  In Everyday plays for the home, school,
    and settlement
Goody Grumble's cottage.   Red Cross. 1
  act
  In Patriotic plays for young people
Grandmother's Cupid.   St. Valentine's
  day. 2 acts
  In Holiday plays for home, school and
    settlement
Key flower.   Juvenile. 3 acts
  In International plays for young people
Lady white and lady yellow.   Juvenile.
  1 act
  In International plays for young people
Little goat lady.   Juvenile. 2 acts
  In International plays for young people
Little homemaker.   Food conservation.
  1 act
  In Patriotic plays for young people
Little invisible guest.   Juvenile. 1 act
  In International plays for young people
Little Jane Patchwork.   Juvenile. 3 acts
  In Patriotic plays for young people
Little people of the autumn.   Nature
  play. 1 act
  In Everyday plays for the home, school,
    and settlement
Night before Christmas.   Juvenile. 2 acts
  In Holiday plays for home, school and
    settlement
On all Souls' eve.   Hallowe'en. 2 acts
  In Holiday plays for home, school and
    settlement
Oneida's dreams.   Patriotic. 1 act
  In Patriotic plays for young people
Poor little boy.   Patriotic. 1 act
  In Patriotic plays for young people
Prayer of the forest spirit.   Arbor Day.
  1 act
  In Holiday plays for home, school and
    settlement
Princess and a chum.   Patriotic. 1 act
  In Patriotic plays for young people
Puritan Christmas.   2 acts
  In Everyday plays for the home, school,
    and settlement
Ruler of the forest.   Animal play. 3 acts
  In Everyday plays for the home, school,
    and settlement
Somebody's princess.   Juvenile. 2 acts
  In International plays for young people
Tina's images.   Juvenile. 2 acts
  In Everyday plays for the home, school,
    and settlement
To London town.   Juvenile. 2 acts
  In International plays for young people

Troll of the mountains. Fairy. 2 acts
In Everyday plays for the home, school,
and settlement
Viva l'Italia. Juvenile. 2 acts
In International plays for young people
Wings of Daedalus. Juvenile. 1 act
In International plays for young people
Wonder-hill. Patriotic. 1 act
In Patriotic plays for young people

Oldenshaw, Lucian
Crabbed age and youth. Comedy. 1 act
In Cranford at home, and other carpet
dramas
Cranford at home (adapted from Mrs.
Gaskell's novel). Provincial life. 3
scenes
In Cranford at home, and other carpet
plays
Italian quarter. Comedy. 1 act
In Cranford at home, and other carpet
plays
Paying guest. Romantic. 2 acts
In Cranford at home, and other carpet
dramas

Oliver, Margaret Scott
Children of Granada. Spain. 1 act
In Six one-act plays
Hand of the prophet. Tragedy. 1 act
In Six one-act plays
Murdering Selina. Comedy. 1 act
In Six one-act plays
Striker. Sociological. 1 act
In Six one-act plays
This youth—gentleman. Fantasy. 1 act
In Six one-act plays
Turtle dove. Chinese. 1 act
In Six one-act plays
Smith, M. M. ed. Short plays of
various types

Oliver, Roland
Little Face. Feminism. 1 act
In Smart Set 44 no 1:131

Oliver, Temple, pseud. *See* Smith, J. O.
D.

O'Neil, George, 1863-
Ladies at twelve. Comedy. 1 act
In Smart Set 55 no 3:73

O'Neill, Eugene Gladstone, 1888-
All God's chillun got wings. N.Y.
Boni. 1920. 12°. 170p. Race pre-
judice. 2 acts
Same in Collected plays (Boni) v 2
[Anna Christie, etc]
Complete works v 2
Amer Merc 1:129
Anna Christie. Melodrama. 4 acts
In Collected plays (Boni) v 2 [Anna
Christie, etc]
Complete works v 1
Hairy ape [and other plays]
Mantle, B. ed. Best plays of 1921-
21 (condensed)
Before breakfast; a play in one act. N.Y.
Shay. 1916. 19p. 25c
Same in Collected plays (Boni) v 1
[Beyond the horizon, etc]
Complete works v 2
Provincetown plays ser 3
Shay, F. ed. Treasury of
plays for women

Beyond the horizon; a play in three acts.
N.Y. Boni. [c1920]. 12°. 165p. Social.
(Pulitzer prize 1920)
Same in Collected plays (Boni) v 1 [Be-
yond the horizon etc]
Complete works v 1
Quinn, A. H. ed. Representa-
tive American plays, 1767-
1923 (1925 ed)
Bound East for Cardiff. Sea. 1 act
In Collected plays (Boni) v 5 [Great
God Brown, etc]
Complete works v 1
Great God Brown, and other plays
Moon of the Caribbees and six other
plays of the sea
Provincetown plays ser 1
Provincetown plays (Stewart Kidd
1921)
Desire under the elms. N.Y. Boni. 1925.
12°. 166. Sex. 3 acts
Same in Collected plays (Boni) v 4
[Desire under the elms, etc]
Complete works v 2
Mantle, B. ed. Best plays of
1924-25 (condensed)
Diff'rent. Mistakes. 2 acts
In Collected plays (Boni) v 2 [Anna
Christie, etc]
Complete works v 1
Emperor Jones, Diff'rent, Straw
Dreamy kid. Psychological. 1 act
In Collected plays (Boni) v 3 [Emperor
Jones etc]
Complete works v 2
Shay, F. ed. Twenty contemporary
one-act plays (American)
Theatre Arts M 4:41
Emperor Jones. Cincinnati. Stewart
Kidd. [c1921]. 12°. 54p. Tragedy. 8
scenes
Same in Collected plays (Boni) v 3
[Emperor Jones, etc]
Complete works v 2
Emperor Jones, Diff'rent,
Straw
Mantle, B. ed. Best plays of
1920-21 (condensed)
Moses, M. J. ed. Representa-
tive American dramas, na-
tional and local
Quinn, A. H. ed. Contempo-
rary one-act plays
Golden Bk 3:517
Theatre Arts M 5:29
First man. Scandal. 4 acts
In Collected plays (Boni) v 3 [Emperor
Jones, etc]
Complete works v 1
Hairy ape [and other plays]
Fog. Sea. 1 act
In Thirst and other one act plays
Fountain. Ponce de Leon. Fantasy. 11
scenes
In Collected plays (Boni) v 5 [Great
God Brown, etc]
Great God Brown, and other plays

Osborn, Laughton, 1809-1878
Bianca Capello; a tragedy. N.Y. More-
head. 1868. 203-419p. 12°. 5 acts
Same in Dramatic works v 1
Calvary. Tragedy. 5 acts
In Calvary
Dramatic works v 1
Cid of Seville. Tragedy. 5 acts
In Dramatic works v 2
Ugo da Este; Uberto; The Cid of
Seville
Double deceit; or, The husband-lovers.
Comedy. 5 acts
In Dramatic works v 4
Silver head; Double deceit
Heart's sacrifice. Tragedy. 5 acts
In Dramatic works v 2
Last Mandeville, etc
Husband-lovers. *See* Osborn, L. Dou-
ble deceit; or, The husband lovers
Last Mandeville. Tragedy. 5 acts
In Dramatic works v 2
Last Mandeville, etc
Magnetiser; or, Ready for anybody.
Comedy. 5 acts
In Magnetiser; The prodigal
Mariamne, being the third of the trag-
edies of Jewish and Biblical his-
tory. . . N.Y. Hinton. 1873. 12°.
p. 167-269. Jewish. 5 acts
Matilda of Denmark. Tragedy. 5 acts
In Dramatic works v 2
Last Mandeville, etc
Meleagros. Tragedy. 5 acts
In Dramatic works v 3
Meleagros; The new Calvary
Monk. Tragedy. 5 acts
In Dramatic works v 2
Last Mandeville, etc
Montanini; comedy. . . 5 acts
Same in Dramatic works v 4
Montanini; School for critics
Natural transformation. *See* Osborn, L.
School for critics; or, a natural trans-
formation
New Calvary. Tragedy. 5 acts
In Meleagros; The new Calvary
Prodigal; or, A vice and virtue. Com-
edy. 5 acts
In Magnetiser; The prodigal
Ready for anybody. *See* Osborn, L.
Magnetiser; or, Ready for anybody
School for critics; or, A natural trans-
formation. Comedy. 5 acts
In Dramatic works v 4
Montanini; School for critics
Silver head. Comedy. 5 acts
In Dramatic works v 4
Silver head; Double deceit
Uberto. Tragedy. 5 acts
In Dramatic works v 2
Ugo da Este; Uberto; The Cid of
Seville
Ugo da Este. Tragedy. 5 acts
In Dramatic works v 2
Ugo da Este; Uberto; The Cid of
Seville

Vice and virtue. *See* Osborn, L. Prodi-
gal; or, A vice and virtue
Virginia. Tragedy. 5 acts
In Dramatic works v 1
Calvary; Virginia
Osborne, Harry
Ann's little affair; a three act comedy.
N.Y. French. c1925. 79p.
Osborne, Hubert
Good men do; an indecorous epilogue.
Shakespearian. 1 act
In Baker, G. P. ed. Plays of the 47
workshop ser 1
O'Shea, Monica Barry
Rush light; a drama in one act. Wash-
ington, D.C. Drama league. 75c.
Character
In Drama 7:602
**Ostrovskiĭ, Aleksandr Nikolaevich, 1823-
1886**
At the jolly spot. Comedy. 3 acts
In Poet Lore 36:1
Bondwomen. Comedy. 4 acts
In Poet Lore 36:475
Domestic picture. Moscow life. 1 act
In Voynich, E. L. Humour of Russia
Enough stupidity in every wise man.
Comedy. 5 acts
In Sayler, O. M. ed. Moscow Art
theatre series of Russian plays
ser 2
Incompatibility of temper. Moscow life.
3 pictures
In Voynich, E. L. Humour of Russia
It's a family affair—we'll settle it our-
selves. Comedy. 4 acts
In Plays
Poverty is no crime. Sociological. 3 acts
In Plays
Protégeé of the mistress. Sociological.
4 acts
In Plays
Sin and sorrow are common to all. Con-
flict of social classes. 4 acts
In Plays
Storm. . . London. Duckworth. 1899. 8°.
119p. Russian patriarchal life. 5
acts
Wolves and sheep. Comedy. 5 acts
In Poet Lore 37:159
Ould, Hermon
Claude. Comedy. 1 act
In Three comedies
One act plays for stage and study
ser 2
Dance of life; a play in nine scenes.
London. Benn. 1924. 12°. 92p.
Discovery. Columbus. 1 act
In Plays of pioneers
Episode. Comedy. 1 act
In Three comedies
Joan the maid; a legend of Joan of Arc.
N.Y. French. c1925. 17p. 1 act
Same in Plays of pioneers
Pathfinder. David Livingston. 1 act
In Plays of pioneers
Thy father and thy mother. Comedy. 1
act
In Three comedies

Overstreet, Harvey Allen, 1875-
Hearts to mend; a fantasy in one act.
Cincinnati. Stewart Kidd. [c1920].
12°. 28p.

Overton, Gwendolen, 1876-
First love—and second. Comi-tragedy. 3
scenes
In Smart Set 3 no 1:141

Owen, Franklin Sanborn, 1897-
Silas Marner; a drama in four acts; adapted from George Eliot's novel. Boston. Baker. 1915. 32p. Social

Owen, Harold, 1872-
Still engaged! a comedy in one act. London. "The Stage" play pub. bureau.
1924. 30p.

Owen, Robert Dale, 1801-1877
Pocahontas: a historical drama in five
acts. N.Y. Geo. Dearborn. 1837.
12°. 240p.

Oxenford, John, 1812-1877
Adrienne Lecouvreur, the reigning favor-
ite. A drama in three acts. London.
Lacy. 12°. 30p. (Lacy's acting edition
of plays. v. 1 no. 4). Historical
Doctor Dilworth. A farce in one act.
Boston. Spencer. [1857?]. 12°. 18p.
Family failing. A farce in one act. . .
Boston. Spencer. [1856?]. 12°. 22p.
My fellow clerk. A farce. In one act. . .
Boston. Spencer. [1856?]. 12°. 16p.

Pacaud, George Washington, 1879-
Social idolatry; a comedy in three acts.
N.Y. French. 1920. 12°. 93p. $1.50

Paget, Violet (Lee, Vernon, pseud.), 1856-
Ariadne in Mantua; a romance in five
acts. Portland. M. Mosher. 1906.
16°. 86p.
Same in Bibelot 12:5
Ballet of the nations; a present-day mor-
ality. . . N.Y. Putnam. 1915. 4°. 25p.
(Part 2 of Satan the waster) 2 acts
Satan the waster; a philosophic war tril-
ogy. . . N.Y. Lane. 1920. 12°. 300p.
$2.50 Allegory. 3 parts
Satan's epilogue to the war. 1 act. Pt. 3
of Satan the waster
In Eng R 29:199
Satan's prologue to the war. 1 act. Pt. 1
of Satan the waster
In Eng R 29:129

Pailleron, Édouard Jules Henri, 1834-1899
Art of being bored (Le monde ou l'on
s'ennuie). . . N.Y. French. [c1914]. 8°.
100p. Comedy. 3 acts
Spark. Comedy in one act. . . Boston.
1879. 12°. 23p.
Triumph of youth; or, The white mouse;
a comedy in three acts. . . Chicago.
Denison. c1907. 12°. 99p.
Washington. A comedy of to-day.
Adapted from the French . . . by
Thomas Earle White and Wm. Henry
Fox. Phila. Allen. 1886. 8°. 30p.

Pain, Mrs. Amelia
Conquest. Comedy. 1 act
In Mine of diamonds, and other plays
Her ladyship's jewels. Comedy. 1 act
In Mine of diamonds, and other plays

Lady typist. Comedy. 1 act
In More short plays
Lost hearts. Fairy play. 1 act
In Mine of diamonds, and other plays
Mrs. Marlowe's case. Romantic. 1 act
In Mine of diamonds, and other plays
Mine of diamonds. Tragedy. 1 act
In Mine of diamonds, and other plays
Pressing engagements. Comedy. 1 act
In Mine of diamonds, and other plays
Quick change. Comedy. 1 act
In More short plays
Reason why. Comedy. 1 act
In More short plays
'Ware wire. Comedy. 1 act
In More short plays

Palamas, Kostes
Royal Blossom; or, Trisevyene. . . New
Haven. Yale Univ. press. 1923. 12°.
163p. $2. Tragedy. 4 parts
Trisevyene. *See* Palamas, K. Royal
Blossom; or, Trisevyene

Pallen, Condé Benoist, 1858-
Aglaë. Poetic. 2 scenes
In Collected poems
Feast of Thalarchus, a dramatic poem.
Boston. Small. 1901. 12°. 73p. Poet-
ic. 1 act
Same in Collected poems

Palm, Carla L.
Perplexing Pirandello. Satirical comedy.
1 act
In Drama 15:102
Schintzleresque. Satire. 1 act
In Drama 14:210

Palmer, Frederick, 1881
Killing them all. War. 2 acts
In Collier's 68:9 O 22 '21

Palmer, Goodrich
Caponsacchi; a play in three acts prologue and epilogue, based upon Robert Browning's "The ring and the
book". . . N.Y. Appleton. 1927. 12°.
185p.

Palmer, H. M.
New Year's day. 1 act
In Harp B 35:43 My '01

Palmer, John
Over the hills. N.Y. Phillips. 1922. 12°.
50c. Comedy. 1 act
Same in Knickerbocker, E. Van B. ed.
Twelve plays
Smart Set 46:227

Palmer, Rose A., joint author. *See* Goodrich, Arthur Frederick, and Palmer,
Rose A.

Palmieri, Aurello, 1870-
On the slopes of Calvary; a religious
drama in three acts . . . dealing with
the Passion of our Lord Jesus
Christ. . . Phila. Palmieri. 1917.
73p. $1

Panella, Antoinette
Red slippers. Chilean. 1 act
In Drama 16:94

Pape, Lee
Bravest thing in the world; a comedy of
childhood in one act. Philadelphia.
Penn Pub. Co. 1917. 12°. 27p.

Parish, Ray
Suburbanism; a play. N.Y. Appleton. 1925. 34p. 1 act

Park, John Edgar, 1879-
Dwarf's spell; a Christmas play. Boston. Pilgrim. c1912. 12°. 55p. 4 acts

Parker, Louis Napoleon, 1852-
Aristocrat; a play. N.Y. Lane. 1917. 12°. 164p. $1. French revolution. 3 acts
Disraeli. N.Y. Lane. 1911. 12°. 114p. Historical. 4 acts
Same in Pierce and Matthews, eds. Masterpieces of modern drama v 1 (abridged)
Drake: a pageant-play in three acts. N.Y. Lane. 1912. 12°. 117p. 75c. Historical
Joseph and his brethren: a pageant play. N.Y. Lane. 1913. 12°. 154p. $1. Biblical. 4 acts
Man in the street. . ., N.Y. French. c1912. 12°. p. 251-262. Comedy. 1 act
Masque of war and peace (1915). [London]. Bickers. 1915. 8°. 30p. War. 1 act
Mavourneen; a comedy in three acts. N.Y. Dodd. 1916. 12°. 208p. $1.25
Mayflower; a play in three acts. [N.Y.?]. Privately printed. [190-?]. 4°. 78p. Historical
Minuet; a little play in verse. N.Y. French. c1922. 12°. 15p. French Revolution. 1 act
Same in One act plays for stage and study ser 1
Thomas, C. S. ed. Atlantic book of junior plays
Cent 89:370
Pomander walk. N.Y. Lane. 1911. 12°. 266p. Comedy. 3 acts
Summer is a-comin' in; a light comedy in three acts. . . N.Y. French. c1922. 12°. 79p.

Parker, Louis Napoleon, 1852-, and Carson, Murray
Rosemary, that's for remembrance; a comedy in four acts. . . N.Y. French. c1924. 12°. 73p.

Parker, Maud May
Louisiana; a pageant of yesterday and to-day. New Orleans. Hauser printing co. [c1917]. 12°. 65p. 5 acts
Missive; a dramatic poem. Boston. Poet Lore Co. 1907. 12°. 48p. Early Christian. 1 act

Parkhurst, Winthrop
Beggar and the king. Supernatural. 1 act
In Leonard, S. A. ed. Atlantic book of modern plays
Shay, F. ed. Treasury of plays for men
Drama 9:62
Getting unmarried. Farce. 1 act
In Smart Set 54 no 4:91
Importance of being early. Comedy. 1 act
In Smart Set 50 no 2:229

It never happens. Comedy. 1 act
In Smart Set 56 no 4:77
Morracca. Biblical. 1 act
In Drama 8 no 32:536

Parmer, Sheldon
Arizona cowboy; a comedy drama of the great Southwest in four acts. Chicago. Denison

Parrish, John
When the clock strikes. Burlesque. 1 act
In Nicholson, K. ed. Appleton book of short plays

Parry, Bernard
Purse-strings; a comedy in four acts. N.Y. French. 1919. 12°. 112p. 60c

Parsons, Mrs Margaret Colby (Getchell), 1891-
April Fool's day. *See* Parsons, M. C. Love lyric of letters
Beauty and the beast. Juvenile. 6 scenes
In Red letter day plays
Birthday cake. Juvenile. 1 act
In In the children's play-house
Boarding school. *See* Parsons, M. C. Play of an oldtime boarding school
Christmas. *See* Parsons, M. C. St. Nicholas
Christmas message. Juvenile. 2 scenes
In Red letter day plays
In the children's play-house
Courtship of Miles Standish. Thanksgiving. 6 parts
In Red letter day plays
Easter lily. Juvenile. 2 scenes
In In the children's play-house
Fire-spirits. Hallowe'en. 1 act
In Red letter day plays
Hallowe'en. *See* Parsons, M. C. Fire-spirits
Hansel and Gretel. Juvenile. 2 scenes
In Red letter day plays
In a valentine box. St. Valentine's day. 1 act
In Red letter day plays
Jack-i'-the-green. May day. 1 act
In Red letter day plays
Little lame prince (from D. M. Muloch's Little lame prince). Juvenile. 5 scenes
In Red letter day plays
Little Rosette. Juvenile. 5 scenes
In Red letter day plays
Love lyric of letters. April Fool's day. 3 acts
In Red letter day plays
Marriage of Sir Gawain. Juvenile. 3 scenes
In Red letter day plays
May day. *See* Parsons, M. C. Potentate of weatherdom
'Neath the scepter of Susan. Boarding school. 2 acts
In Red letter day plays
Play of an oldtime boarding school.
In Red letter day plays
Potentate of weatherdom. May day. 1 act
In Red letter day plays

Parsons, M. C.—*Continued.*
Prophecy. Juvenile. 1 act
In In the children's play-house
St. Nicholas. Christmas. 3 acts
In Red letter day plays
Snow-white and Rose Red. Juvenile. 3 scenes
In Red letter day plays
Thanksgiving dinner dance. Juvenile. 1 act
In In the children's play-house
Thanksgiving pumpkin. Juvenile. 1 act
In In the children's play-house
Trial of the glorious Fourth. Fourth of July. 1 act
In In the children's play-house
Wooden bowl. Japanese. 4 scenes
In Red letter day plays

Pascal, Floy
Facing reality. Farce. 1 act
In Poet Lore 33:451

Paston, George, pseud. *See* Symonds, Emily Morse

Patterson, Marjorie
Pan in ambush; a play in one act. Norman, Remington Co. N.Y. 12°. 1921. 45p. 75c. Poetic

Paul, Howard, 1835-
Lucky hit. A petit comedy in one act. . . Boston. Spencer. [18—]. 12°. 15p.
Mob cup; or, Love's disguises. A domestic drama in two acts. London. Lacy. n.d. 12°. 24p. (Lacy's acting edition of plays. v. 11 no. 153)
Rappings and table movings. An original farce, in one act. London. Lacy. n.d. 12°. 17p. (Lacy's acting edition of plays. v. 11 no. 156)

Paulding, Frederick
Woman's hour, an original comedy of American life, in three acts. N.Y. French. c1926. 12°. 154p.

Paulding, James Kirk, 1778-1860, **and Paulding, William Irving**
Americans in England. *See* Paulding, J. K. and W. I. Bucktails; or, Americans in England
Antipathies; or, The enthusiasts by the ears. Comedy. 5 acts
In American comedies
Bucktails; or, Americans in England. Comedy. 5 acts
In American comedies
Cure for love. *See* Paulding, J. K. and W. I. Madmen all; or, Cure for love
Enthusiasts. *See* Paulding, J. K. and Paulding, W. I. Antipathies; or, The enthusiasts
Madmen all; or, Cure for love. Comedy. 5 acts
In American comedies
Noble exile. Comedy. 5 acts
In American comedies

Paull, H. M.
Bolt from the blue. Problem. 1 act
In 19 Cent 94:843
Other room. Comedy. 1 act
In 19 Cent 90:807
Painter and millionaire. Modern morality. 2 acts
In Fortn 92 (os):1115
Vision. Monastic life. 2 acts
In 19 Cent 89:175

Paull, H. M., and Housman, Lawrence
Unknown star. Christmas mystery. 3 acts
In 19 Cent 86:1065

Paulton, E. A.
Dormitory girls. Washington. Commission on training camp activities. 1918. 12°. 16p. 1 act

Paulton, Edward
Philippa gets there; a farce-comedy in three acts. N.Y. French. c1926. 12°. 128p.

Paulton, Harry, and Paulton, Edward
Noble; a comedy in three acts. N.Y. French. 1912. 12°. 50c

Payne, Fanny Ursula, 1875-
Arbor day. 1 act
In Plays for Anychild
At the gate of peace. Pageant. 1 act
In Plays and pageants of democracy
Christmas day. 1 act
In Plays for Anychild
Columbus day. 1 act
In Plays for Anychild
Conversion of Mrs. Slacker. Patriotic. 1 act
In Plays and pageants of democracy
Decoration day. 1 act
In Plays for Anychild
Dekanawida. Patriotic. 5 episodes
In Plays and pageants of citizenship
Flag day. 1 act
In Plays for Anychild
Golden star. Pageant of victory. 1 act
In Plays and pageants of democracy
Graduation day. 1 act
In Plays for Anychild
Hardships at Valley Forge. Patriotic. 1 act
In Plays and pageants of democracy
Highway of the king. Pageant. 4 episodes
In Plays and pageants of democracy
Humane citizens. Kindness to animals. 1 act
In Plays and pageants of citizenship
Lincoln's birthday. 1 act
In Plays for Anychild
New Year's day. 1 act
In Plays for Anychild
Old Tight-wad and the victory dwarf. 1 act
In Plays and pageants of citizenship
Rich citizens. Government. 1 act
In Plays and pageants of citizenship
Soap-box orator. Patriotic. 1 act
In Plays and pageants of citizenship
Spirit of New England. Patriotic. 5 episodes
In Plays and pageants of citizenship
Thanksgiving day. 1 act
In Plays for Anychild

Triumph of democracy. Patriotic. 5 episodes
In Plays and pageants of citizenship
Victory of the good citizen. Patriotic. 1 act
In Plays and pageants of citizenship
Vision of Columbus; a pageant of democracy. 1 act
In Plays and pageants of democracy
Two war plays for schools
Washington's birthday. 1 act
In Plays for Anychild

Payne, John Howard, 1791-1852
Accusation; or, The family of D'Anglade: a melodrama, in three acts. . . Boston. Richardson. 1818. 12°. 76p.
Ali Pacha; or, The signet-ring. A melodrama in two acts. . . N.Y. Murden. 1823. 12°. 36p.
Same in Cumberland's British theatre v 11 no 2
Brutus; or The fall of Tarquin. An historical tragedy. . . London. White. 1818. 56p.
Same in Moses, M. J. ed. Representative plays by American dramatists from 1765 to the present day v 2
Clari; or, The maid of Milan. A drama in three acts. Boston. Spencer. 1856. 35p. Opera
Same in Cumberland's British theatre v 24 no 6
Fall of Algiers; a comic opera in three acts. . . London. Cumberland. [n.d.]. 12°. 47p. (Cumberland's British theatre. v. 9 no. 6)
Fall of Tarquin. *See* Payne, J. H. Brutus; or, The face of Tarquin
Julia; or, The wanderer; a comedy in five acts. . . N.Y. Longworth. 1806. 70p.
Lancers. An interlude in one act. . . London Cumberland. [n.d.]. (Cumberland's British theatre. v. 19 no. 3)
Love in humble life; a petite comedy in one act. . . London. Davidson. [n.d.]
Same in Cumberland's British theatre v 11 no 5
Lover's vows; a play in five acts. . . Baltimore. Dobbin. 1809. 12°. 90p. Romantic
Maid of Milan. *See* Payne, J. H. Clari; or, The maid of Milan
Richelieu: a domestic tragedy, founded on fact. In five acts. . . N.Y. Murden. 1826. 79p.
Thérèse the orphan of Geneva. 3 acts
In Bates, A. ed. Drama v 19:145
'Twas I! a farce in one act. London. Lacy. n.d. 12°. 15p. (Lacy's acting edition of plays. v. 9 no. 128)
Two galley slaves; a melo-drama in two acts. . . London. Davidson. [n.d.]. 12°. 33p
Same in Cumberland's British theatre v 10 no 7
Wanderer. *See* Payne, J. H. Julia; or, The wanderer

Payne, John Howard, 1736-, and Irving, Washington
Charles the second; or, The merry monarch. A comedy in two acts. . . London. Dolby. [1824]. 12°. 45p.
Same in Cumberland's British theatre v 9 no 3
Quinn, A. H. ed. Representative American plays, 1793-1923 (1925 ed.)

Payson, Stella T.
Society column. Beckley. Chicago. 1923. 12°. 28p. 1 act

Peabody, Josephine P. (Mrs. Lionel Simeon Marks), 1874-1922
Chameleon; a comedy in three acts. N.Y. French. 1918. 12°. 50c
Fortune and men's eyes; a drama in one act. N.Y. French. 1917 12°. 49p. Historical. Shakespeare's sonnets
Same in Fortune and men's eye's, etc
Cohen, H. L. ed. One-act plays by modern authors
Dickinson, A. D. ed. Drama
Marlowe. A drama in five acts. Boston. Houghton. 1901. 156p. Historical
Piper; a play in four acts. Boston. Houghton. 1909. 12°. 201p. Symbolic
Same in Dickinson, T. H. ed. Chief contemporary dramatists ser 2
Moses, M. J. ed. Representative American dramas, national and local
Portrait of Mrs. W.; a play in three acts with an epilogue. Boston. Houghton. 1922. 12°. 150p. Mary Wollstonecraft
Wings; a drama in one act. N.Y. French. 1917. 12°. 28p. 25c. Northumbria. 700 A.D.
Same in Harper's M 110:947
Poet Lore 25:352
Wolf of Gubbio; a comedy in three acts. Boston. Houghton. 1913. 12°. 195p. $1.10

Peacey, Howard
El Dorado; a play in three acts. . . N.Y. French. 1925. 12°. 142p. South American
Fifth of November, a play in three acts. London. Benn. 1924. 12°. 139p. Historical
Magic hours, a play in four acts. London. Benn. 1925. 12°. 109p. Comedy

Peach, L. du Garde
Wind o' the moors. Derbyshire. 1 act
In Clark, A. K. ed. Three one-act plays

Peacock, Thomas Love, 1785-1866
Circle of Loda. Legendary-Scandia. 4 acts
In Plays of Thomas Love Peacock
Dilettanti. Farce. 2 acts
In Plays of Thomas Love Peacock
Three doctors. Musical farce. 2 acts
In Plays of Thomas Love Peacock

Peake, Richard Brinsley, 1792-1847
Amateurs and actors. A musical farce in two acts. . . London. Cumberland. n.d. 12°. 36p. (Cumberland's British theatre. v. 16 no. 5)
Chancery suit! A comedy in five acts. . . Baltimore. Robinson. 1831. 12°. 76p.
Comfortable lodgings, or Paris in 1750: a farce in two acts. . . London. Davidson. n.d. 12°. 36p. (Cumberland's British theatre. v. 29 no. 8)
Court and city. A comedy, in five acts. . . London. Cumberland. n.d. 12°. 72p. (Cumberland's British theatre. v. 42 no. 2)
Day at Boulogne. *See* Peake, R. B. Master's rival; or, a day at Boulogne
Duel; or, My two nephews: a farce in two acts. . . London. Cumberland. n.d. 12°. 43p. (Cumberland's British theatre. v. 22 no. 6)
Haunted inn, a farce in two acts. Boston. Richardson. 1829. 12°. 48p.
Same in Cumberland's British theatre v 30 no 7
Hundred pound note; a farce, in two acts. . . London. Cumberland. n.d. 12°. 43p. (Cumberland's British theatre. v. 34 no. 8)
Master's rival; or, A day at Boulogne: a farce in two acts. . . London. Cumberland. ₁c1829₁. 12°. 46p. (Cumberland's British theatre. no. 152)
Uncle Rip. A farce in two acts. . . London. Cumberland. n.d. 12°. 40p. (Cumberland's British theatre. v. 42 no. 7)
Walk for a wager; or, A bailiff's bet. A musical farce, in two acts. . . London. Fearman. 1819. 12°. 72p.

Pearn, Violet, joint author. *See* Blackwood, Algernon, and Pearn, Violet

Pearse, Padraic H., 1880-1916
Iosagan ₁Child Jesus₁. Religious. 1 act
In Collected works
Singer and other plays
King. Allegory. 1 act
In Collected works
Singer and other plays
Master. Religious. 1 act
In Collected works
Singer and other plays
Singer. Irish patriotism. 1 act
In Collected works
Singer and other plays

Peattie, Mrs. Elia (Wilkinson), 1862-
Family reunion. Comedy. 1 act
In Wander weed, and ₁other plays₁
Great delusion. Spiritualism. 1 act
In Wander weed, and ₁other plays₁
Job's tears. Tragedy. 1 act
In Wander weed, and ₁other plays₁
Love of a Caliban; a romantic opera in one act. Wausau, Wis. Van Vechten. 1898. xxi-xxxxip. 4°
Pity. Tragedy. 1 act
In Wander weed, and ₁other plays₁
Spring cleaning. Marriage. 1 act
In Wander weed, and ₁other plays₁

Sunrise. Peace. 1 act
In Wander weed, and ₁other plays₁
Wander weed. Symbolic. 1 act
In Wander weed, and ₁other plays₁
When the silver bell tree blooms. Character. 1 act
In Wander weed, and ₁other plays₁

Peck, Elizabeth Weller
Nathaniel Hawthorne's Scarlet letter, dramatized. A play in five acts. Boston. Franklin press. 1876. 8°. 72p. Social

Pedder, D. C.
Between two trains. Youth and age. 1 act
In 19 Cent 58:649

Péladan, Joséphin, called Le Sar, 1859-1918
St. Francis of Assisi; a play in five acts. N.Y. Scribner. 1913. 12°. 118p. $1. Historical

Pelée, Lillian Sutton
At the little pipe. Hungarian folk-play. 2 scenes
In Poet Lore 31:422
Ties of blood. Perjury. 1 act
In Poet Lore 32:572

Pellettieri, Guiseppe Mario, 1882-
Love enchained. Comedy. 5 acts
In Love enchained, and other plays
Mater dolorosa. Melodrama. 5 acts
In Love enchained, and other plays
Retribution; a drama in four acts. . . St. Louis. The author. 1922. 12°. 168p. $1.25 Drug habit
Society's victim. Social. 4 acts
In Love enchained, and other plays

Pellico, Silvio, 1788-1854
Esther of Engaddi. A tragedy from the Italian. London. Whittaker. ₁1836₁. 8°. 84p. 5 acts
Euphemio of Messina; a tragedy. . . N.Y. Bancroft. 1834. 12°. 62p. 5 acts
Francesca da Rimini, a tragedy in five acts. London. Francis. 1856. 12°. 75p. *Also.* London. Unwin. ₁1915₁

Pendray, Edward, joint author. *See* Nicholson, Kenyon, and Pendray, Edward

Peple, Edward Henry, 1869-
Girl. 1 act
In One-act plays for stage and study ser 2
Jury of our peers; a comedy in three acts. N.Y. French. 1925. 12°. 120p. 75c
Littlest rebel; a play in four acts. N.Y. French. 1917. 98p. 50c
Pair of sixes; a farce in three acts. N.Y. French. 1917. 171p. 50c
Prince chap; a comedy in three acts. N.Y. French. 1914. 12°. 101p. 50c

Percy, William A., 1885
In April once. New Haven. Yale press. 1920. 12°. 134p. Florentine tragedy. 1 act

Perel'man, Osip Isidorovich (Ossip Dymov, pseud.), 1878-
Nju; an everyday tragedy. . . N.Y. Knopf. 1917. 12°. 96p. 4 acts

Perez, Isaac Loeb, 1851-1915
Champagne. Social. 1 act
In Block, E. tr. One-act plays from
the Yiddish

Peréz Galdós, Benito, 1845-1920
Duchess of San Quentin. Comedy. 3 acts
In Clark, B. H. ed. Masterpieces of
modern Spanish drama
Electra. Fanaticism. 5 acts
In Turrell, C. A. tr. Contemporary
Spanish dramatists
Drama 1 no 2:13
Grandfather (El albruelo). 5 acts
In Poet Lore 21:161

Perkins, Edna Brush
Stage-struck. Comedy. 1 act
In Harp B 36:108 F '02

Perkins, Newton
Fifty-fifty; a comedy in three acts. . .
Chicago. Denison. 1918. 118p.

Pertwee, Roland
Evening dress indispensable; an utterly
nonsensical playlet in one act. N.Y.
French. c1925. 12°. 22p.
Same in Ladies' Home Journal one-act
plays
Ladies H J 41:10 N '24
Loveliest thing. Christmas. 1 act
In Ladies' Home Journal one-act plays
Odd streak; a play in one act. N.Y.
French. 1920. 12°. 24p. 30c
Postal orders; a farce. N.Y. French.
1919. 12°. 28p. 30c. 1 act

Peterson, Agnes E.
Wind. California desert. 1 act
In Drama 15:174

Peterson, Frederick, 1859-
Two doctors at Akragas. Greek medi-
cine. 1 act
In Flutter of the gold-leaf. (*See* Dar-
gan, O. T. and Peterson, F.)
Atlan M 107:816

Peterson, Frederick, joint author. *See*
Dargan Olive Tilford and Peterson,
Frederick

Petrova, Olga, pseud. (Mrs John D. Stew-
art), 1886-
Ghoul; a play in one act. . . Boston. Four
Seas. ɾc1925ɟ. 12°. 24p. Suicide
Hurricane; four episodes in the story of
a life. Boston. Four Seas. 1924.
12°. 104p. $2. Social
White peacock; a play in three acts.
Boston. Four Seas. 1922. 12°. $2.
Melodrama

Pfeiffer, Edward Heyman
Lamp. Fantasy. 1 act
In International (NY) 7:108

Phelps, A. L.
Woman's heart. Romantic. 3 scenes
In Canad M 46:496

Phelps, Elizabeth Stuart (Mrs. H. D.
Ward), 1844-1911
Joy giver. Supernatural. 1 act
In Harp B 38:25 Ja '04
Within the gates. Supernatural. 1 act
In McClure 17:35, 142, 236

Phelps, Pauline
Shakespearian conference (a drama).
N.Y. Warner. 1901. 12°. 15p. 1 act

Phelps, Pauline, and Short, Marion
Belle of Philadelphia town; a colonial
comedy in four acts. N.Y. French.
c1925. 12°. 104p.
Cosy corners; a comedy in four acts.
N.Y. French. c1922. 8°. 107p,
Only me; a modern play in three acts.
N.Y. French. c1924. 96p.

Phelps, S. K.
Fairy prince. Benevolence. 1 act
In 19 Cent 63:138

Phillips, Mrs. Alfred
Master passion. A comedy in two acts.
London. Lacy. n.d. 12°. 30p. (Lacy's
acting edition of plays. v. 7 no. 105)
Organic affection. A farce in one act.
London. Lacy. n.d. 12°. 20p. (Lacy's
acting edition of plays. v. 5 no. 75)
Uncle Crotchet. A farce in one act.
London. Lacy. n.d. 12°. 22p. (Lacy's
acting edition of plays. v. 10 no. 145)

Phillips, David Graham, 1867-1911
Point of law; a dramatic incident. So-
cial. 1 act
In Worth of a woman
Worth of a woman. Social. 4 acts
In Worth of a woman

Phillips, Stephen, 1868-1915
Adversary. Responsibility. 1 act
In Lyrics and dramas
Contemp 102:407
Armageddon; a modern epic drama in a
prologue, series of scenes, and an epil-
ogue, partly in prose and partly in
verse. London. Lane. 1915. 12°. 94p.
World war. 4 scenes
Aylmer's secret. Science. 3 scenes
In Collected plays
Harold. Chronicle. 3 acts
In Poetry Review 7:1, 109
Herod; a tragedy. N.Y. Lane. 1901. 12°.
126p. 3 acts
Same in Pierce and Matthews, eds.
Masterpieces of modern drama v 1
(abridged)
King, a tragedy in a continued series of
scenes. London. Swift. 1912. 12°.
54p. 5 scenes
Same in Lyrics and dramas
Nero. N.Y. Macmillan. 1906. 12°. 200p.
Historical. 4 acts
Same in Collected plays
Nero's mother. Historical. 1 act
In Lyrics and dramas
Paolo and Francesca; a tragedy in four
acts. N.Y. Lane. 1903. 12°. 120p.
Same in Dickinson, T. H. ed. Con-
temporary plays
Pietro of Siena, a drama. N.Y. Mac-
millan. 1910. 12°. 82p. Romantic. 3
acts
Same in Collected plays
Sin of David. N.Y. Macmillan. 1906. 12°.
141p. Biblical. 3 acts
Same in Collected plays

Phillips, Stephen—*Continued.*
Ulysses; a drama . . . in a prologue and
three acts.	N.Y. Macmillan. 1902.
12°. 158p.	Mythological
Same in Collected plays
		Cohen, H. L. ed.	Junior play
		book
Unfinished masterpiece.	Character. 3
scenes
In Eng R 34:21-28
	Strand M 63:450-54

**Phillips, Stephen, 1868-1915, and Carr, J.
Comyns**
Faust; freely adapted from Goethe's
dramatic poem.	N.Y. Macmillan.
1908. 12°. 208p.	Tragedy 4 acts
Same in Collected plays

Phillips, John Franklyn
Honor; a family drama in three acts.
N.Y. 1909. 12°. 53p.
Percy B. Shelley; a vicissitude in four
acts.	N.Y. Printed by the author.
1908. 61p.

Phillpotts, Eden, 1862-
Breezy morning.	London. French.
ₜ18—ₗ. 12°. 16p.	Comedy. 1 act
Carrier-pigeon.	Tragi-comedy. 1 act
In Curtain raisers
Comedy royal, in four acts.	London.
Privately printed for subscribers only
by T. Werner Laurie. 1925. 8°. 166p.
Historical
Devonshire cream.	N.Y. Macmillan.
1925. 12°. 110p. $1.75.	English rural
life. 3 acts
Farmer's wife; a comedy in three acts.
London. Duckworth. ₜ1917.ₗ 16°. 124p.
Hiatus.	Social. 1 act
In Curtain raisers
Mother, a play in four acts.	N.Y.
Brentanos. 1914. 12°. 101p.	Melo-
drama
Same in Three plays
Pair of knickerbockers.	N.Y. French.
1900. 12°. 19p.
Point of view.	Domestic. 1 act
In Curtain raisers
St. George and the dragons; a comedy in
three acts.	London. Duckworth.
1919. 12°. 102p.
Secret woman; a play in five acts.	N.Y.
Brentano's. 1914. 12°. 90p.	Melo-
drama
Same in Three plays
Shadow; a play in three acts.	N.Y.
Brentano's. 1914. 12°. 93p.	Melo-
drama. 3 acts
Same in Three plays

**Phillpotts, Eden, 1862-, and Hastings, B.
M.**
Angel in the house; a comedy in three
acts.	N.Y. French. 1915. 12°. 96p.
Bed rock; a comedy in three acts.	Lon-
don.	Stage play pub. bur. 1924. 12°.
120p.

Pierce, Carl Webster
Breaking Winnie; a comedy in three acts.
N.Y. Fitzgerald Pub. Corp. 1923. 12°.
62p.

Lady to call; a comedy in one act based
upon a story of Madeline Poole.
Boston. Baker. 1918. 10p.
Tip by radio; a play in three acts.	Bos-
ton. Baker. 1923. 12°. 68p.

Pieshkov, Aleksieĭ Maksimovich.	*See*
Gorki, Maxim, pseud.

Pillot, Eugene
Gazing globe.	Tragedy. 1 act
In Lewis, B. R. ed.	Contemporary
one-act plays
	Stratford J 3:26 N '18
Hunger.	Morality. 1 act
In Mayorga, M. G. ed.	Representative
one-act plays
	Stratford J 3:26 N '18
Just two men.	Sea. 1 act
In Clements, C. S. ed.	Sea plays
	Shay, F. ed.	Treasury of plays for
	men
My lady dreams.	Romantic. 1 act
In Shay, F. ed.	Treasury of plays for
	women
Sundial.	1 act
In One-act plays for stage and study
	ser 3
Two crooks and a lady.	Crime. 1 act
In Plays of the 47 workshops ser 1
Young wonder.	A one act play of mod-
ern hero-worship.	Comedy. 1 act
In Drama 11:151-53

Pinero, Sir Arthur Wing, 1855-
Amazons; a farcical romance in three
acts.	Boston. Baker. 1895. 12°. 189p.
3 acts
Benefit of the doubt, a comedy in 3 acts.
Chicago. ₜc1895ₗ. 229p. 12°.
Big drum.	A comedy in four acts. . .
London. Chiswick press. 1915. 12°.
114p.
Cabinet minister; a farce in four acts.
N.Y. Lovell. ₜc1891ₗ. 12°. 188p.
Dandy Dick; a play in three acts.	N.Y.
U.S. Book Co. ₜc1893ₗ. 12°. 162p.
Farce
Dr. Harmer's holidays; a contrast in nine
scenes.	London. Chiswick press.
1924. 82p.
Enchanted cottage; a fable in three acts.
London. Chiswick press. 1921. 12°.
83p.
Fantastics.	*See* Pinero, A. W.	Princess
and the butterfly
Freaks; an idyll of suburbia, in three acts.
London. Chiswick press. 1917. 12°.
99p.
Gay Lord Quex, a comedy in four acts.
N.Y. Russell. 1900. 12°. 186p.
Same in Gay Lord Quex
	Social dramas v 2
	Moses, M. J. ed.	Representa-
	tive British dramas
His house in order; a comedy in four
acts.	Boston. Baker. 1907. 12°. 204p.
Same in Social plays v 3
Hobby-horse; a comedy in three acts.
N.Y. U.S. book co. ₜc1892ₗ. 12°. 168p.

In chancery; an original fantastic comedy in three acts. N.Y. French. c1905. 12°. 72p.

Iris; a drama in five acts. N.Y. Russell. 1902. 12°. 224p. Social
Same in Social plays v 2

Lady Bountiful, a story of years; a play in four acts. London. Heinemann. 16°. 185p. Melodrama

Letty; an original drama in four acts and an epilogue. Boston. Baker. 1905. 12°. 225p. Social
Same in Social plays v 3

Magistrate; a farce in three acts. N.Y. Chicago. United States Book Co. [c1892]. 12°. 164p.

Mid-channel; a play in four acts. Boston. Baker. [c1910]. 12°. 221p. Social
Same in Social plays v 4

"Mind the paint" girl. Boston. Baker. 1910. 12°. 221p. Comedy. 4 acts

Mr. Livermore's dream, a lesson in thrift. London. Chiswick press. 1916. 8°. 25p. 1 act

Money spinner; an original comedy in two acts. N.Y. French. 1900. 12°. 43p.

Notorious Mrs. Ebbsmith. A drama in four acts. Boston. 1895. 12°. 200p. Social
Same in Social plays v 1

Playgoers. A domestic episode. London. Chiswick press. 1913. 8°. 27p. 1 act

Preserving Mr. Panmure. A comic play in four acts. London. Chiswick press. 1910. 8°. 134p.

Princess and the butterfly; or, The fantastics. A comedy in five acts. N.Y. French. [c1897]. 12°. 244p.

Profligate. . . London. Heinemann. 1891. 16°. 123p. Social. 4 acts

Quick work; a story of a war marriage in three acts. London. Chiswick press. 1918. 8°. 77p.

Rocket; an original comedy in three acts. N.Y. French. c1905. 12°. 80p.

Schoolmistress; a farce in three acts. Boston. Baker. 1894. 12°. 177p.

Seat in the park; a warning. N.Y. French. c1922. 12°. 18p. 1 act

Second Mrs. Tanqueray; a play in four acts. Boston. 1894. 12°. 174p. Social
Same in Social plays v 1
Pierce & Matthews, eds. Masterpieces of modern drama v 1 (abridged)

Squire; an original comedy in three acts. N.Y. French. c1905. 12°. 81p.

Sweet lavender; a comedy in three acts. Boston. Baker. [c1893]. 12°. 184p.

Thunderbolt; an episode in the history of a provincial family; in four acts. Boston. Baker. 1909. 12°. 237p. Social
Same in Social plays v 4
Pierce and Matthews, eds. Masterpieces of modern drama v 1 (abridged)

Times; a comedy. N.Y. U.S. Book Co. [c1891]. 12°. 192p. 4 acts

Trelawny of the "Wells"; a comedietta in four acts. Chicago. 1898. 12°. 215p.

Weaker sex; a comedy in three acts. Boston. Baker. 1894. 12°. 133p.

Widow of Wasdale Head. Fantasy. 1 act
In Clark, B. H. ed. Representative one-act plays by British and Irish authors
One act plays for stage and study ser 1
Smart Set 43 no 1:63

Wife without a smile; a comedy in disguise, in three acts. Boston. Baker. 1905. 12°. 166p.

Pinski, David, 1872-
Abigail. Biblical. 1 act
In Goldberg, I. ed. Six plays of the Yiddish theatre
King David and his wives

Abishag. Biblical. 1 act
In King David and his wives

Bathsheba. Biblical. 1 act
In King David and his wives

Beautiful nun. War. 1 act
In Ten plays

Cripples. Comedy. 1 act
In Ten plays

Diplomacy. Satire. 1 act
In Ten plays

Dollar. Symbolic comedy. 1 act
In Ten plays
Lewis, B. R. ed. Contemporary one-act plays
Stratford J 1:25 Je '17

Dumb Messiah. Persecution of Jews. 3 acts
In Three plays

Forgotten souls. Sex. 1 act
In Goldberg, I. ed. Six plays of the Yiddish theatre
Shay, F. and Loving, P. eds. Fifty contemporary one-act plays

God of the newly rich merchant. Religious mania. 1 act
In Ten plays

In the harem. Biblical. 1 act
In King David and his wives

Invention and the king's daughter. Dementia. 1 act
In Ten plays

Isaac Sheftet. Sociological. 3 acts
In Three plays

Last Jew. (Die familie Zwie). Tragedy. 4 acts
In Three plays

Little heroes. World war. 1 act
In Goldberg, I. ed. Six plays of the Yiddish theatre ser 2
Ten plays
Stratford J 1:17 Je '17

Michael. Biblical. 1 act
In King David and his wives
Stratford J 2:25 Ap '18

Phonograph. Comedy. 1 act
In Ten plays

Poland—1919. Historical. 1 act
In Ten plays

Pinsky, D.—*Continued.*
Stranger.   Legendary. 1 act
  In Goldberg, I. ed.   Six plays of the
    Yiddish theatre ser 2
Treasure; a drama in four acts; tr. by
  Ludwig Lewisohn.   N.Y. Huebsch.
  1915. 12°. 194p. $1.   Symbolic
Pirandello, Luigi, 1867-
Each in his own way.   (Ciascuno a suo
  modo).   Comedy. 2 acts
  In Each in his own way and two other
    plays
"Henry IV."   Tragedy. 3 acts
  In Three plays
Man with the flower in his mouth.   Dia-
  log. 1 act
  In Dial 75:313
Naked (Vestire gl'ignudi).   Tragedy. 3
  acts
  In Each in his own way and two other
    plays
Pleasure of honesty.   (Il piacere dell
  'onestà).   Comedy. 3 acts
  In Each in his own way and two other
    plays
Right you are! (If you think so).   Par-
  able. 3 acts
  In Three plays
Sicilian limes.   Romantic. 1 act
  In Goldberg, I. tr.   Plays of the Ital-
    ian theatre
    Theatre Arts M 6:329
Six characters in search of an author.
  Comedy. 3 acts
  In Three plays
Planard, François Antoine Eugène de, 1783-
1855
Is he alive; or, All puzzled!!   A farce in
  two acts. London. White. 1818. 8°.
  32p.
Planché, Mrs. Elizabeth St. George
Handsome husband; a comic drama in
  one act.   London. Lacy. n.d. 12°.
  26p. (Lacy's acting edition of plays.
  v. 11 no. 157)
Planché, James Robinson, 1796-1880
Amoroso, king of Little Britain.   A ser-
  io-comic, bombastic, operatic inter-
  lude in one act. . . London. Cumber-
  land. [n.d.] 12°. 19p. (Cumberland's
  British theatre. v. 43 no. 7)
Beauty and the beast.   Fairy. 2 acts
  In Extravaganzas v 2
Bee and the orange tree; or, The four
  wishes.   Fairy. 1 act
  In Extravaganzas v 3
"Birds" of Aristophanes.   Dramatic ex-
  periment. 1 act
  In Extravaganzas v 3
Blue Beard.   Burletta. 1 act
  In Extravaganzas v 2
Blue Bird of Paradise.   *See* Planché, J.
  R. King charming; or, The blue bird
  of Paradise
Boarded and done for.   *See* Planché, J.
  R. Jenkinses; or, Boarded and done
  for
Bride of the isles.   *See* Planché, J. R.
  Vampire; or, The bride of the isles

Brigand.   A romantic drama in two
  acts. . . London. Cumberland. [n.d.]
  12°. 36p. (Cumberland's British theatre. v. 24 no. 7)
Camp at the Olympic.   A new and original introductory extravaganza and
  dramatic review. London. Lacy. n.d.
  12°. 26p. (Lacy's acting edition of
  plays. v. 12 no. 170). 1 act
  Same in Extravaganzas v 4
Card party.   *See* Planché, J. R. High,
  low, Jack, and the game; or, The card
  party
Charles the Twelfth; an historical drama,
  in two acts. . . London. Davidson.
  [n.d.]. 12°. 52p. (Cumberland's Bri-
  tish theatre. v. 25 no. 2)
Cymon and Iphigenia.   Pastoral. 1 act
  In Extravaganzas v 4
Deep deep sea; or, Perseus and Andro-
  meda.   Burletta. 1 act
  In Extravaganzas v 1
Discreet princess; or, The three glass
  distaffs.   Fairy. 1 act
  In Extravaganzas v 5
Dramas at home; or, An evening with
  Puff.   Extravaganza. 1 act
  In Extravaganzas v 2
Dramas levée; or, A peep in the past.
  Pièce d'occasion. 1 act
  In Extravaganzas v 2
Evening with Puff.   *See* Planché, J. R.
  Drama at home; or, An evening with
  Puff
Fair one with the golden locks.   Fairy.
  1 act
  In Extravaganzas v 2
Fawn, in the forest.   *See* Planché, J. R.
  Price of Happy Land; or, The fawn
  in the forest
Follies of a night.   A vaudeville com-
  edy, in two acts. London. Lacy. n.d.
  12°. 50p. (Lacy's acting edition of
  plays. v. 14 no. 209)
Fortunio and his seven gifted servants.
  Fairy. 2 acts
  In Extravaganzas v 2
    Lewes, G. H. ed.   Selections from
      the modern British dramatists v 2
Four wishes.   *See* Planché, J. R.   Bee
  and the orange tree, or, The four
  wishes
Golden fleece; or, Jason in Colchis; and
  Medea in Corinth.   Extravaganza. 2
  pts.
  In Extravaganzas v 3
Good women in the wood.   A new and
  original fairy extravaganza. In two
  acts. . . London. Lacy. n.d. 12°. 35p.
  (Lacy's acting edition of plays. v. 9
  no. 125)
  Same in Extravaganzas v 4
Graciosa and Percinent.   Fairy. 1 act
  In Extravaganzas v 2
Green-eyed monster: a comedy in two
  acts. . . London. Cumberland. [n.d.].
  12°. 45p. (Cumberland's British thea-
  tre. v. 21 no. 3)

Grist to the mill. A comic drama in two acts. Boston. Spencer. ₁1856?₁. 12°. 34p.

Harlequin out of place. *See* Planché, J. R. New planet; or, Harlequin out of place

High, low, Jack, and the game; or, The card party. Burletta. 1 act
In Extravaganzas v 1

Hit if you like it. *See* Planché, J. R. Success; or, A hit if you like it

Invisible prince; or, The island of tranquil delights. Fairy. 1 act
In Extravaganzas v 3

Island of Calypso. *See* Planché, J. R. Telemachus; or, The island of Calypso

Island of jewels. Fairy. 2 acts
In Extravaganzas v 4

Island of tranquil delights. *See* Planché, J. R. Invisible prince; or, The island of tranquil delights

Jacobite; a comic drama in two acts. . . N.Y. French. ₁1847?₁. 12°. 35p. (Lacy's acting edition of plays. v. 14 no. 201)

Jason in Colchis; and Medea in Corinth. *See* Planché, J. R. Golden fleece; or, Jason in Colchis; and Medea in Corinth

Jenkinses; or, Boarded and done for. A farce in one act. London. Lacy. n.d. 12°. 21p. (Lacy's acting edition of plays. v. 8 no. 120)

Jewess, a grand operatic drama, in three acts, founded on M. Seribe's opera "La juive". . . London. Porter. 1835. 8°. 48p.

King Charming. Fanciful morality. 1 act
In Extravaganzas v 5

King charming; or, The blue bird of Paradise. Fairy. 2 acts
In Extravaganzas v 4

King of the peacocks. Fairy. 2 acts
In Extravaganzas v 3

Knights of the round table. A drama in five acts. London. Lacy. n.d. 12°. 68p. (Lacy's acting edition of plays. v. 15 no. 215)

Lavater the physiognomist; or, Not a bad judge. A comic drama, in two acts. Boston. Spencer. ₁1858?₁. 12°. 35p.

Loan of a lover. A vaudeville. London. Lacy. n.d. 12°. 26p. (Lacy's acting edition of plays. v. 9 no. 124). 1 act

Love and fortune. Dramatic tableau. 1 act
In Extravaganzas v 5

Marriage of Bacchus. *See* Planché, J. R. Theseus and Ariadne; or, The marriage of Bacchus

Merchant's wedding; or, London frolics in 1638; a comedy in five acts, principally founded on Jasper Maynes "City match" and W. Rowley's "Match at midnight". London. Cumberland. 1828. 8°. 79p. (Cumberland's British theatre. v. 19 no. 5)

Mr. Buckstone's ascent of Mount Parnassus: a panoramic extravaganza in one act. London. Lacy. n.d. 12°. 32p. (Lacy's acting edition of plays. v. 10 no. 141)
Same in Extravaganzas v 4

Mr. Buckstone's voyage round the Globe (in Leicester Square). In one act and four quarters. London. Lacy. n.d. 12°. 24p. (Lacy's acting edition of plays. v. 15 no. 211)
Same in Extravaganzas v 5

My daughter, Sir! or, A daughter to marry: a farce in one act. . . London. Cumberland. ₁n.d.₁. 12°. 28p. (Cumberland's British theatre. v. 37 no. 5)

Mysterious lady! or, "Worth makes the man". A comedy in two acts. London. Lacy. n.d. 12°. 32p. (Lacy's acting edition of plays. v. 8 no. 114)

New Haymarket spring meeting. Easter. 1 act
In Extravaganzas v 5

New planet; or, Harlequin out of place. Extravaganza. 1 act
In Extravaganzas v 3

Not a bad judge. A comic drama. In two acts. London. Lacy. n.d. 12°. 32p. (Lacy's acting edition of plays. v. 8 no. 111)

Olympic devils; or, Orpheus and Eurydice. Burletta. 1 act
In Extravaganzas v 1

Olympic revels; or, Prometheus and Pandora. Burletta. 1 act
In Extravaganzas v 1

Once upon a time there were two kings. An original fairy extravaganza in two acts. . . London. Lacy. n.d. 12°. 48p. (Lacy's acting edition of plays. v. 13 no. 186)
Same in Extravaganzas v 4

Orpheus and Eurydice. *See* Planché, J. R. Olympic devils; or, Orpheus and Eurydice

Orpheus in the Haymarket. Opera bouffe. 3 tableaux
In Extravaganzas v 5

Paphian bower; or, Venus and Adonis. Burletta. 1 act
In Extravaganzas v 1

Peep at the past. *See* Planché, J. R. Dramas levée; or, A peep at the past

Perseus and Andromeda. *See* Planché, J. R. Deep deep sea; or, Perseus and Andromeda

Pride of the market; a comic drama in three acts. . . N.Y. Taylor. ₁18—?₁. 12°. 47p.

Prince of the Happy Land; or, The fawn in the forest. Fairy. 2 acts
In Extravaganzas v 4

Prometheus and Pandora. *See* Planché, J. R. Olympic revels; or, Prometheus and Pandora

Puss in boots. Fairy. 1 act
In Extravaganzas v 1

Queen of the frogs. Fairy. 2 acts
In Extravaganzas v 4

Planché, J. R.—*Continued.*
Reputation; or, The state secret.   A play in five acts. . . London.   Andrews. [1883]. 12°. 60p.
Returned "killed"; a farce in two acts. London. 1826. 12°. 40p.
Riquet with the tuft.   Burletta. 1 act
  In Extravaganzas v 1
Seven champions of Christendom.   Spectacle. 2 acts
  In Extravaganzas v 3
Sleeping beauty in the wood.   An original, grand comic, romantic. . .   fairy extravaganza, in three parts. . . London. Lacy. 1864-
  Same in Extravaganzas v 2
Somebody else.   A farce in one act. London. Lacy. n.d. 12°. 26p. (Lacy's acting edition of plays. v. 11 no. 165). *Also* Spencer. Boston. [1856?]
Success; or, A hit if you like it.   Burletta. 1 act
  In Extravaganzas v 1
Telemachus; or, The island of Calypso. Extravaganza. 1 act
  In Extravaganzas v 1
Theseus and Ariadne; or, The marriage of Bacchus.   Extravaganza. 2 acts
  In Extravaganzas v 3
Three glass distaffs.   *See* Planché, J. R. Discreet princess; or, The three glass distaffs
Vampire; or, The bride of the Isles, a romantic melodrama, in two acts. . . London. Davidson. [n.d.]. 12°. 42p.
  Same in Cumberland's British theatre v 27 no 4
Venus and Adonis.   *See* Planché, J. R. Paphian bower; or, Venus and Adonis
White cat.   Fairy. 2 acts
  In Extravaganzas v 2
"Worth makes the man."   *See* Planché, J. R. Mysterious lady; or, "Worth makes the man"
Yellow dwarf and the king of the gold mines.   Fairy. 1 act
  In Extravaganzas v 5
Young and handsome.   Fairy. 1 act
  In Extravaganzas v 5

Pleydell, George
Ware case; a play in four acts.   N.Y. Doran. [c1913]. 16°. 116p.   Melodrama

Pocock, Isaac, 1782-1835
"Auld lang syne".   *See* Pocock; I. Rob Roy MacGregor; or, "Auld lang syne"
Children of the mist.   *See* Pocock, I. Montrose; or, The children of the mist
For England, ho!   A melodramatic opera in two acts. . . London. Cumberland. n.d. 12°. 37p. (Cumberland's British theatre. v. 39 no. 8)
Hit or miss!   A musical farce, in two acts. . . London. Sherwood. 1818. 12°. 40p.
  Same in Cumberland's British theatre v 34 no 3
        Dibdin, T. J. ed.   London theatre v 6 no 1

John of Paris.   A comic opera in two acts. . . London.   Cumberland.   n.d. 12°. 39p. (Cumberland's British theatre. v. 26 no. 5)
Magpie, or the maid?   A melodrama, in three acts. . . Baltimore.   Robinson. 1831. 12°. 48p.
  Same in Cumberland's British theatre v 28 no 2
Miller and his men.   A melo-drama in two acts. London. Davidson. n.d. 12°. 48p. *Also.* Boston. Spencer. 1856
  Same in Cumberland's British theatre v 26 no 6
Montrose; or, The children of the mist. A musical drama in three acts. . . Baltimore. Robinson. 1822. 12°. 60p.
Nigel; or, The crown jewels; a play in five acts. . . London. Wilks. 1823. 8°. 97p.
Omnibus.   A farce in one act.   N.Y. Douglas. 1848. 12°. 23p.
Rob Roy Macgregor; or, "Auld lang syne", an operatic drama in three acts. . . London. Lacy. n.d. 12°. 62p. (Lacy's acting edition of play. v. 3 no. 38)
  Same in Oxberry, W ed.   New English drama v 10 no 5
Robber's wife.   A romantic drama in two acts. Boston. Spencer. 1856. 12°. 27p.
  Same in Cumberland's British theatre v 28 no 1
Robinson Crusoe; or, The bold buccaneers: a romantic drama in three acts. . . London.   Cumberland.   n.d. 12°. 41p. (Cumberland's British theatre. v. 28 no. 9)

Poe, Edgar Allen, 1809-1849
Politian; an unfinished tragedy. . . Menasha, Wis. Banter. 1923. 12°. 89p. 5 scenes
  Same in Poetical works (any complete ed)

Pollock, Channing, 1880-
Enemy; a play in four acts. . . N.Y. Brentano's. [c1925]. 12°. 210p.   World war
  Same in Mantle, B. ed.   Best plays of 1925-26 (abridged)
Fool; a play in four acts.   N.Y. Brentano's. c1922. 12°. 1760   Christ spirit. 4 acts
  Same in Mantle, B. ed. Best plays of 1922-23 (condensed)
Little gray lady; a play without a hero. N.Y. French. 1918. 12°. 105p.   Melodrama. 4 acts
Sign on the door; a play in a prologue and three acts.   N.Y. French. 1924. 12°. 79p. 75c.   Mystery
Such a little queen; a comedy in four acts. . . N.Y. French. c1908. 12°. 113p.

Pollock, John, 1878-
Conchita.   1 act
  In Twelve one-acters
Dream of a winter evening.   1 act
  In Twelve one-acters

For Russia.   1 act
In Twelve one-acters
In the forests of the night
In Twelve one-acters
Invention of Dr. Metzler.   1 act
In Twelve one-acters
King in England.   1 act
In Twelve one-acters
Lolotte (adapted from Meilhac and Halé-
vy).   1 act
In Twelve one-acters
Love of Mrs. Pleasance
In Twelve one-acters
Luck king.   1 act
In Twelve one-acters
Mademoiselle Diana
In Twelve one-acters
On the frontier
In Twelve one-acters
Rosamond.   1 act
In Twelve one-acters

Poole, Evan
Blood royal.   Historical. 1 act
In Age of steel
King's letters.   Historical. 1 act
In Age of steel
Post of honour.   Romantic. 1 act
In Age of steel
Promise.   Historical. 1 act
In Age of steel

Poole, John, 1786?-1872
Atonement; or, The god-daughter.   A
drama in two acts. . . London. Miller.
1836. 44p.   Melodrama
Cock of the walk.   *See* Poole, J. Year in
an hour; or, The cock of the walk
Deaf as a post.   A farce in one act.
London. Lacy. n.d. 12°. 20p. (Lacy's
acting edition of plays. v. 14 no. 207)
Hamlet travestie; in three acts. . . Lon-
don. Lacy. n.d. 12°. 48p. (Lacy's act-
ing edition of plays. v. 10 no. 147).
Also. N.Y. Bradstreet press. 1866.
110p.
Hole in the wall: a farce in two acts. . .
N.Y. Longworth. 1813. 12°. 36p.
Married and single.   A comedy. In three
acts. . . London. J. Poole. 1824. 8°.
67p.
Paul Pry; a comedy in three acts.   N.Y.
Murden. 1826. 40p. 16°.
Scape-goat; a farce in one act. . . Lon-
don. Sherwood. 1826. 12°. 31p.
Same in London stage v 4 no 49
Simpson & Co.; a comedy in two acts. . .
N.Y. Circulating library and drama-
tic repository. 1823. 12°. 48p.
Same in Cumberland's British theatre
v 43 no 10
Soldier's courtship.   A comedy in one
act. Boston. Spencer. [1858?]. 12°.
14p.
They're both to blame.   *See* Poole, J.
Wealthy widow; or, They're both to
blame
Tribulation; or, Unwelcome visitors; a
comedy in two acts. . . London.
Cumberland. n.d. 12°. 42p. (Cumber-
land's British theatre. v. 12 no. 3)
Same in Broadhurst, J. Plays v 12 no 7

Turning the tables; an original farce, in
one act.   London. Duncombe. [18—].
12°. 28p. *Also* Baltimore. Robinson.
1834
'Twould puzzle a conjuror!   A comic
drama in two acts. London. Lacy.
n.d. 12°. 26p. (Lacy's acting edition
of plays. v. 14 no. 206)
Wealthy widow; or, They're both to
blame.   A comedy. In three acts. . .
London. Miller. [1827]. 8°. 61p.
Year in an hour; or, The cock of the
walk.   A farce. London. Miller. 1824.
8°. 28p.

Porter, Arthur Kingsley, 1883-
Seven who slept.   Boston. Marshall
Jones. 1919. 8°. 96p.   Illusion. 4 pts.

Porto-Riche, Georges de, 1849-
Françoise's luck.   Comedy.   1 act
In Clark, B. H. tr.   Four plays of the
Free theatre
Shay, F. and Loving, P. eds.   Fifty
contemporary one-act plays
Loving wife (Amoureuse).   Domestic. 3
acts
In Dickinson, T. H. ed.   Chief con-
temporary dramatists ser 2

Postgate, John William, 1851-
Falstaff in rebellion; or, The mutineers of
Eastcheap; a Shakespearian travesty
of three acts.   Boston. Baker. 1915.
44p. 25c
Retaming the shrew.   Chicago. Denison.
1915. 25c

Potter, Dorothy
Bombast and platitudes.   War. 1 act
In Under the eagle
Under the eagle.   Epilogue. War. 1 act
In Under the eagle
Under the eagle.   Prologue. War. 1 act
In Under the eagle
Watchful waiting.   Mexico. 1 act
In Under the eagle
Yellow yielding.   Preparedness. 1 act
In Under the eagle

Powell-Anderson, Constance
Courting the widow Malone; a comedy in
one act.   N.Y. Phillips. 1922. 12°.
32p. 50c
Heart of a clown; an autumn fantasy in
one act.   N.Y. Phillips. 1921. 12°.
34p. 50c

Powell, Thomas, 1809-1887
Blind wife; or, The student of Bonn.
Tragic romance. 5 acts
In Dramatic poems
Doria.   Tragedy. 5 acts
In Dramatic poems
Puritan.   Tragedy. 5 acts
In Dramatic poems
Shepherd's well.   Tragedy. 5 acts
In Dramatic poems
Student of Bonn.   *See* Powell, T. Blind
wife; or, The student of Bonn
True at last.   A tragedy in five acts.
London. Mitchell. 1844. 12°. 124p.

Power, Tyrone, 1797-1841
Born to good luck; The Irishman's fortune. A farce in two acts. . . London. Lacy. n.d. 12°. 26p. (Lacy's acting edition of plays. v. 2 no. 28)
Married lovers: a petite comedy, in two acts. . . Baltimore. Robinson. 1831. 12°. 42p.
St. Patrick's eve; or, The order of the day. A drama in three acts. . . Phila. Turner. [1838?]. 12°. 54p. *Also* London. Chapman. 1838

Praga, Marco, 1862-
Closed door. Problem. 3 acts
In Sayler, O. M. ed. Eleanora Duse series of plays

Pratt, Theodore
Inside stuff. Gastronomic comedy. 1 act
In Shay, F. ed. Plays for strolling mummers

Presbrey, Eugene Wiley, 1853-
"The barrier"; a clash in four acts, founded on the novel of the same title by Rex Beach. N.Y. Rosenfeld. 1909. 12°. 126p.
Courtship of Miles Standish; adapted from Longfellow's poem. N.Y. French. c1909. 12°. 16p. 1 act
Fool's wisdom; a sketch of 1586. [N.Y.? c1904]. 12°. 26p. Elizabethan drama 1 act

Presland, John, pseud. (Mrs. Gladys Skelton)
Belisarius; general of the east. London. Chatto. 1913. 135p. Historical. 4 acts
King Monmouth. London. Chatto. 1916. 8°. 111p. Historical. 3 acts
Lynton and Lynmouth; a pageant of cliff and moorland. N.Y. Dodd. 1918. 12°. 199p.

Preston, Daniel S.
Columbus; or, A hero of the new world; an historical play. N.Y. Putnam. 1887. 8°. 103p. 5 acts

Price, Graham
Absolution of Bruce. London. Gowans. 1911. 24°. 26p. Historical. 1 act
Capture of Wallace. London. Gowans
Coming of Fair Anne; a ballad play. London. Gowans. 1916. 45p.
Lady Alix Egerton. London. Gowans
Marriages are made in heaven—and elsewhere. London. Gowans. 1914. 12°. 34p.
Masque of the two strangers. London. Gowans
Song of the seal. London. Gowans. 1912. 24°. 25p. Legendary. 1 act

Proctor, Bryan Waller (Barry Cornwall, pseud), 1887-1874
Amelia Wentworth. Tragedy. 2 scenes
In Marcian Colonna
Broken heart. Boccaccio. 2 scenes
In Dramatic scenes
Falcon. Romantic. 2 scenes
In Dramatic scenes

Florentine party. Romantic. 1 scene
In Dramatic scenes
Juan. Tragedy. 1 scene
In Dramatic scenes
Julian the apostate. Historical. 2 scenes
In Marcian Colonna
Ludovico Sforza. Historical. 2 scenes
In Dramatic scenes
Lysander and Ione. Mythological. 1 scene
In Dramatic scenes
Michael Angelo. Historical. 1 scene
In Dramatic scenes
Mirandola; a tragedy. London. Warren. 1821. 8°. 110p. 5 acts
Pandemonium. Biblical. 1 act
In Dramatic scenes
Raffaele and Fornarina. Historical. 2 scenes
In Dramatic scenes
Rape of Proserpine. Mythological. 1 act
In Marcian Colonna
Temptation. Romantic. 2 scenes
In Dramatic scenes
Victim. India. 3 scenes
In Dramatic scenes
Way to conquer. Melodrama. 1 scene
In Dramatic scenes

Prosser, William
Free speech. Farce. 1 act
In Plays of the 47 workshop ser 1

Prydz, Alvida, 1848-
He is coming. Disillusion. 1 act
In Poet Lore 25:230
In confidence; a one-act play tr. from the Norwegian. . . Cincinnati. Stewart Kidd. 1923. 12°. 28p. (Appleton). Comedy
Same in Shay, F. ed. Twenty-five short plays, international

Przybyszeski, Stanilaw. *See* Pshibishevsky, Stanilav

Pshibishevsky, Stanilav, 1868-
For happiness. Emotional. 3 acts
In Poet Lore 23:81
Snow, a play in four acts. . . N.Y. Brown. 1920. 12°. 128p. $1.50

Purdy, Nannie Sutton
Hafed the Persian; a play in four acts. Boston. Badger. c1920. 12°. 87p.

Pushkin, Aleksandr Sergîeevich, 1799-1837
Boris Godunóv; a drama in verse. . . London. Paul. [1918]. 12°. 117p. Historical tragedy. 25 scenes
Same in Bates, A. ed. Drama v 18:75 Turner, C. E. tr. Translations from Poushkin
Gipsies. Poetic. 1 scene
In Turner, C. E. tr. Translations from Poushkin
Mozart and Salieri. Poetic. 2 scenes
In Bechhofer, C. E. ed. Russian anthology in English
Turner, C. E. tr. Translations from Poushkin
Poet Lore 31:297-304
Statue guest. Sketch. 4 scenes
In Turner, C. E. tr. Translations from Poushkin

Purdy, Nina, 1889
Heritage. Juvenile. 1 act
In Jagendorf, M. A. ed. One-act plays for young folks
Putnam, Mrs. Nina Wilcox, 1888-
Orthodoxy [dramatic satire]. N.Y. Kennerly. 1914. 12°. 49p. 60c. 1 act
Same in Forum 51:801
Pryce, Richard
Helen with the high hand. N.Y. French. [1914]. 12°. 103p. Comedy. 3 acts
Pyentsa. Burmese fairy tale. 10 acts
In Shay, F. ed. Twenty-five short plays, international (adapted 3 acts)
J of Asiatic Soc of Bengal 8:531
Quaife, Elise West
Natural incentive. Boston. Cornhill co. c1918. 88p. Social. 4 acts
Querella, David
Rounding the triangle. Social. 1 act
In Smart Set 40 no 1:131
Quick [John] Herbert, 1861-1925
There came two women; a drama in four acts. Indianapolis. Bobbs. 1924. 12°. 122p. $1.25
Quintero, Serafin, and Joaquin. *See* Alvarez Quintero, S. and J.
Quinton, Pauline Brooks
Celibate. Character. 3 acts
In Locust flower, and The celibate
Locust flower. Fantasy. 1 act
In Locust flower, and The celibate
Rabinowitsch, Shalom J., 1859-1916
She must marry a doctor. Comedy. 1 act
In Goldberg, I. ed. Six plays of the Yiddish theatre
Radcliffe, Claude
Borgia; a play of mediaeval Italy in one act. . . N.Y. French. c1926. 12°. 18p.
Rafferty, Ewing
Everyman militant, a modern morality. Boston. Sherman, French. 1916. 12°. 71p. $1. 3 acts
Raisbeck, Kenneth
Torches. Tragedy. 1 act
In Plays of the 47 workshop ser 2
Ramos, José Antonio
When love dies; a worldly comedy. 1 act
In Shay, F. ed. Twenty-five short plays, international
Ramspacher, Anna (Mrs. Albert Lyness)
Agitator. 1 act
In Lady of the Nile, and other plays
Kentucky derby. 1 act
In Lady of the Nile, and other plays
Lady of the Nile. 1 act
In Lady of the Nile, and other plays
Which is the greater man? 1 act
In Lady of the Nile, and other plays
Ramsey, Alice
Henker's Mahlzeit. Reign of Terror. 1 act
In Smart Set 30:123 F '10
Ranck, Edwin Carty
Yellow boots. Tragedy. 1 act
In Stratford J 4:265. My 1919

Randolph, Edith
Lammas eve. Fantasy. 1 act
In Poet Lore 32:288
Raphael, Alice
Dormer windows. Character. 1 act
In Drama 11:418
Interlude in the life of St. Francis
In Drama 11:37
Raphaelson, Samson
Jazz singer; a drama based on his story "The day of atonement", in Everybody's M. Ja '22. N.Y. Brentano's. c1925. p. 17-153
Rapp, William Jourdan
Osman Pasha; a play in four acts. N.Y. Century. c1925. 12°. 145p. $1.25
Rappaport, Solomon, 1863-1920
The dybbuk; a play in four acts. . . N.Y. Boni. 1926. 12°. $2. Spirit possession
Same in Mantle, B. ed. Best plays of 1925-26 (condensed)
Ratcliffe, Dorothy Una
Alison Elizabeth. Seduction. 2 acts
In Dale dramas
Courting of Margaret Ruth. Folk play. 1 act
In Dale dramas
Desormais. Shepherd's play. 1 act
In Dale dramas
Mary of Scotland in Wensleydale. Historical. 2 pts.
In Dale dramas
Price. Jealousy. 1 act
In Dale dramas
Return of Mr. Wiggleswick. Folk play. 1 act
In Dale dramas
Robinetta. Fantasy. 1 act
In Dale dramas
Thieves' gill. Episode. 1 act
In Dale dramas
Time. Juvenile. 1 act
In Dale dramas
Rath, E. J. pseud. (J. Chauncey Cory Bramesal, and Edith Rathbone Brainerd)
Brains of the family; a side-splitting domestic comedy. N.Y. Watt. 1925. 12°. 284p.
Dark chapter; a comedy of class distinctions. N.Y. G. Howard. Watt. 1924. 306p. 4 acts
Gas-drive in; a high-powered comedy-romance that hits on the cylinder. N.Y. Watt. 1925
Ravindranatha Thakura. *See* Tagore, Rabindranath
Rawson, Graham S.
Dangers of peace. Napoleon. 1 act
In Stroke of Marbot and two other plays
Down stream. Politics. 1 act
In Measure, and Down stream
Measure. Comedy. 2 acts
In Measure, and Down stream

Rawson, G. S.—*Continued.*
Pastor of Jena. Napoleon. 1 act
In Stroke of Marbot and two other plays
Stroke of Marbot. Napoleon. 1 act
In Stroke of Marbot and two other plays

Raymond, George Lansing, (Walter Warren, pseud.), 1839-
Aztecs. . . Boston. Arena. 1894. 12°. 126p.
See Raymond, G. L. Aztec god
Aztec god. Mexico. 5 acts
In Aztec god, and other dramas
Cecil the seer. Religious. 3 acts
In Aztec god, and other dramas
Columbus, the discoverer. Boston. Arena pub. co. 1893. 164p. Historical. 5 acts
Same in Aztec god, and other dramas
Dante, a drama in two tableaux and six acts. Washington, D.C. Raymond. [c1908]. 12°. 141p.
Same in Dante, and collected verse
Suffragettes, a play in three acts. Washington, D.C. B. S. Adams. 1908. 53p.

Raymond, Richard John
Castle of Paluzzi; or, The extorted oath; a serious drama in two acts. . . London. 1818. 53p.
Emigrants daughter; a drama in one act. London. Duncombe. [1838?]. 16°. 26p. Melodrama
Extorted oath. *See* Raymond, R. J. Castle of Paluzzi; or, The extorted oath
Mr. and Mrs. Peter White. A farce in one act. . . Phila. Turner. [c1844]. 12°. 26p. (Turner's dramatic library. new ser. no. 83]. *Also* Spencer. [1857?]
Robert the Devil, Duke of Normandy: a musical romance in two acts. . . London. Cumberland. n.d. 12°. 35p. (Cumberland's British theatre. v. 33 no. 6)
Toodles. A domestic drama, in two acts. . . N.Y. French. 1853?. 12°. 28p.

Read, Harriette Fanning
Erminia. Florence. 5 acts
In Dramatic poems
Medea. Tragedy. 5 acts
In Dramatic poems
New world. Tragedy. 5 acts
In Dramatic poems

Read, John
Latter-Lammas. Taunton, Barnicott & Pearce. 1916. 12°. 96p. Wessex. 3 acts

Reade, Charles, 1814-1884
Gold! a drama in five acts. London. Lacy. n.d. 12°. 48p. (Lacy's acting edition of plays. v. 11 no. 15)

Rector, Jessie L. joint author. *See* Cameron, Margaret, and Rector, J.

Rede, William Leman, 1802-1847
Affair of honour: a farce in one act. . . London. Davidson. [n.d.]. 12°. 28p.
Same in Cumberland's British theatre v 44 no 3

Devil and Doctor Faustus: a drama, in three acts. . . London. Davidson. [n.d.]. 12°. 36p.
Same in Cumberland's British theatre v 45 no 2
Flight to America; or, Ten hours in New York! a drama in three acts. . . N.Y. Turner. [184—?]. 12°. 47p.
His first campaign: a farce, in two acts. . . London. Davidson. [n.d.]. 12°. 43p.
Same in Cumberland's British theatre v 44 no 1
Jack in the water; or, The ladder of life: a domestic burletta in three acts. . . Printed for acting. . . London. Davidson. n.d. 12°. 50p.
Same in Cumberland's Minor theatre v 16 no 6
Queen's bench: a farce in two acts. . . London. Davidson. [n.d.]. 12°. 42p.
Same in Cumberland's British theatre v 44 no 7
Rake's progress. A melo-drama, in three acts. . . N.Y. Roorbach. [1856?]. 12°. 51p.
Sixteen-string Jack; a romantic drama in three acts. . . London. Davidson. [n.d.]. 12°. 57p.
Same in Cumberland's Minor theatre v 16 no 10
Two greens. A farce, in one act. . . London. Pattie. [n.d.]. 12°. 20p.
Same in Universal stage v 1 no 8

Reed, John, 1887-
Freedom. Comedy. 1 act
In Provincetown plays ser 2
Shay, F. ed. Treasury of plays for men

Reed, Joseph, 1723-1787
Register office. Farce. 2 acts
In London stage v 4 no 40
Freedom. 1 act
In Provincetown plays ser 2

Reed, Luther, and Hamilton, Hale
Dear me; a comedy in three acts. N.Y. French. 1924. 12°.

Reed, Mark White
She would and she did; a comedy in four acts, a light satire on people as they are. N.Y. French. c1926. 12°. 112p.

Reely, Mary Katharine
Daily bread. Poverty. 1 act
In Daily bread, [and other plays]
Three one-act plays
Early Ohios and Rhode Island reds; a comedy in one act. [Minneapolis. Perine Bk. co. c1921]. 12°. 27p.
Flittermouse. Comedy. 1 act
In Drama 14:104
Lean years. Economy. 1 act
In Daily bread [and other plays]
Three one-act plays
Window to the south. Psychological. 1 act
In Daily bread [and other plays]
Three one-act plays

Rees, Arthur Dougherty
Columbus; a drama. Phila. Winston. [1907]. 12°. 129p. Historical. 5 acts
Double love; a tragedy in five acts. A drama of American life. Phila. Winston. [c1907]. 12°. 85p.
Give up your gods; a drama in three acts of pagan and Christian Russia. Phila. Lippincott. 1908. 12°. 118p.
William Tell; a drama of the origin of Swiss democracy. . . Phila. Lippincott. 1918. 12°. 141p.

Rees, William Guelph
The mayor of Romanstown. N.Y. Cochrane. 1909. 12°. 73p. Comedy. 3 acts

Reid, James Halleck
Confession; a drama in four acts. N.Y. French. 1921. 12°. 92p. 75c. Melodrama

Reizenstein, Elmer L. See Rice, Elmer L.

Remenyi, Joseph
Grotesque children. Fantasy. 1 act
In International (NY) 9:147

Renard, Jules
Good-bye! Comedy. 1 act
In Smart Set 49:81 Je 16

Renfrew, Carolyn
Last of the Strozzi. Historical. 5 acts
In Last of the Strozzi, and The lure
Lure. Allegory. 2 acts
In Last of the Strozzi, and The lure

Rethy, Joseph Bernard
It might happen again. Comedy. 1 act
In International (NY) 10:203

Reynolds, Frederick, 1764-1841
Begone dull care; or, How will it end? A comedy in five acts. . . Boston. Larkin. 1808. 12°. 72p.
Blind bargain; or, Hear it out; a comedy in five acts. . . London. Cumberland. n.d. 12°. 61p. (Cumberland's British theatre. v. 28 no. 8)
Delinquent; or, Seeing company. A comedy in five acts. . . London. Cumberland. n.d. 12°. 58p. (Cumberland's British theatre. v. 40 no. 7)
Dramatist; or, Stop him who can! a comedy. N.Y. Oxford press. 1925. 90p. (Cumberland's British theatre. v. 39 no. 2)
Exile, [or, The deserts of Siberia.] a comedy in three acts. . . Baltimore. Robinson. 1818. 12°. 59p. (Cumberland's British theatre. v. 29 no. 9)
Folly as it flies; a comedy in five acts. . . London. Cumberland. n.d. 12°. 62p. (Cumberland's British theatre. v. 27 no. 9)
How to grow rich; a comedy in five acts. . . London. Cumberland. n.d. 12°. 58p. (Cumberland's British theatre. v. 30 no. 8)
Notoriety; a comedy in five acts. . . London. J. Cumberland. n.d. 12°. 63p. (Cumberland's British theatre. v. 26 no. 1)

Renegade; a grand historical drama, in three acts. . . N.Y. Longworth. 1813. 12°. 54p.
Will: a comedy in five acts. . . London. Robinson. 12°. 72p. (Cumberland's British theatre. v. 21 no. 7)

Rhodes, William Barnes, 1772-1826
Bombastes Furioso; a burlesque tragic opera, in one act. . . London. Bell and Daldy. 1873. 12°. 44p. (Lacy's acting edition of plays. v. 3 no. 43)

Rice, Cale Young, 1872-
Arduin. Alchemy. 1 act
In Collected plays and poems v 1 Immortal lure
Charles di Tocca; a tragedy. N.Y. McClure. 1908. 12°. 134p. 4 acts
In Collected plays and poems v 2
David; a tragedy. N.Y. Doubleday. 1909. 128p. 4 acts
Same in Collected plays and poems v 2 Plays and Lyrics
Earth and new earth. . . Garden City. Doubleday. 1916. 12°. 157p.
Gerhard of Ryle. Tragedy. 1 act
In Earth and new earth
Giorgione. Renaissance. 1 act
In Collected plays and poems v 1 Immortal lure
Immortal lure. Sex awakening. 1 act
Same in Collected plays and poems v 1 Immortal lure
Night in Avignon. N.Y. McClure. 1907. 32p. Renaissance. 1 act
Same in Collected plays and poems v 1
O-Ume's gods. Japan. 1 act
In Collected plays and poems v 1 Immortal lure
Porzia. N.Y. Doubleday. 1913. 12°. 79p. Renaissance. 3 acts
Same in Collected plays and poems v 1
Yolanda of Cyprus. N.Y. McClure. 1908. 134p. 16th Century. 4 acts
Same in Collected plays and poems v 1 Plays and lyrics

Rice, Elmer L. (Reizenstein, Elmer L.), 1892-
Adding machine; a play in seven scenes. . . Garden City. Doubleday. 1923. 12°. 143p. Monotony
In Dickinson, T. H. ed. Contemporary plays
Moses, M. J. ed. Representative American dramas, national and local
Home of the free. Comedy
In Morningside plays
On trial; a domestic composition in four acts. n.d. c1914. 8°. 108p.
Passing of Chow-Chow. 1 act
In One-act plays for stage and study ser 1

Rice, Wallace de Groot Cecil, 1859-
Children of France (about 1778). Pageant
In Illinois centennial plays no 2
Children of the civil war (February, 1862). Pageant
In Illinois centennial plays no 5

Rice, W. de G. C.—*Continued.*
Children of the Illini (about 1673). Pageant. 1 pt.
In Illinois centennial plays no 1
Masque of Illinois. Issued by the Illinois centennial commission. [Springfield, Ill., State printers, 1918]. 8°. 30p. Pageant. 2 pts.
Pageant of the Illinois country. Issued by the Illinois centennial commission. [Springfield, Ill., State printers, 1918]. 8°. 57p. 6 pts.
Pioneer boys and girls (1814). Pageant. 1 pt.
In Illinois centennial plays no 3
Underground railroad (about 1840). Pageant. 1 pt.
In Illinois centennial plays no 4

Rice, Wallace de Groot Cecil, 1859-, and Stevens, Thomas Wood
Chaplet of Pan. A masque. Chicago. Stage Guild. (c1912). 12°. 40p. 1 act

Rice, Walter F.
Winning ways; a farce in one act. Boston. Baker. 1900. 12°. 12p.

Richards, Alfred Bate, 1820-1876
Croesus, king of Lydia; a tragedy, in five acts. . . London. Longman. 1861. 8°. 113p.

Richardson, Marie E.
Children's Barbarossa. Juvenile. 1 act
In Nat'l M 44:795
Jewels of France. Symbolic. 2 scenes
In Nat'l M 43:811
Of others weaving. World war. 2 scenes
In Nat'l M 45:277

Richardson, Pearl
Nifwy the proud; a comedy in prologue, three acts and an epilogue. N.Y. French. c1924. 111p.

Richman, Arthur, 1886-
Ambush. N.Y. Duffield. 1922. 12°. 155p. Social. 3 acts
In Mantle, B. ed. Best plays of 1921-22 (condensed)
Not so long ago; a comedy in prologue, three acts and an epilogue. N.Y. French. c1924. 12°. 111p.

Rideout, Ransom
Boots; a drama in one act. N.Y. Appleton. 1925. 36p.

Ridge, William Pett
Damages for breach. Cockney. 1 act
In London please
Early closing. Cockney. 1 act
In London please
Happy returns. Cockney. 1 act
In London please
Some showers. Cockney. 1 act
In London please

Riggs, Lynn
Knives from Syria. 1 act
In One-act plays for stage and study ser 3

Riley, Mrs. Alice Cushing (Donaldson), 1867-
Black suitcase. Farce. 1 act
In Mandarin coat, etc

Blue prince. Fairy. 2 acts
In Ten minutes by the clock
Brotherhood of man; a pageant of international peace. . . N.Y. Barnes. 1924. 8°. 50p. 8 episodes
Lover's garden. Flower masque. [arranged from Shakespeare]. 1 act
In Drama 5:695
Mandarin coat. Comedy. 1 act
In Mandarin coat, etc
Drama 13:132
Poet's well. Romantic. 1 act
In Ten minutes by the clock
Radio. Comedy. 1 act
In Mandarin coat, etc
Skim-milk. World war. 1 act
In Mandarin coat, etc
Sponge. Comedy. 1 act
In Mandarin coat, etc
Taxi. Comedy. 1 act
In Drama 16:177
Ten minutes by the clock. Comedy. 1 act
In Ten minutes by the clock
Their anniversary. Comedy. 1 act
In Mandarin coat, etc
Drama 12:157
Weathervane elopes. 1 act
In One-act plays for stage and study ser 3
Tom Piper and the pig. Mother Goose. 2 acts
In Ten minutes by the clock

Riley, James Whitcomb, 1849-
Flying islands of the night. . . Indianapolis. Bowen-Merrill. 1892. 12°. 88p. Burlesque epic. 3 acts

Ring, Barbara, 1870-
$100,000 club paper; a comedy in one act. Boston. Baker. 1922. 12°. 34p. 25c

Ritchie, Anna Cord (Mowatt), 1819-1870
Armand; or, The peer and the peasant. Melodrama. 5 acts
In Plays
Fashion; or, Life in New York. London. Newberry. 1850. 12°. 62p. Social satire. 5 acts
In Plays
Moses, M. J. ed. Representative plays by American dramatists from 1765 to the present day
Quinn, A. H. ed. Representative American plays 1767-1923
Life in New York. *See* Ritchie, A. C. Fashion; or, Life in New York
Peer and the peasant. *See* Ritchie, A. C. Armand; or, The peer and the peasant

Rivas, Linares. *See* Linares Rivas, M.

Rives, Amélie. *See* Troubetzkoy, Amélie (Rives) Chanler

Roberts, A. O.
Cloudbreak. Supernatural. 1 act
In Clarke, A. K. ed. Three one-act plays

Roberts, Charles, V. H.
Eagle bound; a drama in two scenes. Boston. Dramatic Arts co. [c1922]. 12°. 42p.

Great conspiracy; an epic drama in nine scenes. . . N.Y. Torch press. 1919. 12°. 130p. (In part a revision of the "Sublime sacrifice")

Louvain; a tragedy in three acts. N.Y. Torch press. 1917. 12°. 84p. $1.25

Myrrha; a tragedy in five acts. Boston. Four seas. 1922. 12°. 140p.

Sublime sacrifice, a drama of the Great War; a tragedy in three acts with prologue. N.Y. Torch press. 1917. 12°. 103p.

Thaisa: a tragedy in prologue and five acts. . . N.Y. Torch press. 1918. 12°. 181p.

Roberts, Lewis Niles

Aftermath; a play in three acts. (Dover, Eng. Griggs & Son). 1914. Privately printed. 12°. 104p.

Lion hunters; or, Modern Dianas; a fantastic farce in three acts. Boston. ₁F. H. Gibson co.₁. 1903. 12°. 206p.

Modern Dianas. *See* Roberts, L. N. Lion hunters; or, Modern Dianas

Roberts, Morley, 1857-

Hour of greatness. Mystery. 1 act
In Four plays

Lamp of God. Social. 1 act
In Four plays

Lay figure. Tragedy. 1 act
In Four plays

White horse. Dramatic fragment. 1 act
In Four plays

Roberts, Myrtle Glenn

Foot of the rainbow. San Francisco. Elder. ₁c1914₁. 8°. 45p. Fantasy. 3 acts

Robertson, Charles Grant, 1869-

Academic saturnalia. Oxford. 1 act
In Voces academicae

Au bonheur des dames. Oxford. 1 act
In Voces academicae

Auto-da-fe. Oxford. 1 act
In Voces academicae

Chez bona dea. Oxford. 1 act
In Voces academicae

Coffee for two. Farce. 1 act
In Voces academicae

Cricket match. Oxford. 1 act
In Voces academicae

Eights. Oxford. 1 act
In Voces academicae

Eternal undergrad. Oxford. 1 act
In Voces academicae

Field night at the Union. Oxford. 1 act
In Voces academicae

Football match. Oxford. 1 act
In Voces academicae

Greater universities. Oxford. 1 act
In Voces academicae

How the other half lives. Oxford. 1 act
In Voces academicae

In the halls of harmony. Oxford. 1 act
In Voces academicae

Morning with the Philistines. Oxford. 1 act
In Voces academicae

New impressions. Comedy. 1 act
In Voces academicae

Twilight of the gods. Oxford. 1 act
In Voces academicae

Une passionnette. Oxford. 1 act
In Voces academicae

Vanity Fair. Oxford. 1 act
In Voces academicae

Water babies. Oxford. 1 act
In Voces academicae

Robertson, Thomas William, 1829-1871

Birds of prey; or, a duel in the dark. A drama. London. Lacy. ₁18—?₁. 12°. 42p. (Lacy's acting edition of plays. v. 93) Comedy. 3 acts

Birth. A new and original comedy in three acts. London. French. 18—. 12°. 47p.
Same in Principal dramatic works v 1

Breach of promise. An extravagant farce in two acts. London. French. ₁18—₁. 12°. 24p.
Same in Principal dramatic works v 1

Cantab! An original farce. London. Lacy. ₁18—₁. 12°. 27p. (Lacy's acting edition of plays. v. 50) 1 act
Same in Evening's entertainment

Caste; an original comedy in three acts. N.Y. Roorbach. c1890. 12°. 51p.
Same in Principal dramatic works v 1
Society, and Caste
Coffmann, G. R. ed. Book of modern plays
Matthews, J. B. & Lieder, P. R. eds. Chief British dramatists
Moses, M. ed. Representative British dramas

David Garrick. A comedy in three acts. Philadelphia. Penn Pub. Co. 1903. 12°. 43p.
Same in Principal dramatic works v 1

Dreams; or, My lady Clara. A drama in five acts. . . N.Y. DeWitt. c1875. 12°. 38p. Comedy
Same in Principal dramatic works v 1

Half caste; or, The poisoned pearl. A. drama. London. French. ₁18—?₁. 12°. 36p. (Lacy's acting edition of plays. v. 97) Melodrama. 3 acts

Home; a comedy in three acts. . . N.Y. Roorbach. c1890. 12°. 40p.
Same in Principal dramatic works v 1

Ladies' battle. Translated from the celebrated French comedy "Un duel en amour". A comedy in three acts. Boston. Spencer. ₁1856?₁. 12°. 35p.
Same in Principal dramatic works v 1

M. P. A comedy in four acts. London. French. ₁18—₁. 12°. p. 323-76
Same in Principal dramatic works v 1

My lady Clara. *See* Robertson, T. W. Dreams; or, My lady Clara

Nightingale. A new and original drama in five acts. London. French. ₁18—₁. 12°. p. 379-418
In Principal dramatic works v 2

Robertson, T. W.—*Continued.*
Noemie! A drama in two acts. From the French of M. M. D'Ennery and Clement. Translated and adapted. N.Y. DeWitt. n.d. 12°. 23p. Romantic
Not at all jealous. A farce in one act. London. Lacy. [18—]. 12°. 20p. (Lacy's acting edition of plays. v. 91)
Our private theatricals. Comedy. 2 acts
In Evening's entertainment
Ours: a comedy in three acts. London. French. [18—]. 12°. 56p.
In Principal dramatic works v 2
Peace at any price; a farce in one act. (Adapted from the French). London. Lacy. 1872. 12°. 12p.
Play. An original comedy in four acts. London. French. [18—]. 12°. p. 491-542
Same in Principal dramatic works v 2
Poisoned pearl. *See* Robertson, T. W. Half caste, or, The poisoned pearl
Progress. Comedy. 3 acts
In Principal dramatic works v 2
Robinson Crusoe. Burlesque. 1 act
In Evening's entertainment
Row in the house. Farce. In one act. London. French. [18—]. 12°. 20p.
Same in Principal dramatic works v 2
"School"; or, The story of Belle Marks. A comedy in four acts. Philadelphia. Penn. pub. co. 1903. 12°. 52p.
Same in Principal dramatic works v 2
Slippers for Cinderella. Juvenile. 1 act
In Moses, M. J. ed. Another Treasury of plays for children
Society. A comedy in three acts. London. Lacy. [18—]. 12°. 66p. (Lacy's acting edition of plays. v. 71)
In Principal dramatic works v 2
Society and Caste
Bates, A. Drama 16:257
War. A drama in three acts. London. French. [18—?]. 12°. p. 745-89.
Same in Principal dramatic works v 2
Robertson, W. G.
Pinkie and the fairies. Juvenile. 1 act
In Moses, M. J. Treasury of plays for children
Robins, Gertrude, d. 1917
Makeshifts. Comedy. 1 act
In Makeshifts, and Realities
Clark, B. H. ed. Representative one-act plays by British and Irish authors
Pot-luck. A farcical fact in one act. N.Y. French. c1911. 12°. 19p.
Realities. Comedy. 1 act
In Makeshifts, and Realities
Robinson, Edwin Arlington, 1869-
Demos and Dionysus. Legendary. 1 act
In Theatre Arts 9:32
Porcupine; a drama in three acts. N.Y. Macmillan. 1915. 12°. 152p. Social
Van Zorn; a comedy in three acts. N.Y. Macmillan. 1914. 12°. 164p.
Robinson, Harriet Jane, 1825-1911
New Pandora; a drama. N.Y. Putnam. 1889. 8°. 151p. Mythological. 5 acts

Robinson, Lennox, 1886-
Clancy name. Melodrama. 3 acts
In Two plays
Crabbed youth and age; a little comedy. N.Y. Putnam. [1924]. 39p. 1 act
Same in Theatre Arts M 8:51
Cross-roads. A play in a prologue and two acts. Dublin. Maunsel. 1909. 59p. Psychological
Dreamers. London. Maunsel. 1915. 68p. Historical. 3 acts
Harvest. Social. 3 acts
In Two plays
Patriots; a play in three acts. Abbey theatre series). Boston. Luce. 1912. 12°. 49p. 75c. Ireland
Round table; a comic tragedy in three acts. N.Y. Putnam. 1924. 12°. 111p.
Whiteheaded boy, a comedy in three acts. Dublin. Talbot. 1922. 12°. 169p.
Robson, Eleanor, 1879-, and Ford, Harriet, 1868-
In the next room; a play in three acts. N.Y. French. c1925. 8°. 67p. (Based on a novel of Burton Stevenson). Mystery
Roddick, Lady Amy Redpath
Birth of Montreal. Chronicle. 4 acts
In Birth of Montreal
Key that unlocks. Tragedy. 3 acts
In Birth of Montreal
Romance of a princess; a comedy, [and other poems]. N.Y. Douguel. 1922. 12°. 94p. $1.50. 5 acts
Seekers, an Indian mystery play. Montreal. Dougall. 1920. 8°. 75p.
Rodwell, George Herbert Buonoparte, 1800-1852
I'll be your second. A farce in one act. London. Lacy. n.d. 13p. (Lacy's acting edition of plays. v. 3 no. 23)
Roelvink, Herman C. J.
Storm bird. Problem. 4 acts
In Poet Lore 24:65
Rogers, John William, jr. 1894-
Bumblepuppy. Comedy of climate. 1 act
In Theatre Arts M 10:604
Judge Lynch; a drama in one act. N.Y. French. c1924. 22p.
In One-act plays for stage and study ser 1
Mary means what she says. 1 act
In One-act plays for stage and study ser 3
Saved
In One act plays for stage and study ser 2
Rogers, Margaret Douglas
Echo and Narcissus; a play in one act. Piqua, O. Little classics press. c1924. 12°. 23p.
Gift; a poetic drama. Cincinnati. Stewart. 1914. 12°. 47p. Mythological. 2 acts
Kiss of Aphrodite; a play in two acts, a prologue and an epilogue. Piqua, O. Little classics press. c1925. 12°. 48p.

Rogers, Robert Emmons
Behind a Watteau picture; a fantasy in verse, in one act. Boston. Baker. 1918. 12°. 66p. 75c
Boy Will. Shakespeare. 1 act
In Cohen, H. L. ed. One-act plays by modern authors
Rogers, Thomas Badger
Eyes to the blind. Character. 1 act
In Five plays
Forfeit. Character. 1 act
In Five plays
Cohen, H. L. ed. Junior play book
Knickerbocker, E. Van B. ed. Twelve plays
Hall of laughter. Comedy. 1 act
In Five plays
Heirloom. Romantic. 1 act
In Five plays
Saint-king. Tragedy. 1 act
In Five plays
Rolland, Romain, 1866-
Danton. French revolution. 3 acts
In Fourteenth of July; and Danton
Fourteenth of July. French revolution. 3 acts
In Fourteenth of July; and Danton
Liluli. . . N.Y. Boni. c1920. 12°. 127p. Farce. 1 act
Montespan ɾdrama in three actsɿ. . . N.Y. Huebsch. 1923. 12°. 130p.
Wolves. French revolution. 3 acts
In Drama 8:578
Rolt-Wheeler, Francis William, 1876-
Beyond; a play. Boston. Lothrop. 1923. 12°. 78p.
Nimrod; a drama. Boston. Lothrop. ɾ1912ɿ. 12°. 90p. Biblical. 3 acts
Romains, Jules, 1885-
Doctor Knock; a comedy in three acts, in an English version by Harley Granville-Barker. London. Benn. 1925. 95p.
Roman, Ronettl
New lamps for old; authorized adaptation from the Roumanian by Oscar Leonard. Boston. Stratford. 1920. 12°. $1.50
Roof, Katharine Metcalf
Christmas tryst. 1 act
In Touchstone 6:83
Edge of the wood. Fantasy. 1 act
In Drama 10:196
Man under the bed, a farce-comedy in one act. Boston. Baker. 1924
Mirror; an original play in one act. N.Y. French. 1924. 28p.
Stone Venus. Superstition. 7 scenes
In Poet Lore 37:124
World beyond the mountain. Fantasy. 1 act
In International (NY) 7:322
Rose, Edward Everett, 1862-
Cappy Ricks; a comedy in three acts; adapted from the story of Peter B. Kyne. N.Y. French. 12°. 130p.
Penrod; a comedy in four acts, adapted . . . from Booth Tarkington's Penrod stories. N.Y. French. c1921. 12°. 126p.

Rosenberg, James Naumberg, 1874-
Punchinello; a ballet. N.Y. Kennerley. 1923. 12°. 92p. 3 acts
Return to mutton. N.Y. Kennerley. 1916. 12°. 53p. Comedy. 2 acts
Rosener, George M.
"True hearts of Erin", an Irish comedy drama in three acts. . . N.Y. Stagelore play. c1922. 12°. 59p.
Rosenfeld, Sydney, 1855-
At the White Horse tavern; a comedy in three acts . . . being an English version of "Im Weissen roess'l", by Messrs. Blumenthal & Kadelburg. N.Y. Kauser. ɾc1907ɿ. 12°. 63p.
Children of destiny; a play in four acts. N.Y. Dillingham. ɾc1910ɿ. 12°. 127p. Social
Club friend; or, A fashionable physician, an original comedy in four acts. . . New York; DeWitt. 1897. 12°. 89p.
Fashionable physician. *See* Rosenfeld, S. Club friend, or, A fashionable physician
Mr. X. A farce in one act. . . N.Y. DeWitt. c1875. 12°. 17p.
My daughter! oh! my daughter! *See* Rosenfeld S. Rosemi Shell; or, My daughter! oh! my daughter
Off the stage. An original comedietta, in one act. N.Y. DeWitt. c1875. 12°. 26p.
On bread and water. A musical farce, in one act. . . N.Y. DeWitt: c1875. 12°. 12p.
Pair of shoes. A farce in one act. . . N.Y. DeWitt. c1882. 12°. 12p.
Rosemi Shell; or, My daughter! oh! my daughter. . . N.Y. DeWitt. c1876. 12°. 19p.
Ulster. A farcical comedy, in three acts In part adapted from the German. . . N.Y. DeWitt. c1882. 12°. 46p.
Rosett, Joshua
Middle class; a play in four acts. Baltimore. Phoenix. ɾ1912ɿ. 12°. 124p. Sociological
Quandary; a play in three acts. Baltimore. Phoenix. ɾc1913ɿ. 12°. 173p.
Roskoten, Robert
Carlotta; a tragedy in five acts. Peoria, Ill. (J. W. Franks). 1880. 8°. 123p.
Rosmer, Ernst, pseud. *See* Rerstein, Elsa
Ross, Clarendon
Avenger. Fantasy. 1 act
In Drama 8:329
Derelict. Fantasy. 1 act
In Poet Lore 30:601
Murderer. Miracle. 1 act
In Poet Lore 30:596
Prisoner. Fantasy. 1 act
In Poet Lore 29:590
Reconsiderations. 2 plays. 1. Murderer. 2. Derelict
In Poet Lore 30:596
Rostand, Edmond, 1868-
L'Aiglon; (Eaglet) a play in six acts; adapted into English by L. N. Park-

Rostand, E.—*Continued.*
　er.　N.Y. Russell. 1900. 8°. 261p. $1.50
　Tragedy. 6 acts
　Same in Plays v 2
Chanticler; a play in four acts. tr. by Gertrude Hall.　N.Y. Duffield. 1910. 12°. 289p.　Animal
　Same in Plays v 2
Cyrano de Bergerac; an heroic comedy in five acts.　N.Y. Holt. 1925. 12°. 256p.　Romantic
　Same in Plays v 1
　　　Dickinson, T. H. ed.　Chief contemporary dramatists
　　　Moses, M. J. ed.　Representative continental dramas
　　　Pierce and Matthews, eds. Masterpieces of modern drama v 2 (abridged)
Eaglet.　*See* Rostand, E.　L'Aiglon
Fantasticks; a romantic comedy in three acts. . .　N.Y. Russell. 1900. 12°. 146p.
Far princess (La princesse lointaine); a drama in four acts.　N.Y. Holt. 1925. 12°. 169p. *also.* Stokes. c1899.　Romantic
　Same in Plays v 1
Princess Far-away.　*See* Rostand, E.　Far princess
Romancers (Romantics); a comedy in three acts. . .　N.Y. Doubleday. 1899. 12°. 134p. *also.* French. 1915
　Same in Plays v 1
　　　Coffman, G. R. ed.　Book of modern plays
　　　Smith, M. M. ed.　Short plays of various types
　　　Poet Lore 32:520
Woman of Samaria.　Biblical. 3 pts.
　In Plays v 1

Rostetter, Alice
Mable and Maisie.　*See* Rostetter, A. Which is witch? or, Mable and Maisie
Queen's lost dignity.　Marionette. 5 scenes
　In Cohen, H. L. ed.　Junior play book
Which is witch? or, Mable and Maisie. Juvenile. 1 act
　In Jagendorf, M. A. ed.　One-act plays for young folks
Widow's veil; a comedy in one act . . . as played by the Provincetown players. N.Y. E. Arens. 1920. 12°. 31p. (Flying stag plays for the little theatre. no. 9)
　Same in Provincetown plays (Stewart Kidd 1921)

Rouveyrol, Aurania
Price of love.　Satirical comedy. 1 act
　In Drama 16:219
Skidding; a comedy in three acts.　Los Angeles. Playshop. c1925. 8°. 157p.
When's your birthday? a comedy in three acts. . .　Los Angeles.　Playshop. 1924. 8°. 131p.

Rowell, Adelaide C.
Beloved it is morn.　Fantasy. 1 act
　In Poet Lore 36:101

Last frontier.　Psychological. 1 act
　In Drama 15:157
Silly ass.　Comedy. 1 act
　In Drama 12:344

Rowley, Anthony
Probationer; a play in four acts.　London. Gowans. 1911. 12°. 160p.　Melodrama

Royle, Edwin Milton, 1862-
Squaw man.　Melodrama. 1 act
　In Cosmopol 37:41

Rubin, William Benjamin, 1873-
Bolshevists; a comedy drama.　Boston. Cornhill. 1921. 12°. 87p. $1.50. 4 acts

Rubinstein, Harold F., 1892-
Arms and the drama.　World war. 1 act
　In What's wrong with the drama?
Grand Guignol.　Satire. 1 act
　In What's wrong with the drama?
House, a play in three acts.　London. Benn. 1920. 12°. 97p.
Insomnia.　1 act
　In Baker's anthology of one-act plays
Old boyhood; a comedy in one act.　London.　"The Stage". 1924. 16°. 40p.
Peter & Paul; a play in three acts.　London. Benn. 1924. 12°. 66p.　Psychological
Repertory.　Comedy. 1 act
　In What's wrong with the drama?
"Revanche"—A mystery.　1 act
　In New Coterie N '25:p 71
Specimen.　Authorship. 1 act
　In What's wrong with the drama?
Theatre.　Curtain raiser. 1 act
　In What's wrong with the drama?

Rubinstein, Harold F., 1892, **and Bax, Clifford**
Shakespeare; a play.　Boston. Houghton. 1921. 12°. 117p.　Historical. 5 episodes

Rubinstein, Harold F., 1892, **and Glover, Halcott**
Exodus; a dramatic sequence in five episodes.　London. Benn. 1923. 12°. 109p.　Biblical

Rubinstein, Harold F., 1892, **and Talbot, A. J.**
Churchill; a chronicle comedy, in eight scenes.　London. Benn. 1925. 12°. 114p. (Contemporary British dramatists. v. 29)

Rusiñol, Santiago, 1861-
Prodigal doll.　Comedy. 1 act
　In Drama 7:no 25:90

Rueda, Jiménez Julio.　*See* Jiménez Rueda, Julio

Ruschke, Egmont W., 1898-
Death speaks.　Fantasy. 1 act
　In Echo, and A bit of verse
Echo.　Comedy. 1 act
　In Echo, and A bit of verse
Intangible.　Wealth. 1 act
　In Echo, and a bit of verse

Russell, Phillips
Course in piracy.　Burlesque comedy. 1 act
　In Shay, F. ed.　Plays for strolling mummers

Ruthenberg, G. Hutchinson
Children. Social. 1 act
In Drama 15:131
Solomon. Biblical. 1 act
In Poet Lore 36:600
Rutherford, Mayne, pseud. *See* Waddell, Samuel
Ryerson, Florence
Letters. Comedy. 1 act
In Drama 16:253
Ryley, Mrs. Madeleine Lucette, 1868-
Mrs. Grundy; a play in four acts. London. "The Stage" pub. bureau. 1924. 138p.
Ryves, Evangeline
House· of man. Supernatural. 5 scenes
In Running fires
Running fires. Supernatural. 6 scenes
In Running fires
Zöe. Supernatural. 5 scenes
In Running fires
Saavedra y Bessey, Rafael M.
La Chinta. Panorama of Uruapan. 2 scenes
In Poet Lore 37:107
Sabatini, Rafael, 1875-
Tyrant: an episode in the career of Cesare Borgia; a play in four acts. London. Hutchinson. 1925. 138p.
Sackville, Lady Margaret, 1881-
Hildris the Queen; a play in four acts. London. Sherratt. 1908. 115p. 12°. Legendary
Saddler, Harry Dean
Outsider; a play in one act. N.Y. French. c1926. 12°. 22p.
Sage, Selwin, and Jones, Howard Mumford
Fascinating Mr. Denby. Comedy. 1 act
In Drama 14:175
St Cyres, Dorothy, viscountess
Holy city; a tragedy and allegory in three acts. N.Y. Longmans. 1922. 12°. 91p. $1.75
Salmonsen, Morris, 1843-
We mortals; a play in three acts. Chicago. J. M. W. Jones. 1897. 12°. 147p. Romantic
Saltykov, (Saltinkoff-Shchedrin), Mikhail Evgrafovich, 1826-1889
Death of Pazukhin; a play in four acts... N.Y. Brentano. c1924. 55p.
Salzburg, Sidney S.
Lucrezia Borgia; a drama. Phila. Dorrance. 1922. 12°. 74p.
Sammis, Edward R.
Outcasts. Fantasy. 1 act
In Poet Lore 36:306
Poet's paradise. Romantic. 1 act
In Poet Lore 36:569
Samuels, Maurice Victor, 1873-
Florentines; a play. N.Y. Brentano. 1904. 12°. 153p. Historical. 3 acts
Pageant of the strong. N.Y. Jarvis Maxwell. 1923. 8°. 58p. 5 scenes
Sanborn, Arthur W.
Clerks of Kittery; a comedy in seven acts. Boston. Baker. [1912]. 8°. 77p.
Young American in the hands of his friends, a political drama. Boston. West. [1904]. 12°. 82p. 1 act

Sandiford, B. P.
Crows. Character. 1 act
In Canad M 58:397
Santayana, George, 1863-
Lucifer; a theological tragedy. N.Y. Stone. 1899. 12°. 187p. 5 acts
Sapte, William
Actor. Domestic. 1 act
In Curtain raisers and sketches v 3
After many years. Romantic. 1 act
In Curtain raisers and sketches v 4
Afternoon call. Duologue. 1 act
In Curtain raisers and sketches v 4
Conway-chauffeur. Comedy. 1 act
In Curtain raisers and sketches v 4
Daddy. Farce. 1 act
In Curtain raisers and sketches. v 1
Harmony. Comedy. 1 act
In Curtain raisers and sketches v 3
His girl and his guv'nor. Comedy. 1 act
In Curtain raisers and sketches. v 1
James and the telephone. Comedy. 1 act
In Curtain raisers and sketches v 2
Leasehold marriage. Comedy. 1 act
In Curtain raisers and sketches v 3
Lesson in proposing. Farce. 1 act
In Curtain raisers and sketches. v 1
Lioness. Melodrama. 1 act
In Curtain raisers and sketches v 4
Mesalliance. Farce. 1 act
In Curtain raisers and sketches. v 1
Mortara; or, The poisoned chalice. Melodrama. 1 act
In Curtain raisers and sketches v 3
Photograph. Farce. 1 act
In Curtain raisers and sketches v 2
Poisoned chalice. *See* Sapte, W. Mortara; or, The poisoned chalice
Rightful heir. Farce. 1 act
In Curtain raisers and sketches v 2
Sample versus pattern. Farcical duologue. London. French. [18—]. 12°. 9p.
Step-sister. Domestic play in one act. London. French. [18—]. 12°. 12p.
Waiting for the truth. Comedy. 1 act
In Curtain raisers and sketches v 2
Sardou, Victorien, 1831-1908
Black pearl (La perle noir); a comedy in three acts... tr. by B. H. Clark. N.Y. French. [c1915]. 49p.
Daniel Rochat. A comedy in five acts... London. French. [c1880]. 12°. 76p.
Diplomates; a comedy in four acts; tr. by H. L. Williams. Chicago. Denison. [1894]. 84p.
Duty; a comedy in four acts... Adapted from... "Les bourgeois de Pont Arcy". London. French. [188—?]. 16°. 75p.
Fedora. A lyric drama in three acts... N.Y. Rullman. c1906. 8°. 77p.
Fernanda; or, Forgive and forget. A drama in three acts. Adapted to the English stage by H. L. Williams, jr... N.Y. DeWitt. c1870. 54p.
Forgive and forget. *See* Sardou, V. Fernanda; or, Forgive and forget
Friends or foes? A comedy in four acts... Adapted. London. Lacy.

Sardou, V.—*Continued.*
   [1862?]. 12°. 68p. (Lacy's acting edi-
      tion of plays. v. 54 no. 805)
   Love and science; a comedy in three acts.
      Tr. by C. H. Bellow. [Baltimore].
      1887. 56p.
   Our friends (Nos intimes); a comedy-
      drama in four acts. . . Adapted. . .
      London. French. [1872?]. 12°. 90p.
   Patrie! an historical drama in five acts
      (eight scenes); tr. by B. H. Clark.
      Garden City. Doubleday. 1915. 202p.
      75c.
   Pattes de mouches.   *See* Sardou, V.
      Scrap of paper
   Progress.   A comedy in three acts.
      (Founded on "Les Ganaches").
      Adapted. . . London. French. [18—?].
      12°. p. 545-601.
   Scrap of paper; (Pattes de mouches); a
      comedy in three acts; tr. and adapted
      by J. P. Simpson, from "Pattes de
      mouche." Boston. Baker. 1911. 68p.
      Same in Pierce   and   Matthews, eds.
         Masterpieces   of   modern
         drama v 2 (abridged)
      World's great classics Drama
         v 2
   Sorceress, a drama in five acts. . . Bos-
      ton. Badger. 1917. 136p.   Historical.
      Granada. 5 acts

**Sardou, Victorien, 1831-1908, and Moreau,
   Émile, 1852-**
   Dante; drama in a prologue and four
      acts. . . N.Y. Ciocia. [1903]. 66p.
   Madame   Sans-Gêne (Madame   Don't
      Care). . . N.Y.   Street & Smith.
      [1900]. 256p.   Comedy. 3 acts

**Sardou, Victorien, 1831-1908, and Najac,
   Émile de, 1828-1889**
   Divorçons, a comedy in three acts. N.Y.
      Dramatic pub. co. [c1909]. 116p.
      Same in Pierce   and   Matthews, eds.
         Masterpieces of modern drama v 2
         (abridged)

Sarg, Tony, joint author. *See* Williamson,
   H. and Sarg, T.

Sargent, Epes, 1813-1880
   Velasco; a tragedy in five acts.   N.Y.
      Harper. 1839. 12°. 110p.

Sargent, Herbert C.
   Always polite.   Comedy. 1 act
      In Bits and pieces
   Brighten Dartmoor.   Farce. 1 act
      In Bits and pieces
   Busy bee.   Comedy. 1 act
      In Bits and pieces
   Buying a sewing machine.   Farce. 1 act
      In Pierrotechnics
   Comforts.   Comedy. 1 act
      In Bits and pieces
   Few remarks
      In Pierrotechnics
   Footsteps.   Melodrama. 1 act
      In Bits and pieces
   Geysers, Ltd.   Comedy. 1 act
      In Bits and pieces
   Grain of truth.   Comedy. 1 act
      In Bits and pieces

Great snakes
   In Pierrotechnics
Income tax
   In Pierrotechnics
Mrs. Hamblett records her vote.   1 act
   In Pierrotechnics
Mug.   1 act
   In Pierrotechnics
Out of sight.   1 act
   In Pierrotechnics
Raising the wind.   Comedy. 1 act
   In Bits and pieces
Revueitis
   In Pierrotechnics
Strong situation
   In Pierrotechnics
Winner.   Comedy. 1 act
   In Bits and pieces

Sarkadi, Leo
   Lure of life.   Symbolic. 1 act
      In International (NY) 10:341
   Passing shadow.   Pathological. 1 act
      In International (NY) 10:237
   Vision of Paganini.   Allegory. 1 act
      In International (NY) 10:54

Saunders, Lilian
   Bee.   Triangle. 1 act
      In Drama 14:170
   Night brings a counselor.   Psycholog-
      ical. 1 act
      In Drama 13:251
   Sob sister.   Character. 1 act
      In Drama 11:354

Saunders, Louise
   Figureheads.   Romantic. 1 act
      In Magic lanterns
   King and commoner.   Comedy. 1 act
      In Magic lanterns
   Knave of hearts.   Comedy. 1 act
      In Leonard, S. A. ed.   Atlantic book
         of modern plays
   Our kind.   Comedy. 1 act
      In Magic lanterns
         Smart Set 64:73
   Poor Maddalena.   Fantasy. 3 scenes
      In Magic lanterns
         Knickerbocker,   E.   Van   B.   ed.
            Twelve plays
   See-saw.   Comedy. 1 act
      In Magic lanterns
   Woodland princess; a play for young peo-
      ple.   N.Y. French. [1909]. 12°. 28p.

Sauter, Edwin
   As 'twas done in Italy.   *See* Sauter, E.
      Poisoners, or, As 'twas one in Italy
   Death of Gracchus; a tragedy.   Private
      ed. St. Louis. 1908. 16°. 75p. 5 acts
   Faithless favorite.   A mixed tragedy. : .
      St. Louis. The author. 1905. 16°. 238p.
      5 acts
   Poisoners; or, As 'twas done in Italy. A
      tragedy. St. Louis. The author. 1906.
      24°. 72p. 5 acts

Savage, Dorothy O.
   Jon.   1 act
      In Baker's anthology of one-act plays

Savage, John, 1828-1888
   Dreaming by moonlight.   Poetic. 1 act
      In Poems, lyrical, dramatic and roman-
         tic

Sybil; a tragedy in five acts. N.Y. Kirker. 1865. 12°. 105p.
Same in Poems, lyrical, dramatic and romantic

Saward, William T.
Glastonbury; an historical drama in four acts. London. Kingsgate press. 1911. 78p

Sawyer, Ruth, 1880-
Sidhe of Ben-Mor; an Irish folk play. Boston. Badger. 1910. 1 act
Same in Poet Lore 21:300

Sax, C., and Christie, M.
Questions. Character. 1 act
In Touchstone 5:111

Scharrelmann, Wilhelm, joint author. *See* Wiegand, J. and Scharrelmann, Wilhelm

Scheffauer, Herman George, 1876-
Hollow head of Mars; a modern masque in four phases. London. Simpkin. 1915. 12°. 80p.
Sons of Baldur, a forest music drama. . . San Francisco. Hauser. 1908. 8°. 41p.

Schiller, Johann Christoph Friedrich von, 1759-1805
Bride of Messina. Historical. 1 act
In Works (Bohn) Historical dramas
  Works (Cambridge) v 6
  Works (Dole) v 4
Camp of Wallenstein. Tragedy. 5 acts
In Works (Bohn) Historical and dramatic
  Works (Cambridge) v 4
  Works (Dole) v 4
  Bates, A. ed. Drama v 16
Death of Wallenstein. Historical. 5 acts
In Works (Bohn). Historical and dramatic
  Works (Cambridge) v 4
  Works (Dole) v 4
  German classics 3:84
Demetrius. Historical. 2 acts
In Works (Bohn) Early dramas and romances
  Works (Cambridge) v 5
  Works (Dole) v 4
Don Carlos, infant of Spain. Tragedy. 5 acts
In Works (Bohn) Historical dramas
  Works (Cambridge) v 5
  Works (Dole) v 3
  Thompson, B. German theatre v 5
Fiesco. Tragedy. 5 acts
In Works (Bohn). Early dramas and romances
  Works (Cambridge) v 3
  Works (Dole) v 3
Love and intrigue (Cabal and love). Tragedy. 5 acts
In Works (Bohn) Early dramas and romances
  Works (Cambridge) v 3
  Works (Dole) v 3
Maid of Orleans. Historical. 5 acts
In Works (Bohn) Historical and dramatic
  Works (Cambridge) v 6
  Works (Dole) v 4
Mary Stuart. Historical. 5 acts
In Works (Bohn) Historical dramas

  Works (Cambridge) v 6
  Works (Dole) v 3
Piccolomini. Tragedy. 5 acts
In Works (Bohn) Historical and dramatic
  Works (Cambridge) v 4
  Works (Dole) v 4
  Bates, A. ed. Drama v 10:108
Robbers. Tragedy. 5 acts
In Works (Bohn) Early dramas and romances
  Works (Cambridge) v 3
  Works (Dole) v 3
  Thompson, B. ed. German theatre v 5
Wilhelm Tell. Historical. 5 acts
In Works (Bohn) Historical and dramatic
  Works (Cambridge) v 5
  Works (Dole) v 4
  German classics 3:245

Schlumberger, J.
Césaire. Retaliation. 1 act
In Liv Age 312:106

Schmidt, Godfrey P., jr.
I did but jest. Tragedy. 1 act
In Poet Lore 35:130

Schmidt, Otto Ernst (Otto Ernst, pseud)., 1862-
Master Flachsmann (Flachsmann als Erzieher). A comedy in three acts. . . N.Y. Duffield. [191—?]. 12°. 155p.

Schmithof, E.
Six cups of chocolate; a piece of gossip in one act. . . N.Y. Harper. [c1897]. 16°. 32p.

Schnittkind, Henry T.
Shambles. World war. 1 act
In Poet Lore 25:559

Schnitzler, Arthur, 1862-
Anatol; a sequence of dialogues paraphrased for the English stage by Granville Barker. N.Y. Kennerley. 1911. 125p. *Also* Boni. 8 pts. Romantic
Ask no questions and you'll hear no stories. (dialogue in Anatol). *q.v.*
Big scene. Comedy. 1 act
In Comedies of words and other plays
Christmas present (dialogue in Anatol)
In Anatol
  International (NY) 4:6-7
Comedies of words. Comedy
In Comedies of words and other plays
Countess Mizzi; or, The family reunion (Komtesse Mizzi). Boston. Little. 1907. Comedy. 1 act
Same in Lonely way
    Moses, M. J. ed. Representative one-act plays by continental authors
Duke and the actress. *See* Schnitzler, A. Green cockatoo
Dying pangs (dialogue in Anatol). *q.v.*
Episode (dialogue in Anatol). Satire
In Anatol
  International (NY) 4:23-24
Family reunion. *See* Schnitzler, A. Countess Mizzi; or, The family reunion

Schnitzler, A.—*Continued.*
Farewell supper (dialogue in Anatol). *q.v.*
Festival of Bacchus. Comedy. 1 act
In Comedies of words and other plays
Shay, F. ed.   Twenty-five short
plays, international
International (NY) 10:303-10
Free game; (Freiwild); a drama in three
acts. Boston. Badger. 1913. $1.25.
Duelling
Gallant Cassian, a puppet-play in one act;
tr. . . by Adam L. Gowans London.
1914. 12°. 45p.
Green cockatoo (Duke and the actress;
Der grüne Kakadu).   Grotesque. 1
act
In Green cockatoo and other plays
German classics 20:289
Poet Lore 1:257
Golden Bk 4:637
His helpmate (Mate. Die Gefährten).
Domestic. 1 act
In Comedies of words and other plays
Green cockatoo and other plays
Mate
International (NY) 9:207-11
Hour of recognition. Comedy. 1 act
In Comedies of words and other plays
International (NY) 10:167
Hours of life. *See* Schnitzler, A. Liv-
ing hours
Intermezzo. Comedy. 3 acts
In Lonely way and other plays
Keepsakes (dialogue in Anatol). *q.v.*
Lady with the dagger (Woman with the
dagger; Die Frau mit dem dolche).
Reincarnation. 1 act
In Fortn 91:1179
International (NY) 4:92
Poet Lore 15 no 2:1
Legacy (Das vermächtnis); a drama in
three acts. . . Boston. Badger. c1911.
Social
Same in Poet Lore 22:241
Light o'love. *See* Schnitzler, A. Play-
ing with love
Literature (Literatur). Comedy. 1 act
In Comedies of words and other plays
German classics 20:332
Shay, F. and Loving, P. eds.   Fifty
contemporary one-act plays
International (NY) 9:330
Living hours (Vivid hours; Hours of life;
Lebendige Stunden). 1 act. Sacri-
fice
In Living hours
Dickinson, T. M. ed.   Chief con-
temporary dramatists ser 2
Loving, P. ed.   Ten minute plays
Poet Lore 17, no 1:36
Stratford J 4:155 Mr '19
Lonely way (Der einsame weg). Bos-
ton. Little. 1904. 5 acts
Same in Lonely way [and other plays]
Moses, M. J. ed.   Representa-
tive continental dramas
Mate. . . Chicago. McClurg. 1913. *See*
Schnitzler, A. His helpmate

Paracelsus. . . Chicago. McClurg. 1913.
Comedy. 11 scenes
Same in Green cockatoo and other
plays
Playing with love. (Light o'love; Lie-
belei). . . The prologue to Anatol; by
H. von Hoffmansthal. . . London.
Gay. 1914. 101p. Comedy. 3 acts
Same in Drama 2 no 7:15
Professor Bernhardi; a comedy. . . San
Francisco. Elder. [c1913]. 64p. $1. 4
acts
Questioning the irrevocable (Die frage
an das schicksal). Hypnotism. 1 act
In Bates, A. ed. Drama 12:329
Vast domain (Das weite land) Tragi-
comedy. 5 acts
In Poet Lore 34:317
Vital moments. Ideas. 1 act
In International (NY) 3:7
Wedding morning (dialogue in Anatol).
q.v.
Wife. Emotional. 1 act
In Cur Lit 39:553 (abridged)
Woman with the dagger. *See* Schnitzler,
A. Lady with the dagger
Schönherr, Karl, 1869-
Faith and fire side (Glaube und Heimat).
Tragedy. 2 acts
In German classics 16:417
Schoenthan, Franz von, 1849-1912
Hurly-burly; or, Number seven-twenty-
eight. A farcical comedy in three
acts. . . N.Y. French. [1884?]. 12°.
48p.
Kettle of fish. A farcical comedy in
three acts. . . Boston. Baker. [c1890].
12°. 53p.
Last word; a comedy in four acts . . .
[adapted]. . . N.Y. Privately printed.
1891. 4°. 71p.
Night off; or, A page from Balzac. A
comedy in four acts. . . N.Y. Printed
for the author. 1885. 8°. 75p.
Railroad of love; a comedy in four
acts. . . N.Y. Privately printed. 1887.
8°. 72p.
Schofield, Stephen
Bruiser's election; a political farce in one
act. London. Labour pub. co. [1925].
24p.
Schoonmaker, Edwin Davies, 1873-
Americans. N.Y. Kennerley. 1913. 12°.
304p. Sociological. 5 acts
Saxons; a drama of Christianity in the
north. Chicago. Hammersmark pub.
co. 1905. 8°. 214p. 5 acts
Schrader, George Morrison, von, 1862-
Salambo; a tragedy in four acts. N.Y.
French. 1914. 12°. 108p. $1
Schroeder, Friedrich Ludwig
Ensign. A comedy in three acts. . .
London. Vernor. 1800. 8°. 87p.
Schütze, Martin, 1866-
Hero and Leander; a tragedy. N.Y.
Holt. 1908. 12°. 176p. 5 acts
Judith: a tragedy in five acts. N.Y.
Holt. 1910. 8°. 306p.

Schwartz, Esther Dresden
Three souls in search of a dramatist. Farce. 1 act
In Drama 16:247

Schwartz, T. G.
Monster. Comedy. 1 act
In Poet Lore 37:597

Scott, Mansfield
Submarine shell; a war play in four acts. Boston. Baker. 1918. 79p.

Scott, Margretta
Bag o'dreams. Juvenile. 1 act
In Drama 11:131
Heart of Pierrot. Juvenile. 1 act
In Schafer, B. L. ed. Book of one-act plays
Drama 10:200
Three kisses. Heaven. 3 scenes
In Drama 10:15

Scott, Sir Walter. *See* Dibdin, T. J. for adaptations of Heart of Midlothian; Ivanhoe; Kenilworth; Lady of the lake; Pirate

Scott, William Wiley
Crowning; a play in four acts. Boston. Gorham. 1918. 12°. 40p. Peace
Downfall of humanity; a drama in three acts. Boston. Badger. 1918. 8°. $1.25. 50p. Prophetic

Scott-Maxwell, Mrs. Florida
Flash-point; a play in three acts. London. Sidgwick. 1914. 12°. 127p. Problem

Scribe, Augustine Eugéne, 1791-1861
Glass of water . . . a comedy in two acts. Freely adapted from "Verre d'eau". . . London. Lacy. n.d. 12°. 54p. (Lacy's acting edition of plays. v. 79 no. 1181)
Marco Spado. *See* Simpson, J. P. Marco Spado; altered and adapted from M. Scribe
Russian honeymoon; a comedy in three acts. . . N.Y. DeWitt. 1890. 12°. 68p.
School for politicians (Bertrand et Raton, ou, L'Art de conspirer). Comedy in five acts. N.Y. Carvill. 1840. 8°. 179p. (adapted)

Scribe, Augustine Eugéne 1791-1861, and Legouvé, Ernest
Adrienne Lecouvreur, a drama in five acts. . . N.Y. Darcie. 1855. 4°. 79p. Comedy
Ladies' battle (La bataille des dames), a comedy in three acts. . . London. Lacy. n.d. 12°. 43p. (Lacy's acting edition of plays. v. 4 no. 47)
Lost husband. A drama in four acts. . . London. n.d. 12°. 36p. (Lacy's acting edition of plays. v. 6 no. 86)

Searle, Katharine
Game! Comedy. 3 acts
In Two plays
Roderick's career. Marriage. 3 acts
In Two plays

Searle, Margaret Cassie
Bad debts; a drama in one act. N.Y. French. 1921. 12°. 36p. 35c. Psychological

Seavey, Martha M.
Judith of Tyre; a drama in three acts N.Y. J. T. White. 1924. 12°. 121p. $1.25. Poetic

See, Edmund, 1875-
Friend of his youth. Friendship. 1 act
In Poet Lore 36:159

Seiler, Conrad
Crime. Comedy. 1 act
In Suicide, and other one-act comedies
Eye for an eye. Comedy. 1 act
In Suicide, and other one-act comedies
Fantasia. Grotesque for marionettes. 1 act
In Suicide, and other one-act comedies
Poets all. Dramatic intermezzo. 1 act
In Suicide, and other one-act comedies
Suicide. Comedy. 1 act
In Suicide, and other one-act comedies
Time will tell. Comedy. 1 act
In Suicide, and other one-act comedies

Selby, Charles, 1802?-1863
Anthony and Cleopatra. A burletta in one act. Boston. Spencer. [1856?]. 12°. 15p.
Catching an actress; an original petite comedy in one act. . . London. Duncombe. [18—?]. 12°. 38p.
Fire-eater! a farce. In one act. London. Lacy. n.d. 12°. 15°. (Lacy's acting edition of plays. v. 4 no. 52)
Hotel charges; or, How to cook a biffin! An original farcical sketch. In one act. London. (Lacy's acting edition of plays. v. 12 no. 169)
How to cook a biffin! *See* Selby, C. Hotel charges; or, How to cook a biffin!
Hunting a turtle; an original farce in one act. . . London. Duncombe. [18—?]. 12°. 26p.
Husband of my heart. A comic drama in two acts. London. Lacy. n.d. 12°. 32p. (Lacy's acting edition of plays. v. 2 no. 30)
Lady and gentleman, in a peculiarly perplexing predicament A burletta in one act. . . Boston. Spencer. [1857?]. 12°. 21p.
Last of the pigtails. An original petite comedy. In one act. Boston. Spencer. [1858?]. 12°. 23p.
Marble heart; or, The sculptor's dream. A romance of real life. In five chapters. London. Lacy. n.d. 12°. 54p. (Lacy's acting edition of plays. v. 15 no. 214)
Married rake; an original interlude in one act London. Duncombe. [1835]. 22p. 24°.
Mysterious stranger. *See* Selby, C. Satan in Paris; or, The mysterious stranger
Robert Macaire; or, The two murderers. A melo-drama in two acts. N.Y. French. [18—?]. 12°. 38p.
Satan in Paris; or, The mysterious stranger; a drama in two acts. . . Boston. Spencer. 1855. 12°. 70p.

Selby, C.—*Continued.*
Two murderers. *See* Selby, C. Married rake; or, The two murderers
Valet de sham. A farce in one act. Boston. Spencer. ₁1858?₁. 12°. 21p.

Sellers, Irma Peixotto
Adored one. Historical. (France. Louis XV.) 1 act
In Drama 13:253

Selwyn, Edgar, 1875-
Country boy; a comedy in four acts. N.Y. French. 1917. 101p.
Nearly married; a farce in three acts. N.Y. French. c1918. 136p.
Rolling stones; a comedy in four acts. N.Y. French. 1917. 130p.
When Danny comes marching home; a farce in one act. Washington. Commission on training camp activities. . . War Dept. 1918

Selwyn, Edgar, and Goulding, Edmund
Dancing mothers. Modern life. 4 acts
In Mantle, B. ed. Best plays of 1924-25 (condensed)

Selwyn, Mrs. Edgar. *See* Mayo, Margaret

Serle, Thomas James
Merchant of London; a play in five acts. London. Sams. 1832. 8°. 115p. Melodrama
Tender precautions; or, The romance of marriage. A new and original comedy in one act. London. Lacy. n.d. 12°. 28p. (Lacy's acting edition of plays. v. 5 no. 71)

Shairp, Mordaunt
Offence; a play in three acts. London. Benn. 1925. 12°. 84p. Psychological

Shaler, Nathaniel Southgate, 1841-1906
Armada days. Boston. Houghton. 1903. 8°. 116p. Historical. 5 acts. Pt. 3 of Elizabeth of England
Coronation. Boston. Houghton. 1903. 8°. 173p. Historical. 5 acts. Pt. 1 of Elizabeth of England
Death of Essex. Boston. Houghton. 1903. 203p. Historical. 5 acts. Pt. 4 of Elizabeth of England
Elizabeth of England; a dramatic romance in five pts. Boston. Houghton. 1903. 8°. 5v. Pt. 1 Coronation; Pt. 2. Rival queens; Pt. 3. Armada days; Pt. 4. Death of Essex; Pt. 5. Passing of the Queen
Passing of the queen. Boston. Houghton. 1903. 8°. 149p. 5 acts. Pt. 5 of Elizabeth of England
Rival queens. Boston. Houghton. 1903. 8°. 184p. Historical. 5 acts. Pt. 2 of Elizabeth of England

Shapleigh, Mabelle, and Kahn, Alfred, 1882-
Bird and the fish; a romantic play on the marriage problem, in four acts. ₁N.Y.₁. c1924. 64p.

Sharp, H. Sutton
Germs. Physiological. 1 act
In Drama 16:167

Sharp, William (Fiona Macleod, pseud)
House of Usna; a drama. Mosher. Portland, Me. 1903. 75p. Celtic legend. 1 act
Same in Poems and dramas
    National 35:773
Immortal hour; a drama in two acts. Mosher. Portland, Me. 1907. 47p. Celtic legend
Same in Poems and dramas
    Fortn 74:867

Shaw, F.
Person in the chair. Character. 1 act
In Drama 11:171

Shaw, Alexander Wilson
Girl in the picture; a play in two acts. Boston. Badger. 1914. 12°. 87p. Comedy

Shaw, George Bernard, 1856-
Admirable Bashville; or, Constancy unrewarded . . . being the novel of Cashel Byron's profession done into a stage play. . . N.Y. Brentano's. 1909. 74p.
Androcles and the lion. Comedy. 1 act
In Androcles and the lion ₁and other plays₁
    Everybody's 31:289
Annajanska the Bolshevik empress. Satire. 1 act
In Heartbreak house
Arms and the man. (a pleasant play) N.Y. Brentano's. 1913. 80p. Comedy. 3 acts
Same in Plays, pleasant and unpleasant v 2
Augustus does his bit. Comedy. 1 act
In Heartbreak house
Back to Methuselah. A metabiological pentateuch. N.Y. Brentano's. 1921. 12°. 300p. 5 pts.
Caesar and Cleopatria, a page of history. N.Y. Brentano's. 1913. 124p. Comedy. 5 acts
In Three plays for Puritans
    Pierce and Matthews, eds. Masterpieces of modern drama v 1 (abridged)
Candida. (a pleasant play). N.Y. Brentano's. 1913. 79p. Psychological. 3 acts
Same in Plays, pleasant and unpleasant v 2
Captain Brassbound's conversion; a play of adventure. N.Y. Brentano's. 1913. 95p. Comedy. 3 acts
Same in Three plays for Puritans
Constancy unrewarded. *See* Shaw, G. B. Admirable Bashville, or, Constancy unrewarded
Dark lady of the sonnets. Shakespeare. 1 act
In Misalliance
    Eng R 7:258
    Red Book 16:417
Devil's disciple, a melodrama. N.Y. Brentano's. 1913. 86p. 3 acts
Same in Three plays for Puritans

Doctor's dilemma, with a preface on doctors. N.Y. Brentano's. 1913. 116p. Satire. 5 acts
Same in Doctor's dilemma [and other plays]
Fanny's first play. Comedy. 3 acts
In Misalliance
Fatal gazogene. *See* Shaw, G. B. Passion, poison, and petrifaction
Getting married. N.Y. Brentano's. 1913. 205p. Comedy. 1 act
Same in Doctor's dilemma [and other plays]
Great Catharine. Comedy. 4 scenes
In Heartbreak house
Everybody's 32:193 (excerpts)
Heartbreak house. English society. 3 acts
In Heartbreak house, etc
How he lied to her husband. 1 act
In John Bull's other island
Man of destiny, and How he lied to her husband
Inca of Perusalem. William II of Germany. 1 act
In Heartbreak house, etc
John Bull's other island, with preface for politicians. N.Y. Brentano's. 1913. 126p. Comedy. 4 acts
Same in John Bull's other island, and Major Barbara
Major Barbara, with an essay as first aid to critics. N.Y. Brentano's. 1913. 159p. Comedy. 3 acts
Same in John Bull's other island, and Major Barbara
Man and superman; a comedy and a philosophy. N.Y. Brentano's. 1905. 244p. Social. 4 acts
Man of destiny (pleasant play). Napoleon. 1 act
In Man of destiny, and How he lied to her husband
Plays, pleasant and unpleasant v 2
Misalliance. Comedy. 1 act
In Misalliance
Mrs. Warren's profession (an unpleasant play). N.Y. Brentano's. 1913. 84p. Social. 4 acts
Same in Plays, pleasant and unpleasant v 1
O'Flaherty, V. C.—an interlude of the Great war. 1 act
In Heartbreak house
Cur Op (excerpts) 63:167
Hearst's M Ag 16
Overruled. Comedy. 1 act
In Androcles and the lion
Eng R 14:179
Hearst's M 23:680
Passion, poison, and petrifaction; or, The fatal gozogene. A tragedy. N.Y. Claflin. c1905. 11p. Comedy
Philanderer; (an unpleasant play). N.Y. Brentano's. 1913. 90p. Character. 4 acts
Same in Plays, pleasant and unpleasant v 1

Press cuttings. . . N.Y. Brentano's. 1909. 45p. Comedy. 1 act
Pygmalion. Romantic. 5 acts
In Androcles and the lion
Everybody's 31:577
Saint Joan; a chronicle play in six scenes and an epilogue. N.Y. Brentano's. 1924. 12°. 163p. Historical
Shewing up of Blanco Posnet; a sermon in crude melodrama. N.Y. Brentano's. 1909. 36p. 1 act
Same in Doctor's dilemma, and other plays
Widowers' houses (an unpleasant play). N.Y. Brentano's. 1913. 73p. Social. 3 acts
Same in Plays, pleasant and unpleasant v 1
You never can tell (a pleasant play). N.Y. Brentano's. 1913. 125p. Comedy. 4 acts
Same in Plays, pleasant and unpleasant v 2
Pierce and Matthews, eds. Masterpieces of modern drama v 2 (abridged)
Shay, Frank, ed.
Pyentsa. 3 acts
In Shay, F. ed. Twenty-five short play, international
Sheldon, Edward Brewster, 1886-
Boss. Politics. 4 acts
In Quinn, A. H. ed. Representative American plays 1767-1923
Garden of paradise . . . based on the "The little mermaid" by Hans Anderson. N.Y. Macmillan. 1915. 12°. 244p. $1.25. Fantasy. 9 scenes
"The nigger", an American play in three acts. N.Y. Macmillan. 1910. 12°. 269p. $1.25. Sociological
Romance. . . N.Y. Macmillan. 1914. 12°. 232p. Romantic. 3 acts and epilogue
Same in Baker, G. P. ed. Modern American plays
Salvation Nell; a play in three acts. N.Y. Kauser. [c1908]. 12°. 99p. Melodrama
Shelley, Percy Bysshe, 1792-1822
Cenci. Tragedy. 5 acts
In Poems (any complete edition)
Charles the First. Historical. 5 scenes
In Poems (any complete edition)
Hellas. Lyrical drama. 1 act
In Poems (any complete edition)
Shen Hung
Cow-herd and the weaving maid. Chinese folk-lore. 1 act
In Drama 11:404
Wedded husband. Chinese. 3 acts
In Poet Lore 32:110
Shephard, Esther
Pierrette's heart; a play in one act. N.Y. French. 1924. 20p.
Sheridan, Frances Chamberlaine, 1724-1766
Discovery; a comedy in five acts. N.Y. Doran. 1925. 12°. 121p. $2. (Adapted for the modern stage by Aldous Huxley)

Sheridan, Richard Brinsley Butler, 1751-
1816
  Camp.   Musical entertainment. 1 act
    In Works
  Critic; or, a tragedy rehearsed.   Comedy.
    2 acts
    In Dramatic works
      Works
  Duenna.   Comedy. 3 acts
    In Dramatic works
      Works
  Pizarro.   Comedy. 5 acts
    In Dramatic works
      Works
  Rivals.   Comedy. 5 acts
    In Dramatic works
      Works
  St. Patrick's day; or, The scheming lieu-
    tenant.   Farce. 2 acts
    In Dramatic works
      Works
  School for scandal.   Comedy. 5 acts
    In Dramatic works
      Works
      Matthews, J. and Lieder, P. R. eds.
        Chief British dramatists
  Trip to Scarborough.   Comedy. 5 acts
    In Dramatic works
      Works
Sheridan, Richard B., 1751-1816, and Col-
man, George
  Forty thieves: a grand operatical ro-
    mance and brilliant spectacle in two
    acts. Boston. Turner. 1810. 32°. 52p.
Sherman, Sylvia
  Pipes o'Pan; a wood dream. . . Boston.
    Badger. [c1916]. 8°. 81p.   Fantasy.
    3 acts
Sherry, Mrs. Laura Case
  On the pier.   Character. 1 act
    In Wisconsin plays ser 2
Sherwood, Margaret, 1864-
  Vittoria.   Romantic. 1 act
    In Scrib M 37:497
Shields, Charles Woodruff, 1825-1904
  Reformer of Geneva; an historical drama.
    N.Y. Putnams. 1898. 8°. 125p. 5 acts
Shigeyoshi, Obata
  Melon thief.   Farce. 1 act
    In Drama 10:104
Shipley, Joseph T.
  Echo.   Psychological. 1 act
    In Loving, P. ed.   Ten minute plays
  Mother goose drops in.   Juvenile. 1 act
    In Jagendorf, M. A. ed.   One-act plays
      for young folks
Shipman, Louis Evan, 1869-
  D'Arcy of the guards; a play in four acts.
    N.Y. French. 1915. 12°. 76p.
  Fools errant.   Comedy. 4 acts
    In Three comedies
  Fountain of youth.   Comedy. 3 acts
    In Three comedies
  On parole.   Comedy. 4 acts
    In Three comedies
Shipman, Samuel, 1883, and Hoffman,
Aaron, 1880-
  Friendly enemies; a play in three acts.
    N.Y. French. c1923. 12°. 100p. Com-
    edy

Shipman, Samuel, 1883-, and Hymer, John
B.
  East is west; a comedy in three acts and
    a prologue. N.Y. French. 1924. 12°.
    96p. 75c.
Shipman, Samuel, 1883-, and Lipman, Clara,
1869-
  Children of today; a satirical comedy-
    drama. N.Y. French. c1926. 12°. 95p.
Shore, Louisa Catherine
  Hannibal; a drama.   London. Richards.
    1898. 12°. 226p. Historical. 2 pts. 5
    acts ea.
Short, Marion
  Rose of the Southland; a comedy in three
    acts. N.Y. French. c1924. 75p.
Shpazhínsky, Ippolít Vasílievich
  Madame Major.   Emotional. 5 acts
    In Poet Lore 28:257
Shumway, Merline Henderson, 1892-
  Back to the farm.   Bulletin of the Uni-
    versity of Minnesota.   General series
    no. 12. Agric. Extension division.
    Minneapolis. Colwell press. 1914. 45p.
    Rural. 1 act
Sierra.   *See* Martínez Sierra, G.
Sigurjónsson, Jóhann, 1880-
  Eyvind of the hills.   Tragedy. 4 acts
    In Modern Icelandic plays
  Hraun farm.   Romantic. 3 acts
    In Modern Icelandic plays
      Smith, A. M. ed.   Short plays by
        representative authors
Simmonds, Mattie F.
  Grown-up children.   Comedy. 1 act
    In Poet Lore 36:434
Simmons, Maude Evangeline, 1875-
  Geraldine's treachery; a play in five acts.
    N.Y. Shakespeare press. 1913. 12°.
    61p.
Simms, William Gilmore, 1806-1870
  Atalantis; a story of the sea. . . Phila.
    Carey. 1848. 144p. 12°. 3 acts
  Man of the people. *See* Simms, W. G.
    Norman Maurice; or, The man of the
    people
  Norman Maurice; or, The man of the
    people. An American drama. In five
    acts. Richmond. Jno R. Thompson.
    1851. 8°. 31p.
Simonson, Gustav
  Horace Walpole: a romantic drama in
    four acts. N.Y. Moffatt. 1913. 12°.
    64p. 75c.
Simonson, Jules, joint author. *See* Coving-
ton, Zellah and Simonson, Jules
Simpson, Helen
  Pan in Pimlico.   Fantasy. 1 act
    In Double demon and other one-act
      plays
      Four one-act plays
      Shay, F. ed. Twenty-five short plays,
        international
Simpson, John Palgrave, 1807-1887
  Broken ties.   Domestic drama in two
    acts. . . N.Y. French. n.d. 12°. 41p.
    (Lacy's acting edition of plays. no.
    1439)

Dreams of delusion. A drama, in one act. Adapted from the French drama "Elle est folie". . . Boston. Spencer. [1857?]. 12°. 28p.

Heads or tails? A comedietta in one act. London. Lacy. n.d. 12°. 36p. (Lacy's acting edition of plays. v. 15 no. 221)

Marco Spado. A drama in three acts. Altered and adapted from the French of M. Scribe. London. Lacy. n.d. 12°. 44p. (Lacy's acting edition of plays. v. 10 no. 138)

Matrimonial propectuses! A comedietta in one act. London. Lacy. n.d. 12°. 21p. (Lacy's acting edition of plays. v. 6 no. 81)

Poor Cousin Walter. A drama in one act. London. Lacy. n.d. 12°. 22p. (Lacy's acting edition of plays. v. 2 no. 19)

Second love. An original comic drama, in three acts. . . Boston. Spencer. [1856]. 12°. 40p.

Two gentlemen at Mivarts. A dramatic duologue in one act
In Scott, C. ed. Drawing-room plays

Very suspicious! An original comedietta in one act. London. Lacy. n.d. 12°. 22p. (Lacy's acting edition of plays. v. 6 no. 90)

Without incumbrances. A farce in one act. London. Lacy. n.d. 12°. 24p. (Lacy's acting edition of plays. v. 2 no. 25)

Simpson, John Palgrave, and Wray, Charles
Ranelagh. A comic drama in two acts. London. Lacy. n.d. 12°. 48p. (Lacy's acting edition of plays. v. 13 no. 192)

Sinclair, Upton Beall, 1878-
Bill Porter; a drama of O. Henry in prison. Pasadena. Cal. The author. [c1925]. 8°. 58p. 4 acts

Hell; a verse drama and photoplay. Pasadena. Author. 1923. 12°. 128p. Satire. Act 4

Indignant subscriber. Comedy. 1 act
In Socialist R 4:389

"John D." Socialism. 1 act
In Socialist R 4:463

Machine. Tammany. 3 acts
In Plays of protest

Naturewoman. Social. 4 acts
In Plays of protest

Prince Hagen; a fantasy. Boston. Page. 1903. 12°. p. 11-249. Politic. 4 acts
Same in Plays of protest

Second-story man. Socialism. 1 act
In Plays of protest
Socialist R 4:91

Singing jailbirds; a drama in four acts. Pasadena. The author. 1924. 12°. $1 Expressionism. 4 acts

Siraudin, Paul, 1813-1883
Left the stage; or, Grassot tormented by Ravel. A personal experiment in one act. . . London. Lacy. n.d. 12°. 14p. (Lacy's acting edition of plays. v. 7 no. 91)

Siraudin, Paul, 1813-1883, and Thiboust, Lambert, 1826-1867
What tears can do! A comedietta in one act. Tr. from "Les femmes qui pleurent." N.Y. DeWitt. [1883]. 12°. 18p. *also* 1892 under title Weeping wives

Skelton, Mrs. Gladys. *See* Presland, John, pseud.

Slinsby, Lawrence, pseud. *See* Lewes, George Henry

Smith, Albert
Alhambra; or, The three beautiful princesses. A new and original burlesque extravaganza. London. Lacy. n.d. 12°. 25p. (Lacy's acting edition of plays. v. 3 no. 45). 1 act

Esmeralda. An entirely new and original operatico-terpscichorean burlesque. In two acts. London. Lacy. n.d. 12°. 36p. (Lacy's acting edition of plays. v. 2 no. 1)

Smith, Edward H.
Release; a tragedy in one act. N.Y. Norman. 1921. 12°. 50p. 75c.
Same in Shay, F. ed. Treasury of plays for men

Smith, Edward Percy, 1891-
Merry widow Welcome; or, The treasure hunters; an early Victorian frolic. N.Y. French. c1924. 12°. 27p. 1 act

Peer and the paper girl, twenty minutes. N.Y. French. c1924. 16p. 1 act

Rigordans, a play in three acts. London. Benn. 1924. 12°. 100p.

Smith, Edward Percy, and Nichols, W. B.
Coloman; a play in five acts. N.Y. Gomme. [c1916]. 12°. 136p. Tragedy

Smith, Francis Sladen, 1886-
St. Simon Stylites. Historical. 1 act
In Double demon and other one-act plays
Four one-act plays

Smith, George Jay, 1866-
Forbidden fruit. Comedy. 1 act
In Shay, F. ed. Contemporary one-act plays of 1921
Shay, F. ed. Twenty contemporary one-act plays. (American)

Smith, Glenna Smith, joint author. *See* Brown, Katharine S. and Tinnin, G. S.

Smith, Harry James, 1880-1918
Mrs. Bumpstead-Leigh; a comedy in three acts. N.Y. French. c1917. 100p. 12°.
Same in Moses, M. J. ed. Representative American dramas, national and local

Smith, Howard Forman
Blackberryin'. Comedy. 1 act
In Shay, F. ed. Treasury of plays for women

Rusty door. Sea. 1 act
In Clements, C. C. ed. Sea plays
Shay, F. ed. Treasury of plays for men. (In this volume the play is attributed to Howard Southgate)

Smith, Hyacinth Stoddart
Cordia. Love. 3 acts
In Poet Lore 19:165

Smith, Jeanne Oliver Davidson (Mrs. Horace E. Smith) (Temple Oliver, pseud.), d. 1925
Seal of Hellas; a classical drama. Boston. Sherman. 1915. 12°. $1
Smith, Jessica Welborn (Mrs. Lewis Worthington Smith)
Lamp of heaven; a Chinese play in one act. Boston. Four Seas. 1920. 12°. 25p. 75c.
Smith, Mrs. L. Worthington. See Smith, Jessica W.
Smith, Marion
Comedietta. Juvenile. 1 act
In Canad M 19:40
Smith, Marion Spencer
American grandfather. Immigrants. 1 act
In Poet Lore 35:443
Good night. Romantic. 1 act
In Drama 16:174
Hamburger king. Character. 3 scenes
In Drama 15:125
Oft in the stilly night. Comedy. 1 act
In Drama 15:75
Slow but sure. Comedy. 1 act
In Drama 17:138
Smith, Nora Del
Cave. Comedy. 3 acts
In Cave, and The woman's masquerade
Woman's masquerade. Comedy. 1 act
In Cave, and The woman's masquerade
Smith, Richard Penn, 1799-1854
Deformed, or, Woman's trial, a play in five acts. Phila. Alexander. 1830. 12°. 87p. Melodrama
Same in McCullough, B. W. Life and writings of Richard Penn Smith
Disowned; or, The prodigals; a play in three acts. Phila. Alexander. 1830. 67p.
Eighth of January, a drama in three acts. . . Phila. Neal & MacKenzie. 1829. 54p.
Triumph at Plattsburg. Historical. War of 1812. 2 acts
In Quinn, A. H. ed. Representative American plays, 1767-1923 (1925 ed)
Smith, Rita Creighton
Rescue. Psychological. 1 act
In Plays of the Harvard dramatic club ser 1
Smith, S. Decatur
Grandpa; a farce-comedy in one act. Philadelphia Penn. pub. co. 1912. 12°. 15p.
Man's honor. A drama in one act. Philadelphia. Penn publishing co. 1907. 12°. 12p. Triangle
Mother Goose Christmas. Juvenile. 1 act
In Ladies' H J 25:19, 75 D '07
"Princess Aline" play. Comedy. 2 acts
In Ladies' H J 18:3, 40 Ap '01
Restville auction sale. A farce in one act. Philadelphia. Penn. pub. co. 1907. 12°. 16p.

Smith, W. H., and A gentleman
Drunkard. A moral domestic drama of American life, in four acts. London. Lacy. n.d. 12°. 38p. (Lacy's acting edition of plays. v. 7 no. 102)
Smith, Winchell, 1871-
Fortune hunter, a comedy in four acts. N.Y. French. c1909. 12°. 116p.
Smith, Winchell, and Abbott, George
Holy terror; a none-too-serious drama. N.Y. French. c1926. 12°. 167p.
Smith, Winchell, 1871-, and Bacon, Frank
Lightnin'; a play in prologue and three acts. N.Y. French. c1918. 8°. 130p. Comedy
Going crooked; a comedy in three acts, from a tale of Hoffman's (Aaron's). . . N.Y. French. c1926. 12°. 99p. (Copyright 1925. . . under title "Re: Ward")
Smith, Winchell, 1871-, and Cushing, Tom
"Thank you"; a play in three acts. N.Y. French. 1922. 12°. 129p. 75c. Comedy
Smith, Winchell, 1871-, and Hazzard, John E.
Turn to the right, a comedy in a prologue and three acts. N.Y. French. c1916. 12°. 140p.
Smith, Winchell, 1871-, and Mapes, Victor
Boomerang; a comedy in three acts. N.Y. French. c1915. 12°. 112p.
Smith, Winchell, 1871-, and Ongley, Byron
Brewster's millions; a comedy in four acts, dramatized from the novel . . . by George Barr McCutcheon. N.Y. French. c1925. 12°. 113p.
Snowe, Lucy
Bondage. Social. 3 acts
In Two stage plays
Denzild Herbert's atonement. Melodrama. 3 acts
In Two stage plays
Paying guest; a problem farce in two acts. London. Johnson. 1901. 24°. 72p.
Snyder, Margaret I.
Nativity. A Christmas pageant. N.Y. Abingdon press. 1925. 12°. 22p. 25c.
Sobel, Bernard
Jennie knows. Comedy. 1 act
In Three plays
Mrs. Bompton's dinner party. Comedy. 1 act
In Three plays
Phoebe Louise. Comedy. 1 act
In Schafer, B. L. comp. Book of one-act plays
There's always a reason. Comedy. 1 act
In Three plays
Sollenberger, Judith K.
Marriage gown. Sea. 1 act
In Indiana prize plays, 1922-23
Sollohub, Count W.
His hat and cane. Comedy. 1 act
In Bellevue dramatic club: Plays for private acting

Sologub, Feodor, pseud. (Teternikov, Fedor Kuzmich), 1863-
Trumph of death.   Tragedy. 3 acts
In Drama 6:346
Solon, Israel
Biteless dog.   Sex. 1 act
In Smart Set 42 no 1:97
Somers, Dene
Goodness gracious! what next? a comedy.
Boston. Baker. c1925. 95p.
Somerset, Charles A.
Crazy Jane.   A romantic play in three acts. . . London. Cumberland. n.d. 12°. 57p. (Cumberland's minor theatre. v. 2 no. 4)
Day after the fair.   A burletta in one act. . . N.Y. Elton's dramatic repository. 1828. 8°. 24p. (Cumberland's minor theatre. v. 3 no. 9)
Mistletoe bough; or, Young Lovel's bride: a legendary drama in two acts. . . London. Davidson. n.d. 12°. 36p. (Cumberland's minor drama. v. 12 no. 9)
Shakespeare's early days: a historical play, in two acts. . . London. Cumberland. n.d. 12°. 48p. (Cumberland's British theatre. v. 28 no. 3)
Tower of London; or, The rival queens: a grand historical spectacle, in two acts. . . London. Pattie. n.d. 12°. 38p.
Same in Universal stage. v. 2 no. 5
"Yes!"   An operatic interlude, in one act. . . London. Davidson. n.d. 12°. 24p. (Cumberland's minor theatre. no. 15 (v. 2 no. 6))
Zelina; or, The triumph of the Greeks. A grand war-like Grecian drama in three acts. . . Boston. Spencer. [1856?]. 12°. 27p.
Sorlin, Daniel Bror
Her brother's code; a drama of life in four acts.   Boston. Cornhill. [c1918]. 105p.   Melodrama
Soumet, Alexandre, 1788-1845
Jeanne D'Arc.   A tragedy in five acts. . . N.Y. Darcie & Corbyn. 1855. 4°. 36p.
Soutar, Robert, joint author.   *See* Claridge, C. J. and Soutar, Robert
South, Robert
Divine Aretino.   Comedy
In Divine Aretino, and other plays
Sabado.   Early renaissance
In Divine Aretino, and other plays
Savonarola.   Tragedy
In Divine Aretino, and other plays
Smithy; a drama.   London. Constable. 1905. 12°. 181p.   Domestic. 4 acts
Sir Walter Raleigh; a prose drama for the stage and study.   London. Long. 1904. 8°.
White rose
In Divine Aretino, and other plays
Southgate, Howard
Rusty door.   Sea. 1 act
In Clements, C. C. ed.   Sea plays. (In this collection the play is attributed to H. F. Smith)
Shay, F. ed. Treasury of plays for men

Sowerby, Githa
Rutherford and son; a play in three acts. N.Y. Doran. c1912. 12°. 123p.   Domestic. 3 acts
Same in Dickinson, T. H. ed.   Contemporary plays
Pierce and Matthews, eds. Masterpieces of modern drama. v. 1 (abridged)
Speenhoff, J. H.
Louise.   Character. 1 act
In Shay, F. and Loving, P. eds.   Fifty contemporary one-act plays
Spencer, Francis P.
Dregs.   Melodrama. 1 act
In Mayorga, M. G. ed.   Representative one-act plays
Spencer, Willard
Carrying out a theory; a farce comedy in one act.   Phila. Penn. 1921. 12°. 25c.
Speyer, Lady
Love me, love my dog.   Comedy. 1 act
In Smart Set 58 no 1:73
Spiers, Kaufmann Charles
If youth but knew! a play in three acts. . . London. Adelphi pub. co. [c1924]. 12°. 110p.
Lighthouse; or, "Mother of pearl"; a play in three acts. London. Adelphi pub. co. c1925. 130p.
Springer, Thomas Grant, 1873-
Secrets of the deep.   Tragedy. 1 act
In Smart Set 43:no 2:133
Squire, John Collings, 1884-
Clown of Stratford.   Comedy. 1 act
In Lond Mercury 7:18
Šrámek, Fraňa
June; a play in one act
In Selver, P. ed.   Anthology of modern Slavonic literature
Sri Hersha Deva.   *See* Harshadeva
Staff of the Big Brother movement
Fingers; a gripping drama of boy life, in four acts.   N.Y. French. c1924. 56p.
Stafford, John Kendrick
It's turrible to be popular; a farce in three acts.   N.Y. French. 1924. 12°. 30c.
Poor father; a three-act farce.   Chicago. Denison. c1924. 12°. 62p.
Stahl, Clarence Victor, 1885-
Zorabella; a poetic tragedy in five acts. N.Y. Neale. 1915. 12°. 77p. $1.
Stallings, Lawrence, 1894, and Anderson, M.   *See* Anderson, Maxwell and Stallings, L.
Stange, Hugh Stanislaus; Mears, Stannard, and Walker, Stuart
Booth Tarkington's Seventeen; a play of youth and love and summertime, in four acts.   N.Y. French. 1924. 12°. 111p. 75c.
Stanwood, L. R.
Progress of Mrs. Alexander.   Comedy. 3 acts
In New Eng M ns 43:529
Stapp, Emilie Blackmore, and Cameron, Eleanor
December play: The holly wreath.   1 act
In Happyland's fairy grotto plays

Stapp, E. B., and Cameron E.—*Continued.*
February play: Mr. February Thaw. 1 act
In Happyland's fairy grotto plays
Janaury play: Molly's New Year's party. 1 act
In Happyland's fairy grotto plays
November play: The little gray lady. 1 act
In Happyland's fairy grotto plays
October play. The lost firewood.   1 act
In Happyland's fairy grotto plays
September play. The tadpole school.   1 act
In Happyland's grotto plays

Starling, Lynn
In his arms; a comedy.   N.Y. French. c1925. 12°. 103p. 3 acts

Stechhan, H. O., and Terrell, Maverick
Branded Mavericks.   Texas. 1 act
In Smart Set 42 no 3:133
You never can tell about a woman.   Rascality. 1 act
In Smart Set 37 no 4:135

Stedman, Adelaide
Substitute bride.   Episode. 1 act
In Smart Set 35 no 2:129

Steele, Rufus, 1877-
Fall of Ug; a masque of fear. . . San Francisco. Howell. 1913. 12°. 50p. 1 act
Same in Grove plays of the Bohemian club v 3

Steele, Wilbur Daniel, 1886-
Giants' stair; a play in one act.   N.Y. Appleton. 1924. 12°. 39p.   Fear. 1 act
Same in Terrible woman and other one-act plays
Not smart.   Parlor radicalism. 1 act
In Terrible woman and other one-act plays
Provincetown plays (Stewart Kidd 1921)
Ropes.   Lighthouse. 1 act
In Terrible woman and other one-act plays
Harper 142:193
Terrible woman.   N. E. comedy. 1 act
In Terrible woman, and other one-act plays
Pict R 26:6 N '24

Steell, Willis, 1866-
Bride from home.   1 act
In Plays with a punch
Brother Dave.   1 act
In Plays with a punch
Death of the discoverer.   Philadelphia. Murray. [1892]. 12°. 89p.   Historical. 2 acts
Juliet of the people.   [N.Y. McEvoy]. c1919. 12°. 36p.   Tragedy. 1 act
Same in Parerga
Faro Nell.   1 act
In Plays with a punch
Parerga.   N.Y. McEvoy. 1920. 12°. 142p.

Steiner, Rudolph, 1861-1925
Guardian of the threshold.   Mystery. 10 scenes
In Four mystery plays v 2
Portal of initiation.   Mystery. 11 scenes
In Four mystery plays v 1
Soul's awakening.   Mystery. 15 scenes
In Four mystery plays v 2
Soul's probation.   Mystery. 13 scenes
In Four mystery plays v 1

Stephenson, Ann, and Macbeth, Allan
Life's little sideshows, for a "he" and a "she".   N.Y. French. c1925. 12°. 52p.

Stepniak, pseud. *See* Kravchinskii, Sergiei Mikhailovich, 1852-1895

Sterling, George, 1869-
Dryad.   Fantasy. 1 act
In Overland ns 84:293
Lilith; a dramatic poem.   N.Y. Macmillan. 1926. 12°. 116p.   Tragedy. 4 acts
Rosamund; a dramatic poem.   N.Y. Robertson. 1920. 12°. 120p. $1.50. Historical. 3 acts
Triumph of Bohemia.   A forest play. 1 act
In Grove plays of the Bohemian club v 1
Truth.   Chicago.   Bookfellows. 1923. 12°. 124p. $3.75.   Supernatural. 3 acts

Sterling, John, 1806-1844
Strafford; a tragedy.   London. Moxon. 1843. 12°. 223p. 5 acts

Sterry, Joseph Ashby
Katharine and Petruchio; or, The shaming of the true.   Parody. 1 act
In Scott, C. ed.   Drawing-room plays

Stevens, Caroline D.
Elopements while you wait.   Farce. 1 act
In Drama 13:184

Stevens, Henry Bailey
Bolo and Babette the voice of beauty. Symbolic. 1 act
In Cry out of the dark
City rubes; a play in one act. . . Durham, N.H. University of N.H. Extension service. [c1924]. 8°. 28p.   Comedy
Madhouse; the voice of reason.   War. 2 scenes
In Cry out of the dark
Meddler; the voice of love.   Social. 1 act
In Cry out of the dark

Stevens, James Stacy, 1864-
Dramatization of the book of Job; the problem of human suffering.   Boston. Stratford. 1917. 12°. 41p.

Stevens, Thomas Wood 1880-
Adventure, a pageant-drama of life and change.   N.Y. National Bur. of Casualty & Surety Underwriters. 1923. 8°. 114p. 50c.   Safety. 25 scenes
Book of words; a pageant of the Italian renaissance. . . Chicago. Society of the antiquarians. c1909. 8°. 85p.   Pageant. 12 scenes
Book of words; an historical pageant of Illinois. . . Chicago. Alderbrink press. c1909. 8°. 67p.

Book of words; the pageant of Newark . . . Newark. Committee of one hundred. 1916. 8°. 112p. 4 movements

Book of words; the pageant of Virginia. . . . Richmond. Virginia historical pageant association. 1922. 12°. 144p.

Drawing of the sword. Masque. 1 act
In Drawing of the sword, etc

Dunes under four flags; an historical pageant of the dunes of Indiana . . . in Port Chester, Ind. May 30 and June 3, 1917. n.p. c1917. 8°. 40p.

Duquesne Christmas mystery. Nativity. 1 act
In Nursery-maid of heaven, etc

"Fighting for freedom," Independence day pageant. . . St. Louis. Britt. 1918. 4°. 48p. 2 pts.

Friend Mary. Lincoln's birthday. 1 act
In Nursery-maid of heaven, etc

Gold circle. Fantasy. 1 act
In Shay, F. ed. Treasury of plays for men

Highways cross. Comedy. 1 act
In Nursery-maid of heaven, etc

Historical pageant of Madison County. . . Madison Co. Centennial assn. [Edwardsville? Ill. 1912]. 8°. 10p.

Missouri one hundred years ago. [St. Louis]. Saint Louis, Missouri centennial association. [c1921]. 12°. 96p. Historical. 2 acts

National Red Cross pageant. 1 episode
In Drawing of the sword, etc

Nursery maid of heaven. Miracle. 1 act
In Shay, F. and Loving, P. eds. Fifty contemporary one-act dramas Nursery-maid of heaven, etc

Pageant of Charlotte and old Mecklenberg; written for the sesquicentennial of the Mecklenburg Declaration of Independence May 20, 1775. Charlotte, N.C. Charlotte pageant assoc. [1925]. 8°. 121p. 9 episodes

Pageant of Saint Louis. 3 movements
In Stevens, T. W. and Mackaye, P. Books of words of the pageant and masque of Saint Louis

Pageant of victory and peace, with a threnody of those who fell. . . Boston. Burchard. 1919. 8°. 29p.

Three wishes; a comedy in one act. N.Y. Shaw. [c1920]. 12°. 10p.
Same in Shay, F. ed. Treasury of plays for men Nursery-maid of heaven, etc

Trumph of Punchinello. Pantomine. 1 act
In Nursery-maid of heaven, etc

Stevens, Thomas Wood, 1880-, **joint author.**
See Goodman, Kenneth S. and Wood, Thomas

Stevens, Thomas Wood, joint author. *See* Mackaye, P. and Stevens, T. W.

Stevens, Thomas Wood, 1880-, **joint author.**
See Rice, W. de G. and Stevens, T. W.

Stevens, Wallace
Carlos among the candles. Symbolic. 1 act
In Poetry 11:115

Three travelers watch a sunrise. Poetic. 1 act
In Shay, F. and Loving, P. eds. Fifty contemporary one-act dramas Poetry 8:163

Stevenson, Augusta
Beautiful song. Juvenile. 1 act
In Children's classics bk 1

Bernard Palissy, enameller to His Majesty. Historical. 3 scenes
In Children's classics bk 4

Blind men and the elephant. From the folk-story, The blind men. Juvenile. 1 act
In Children's classics bk 2

Cat and the mouse. Suggested by Grimm's The cat and the mouse. Juvenile. 1 act
In Plays for the home
   Children's classics bk 3

Cat that waited. Juvenile. 4 scenes
In Children's classics bk 1

Christmas pitcher. Suggested by Hawthorne's The Miraculous pitcher. Juvenile. 1 act
In Children's classics bk 1

Christopher Columbus. Historical. 3 scenes
In Plays for the home
   Children's classics bk 3

Clever cock. Suggested by Aesop's Dog, the cock and the fox. Juvenile. 2 scenes
In Children's classics bk 1

Clever kid. Suggested by Aesop's The wolf and the goat. Juvenile. 1 act
In Children's classics bk 2

Crow and the fox. Suggested by Aesop's The Crow and the fox. Juvenile. 1 act
In Plays for the home
   Children's classics bk 3

Daniel Boone. Historical. 3 scenes
In Children's classics bk 4

Don Quixote. Based on incidents in Cervantes romance. Juvenile. 4 scenes
In Children's classics bk 4

Each in his own place. Suggested by Grimm's The mouse, the bird and the sausage. Juvenile. 1 act
In Plays for the home
   Children's classics bk 3

Emperor's test. Juvenile. 3 scenes
In Plays for the home
   Children's classics bk 3

Endless tale. Juvenile. 1 act
In Children's classics bk 2

Fairy and the cat. Suggested by Aesop's Venus and the cat. Juvenile. 1 act
In Children's classics bk 1

Fishing on dry land. Suggested by Grimm's The peasant's clever daughter. Juvenile. 1 act
In Children's classics bk 2

Girl who trod on the loaf. Suggested by Hans Andersen's. The girl who trod on the loaf. Juvenile. 4 scenes
In Plays for the home
   Children's classics bk 3

Stevenson, A.—*Continued*

Goblin and the huckster's jam. Suggested by Hans Andersen's. The nis at the huckster's. Juvenile. 2 scenes
In Children's classics bk 4

Golden bucket. Juvenile. 1 act
In Children's classics bk 1

Hare and the hedgehog. Suggested by Grimm's The hare and the hedgehog. Juvenile. 1 act
In Children's classics bk 2

Hare and the tortoise. Based on Aesop's The hare and the tortoise. Juvenile. 1 act
In Children's classics bk 1

Henry Hudson. Historical. 3 scenes
In Children classics bk 4

Hole in the dike. Juvenile. 2 scenes
In Children's classics bk 2

Honest critic. Historical. 1 act
In Children's classics bk 4

Honest woodman. Suggested by Aesop's Mercury and the woodman. Juvenile. 1 act
In Children's classics bk 1

House of brick. Based on the old English tale of The three little pigs. Juvenile. 1 act
In Children's classics bk 1

How a prince was saved. Based on a tradition of Mohammed. Juvenile. 1 act
In Children's classics bk 1

How they saved the fort. Historical. 2 scenes
In Children's classics bk 4

In bad company. Suggested by Aesop's The husbandman and the stork. Juvenile. 1 act
In Children's classics bk 1

Indian boy's pet. Juvenile. 2 scenes
In Children's classics bk 1

Keys of Calais. Historical. 3 scenes
In Children's classics bk 4

King Alfred and the cakes. Juvenile. 1 act
In Children's classics bk 2

King's good friend. Based on the Bidpai fable of The king, the falcon and the cup. Juvenile. 1 act
In Children's classics bk 1

Lafayette's toast. Based on the incident of the Conway Cobal. Historical. 1 act
In Children's classics bk 4

Lark's nest. Juvenile. 3 scenes
In Children's classics bk 1

Lazy Kate. Suggested by the German folk-story Lazy Lizette. Juvenile. 3 scenes
In Children's classics bk 2

Little fish. Suggested by Aesop's The angler and the little fish. Juvenile. 1 act
In Children's classics bk 1

Little jackal and the camel. Suggested by the Oriental legend The jackal and the camel. Juvenile. 3 scenes
In Children's classics bk 2

Man and the alligator. From a folktale of Spanish Honduras. Juvenile. 2 scenes
In Plays for the home
Children's classics bk 3

Mill that ground hot porridge. Suggested by Grimm's The porridge mill. Juvenile. 1 act
In Children's classics bk 1

Miller, his son and their donkey. Suggested by Aesop's fable, The miller, his son, and their ass. Juvenile. 1 act
In Plays for the home
Children's classics bk 3

Moon's silver cloak. Suggested by Aesop's Moon and her mother. Juvenile. 3 scenes
In Children's classics bk 1

Old man and his grandson. Adapted from Grimm's The old man and his grandson. Juvenile. 1 act
In Plays for the home
Children's classics bk 3

Pen and the inkstand. Suggested by Hans Andersen's The pen and the inkstand. Juvenile. 1 act
In Children's classics bk 4

Persephone. Mythological. 3 scenes
In Children's classics bk 4

Peter the Great's school. Historical. 2 scenes
In Children's classics bk 4

Piece of cheese. Suggested by Aesop's The cats and the monkey. Juvenile. 1 act
In Children's classics bk 1

Pocahontas and Captain Smith. Juvenile. 2 scenes
In Children's classics bk 2

Pocahontas saves Jamestown. Juvenile. 2 scenes
In Children's classics bk 2

Pot of gold. Suggested by Aesop's The farmer and his sons. Juvenile. 3 scenes
In Children's classics bk 2

Proud ring-finger. Suggested by the German folk-story, The proud ring-finger. Juvenile. 1 act
In Children's classics bk 2

Puppet princess; or, The heart that squeaked; a Christmas play for children. Boston. Houghton. [1915]. 12°. 58p.

Red shoes. Suggested by Hans Andersen's The red shoes. Juvenile. 4 scenes
In Plays for the home
Children's classics bk 3

Return of the spring. Suggested by Browning's The Pied piper. Juvenile. 2 scenes
In Children's classics bk 1

Romantic Indiana; a dramatic pageant. Seven episodes with prologue and tableaux. Indianapolis. Bobbs-Merrill. [c1916]. 12°. 185p.

Sandalwood box. Suggested by The legend of the Moor's legacy from Irving's Alhambra. Juvenile. 3 scenes
In Children's classics bk 4
Selfish woman. Suggested by the folk-story, The redheaded woodpecker. Juvenile. 1 act
In Children's classics bk 2
Shepherd-boy who called wolf. Suggested by Aesop's The shepherd-boy and the wolf. Juvenile. 3 scenes
In Children's classics bk 2
Sick deer. Suggested by Aesop's The sick stag. Juvenile. 1 act
In Children's classics bk 1
Sir Percivale, the boy knight from the forest. Based on the story of Peredur in the Mabinogian. Juvenile. 3 scenes
In Children's classics bk 4
Song in the heart. Suggested by Grimm's The three spinners. Juvenile. 2 scenes
In Plays for the home
Children's classics bk 3
Sparrows in the hat. Juvenile. 2 scenes
In Children's classics bk 1
Stag and the fawn. Suggested by Aesop's The stag at the pool. Juvenile. 2 scenes
In Children's classics bk 2
Story of Ali Cogia. Adapted from The story of Ali Cogia from the Arabian Nights' entertainments. Juvenile. 2 scenes
In Plays for the home
Children's classics bk 3
Torn dresses. Juvenile. 3 scenes
In Children's classics bk 1
Tracks to the den. Suggested by Aesop's The sick lion. Juvenile. 1 act
In Children's classics bk 1
Travellers and the hatchet. Adapted from Aesop's fable, The travellers and the hatchet. Juvenile. 1 act
In Plays for the home
Children's classics bk 3
Two countrymen. Suggested by an oriental legend. Juvenile. 2 scenes
In Plays for the home
Children's classics bk 3
Two holes. Juvenile. 1 act
In Children's classics bk 1
Two millers. Suggested by the German folk-story, The two millers. Juvenile. 2 scenes
In Children's classics bk 2
Two questions. Juvenile. 3 scenes
In Children's classics bk 2
Ugly duckling. Suggested by Hans Andersen's Ugly duckling. Juvenile. 3 scenes
In Plays for the home
Children's classics bk 3
Vain jackdaw. Suggested by Aesop's The vain jackdaw. Juvenile. 1 act
In Children's classics bk 2

What the goodman does is always right. Adapted from Hans Andersen's What the goodman does is always right. Juvenile. 3 scenes
In Plays for the home
Children's classics bk 3
White canoe. Based on an episode in William Trumbull's The white canoe. Juvenile. 3 scenes
In Children's classics bk 4
Wild swans. Suggested by Hans Andersen's The wild swans. Juvenile. 4 scenes
In Plays for the home
Children's classics bk 3
William Tell. Juvenile. 4 scenes
In Children's classics bk 4
Wise crow. Suggested by Aesop's The crow and the pitcher. Juvenile. 1 act
In Children's classics bk 2
Wise men of Gotham. Juvenile. 2 scenes
In Children's classics bk 2
Wish-bird. Juvenile. 1 act
In Children's classics bk 2
Wolf and the horse. Suggested by Aesop's The wolf and the horse. Juvenile. 1 act
In Children's classics bk 2
Wolf and the lamb. Suggested by Aesop's The wolf and the lamb. Juvenile. 1 act
In Children's classics bk 2

Stevenson, Mabel B.
Brown mouse; a rural play in four acts. N.Y. French. 1922. 12°. 30c.

Stevenson, Margaretta
Two dollars, please! Comedy. 1 act
In Indiana prize plays, 1922-23

Stevenson, Robert Louis. *See* Henley, W. E. and Stevenson, R. L.

Stewart, Mrs. John D. *See* Petrova, Olga, pseud.

Stigler, W. A.
Soup stone. Comedy. 1 act
In Poet Lore 35:91

Stimson, Frederic Jessup (J. S. of Dale, pseud), 1855-
Light of Provence; a dramatic poem. N.Y. Putnam. 1917. 12°. 115p. $1.25. Troubadours. 5 acts

Stirling, Edward, 1807-1894
Cheap excursion. An original farce, in one act. London. Lacy. 12°. n.d. 14p. (Lacy's acting edition of plays. v. 4 no. 49)
Left in a cab. An original farce, in one act. London. Lacy. n.d. 12°. 12p. (Lacy's acting edition of plays. v. 4 no. 59)
Nicholas Nickleby. A farce in two acts. . . Boston. Spencer. [1858?]. 12°. 32p.
Norah Creina. A drama in one act. Boston. Spencer. [1856?]. 12°. 14p.
Pet of the public. A farce. In one act. London. Lacy. n.d. 12°. 13p. (Lacy's acting edition of plays. v. 12 no. 180)

Stirling, E.—*Continued.*
Teddy Roe; a farce.   In one act. . .
Boston. Spencer. [1856?]. 12°. 15p.
Woodman's spell; a serio-comic drama.
In one act. London. Lacy. n.d. 12°.
15p. (Lacy's acting edition of plays.
v. 2 no. 23)
Young scamp; or, My grandmother's pet.
A farce. In one act. . . Boston. Spen-
cer. [1856?]. 12°. 17p.
Stockbridge, Dorothy
Jezebel.   Biblical. 1 act
In Shay, F. ed.   Contemporary one-
act plays of 1921
Shay, F. ed.   Twenty contemporary
one-act plays (American)
Stoddard, Anne, and Sarg, Tony
Don Quixote.   1 act
In Moses, M. T. ed.   Another treasury
of plays for children
Stokes, C. W.
Door.   Comedy. 1 act
In Canad M 58:498
Stokes, Rose Pastor, 1879-
Woman who wouldn't.   N.Y. Putnams.
1916. 183p. $1.25.   Social. 3 acts
Stone, John
Great Kleopatra; a tragedy in three acts.
London. Richards. [1911]. 8°. 86p.
Stone, John Augustus, 1801-1834
Tancred; or, The siege of Antioch.   A
drama in three acts. Phila. Printed
for the proprietor. 1827. 16°. 45p.
Historical
Stopes, Marie Charlotte Carmichael, 1880-
Conquest; or, A piece of jade. . . N.Y.
French. 1917. 12°. 94p.   Romantic. 3
acts
Gold in the wood.   Comedy. 1 act
In Gold in the wood, and The race
Our ostriches; a play of modern life in
three acts.   London. Putnam. c1923.
12°. 105p.   Social
Race.   Social. 3 acts
In Gold in the wood, and The race
Vectia.   Problem. 3 acts
In Banned play
Storer, Edward
Helen.   Mythological. 1 act
In International (NY) 9:17
Story, William Wetmore, 1819-1895
Nero. London. Blackwood. 1875. 16°.
275p.   Historical. 5 acts
Stephania, a tragedy in five acts; with a
prologue.   Edinburgh. Blackwood.
[c1875]. 12°. 109p. (For private cir-
culation only)
Stow, Clara
Party of the third part.   Comedy. 1 act
In Drama 15:110
Stowe, Harriet Beecher, 1811-1896
Uncle Tom's cabin.   A drama of real
life. In three acts. Adapted from the
novel. London. Lacy. n.d. 12°. 30p.
(Lacy's acting edition of plays. v. 12
no. 178).   Slavery

Strachey, Amabel
Sea-power of England.   A play for a
village audience, with a chorus by
Mrs. St. Loe Strachey. Oxford press
1913. 16°. 83p. 5 episodes
Stramm, August
Bride of the moor.   Fantasy. 4 scenes
In Poet Lore 25:499
Sancta Susanna; the song of a May night.
1 act
In Poet Lore 25:514
Stratton, Charles
Coda.   Social. 1 act
In Drama 8:215
Stratton, Clarence
Ruby red.   Oriental satire. 1 act
In Drama 10:192
Strindberg, August, i.e. Johan August, 1849-
1912
Advent, a play in five acts. . . Badger.
Boston. 1914. 110p.   Miracle play
Same in Plays ser 3 (Scribner 1913)
Plays v 3 (Swanwhite, etc)
(Luce 1914)
After the fire (Brända tomten).   Sus-
picion. 2 scenes
In Plays ser 3 (Scribner 1913)
Bridal crown (Kronbruden).   Folk-play.
4 acts
In Plays ser 4 (Scribner 1916)
Comrades (Kamraterna).   Comedy. 4
acts
In Plays v 2 (Comrades, etc) (Luce
1912)
Countess Julia (Julie) (Fröken Julie); a
naturalistic tragedy in one act. . .
Phila. Brown. 1912. 151p.
Same in Miss Julie, and other plays
Plays v 1 (The father, etc)
(Luce, 1912)
Plays ser 2 (Miss Julia, etc)
(Scribner 1912)
Poet Lore 22:161
Creditor.   *See* Strindberg, A.   Creditors
Creditors (Creditor) (Forddringsägare); a
tragic comedy. . . Phila. Brown. 1910.
118p. 1 act
In Miss Julie, and other plays
Plays ser 2 (Scribner)
Plays (Creditors, Pariah) (Scribner
1912)
Shay, F. and Loving, P. eds.   Fifty
contemporary one-act plays
Poet Lore 22:81
Dance of death (Döds dansen).   Pts. 1
and 2.   Life's enigma
In Plays (Dream play, etc) (Scribner
1912)
Debit and credit (Debet och Kredit).
Character. 1 act
In Plays ser 3 (Scribner 1913)
Poet Lore 17 no 3:28
Dream play (Drömspelet).   Fairy. 1 act
In Plays ser 1 (Dream play, etc)
(Scribner 1912)

Easter (Påsk) a play in three acts, and stories from the Swedish. . . Cincinnati. Stewart Kidd. 1912. 269p. $1.50. Symbolic
In Plays v 2 (Comrades, etc) (Luce 1912)
Facing death (Infor döden), a drama in one act. Easton, Pa. c1911. 8°. 16p. Suicide
Same in Plays v 2 (Comrades, etc) (Luce 1912)
Dramatist 2:173
Father (Fadren); a tragedy. . . Boston. Luce. 1907. 99p. 3 acts
Same in Plays v 1 (The father, etc) (Luce 1912)
Dickinson, T. H. ed. Chief contemporary dramatists
Pierce and Matthews, eds. Masterpieces of modern drama v 2 (abridged)
Hearst's M 22:111 Jl
First warning. Comedy. 1 act
In Plays ser 4 (Scribner 1916)
Gustavus Vasa. Historical. 5 acts
In Plays ser 4 (Scribner 1916)
Julie. *See* Strindberg, A. Countess Julia
Link (Lenken). Tragedy. 1 act
In Plays ser 1 (The dream play, etc) (Scribner 1912)
Lucifer or God? Mystery. 6 acts
In International (NY) 3:85
Lucky Pehr (Lycko Pers resa). . . Cincinnati. Stewart. 1912. 181p. $1.50. Allegorical. 5 acts
Master Olof, a drama in five acts. . . N.Y. Amer. Scand. foundation. 1915. 125p. Historical
Miss Julia. *See* Strindberg, A. Countess Julia
Motherlove (Motherly love) (Moderskärlek); an act. . . Phila. Brown. 1910. 41p.
In Miss Julie, and other plays
Shay, F. ed. Treasury of plays for women
Motherly love. *See* Strindberg, A. Motherlove
Outcast. *See* Strindberg, A. Pariah
Outlaw (Den fredlöse). 1 act
In Plays v 1 (The father, etc) (Luce 1912)
Paria. *See* Strindberg, A. Pariah
Pariah (Outcast, Paria). Psychological. 1 act
In Miss Julie and other plays
Pariah, Simoom
Plays v 2 (Comedies, etc) (Luce 1912)
Plays (Creditors, etc) (Scribner 1912)
Plays ser 2 (Scribner 1913)
Poet Lore 17 no 3:8
Simoom (Samun). Algiers. 1 act
In Miss Julie, and other plays
Pariah; Simoom
Plays ser 3 (Scribner 1913)

Moses, M. J. ed. Representative one-act plays by continental authors
Poet Lore 17 no 3:21
Smart Set 40:135 Jl '13
Spook sonata (Spök-sonaten). Chamber play. 1 act
In Plays ser 4 (Scribner 1916)
Storm. *See* Strindberg, A. Thunderstorm
Stronger (Stronger woman) (Den starkare). Two women. 1 scene
In Miss Julie, and other plays
Plays ser 2 (Scribner 1913)
Plays v 1 (The father, etc) (Luce 1912)
Plays: Miss Julia, etc (Scribner 1912)
Lewis, B. R. ed. Contemporary one-act plays
Loving, P. ed. Ten minute plays
Shay, F. ed. Treasury of plays for women
Poet Lore 17 no 1:47
Stronger woman. *See* Strindberg, A. Stronger
Swanwhite (Svanehvit); a fairy drama. . . Phila. Brown. 1909. 107p. 1 act
Same in Plays ser 3 (Scribner 1913)
Plays v 3 (Swanwhite, etc) (Luce 1914)
There are crimes and crimes. (Brott och brott); a comedy. . . N.Y. Scribner. 1912. 86p. 4 acts
In Plays ser 2 (Scribner 1913)
Thunderstorm (Storm) (Oväder). 3 scenes
In Plays ser 3 (Scribner 1913)
Plays v 3 (Swanwhite etc) (Luce 1914)
Strong, Austin, 1881-
Drums of Oude. Indian uprising. 1 act
In Drums of Oude, and other one-act plays
One-act plays for stage and study ser 2
Little father of the wilderness. *See* Strong, Austin, and Osbourne, Lloyd (Lloyd Osbourne). 1 act
Popo. 1 act
In Drums of Oude, and other one-act plays
Seventh heaven; a play in three acts. N.Y. French. c1922. 8°. 92p.
Three wise fools; a comedy in three acts. N.Y. French. 1923. 12°. 121p. 75c.
Toymaker of Nuremberg; a play in three acts and two scenes. N.Y. French. c1921. 12°. 77p. Juvenile
Same in Moses, M. J. Treasury of plays for children
Strong, Austin, 1881-, and Osbourne, Lloyd
Little father of the wilderness; a play in one act. N.Y. French. c1924. 12°. 24p. Comedy
Same in Drums of Oude, and other one-act plays
Cohen, H. L. ed. More one-act plays by modern authors
One-act play for stage and study ser 1

Sturgis, Granville Forbes, 1880-
Butcher's daughter; or, His first courting.
    Comedy. 2 scenes
    In Little plays for all occasions
College joke. Comedy. 1 act
    In Little plays for all occasions
Fatal pill. Comedy. 1 act
    In Little plays for all occasions
His first courting. *See* Sturgis, G. F.
    Butcher's daughter; or, His first
    courting
Just before dawn. Historical. 1 act
    In Little plays for all occasions
Little Colombine. Romantic. 1 act
    In Little plays for all occasions
Madame. Romantic. 1 act
    In Little plays for all occasions
Our Mary. Comedy. 1 act
    In Little plays for all occasions
Red roses. Tragedy. 1 act
    In Little plays for all occasions
Two of a kind. Comedy. 1 act
    In Little plays for all occasions
Widow Sabrina. Comedy. 1 act
    In Little plays for all occasions
Winning a husband. Comedy. 1 act
    In Little plays for all occasions

Sturgis, Julian, 1848-1904
Apples. Comedy. 1 act
    In Little comedies
Cross-roads. Comedy. 1 act
    In Blackw 171:194
Fire-flies. Comedy. 1 act
    In Little comedies
Half way to Arcady. Comedy. 1 act
    In Little comedies
Heather. Comedy. 1 act
    In Little comedies
Mabel's holy day. Comedy. 1 act
    In Little comedies
Picking up the pieces. Comedy. 1 act
    In Little comedies

Sturgis, Rebecca Forbes
Our war babe. War. 1 act
    In Sturgis, G. F. Little plays for all
    occasions

Subert, Frantisek Adolf, 1849-
Awakening. Serfdom. 5 acts
    In Poet Lore 33:159
Four bare walls; Labor oppression. 4
    acts
    In Poet Lore 28:497
Great freeholder. Public and private
    duty. 3 acts
    In Poet Lore 35:317
Jan Výrava. Feudalism. 5 acts
    In Poet Lore 26:281
Petr Vok Rozmberk. Historical. 1 act
    In Poet Lore 31:1

Sudermann, Hermann, 1857-
Eternal masculine (Das ewigmännliche).
    Satire. 1 act
    In Morituri
Far-away princess. A comedy in one
    act. N.Y. Scribner. [c1909]. 12°. 183p.
    Same in Roses
           Lewis, B. R. ed. Contempo-
           rary one-act plays

Fires of St. John (St John's fire); a drama
    in four acts. . . Boston. Luce. 1904.
    139p. *Also.* Badger. 1911
    Same in Moses, M. J. ed. Representa-
          tive continental dramas
Johannes. *See* Sudermann, H. John
    the Baptist
John the Baptist (Johannes). . . Tr. by
    Beatrice Marshall. London. 1909. 12°.
    202p. N.Y. Lane. Tragedy. 5 acts
    Same in German classics 17:167
          Pierce and Matthews, eds.
          Masterpieces of modern
          drama v 2 (abridged)
          Poet Lore 11:161
Joy of living (Es lebe das leben); a play
    in five acts. . . N.Y. Scribner. 1902.
    185p. Problem. 5 acts
Last visit. Social. 1 act
    In Roses
Magda. (Die heimat); a play in four
    acts. . . Boston. Lawson. 1896. 161p.
    Also French. Social
Margot. Psychological. 1 act
    In Roses
Regina; or, The sins of the fathers. . .
    N.Y. Lane. 1910. 12°. 347p.
St. John's fires. *See* Sudermann, H.
    Fires of St. John
Sins of the fathers. *See* Sudermann, H.
    Regina, or, The sins of the fathers
Streaks of light. Social. 1 act
    In Roses
Teja [Teias]. . . Boston. Heath. [c1906].
    12°. 69p. Goths. 1 act
    Same in Morituri
          Moses, M. J. ed. Representa-
          tive one-act plays by con-
          tinental authors
          Poet Lore 9:330
Three heron's feathers (Die drei reiher-
    federn). Symbolic. 5 acts
    In Poet Lore 12:161
Vale of content. (Das glück in winkel); a
    drama in three acts. . . [Boston?
    c1915]. 8°. Social
    Same in Dickinson, T. H. ed. Chief
          contemporary dramatists

Sulivan, Robert
Elopements in high life. A comedy in
    five acts. London. Lacy. n.d. 12°. 54p.
    (Lacy's acting edition of plays. v. 10
    no. 143)

Sullivan, Elizabeth (Higgins), 1874-
Strongest man. Triangle. 1 act
    In Plays of the 47 workshop ser 4

Sumarokov, Aleksandr
Demetrius the imposter; a tragedy. Lon-
    don. Nichols. 1806. 8°. 76p. 5 acts

Sundulkianz, Kapriel
Ruined family. Armenian. 3 acts
    In Armenian literature p 81

Supersac, Léon
Door is closed. Monologue.
    In Bellevue dramatic club: Plays for
    private acting

Surguchev, Ilya Dmitrievich
Autumn, a play in four acts. N.Y.
    Appleton. 1924. 12°. 86p. 50c. Com-
    edy

Susman, Harold
In the Ballinger's box. Farce. 1 act
In Smart Set 30:65 Ap '10

Sutherland, Evelyn Greenleaf, 1855-1908
At the barricade. Episode of the com-
mune. 1 act
In Po' white trash, and other one-act
dramas
Bit of instruction. Comedy. 1 act
In Po' white trash, and other one-act
dramas
Comedie royall. Comedy. 1 act
In Po' white trash, ·and other one-act
plays
Smith, M. M. ed. Short plays of
various types
End of the way. Robin Hood days. 1
act
In Po' white trash, and other one-act
plays
Galatea of the toy-shop. Fantasy. 1 act
In Po' white trash, and other one-act
plays
In far Bohemia. Romantic. 1 act
In Po' white trash, and other one-act
plays
Po' white trash. Negro. 1 act
In Po' white trash, and other one-act
dramas
Rohan the Silent. Romantic. 1 act
In Po' white trash, and other one-act
plays
Song at the castle. Comedy. 1 act
In Po' white trash, and other one-act
plays

**Sutherland, Evelyn G., and Dix, Beulah
Marie**
Road to yesterday; a comedy of fantasy.
N.Y. French. c1925. 12°. 92p. 4 acts
Rose o' Plymouth-town. A romantic
comedy in four acts. Boston. For-
tune press. 1903. 8°. 111p.

Sutherland, Howard Vigne
Woman who could; a play with a pur-
pose. N.Y. Fitzgerald. 1911. 191p.
Social. 4 acts

Sutton, George W. jr.
Yellow triangle; a play in one act. N.Y.
French. c1925. 12°. 28p. (Winner of
the second Samuel French prize 1925)

Sutphen, William Gilbert Van-Tassell, 1861-
House of cards. Comedy. 1 act
In Harper 109:901
Special delivery. Monologue. 1 act
In Harper 108:458

Sutro, Alfred, 1863-
Barriers; a new and original play in four
acts. N.Y. French. [c1908]. 8°. 112p.
Social
Bracelet; a play in one act. N.Y.
French. 1912. 12°. 24p. Comedy
Same in Five little plays
Builder of bridges; a play in four acts.
N.Y. French. c1909. 12°. 95p. Ro-
mantic
Choice; a play in four acts. London.
Duckworth. [1917]. 12°. 107p. Roman-
tic

Correct thing. A one act play. London.
French. c1905. 12°. 15p. Problem
Desperate lovers; a frivolous comedy in
three acts. London. Duckworth.
c1926. 12°. 109p.
Ella's apology. A duologue. London.
French. [1907]. 12°. 11p. 1 act
Far above rubies; a comedy in three
acts. . . London. Duckworth. [1924].
12°. 119p.
Fascinating Mr. Vanderveldt; a comedy
in four acts. N.Y. French. c1906.
12°. 90p.
Fire screen; a comedy in four acts. Lon-
don. N.Y. French. c1912. 12°. 109p.
Freedom; a play in three acts. N.Y.
Brentano. 1916. 16°. 106p. Social
Game of chess. A duologue. London.
French. [1905]. 12°. 15p. 1 act
Great well; a play in four acts. Lon-
don. Duckworth. 1923. 12°. 126p.
Problem
Gutter of time. A duologue. London.
French. [1905]. 12°. 16p. 1 act
John Glayde's honour. A new and orig-
inal play in four acts. N.Y. French.
c1907. 12°. 95p. Social
Same in Dickinson, T. H. and Craw-
ford, J. R. eds. Contemporary
plays
Laughing lady; a comedy in three acts.
London. Duckworth. c1922. 12°. 111p.
Maker of men. A duologue. London.
French. [1905]. 12°. 15p. 1 act
Man in the stalls. N.Y. French. c1911.
12°. 24p. Social. 1 act
Same in Five little plays
Clark, B. H. ed. Representa-
tive one-act plays by British
and Irish authors
Man on the kerb. A duologue. London.
French. c1908. 16°. 14p. Ethical. 1
act
Same in Five little plays
Smith, A. M. ed. Short plays
by representative authors
Man with a heart; a play in four acts.
London. Duckworth. [1924]. 12°. 122p.
Problem
Marriage . . . will not take place; a play
in one act. London. French. c1917.
12°. 24p. Comedy
Marriage has been arranged; a duologue;
a comedy in one act. N.Y. French.
c1904. 12°. 14p.
Same in Five little plays
Marriott, J. W. ed. One-act
plays of to-day ser 2
Mollentrave on women; a comedy in three
acts. N.Y. French. c1905. 12°. 86p.
Mr. Steinmann's corner. London.
French. [1907]. 12°. 15p. Finance. 1
act
Open door, a duologue in one act. N.Y.
French. c1912. 12°. 15p.
Same in Five little plays
Perplexed husband; a comedy in four
acts. N.Y. French. c1913. 12°. 100p.

Sutro, A.—*Continued.*
Price of money; a play in four acts.
N.Y. French. c1906. 12°. 106p.   So-
cial

Salt of life.   London.   French.   [1907].
12°. 11p.   Problem. 1 act

Two virtues; a comedy in four acts.
London. Duckworth. 1914. 12°. 110p.

Walls of Jericho; a play in four acts.
N.Y. French. c1906. 12°. 95p.   Social

Sutton, V. R.
Mantle of the virgin.   Miracle play. 1
act
In Drama 12:71

Swan, Mark Elbert, 1871-
Brown's in town, a farcical comedy in
three acts.   N.Y. French. c1915. 12°.
95p.

Her own money; a comedy in three
acts. . . N.Y. French. 1915. 8°. 94p.

Swartout, Norman Lee
Arrival of Kitty; a farce in three acts.
Boston. Baker. 1914. 12°. 181p.

Close to nature; a farcical episode in the
life of an American family, in four
acts. . . Boston. Baker. 1915. 12°.
180p.

Swears, Herbert
Captain X; a farcical comedy in three
acts.   N.Y. French. c1920. 12°. 95p.

Granny's Juliet; an impression.   N.Y.
French. c1911. 12°. 24p.

Hero and heroine; a melodramatic ab-
surdity in one act.   N.Y. French.
c1911. 12°. 19p.

Tight corner; a farcical comedy in three
acts.   N.Y. French. 1910. 12°. 92p.

Woman's crowning glory; a comedy in
one act.   N.Y. French. c1926. 12°.
44p.

Swift, Fletcher Harper, 1876-
Joseph, a drama for children, in one act
and three scenes. . . N.Y. Harrison.
c1907. 12°. 31p.

Swinburne, Algernon C., 1837-1909
Atalanta in Calydon; a tragedy.   Lon-
don. Chatto. 1896. 12°. 98p. 1 act
Same in Poems v 4
Works (Poems)

Bothwell: a tragedy.   London. Chatto.
1874. 12°. 532p. 5 acts
Same in Tragedies v 2 and 3
Works (Tragedies)

Chastelard; a tragedy.   N.Y. Hurd &
Houghton. 1866. 16°. 178p. 5 acts
Same in Tragedies v 2
Works (Tragedies)

Duke of Gandia.   N.Y. Harper. 1908. 8°.
57p.   Tragedy. 4 scenes

Erectheus.   London. Chatto. 1876. 12°.
105p.   Tragedy. 1 act
Same in Poems v 4
Works (Poems)

Locrine; a tragedy.   London. Chatto.
1887. 12°. 138p. 5 acts
Same in Tragedies v 5
Works (Tragedies)

Marino Faliero; a tragedy.   London.
Chatto. 1885. 12°. 151p. 5 acts
Same in Tragedies v 5
Works (Tragedies)

Mary Stuart; a tragedy.   London.
Chatto. 1881. 12°. 203p. 5 acts
Same in Tragedies v 4
Works (Tragedies)

Masque of Queen Bersabe.   Miracle. 1
act
In Works (Poems)

Pan and Thalassius.   Mythological. 1 act
In Works (Poems)

Phaedra.   Mythological. 1 act
In Works (Poems)

Queen mother.   Tragedy. 5 acts
In Queen mother and Rosamund
Tragedies v 1
Works (Tragedies)

Rosamond.   Tragedy. 5 acts
In Tragedies v 1
Works (Tragedies)

Rosamund, queen of the Lombards; a
tragedy.   London. Chatto & Windus.
1899. 12°. 88p. 5 acts
Same in Queen mother, and Rosamund
Tragedies v 5

Sisters; a tragedy.   London. Chatto &
Windus. 1892. 12°. 107p. 5 acts
Same in Tragedies v 5
Works (Tragedies)

Symon, James David
Conscript fathers: a forecast.   War. 1
act
In Eng R 27:208

**Symonds, Emily Morse (George Paston,
pseud.)**
Clothes and the woman; a comedy in
three acts. . . N.Y. French. c1922. 8°.
62p.

Nobody's daughter; a play in four acts. . .
London. "Stage" play pub. bureau.
1924. 12°. 127p.

Stars; a comedy by George Paston
[pseud.]. . . N.Y. French. c1925. 12°.
23p.

**Symonds, Emily Morse, and Maxwell, W.
B.**
Naked truth; a farcical comedy in three
acts. . . N.Y. French. 1910. 12°. 122p.

Symons, Arthur, 1865-
Barbara Roscorla's child.   Tragedy. 1
act .
In Little R 4:25 O '17

Cesare Borgia.   Tragedy. 1 act
In Cesare Borgia, etc

Cleopatra in Judaea.   Tragedy. 1 act
In Collected works v 7
Tragedies
Forum 55:643

Dance of the seven deadly sins.   Alle-
gory. 1 act
In Collected works v 3
Eng R 30:481

Death of Agrippina. Tragedy. 1 act
In Collected works v 7
  Tragedies
Faustus & Helen. Poetic. 1 act
In Collected works v 2
Fool of the world. Morality. 1 act
In Collected works v 2
Harvesters. Tragedy. 3 acts
In Collected works v 6
  Tragedies
Iseult of Brittany. Legendary. 1 act
In Cesare Borgia, etc
Lover of the Queen of Sheba. Poetic.
  1 act
In Collected works v 2
Mary in Bethlehem. A nativity. 1 act
In Collected works v 2
Nero. Historical. 2 scenes
In Collected works v 3
Otho and Poppaea. Poetic. 1 act
In Collected works v 2
Toy cart; a play in five acts. Dublin.
  Maunsel. 1919. 12°. 114p. India
Same in Collected works v 7
  Cesare Borgia, etc
Tristan and Iseult; a play in four acts.
  N.Y. Brentano's. 1917. 12°. 108p.
  Tragedy
Same in Collected works v 6

Synge, John Millington, 1871-1909
Deirdre of the sorrows, a play. Boston.
  Luce. 1911. 93p. Tragedy. 3 acts
In Works (Luce 1912) v 2 (1913) v 2
  Works (Maunsel 1910) v 2
  Plays (Allen 1924)
  Two plays
In the shadow of the glen. Boston.
  Luce. 1911. 40p. *See* Synge, J. M.
  Shadow of the glen
Playboy of the western world. A com-
  edy in three acts. Dublin. Maunsel.
  ₁1909₁. 12°. 86p.
Same in Works (Luce 1912) v 2 (1913)
  v 1
  Works (Maunsel 1910) v 2
  Plays (Allen 1924)
  Two plays
  Golden Bk 4:513
Riders to the sea. Boston. Luce. 1911.
  12°. 45p. Tragedy. 1 act
Same in Works (Luce 1912) v 1 (1913)
  v 4
  Works (Maunsel 1910) v 1
  Four plays
  Shadow of the glen and Riders
    to the sea
  Clark, B. H. ed. Representa-
    tive one-act plays by British
    and Irish authors
  Coffman, G. R. ed. Book of
    modern plays
  Cohen, H. L. ed. One-act
    plays by modern authors
  Dickinson, T. H. ed. Chief
    contemporary dramatists
  Leonard, S. A. ed. Atlantic
    book of modern plays
  Bibelot 19:249
  Poet Lore 16 no 1
  Samhain S '03:24

Shadow of the glen (In the shadow of
  the glen). Comedy. 1 act
In Works (Luce 1912) v 1 (1913) v 4
  Works (Maunsel 1910) v 1
  Four plays
  Plays (Allen 1924)
  Shadow of the glen, and Riders to
    the sea
  Bibelot 19:27
  Samhain D '04:34
Tinker's wedding; a comedy in two acts.
  Dublin. Maunsel. 1907. 50p.
Same in Works (Luce 1912) v 1 (1913)
  v 4
  Works (Maunsel 1910) v 1
  Four plays
  Plays (Allen 1924)
Well of the saints. . . London. Bullen.
  1905. 91p. Comedy. 3 acts
Same in Works (Luce 1912) (1913 v 3
  Works (Maunsel 1910) v 1
  Four plays
  Plays (Allen 1924)

Tadema, Laurence Alma. *See* Alma Tadema, Laurence

Taft, Grace Ellis
Chimalman. Indian myth. 1 act
In Chimalman, and other poems
Tecpancaltzin. Mexican. 1 act
In Chimalman, and other poems
Testeuctli. Mexican. 1 act
In Chimalman, and other poems

Taft, Linwood
He is the Son of God; a play for Holy
  week. . . Boston. Pilgrim press.
  c1923. 12°. 32p.
Joseph; a play in five acts based upon
  the story of Joseph as found in Genesis. N.Y. Century. c1925. 80p.

**Tagore, Rabindranath (Ravīndranātha
  Thākura),** 1861-
Ascetic. *See* Tagore, R. Sanyasi; or,
  The ascetic
Car of time. Symbolic. 1 act
In Visva-Bharati quar 1:321
Chitra; a play in one act. London.
  India Society. 1913. 12°. 34p. From
  the Mahabharata
Cycle of spring. N.Y. Macmillan. 1917.
  12°. 139p. Spring. 4 acts
King and the queen. Tragedy. 2 acts
In Sacrifice, and other plays
King of the dark chamber. . . N.Y.
  Macmillan. 1914. 12°. 206p. Sym-
  bolic. 20 scenes
Same in Drama 4:177
Malini. Religious. 2 acts
In Sacrifice, and other plays
Post office. N.Y. Macmillan. 1915. 12°.
  195p. Childhood. 2 acts
Same in Smith, A. M. ed. Short plays
  by representative authors
  Forum 51:455
Red oleanders; a drama in one act. Lon-
  don. Macmillan. 1925. 12°. 181p.
  Oriental
Same in Visva-Bharati quar. 1924,
  special Sharadiya (autumn no.) p 1

Tagore, R. —*Continued.*
Sacrifice. War. 1 act
In Sacrifice, and other plays
Sanyasi; or, The ascetic. Religious. 4 acts
In Sacrifice, and other plays

Taketomo, Torao
Mulan. War. 1 act
In Asia 19:1258

Talfourd, Francis
Chain of roses. *See* Talfourd, F. Thetis and Peleus; or, The chain of roses
Ganem, the slave of love. An original extravaganza. . . Lacy. London. n.d. 12°. 29p. (Lacy's acting edition of plays. v. 6 no. 88) 1 act
Godiva; or, Ye ladye of Coventrye and ye exyle fayrie. A burlesque historic fancy, in one act. (Lacy's acting edition of plays. v. 4 no. 56)
Macbeth, somewhat removed from the text of Shakespeare. In two acts. London. Lacy. n.d. 12°. 37p. (Lacy's acting edition of plays. v. 8 no. 108)
Mandarin's daughter! being the simple story of the Willow-pattern plate. A Chinese tale. London. Lacy. n.d. 12°. 28p. (Lacy's acting edition of plays. v. 5 no. 74)
Match for Lucifer. *See* Talfourd, F. Princesses in the tower; or, a match for Lucifer
Princesses in the Tower; or, A match for Lucifer! A piece of extravagance in one act. London. Lacy. n.d. 12°. 24p. (Lacy's acting edition of plays. v. 2 no. 26)
Shylock; or, The merchant of Venice preserved. An entirely new reading of Shakespeare. . . London. Lacy. n.d. 12°. 30p. Farce. 1 act (Lacy's acting edition of plays. v. 11 no. 159)
Thetis and Peleus; or, The chain of roses. A mythological love story, told in one act. . . London. Lacy. n.d. 12°. 21p. (Lacy's acting edtiion of plays. v. 5 no. 66)
Ye ladye of Coventrie and ye exyle fayrie. *See* Talfourd, F. Godiva, or, Ye ladye of Coventrye and ye exyle fayrie

Talfourd, Sir Thomas Noon, 1795-1854
Athenian captive. A tragedy in five acts. N.Y. Langley. 1838. 12°. 81p.
In Dramatic works
Tragedies
Castilian. An historical tragedy. In five acts. London. Moxon. 1853. 12°. 191p.
Fate of the MacDonalds. *See* Talfourd, T. N. Glencoe; or, The fate of the MacDonalds
Glencoe; or, The fate of the MacDonalds. Tragedy. 5 acts
In Dramatic works
Tragedies
Ion, a tragedy in five acts. . . N.Y. Dearborn. 1837. 12°. 109p.
Same in Dramatic works
Tragedies

Tamaya y Baus, Manual, 1829-1898
New drama; a tragedy in three acts. . . N.Y. Hispanic Soc. of America. 1915. 152p.

Tarkington, Booth, 1869-
Beauty and the Jacobin; an interlude of the French revolution. N.Y. Harper. 1912. 12°. 99p. 1 act
Same in Cohen, H. L. ed. One-act plays by modern authors
Dickinson, A. D. ed. Drama
Harper 125:390
Bimbo the pirate; a comedy. N.Y. Appleton. 1926. 12°. 39p. 1 act
Same in Ladies' Home Journal one-act plays
Ladies' H J 4:18 Je '24
Clarence; a comedy in four acts. N.Y. French. [c1921]. 12°. 124p.
Ghost story; a one-act play for persons of no great age. Cincinnati. Kidd. [c1922]. 12°. 42p. Comedy
Same in Nicholson, K. ed. Appleton book of short plays
Ladies' H J 39:6 Mr '22
Intimate strangers. N.Y. French. 1921. 12°. 116p. 75c. Comedy. 3 acts
In Cohen, H. L. ed. Longer plays by modern authors
Harper 144:599, 761; 145:75
Monsieur Beaucaire. *See* Freeman, Ethel H. Dramatization of Monsieur Beaucaire
Mister Antonio. Comedy. 4 acts
In Harper 134:187, 375
Seventeen. Boston. Baker. 1924. 12°. 111p. 75c. *See also* Stange, H. S. et al. Booth Tarkington's Seventeen. Romantic. 4 acts
Station YYYY. 1 act
In Ladies' H J 43:6 My '26
Travelers. 1 act
In Ladies' H J 43:16
Trysting place; a farce in one-act. Cincinnati. Stewart. 1923. 12°. 51p. 50c.
Same in Cohen, H. L. ed. Junior play book
Ladies' H J 39:36 S '22
Wren; a comedy in one act. N.Y. French. c1922. 8°. 109p.

Tarkington, Booth, 1869-, and Street, Julian
Country cousin; a comedy in four acts. N.Y. French. 1921. 12°. 141p. 75c. (Published 1916 under title: Ohio lady)

Tarkington, Booth, and Wilson, Harry Leon
Gibson upright. N.Y. Doubleday. 1919. 12°. 117p. Sociological. 3 acts
Man from home. N.Y. Harper. 1908. 8°. 176p. Romantic. 4 acts
Tweedles; a comedy. N.Y. French. 1924. 12°. 112p. 75c. 3 acts

Tassin, Algernon de Vivier, 1869-
Craft of the tortoise; a play in four acts. N.Y. Boni. 1919. 12°. 157p. Femininism
Rust; a play in four acts. N.Y. Broadway pub. co. [c1911]. 12°. 172p. Social

Tayleure, Clifton W.
Battle of King's Mountain. *See* Tayleure, C. W. Horseshoe Robinson: or, The battle of King's Mountain
Boy martyrs of Sept. 12, 1814. A local historical drama in three acts. N.Y. French. [187—?]. 12°. 30p.
Horseshoe Robinson: or, The battle of King's Mountain. A legendary patriotic drama. N.Y. French. c1858. 16°. 40p. 3 acts
Same in Moses, M. J. ed. Representative plays by American dramatists from 1765 to the present day v 2
Won back. A play in four acts. N.Y. DeWitt. c1892. 12°. 48p. Comedy

Taylor, Bayard, 1825-1878
Masque of the gods. Boston. Osgood. 1872. 48p. 12°. 3 scenes

Taylor, Frank
Carthaginian; a tragedy in three acts. London. Murray. 1916. 8°. 105p.

Taylor, Sir Henry, 1800-1886
Edwin the Fair; an historical drama. Isaac Commenus, a play. . . London. Moxon. 1852. 12°. 416p. 5 acts
Same in Works v 2
Isaac Commenus. Tragedy. 5 acts
In Edwin the Fair, etc
Works v 2

Philip van Artevelde. A dramatic romance. In two parts. . . Phila. Lippincott. [18—]. 16°. 456p. ea. part. 5 acts
Same in Works v 1

St. Clement's eve. A play. London. Chapman. 1862. 16°. 180p. Historical. France. Charles the Sixth. 5 acts
Same in Works v 3

Virgin widow. A play. London. Longman. 1850. 12°. 192p. Romantic comedy. 5 acts
Same in Works v 3

Taylor, L. M.
Cockcrow. Vengeance. 1 act
In Poet Lore 33:118

Taylor, Laurette
Dying wife. 1 act
In One-act plays for stage and study ser 1
Moonshine. 1 act
In One-act plays for stage and study ser 1

Taylor, Rica B.
Bitter end. 1 act
In Baker's anthology of one-act plays

Taylor, Tom, 1817-1880
Anne Boleyn. Historical. 5 acts
In Historical dramas
Arkwright's wife. Domestic. 3 acts
In Historical dramas
Babes in the wood. An original comedy. London. Lacy. [18—]. 12°. 71p. (Lacy's acting edition of plays. v. 50) 3 acts
Blighted being. A farce in one act. . . Boston. Spencer. [1857?]. 12°. 18p.

Contested election: a comedy in three acts. Manchester. Chambers. 1868. 8°. 60p.
Court and the stage. *See* Taylor, T. King's rival; or, The court and the stage
Daughter's trial. *See* Taylor, T. Henry Dunbar; or, A daughter's trial
Diogenes and his lantern; or, A hue and cry after honesty. . . Extravaganza. London. Lacy. 1850. 12°. 32p. 1 act (Lacy's acting edition of plays. v. 1 no. 15)
Fool's revenge: a drama. N.Y. French. [1863?]. 16°. 46p. Historical. 3 acts
In Historical dramas
Going to the bad: an original comedy in two acts. London. Lacy. [18—]. 12°. 71p. (Lacy's acting edition of plays. v. 37)
Helping hands. A domestic drama in two acts. Boston. Spencer. [1856?]. 12°. 48p.
Henry Dunbar; or, A daughter's trial. A drama . . . founded on Miss Braddon's novel of the same name. London. Lacy. [18—?]. 12°. 59p. (Lacy's acting edition of plays. v. 76) Melodrama. 4 acts
House or the home? A comedy in two acts. London. Lacy. [18—]. 12°. 46p. (Lacy's acting edition of plays. v. 42)
Hue and cry after honesty. *See* Taylor, T. Diogenes and his lantern; or, A hue and cry after honesty
Jeanne D'arc. Historical. 5 acts
In Historical dramas
King's rival; or, The court and the stage. A drama in five acts. London. Bentley. 1854. 12°. 72p. Nell Gwynne
Lady Clancarty; or, Wedded and wooed. A tale of the assassination plot, 1696. An original drama in four acts. London. French. [187—?]. 12°. 68p. Historical
In Historical dramas
Lady Elizabeth. *See* Taylor, T. Twixt axe and crown; or, The Lady Elizabeth
Love levels all. *See* Taylor, T. Serf; or, Love levels all!
Nice firm. An original comic drama. . . London. Lacy. [18—]. 12°. 30p. (Lacy's acting edition of plays. v. 13) 1 act
Nine points of the law. An original comedietta in one act. London. Lacy. [18—]. 12°. 36p. (Lacy's acting edition of plays. v. 40)
No. 3, Fig Tree Court, Temple. *See* Taylor, T. Our clerks; or, No. 3, Fig Tree Court, Temple
Our clerks; or, No. 3, Fig Tree Court Temple; an original farce, in one act. London. Lacy. n.d. 12°. 26p. (Lacy's acting edition of plays. v. 6 no. 80)
Overland route. A comedy in three acts. London. French. [18—]. 12°. 66p. (French's acting edition of plays. v. 124)

Taylor, T.—*Continued.*
"Payable on demand." An original domestic drama. London. Lacy. ₁18—₁. 12°. 53p. (Lacy's acting edition of plays. v. 41) 2 acts

Philosopher's stone. An entirely new and original satirical and politics—economical Whitsun morality, extremely serious and very comical. London. Lacy. n.d. 12°. 35p. 3 morals. (Lacy's acting edition of plays. v. 1 no. 14)

Plot and passion. An original drama in three acts. London. Lacy. n.d. 12°. 56p. (Lacy's acting edition of plays. v. 13 no. 191)   Melodrama
Same in Historical dramas

Prince Dorus; or, The romance of the nose. . . A new and original aerial, floreal and conchological fairy tale. London. Lacy. n.d. 12°. 35p. (Lacy's acting edition of plays. v. 3 no. 35) 10 scenes

Retribution: a domestic drama in four acts. London. Lacy. ₁18—₁. 12°. 41p. (Lacy's acting edition of plays. . . v. 27)

Romance of the nose. *See* Taylor, T. Price Dorus; or, The romance of the nose

Sense and sensation; or, The seven sisters of Thule. A new and original morality in a prologue and seven scenes. London. Lacy. ₁18—₁. 12°. 63p. (Lacy's acting edition of plays. v. 63)

Serf; or, Love levels all. An original drama. London. Lacy. ₁18—?₁. 12°. 53p. (Lacy's acting edition of plays. v. 68)   Melodrama

Settling day. A story of the time, in five acts. London. Lacy. ₁18—₁. 12°. 84p. (Lacy's acting edition of plays. v. 82)   Melodrama

Seven sisters of Thule. *See* Taylor, T. Sense and sensation; or, The seven sisters of Thule

Seven swan princes and the fair Melusine. *See* Taylor, T. Wittikind and his brothers, or, The seven Swan princes, and the fair Melusine

Sheep in wolf's clothing. A domestic drama in one act. London. Lacy. ₁18—₁. 12°. 34p. (Lacy's acting edition of plays. v. 37)

Sir Roger de Coverley; or, The widow and her wooers. A new and original drama in three acts. London. Lacy. n.d. 12°. 58p.   Comedy. (Lacy's acting edition of plays. v. 4 no. 46)

Still waters run deep. An original comedy in three acts. . . Boston. Spencer. ₁1856?₁. 12°. 58p.

Tale of two cities. A drama . . . adapted from the story of that name by C. Dickens. London. Lacy. ₁18—₁. 12°. 56p. (Lacy's acting edition of plays. v. 45) 2 acts

Ticket-of-leave man. A drama in four acts. London. Lacy. ₁18—₁. 12°. 84p. (Lacy's acting edition of of plays. v. 59)   Melodrama

To oblige Benson. A commedietta in one act. . . London. Lacy. n.d. 12°. 28p. (Lacy's acting edition of plays. v. 14 no. 208)

"To parents and guardians! At Jubilee House establishment, Clapham, young gentlemen are—". An original and comic drama in one act. London. Lacy. n.d. 12°. 23p. (Lacy's acting edition of plays. v. 13 no. 181)

'Twixt axe and crown; or, The lady Elizabeth. London. French. ₁18—₁. 12°. 72p. Historical. 5 acts
In Historical dramas

Unequal match. A comedy in three acts. London. French. ₁18—₁. 12°. 66p. (French's acting edition of plays. v. 118)

Up at the hills. An original comedy of Indian life. London. Lacy. ₁18—₁. 12°. 60p. (Lacy's acting edition of plays. v. 50) 2 acts

Victims. An original comedy. London. Lacy. ₁18—?₁. 12°. 60p. (Lacy's acting edition of plays. v. 32) 3 acts

Wedded and wooed. *See* Taylor, T. Lady Clancarty; or, Wedded and Wooed

Widow and her wooers. *See* Taylor, T. Sir Roger de Coverley, or, The widow and her wooers

Wittikind and his brothers; or, The seven swan princes and the fair Melusine. An original fairy tale. In two acts. London. Lacy. n.d. 12°. 28p. (Lacy's acting edition of plays. v. 6 no. 85)

Taylor, Tom, joint author. *See* Dubourg, A. W. and Taylor, Tom

Taylor, Tom, 1817-1880, and Reade, Charles
Before and behind the curtain. *See* Taylor, T. and Reade, C. Masks and faces; or, Before and behind the curtain

Masks and faces; or, Before and behind the curtain. A comedy. In two acts. Boston. Spencer. 1855. 12°. 60p.

Two loves and a life. A drama in four acts. Boston. Spencer. ₁1856?₁. 12°. 48p.

Tchekhov, A. P. *See* Chekhov, A. P.

Tchirikow, Eugen. *See* Chirikov, Eugen

Teeple, L. R.
Spartan Dorothy and her fox. Farce. 1 act
In Overland ns 39:548

Tefft, Nathan Appleton
Daughters of fate; a three act play of a once great war. Boston. Badger. 1918. 89p.   American Revolution

Teller, Charlotte
Higginbotham. Ethical. 3 acts
In International (NY) 10:74

Temple, Joan
Widow's cruise; a comedy in three acts. London. Benn. 1926. 12°. 116p.

Temple, Paul Prester
Too many crooks; a comedy in three acts. Chicago. Denison. 1923. 12°. 127p.

Ten Eyck, Cora
Their lives translated; an original play in three acts, with prologue and epilogue. Boston. Badger. 1919. 12°. 43p. $1.25 Symbolic

Tennyson, Alfred Lord, 1809-1892
Becket. Tragedy. 5 acts
In Complete poems (any edition)
Cup. Tragedy. 2 acts
In Complete poems (any edition)
Falcon. Romantic. 1 act
In Complete poems (any edition)
Smith, M. M. ed. Short plays of various types
Foresters. Robin Hood. 3 acts
In Complete poems (any edition)
Promise of May. Melodrama. 3 acts
In Complete poems (any edition)
Queen Mary. Historical. 5 acts
In Complete poems (any edition)

Tennyson, Jesse Fryniwyd, and Harwood, H. M.
Billeted; a comedy in three acts. . . N.Y. French. c1900. 12°. 73p.

Terrell, Maverick
Honi soit. Satire. 1 act
In Smart Set 54 no 1:71
Temperament. Comedy. 1 act
In Smart Set 50 no 1:215

Terry, Joseph Edward Harold, 1885-
General Post; a comedy in three acts. N.Y. Dutton. 1918. 16°. 128p.

Terry, Joseph Edward Harold, 1885-, and Worrall, Lechmere
Man who stayed at home; a play in three acts. . . N.Y. French. 1916. 12°. 155p. 50c.

Teternikov, Feodur Kuźmich. *See* Sologub, F. T., *pseud.*

Thackeray, William Makepeace
Wolves and the lamb. 2 acts
In Complete works (any edition)
Golden Bk 3:216

Thanhouser, Lloyd F.
Biddie sweeps out. Comedy. 1 act
In Yale playcraftsmen plays
End of the rope. Suicide. 1 act
In Yale playcraftsmen plays
Tie game. 1 act
In Baker's anthology of one-act plays
Trash. Comedy. 1 act
In Yale playcraftsmen plays

Thanhouser, Lloyd F., and Foster, Thomas J. jr.
Man without a head. Supernatural. 1 act
In Yale playcraftsmen plays

Theis, Grover
Between fires. Romantic. 1 act
In Numbers
Crack in the bell. Problem. 1 act
In Numbers

Like a book. Farce. 1 act
In Numbers
Numbers. World war. 1 act
In Numbers
There's a difference. Farce. 1 act
In Numbers

Theuriet, André, 1833-1907
Jean Marie; a play in one act. . . N.Y. French. [c1915]. 12°. 16p. Domestic tragedy
Old homestead. Romantic. 1 act
In Bellevue dramatic club: Plays for private acting

Thibault, Jacques Anatole. *See* France, Anatole, pseud.

Thoma, Ludwig, 1867-1921
"Moral"; a comedy in three acts. . . N.Y. Knopf. 1916. 12°. 94p.
Same in Dickinson, T. H. ed. Chief contemporary dramatists ser 2

Thomas, Albert Ellsworth, 1872-
Champion. *See* Louden, T. joint author
Come out of the kitchen; a comedy in three acts . . . made from the story of Alice Duer Miller. . . N.Y. French. [c1921]. 12°. 98p.
Her husband's wife; a comedy in three acts, with an introduction by Walter Prichard Eaton. N.Y. Doubleday. 1914. 133p. *also.* French. [1908]. 12°. 132p.
Just suppose; a comedy in three acts. N.Y. French. 1923. 12°. 98p.
Only 38; a comedy in three acts. . . N.Y. French. 1923. 12°. 109p. 75c.
Rainbow; a comedy in three acts. . . N.Y. French. c1919 12°. 111p.

Thomas, Albert Ellsworth, 1872-, and Hamilton, Clayton Meeker, 1881-
Better understanding; a drama in three acts. Boston. Little. 1924. 12°. 153p. American life
Big ideas; an unusual play in three acts. N.Y. French. [c1917]. 94p. Copyrighted 1914 . . . under title "To be or not to be"
Thirty days; a farce in three acts. N.Y. French. 1923. 12°. 109p.

Thomas, Augustus, 1857-
Alabama; a drama in four acts. Chicago. Dramatic Pub. co. 1905. 8°. 148p. Romantic
Arizona, a drama in four acts. Chicago. Dramatic Pub. co. 1904. 8°. 155p. Romantic
As a man thinks. N.Y. Duffield. 1911. 12°. 213p. Romantic. 4 acts
Same in Baker, G. B. ed. Modern American plays
Pierce and Matthews: Masterpieces of modern drama v 1 (abridged)
Copperhead . . . a drama in four acts. N.Y. French. 1922. 12°. 92p. 75c. Historical. Civil war and later
Same in Cohen, H. L. ed. Longer plays by modern authors

Thomas, A.—*Continued.*
Earl of Pawtucket; a comedy in three
acts. N.Y. French. 1917. 12°. 130p.
50c.
Harvest moon; a play in tour acts. N.Y.
French. [c1922]. 12°. 107p. Psycho-
logical
In Mizzoura, a play in four acts. N.Y.
French. c1916. 12°. 80p. Western
life
Man upstairs; a comedy in one act.
Washington. Committee on training
camp activities. . . (War dept. service
ed. no. 6) 1918. 12°. 16p.
Same in One act plays for stage and
study ser 1
Mrs. Leffinwell's boots, a farcical com-
edy in three acts. N.Y. French.
c1916. 12°. 121p. 50c.
Nemesis. Crime. 5 acts
In Everybody's 45:106
Oliver Goldsmith; a comedy in three acts.
N.Y. French. [c1916]. 12°. 107p. 50c.
Other girl; a comedy in three acts. . .
N.Y. French c1917. 12°. 134p.
Still waters; a play in three acts. N.Y.
French. [c1926]. 12°. 214p.
Witching hour; a drama in four acts.
N.Y. French. c1916. 12°. 111p. Hy-
notism
Same in Dickinson, T. H. ed. Chief
contemporary dramatists
Moses, M. J. ed. Representa-
tive American dramas, na-
tional and local
Quinn, A. H. ed. Representa-
tive American plays 1767-1923
Pierce and Matthews, eds.
Masterpieces of modern
drama v 1 (abridged)

Thome, J. Frederic
Six senses. Satire. 1 act
In Smart Set 54 no 1:3

Thompson, Alice Callender
Auction at Meadowville; comedy. Baker.
Boston. 15c. 1 act
Aunt Matilda's birthday party. A play
for girls. Chicago. Denison. [c1908].
12°. 19p. Commedietta. 1 act
Broken engagement; comedy. N.Y.
French. 23c. 1 act
Fudge and a burglar; a farce for girls.
Chicago. Denison. 1907. 12°. 8p. 15c.
1 act
Good old days; a comedy in one act.
Philadelphia. Penn pub. co. 1916. 12°.
14p.
Hannah gives notice; a comedy. N.Y.
French. 25c. 1 act
Her scarlet slippers; a comedy in one
act. Philadelphia. Penn pub. co.
1908. 12°. 14p.
In the absence of Susan; a comedy.
N.Y Dick. 3 acts
Just like Percy; a comedy. Baker. Bos-
ton. 3 acts
Knot of white ribbon; a comedy in one
act. Philadelphia. Penn pub. co.
1910. 12°. 16p.

Miss Deborah's pocketbook; a play in
one act. Philadelphia. Penn pub.
co. 1914. 12°. 14p. Comedy
Miss Susan's fortune; a comedy in one
act. Philadelphia Penn pub. co.
1916. 12°. 18p.
Molly's way; a comedy in three acts.
Philadelphia. Penn pub. co. 1915.
12°. 51p.
Oysters; a farce. Boston. Baker. 1 act
Return of Letty; a comedy in one act.
Philadelphia Penn pub. co. 1915. 12°.
18p.
Romantic Mary; a comedy. Boston.
Baker. 3 acts
Suffragette baby; a comedy in one act.
Philadelphia. Penn pub. co. 1912. 12°.
18p.
Susan's finish; a comedy. Boston.
Baker. 1 act
Truth about Jane; a comedy. Boston.
Baker. 1 act
Wrong baby; a farce. Chicago. Deni-
son. 1907. 12°. 13p. 1 act

**Thompson, Denman, 1833-1911, and Ryer,
George W.**
Our new minister; a comedy drama in
three acts. . . N.Y. French. 1916. 12°.
111p. 50c.

Thompson, Harlan
Man hunt. Farce. 1 act
In Smart Set 59 no. 2:87
One by one. Morality play more or less.
1 act
In Smart Set 59 no 1:93

Thorp, Josephine
Answer. Patriotic. 1 act
In Patriotic pageants of today
Torch. Pageant of democracy. 1 act
In Patriotic pageants of today
Treasure chest, a children's fairy play.
Chicago. Old Tower press. [c1922].
12°. 30p. 1 act
When liberty calls. Pageant of the al-
lies. 1 act
In Patriotic pageants of today

Thurston, Althea
Exchange. Farce-comedy. 1 act
In Lewis, B. R. ed. Contemporary
one-act plays
Schafer, B. L. comp. Book of one-
act plays
Pageant of spring. Pageant. 3 episodes
In Drama 12:251

Thurston, Ernest Temple, 1879-
Cost; a comedy in four acts. London.
Chapman. 1914. 134p.
Driven; a play in four acts. London.
Chapman. 1914. 144p.
Judas Iscariot; a play in four acts. N.Y.
Putnam. 1923. 12°. 122p. Biblical
Roof and four walls a comedy in four
acts. N.Y. Putnam. [1923]. 12°. 142p.
Snobs; a farcical comedy in one act.
N.Y. French. c1925. 12°. 24p.
Wandering Jew; a play in four phases.
N.Y. Putnam. 1921. 12°. 156p. $1.75

Tietzelieve, Julius Tietze
Francisco Ferrer; a tragedy in five acts.
N.Y. Dramatological pub. co. 1912.
12°. 83p.
Goldie Pride; a play in five acts. N.Y.
Ewald Bros. 1906. 16°. 75p. Romantic
Robert Emmet, Ireland's patriot martyr.
A political tragedy in 5 acts. N.Y.
Auerbach. 1902. 12°. 78p.

Tiffany, Esther Brown
Anita's trial; or, Our girls in camp, a
comedy in three acts for female characters only. Boston. Baker. 1889.
42p.
Autograph letter; a comedy in three acts.
Boston. Baker. 1889. 42p.
Model lover, a comedy in two acts. Boston. Baker. 1893. 22p.
Our girls in camp. *See* Brown, E. B.
Anita's trial; or, Our girls in camp
Rice pudding, a comedy in two acts.
Boston. Baker. 1889. 30p.
Tocsin; a drama of the renaissance. . .
San Francisco. Elder. [c1909]. 72p.

Tighe, Harry, 1877-
Silent room; a rustling comedy with an
undercurrent of seriousness. London. Westall. 1918. 12°. 324p.

Tilden, Freeman, 1883-
Enter Dora—exit dad. Comedy. 1 act
In Ladies' H J one-act plays

Titheradge, Dion, 1889-
The "altogether". Comedy. 1 act
In Out of the box
Company will recite. Farce. 1 act
In Out of the box
Cure. Comedy. 1 act
In From the prompt corner
Difference. Comedy. 1 act
In From the prompt corner
Dogs' life. Comedy. 1 act
In From the prompt corner
Domestic bliss. Comedy. 1 act
In From the prompt corner
Eighth wonder. Farce. 1 act
In From the prompt corner
Essential to the action. Comedy, 1 act
In Out of the box
Green-eyed monster. Farce. 1 act
In From the prompt corner
Indicator. Comedy. 1 act
In Out of the box
New Portia. Comedy. 1 act
In Out of the box
Props. Comedy. 1 act
In From the prompt corner
Sense of humour. Comedy. 1 act
In Out of the box
Sleeping out. Comedy. 1 act
In Out of the box
Stoic. Comedy. 1 act
In From the prompt corner
Tea-shop tattle. Comedy. 1 act
In Out of the box
Unwritten law. Comedy. 1 act
In Out of the box
Waiting. Comedy. 1 act
In From the prompt corner

Todhunter, John, 1839-1916
Black cat. A play in three acts. . .
London. Henry & Co. 1895. 97p.
Tragedy
How dreams come true. A dramatic
sketch in two scenes. . . London.
Bemrose & Sons. [1890]. 46p.
Sicilian idyll; a pastoral play in two
scenes. London. Mathews. 1890.
12°. 40p.

Toler, Sidney
Agatha's aunt; a comedy in three acts,
adapted from the novel by H. L.
Smith. N.Y. French. 1923. 12°. 95p.

Toler, Sidney, and Short, Marion
Golden days; a comedy in four acts.
N.Y. French. [1922]. 8°. 134p.

Toller, Ernst, 1893-
Machine-wreckers; a drama of the English Luddites in a prologue and five
acts. . . N.Y. Knopf. 1925. 113p.
Man and the masses (Masse mensch); a
play of the social revolution, in seven
scenes. . . Garden City. Doubleday.
1924. 12°. 109p. $2

Tolstoi, Alexei, 1817-1875
Tsar Fyodor Ivanovitch. Historical. 5
acts
In Sayler, O. M. ed. Moscow art
theatre plays

Tolstoi, Count Lyof N., 1828-1910
"And a light shineth in darkness." *See*
Tolstoi, L. N. Light that shines in
darkness
Cause of it all (Root of all evil). Temperance. 1 act. (Dramatization of
How the little devil earned a crust of
bread)
In Dramatic works (Crowell)
Forged coupon, and other stories
and dramas
Hadji Murad
Man who was dead, etc
Plays (Funk and Wagnalls, 1923)
Posthumous works v 3
Contaminated family. Comedy. 5 acts
In Stories and dramas (Dent)
Dramatic scenes about Pan who became
a beggar. 10 tableaux
In Stories and dramas (Dent)
First distiller. Temperance. 6 acts
In Dramatic works (Crowell)
Plays (Funk and Wagnalls)
Fruits of culture. *See* Tolstoi L. N.
Fruits of enlightenment
Fruits of enlightenment (Fruits of culture); Boston. Tucker. 1891. 12°. 185p.
Comedy. 4 acts *Also*. Luce. Boston.
1911. 12°. 149p.
Same in Works v 9
Dramatic works (Crowell)
Novels and other works (Scribner) v 16
Plays (Funk and Wagnalls)
Redemption and two other
plays v 2

Tolstoi, L. N.—*Continued.*
Light that shines in darkness (And a light
shineth in darkness). N.Y. Dodd.
1912. 12°. 205p. Christianity. 5 acts
Same in Dramatic works (Crowell)
    Hadji Murad
    Plays (Funk and Wagnalls,
      1923)
    Posthumous works v 2
Live corpse. *See* Tolstoi, L. N. Man
  who was dead
Living corpse. Phila. Brown. 1912. 8°.
  125p. *See also* Tolstoi, L. M. Man
  who was dead
Living dead. *See* Man who was dead
Man who was dead (Living corpse, Liv-
  ing dead, Live corpse, Reparation,
  Redemption). Conjugal. 6 acts
In Dramatic works (Crowell)
    Forged coupon, and other stories
      and dramas
    Hadji Murad
    Living corpse (E. M. Brown, tr)
    Man who was dead, etc
    Plays (Funk and Wagnalls 1923)
    Posthumous works v 2
    Redemption, and two other plays
      (abridged) v 1
    Golden bk 1:395
Nihilist. Farce. 3 acts
In Stories and dramas (Dent)
Peter the publican. Biblical. 5 acts
In Stories and dramas (Dent)
Power of darkness (Dominion of dark-
  ness). Chicago. Sergel. [c1890]. 12°.
  116p. Social revolt. 5 acts
Same in Complete works (Estes) v 18
    Works (Estes. 1904)
    Novels and other works
      (Scribner) v 16
    Father Sergius and other
      stores and plays
    Plays (Funk and Wagnalls)
    Redemption and two other
      plays v 1
    Pierce and Matthews, eds.
      Masterpieces of modern
      drama v 1 (abridged)
Reparation. *See* Tolstoi, L. M. Man
  who was dead
Traveller and peasant. Christian life. 1
  act
In Eng R 5:617
What men live by (adapted). Religious.
  3 scenes
In Malleson, M. ed. Young heaven and
    three other plays. (Play called
    Michael)
    Thomas, C. S. ed. Atlantic book
      of junior plays
Wisdom of children. Child life. 21
  scenes
In Dramatic works (Crowell)
    Father Sergius, and other stories
      and plays
    Posthumous works v 3

Tompkins, Eugene
André Fortier, the hero of the Calaveras.
  A drama in 4 acts and 6 tableaux.

By Eugene Tompkins. A translation
and adaptation of "La poudre d'or."
Boston. 1879. 12°.

Tompkins, Frank Gerow, 1879-
In front of Potter's. Dual personality.
  1 act
In Shay, F. ed. Treasury of plays for
  men
Letters. Cincinnati. Stewart Kidd. 1923.
  12°. 32p. Character. 1 act
Philanthropy. Comedy. 1 act
In Loving, P. ed. Ten minute plays
Sham; a social satire. Cincinnati. Ste-
  wart Kidd. [1920]. 12°. 31p. *also* Ap-
  pleton. 1 act
Same in Dickinson, A. D. ed. Drama
    Shay, F. and Loving, P. eds.
    Fifty contemporary one-act
    plays

Tooker, Gertrude Fulton
Everychild; a play in three acts. In-
  dianapolis. Bobbs-Merrill. [1914]. 142p.
  Fantasy

Tompkins, Juliet Wilbur, 1871-
Tired; a comedy in one act. N.Y.
  French. c1924. 17p.

Topelius, Zakarias, 1818-1898
Bride's crown. Fairy. 1 act
In Poet Lore 28:595
Field of enchantment. Fairy. 1 act
In Poet Lore 28:584
Stolen prince. Fairy. 1 act
In Poet Lore 28:567
Troll king's breakfast. Fairy. 1 act
In Poet Lore 28:589

Torrence, Frederic Ridgely, 1875-
Abelard and Heloise. N.Y. Scribner.
  1907. 215p. Romantic. 4 acts
El Dorado; a tragedy. N.Y. Lane. 1903.
  132p. 5 acts
Granny Maumee. Negro. 1 act
In Granny Maumee, etc
Rider of dreams. Negro. 1 act
In Granny Maumee, etc
    Smith, A. M. ed. Short plays by
    representative authors
Simon the Cyrenian. Christ play. 1 act
In Granny Maumee, etc

Totheroh, Dan W.
In the darkness. Blindness. 1 act
In Loving, P. ed. Ten minute plays
Kelly kid. (with K. Norris). Boston.
  Baker. 1926. 12°. 24p.
Pearls. 1 act
In Cohen, H. L. More one-act plays
  by modern authors
Stolen prince. Chinese-juvenile. 1 act
In Drama 15:30 O '24
    Webber, J. P. and Webster, H. H.
    eds. Short plays for young people
Tune of a tune. Comedy. 1 act
In Drama 10:184
While the mushrooms bubble. Fantasy.
  1 act
In Poet Lore 32:251
Widdy's mite. Comedy. 1 act
In Drama 13:13

Wild birds; a play in three acts.   Garden City. Doubleday. 1925. 12°. 124p. $1.   Prairie   country.   Tragedy. (California prize play)
Same in Mantle, B. ed.   Best plays of 1924-25 (condensed)

Towne, Charles H.
Aliens.   Art. 1 act
In McClure 47:12 My '16

Townley, Morris MacDonald
Caught.   Comedy. 1 act
In Two plays
Nothing else to do.   Comedy. 3 acts
In Two plays

Townsend, George Alfred, 1841-1914
President Cromwell; a drama in four acts. N.Y. Bonaventure. [c1884]. 94p. 8°. Historical

Traill, Peter, joint author.   *See* Morton, Michael and Traill, Peter

Trask, Mrs. Kate, 1853-
In the vanguard.   N.Y. Macmillan. 1914. 12°. 148p.   War. 3 acts
King Alfred's jewel (a drama) by the author of Mors et Vitoria.   N.Y. Lane. 1908. 12°. 180p.   Historical. 3 acts
Mors et victoria (a drama). N.Y. Longmans. 1903. 12°. 116p.   Historical. 3 acts
Without the walls; a reading play.   Macmillan. N.Y. 1919. 12°. 196p.   Christ play. 3 acts

Travis, John Coleridge, 1871-, and Huntington, Marie
Simple life.   An American play in four acts.   [Peekskill. N.Y. Highland Democrat Print]. 1908. 12°. 107p. Romantic

Trench, Herbert, i.e. Frederick Herbert, 1865-1923
Napoleon; a play.   N.Y. Oxford. 1919. 8°. 102p.   Historical. 4 acts
Same in Collected works v 3

Trent, John Jason
Owin' to Maggie; a comedy in one act. . . Boston. Baker. 1904. 8°. 28p.

Trevelyan, Robert Calvery, 1872-
Birth of Parsival.   N.Y. Longmans. 1905. 12°. 109p.   Legendary. 4 acts
Bride of Dionysus.   N.Y. Longmans. 1912. 8°. 77p.   Music. 3 acts
New Parsival; an operatic fable.   London. Chiswick press. 1914. 8°. 75p. 2 acts
Pterodamozels; an operatic fable.   London. Printed for the author at the Pelican press. [1917]. 8°. 64p. 2 acts

Trollope, Anthony, 1815-1882
Noble jilt; a comedy. . . London. Constable. 1923. 12°. 181p. 5 acts

Troubetzkoy, Amelie (Rives) Chanler, 1863-
Athelwold.   N.Y. Harper. 1893. 16°. 117p. Tragedy. 5 acts
Augustine the man.   N.Y. Lane. 1906. 12°. 83p.   Historical. 4 acts
Herod and Mariamne.   Tragedy. 5 acts
In Lippinc 42:305 S '88

November eve.   Tragedy. 3 acts
In Sea-woman's cloak, and November eve
Out of the midst of hatred.   World war. 1 act
In Virginia quarterly review 2:226
Sea-woman's cloak.   Sea. 3 acts
In Sea-woman's cloak, and November eve

True, Emma J.
Listen, ladies! a comedy in two acts. Boston. Baker. 1922. 12°. 35p.

Trumbull, Annie Eliot, 1857-
Green-room rivals.   A comedietta in one act. Boston. Baker. 1894. 12°. 16p.
Masque of culture.   Hartford, Conn. Case, Lockwood & Brainard. 1893. 16°. 54p.   Masque. 1 act

Tubbs, Arthur Lewis, 1867-
Beaten paths; a rural play in three acts. . . Phila. Penn. 1925. 12°. 73p.
Double deception; a comedy in one act. . . Boston. Baker. 1901. 12°. 24p.
Finger of scorn; a play in four acts. Phila. Penn. 1901. 12°. 57p.
Followed by fate; a melodrama in four acts. . . Phila. Penn. 1903. 12°. 54p.
For the old flag; a patriotic play in three acts. . . Phila. Penn. 1918. 12°. 94p.
Fruit of his folly; a society drama in five acts. . . Phila. Penn. 1894. 12°. 58p.
Willowdale; a play of country life in three acts. . . Boston. Baker. 1904. 12°. 59p.

Tull, Maurice Carter
Treason.   World war. 3 acts
In Indiana prize plays 1922-23

Tupper, Martin Farquhar, 1810-1889
Alfred.   A patriotic play in five acts. Printed not published Westminster. Brettell. 1858. 8°. 51p.   Historical
Washington: a drama in five acts. . . N.Y. Miller. 1876. 12°. 67p.   Historical

Tupper, Wilbur S.
Bargain.   Tragi-comedy. 1 act
In Six short plays
Figs and thistles.   Morality. 1 act
In Six short plays
In Toscana tavern.   Tragedy. 1 act
In Six short plays
Mr. Fraser's friends.   Satire. 1 act
In Six short plays
Onesimus.   Biblical. 1 act
In Six short plays
Wise men of Nineveh.   Oriental. 2 acts
In Six short plays

Turgenev, Ivan Sergíeevich, 1818-1883
Amicable settlement.   Comedy. 1 act
In Plays of Ivan S. Turgenev
Bachelor.   Comedy. 3 acts
In Plays of Ivan S. Turgenev
Broke.   Comedy. 1 act
In Plays of Ivan S. Turgenev
Carelessness.   Comedy. 1 act
In Plays of Ivan S. Turgenev
Conversation on the highway.   Comedy. 1 act
In Plays of Ivan S. Turgenev
Country woman.   Comedy. 1 act
In Plays of Ivan S. Turgenev

Turgenev, I. S—*Continued.*
Evening in Sorrento.   Comedy. 1 act
  In Plays of Ivan S. Turgenev
Family charge.   Comedy. 2 acts
  In Plays of Ivan S. Turgenev
Month in the country.   Comedy. 5 acts
  In Plays of Ivan S. Turgenev
One may spin a thread too finely. *See*
  Turgenev, I. S.   Where it is thin
  there it breaks
Where it is thin, there it breaks. (One
  may spin a thread too finely) Com-
  edy. 1 act
  In Plays of Ivan S. Turgenev
    Fortn 91:786

Turner, John Hastings
Lilies of the field; a comedy in three acts.
  N.Y. Appleton. 1924. 199p.

Turner, W. J., 1889-
Man who ate the popomack; a tragi-comedy of love in four acts.   N.Y. Brentano's. 1923. 12°. 90p.

Tyler, Royall, 1757-1826
Contrast; a comedy. . . N.Y. Dunlap So-
  ciety. (Pub. no. 1). 1887. 107p. New
  England. Comedy. 5 acts. ₍Boston.
  Houghton. 1920₎
  Same in Bates, A. ed.   Drama v 19
          Quinn, A. H. ed.   Representa-
          tive American plays, 1767-
          1923

Tynan, Brandon
Behold the man; a play in one act . . .
  based upon a story "The unbroken
  seal", by F. C. Kelley. . . N.Y.
  French. c1925. 12°. 23p.   Strike
Melody of youth; a comedy of the thirties
  in three acts.   N.Y. French. c1925.
  12°. 120p.
Northeast corner; a play in one act.
  N.Y. French. c1925. 20p. 12°.   Irish
  independence

Tzitlonok, Schevel
The children of the universe; a play, prolog, five acts, epilog.   N.Y. The author. 1921. 12°. 102p.   Symbolic

Ukráinka, Lésya, pseud.   (Laissa Petrovna
  Kossatch)
Babylonian captivity.   Ukraine. 1 act
  In Bechhofer, C. E. tr.   Five Russian
    plays
    Bechhofer, C. E. ed.   Russian an-
    thology in English

Ullmann, Margaret, 1882-
Pocahontas; a pageant.   Boston. Poet
  Lore. ₍c1912₎. 86p. 4 acts

Ulrich, Charles Kenmore
Altar of riches; a comedy of American
  finance in four acts.   Chicago. Denison. ₍c1909₎. 12°. 79p. 4 acts
Daughter of the desert; a comedy drama
  of the Arizona plains in four acts.
  Chicago. Denison. ₍c1908₎. 12°. 70p.
Dawn of liberty, a colonial comedy drama
  in four acts.   Chicago. Dramatic
  pub. co. c1905. 12°. 73p.
Deserter; a dramatic playlet.   Chicago.
  Denison. ₍c1912₎. 12°. 20p.   Army. 1
  act

Editor-in-chief; a farce comedy of newspaper life.   Chicago. Denison. ₍c1909₎.
  12°. 30p. 1 act
Hebrew; a dramatic sketch.   Chicago.
  Denison. ₍c1910₎. 12°. 17p.   Melodrama. 1 act
High school freshman; a comedy for boys
  in three acts.   Chicago. Denison. 12°.
  ₍c1909₎. 54p.
Honor of a cowboy; a comedy drama in
  four acts.   Chicago. Denison. ₍c1906₎.
  12°. 76p.
In Plum Valley; a rural comedy drama in
  four acts.   Chicago. Denison. ₍c1910₎.
  12°. 64p.
Man from Nevada; a comedy drama in
  four acts.   Chicago, Denison. ₍c1905₎.
  12°. 77p.
Nugget, a Western play in four acts.
  Chicago. Chicago pub. co. ₍c1905₎. 12°.
  51p.
On the Little Big Horn; a comedy drama
  of the west.   In four acts. Chicago.
  Denison. ₍c1907₎. 12°. 82p.
Political editor; a comedy of newspaper
  and political life.   Chicago. Denison.
  ₍c1912₎. 12°. 19p. 1 act
Road agent; a Western playlet.   Chicago, Denison. ₍c1912₎. 16°. 21p. 1 act
Royal highway; a comedy drama in four
  acts.   Chicago. Denison. ₍c1914₎. 12°.
  94p.
Town marshall; a comedy drama of the
  rural Northwest.   Chicago. Denison.
  ₍c1910₎. 12°. 68p. 4 acts
Tramp and the actress; a vaudeville
  sketch.   Chicago. Denison. ₍c1909₎.
  12°. 11p. 1 act

Unger, Gladys
Our Mr. Hepplewhite; a comedy in three
  acts.   London. French. c1919. 12°.
  106p.
Son and heir; or, The English; an original comedy in four acts.   N.Y.
  French. c1913. 111p.

Upward, Allen, 1863-
Paradise found; or, The superman found
  out. In three acts. Boston. Houghton.
  1915. 12°. 99p.   Prophetic

Vachell, Horace Annesley, 1861-
Case of Lady Camber.   London. Murray.
  1916. 12°. 131p.   Character. 4 acts
Evarannie; a play in one act.   Boston.
  Baker. 1925. 16p.
  Same in Baker's anthology of one-act
    plays
Jelf's; a comedy in four acts.   N.Y. Hod-
  der. 1912. 12°. 154p.
Quinney's; a comedy in four acts.   N.Y.
  Doran. 1916. 12°. 140p.
Searchlights; a play in three acts.   Lon-
  don. Murray. 1915. 12°. 136p.   So-
  cial

Vajda, Ernö (Ernest), 1887-
Fata Morgana (Mirage); a comedy in
  three acts. . . Garden City. Doubleday. 1924. 12°. 194p. $2

Valle-Inclán, Ramon del, 1870-
Dragon's head; a fantastic farce. . . 1 act
In Poet Lore 29:531

Van Druten, John
Young Woodley. N.Y. Simon. 1926. 12°.
164p. English public school. 3 acts
Same in Mantle, B. ed. Best plays of
1925-26 (abridged)

Van Dyke, Henry, 1852-
House of Rimmon. N.Y. Scribner. 1908.
121p. Damascus. 4 acts
Same in Scrib M 44:129

Vane, Sutton
Outward bound. N.Y. Boni. 1924. 12°.
171p. $1.75. Immortality. 3 acts
In Mantle, B. ed. Best plays of 1923-
24

Vanzyke, Gustave
Mother Nature (La souveraine). Bel-
gium. 3 acts
In Mother Nature; Progress
Progress (Les étapes). Belgium. 3 acts
In Mother Nature; Progress

Varesi, Gilda, and Byrne, Dolly
Enter Madame; a play in three acts.
N.Y. Benda. 1921. 12°. 177p. $1.75
Comedy
Same in Mantle, B. ed. Best plays of
1920-21 (abridged)

Vasquez, José Andrés
With chains of gold. Wealth. 1 act
In Poet Lore 34:417

Vaughan, Virginia
New era; a dramatic poem. . . London.
Chapman. 1880. 12°. 238p. Utopia.
4 scenes

Veiller, Bayard
Thirteenth chair; a play in three acts.
N.Y. French. 1922. 12°. 110p. 75c.
Mystery
Within the law; a melodrama in four acts.
N.Y. French. 1917. 12°. 156p. 50c.

Verconsin, Eugène, 1823-1892
Fond delusion; a farce. . . Phila. Penn.
1908. 12°. 12p. 1 act

Verga, Giovanni, 1840-1922
Wolf-hunt. Triangle. 1 act
In Goldberg, I. tr. Plays of the
Italian theatre

Verhaeren, Emile, 1855-1916
Cloister; a play in four acts. . . London.
Constable. 1915. 66p.
Same in Plays
Dawn (Les aubes). London. Duck-
worth. 1898. 12°. 110p. Problem. 4
acts. *also* Boston. Small
Same in Plays
      Moses, M. J. ed. Representa-
      tive continental dramas
Helen of Sparta. Tragedy. 4 acts
In Plays
Philip II. Tragedy. 4 acts
In Plays

Vermilye, Kate Jordan
Pompadour's protégé. Court of Louis
XV. 1 act
In Smart Set 11 no 1:75

Vernon, Harry M., 1878-
All men are fools
In Four plays for male characters
Case of Johnny Walker
In Four plays for male characters
"Something" in the city
In Four plays for male characters
Squeaky
In Four plays for male characters

Vernon, Leicester Viney
Lancers. A drama. In three acts.
(Adapted from the French). London.
Lacy. n.d. 12°. 46p. (Lacy's acting
edition of plays. v. 13 no. 187)

Viaud, Louis Marie Julien. *See* Loti,
Pierre, pseud.

Vidler, Edward A.
Rose of Ravenna. Melbourne. Robertson. 1914. 12°. 135p. Romantic
tragery. 5 acts

Viereck, George Sylvester, 1884-
Butterfly. Morality. 1 act
In Game at love, and other plays
International (NY) 11:156
From death's own eyes. Passion. 1 act
In Game at love, and other plays
International (NY) 11:80
Game at love. Psychological. 1 act
In Game at love, and other plays
International (NY) 11:48
Mood of a moment. Psychological. 1 act
In Game at love, and other plays
International (NY) 11:13
Question of fidelity. Social. 1 act
In Game at love, and other plays
International (NY) 11:121

Vildrac, Charles
Steamer Tenacity. Comedy. 3 acts
In Poet Lore 32:463

**Villiers de L'Isle Adam, Jean Marie ⌊Mat-
thias Philippe Auguste⌋, Comte de,**
1838-1889
Escape. Character. 1 act
In The revolt, and The escape
Revolt. Social. 1 act
In The revolt, and The escape

Vilsack, Gladys Brace. *See* Brace, Gladys,
pseud.

Vizin, Denis von
Brigadier's visit. Domestic. 1 act
In Bechhofer, C. E. ed. Russian an-
thology in English
Choice of a tutor. Farce. 1 act
In Bechhofer, C. E. ed. Five Russian
plays

Voigt, Bernhard, joint author. *See* Hamilton, Clayton M. and Voigt, Bernhard

Vollmer, Lula
Sun-up; a play in three acts. N.Y.
Brentano's. 1924. 12°. 80p. $1. Com-
edy
Same in Mantle, B. ed. Best plays of
1923-24 (condensed)
      Quinn, A. H. ed. Representa-
      tive American plays, 1767-
      1923 (1925 ed)

Vollmoeller, Karl, pseud. (Carlo Gozzi),
1848-
Turandot, princess of China.   A chin-
oiserie in three acts. . . N.Y. Duffield.
$1
Vorse, Mary Heaton
I've come to stay; a love comedy of Bo-
hemia.   N.Y.   Century.   1918.   12°.
190p. $1.25
**Vorse, Mary Heaton, and Clements, Colin
Campbell**
Wreckage; a play in one act.   N.Y.
Appleton. 1924. 12°. 31p.   Tragedy
Vosburgh, Mrs. Maude (Batchelder)
Health champions; a modern health cru-
sade play. . . Boston, Mass. tuber-
culosis league. 1921. 8°. 16p. 1 act
The home-makers; a play of the Pil-
grims, in three acts. . . N.Y. S.
French. c1920. 12°. 69p.
Miss Maria; a comedy in one act; drama-
tized from Old Chester tales by
Margaret Deland.   N.Y. French.
1918. 12°. 25c.
Vojnovich, Ivo, 1857-
Resurrection of Lazarus.   Historical
(Serbian). 4 acts
In Poet Lore 37:318
**Vrchlicky, Jaroslav, pseud. (Frida, Emil
Bohuslav)**
At the chasm.   Artist. 1 act
In Poet Lore 24 no 5:289
Vengeance of Catullus.   Historical. 1 act
In Poet Lore 25:536
Witness.   Infidelity. 1 act
In Shay, F. ed.   Twenty-five short
plays, international
Poet Lore 25:546
**Waddell, Samuel (Rutherford Mayne,
pseud.), 1878-**
Drone; a play in three acts. . . Dublin.
Maunsel. 1909. 12°. 68p.   Comedy
Same in Drone, and other plays
Phantoms.   Tragedy. 1 act
In Dublin M 1:382
Red turf.   Tragedy. 1 act
In Drone, and other plays
Troth; a play in one act.   Dublin.
Maunsel. 1909. 12°. 14p.   Tragedy
Same in Drone, and other plays
Turn of the road; a play in two scenes
and an epilogue.   Dublin. Maunsel.
1907. 12°. 71p.   Music
Same in Drone, and other plays
Wagstaff, Blanche Shoemaker, 1888-
Colonial Virginia.   Historical. 1 act
In Colonial plays for the school-room
Columbus story.   Historical. 1 act
In Colonial plays for the school-room
Eris; a dramatic allegory.   N.Y. Moffat.
1914. 12°. 41p. 3 scenes
First Thanksgiving.   Historical. 1 act
In Colonial plays for the school-room
Georgia debtors.   Historical. 1 act
In Colonial plays for the school-room
Indian story.   1 act
In Colonial plays for the school-room
Life in New York.   Historical. 1 act
In Colonial plays for the school-room

Pennsylvania incident.   Historical. 1 act
In Colonial plays for the school-room
Revolutionary days.   Historical. 1 act
In Colonial plays for the school-room
Witchcraft story.   Historical. 1 act
In Colonial plays for the school-room
Waight, James F.
Edward I.   London.   Allen & Unwin.
[1922]. 12°. 109p.   Historical. 2 acts.
Pt. 2 of his: Trilogy of freedom
Godwine.   London. Allen.   [1917]. 12°.
123p.   Historical. 3 acts. Pt. 1 of
Godwine trilogy
Harold.   London. Allen. [1918]. 12°. 127p.
Historical. 4 acts. Pt. 3 of Godwine
trilogy
Henry III.   London. Allen & Unwin.
[1920]. 12°. 123p.   Historical. 4 acts.
Pt. 1 of his: Trilogy of freedom
Richard II.   London. Allen & Unwin.
[1920]. 12°. 109p.   Historical. 2 acts.
Pt. 3 in his: Trilogy of freedom
Swegen.   London. Allen & Unwin. [1916].
12°. 94p.   Historical. 3 acts. Pt. 2 of
Godwine trilogy
Waite, Arthur Edward
Further side of the portal.   Religious. 2
pts.
In Collected poems v 2
Morality of the lost word.   Religious. 3
acts
In Collected poems v 2
Soul's comedy.   Religious. 3 pts.
In Collected poems v 2
Walker, Alice Johnstone, 1871-
At the White House—1863.   Historical.
1 act
In Little plays from American history
Christopher Columbus.   Historical. 4
acts
In Lafayette, etc
Hiding the regicides.   Historical. 7
scenes
In Little plays from American history
In Boston, 1864.   Historical. 1 act
In Little plays from American history
Lafayette. · Historical. 3 acts
In Lafayette, etc
Long knives of Illinois.   Historical. 3
acts
In Lafayette, etc
Mr. Lincoln and the little girl.   Histori-
cal. 1 act
In Little plays from American history
Mrs. Murray's dinner party.   Historical.
3 acts
In Little plays from American history
On a plantation, 1863.   Historical. 1 act
In Little plays from American history
Walker, C. C.
Caswallon; or, The Briton chief.   A
tragedy in five acts. Baltimore. Rob-
inson. 1829. 8°. 68p.
Wallace: a historical tragedy in five
acts. . . London. Miller. 1820. 8°. 69p.
Same in Oxberry, W. ed.   New Eng-
lish drama v 18 no 1

Warlock of the glen. A melodrama in two acts. . . Boston. Spencer. ₁1856?₁. 12°. 20p.

Walker, Stuart
Birthday of the infanta (Oscar Wilde). Tragedy. 1 act
In Portmanteau adaptations
Moses, M. J. ed. Another treasury of plays for children
Thomas, C. S. ed. Atlantic book of junior plays
Gammer Gurton's needle. Comedy. 5 acts
In Portmanteau adaptations
Jonathan makes a wish. Comedy. 3 acts
In More portmanteau plays
King's great aunt sits on the floor. N.Y. Appleton. 1925. 12°. 41p. Comedy. 1 act
Lady of the weeping willow tree. Japan. 3 acts
In More portmanteau plays
Drama 8 no 29:10
Medicine show. Character. 1 act
In Portmanteau plays
Dickinson, A. D. ed. Drama
Shay, F. and Loving, P. eds. Fifty contemporary one-act plays
Nellijumbo. Comedy. 1 act
In Portmanteau adaptations
Nevertheless. Cincinnati. Stewart Kidd. 1923. 12°. 34p. Comedy. 1 act
Same in Portmanteau plays
Schafer, B. L. comp. Book of one-act plays
Sir David wears a crown (Sequel to Six who pass while the lentils boil). Cincinnati. Stewart. 1922. 12°. 47p. 50c. Fantasy. 1 act
Same in Portmanteau adaptations
Shay, F. ed. Contemporary one-act plays of 1921
Shay, F. ed. Twenty contemporary one-act plays (American)
Six who pass while the lentils boil. Cincinnati. Stewart Kidd. ₁c1921₁. 12°. 54p. Social. 1 act
Same in Portmanteau plays
Mayorga, M. G. ed. Representative one-act plays
Moses, M. J. ed. Treasury of plays for children
Smith, A. M. ed. Short plays by representative authors
Trimplet. Symbolic. 1 act
In Portmanteau plays
Very naked boy. Interlude. 1 act
In More portmanteau plays

Wallace, William
Divine surrender; a mystery play. London. Stock. 1895. 12°. 77p. 3 pts.

Walsh, Ignatius
House of sand; a mediated tragedy in four acts. Chicago. Loyola press. 1916. 43p.

Walter, Eugene
Easiest way . . . in four acts and four scenes. N.Y. Goerck Art press. 1908. 12°. 85p. (Privately printed). Problem
Same in Dickinson, T. H. ed. Chief contemporary dramatists ser 2

Ward, W. D.
Babes in the wood. After Maeterlinck. 1 act
In Touchstone 5:281

Warren, Algernon
Taking of Capri. A drama in three acts. London. Stockwell. ₁1906₁. 12°. 51p. Historical

Warren, Marie Josephine
Substance of ambition. 1 act
In Plays with a punch
Tommy's wife; a farce in three acts. Boston. Baker. ₁c1905₁. 12°. 30p.
Twig of thorn; an Irish fairy play in two acts. Boston. Baker. 1910. 12°. 96p.

Warren, Thomas Herbert, 1853-
Death of Virgil. A dramatic narrative. Oxford. Blackwell. Historical. 5 scenes

Warren, Walter, pseud. *See* Raymond, George Lansing

Watson, Sir William, 1858-
Heralds of the dawn; a play in eight scenes. N.Y. Lane. 1912. 12°. 93p. Prophetic. 8 scenes

Watson-Taylor, George, d. 1841
England preserved: an historical play, in five acts. London. Printed for T. N. Longman. 1795. 8°. 80p.
Same in Inchbald, E. S. Modern theatre v 8
King Henry the third; or, The expulsion of the French. Historical. v 1
In Pieces of poetry; with two dramas
Profligate; a comedy. . . London. Bulmer & Nicol. 1820. 4°. 153p. (Privately printed). 5 acts
Same in Pieces of poetry; two dramas

Watts, Mary Stanbery, 1868-
Ancient dance. Domestic tragedy. 2 acts
In Three short plays
Civilization. Social. 1 act
In Three short plays
Wearin' o' the green. Farce. 1 act
In Three short plays

Watts, William
Adrianwona; a play in four acts. N.Y. Boyle. c1924. 8°. 62p. Poetic
King Philip IV. Historical. 4 acts
In Plays and poems

Weaver, John Van Alstyne, 1893-
So that's that. N.Y. Appleton. 1926. 12°. 22p. Comedy. 1 act

Weaver, John V. A., joint author. *See* Abbott, George and Weaver, John V. A.

Weaver, Wyn, and Leycester, Laura
Rising generation; a comedy in three acts. N.Y. French. 1924. 12°. 95p. 75c.

Webster, Jean i.e. **Alice Jean Chandler (Mrs. Glenn Ford McKinney)**, 1876-1916
Daddy-Long-Legs; a comedy in four acts. N.Y. French. 1922. 12°. 128p. 75c.

Wedekind, Frank, 1864-1918
Awakening of spring (Spring's awakening). Phila. Brown. 1910. 12°. 161p. Tragedy of childhood. 3 acts
Same in Tragedies of sex
Court singer (Tenor; Heart of a tenor). Artistic temperament. 1 act
In German classics 20:360
Moses, M. J. ed. Representative one-act plays by continental authors
Shay, F. and Loving P. eds. Fifty contemporary one-act plays
Golden Bk 5:65
Smart Set 40 no 2:129 (adapted)
Damnation. A death-dance in three scenes
In Tragedies of sex
Erdgeist (Earth spirit) a tragedy in four acts. . . N.Y. Boni. 1914. 12°. 93p.
Same in Tragedies of sex
Heart of a tenor. *See* Wedekind, F. Court singer
Pandora's box; a tragedy in three acts. . . N.Y. Boni. 1918. 12°. 79p.
Same in Tragedies of sex
Glebe 2:no 4
Spring's awakening. *See* Wedekind, F. Awakening of spring
Such is life; a play in 5 acts. Phila. Brown. 1912. 12°. 127p. Mediaeval Italy
Tenor. *See* Wedekind, F. Court singer
Virgin and the white slaver. Sex. 1 act
In International (NY) 7:279

Weeks, Kenneth
Beacon. Japanese in California. 3 acts
In Esau, and The beacon
Cardor's duel. Comedy. 1 act
In Esau, and The beacon
Esau. Sociological. 3 acts
In Esau, and The beacon
Involution. Romantic. 3 acts
In Five impractical plays
Man of principle. Tragedy. 1 act
In Five impractical plays
Phélysmort. Tableau. 1 act
In Esau, and The beacon
Sara. Tragedy. 10 scenes
In Esau, and The beacon
Substitute. Dialogue. 1 act
In Five impractical plays
Susanna and the elders. Vaudeville. 3 acts
In Five impractical plays
Tonrehl and Ylande. Improvisation. 3 acts
In Five impractical plays

Weinberg, Anita, and Weinberg, Albert
Philosophy of the tooth brush. Comedy. 1 act
In Poet Lore 36:615

Weinberger, Mildred
Elaine. Poetic. 1 act
In Poet Lore 34:72

Welch, Livingston
Victim of rest; a play. Boston. Four Seas co. 1924. 24p.

Welcker, Adair
Bitter end. Tragedy. 5 acts
In Romer, King of Norway, and other dramas
Dream of realms beyond us. Romantic. 3 acts
In Romer, King of Norway, and other dramas
Flavia. Historical. 5 acts
In Romer, King of Norway, and other dramas

Wellman, Rita, 1890-
Dawn. "The dawn is wiser than the eve."—Slav proverb. War. 1 act
In Drama 9:89
For all time. Melodrama. 1 act
In Shay, F. and Loving, P. eds. Fifty contemporary one-act plays
Funiculi Funicula. Tragedy. 1 act
In Mayorga, M. G. ed. Representative one-act plays
Gentile wife; a play in four acts. N.Y. Moffatt. 1919. 12°. 128p. Race
Lady with the mirror. Allegory. 1 act
In Drama 8:299
String of the Samisen. 1 act
In Provincetown plays (Stewart Kidd 1921)

Wells, Carolyn
Christmas gifts for all nations. Juvenile. 1 act
In Jolly plays for holidays
Day before Christmas. Christmas. 1 act
In Jolly plays for holidays
Greatest day in the year. Christmas. 1 act
In Jolly plays for holidays
Greatest gift. Christmas. 1 act
In Jolly plays for holidays
Is Santa Claus a fraud? Christmas. 1 act
In Jolly plays for holidays
Substitute for Santa Claus. Christmas. 1 act
In Jolly plays for holidays

Wells, William H.
Brotherhood. Strike. 1 act
In Plays of the 47 workshop ser 4

Welsh, Robert Gilbert
Jezebel. Israel. 1 act
In Forum 51:647

Wendell, Barrett, 1855-
Christmas masque. 3 pts.
In Raleigh in Guiana [and other plays]
Raleigh in Guiana. 2 pts.
In Raleigh in Guiana [and other plays]
Rosamond. Historical. 1 act
In Raleigh in Guiana [and other plays]

Wentworth, Marion Craig, 1872-
Flower shop; a play in three acts. Boston. Badger. 1912. 117p. Social
War brides; a play in one act. . . N.Y. Century. 1915. 12°. 71p. 50c. World war
Same in Cent 89:527

Werner, Friedrich Ludwig Zacharias, 1768-1823
Templars in Cyprus A dramatic poem. . . London. Bell. 1886. 12°. 262p.
24th of February. Fate. 3 scenes
In Bates, A. ed. Drama v 10:305

West, Duffy R.
Society notes; a play in one act. Cincinnati. Kidd. ɪc1922ɪ. 12°. 41p. Comedy
Same in Nicholson, K. ed. Appleton book of short plays

Westerfelt, George Conrad, 1879-
Not so fast; or, The blimp; a comedy in three acts. N.Y. French. 1924. 12°. 93p. 75c.

Westerfelt, Leonides, 1875-, and others
Under twenty; a comedy in three acts. . . N.Y. French. c1926. 8°. 90p.

Wheeler, Francis William Rolt. *See* Rolt-Wheeler, Francis William

Whiffen, Edwin Thomas
Dinah. Biblical. 1 act
In Jephtha sacrificing, and Dinah Tamar, and other poems
Jephtha sacrificing. Biblical. 1 act
In Jephtha sacrificing, and Dinah Tamar, and other poems
Samson at Timnah. Biblical. 1 act
In Samson marrying, etc Tamar, and other poems
Samson blinded. Biblical. 1 act
In Samson marrying, etc Tamar, and other poems
Samson hybristes. Biblical. 1 act
In Samson marrying, etc Tamar, and other poems
Samson marrying. Biblical. 1 act
In Samson marrying, etc Tamar, and other poems
Tamar. Biblical. 1 act
In Tamar and other poems

White, Arthur Corning
Maze. Duty. 1 act
In Poet Lore 36:147
Two black sheep. Satire. 1 act
In Poet Lore 35:464

White, Clematis
A convert. Intrique. 1 act
In Smart Set 35 no 3:103

White, Hervey, 1866-
Assassis; a tragedy in four acts. Woodstock, N.Y. Maverick press. ɪc1911ɪ. 12°. 55p.
Green peppers. Woodstock, N.Y. Maverick press. ɪc1913ɪ. 12°. 70p. Comedy. 3 acts

White, James, 1803-1862
Earl of Glowrie; a tragedy. London. Newby. 1845. 8°. 198p. 5 acts
John Savile of Haysted. A tragedy in five acts. . . London. Newby. 1847. 8°. 108p.
King of the commons; a drama. . . London. Newby. 1846. 8°. 100p. Historical. 5 acts

White, Jessie B.
Snow white and seven dwarfs
In Moses, H. T. ed. Another treasury of plays for children

White, Leonard C.
Greater law; a comedy in one act. London. "The Stage" pub. bureau. 1924. 8°. 38p.

White, Lucy
Bird child. Social. 1 act
In International (NY) 8:337

Whitehouse, Josephine Henry
Canary. World war. 1 act
In Poet Lore 37:589

Whiting, Eleanor Custis
Ashes. Psychological. 1 act
In Poet Lore 33:423
Common ground. Emotional. 1 act
In Poet Lore 32:140

Whiting, Evelyn G.
Confidence game; a comedy in two acts. Boston. Baker. 1900. 12°. 26p.

Whitman, Eleanor Wood
Drama of Isaiah. Chicago. Pilgrim press. 1917. 12°. 64p. 75c.
Jeremiah; a drama in five acts, based upon the story of Jeremiah as found in the Bible. N.Y. Century. ɪc1925ɪ. 12°. 125p.

Whitman, John Pratt
Sympathy of the people; a drama of today. Boston. Four Seas. 1921. 12°. 39p. 75c. Capital and labor. 4 acts

Whitney, Alfred Carpenter, 1881-
Pontiac; a drama of old Detroit, 1763. Boston. Badger. 1910. 12°. 111p. 5 acts

Wied, Gustav Joannes, 1858-1914
Autumn fires. Comedy. 1 act
In Shay, F. and Loving, P. eds. Fifty contemporary one-act plays
2 x 2=5; a comedy in four acts. . . N.Y. Brown. 1923. 12°. 146p.

Wiegand, Charmion von
Emilia Viviani. Romantic. 1 act
In Poet Lore 36:552
Jasmine and the poet. Comedy. 1 act
In Poet Lore 37:418

Wiegand, Johannes and Scharrelmann, Wilhelm
Wages of war. War. 3 acts
In Poet Lore 19:129

Wiers-Jenssen, Hans, 1866-1925
Anne Pedersdotter; a drama in four acts. Boston. Little. 1917. 12°. 92p. $1. Witchcraft
Saul. Kristiania. Aschehoug. 1916. 194p.
Witch; a drama in four acts. . . N.Y. Brentano. 1926. 12°. 93p. (Published in 1917 under title of Anne Pedersdotter, *q.v.*

Wiggin, Kate Douglas, 1857-
Bird's Christmas carol; dramatic version. In collaboration with Helen Ingersoll. Boston. Houghton Mifflin. 1914. 12°. 103p. 3 acts
Old Peabody pew. N.Y. French. c1917. 12°. 45p. Romantic. 1 act
In Ladies' H J 34:21

Wiggin, K. D.—*Continued.*
Thorn in the flesh.   Monologue. 1 scene
In Poet Lore 36:191

Wiggin, Kate Douglas, 1857- and Crothers, Rachel
Mother Carey's chickens; a little comedy of home, in three acts.   N.Y. French. c1925. 12°. 99p.

Wigginton, May Wood
Love and friendship; a play in five acts, dramatized from the novel of Jane Austen. . . N.Y. French. c1925. 12°. 46p.

Wilbrandt, Adolph von, 1837-1911
Master of Palmyra.   Philosophic. 5 acts
In German classics 16:10
Poet Lore 13:161

Wilcox, Constance Grenelle
Blue and green mat of Abdul Hasson. An Arabian adventure.   N.Y. Appleton. 1925. 12°. 36p. 1 act

Egypt's eyes; a three act play with an epilogue.   N.Y. French. c1924. 12°. 94p.   Egyptian

Four of a kind; a play for a boat in one act.   N.Y. French. 1920. 12°. p. 93-126.   Aquatic
Same in Told in a Chinese garden, etc

Heart of Frances; a one-act play.   N.Y. Appleton. 1925. 12°. 22p.

Mah-jongg; the play of one hundred intelligences, in a prologue and one act. . . Boston. Birchard. c1923. 12°. 75p.   Chinese

Mother Goose garden.   Fantasy. 1 act
In Told in a Chinese garden

Pan pipes; a woodland play in one act. N.Y. French. c1920. 12°. p. 63-90
In Told in a Chinese garden

Princess in the fairy tale; a garden fairy story for children in one act.   N.Y. French. c1920. 12°. p. 129-168
In Told in a Chinese garden

Told in a Chinese garden.   Play pageant for a garden. 1 act
In Told in a Chinese garden
Drama 9:116 My '19

Wilde, Oscar (Fingall O'Flahertie Wills), 1856-1900
Birthday of the infanta.   Psychological. 1 act
In Thomas, C. S. ed.   Atlantic book of junior plays
Duchess of Padua.   Tragedy. 5 acts
In (Complete works) (Ross ed) v 10
Plays (Nichols)
Works (Sunflower ed) v 7
Writings (Uniform ed) v 11
Florentine tragedy.   Luce. Boston. 1908. 1 act
Same in (Complete works) (Ross ed) v 6
For love of the king.   Fairy. 3 acts
In Cent 103:225

Happy prince. (story dramatized).   Allegory. 1 scene
In Poet Lore 27:406
Ideal husband.   London. Methuen. 1910. 246p.   Comedy. 4 acts
Same in (Complete works) (Ross ed) v 9
Works (Sunflower ed) v 6
Writings (Uniform ed) v 7
Plays (Luce)
Plays (Nichols)
Importance of being earnest, a trivial comedy for serious people.   London. Methuen. 1910. 181p. 3 acts
Same in (Complete works) (Ross ed) v 7
Works (Sunflower ed) v 5
Writings (Uniform ed) v 2
Importance of being earnest
Plays (Nichols)
Moses, J. M. ed.   Representative British dramas
Pierce and Matthews, eds. Masterpieces of modern drama v 1 (abridged)
Lady Windermere's fan; a play about a good woman.   London. Methuen. 1910. 157p.   Comedy.
Same in Lady Windermere's fan (Complete works) (Ross ed) v 7
Works (Sunflower ed) v 5
Writings (Uniform ed) v 2
Plays (Luce)
Plays (Nichols)
Matthews, B. and Lieder, P. R. eds. Chief British dramatists
Pierce and Matthews, ed. Masterpieces of modern drama v 1 (abridged)
Nihilists.   *See* Wilde, O. Vera; or, The nihilists
Salomé; a tragedy in one act.   N.Y. Caldwell. [c1907]. 117p. (Originally written in French. Translated by Aubrey Beardsley)
Same in (Complete works) (Ross ed) v 6
Works (Sunflower ed) v 7
Writings (Uniform ed) v 11
Plays (Luce)
Plays (Nichols)
Clark, B. H. ed.   Representative one-act plays by British and Irish authors
Poet Lore 18:189
Golden Bk 1:207
Vera; or, The nihilists; a drama in prologue and four acts. [n.p.].   Tragedy. Privately printed. 1902. 75p.
Same in (Complete works) (Ross ed) v 6
Works (Sunflower ed) v 7
Writings (Uniform ed) v 11
Plays (Nichols)
Vera; or, The nihilists

Woman of no importance. London.
Methuen. [1910]. 182p. Comedy. 4
acts
Same in (Complete works) (Ross ed)
v 8
Works (Sunflower ed) v 6
Writings (Uniform ed) v 7
Woman of no importance
(Methuen)

Wilde, Percival, 1887-
According to Darwin. Ethical. 1 act
In Confessional and other American
plays
Question of morality, and other
plays
Forum 54:488
Alias Santa Claus. Christmas. 1 act
In Pict R 28:16
Ashes of romance. Fantasy. 1 act
In Inn of discontent, and other fantas-
tic plays
Beautiful story. Christmas. 1 act
In Confessional and other American
plays
Question of morality, and other
plays
Catesby. Comedy. 1 act
In Eight comedies for little theatres
Confessional. Ethical. 1 act
In Confessional and other American
plays
Question of morality, and other
plays
Dawn. Supernatural. 1 act
In Dawn, The noble lord, etc
Smart Set 44 no 3:115
Dyspeptic ogre. Comedy. 1 act
In Eight comedies for little theatres
Thomas, C. S. ed. Atlantic book of
junior plays
Embryo. Comedy. 1 act
In Eight comedies for little theatres
Enchanted Christmas tree, a Yuletide
play. N.Y. Appleton. 1925. 12°. 50p.
1 act
Finger of God. Ethical. 1 act
In Dawn, The noble lord, etc
Shay, F. and Loving, P. eds. Fifty
contemporary one-act plays
His return. Comedy. 1 act
In Eight comedies for little theatres
House of cards. Domestic tragedy. 1 act
In Dawn, The noble lord, etc
In the net. Comedy. 1 act
In Eight comedies for little theatres
In the ravine. War. 1 act
In Unseen host, and other war plays
Inn of discontent. Fantasy. 1 act
In Inn of discontent, and other fantas-
tic plays
Lady of dreams. Fantasy. 1 act
In Inn of discontent, and other fantas-
tic plays
Luck-piece. Fantasy. 1 act
In Inn of discontent, and other fantas-
tic plays
Mothers of men. War. 1 act
In Unseen host and other war plays

Noble lord. Comedy. 1 act
In Dawn, The noble lord, etc
Nocturne. Fantasy. 1 act
In Inn of discontent, and other fantas-
tic plays
Pawns. War. 1 act
In Unseen host and other war plays
Playing with fire. Comedy. 1 act
In Dawn, The noble lord, etc
Knickerbocker, E. Van B. ed.
Twelve plays
Previous engagement. Comedy. 1 act
In Eight comedies for little theatres
Question of morality. Comedy. 1 act
In Confessional and other American
plays
Question of morality, and other
plays
Mayorga, M. G. ed. Representative
one act plays
Century 90:609
Reckoning; a play in one act. Boston.
Baker. 1922. 12°. 28p. Comedy
Reverie. Boston. Baker. 1924. 12°. 54p.
Christmas. 1 act
Saved! Boxer uprising. 1 act
In Smart Set 46 no 3:397
Sequel. Comedy. 1 act
In Eight comedies for little theatres
Toy shop. Boston. Baker. 1924. 12°.
47p. Christmas. 1 act
Same in Webber, J. P. and Webster,
H. H. eds. Short plays for young
people
Traitor. Boer war. 1 act
In Dawn, The noble lord, etc
Unseen host. War. 1 act
In Unseen host and other war plays
Valkyrie. War. 1 act
In Unseen host and other war plays
Villain in the piece. Comedy. 1 act
In Confessional, and other American
plays
Question of morality, and other
plays
Wonderful woman. Comedy. 1 act
In Eight comedies for little theatres
Smart Set 67:79

Wildenbruch, Ernst von, 1845-1909
Harold, a play in five acts. . . Boston.
Heath. 1909. 12°. 145p. Historical
Same in Poet Lore 3:393
King Henry [IV of Germany]. His-
torical. 4 acts
In German classics 11:9
Drama 5:12

Wilkins, John H.
Civilization. A play. In five acts. London. Lacy. n.d. 12°. 64p. (Lacy's acting edition of plays. v. 10 no. 137)
Egyptian. A play in two acts. London.
Lacy. n.d. 12°. 54p. (Lacy's acting
edition of plays. v. 12 no. 174)

Wiley, Sara King, 1871-1909
Coming of Philibert. N.Y. Macmillan.
1907. 12°. Historical. 3 acts
Football game; a comedy in one act.
N.Y. French. c1904. 12°. 15p.

Wilkes, Thomas Egerton, 1812-1854
Cross-bow letter. *See* Wilks, T. E. Miller of Whetstone; or, The cross-bow letter
Fayre lass of Lichfield. *See* Wilks, T. E. Michael Erle, the maniac; or, The fayre lass of Lichfield
Michael Erle, the maniac; or, The fair lass of Lichfield. A romantic original drama in two acts. Boston. Spencer. ₁1856?₁. 12°. 24p.
Raffaelle the reprobate; or, The secret mission and the signet ring. A drama in two acts. London. Lacy. n.d. 12°. 31p. (Lacy's acting edition of plays. v. 10 no. 140)
Secret mission and the signet ring. *See* Wilks, T. E. Raffaelle the reprobate; or, Secret mission and the signet ring
Sudden thoughts. An original farce in one act. . . Boston. Spencer. ₁1857?₁. 12°. 19p.
Woman's love; or, Kate Wynsley, the cottage-girl; an entirely original drama in two acts. London. Lacy. n.d. 12°. 34p. (Lacy's acting edition of plays. v. 4 no. 50)

Willard, John
Cat and the canary; a melodrama in three acts. N.Y. French. c1927. 12°. 103p.

Williams, Eliot Crawshay, 1879-
Amends. 1 act
In Five Grand Guignol plays
Cupboard love. 1 act
In Five Grand Guignol plays
E. & O. E. 1 act
In Five Grand Guignol plays
Nutcracker suite. 1 act
In Five Grand Guignol plays
Rounding the triangle. 1 act
In Five Grand Guignol plays

Williams, Emily Coddington
Pals; a one-act play. N.Y. 1925. 12°. 64p.

Williams, Francis Howard, 1844
Princess Elizabeth; a lyric drama. Phila. Claxton. 1880. 12°. 212p. Historical. 4 acts

Williams, Jesse Lynch, 1871-
"And so they were married"; a comedy of the new woman. N.Y. Scribner. 1914. 242p. *See* Williams, J. L. Why marry? 3 acts
Why marry? N.Y. Scribner. 1918. 12°. 242p. $1.50. Comedy. 3 acts. (Originally published under title "And so they were married")
In Mantle, B. ed. Best plays of 1922-23 (condensed)
Quinn, A. H. ed. Contemporary American plays
Golden Bk 3:789
Why not? A comedy in three acts. Boston. Baker. 1924. 12°. 130p. 75c.

Williams, Oscar, and Brady, Jack
King who scoffed. Tragedy. 1 scene
In Poet Lore 34:139

Williams, Thomas, 1891-
In the hands of men; a romantic tragedy in five acts together with a prologue. London. Macdonald. ₁1925₁. 139p.

Williamson, Harold
Peggy, a tragedy of the tenant farmer. 1 act
In Carolina folk-plays ser 1

Williamson, Harold and Sarg, Tony
Three wishes. Juvenile
In Moses, M. T. ed. Treasury of plays for children

Willis, Nathaniel Parker, 1806-1867
Bianca Visconti; or, The heart overtasked. N.Y. Colman. 1839. 12°. 108p. Tragedy. 5 acts
In Tortesa the usurer (and Bianca Visconti)
Tortesa the usurer. A play. N.Y. Colman. 1839. 12°. 148p. Comedy. 5 acts
Same in Tortesa the usurer, etc
Moses, M. J. ed. Representative plays by American dramatists from 1765 to the present day v 2
Quinn, A. H. ed. Representative plays, 1767-1923

Wilson, Clara, joint author. *See* Buchanan, Fannie R. and Wilson, Clara

Wilson, Harry Leon, 1867-, joint author. *See* Tarkington, Booth and Wilson, Harry Leon

Wilson, Huntington, 1875-
Stultilia; a nightmare and an awakening in four discussions. N.Y. Stokes. c1915. 12°. 180p. (also published under title 'Save America'). World war. 4 pts.

Wilson, Leila Weekes
Like father, like son. Domestic. 1 act
In Drama 13:188

Wilson, Lillian P.
Being a fly. Social. 1 act
In Fruit of toil, and other one-act plays
Empty shrine. Tragedy. 1 act
In Fruit of toil, and other one-act plays
Episode. Character. 1 act
In Fruit of toil, and other one-act plays
Fruit of toil. Tragedy. 1 act
In Fruit of toil, and other one-act plays
Living. Death. 3 pts.
In Fruit of toil, and other one-act plays
This is law. Justice. 1 act
In Fruit of toil, and other one-act plays
Voice on the stair. Tragedy. 1 act
In Fruit of toil, and other one-act plays
Weight of wings. Death. 1 act
In Fruit of toil, and other one-act plays

Wilstach, Paul, 1870-
Thais "the story of a sinner who became a saint and a saint who sinned." A play in four acts. Founded on Anatole France's novel of the same name. Indianapolis. Bobbs-Merrill. ₁c1911₁. 149p.

Winbolt, Frederick
Philip of Macedon. Tragedy. London. Alex. Moring. 1904. 98p. 4 acts

Winser, Charles
Alberto della Scala: an historical tragedy.
London. Rodwell. 1839. 8°. 169p. 5
acts
Winter, Mary
Ruling class. Comedy. 1 act
In Drama 15:150 Ap 25
Winter, William Harris
Queen Elizabeth; an epic drama. Lon-
don. Long. [1913]. 12°. 149p. 5 acts
Wister, Owen, 1860-
Watch your thirst; a dry opera in three
acts. . . N.Y. Macmillan. 1923. 12°.
175p.
Witney, Frederick
All's fair in love? A comedy in three
acts. London. "The Stage" pub.
bureau. 1924. 8°. 144p.
Wolfe, Thomas Clayton
Return of Buck Gavin, the tragedy of a
mountain outlaw. 1 act
In Koch, F. H. ed. Carolina folk-plays
ser 2
Wolff, Oscar M.
Where but in America? Comedy. 1 act
In Knickerbocker, E. Van B. ed.
Twelve plays
Lewis, B. R. ed. Contemporary
one-act plays
Mayorga, M. G. ed. Representative
one-act plays
Smith, M. M. ed. Short plays of
various types
Smart Set 54 no 3:79
Wolff, Pierre
Unhoodwinkable. Comedy. 1 act
In Smart Set 58 no 3:85
Wolfrom, Anna
Albion and Rosamond. Historical. 4
acts
In Albion and Rosamond, and The liv-
ing voice
Danny. Tragedy. 1 act
In Human wisps
Living voice. Problem. 3 acts
In Albion and Rosamond, and The liv-
ing voice
Marriage certificate. Sociological. 1 act
In Human wisps
New race. Symbolic. 1 act
In Human wisps
Old shoes. Character. 1 act
In Human wisps
Ripening wheat. Tragedy. 1 act
In Human wisps
Will-o'-wisp. Social. 1 act
In Human wisps
Wood, Cora Antoinette, 1867-
Buying culture. Comedy. 1 act
In Boston theatre guild plays, 1924
Wood, Ellen Price, 1814-1887
East Lynne; a drama in five acts; adapted
from the famous novel of that name.
Phila. Penn. pub. co. 1894. 12°. 52p.
Woodhouse, Vernon Herslake, 1874-, and
MacClure, Victor
Limpet; a comedy in three acts. Lon-
don. "The Stage" pub. bureau. 1924.
107p.

Woodruff, Robert W.
Death. A discussion. 1 scene
In Smart Set 44 no 4:213
Woods, Mrs. Margaret Louisa, 1856-
Death of Edward III. Historical. 4
scenes
In Return, and other poems
Princess of Hanover. N.Y. Holt. 1903.
12°. 144p. Historical. 5 acts
Wormser, Florine R.
Portrait. Domestic. 1 act
In Smart Set 28 no 2:76
Wright, R.
Five ghosts. Juvenile. 1 act
In Jagendorf, M. A. ed. One-act plays
for young folks
Yates, Elizabeth Hall
Blind. Comedy. 1 act
In Small plays for small casts
Coral beads. Comedy. 1 act
In Small plays for small casts
Laughing child. Parable. 1 act
In Small plays for small casts
Millenium morning. Farce. 1 act
In Small plays for small casts
Rich young lady. Satire. 1 act
In Small plays for small casts
Slave. Tragedy. 1 act
In Small plays for small casts
Spot cash. Comedy. 1 act
In Small plays for small casts
Yeats, William Butler, 1865-
At the Hawk's well. Legendary. 1 scene
In Four plays for dancers
Plays and controversies
Wild swans at Coole. . .
Calvary. Biblical. 1 act
In Four plays for dancers
Plays and controversies
Cat and the moon. Ireland. 1 act
In Dial 77:23
Cathleen ni Houlihan; a play in one act.
London. Bullen. 1902. 34p. Ireland.
(with Lady Gregory)
In Collected works v 4
Hour glass and other plays
Plays for an Irish theatre
Plays in prose and verse
Unicorn from the stars, and other
plays
Countess Cathleen (Countess Kathleen).
Famine. 4 acts
In Collected works v 3
Countess Kathleen, and various le-
gends
Plays and controversies
Poems
Poetical works v 2
Countess Kathleen. *See* Yeats, W. B.
Countess Cathleen
Deirdre. . . London. Bullen. 1907. 8°. 47p.
Tragedy. 1 act
In Collected works v 2
Plays for an Irish theatre
Plays in prose and verse
Poetical works v 2

Yeats, W. B.—*Continued.*
Dreaming of the bones.   Legendary. 1
act
In Four plays for dancers
Plays and controversies
Little R 6 no 9:1
Golden helmet.   N.Y. Quinn. 1908. 12°.
32p.   Legendary. 1 act
Same in Collected works v 4
Green helmet.   Legendary. 1 act
In Green helmet
Plays for an Irish theatre
Plays in prose and verse
Forum 46:301
Hour glass.   Morality. 1 act
In Collected works v 4
Hour-glass and other plays
Plays for an Irish theatre
Plays in prose and verse
Responsibilities and other poems
Unicorn from the stars and other
plays
Golden Bk 3:641
Mask 5:327
No Am 177:445
King's threshold.   Irish romance. 1 act
In Collected works v 2
King's threshold
Plays for an Irish theatre
Plays in prose and verse
Poetical works v 2
Land of heart's desire.   Chicago. Stone.
1894. 43p.   Symbolic. 1 act
Same in Collected works v 3
Land of heart's desire
Plays and controversies
Poems
Poetical works v 2
Clark, B. H. ed.   Representa-
tive one-act plays by Brit-
ish and Irish authors
Leonard, S. A. ed.   Atlantic
book of modern plays
Mosada; a dramatic poem. . . Dublin.
Sealy. 1886. 1 act
Same in Wanderings of Oisin, and
other poems
Dublin Univ R Je '86
On Baile's strand.   Tragedy. 1 scene
In the seven woods
King's threshold (Bullen)
Same in Collected works v 2
Plays for an Irish theatre
Plays in prose and verse
Poetical works v 2
Only jealousy of Emer.   Legendary. 1
act
In Four plays for dancers
Plays and controversies
Player queen.   Comedy. 2 scenes
In Plays in prose and verse
Dial 73:486
Pot of broth.   Comedy. 1 act
In Hour glass and other plays
Plays and prose and verse
Seeker.   Dramatic poem. 2 scenes
In Wanderings of Oisin
Dublin Univ R S '85

Shadowy waters.   N.Y. Dodd. 1901. 8°.
62p.   Symbolic. 1 act
Same in Collected works v 2
Plays for an Irish theatre
Plays in prose and verse
Poetical works v 2
No Am 170:711
Unicorn from the stars.   Tragedy. 3
acts (with Lady Gregory)
In Collected works v 3
Plays in prose and verse
Unicorn from the stars and other
plays
Moses, M. J. ed.   Another treasury
British dramas
Samhain '02
Where there is nothing, being volume
one of plays for an Irish theatre.
N.Y. Macmillan. 1903. 12°. 212p.
Idealism. 5 acts. *Also.* Dodd. 1901

Yehoash
Shunamite.   Biblical. 1 act
In Shay, F. ed.   Twenty-five short
plays, international
Stratford J 4:313 Je '19

Young, Pauline Rogers
Off the road.   Loneliness. 1 act
In Poet Lore 36:300

Young, Rida Johnson, 1864-1926
Captain Kidd, jr; a farcical adventure in
three acts.   N.Y. French. 1920. 12°.
89p. 60c.
Girl and the pennant, a baseball comedy
in three acts.   N.Y. French. 1917.
12°. 95p. 50c.
Lottery man; a comedy in three acts.
N.Y. French. 1924. 12°. 87p. 75c.

Young, Stark, 1881-
Addio.   Romantic. 1 act
In Addio, Madretta and other plays
Three one-act plays
All eyes.   Juvenile. 1 act
In Sweet times and The blue policeman
At the shrine.   Problem. 1 act
In Three one-act plays
Theatre Arts M 3:196
Blessed bird.   Juvenile. 1 act
In Sweet times and The blue policeman
Blue policeman.   Juvenile. 1 act
In Sweet times and The blue policeman
Colonnade.   Theatre Arts. N.Y. 1924.
16°. 121p. $1.   Ethical. 4 acts
Same in Theatre Arts M 8:521
Dead poet.   Poetic. 1 act
In Addio, Madretta and other plays
Flower tree.   Juvenile. 1 act
In Sweet times and The blue policeman
Glove of gold.   Juvenile. 1 act
In Sweet times and The blue policeman
Guenever; a play in five acts.   N.Y.
Grafton. 1906. 12°. 82p.   **Legendary**
King with the iron heart.   Juvenile. 1
act
In Sweet times and The blue policeman
Moses, M. J. ed. Another treasury
of plays for children
Laughing doors.   Juvenile. 1 act
In Sweet times and The blue policeman

Madretta. Tragedy. 1 act
In Addio, Madretta and other plays
Three one-act plays
Magic sea. Juvenile. 1 act
In Sweet times and The blue policeman
Naughty duck. Juvenile. 1 act
In Sweet times and The blue policeman
Prince of the moon. Juvenile. 1 act
In Sweet times and The blue policeman
Queen of Sheba. Insanity. 1 act
In Addio, Madretta and other plays
Theatre Arts M 6:152
Rose windows. Comedy. 1 act
In Theatre Arts M 9:682
Saint; a play in four acts. N.Y. Boni.
1925. 12°. 143p. Psychological
Seven kings and the wind. Philosophi-
cal. 1 act
In Addio, Madretta and other plays
Shepherd's dream. Juvenile. 1 act
In Sweet times and The blue policeman
Star in the trees. Poetic. 1 act
In Addio, Madretta and other plays
Sweet times. Juvenile. 1 act
In Sweet times and The blue policeman
Twilight saint; a play in one act. N.Y.
French. c1925. 12°. 17p. St. Francis
of Assisi
In Addio, Madretta and other plays
Cohen, H. L. ed. One-act plays
by modern authors
Wild manners. Juvenile. 1 act
In Sweet times and The blue policeman
Zamacois, Eduardo, 1866-
Jesters; a simple story in four acts of
verse. . . N.Y. Brentano. 1908. 12°.
175p.
Passing of the magi
In Turrell, C. A. tr. Contemporary
Spanish dramatists
Zangwill, Israel, 1864-1926
Cockpit; romantic drama in three acts.
N.Y. Macmillan. 1921. 12°. 264p. $1.60

Forcing house; or, The cockpit continued:
a tragi-comedy in four acts. N.Y.
Macmillan. 1923. 12°. 310p. $2
Melting pot; a drama in four acts. N.Y.
Macmillan. 1914. 12°. 215p. $1.25.
Immigrants
Merely Mary Ann; a comedy in four acts.
N.Y. French. 1921. 12°. 80p. 75c.
Next religion; a play in three acts. Lon-
don. Heineman. 1912. 12°. 192p.
Religious
Plaster saints; a high comedy in three
movements. N.Y. Macmillan. 1915.
12°. 211p. $1.25
Promise; a play in one act. Printed for
private circulation only. N.Y. De
Vinne press. 1886. 40p.
"Six persons". London. French. c1898.
12°. 14p. Comedy. 1 act
Too much money; a farcical comedy in
three acts. N.Y. Macmillan. 1925.
12°. 102p. $1.50
War god; a tragedy in five acts. Lon-
don. Heinemann. 1911. 12°. 163p.
We moderns; a post-war comedy in three
movements. London. Heinemann.
1926. 8°. 229p.
Zechmeister, Alexander Victor, 1817-1877
One of you must marry. A comic drama
in one act. Adapted. . . London.
French. [18—?]. 12°. 20p.
Zeyer, Julius
Raduz and Mahulena. Slovakian. 4 acts
In Poet Lore 44:1
Zietz, Edward Shrubb
Reformers; a drama of modern life. In
Three acts. N.Y. Bookery. [1912]. 12°.
94p.
Zschokke, Heinrich, 1771-1848
Aboellino, the great bandit. A grand
dramatic romance. In five acts. . .
N.Y. Longworth. 1807. 24°.
Zweig, Stefan, 1881-
Jeremiah; a drama in nine scenes. . . N.Y.
Seltzer. 1922. 12°. 336p. $2.50

TITLE AND SUBJECT INDEX

Title and Subject Index

A. S. S.   Maddox, J. M.
Aaron Boggs, freshman.   Hare, W. B.
Abbé de l'Epée.   Kotzebue, A. F. F. von
Abbu San of old Japan.   Hare, W. B.
Abe Lincoln and little A. D.   Merington, M.
Abelard and Heloise.   Torrence, F. R.
Abigail.   Pinski, D.
Abishag.   Pinski, D.
Aboellino, the great bandit.   Zschokke, H. (Dunlap, W. trs.)
Above the clouds.   Baker, G. M.
Abraham Lincoln.   Bird, G. E. and Starling, M.
Abraham Lincoln.   Drinkwater, J.
Abraham Lincoln.   Mackay, C. D'A.
Abraham Lincoln; or, The rebellion.   Norton, F. P.
Abie's Irish rose.   Nichols, A.
Absolution of Bruce.   Price, G.
Abu Bakar.   Kiesing, M. R.
Acacia cottage.   Orange, B.
Academic saturnalia.   Robertson, C. G.
Accomplice.   Marshall, A.
According to Darwin.   Wilde, P.
Accusation; or, The family of D'Anglade.   Payne, J. H.
Accuser.   Field, M.
Achilles in Scyros.   Bridges, R. S.
Acid drops.   Jennings, G.
Acorn-planter.   London, J.
Across the border.   Dix, B. M.
Acting edition of Ariadne; or, Business first.   Milne, A. A.
Action!   Hudson, H.
Actor.   Sapte, W.
Actor of all work; or, The first and second floor.   Colman, G.
Actress.   Molnár, F. and Teleki, J.
Adam and Eva.   Bolton, G. R. and Middleton, G.
Adam's apple.   Dalton, T.
Adapted for amateurs.   Eckersley's A.
Adder.   Abercrombie, L.
Adding machine.   Rice, E. L.
Addio.   Young, S.
Adelaide of Wulfingen.   Kotzebue, A. F. F. von
Admetus.   *See* Housman, L.   Doom of Admetus
Admirable Bashville, or Constancy unrewarded.   Shaw, G. B.
Admirable Crichton.   Barrie, J. M.
Admiral Guinea.   Henley, W. E. and Stevenson, R. L.
Admiral Peters.   Jacobs, W. W. and Mills, H.
Adopted son.   Hurwitz, B.
Adoration of the soldiers.   Cammaerts, E.
Adored one.   Sellers, I. P.
Adrian and Orrila.   Dimond, W.

Adrianwona.   Watts, W.
Adrienne Lecouvreur.   Oxenford, J.
Adrienne Lecouvreur.   Scribe, A. E. and Legouvé, E.
Advent.   Coxe, A. C.
Advent.   Strindberg, A.
Advent of spring in the south.   Novak, A.
Adventure.   Binns, H. B.
Adventure.   Stevens, T. W.
Adventure of Lady Ursula.   Hawkins, A. H.
Adventurer.   Capus, A.
Adventuress.   Augier, E.
Adverbs.   Kreymborg, A.
Adversary.   Phillips, S.
Advertising April; or, The girl who made the sunshine.   Farjeon, H. and Horsnell, H.
Advertisement.   Hastings, B. M.
Adzuma; or, The Japanese wife.   Arnold, E.
Aethiop; or, The child of the desert.   Dimond, W.
Affair of honour.   Rede, W. L.
Afranius.   Leavitt, J. M.
African love.   Merimée, P.
Africans; or, War, love and duty.   Colman, G.
After a storm comes a calm.   Morton, J. M.
After all.   Monroe, H.
After Euripides' "Electra".   Baring, M.
After glow.   Corbett, E. F.
After many years.   Sapte, W.
After the fire.   Strindberg, A.
After the game.   Barbee, L.
After the honeymoon.   Gyalin, F.
After the requiem.   Draper, J. W.
After the theatre.   Morton, M. and Traill, P.
After twenty-five years.   Firkins, O. W.
Afterglow.   Fuller, H. B.
Aftermath.   Glynn-Ward, H.
Aftermath.   Roberts, L. N.
Afternoon call.   Sapte, W.
Afternoon orator.   Crowell, C. T.
Afternoon walk.   Lavedan, H.
Agamemnon.   Galt, J.
Agatha Steel.   Gibson, W. W.
Agatha's aunt.   Toler, S.
Age of folly.   Lavedan, H.
Aged forty.   Courtney, J.
Aggression won.   Chapin, H. L.
Agitator.   Ramspacher, A.
Aglaë.   Pallen, C. B.
Aglavaine and Selysette.   Maeterlinck, M.
Agnes Bernauer.   Hebbel, F.
Agnes De Vere; or, The wife's revenge.   Buckstone, J. B.
Agonists.   Hewlett, M.

Balboa.   MacNutt, F. A.
Balboa, Vaco Nunez de.   Bird, G. E. and Starling, M.
Balcony.   Heiberg, G.
Ball and chain.   Cowan, S.
Ballet of the nations.   Paget, V.
Balm.   Dennison, M.
Bank account.   Brock, H.
Bank robbery.   Ehrmann, M.
Banker's daughter.   Howard, B.
Bankrupt.   Bjørnson, B.
Banks of the Hudson; or, The congress trooper.   Dibdin, T. J.
Banquet gallery.   *See* Colman, G. Feudal times; or, The banquet-gallery
Banquet of Palacios.   Moore, C. L.
"Bantam, V. C."   Brighouse, H.
Barabbas.   Mitchell, S. W.
Barbara.   Baron, H. S.
Barbara.   Goodman, K. S.
Barbara Frietchie.   Fitch, C.
Barbara grows up.   Hamlen, G. J.
Barbara Roscorla's child.   Symons, A.
Barbara's wedding.   Barrie, J. M.
Barberine.   Musset, A. de
Bargain.   Tupper, W. S.
Bard of Mary Redcliffe.   Lacy, E.
Barrack room.   Bayly, T. H.
Barrier.   Presbrey, E. W.
Barriers.   Sutro, A.
Barringtons' "At Home".   Bangs, J. K.
Baseball
   Young, R. J.   Girl and the pennant
Bashful man.   Moncrieff, W. T.
Bashful Mr. Bobbs.   Hare, W. B.
Basil.   Baillie, J.
Basket.   Jacob, F.
Bath road.   Neilson, F.
Bathroom door.   Jennings, G.
Bathsheba.   Pinski, D.
Battle of Hexham.   Colman, G.
Battle of King's Mountain.   *See* Tayleure, C. W. Horseshoe Robinson; or, The battle of King's Mountain
Battle of Samurai and Christian spirits.   Okamoto, K.
Battle of the millionaires.   *See* Chaloner, J. A.   Robbery under law; or, The battle of the millionaires.
Battle of Tinderley Down.   *See* Munro, C. K.   Storm; or, The battle of Tinderley Down.
Battle of Waterloo.   Amherst, J. H.
"Be calm, Camilla!"   Kummer, C. B.
Beacon.   Baillie, J.
Beacon.   Weeks, K.
Beaded buckle.   Gray, F.
Bear.   *See* Chekhov, A. P.   Boor.
Bear leaders.   Critchett, R. C.
Beaten paths.   Tubbs, A. L.
Beat of the wing.   Curel, F. de
Beatrice Eden.   Mayo, P.
Beau Austin.   Henley, W. E. and Stevenson, R. L.
Beau Brummell.   Fitch, C.
Beau of Bath.   Mackay, C. D'A.
Beau's comedy.   Dix, B. M. and Harper, C. A.
Beautiful despot.   Evreinov, N. N.

Beautiful nun.   Pinski, D.
Beautiful song.   Stevenson, A.
Beautiful story.   Wilde, P.
Beautiful thing.   Leinster, M. and Jenkins, G. B.
Beauty; a Chinese drama.   Macgowan, J. tr.
Beauty and the barge.   Jacobs, W. W. and Parker, L. N.
Beauty and the beast.   Parsons, M. C.
Beauty and the beast.   Planché, J. R.
Beauty and the Jacobin.   Tarkington, B.
Beauty versus the beast.   Morley, M.
Beaver coat.   Hauptmann, G.
Because he loved David so.   Kraft, I.
Becket.   Tennyson, A.
Becky Sharp.   Conway, O.
Bed rock.   Phillpotts, E. and Hastings, M.
Bedroom suite.   Morley, C. D.
Bee.   Saunders, Lilian
Bee and the orange tree; or, The four wishes.   Planché, J. R.
Bee-hive.   Millingen, J. G.
Beethoven deaf.   Lamb, J. L.
Before and behind The curtain.   *See* Taylor, T. and Reade, C. Masks and faces; or, Before and behind the curtain.
Before breakfast.   O'Neill, E. G.
Before dawn.   Hauptmann, G.
Before the fairies came to America.   Griffith, W.
Before the play begins.   Earle, G.
Beggar and the king.   Parkhurst, W.
Beggar maid.   Aber, L. A.
Beggar of Bethnal Green.   Knowles, J. S.
Beggar on horseback.   Kaufman, G. and Connelly, M.
Begone dull care; or, How will it end.   Reynolds, F.
Behind a curtain.   Harrison, C. C.
Behind a Watteau picture.   Rogers, R. E.
Behind the black cloth.   Goodman, K. S.
Behind the lines.   Bagg, H.
Behind the purdah.   Gardener, E.
Behold the man.   Tynan, B.
Being a fly.   Wilson, L. P.
Belgian baby.   Elkins, F. B.
Belgian Christmas eve.   ("Rada" rewritten).   Noyes, A.
Belgium
   Andreev, L.   Sorrows of Belgium
   Leeman, J.   Martyr; a tragedy of Belgium
   Vanzype, G.   Mother Nature
   —— Progress
Believe me, Xantippe.   Ballard, F.
Belinda.   Milne, A. A.
Belisarius; general of the East.   Presland, J.
Bell Haggard (Pt. 2 of Kringleslyke).   Gibson, W. W.
Bella Marks.   *See* Robertson, T. W.   "School"; or, The story of Bella Marks.
Belle of Philadelphia town.   Phelps, P. and Short, M.
Bellman of Mons.   Googins, D. R.
Bells; or, The Polish Jew.   Erckmann, E. and Chatrian, A.
Bells. (adapted from Erckmann-Chatrian).   Lewis, L.

Beloved it is morn. Rowell, A. C.
Belphegor; or, The mountebank. D'En-
nery. A. and Fournier, M. J. J.
Belshazzar. Dumas, W. C.
Ben Bolt. Johnstone, J. B.
Ben of Broken Bow. Ellis, E.
Bending of the bough. Moore, G.
Benefit of the doubt. Pinero, A. W.
Benjamin Franklin. Bird, G. E. and Star-
ling, M.
Benjamin Franklin episode. Mackay, C.
D'A.
Berenice. Masefield, J.
Berlin, July 24-31, 1914-
Barclay, Sir T. Sands of fate
Bicyclers. Bangs, J. K.
Biddie sweeps out. Thanhouser, L. F.
Big drum. Pinero, A. W.
Big idea. Thomas, A. E. and Hamilton,
C.
Big Kate. Nirdlinger, C. F.
Big scene. Schnitzler, A.
Bill of divorcement. Dane, C.
Bill Porter. Sinclair, U. B.
Billeted. Tennyson, J. F.
Billy. Cameron, G.
Billy's little love affair. Esmond, H. V.
Bimbo and Scrumbo and Blinko. Jagen-
dorf, M. A.
Bimbo the pirate. Tarkington, B.
Binks the bogman. Coyne, J. S.
Bird and the fish. Kahn, A.
Bird child. White, Lucy.
Bird in hand. Housman, L.
Bird's Christmas carol. Wiggin, K. D.
Birds of a feather. Dickinson, L. A. H.
Birds of a feather. Gaffney, T.
"Birds" of Aristophanes. Planché, J. R.
Birds of prey. Robertson, T. W.
Birth. Robertson, T. W.
Birth and death of the prince. Block, L.
J.
Birth of America. Andrews, M. P.
Birth of Galahad. Hovey, R.
Birth of God. Heidenstam, V. von
Birth of Montreal. Roddick, A. R.
Birth of Parsival. Trevelyan, R. C.
Birthday. Dibdin, T. J.
Birthday. Kotzebue, A. F. F. von
Bernard Palissy, enameller to His Majesty.
Stevenson, A.
Bernice. Glaspell, S.
Berquin. Crane, E. G.
Bethlehem. Housman, L.
Betrayal. Colum, P.
Betrothal. Boker, G. H.
Betrothal. Maeterlinck, M.
Betrothed. Gibson, W. W.
Betsy Baker! or, Too attentive by half.
Morton, J. M.
Better late than never. Cannon, C. J.
Better son. Goldberg, I.
Better than gold. Baker, G. M.
Better understanding. Thomas, A. E. and
Hamilton, C.
Bettine. Musset, A. de.
Betty, the girl o' my heart. Kavanaugh, K.
Betty's degree. Gerstenberg, A.
Betty's last bet. Ellis, E.
Between fires. Theis, G.

Between the soup and the savoury. Jen-
nings, G.
Between two thorns. Heermans, F.
Between two trains. Pedder, D. C.
Beyond. Gerstenberg, A.
Beyond. Rolt-Wheeler, F. W.
Beyond human might. *See* Bjørnson, B.
Beyond human power II.
Beyond human power II. Bjørnson, B.
Beyond our power. Bjørnson, B.
Beyond the horizon. O'Neill, E. G.
Bianca Capello. Osborn, L.
Bianca Visconti; or, The heart overtasked.
Willis, N. P.
Biblical
Allotte de la Fuije. Lord of death
Benton, R. Burning fiery furnace
—— Call of Samuel
—— Christmas story
—— Coming down the mount
—— Daniel
—— Daughter of Jepthah
—— David and Goliath
—— Esther
—— Golden calf
—— Good Samaritan
—— Joseph and his brethren
—— Judgment of Solomon
—— Manger service
—— Moses in the bulrushes
—— Noah's flood
—— Proving of Abraham
—— Ruth and Boaz
—— Up, up from Egypt to the promised
land
Bloomgarden, S. Shunamite
Burton, R. Rahab
Carpenter, E. Moses
Cayzer, C. W. David and Bathshua
Chaloner, J. A. Saul
—— Saul and David
Coxe, A. C. Saul
Crigler, G. F. Saul of Tarsus
Cromer, J. M. Jeptha's daughter
Crowley, A. Jephthah
Ehrmann, M. David and Bathsheba
—— Jesus
Evans, F. W. David of Bethlehem
—— Mary Magdalen
Frank, F. K. Jael
Greene, H. C. Pontius Pilate
Gregory, O. Jesus
Harnwell, A. J. Sin of Ahab
Heaton, A. G. Heart of David the psal-
mist king.
Hebbel, F. Herod and Mariamne
Hertz, B. R. Son of man
Heyse, P. Mary of Magdala
Heywood, J. C. Herodias
—— Salome
Hinkson, K. T. Annunciation
—— Finding in the temple
—— Flight into Egypt
—— Nativity
—— Presentation in the temple
—— Visitation
Hobbs, M. and Miles, H. David **and**
Jonathan
—— Esther

Byron, Lord
  Ferber, M.   Lord Byron
  Glick, C. and Sobel, B.   Immortal
Cabestaing.   Cawein, M. J.
Cabin call.   Larrimer, W.
Cabin courtship.   Crandall, I. J.
Cabinet.   Dibdin, T. J.
Cabinet minister.   Pinero, A. W.
Caesar and Cleopatra.   Shaw, G. B.
Caesar's apostasy.   *See* Ibsen, H. Emperor
  and Galilean. pt. 1
Caesar's goods.   Goodman, K. S. and Ste-
  vens, T. W.
Caesar's wife.   Maugham, W. S.
Cagliostro.   Doyle, E.
Cain.   Lodge, G. C.
Caius Gracchus   Gregory, O.
Caius Gracchus.   Knowles, J. S.
Cake.   Bynner, W.
Calais to Dover.   Jennings, G. E.
Calaynos.   Boker, G. H.
Caleb Stone's death watch.   Flavin, M. A.
Caliban by the yellow sands.   MacKaye,
  P. W.
Caligula's picnic.   Baring, M.
Call.   Gibson, W. W.
Call from the sea.   Cook, W. A.
Call of Samuel.   Benton, R.
Call of the colors.   Barbee, L.
Call to the youth of America.   Kimball,
  R.
Call of the ninth wave.   Jast, L. S.
Callirhoë.   Field, M.
Calpurnia's dinner-party.   Baring, M.
Calvary.   Osborn, L.
Calvary.   Yeats, W. B.
Calypso.   Kemp, H. H.
Camberley triangle.   Milne, A. A.
Camille.   Dumas, A., *fils*
Camma.   Montanelli, G.
Camp.   Sheridan, R. B.
Camp at the Olympic.   Planché, J. R.
Camp of Wallenstein.   Schiller, F. von
Campbell of Kilmhor.   Ferguson, J. A.
Campden wonder.   Masefield, J.
Canada
  Denison, M. Brothers in arms
  —— From their own place
  —— Marsh hay
  —— Weather breeder
Canary.   Whitehouse, J. H.
Canavans.   Gregory, I. A.
Candida.   Shaw, G. B.
Candle flame.   Howard, K.
Canonicus.   Hamilton, A.
Cantab.   Robertson, T. W.
Canterbury pilgrims.   Mackaye, P. W.
Capital match.   Morton, J. M.
Caponsacchi.   Goodrich, A. F. and Palm-
  er, Rose A.
Cappy Ricks.   Rose, E. E.
Capri
  Warren, A.   Taking of Capri
Caprice.   Musset, A. de
Captain Brassbound's conversion.   Shaw,
  G. B.
Captain Drew on leave.   Davies, H. H.
Captain Firnewald.   Amalie of Saxony
Captain Jack.   Moore, B. J.

Captain Jinks of the Horse Marines.
  Fitch, C.
Captain Joe.   Gerstenberg, A.
Captain Kidd.   Young, R. J.
Captain Kyd; or. The wizard of the sea.
  Jones, J. S.
Captain Letterblair.   Merington, M.
Captain of the gate.   Dix, B. M.
Captain of the host.   Hyde, F. E.
Captain Swift.   Chambers, C. H.
Captain X.   Swears, H.
Captive.   Bourdet, E.
Captive.   Mapes, V.
Captive.   Mitford, M. R.
Captive queen.   Hanning, S. C.
Capture of Wallace.   Price, G.
Car of time.   Tagore, R.
Card party.   Planché, J. R.   High, low,
  Jack and the game; or, The card party
Cardinal's illness.   Droz, G.
Cardor's duel.   Weeks, K.
Carelessness.   Turgenev, I. S.
Carlos among the candles.   Stevens, W.
Carlotta.   Dargan, O. T.
Carlotta.   Roskoten, R.

Carlyle, Thomas
  Firkins, O. W.   Two passengers for
  Chelsea
Carlyon Sahib.   Murray, G.
Carmosine.   Musset, A. de
Carnac Sahib.   Jones, H. A.
Carnival at Naples.   Dimond, W.
Carpenter of Rouen.   Jones, J. S.
Carrier-pigeon.   Phillpotts, E.
Carrying out a theory.   Spencer, W.
Carthaginian.   Taylor, F.
Carthon.   Cook, W. P.
Cartouche, the French robber.   D'Ennery,
  A. and Dugue, F.
Casanova.   Azertis, L. de
Case of Becky.   Locke, E.
Case of Johnny Walker.   Vernon, H. M.
Case of Lady Camber.   Vachell, H. A.
Case of Mrs. Kantsey Know.   Jarrell, M.
  W.
Case of rebellions Susan.   Jones, H. A.
Case of Teresa.   John, G.
Cash, $2,000.   Chatterton, N. G.
Casino gardens.   Nicholson, K.
Cassilis engagement.   Hankin, St. J.
Castaway.   Jacobs, W. W. and Sargent,
  H. C.
Caste.   Robertson, T. W.
Castilian.   Talfourd, T. N.
Castle Adamant.   *See* Gilbert, W. S. Prin-
  cess Ida; or, Castle Adamant.
Castle of Andalusia.   O'Keeffe, J.
Castle of Paluzzi; or, The extorted oath.
  Raymond, R. J.
Caswallon; or, The Briton chief.   Walker,
  C. E.
Casualties.   Flavin, M. A.
Cat.   Cowan, S.
Cat and the canary.   Willard, J.
Cat and the cherub.   Fernald, C. B.
Cat and the moon.   Yeats, W. B.
Cat and the mouse.   Stevenson, A.
Cat-bird.   Hughes, R.
Cat-boat.   Mackaye, P. W.

Chili
Panella, A.   Red slippers
Chimalman.   Taft, G. E.
China
Hazelton, G. C. and Benrimo; J. N.
  Yellow jacket
Justema, W.,   Chi-Fu
Knevels, G.   Dragon's glory
Loti, P.   Daughter of heaven
Macgowan, J. tr.   Beauty
Sacrifice of the soul of Ho Man-San.
  Chinese   3 scenes.
  In Stanton, W.   Chinese drama
    China Review 17:152
China pig.   Emig, E.
Chinese drama
Borrowed boots.   Translated from Pi-
  pa-ke.   Farce, 1 act
  In China Review 2:325
Chinese farce [A-lan's pig]. 1 act
  In China Review 1:26
Compared tunic by Chang Kwohpin.
  Chinese.   4 acts
  In Chinese Repertory 18:116
Flowery ball.   Chinese.   1 act
  In Giles, H. A. History of Chinese lit-
    erature.   p 264
Golden leafed chrysanthemum.   Chinese
  5 acts.
  In Stanton, W.   Chinese drama of
    Hongkong
    China Review 22:651, 697
Han Koong Tsew; or, The sorrows of
  Han.   Tragedy.   4 acts
  In World's great classics.   Oriental
    literature   4:279
Willow lute.   Chinese.   5 acts
  In Stanton, W.   Chinese drama of
    Hongkong
    Chinese Review 17:311
Chinese lantern.   Housman, L.
Chinese lily.   Jacobi, P.
Chinese love.   Kummer, C. B.
Chintamini.   Ghose, G. C.
Chita.   Tagore, R.
Chocolate cake and black sand.   Cauld-
  well, S. M.
Chocorua.   Coverly, R. B.
Choice.   Monkhouse, A. B.
Choice.   Sutro, A.
Choice of a tutor.   Vizin, D. von
Choice of Gianneta.   Applegate, A.
Choir rehearsal.   Kummer, C. B.
Choosing a career.   Caillevet, G. A. de.
Chorus lady.   Forbes, J.
Chosen people.   Chirikov, E.
Christmas
Austin, M. H.   Man that didn't believe
  in Christmas
Bangs, J. K   Return of Christmas.
Bell, J. K.   Come Michaelmas
Blanchard, E. L. Harlequin Hudibras! or,
  Old dame Durden and the merry days
  of the merry monarch
Cheltnam, C. S.   Christmas eve in a
  watchhouse
Clements, C. E.   Troubadour's dream
Cleugh, D.   Violet under the snow
Coleridge, S. T.   Zapolya

Converse, F.   Blessed birthday
Creagh-Henry, M.   Star
Fawcett, E.   When the clock struck
  twelve
Goodman, K. S.   Dust of the road
—— Ephraim and the winged bear
Greene, C. M.   Star of Bethlehem
—— Through Christmas bells
Greene, K. C.   First Christmas eve
Hare, W. B. Anita's secret; or Christmas
  in the steerage
—— Her Christmas hat
—— Wishing man
Howells, W. D.   Night before Christmas
Jackson, M. B. S.   Meg, the match girl
Jones, G. L.   What makes Christmas
  Christmas
Kemp, H. H.   Don Juan's Christmas
  eve
Laffan, B. J.   One Christmas eve
Lord, D. A.   Peageant of peace
—— Mistress Castlemaine's Christmas
  dinner
Lord, K.   Greatest gift
—— Yule-tide rose-miracle play
Loving, P.   Drift flake
McChesney, D. G.   Outside the gate
McFadden, E. A.   Why the chimes rang
Mackay, C. D'A.   Gift of time.   Chris-
  tmas masque
—— Masque of Christmas
—— On Christmas eve
MacKaye, P.   Evergreen tree a masque
Macmillan, M.   Shadowed star
Mathews, F. A.   Lady June's highway-
  man
Mixon, A.   Peace on earth
Nichols, A.   Shepherd's pipe
Noyes, A.   Belgian Christmas eve
O'Brien, E. J. N.   At the flowing of the
  tide
Olcott, V.   Night before Christmas
—— Puritan Christmas
Park, J. E.   Dwarf's spell
Parsons, M. C.   St. Nicholas
Paull, H. M. and Housman, L.   Un-
  known star
Pertwee, R.   Loveliest thing
Snyder, M. I.   Nativity; a Christmas
  pageant
Stevens, T. W.   Duquesne Christmas
  mystery
Wells, C.   Day before Christmas
—— Is Santa Claus a friend?
—— Night-before-Christmas dream
—— Substitute for Santa Claus
Wilde, P.   Beautiful story
—— Enchanted Christmas tree
Christmas carol; or, The miser's Yuletide
  dream.   Hare, W. B.
Christmas chime.   Cameron, M.
Christmas day.   Payne, F. U.
Christmas elves.   Baldwin, S.
Christmas eve.   Baldwin, S.
Christmas eve in a watchhouse.   Chelt-
  nam, C. S.
Christmas eve with Charles Dickens.
  Frank, W. M.
Christmas gifts for all nations.   Wells, C.
Christmas guest.   Kingsbury, S.

Colomon. Smith, Edward P. and Nichols, W. B.
Colonial Virginia. Wagstaff, B. S.
Colonnade. Young, S.
Color blind. Applegarth, M. T.
Columbine. Clements, C. C.
Columbine in business. Field, R. L.
Columbus. Raymond, G. L.
Columbus. Rees, A. D.
Columbus; or, A hero of the new world. Preston, D. S.
Columbus; or, A world discovered. Morton, T.
Columbus, Christopher. Bird, G. E. and Starling, M.
Columbus, Christopher. *See also* Christopher Columbus
  Lord, A. E. Visions quest
  Moore, F. F. Discoverer
Columbus day. Payne, F. U.
Columbus story. Wagstaff, B. S.
Columbus the discover. See Raymond, G. L. Columbus
Combat. Duhamel, G.
Come Michaelmas. Bell, J. K.
Come out of the kitchin. Thomas, A. E.
Come what may France, A.
Comedie royall. Sutherland, E. G.
Comedies of words. Schnitzler, A.
Comedietta. Smith, M.
Comedy and tragedy. Gilbert, W. S.
Comedy of death. Harris, G. E.
Comedy of good and evil. Hughes, R. A. W.
Comedy of love. *See* Ibsen, H. Love's comedy
Comedy of marriage. Maupassant, G. de
Comedy royal. Phillpotts, E.
Comet. Doyle, E.
Comfortable lodgings; or, Paris in 1750. Peake, R. B.
Comfortable service. Bayly, T. N.
Comforter. Housman, L.
Comforts. Sargent, H. C.
Comical countess. Brough, W.
Coming down the Mount. Benton, R.
Coming of Fair Anne. Price, G.
Coming of peace. Hauptmann, G.
Coming of Gabrielle. Moore, G.
Coming of Philibert. Drummond, S. K. W.
Coming of Philibert. Wiley, S. K.
Commandant pro tem. Moreton, A. H.
Commemoration masque. Hauptmann, G.
Committee on matrimony. Cameron, M.
Common clay. Kinkead, C.
Common ground. Whiting, E. C.
Commune
  Sutherland, E. At the barricade.
Commuters. Forbes, J.
Company will recite. Titheradge, D.
Compared tunic. Cháng Kwohpin
Compromise of the king of the Golden isles. Dunsany, E.
Compromising Martha. Bell, J. K.
Comrades. Holt, F. T.
Comrades. Strindberg, A.
Comrades courageous. Barbee, L.
Concert. Bahr, H.
Conchita. Pollock, J.

Confederates. Harwood, H. M.
Confession. Nicholson, K.
Confession. Reid, J. H.
Confessional. Wilde, P.
Confidence game. Whiting, E. G.
Conflagration. Hauptmann, G.
Conflagration of Moscow. *See* Amherst, J. H. Napoleon Bonaparte's invasion of Russia; or, The conflagration of Moscow
Conflict. McCauley, C. V.
Conflict. Malleson, M.
Congratulations. Jackson, M. B. S.
Conquering and to conquer. Hobart, M. E.
Conquering hero. Monkhouse, A. N.
Conquest. Pain, A.
Conquest, or a piece of jade. Stopes, M. C. C.
Conquest of Taranto; or, St. Clara's eve. Dimond, W.
Conscript fathers. Symon, J. D.
Conspiracy. *See* Bulwer-Lytton, E. G. Richelieu; or, The conspiracy
Conspirators. Flattery, M. D.
Conspirators. Mérimeé, P.
Constancy unrewarded. *See* Shaw, G. B. Admirable Bashville, or Constancy unrewarded
Constant lover. Hankin, St. J.
Constant nymph. Kennedy, M. and Dean, B.
Constant wife. Maugham, W. S.
Constantine Palelogus. Baillie, J.
Constantine the great. Howard, H. N.
Contaminated family. Tolstoi, L. N.
Contents unknown. Barbee, L.
Contested election. Taylor, T.
Contrary Mary. Ellis, E.
Contrast. Tyler, R.
Conversation on the highway. Turgenev, I. S.
Conversion of Mrs. Slacker. Payne, F. U.
Converted suffragist. Kavanaugh, K.
Converts. Brighouse, H.
Convict on the hearth. Fenn, F.
Convolvulus. Norton, A.
Conway-chauffeur. Sapte, W.
Cooks and cardinals. Lindau, N. C.
Cool as a cucumber. Jerrold, W. B.
Coom-na-goppel. Carleton, J. L.
Coontown millionaire. Hare, W. B.
Cophethua. Drinkwater, J.
Copperhead. Thomas, A.
Coral beads. Yates, E. H.
Cordia. Smith, H. S.
Corinna; or, The strenuous life. John, G.
Cormorant fisher. Noguchi, Y.
Corner lot chorus. Furniss, G. L.
Coronation. Shaler, N. S.
Cornwall
  Symon, A. Harvesters
Corp'. Moon, L.
Corporal's wedding! or, A kiss from the bride. Morton, J. M.
Correct thing. Sutro, A.
Corsican lieutenant. Housum, R.
Corsicans. Kotzebue, A. F. F. von
Cosher! Mosley, M.
Cost. Thurston, E. T.

Cost of a hat. Crocker, B.

Cost of a crown. Binson, R. H.

Costa's daughter. Bercovici, K.

Council of Trent. *See* Moncrieff, W. T. Jewess; or, The council of Trent

Counsel retained. Mackay, C. D'A.

Count Benyowsky; or, The conspiracy of Kamschatka. Kotzebue, A. F. F. von

Count Julian. Calvert, G. H.

Count of Burgundy. Kotzebue, A. F. F. von

Counter-charm. Duffy, B.

Counterfeit presentment. Howells, W. D.

Countess Cathleen. Yeats, W. B.

Countess for an hour. *See* Coyne, J. S. Pas de fascination; or, Catching a governor

Countess Julia. Strindberg, A.

Countess Kathleen. *See* Yeats, W. B. Countess Cathleen

Countess Mizzi; or, The family reunion. Schnitzler, A.

Country boy. Selwyn, E.

Country boy scout. Hare, W. B.

Country cousin. Amalie of Saxony

Country cousin. Tarkington, B. and Street, J.

Country dressmaker. Fitzmaurice, G.

Country fair. Barnard, C.

Country inn. Baillie, J.

Country justice. Denison, T. S.

Country woman. Turgenev, I. S.

County chairman. Ade, G.

County fair. Barnard, C. and Burgess, N.

Courier of Lyons; or, The attack upon the mail. Moreau, P. *et al*

Course in piracy. Russell, P.

Court and city. Peake, R. B.

Court and the stage. Taylor, T.

Court singer. Wedekind, F.

Courtin' Christina. Bell, J. J.

Courting of Margaret Ruth. Ratcliffe, D. U.

Courtin' of Sally Ann. Moon, L.

Courting the widow Malone. Powell-Anderson, C.

Courtship (Miles Standish). Garnett, L. A.

Courtship of Miles Standish. Parsons, M. C.

Courtship of Miles Standish. Presbrey, E. W.

Courtship with variations. Bunner, H. C.

Cousin Kate. Davies, H. H.

Covenanters. Dibdin, T. J.

Covered fire. Lambe, J. L.

A couvert. White, C.

Cowards. Lovett, R. M.

Cowboy and the lady. Fitch, C.

Cow-herd and the weaving maid. Shen Hung

Crabbed age and youth. Oldenshaw, L.

Crabbed youth and age. Robinson, L.

Crack in the bell. Theis, G.

Cradle song. Martínez Sierra, G.

Craft of the tortoise. Tassin, A. de V.

Craig's wife. Kelly, G.

Crainquebille. France, A.

Cramond brig. Murray, W. H. W.

Crawford. Merington, M.

Cranford at home. Oldenchaw, L.

Crazy Jane. Somerset, C. A.

Creation. Oppenheim, J.

Creatures of impulse. Gilbert, W. S.

Creditor. *See* Strindberg, A. Creditors

Creditors. Strindberg, A.

Creole; or Love's fetters. Brooks, S.

Crepuscule. Louys, P.

Cricket match. Robertson, C. G.

Crier by night. Bottomley, G.

Crime

Abbott, A. Mr. Enright entertains

Aidé, H. Gleam in the darkness

Brieux, E. Red robe

Brown, A. Web

Cheltnam, C. S. Shadow of a crime

Davies, R. H. Orator of Zepata City

Enander, H. L. On the trail

Frost, R. Way out

Galsworthy, J. Show

Jacobs, W. W. and Sargent, H. C. In the library

Pillot, E. Two crooks and a lady

Thomas, A. Nemesis

Crime. Seiler, C.

Criminals. Geijerstam, G.

Criminals. Middleton, G.

Crimson cocoanut. Beith, I. H.

Crimson Lake. Brown, A.

Crinoline. Brough, R. B.

Cripples. Pinski, D.

Cristilinda. Hoffe, M.

Cristina's journey home. Hofmannsthal, H. von

Critic; or, A tragedy rehearsal. Sheridan, R. B.

Critics. Ervine, St. J. G.

Croesus, king of Lydia. Richards, A. B.

Cromwell. Duckworth, W.

Cromwell. Hamilton, A.

Cromwell. Hugo, V.

Cromwell, Oliver

De Lessehue, L. Two Cromwells

Cromwell: mall o' monks. Calderon, G.

Crooked man and his crooked wife. Andrews, K. L.

Crooks. Kussy, N.

Cross-bow letter. Wilkes, T. E.

Cross of sorrow. Akerman, W.

Cross-roads. Robinson, S. L.

Cross-roads. Sturgis, J.

Crossings. De La Mare, W. J.

Crow and the fox. Stevenson, A.

Crowding the season. Hardy, E. T.

Crown for a song. Lomas, B. A.

Crowning. Scott, W. W.

Crows. *See* Becque, H. Vultures

Crows. Sandiford, B. P.

Crowsnest. Manley, W. F.

Crusade of the children. Morris, E. W.

Crusaders. Jones, H. A.

Crusades

Hemans, F. De Chatillon

Cuchulainn. Gray, T.

Cuckoo. Goldring, D.

Cul-de-sac. Dane, E.

Cult of content. Leslie, N.

Cunigunda's vow. Mitford, M. R.

Cup. Tennyson, A.
Cup of youth. Mitchell, S. W.
Cupboard love. Williams, E. C.
Cupid and commonsense. Bennett, A.
Cupid and Psyche. Chapman, J. J.
Cupid in Claphan. Baker, E.
Cupid mixes things. Henderson, S.
Cure. Titheradge, D.
Cure for jealousy. Hobart, G. V.
Cure for love. See Paulding, J. K. and W.
  I. Madmen all; or, Cure for love
Cure for the heartache. Morton, T.
Cure of souls. Fuller, H. B.
Cure of souls. Housman, L.
Curious case. Maddox, J. M.
Curious herbal. Armfield, A. C.
Curse of the country. Moylan, T. K.
Curtain. Flanagan, H. F.
Curtains. Head, C. and Gavin, M.
Custodian. Eyre, A.
Cycle. Bynner, W.
Cycle of spring. Tagore, R.
Cymon and Iphigenia. Planché, J. R.
Cynthia, a suffragette. Newmarch, E.
Cyrano de Bergerac. Rostand, E.
'D' Company. Malleson, M.
Daddy. Sapte, W.
Daddy Long-legs. Webster, J.
Daddy's gone-a-hunting. Akins, Z.
Dagobert king of the Franks. Babo, J. N.
Daily bread. Reely, M. K.
Daimio's head. Goodman, K. S. and
  Stevens, T. W.
Daimyo. See Japanese plays
Daisy Mayme. Kelly, G. E.
Daisy Miller. James, H.
Dakota widow. Furness, G. L.
Damaged goods. Brieux, E.
Damages for breach. Ridge, W. P.
Damascus
  Van Dyke, H. House of Rimmon
Dame Greel o' Portland town. Mackay,
  C. D'A.
Dame Julian's window. Lyttelton, E. S.
Dame school holiday. Edgeworth, M.
Damer's gold. Gregory, I. A.
Damnation. Wedekind, F.
Dance diurnal. Carman, B. and King, M.
  P.
Dance of death. Strindberg, A.
Dance of life. Ould, H.
Dance of the seven deadly sins. Symons,
  A.
Dancing dolls. Goodman, K. S.
Dancing girl. Jones, H. A.
Dancing mothers. Selwyn, E. and Gould-
  ing, E.
Dandy Dick. Pinero, A. W.
Dandy dolls. Fitzmaurice, G.
Danger. Hughes, R. A. W.
Danger signal. Denison, T. S.
Dangers of peace. Rawson, G. S.
Daniel. Benton, R.
Daniel Boone. Stevenson, A.
Daniel Boone, patriot. Mackay, C. D'A.
Dan'l Druce. Gilbert, W. S.
Daniel Rochat. Sardou, V.
Daniela. See Guimerá, A. La pecadora
Danites in the Sierras. Miller, J.

Danny. Wolfram, A.
Dante. Raymond, G. L.
Dante. Sardou, V. and Moreau, E.
Dante
  Kerley, R. Wedding guest.
  Kirker, K. Lady compassionate
  Klauber, A. J. Exile
Danton. Rolland, R.
Daphne. Merrington, M.
Darby's return. Dunlap, W.
D'Arcy of the guards. Shipman, L. E.
Dark chapter. Rath, E. J.
Dark doings in the cupboard. Coyne, J. S.
Dark hours. Marquis, D.
Dark lady of the sonnets. Shaw, G. B.
Dark of the dawn. Dix, B. M.
Daughter. Bayly, T. H.
Daughter. See Kotzebue, A. F. F. von
  Sighs; or, The daughter
Daughter. Knowles, J. S.
Daughter of heaven. Loti, P. and
  Gautier, J.
Daughter of Jephthah. Benton, R.
Daughter of Jorio. Annunzio, G. d'
Daughter of the desert. Ulrich, C.
Daughters of dawn. Carman, B. and
  King, M. P.
Daughters of fate. Tefft, N. A.
Daughters of men. Klein, C.
Daughter's trial. See Taylor, T. Henry
  Dunbar; or, A daughter's trial
Dave. Gregory, I. A.
David. Lawrence, D. H.
David. Rice, C. Y.
David. Lawrence, D. H.
David and Bathsheba. Ehrmann, M.
David and Bathshua. Cayzer, C. W:
David and Goliath. Benton, R.
David and Jonathan. Hobbs, M. and
  Miles, H.
David Ballard. McEvoy, C.
David Garrick. Robertson, T. W.
David of Bethlehem. Evans, F. W.
Dawn. Verhaeren, E.
Dawn. Wellman, R.
Dawn. Wilde, P.
Dawn of liberty. Ulrich, C. K.
Dawn of music. Denison, E. H.
Day after the fair. Somerset, C. A.
Day at Boulogne See Peake, R. B.
  Master's rival; or, A day at Boulogne
Day before Christmas. Wells, C.
Day before commencement. Neilson, F.
Day before Thanksgiving. Olcott, V.
Day dream in Japan. Burton, P.
Day of days. Block, L. J.
Day of dupes. Manners, J. H.
Day Will Shakespeare went to Kenilworth.
  Lord, K.
Day's fishing. Morton, J. M.
Days of Magnificat. Maquarie, A.
Days of Thanksgiving. Larrimer, M.
Deacon. Jones, H. A.
Deacon Brodie. Henley, W. E. and
  Stevenson, R. L.
Deacon Dubbs. Hare, W. B.
Deacon's hat. Marks, J. A.
Dead alive; or The double funeral.
  O'Keeffe, J.

Devil and Doctor Faustus.   Rede, W. L.
Devil looks after his own.   *See* Nesbitt,
C. M. Demshur man; or, The devil
looks after his own
Devil's bridge.   Arnold, S. J.
Devil's disciple.   Shaw, G. B
Devil's field.   Nichols, A.
Devil's gold.   Curry, S. J.
Devonshire cream.   Phillpotts, E.
Dhord Fhiam.   *See* Craig, A. T. Book of
the Irish historic pageant
Diabolical circle.   Bornstead, B.
Diamond cut diamond.   Murray, W. H.
Diamond chip.   Kavanaugh, K.
Diana of Dobson's.   Hamilton, C. M.
Dick and the Marchioness.   Fitzgerald,
S. J. A.
Dickens Charles
Frank, M. M.   Christmas eve with
Charles Dickens
Dickey bird.   Ford, H. and O'Higgins, H.
J.
Dictator.   Davis, R. H.
Did it really happen?   Brand, A.
Did you ever send your wife to Brooklyn?
Coyne, J. S.
Dierdre.   *See also* Deirdre
Dierdre.   Field, M.
Dierdri.   Hanning, S. C.
Difference.   Titheradge, D.
Difficult border.   Halman, D. F.
Diff'rent.   O'Neill, E. G.
Dilettanti.   Peacock, T. L.
Dinah.   Whiffen, E. T.
Dinner.   Molnár, F.
Dinner for six.   *See* Morton, J. M.   Who
stole the pocket book? or, A dinner for
six
Dinah, queen of the Berbers.   McCauley,
C. V.
Dinner for nothing.   Cheltnam, C. S.
Dinner's served!   Hill, F. T.
Diogenes and his lantern or, A hue and
cry after honesty.   Taylor, T.
Diplomacy.   Pinski, D.
Diplomates.   Sardou, V.
Discoverer.   Moore, F. F.
Discovery.   Ould, H.
Discovery.   Sheridan, F. C.
Discovery of America.   Coakley, T. F.
Discreet princess; or, The three glass dis-
taffs.   Planché, J. R.
Disenchanted.   Izzet-Mehyh.
Disengaged.   James, H.
Disowned; or, The prodigals.   Smith, R.
P.
Dispensation.   Greene, C. M.
Disraeli.   Parker, L. H.
Distinguished villa.   O'Brien, K.
Distress.   Lavedan, H.
District visitor.   Middleton, R. B.
Ditch.   Andrews, M. R. S.
Divine Aretino.   South, R.
Divine gift.   Jones, H. A.
Divine surrender.   Wallace, W.
Divorce.   Daly, A.
Divorçons.   Sardou, V. and Najac, É. de.
Dobromila Rettig.   Jirásek, A.
Doctor Auntie.   Brown, A.

Doctor Dilworth.   Oxenford, J.
Dr. Harmer's holidays.   Pinero, A. W.
Doctor Johnson, Newton, A. E.
Dr. Jonathan.   Churchill, W.
Doctor Knock.   Romains, J.
Doctor's dilemma.   Shaw, G. B.
"Dod gast ye both".   Heffner, H.
Dog.   Crocker, B.
Dog.   Halman, D. F.
Dog's life.   Titheradge, D.
Dollar.   Pinski, D.
Dollars and chickens.   Ballard, E.
Dollars and sense; or, The heedless ones.
Daly, A.
Dollars and sense.   Kraemer, O. J. and
Humphreys, L. W.
Dolls and toy-ballons.   Jenkins, Y., Mc-
Graw, D. and Darrow, R. P.
Doll's house.   Ibsen, H.
Dolly Madison
Nirdlinger, C. F.   First lady of the land
Dolly Madison's afternoon tea.   Denison,
E. H.
Dolly reforming herself.   Jones, H. A.
Dolly's little bells.   Jones, H. A.
Dolores.   Cannon, C. J.
Dolores of the Sierra.   Haslett, H. H.
Domestic bliss.   Titheradge, D.
Domestic dilemma.   Irwin, G. L.
Domestic dilemma.   Jackson, M. B. S.
Domestic economy.   Lemon, M.
Domestic picture.   Ostrovskii, A. N.
Dominant sex.   Meyer, A. N.
Don.   Besier, R.
Don Carlos, infant of Spain.   Schiller, F.
von
Don Giovanni; or, a spectre on horseback.
Dibdin, T. J.
Don Juan.   Flecker, J. E.
Don Juan duped.   Boyesen, A.
Don Juan in a garden.   Kemp, H. H.
Don Juan's Christmas eve.   Kemp, H. H.
Don Juan's failure.   Baring, M.
Don Luca sperante.   Flamma, A.
Don Quixote.   Dearmer, M. W.
Don Quixote.   Stevenson, A.
Donna Diana.   Marston, J. W.
Done on both sides.   Morton, J. M.
Donna Marina.   Cayzer, C. W.
Don't tell Timothy.   Arundel, M.
Don't judge by appearances.   Morton, J.
M.
Doom of Admetus.   Housman, L.
Doom of Barostein.   *See* Lemon, M. An-
cestress! or, The doom of Barostein
Door.   Stokes, C. W.
Door is closed.   Supersac, L.
Door must be either open or shut.   Mus-
set, A. de
Doormats.   Davies, H. H.
Dora Dimple's beau.   Norton, F. P.
Dora, her flag.   Olcott, V.
Doria.   Powell, T.
Dorinda dares.   Morris, A.
Doris and the dinosaur.   Booth, N.
Dormer windows.   Raphael, A.
Dormitory girls.   Paulton, E. A.
Dorothy's fortune.   *See* Jerrold, D. W. St.
Cupid, or, Dorothy's fortune

Dust in the eyes. *See* Labiche, E. M. and Martin, E. Bluffers, or, Dust in the eyes
Dust of the road. Goodman, K. S.
Dutch Pilgrims
Harnwell, A. and Meeker, I. Sojourners.
Duty. O'Brien, S.
Duty. Sardou, V.
Dwarf's spell. Park, J. E.
Dybbuk. Rappoport, S.
Dylan, son of the wave. Howard de Walden, T. E. E.
Dying for love. Morton, J. M.
Dying pangs. Schnitzler, A.
Dying wife. Taylor, L.
Dynasts. Hardy, T.
Dyspeptic ogre. Wilde, P.
E. and O. E. Williams, E. C.
Each in his own place. Stevenson, A.
Each in his own way. Pirandello, L.
Eagle bound. Roberts, C. V. H.
Eaglet. *See* Rostand, E. L'aiglon
Earl of Glowrie. White, J.
Earl of Pawtucket. Thomas, A.
Early closing. Ridge, W. P.
Early Ohios. Reely, M. K.
Earning a living. McCracken, J. L. H.
Earth. Fagan, J. B.
Earth and new earth. Rice, C. Y.
Earth deities. Carman, B. and King, M. P.
Earth spirit. Wedekind, F.
Easiest way. Walter, E.
East Indian. Kotzebue, A. F. F. von
East is west. Shipman, S. and Hymer, J. B.
East Lynne. Wood, E. P.
East of Eden. Morley, C. D.
East of Suez. Maugham, W. S.
East wind's revenge. Janney, S.
Easter. Strindberg, A.
Easter
Clinton, I. F. Resurrection of Peter
Converse, F. Thy kingdom come
Olcott, V. Flower of the ages
Planché, J. B. New Haymarket spring morning
Easter eggs. Henderson, S.
Easter lily. Parsons, M. C.
Easter recess. Morgan, S. O.
Easy come, easy go. Davis, O.
Easy Dawson. Kidder, E. E.
Easy mark. Larric, J.
Easy terms. Kavanaugh, K.
Easy virtue. Coward, N. P.
Eccentric philosopher. Chapin, H. L.
Echo. Ruschke, E. W.
Echo. Shipley, J. T.
Echo and Narcissus. Rogers, M. D.
Eclogue of the downs. Davidson, J. Anglo-Saxon R 5:196
Edendale. Cheltnam, C. S.
Edge o' dark. John, G.
Edge of the wood. Roof, K. M.
Edged tools. Matthews, J. B.
Editor. Bjørnson, B.
Editor-in chief. Ulrich, C.
Educatin' Mary. Fischer, N. L.
Education. Morton, T.
Education of Mr. Surrage. Monkhouse, A. N.

Edward. Eckersley, A.
Edward I. Waight, J. F.
Edwin the fair. Taylor, H.
Efficiency. Brooker, B.
Efficiency. Davis, R. H. and Sheehan, P. P.
Eglantina. Freeman, M. W.
Egmont. Goethe, J. W.
Egotist and pseudo-critic. Kotzebue, A. F. F. von
Egyptian. Wilkins, J. F.
Egypt's eyes. Wilcox, C. G.
Eight hours at the sea-side. Morton, J. M.
Eight hundred rubles. Neihardt, J. G.
Eight o'clock. Berkeley, R.
Eighth of January. Smith, R. P.
Eighth wonder. Titheradge, D.
Eights. Robertson, C. G.
El Cid Campeador. Lee, H. W.
El Cristo. Larkin, M.
El Dorado. Peacey, H.
El Hyder. Barrymore, W.
Elaine. Chapin, H.
Elaine. Weinberger, M.
Eldest. Ferber, E.
Eldest son. Galsworthy, J.
Eldorado. Gilbert, B.
El Dorado. Torrence, F. R.
Election. Baillie, J.
Election of the roulette. Mowery, W. B.
Electra. Hofmannsthal, H. von
Electra. Pérez-Galdós, B.
Electricity. Gillette, W. H.
Elegant Edward. Jennings, G. E.
Elevator. Howells, W. D.
Elf child. Mackay, C. D'A.
Elga. Hauptmann, G.
Eligible Mr. Bangs. Housum, R.
Eliza come to stay. Esmond, H. V.
Elizabeth Cooper. Moore, G.
Elizabeth of England. Shaler, N. S.
Ella's apology. Sutro, A.
Ellis Island
Fagin, M. Room 226
Elopement. Brunner, E. H.
Elopement. Jones, H. A.
Elopements in high life. Sulivan, R.
Elopements while you wait. Stevens, C. D.
Eloquent Dempsy. Boyle, W.
Embarrassed butler. Bell, J. K.
Embers. Middleton, G.
Embryo. Wilde, P.
Emergency case. Flavin, M. A.
Emigrant's daughter. Raymond, R. J.
Emilia Viviani. Wiegand, C. von
Emily. Mitford, M. R.
Empedocles on Etna. Arnold, M.
Emperor and Galilean. Ibsen, H.
Emperor Jones. O'Neill, E.
Emperor Julian. *See* Ibsen, H. Emperor and Galilean. Pt. 2
Emperor's test. Stevenson, A.
Empire of Talinis. Bartlett, A. E.
Empty house. Barbee, L.
Empty shrine. Wilson, L. P.
Empty stockings. Applegarth, M. T.
Enchanted Christmas tree. Wilde, P.

Facing death. Strindberg, A.
Facing reality. Pascal, F.
Failures. Forrest, B.
Failures. Lenormand, H. R.
Failures. Middleton, G.
Fair one with the golden locks. Planché,
  J. R.
Fair Rosamond. Mitford, M. R.
Fair Rosamund. Field, M.
Fairies' plea (adapted from Thomas
  Hood's Plea of the midsummer fairies)
  Frank, M. M.
Fairy. Feuillet, O.
Fairy bride. O'Conor, N. J.
Fairy
  Wilcox, C. G.   Pan pipes
  —— Princess in the fairy tale
Fairy and the cat. Stevenson, A.
Fairy prince. Phelps, S. K.
Fairyland. Hooker, B.
Fairy's dilemma. Gilbert, W. S.
Fairy's father. Cheltnam, C. S.
Faith. Candler, M.
Faith. Evans, M.
Faith and fireside. Schönherr, K.
Faith cure
  Gilbert, H.   Good Sainte Anne
  Hagedorn, H.   Pool of Bethesda
  Moody, W. V.   Faith healer
Faith healer. Moody, W. V.
Faith of the fathers. Berman, H.
Faithful. Masefield, J.
Faithless favorite. Sauter, E.
Falcon. Proctor, B. W.
Falcon. Tennyson, A.
Fall guy. Abbott, G. and Gleason, J.
Fall of Algiers. Payne, J. H.
Fall of Jerusalem. Milman, H. H.
Fall of Robespierre. Coleridge, S. T.
Fall of Tarquin. See Payne, J. H. Brutus;
  or, The fall of Tarquin
Fall of Ug. Steele, R.
Fallen angels. Coward, N. P.
Fallen fairies; or, The wicked world. Gil-
  bert, W. S.
False delicacy. Kotzebue, A. F. F. von
False gods. Brieux, E.
False pretenses. Mathews, C.
False pretensions. Fuller, H. W.
False saint. Curel, F. de
False shame. Kotzebue, A. F. F. von
False step (adapted). Augier, E.
Falsehood and truth. Amalie of Saxony
Falstaff in rebellion. Postgate, J. W.
Fame and the poet. Dunsany, E.
Familiar friend. Lemon, M.
Family catastrophe. See Hauptmann, G.
  Reconciliation
Family charge. Turgenev, I. S.
Family distress; or, Self-immolation. Kot-
  zebue, A. F. F. von
Family exit. Langner, L.
Family failing. Boyle, W.
Family failing. Oxenford, J.
Family jars. Lunn, J.
Family legend. Baillie, J.
Family man. Galsworthy, J.
Family quarrel. Chapman, J. J.
Family quarrels. Dibdin, T. J.

Family reunion. Peattie, E. W.
Family reunion. See Schnitzler, A.
  Countess Mizzi; or, The family reunion
Family strike. Denison, T. S.
Family upstairs. Delf, H.
Family's pride. Gibson, W. W.
Famine
  Colum, P.   Miracle of the corn
Famine and the ghost. Halman, D. F.
Famous Mrs. Fair. Forbes, J.
Famous tragedy of the Queen of Cornwall.
  Hardy, T.
Fan and two candlesticks. MacMillan, M.
Fan-Fan. Meurice, Paul
Fanatics. Malleson, M.
Fancy free. Houghton, S.
Fanny's first play. Shaw, G. B.
Fanny's second play. Nathan, G. J.
Fantasia. Seiler, C.
Fantasio. Musset, A. de
Fantasticks. Rostand, E.
Fantastics. See Pinero, A. W. Princess
  and the butterfly
Fantasy. Dickinson, L. A. H.
Far above rubies. Sutro, A.
Far-away princess. Sudermann, H.
Far princess. Rostand, E.
Farce of the worthy Master Pierre Patelin.
  Jagendorf, M.
Fare please. Applegarth, M. T.
Farewell supper (dialogue in Anatol).
  Schnitzler, A.
Farewell to the theatre. Barker, H. G.
Farmer. O'Keeffe, J.
Farmer forsworn. Anzengruber, L.
Farmer's wife. Phillpotts, E.
Faro Nell. Steell, W.
Fascinating Mr. Denby. Sage, S. and
  Jones, H. M.
Fascinating Mr. Vanderveldt. Sutro, A.
Fashion; or, Life in New York. Ritchie,
  A. C.
Fashionable physician. See Rosenfeld, S.
  Club friend; or, A fashionable physician
Fashionable follies. Hutton, J.
Fashions for men. Molnár, F.
Fast coach. Claridge, C. J. and Soutar, R.
Fast train! High pressure!! Express!!!
  Maddox, J. M.
Fat kine and lean. Cannan, G.
Fata deorum. Guske, C. W.
Fata morgana. Vajda, E.
Fatal gazogene. See Shaw, G. B. Pas-
  sion, poison and petrification
Fatal message. Bangs, J. K.
Fatal pill. Sturgis, G. F.
Fatal rubber. Baring, M.
Fate of Calas. Dibdin, T. J.
Fate of Calas. Du Cange, V. H. J. B.
Fate of Ivan. Kitching, H. St. A.
Fate of the MacDonalds. See Talfourd,
  T. N.   Glencoe; or, The fate of the
  MacDonald's
Father. Clements, C. C.
Father. Greene, H. C.
Father. Strindberg, A.
Father and mother. Howells, W. D.
Father and the boys. Ade, G.
Father Junipero Serra. Miller, C. G.

Fountain of youth. Mackay, C. D'A.
Fountain of youth. Shipman, L. E.
Four adventurers. Kavanaugh, K.
Four bare walls. Subert, F. A.
Four fairy plays. Stolen prince; Bride's crown; Tall king's breakfast; Field of enchantment. Topelius, Z.
Four-fifteen express. Edwards, A. A. B.
Four-flusher. Dunn, C.
Four-flushers. Kinkead, C.
Four of a kind. Wilcox, C.
Four who were blind. Clements, C. C.
Four wishes. *See* Planché, J. R. Bee and the orange tree; or, The four wishes
Fourteen. Gerstenberg, A.
Fourteenth of July. Rolland, R.
Friday for luck. Mountford, G. F.
Friend. Lavedan, H.
Friend husband. Dale, I.
Friend indeed. Hamilton, C. M. and Voigt, B.
Friend Mary. Stevens, T. W.
Friend of his youth. See, E.
Friend of the family. Fitzgerald, S. J. A.
Friend of the people. Bonnet, T. F.
Friend Waggles. Morton, J. M.
Friendly enemies. Shipman, S. and Hoffman, A,
Friendly tip. Kavanaugh, K.
Friends. Farjeon, H.
Friends or foes. Sardou, V.
Franklin. Mackay, C. D'A.
Fraternal discord. Kotzebue, A. F. F. von
Fraternal discord. Dunlap, W.
Fraud and its victims. Coyne, J. S.
Freaks. Pinero, A. W.
Fredegonde, Queen of the Franks. Clark, J.
Free. Mann, H.
Free and easy. Arnold, S. J.
Free game. Schnitzler, A.
Free love
Marcy, E. Free union
Free speech. Prosser, W.
Free union. Marcy, E.
Free woman. Donnay, M. C.
Freedom. Reed, J.
Freedom. Sutro, A.
Freischutz; or, The seven charmed bullets. Amherst, J. H.
French leave. Berkeley, R. C.
Fourth of July
Dunlap, Wm. Glory of Columbia
Goodman, K. S. and Stevens, T. W. Pageant for Independence Day
Merington, M. First flag
Parsons, M. C. Trial of the glorious Fourth
Stevens, T. W. Fighting for freedom
Francesca da Rimini. Annunzio, G d'
Francesca da Rimini. Boker, G. H.
Francesca da Rimini. Crawford, F. M.
Francesca da Rimini. Pellico, S.
Francis Drake. Mitchell, S. W.
Franciscans. *See also* St. Francis of Assisi
Heald, L. Love in Umbria
Francisco Ferrer. Tietzelieve, J. T.
Francois Villon. Mitchell, S. W.

Françoise's luck. Porto-Riche, G.
Frank Wylde. Matthews, J. B.
Franklin. Benton, R.
Franklin, Benjamin. Bird, G. E. and Starling, M.
French Revolution
Courtney, J. Wicked wife
Parker, L. N. Aristocrat
—— Minuet
Rolland, R. Danton
—— Fourteenth of July
—— Wolves
Tarkington, B. Beauty and the Jacobin
French without a master. Bernard, T.
Freshman. • Morris, E. B.
Freud
Glaspell, S. and Cook, C. C. Suppressed desires
Jacobs, W. W. Establishing relations.
Fritzchen. Sudermann, H.
From death's own eyes. Viereck, G. S.
From frowns to smiles. Henderson, S.
From morn to midnight. Kaiser, G.
From president to postman. *See* Fitzgerald, F. S. K. Vegetable; or, From president to postman
From their own place. Denison, M.
From village to court. Morton, J. M.
Frou-frou. Daly, A.
Frou frou. Meilhac, H. and Halévy, L.
Fruit of his folly. Tubbs, A. L.
Fruit of toil. Wilson, L. P.
Fruits of culture. *See* Tolstoi, L. Fruits of enlightenment
Fruits of enlightenment. Tolstoi, L.
Fudge and a burglar. Thompson, A. C.
Führman Henschel. Hauptmann, G.
Fugitive. Galsworthy, J.
Full house. Jackson, F.
Full moon. Gregory, I. A.
Full of the moon. Herrick, G.
Funeral march of a marionette. Nethercot, A. H.
Funiculi Funicula. Wellman, R.
Furnace. Gibson, W. W.
Further side of the postal. Waite, A. E.
Futurists. MacMillan, M.
Gabriel Schilling's flight. Hauptmann, G.
Gainsborough lady. Merington, M.
Gaius and Gaius, Jr. Cobb, L. M.
Galahad Jones. Adams, A. H.
Galatea of the toy-shop. Sutherland, E. G.
Galatea takes a lease on life. Applegarth, M. T.
Gale Breezely; or, the tale of a tar. Johnstone, J. B.
Galilean's victory. Jones, H. A.
Gallant Cassian. Schnitzler, A.
Galloper. Davis, R. H.
Gambetta's story. Barclay, T.
Gamblers. Klein, C.
Game. Brighouse, H.
Game. Bryant, L. S.
Game. Searle, K.
Game at love. Viereck, G. S.
Game called kiss. Kemp, H. H.
Game of chess. Goodman, K. S.
Game of chess. Sutro, A.

How the other half lives. Robertson, C. G.

How the note was won. Hamilton, C. M. and Marshall, C.

How the weather is made. Brighouse, H.

How they saved the fort. Stevenson, A.

How to cook a biffin! *See* Selby, C. Hotel charges; or, How to cook a biffin!

How to die for love; or, The rival captains. Kotzebue, A. F. F. von

How to grow rich. Reynolds, F.

How to make home happy. Brough, W.

How to take up a bill; or, The village Vauxhall. Moncrieff, W. T.

How to try a lover. Barker, J. N.

Hraun farm. Sigurjónsson, J.

Hudson, Henry. Bird, G. E. and Starling, M.

Hue and cry after honesty. *See* Taylor, T. Diogenes and his lantern; or, A hue and cry after honesty

Hugger-Mugger. Clarke, H. S.

Human nature. Dell, F.

Human nature. Downing, H. F.

Humane citizens. Payne, F. U.

Humours of the court. Bridges, R. S.

Humpty Dumpty. Bloch, B.

Hunchback. Knowles, J. S.

Hundred pound note. Peake, R. B.

Hundred years ago. *See* Buckstone, J. B. The green bushes; or, A hundred years ago

Hundreth trick. Dix, B. M.

Hunger. Pillot, E.

Hunter. Frederick, J. T.

Hunter of the Alps. Dimond, W.

Hunting a turtle. Selby, C.

Hurly-burly; or, Number seven-twenty-eight. Schoenthan, F. von

Hurricane. Petrova, O.

Hurricane wooing. Giles, W. and Giles, J.

Husband. Corbin, J.

Husband-lovers. *See* Osborn, L. Double deceit; or, The husband lovers!

Husband of my heart. Selby, C.

Husband to order. Morton, J. M.

Husbands are a problem. Deans, H.

Husbands on approval. Blatt, W. M.

Hut. Linsky, F. B.

Hut of the Red Mountain; or, Thirty years of a gamester's life. Du Cange, V. H. J. B.

Huzza for the constitution! *See* Dunlap, W. Yankee chronology; or, Huzza for the constitution

Hyacinth Halvey. Gregory, I. A.

Hyacinths. Hanna, T. M.

Hyllus. Dunning, R. C.

Hypocrites. Jones, H. A.

Hypnotism
Schnitzler, A. Questioning the irrevocable.

Hypolympia; or, The gods in the island. Gosse, E.

I did but jest. Schmidt, G. P. jr.

"I shall invite the major." Moser, G. von

I'm going! Bernard, T.

"I'm sorry—it's out!". Jennings, G. E.

I've come to stay. Vorse, M. H.

I'll be your second. Rodwell, G. H.

"I'll leave it to you." Coward, N. P.

I'll tell you what. Inchbald, E. S.

Iberian. Lamb, O. R.

Ibsen revisited. Dell, F.

Icebound. Davis, O.

Iceland
Einarsson, I. Sword and crozier
Garnett, E. Feud

Ice lens. Gundelfinger, G. F.

Ideal husband. Wilde, O.

Idealist. Down, O.

Idealists. Hull, H. R.

Idiot. Lodovici, C.

Idler. Chambers, C. H.

Idol breaker. Kennedy, C. R.

Idumean. Leavitt, J. M.

Idyll. Grahn, M.

Idyll. Hofmannsthal, H. von

Idyll of the shops. Goodman, K. S. and Hecht, B.

If. Dunsany, E.

"If don't-believe is changed to believe". Barbee, L.

If I had a thousand a year. Morton, J. M.

If men played cards as women do. Kaufman, G. S.

If youth but knew! Spiers, K. C.

If Shakespeare lived to-day. Dunsany, E.

Il bondocani; or, The caliph robber. Dibdin, T. J.

Il nano Italiano. Heywood, J. C.

Il pescaballo. Child, F. J.

Ile. O'Neill, E. G.

Ill-beloved. *See* Benavente y Martinez, J. La malquerida

Illuminatti in drama libre. Gerstenberg, A.

Image. Gregory, I. A.

Imaginary conversation. O'Riordan, C. O'C.

Immigrants. MacKaye, P. W.

Immortal. Glick, C. and Sobel, B.

Immortal hour. Sharp, W.

Immortal lure. Rice, C. Y.

Immortality. MacInnis, C. P.

Immortals. Dobie, C. C.

Imperial republic. Crane, E. G.

Impertinence of the creature. Gordon-Lennox, C.

Importance of being a woman. Crothers, R.

Importance of being a roughneck. Garland, R.

Importance of being clothed. Crothers, R.

Importance of being early. Parkhurst, W.

Importance of being earnest. Wilde, O.

Importance of being married. Crothers, R.

Importance of being nice. Crothers, R.

Impossible. Howells, W. D.

Impossible philanthropist. Neilson, F.

Impromptu; drama. Burnet, D.

In a garden. Barry, P.

In a street-car. Cameron, M.

Innocent villain. Irwin, G. L.
Ins and outs. Lemon, M.
Insanity. *See* Dementia
Insects
  Capek, K. U. and J. "And so ad infinitum"
Inside stuff. Pratt, T.
Inside the lines. Biggers, E. D.
Insomnia. Rubinstein, H. F.
Inspector-general. Gogol, N. V.
Instrument. Housman, L.
Intangible. Ruschke, E. W.
Interior. Maeterlinck, M.
Interlude. More, F.
Interlude in the life of St. Francis. Raphael, A.
Intermezzo. Schnitzler, A.
Interpolated. Brookman, K. B.
Intervention of Miss Watson. Eyre, A.
Interviewed. Megrue, R. C.
Intimate acquaintance. Irwin, G. L.
Intimate strangers. Tarkington, B.
Intruder. Harcourt, C.
Intruder. Maeterlinck, M.
Inventor and the king's daughter. Pinski, D.
Invention of Dr. Metzler. Pollock, J.
Invention of the rat trap. Cauldwell, S. M.
Inventor. Haslett, H. H.
Invincible ship. Kosor, J.
Invincibles. Morton, T.
Invisible prince; or, The island of tranquil delights. Planché, J. R.
Involution. Weeks, K.
Inward light. Davis, A. and Stratton, A. R.
Iolanthe. Gilbert, W. S.
Iolanthe. *See* Hertz, H. King René's daughter.
Ion. Talfourd, T. N.
Iosagan. Pearse, P. H.
Iphigenia in Tauris. Bynner, W. *trans.*
Iphigenia in Tauris. Goethe, J. W.
Ireland
  Byrne, S. Silken Thomas
  Colum, P. Fiddler's house
  —— Thomas Muskerry
  Corkery, D. Clan Falvey
  —— King and hermit
  —— Resurrection
  —— Yellow bittern
  Craig, A. T. Passing of Dana's people
  Fitzmaurice, G. Pie-dish
  Gregory, I. A. *See* author entry
  Herrick, G. Full of the moon
  Hyde, D. Lost Saint
  —— Marriage
  —— Righ Seumas
  Marsh, A. Ulstermen
  MacSwiney, T. J. Revolutionist
  Moylan, T. K. Curse of the country
  Muldoon, J. & J. M. For Ireland's sake; or, Under the green flag
  Murray, T. C. Birthright
  O'Riordan, C. O'C. Piper
  Pearse, P. H. Singer
  Robinson, L. Patriots
  Rosener, G. M. "True hearts of Erin"
  Sawyer, R. Sidhe of Ben-Mor

Tietzelieve, J. T. Robert Emmet
Yeats, W. B. Cat and the moon
  —— Cathleen ni Houlihan
  —— King's threshold
Ireland as it is. Amherst, J. H.
Irene obliges. Millward, F. M.
Iris. Pinero, A. W.
Irish agent. Moore, B. F.
Irish diamond. *See* Boucicault D. Andy Blake; or, The Irish diamond
Irish heiress. Boucicault, D.
Irish outlaw. *See* Moore, B. F. Captain Jack; or, The Irish outlaw
Irish rebel. Moore, B. F.
Irish tiger. Morton, J. M.
Irishman in London. Macready, W.
Irishman's fortune. *See* Power, T. Born to good luck; or, The Irishman's fortune
Iron chest. Colman, G. (younger)
Iron manufacturer. *See* Ohnet, G. Forge master
Irresistible Marmaduke. Denny, E.
Is he alive or, All puzzled!! Planard, F. A. E. de
Is Santa Claus a fraud? Wells, C.
Is she his wife? or, Something singular. Dickens, C.
Is your name Smith? Dunton, E. K.
Isaac Commenus. Taylor, H.
Isaac Sheftel. Pinski, D.
Isabel, Edward and Anne. Jennings, G. E.
Isaiah. *See* Whitman, E. W. Drama of Isaiah
Iseult of Brittany. Symons, A.
Island of Calypso. *See* Planché, J. R. Telemachus; or, The island of Calypso
Island of jewels. Planché, J. R.
Island of tranquil delights. *See* Planché, J. R. Invisible prince; or, The island of tranquil delights
It ain't my fault. Kavanaugh, K.
It behooves us. Halman, D. F.
It can be done. Feldhake, J. A.
It is a strange house. Burnet, D.
It isn't done. Glick, C.
It might happen again. Rethy, J. B.
It never happens. Parkhurst, W.
It passes by. Monroe, H.
It pays to advertise. Megrue, R. C. and Hackett, W.
It's a family affair—we'll settle it ourselves. Ostrovskiĭ, A. N.
It's all in the pay streak. Denison, T. S.
It's spring. Harris, C. L.
It's the poor that 'elps the poor. Chapin, H.
It's time something happened. Doyle, A.
It's turrible to be popular. Stafford, J. K.
'Twas I! Payne, J. H.
'Twould puzzle a conjurer. Poole, J.
Italian father. Dunlap, W.
Italian quarter. Oldenshaw, L.
Ivanhoe, or, The Jew's daughter. Dibdin, T. J.
Ivanhoff. *See* Chekhov, A. P. Ivanhov
Ivanhov. Chekhov, A. P.
I've come to stay. Vorse, M. H.

Ivory tower.   Macintire, E. and Clements, C.
Jack and Jack's brother.   *See* Johnstone, J. B. Gipsy farmer; or, Jack and Jack's brother
Jack and Jill and a friend.   Hamilton, C. M.
Jack and the beanstalk.   Barbee, L.
Jack Cade.   Conrad, R. T.
Jack in the Green.   Lemon, M.
Jack-i'-the-green.   Parsons, M. C.
Jack in the water; or, The ladder of life. Rede, W. L.
Jack Straw.   Maugham, W. S.
Jack the giant-killer.   Applegarth, M. T.
Jack Trust.   Furniss, G. L.
Jackdaw.   Gregory, I. A.
Jack's house.   Kreymborg, A.

Jackson, Andrew
   Anderson, M. and Stallings, L.   First flight

Jacob Leisler.   Bates, W. O.
Jacobite.   Planché, J. R.
Jael.   Frank, F. K.
James and John.   Cannan, G.
James and the telephone.   Sapte, W.
James Wolfe.   Bird, G. E. and Starling, M.
Jan Výrava.   Subert, F. A.
Jane Clegg.   Ervine, St. J. G.
Jane, Jean and John.   Kreymborg, A.
January play: Molly's New Year's party. Stapp, E. B. and Cameron, E.

Japan
   Lengyel, M.   Typhoon
   Lord, K.   Honorable miss

Japanese plays
   Banchô Sarayaskiki.   *See* Japanese plays: Haunted mansion
   Clements, C C.   Seven plays of old Japan
   Daimyo
      In Duran, L. tr.   Plays of old Japan
   Death-stone; lyric drama.   From the Nō-no-utai)
      In Bates, A.   Drama 3:241
         Chamberlain, B. H.   Japanese poetry
   Demon's mallet.   *See* Noguchi, Y. Demon's mallet
   Enchanted palace.   (From Saiyuki)
      In McClatchie, T. R. H.   Japanese plays versified
   Fatal error (from the Kaga-Sôdô). 1 act
      In Bates, A. ed.   Drama 21:221
         McClatchie, T. R. H.   Japanese plays versified
   Fencing master (from "Nikgaigasa")
      In McClatchie, T. R. H.   Japanese plays versified
   Forsaken love (a poetical comedy)
      In Duran, L. tr.   Plays of old Japan
   Hagoromo.   1 act
      In Fenollosa E. and Pound, E. Britain Noble plays of Japan

Hands in the box
   In Duran, L. tr. Plays of old Japan
Haunted mansion (Banchô Sarayashiki)
   In McClatchie, T. R. H.   Japanese plays versified
Hayano Kampei (from the "Chiushin-gura)
   In McClatchie, T. R. H.   Japanese plays versified
Honor of Danzo
   In Duran, L tr.   Plays of old Japan
Horns
   In Duran, L. tr.   Plays of old Japan
Kagekiyo.   *See* Motokiyo, Kagekiyo
Kakitsuhata
   In Fenollosa, E. and Pound, E. "Noh" Drama 1916 p 428
Kayoi Komachi.   *See* Minoru
Kumasaka.   *See* Ujinobu Kumasaka
Lady Kokonoyé
   In McClatchie, T. R. H.   Japanese plays versified
Life is a dream; lyric drama (From the Nō-no-utai)
   In Chamberlain, B. H.   Japanese poetry
Maiden's tomb
   In Stopes, M. C. C.   Plays of old Japan
Moon night-bell.   *See* Noguchi, Y. Moon night-bell
Nakamitsu, lyric drama.   (from the Nō-no-utai).
   In Chamberlain, B. H.   Japanese poetry
Noguchi, Y.   "Bussu"
—— Cormorant fisher
—— Delusion of a human cup
—— Demon's mallet
—— Everlasting sorrow
—— Mountain she-devil
—— Shower: the moon
—— Tears of the birds
—— Two blind men
Parsons, N. C. Wooden bowl
Piece of jade
   In Stopes, M. C. C.   Conquest; or, A piece of jade
Resumé of Tamura
   In Stopes, M. C. C.   Plays of old Japan
Shojo
   In Drama 5:239
Sotoba Komachi   *See* Kiyotsugu
Suma Genji.   *See* Manzaburo
Sumida Gawa (Sumida river).   Adapted from the Nō drama by Motomasa.
   In Royal Soc. of Literature. Lond. Trans. Ser 2 v. 29:165
      Stopes, M. C. C.   Plays of old Japan
      Stratford, J. (Bost.) 2:29 Ja '18
Stopes, M. C. C.   Conquest; or, A piece of jade

Lady of Lyons; or, Love and pride. Bulwer-Lytton, E. G.
Lady of Munster. Bayly, T. H.
Lady of the camellias. *See* Dumas, A. *fils.* Camille
Lady of the lake. Dibdin, T. J.
Lady of the Nile. Ramspacher, A.
Lady of the rose. Flavin, M.
Lady of the swamp. Norton, F. P.
Lady of the weeping willow tree. Walker, S.
Lady Patricia. Besier, R.
Lady to call. Pierce, C. W.
Lady typist. Pain, A.
Lady white and lady yellow. Olcott, V.
Lady-who-hoarded Easter. *See* Applegarth, M. T. Strictly private
Lady Windemere's fan. Wilde, O.
Lady with the dagger. Schnitzler, A.
Lady with the mirror. Wellman, R.
Lafayette. Chapman, J. J.
Lafayette. Walker, A. J.
Lafayette; or, The maid and the Marquis. Morrison, G. A. jr.
Lafayette's toast. Stevenson, A.
L'aiglon. Rostand, E.
Lammas Eve. Randolph, E.
Lamp. Calderon, G.
Lamp. Pfeiffer, E. H.
Lamp and the bell. Millay, E. St.V.
Lamp of God. Roberts, M.
Lamp of heaven. Smith, J. W.
Lamplighter. Dickens, C.
Lancers. Payne, J. H.
Lancers. Vernon, L. V.
Land. Colum, P.
Land and love. Dubourg, A. W.
Land of heart's desire. Yeats, W. B.
Land of promise. Maugham, W. S.
Land of the "Free." Graham, B. M.
Land where lost things go. Halman, D.
Landed gentry. Maugham, W. S.
Lantern. Jirásek, A.
Laodice and Danaë. Bottomley, G.
La princesse Georges. Dumas, A. *père*
Larkin v. Fitzhugh. Barringer, E. F.
Lark's nest. Stevenson, A.
La Salle. Bird, G. E. and Starling, M.
Lass that loved a sailor. *See* Gilbert, W. S. H. M. S. Pinafore; or, The lass that loved a sailor
Lassoo. Mapes, V.
Last cache. Mackay, I. E.
Last disciple. Housman, L.
Last frontier. Rowell, A. C.
Last Jew. Pinski, D.
Last judgment. Bartlett, A. E.
Last lily. Dandet. A. and E. L. V. J.
Last man. Beddoes, T. L.
Last man in London. Maxwell, W. B.
Last Mandeville. Osborn, L.
Last night of a nation. Caverly, R. B.
Last of Mrs. Cheyney. Lonsdale, F.
Last of the De Mullins. Hankin, St.J.
Last of the English. Craven, A. S.
Last of the Lowries. Green, P.
Last of the pigtails. Selby, C.
Last of the Strozzi. Renfrew, C.
Last sitting. Merington, M.

Last straw. Crocker, B.
Last visit. Sudermann, H.
Last wish. Fitzgerald, S. J. A.
Last word. Schoenthan, F. von
Late delivery. Beith, J. H.
Late Mr. Castello. Grundy, S.
Latest Victor record. Applegarth, M. T.
Last wish. Fitzgerald. S. J. A.
Late delivery. Beith, J. H.
Latter-Lammas. Read, J.
Laughing Anne. Conrad, J.
Laughing child. Yates, E. H.
Laughing doors. Young, S.
Laughing gas. Dreiser, T.
Laughing lady. Sutro, A.
Laughing mind. Brighouse, H.
Laughter of the gods. Dunsany, E.
Launcelot and Guenevere. Hovey, R.
Laura Dibalzo; or, The patriot martyrs. Horne, R. H.
Laurette's wedding. *See* Musset, A. de. Venetian night; or, Laurette's wedding
Lavator the physiognomist. Planché, J. R.
Law divine. Esmond, H. V.
Law of Java. Colman, G.
Law of the land. Broadhurst, G. H.
Law of the savage. Artsybashev, M. P.
Law-suit. Benedix, R.
Lawyers. Lewes, G. H.
Lawyer's legend. *See* Johnstone, J. B. Tufelhausen; or, The lawyer's legend.
Lawyer's mistake. Burghlie, J.
Lay figure. Roberts, M.
Layla-Majnu. Mukerji, D. G.
Lazy Kate. Stevenson, A.
Le procureur Hallers. Gosse, H. de. and Forest, L.
Leading lady. Eyre, A.
League of youth. Ibsen, H.
Leah Kleschna. McLellan, C. M. S.
Lean years. Reely, M. K.
Leasehold marriage. Sapte, W.
Leatherlungos the great, how he stormed, reign'd and mizzled. Cheltnam, C. S.
Leave the woman out. Gordon, L.
Led astray. Boucicault, D.
Left in a cab. Stirling, E.
Left the stage. Siraudin, P.
Legacy. Schnitzler, A.
Legend. Dell, F.
Legend of "Norwood"; or, Village life in New England. Daly, A.
Legend of St. Nichola. Dix, B. M.

Legendary
Aber, L. A. Beggar maid
Baring, M. King Alfred and the neatherd
Betts, F. Ingiald Evil-heart
—— Passing of Sinfiotli
Block, L. J. Birth and death of the prince
—— On the mountain top
Carr, J. W. C. King Arthur
—— Tristram and Iseult
Craig, A. T. Passing of Dana's people (Irish)
Crane, E. G. Necken
Davidson, J. Godfrida

Mable and Maisie. *See* Rostetter, A. Which is witch? or, Mable and Maisie

Macaire. Henley, W. E. and Stevenson, R. L.

Macbeth, somewhat removed from the text of Shakespeare. Talfourd, P.

Maccabean cure. Kraft, I.

MacDaragh's wife. *See* Gregory, I. A. McDonough's wife

McDonough's wife. Gregory, I. A.

Machiavelli. Norton, F. P.

Machine. Sinclair, U. B.

Machine-wreckers. Toller, E.

Madame. Sturgis, G. F.

Madame Butterfly. Belasco, D. and Long, J. L.

Madame Major. Shpazhinsky, I. V.

Madame Pepita. Martinez Sierra, G.

Madame Princeton's temple of beauty. Denison, T. S.

Madame Sand. Moeller, P.

Madame Sans-Gêne. Sardou, V. and Moreau, E.

Maddalen. Galt, J.

Mademoiselle de Belle Isle. Dumas, A. *père*

Mademoiselle Diana. Pollock, J.

Mademoiselle Merowsky. Dagney, J. P.

Madhouse; the voice of reason. Stevens, H. B.

Madman divine. Echegaray, J.

Madman on the roof. Kikuchi, K.

Madman or saint. Echegaray, J.

Madmen all; or, Cure for love. Paulding, J. K. and W. I.

Madonna. Middleton, G.

Madonna and the scarecrow. Kaplan, J. De W.

Madonna Dianora. Hofmannsthal, H. von

Madras house. Barker, H. G.

Madretta. Young, S.

Maeve. Martyn, E.

Magda. Sudermann, H.

Magellan, Ferdinand. Bird, G. E. and Starling, M.

Maggie Pepper. Klein, C.

Maggie's situation. Morton, J. M.

Magi. Lunarsharski, A. V.

Magic. Chesterton, G. K.

Magic
Jacobs, W. W. and Parker, L. N. Monkey's paw

Magic glasses. Fitzmaurice, G.

Magic hours. Peacey, H.

Magic of an hour. Benavente, J.

Magic sea. Young, S.

Magic sea shell. Farrar, J. C.

Magical city. Akins, Zoe

Magistrate. Pinero, A. W.

Magnanimity. O'Brien, S.

Magnanimous lover. Ervine, St. J. G.

Magnetism; or, Ready for everybody. Osborn, L.

Magpie; or, the maid? Caigniez, L. C.

Magpie; or, the maid? Pocock, I.

Mah-jongg. Gerstenberg, A.

Mah-jongg. Wilcox, C. G.

Maharani of Arakan. Calderon, G.

Mahasena. Baring, M.

Maid Marian; or, The huntress of Arlingford. Planché, J. R.

Maid of France. Brighouse, H.

Maid of honour. Hemmerde, E. G.

Maid of Mariendorpt. Knowles, J. S.

Maid of Milan. *See* Payne, J. H. Clari; or, The maid of Milan

Maid of Northumberland; or, The blockade runner. Lucas, D. B.

Maid of Orleans. Benson, R. H.

Maid of Orleans. Calvert, G. H.

Maid of Orleans. Schiller, F. von

Maid who wouldn't be proper. Mick, H. L.

Maid with the milking pail. Buckstone, J. B.

Maiden over the wall. Bloch, B.

Maiden's oath. Lawson, J.

Maidens of the Mount. Hauptmann, G.

Maid's forgiveness. Chapman, J. J.

Major Barbara. Shaw, G. B.

Major John André. Haid, L.

Make-believe. Milne, A. A.

Maker of dreams. Down, O.

Maker of men. Sutro, A.

Makers of light. Day, F. L.

Makers of madness. Hagedorn, H.

Makeshifts. Robins, G.

Making a man. Brunner, E. B.

Makropoulos secret. Capek, K.

Malachi and Miranda. Monroe, J. R.

Malini. Tagore, R.

La Malquerida. Benavente, J.

Malvaloca. Alvarez Quintero, S. and J.

Mamma's affair. Butler, R. B.

Mammy. Babcock, B.

Man and his wife. Clements, C. C.

Man about the place. Brighouse, H.

Man and superman. Shaw, G. B.

Man and the alligator. Stevenson, A.

Man and the masses. Toller, E.

Man and wife; or, More secrets than one. Arnold, S. J.

Man born to be hanged. Hughes, R. A. W.

Man can only do his best. Goodman, K. S.

Man from Denver. Bernard, F. H.

Man from home. Tarkington, B. and Wilson, H. L.

Man from Mexico. Du Souchet, H. A.

Man from Nevada. Ulrich, C.

Man from Toronto. Murray, D.

Man higher up. De Mille, W. C.

Man hunt. Thompson, H.

Man in black. Echegaray, J.

Man in the bowler hat. Milne, A. A.

Man in the stalls. Sutro, A.

Man in the street. Parker, L. N.

Man masterful. Middleton, G.

Man of business. Housman, L.

Man of destiny. Shaw, G. B.

Man of forty. Kotzebue, A. F. F. von

Man of honour. Maugham, W. S.

Man of ideas. Malleson, M.

Man of Kerioth. Norwood, R. W.

Man of many friends. Coyne, J. S.

Man of principle. Weeks, K.

Man of the hour. Broadhurst, G. H.

Much ado about Betty.   Hare, W. B.
Mud.   McKinney, I.
Muddle-Annie.   Chapin, H.
Muffins.   Garnett, L. A.
Mug.   Sargent, H. C.
Mulan.   Taketomo, T.
Muleteer of Toledo; or, King, queen and knave.   Morton, J. M.
Mumbo Jumbo.   Clews, H. jr.
Murder will out.   See Buckstone, J. B. Presumptive evidence; or, Murder will out
Murderer.   Ross, C.
Murdering Selina.   Oliver, M. S.
Mushrooms.   Home, E.
Music hath charms.   Irwin, G. L.
Musotte.   Maupassaut, G. de
My aunt.   Arnold, S. J.
My bachelor days.   Morton, J. M.
My daughter! oh! my daughter.   See Rosenfeld, S. Rosemi Shell; or, My daughter! oh! my daughter
My daughter's dowry.   See Legouvé, E. Foresight; or, My daughter's dowry
My daughter, Sir! or, A daughter to marry.   Planché, J. R.
My dear!   O'Connor, P.
My fellow clerk.   Oxenford, J.
My first fit of the gout.   Morton, J. M.
My friend from India.   Du Souchet, H. A.
My friend's in town.   Denison, E. H.
My husband's ghost.   Morton, J. M.
My Irish rose.   Hare, W. B.
My Lady Clara.   See Robertson, T. W. Dreams; or, My Lady Clara
My lady dreams.   Pillot, E.
My lady's dress.   Knoblock, E.
My little girl.   Boucicault, D.
My precious Betzy!   Morton, J. M.
My son Diana.   Harris, A. G.
My tailor.   Capus, A.
My wife's bonnet.   Morton, J. M.
My wife's come!   Morton, J. M. and Morton, E.
My wife's daughter.   Coyne, J. S.
My wife's second floor.   Morton, J. M.
Myriad-minded man.   Block, L. J.
Myrrha.   Roberts, C. V. H.
Mysterious lady!   or; Worth makes the man.   Planché, J. R.
Mysterious stranger.   See Selby, C. Satan in Paris; or, The mysterious stranger
Mystery of Beacon Hill.   Denison, E. H.
Mystery play.   Benson R. H.

Mystery
Cawein, M. J.   House of fear
John, G.   Mr. Jardyne
Johnson, F. G.   Am I intruding?

Mythological
Baring, M.   Jason and Medea
—— Pious Æneas
Binyon, L.   Paris and Oenone
Bridges, R. S.   Feast of Bacchus
—— Return of Ulysses
Chapman, J. J.   Cupid and Psyche
—— Hector's farewell
—— Romulus and Remus
—— Wrath of Achilles
Creamer, E. S.   Orphean tragedy

Fields, A. A.   Orpheus and Eurydice
Galt, J.   Agamemnon
Goodloe, A. C.   Antinoüs
Grant, P. S.   Return of Odysseus
Hofmannstahl, H. von.   Electra
Hole, W. G.   Paris and Oenone
Housman, L.   Death of Orpheus
Le Gallienne, R.   Orestes
Legouvé, E.   Medea
Lodge, H. C.   Herakles
Miller, M. M.   Return of Odysseus
Montenegro.   Alcestis
Moody, W. V.   Fire bringer
Moore, T. S.   Orpheus and Eurydice
Murray, G.   Andromache
Pérez-Galdós, B.   Electra
Phillips, S.   Ulysses
Planché, J. R.   Olympic devils
—— Olympic revels
—— Theseus and Ariadne
—— Venus and Adonis
Proctor, B. W.   Lysander and Ione
—— Rape of Proserpine
Read, H. F.   Medea
Robinson, H. J.   New Pandora
Rogers, M. D.   Echo and Narcissus
Schnitzler, A.   Festival of Bacchus
Schütze, M.   Hero and Leander
Smith, J. O. D.   Seal of Hellas
Talfourd, F.   Thetis and Peleus
Naboclish.   Moylan, T. K.
Naboth's vineyard.   Dane, C.
Naked.   Pirandello, L.
Naked truth.   Symonds, E. M. and Maxwell, W. B.
Nameless.   Gray, T.
Nameless one.   Cheney, A. C.
Nancy and company.   Daly, A.
Il nano Italiano.   Heywood, J. C.
Napoleon.   Trench, H.

Napoleon
Claudel, P.   Hostage
Durant, H.   Man within
Lavelle, A. E.   Puppets of fate
Rawson, G. S.   Dangers of peace
—— Pastor of Jena
—— Stroke of Marbot
Rostand, E.   L'aiglon
Sardou, V.   Madame Sans-Gène
Shaw, G. B.   Man of destiny
Napoleon Buonoparte's invasion of Russia.   Amherst, J. H.
Napoleon crossing the Rockies.   MacKaye, P.
Napoleon's barber.   Caesar, A.
Nari-kin.   Iwasaki, Y. T.
Narrow squeak.   Morton, J. M.
Nathan Hale.   Cushing, C. C.
Nathan Hale.   Fitch, C.
Nathaniel Hawthorne's Scarlet letter, dramatized.   Peck, E. W.
National anthem.   Manners, J. H.
National Red Cross pageant.   Stevens, T. W.
Nativity.   Hinkson, K. T.
Nativity.   Hyde, D.
Nativity.   Snyder, M. I.

Nativity
Benson, R. H.   Mystery play in honour of the nativity
Brown, K. S. and Tinnin, G. S.   One night in Bethlehem
Housman, L.   Bethlehem
Stevens, T. W.   Duquesne Christmas mystery
Symons, A.   Mary in Bethlehem
Natural incentive.   Quaife, E. W.
Natural son.   Kotzebue, A. F. F. von
Natural transformation.   See Osborn, L. School for critics; or, A natural transformation
Naturewoman.   Sinclair, U. B.
Naughty duck.   Young, S.
Naughty wife.   Jackson, F.
Naval pillar.   Dibdin, T. J.
Nazareth.   Housman, L.
Nearly married.   Selwyn, E.
'Neath the scepter of Susan.   Parsons, M. C.
Necessary evil.   Kennedy, C. R.
Necken.   Crane, E. G.
Ned McCobb's daughter.   Howard, S.
Needles and pins.   Daly, A.
Negro slaves.   Kotzebue, A. F. F. von
Negroes
Culbertson, E. H.   Goat Alley
Dransfield, J.   Blood o' kings
Green, P.   See Lonesome road
O'Neill, E.   Emperor Jones
Sutherland, E. G.   Po' white trash
Torrence, F. R.   Granny Maumee
—— Rider of dreams
Neighbors.   Gale, Z.
Nell Gwynne; or, The prologue.   Jerrold, D. W.
Nellijumbo.   Walker, S.
Nelson touch.   Fenn, F.
Nemesis.   Thomas, A.
Neptune's isle.   Chapman, J. J.
Nero.   Bridges, R. S.
Nero.   Phillips, S.
Nero.   Story, W. W.
Nero.   Symons, A.
Nero
Cecil, K. H. D.   Historical tragedy of Nero
Nero's mother.   Phillips, S.
Nerves.   Farrar, J.
Nervous set.   Barrière, T. and Sardou, V.
Nervous wreck.   Davis, O.
Nest.   Geraldy, P.
Nest.   Jex, J.
Nettie.   Ade, G.
Nevertheless.   Walker, S.
New Americans.   See Applegarth, M. T. Fare, please
New brooms.   Craven, F.
New Calvary.   Osborn, L.
New convert.   Kravchinskiŭ, S. M.
New drama.   Tamàyo v Baus, M.
New England
Caverly, R. B.   King Philip
—— Regicides
Cochran, E. O.   Wilderness rose
Daly, A.   Legend of "Norwood"
New England fable.   Lewisohn, L.

New era.   Vaughan, V.
New-fangled notions.   Harrington, H.
New hay at the old market.   See Colman, G. Sylvester Daggerwood; or, New hay at the old market
New Haymarket spring meeting.   Planché, J. R.
New impressions.   Robertson, C. G.
New King Arthur.   Fawcett, E.
New lamps for old.   Roman, R.
New lights.   Mann, H.
New Magdalen.   Field, A. N.
New men and old acres.   Dubourg, S. W. and Taylor, T.
New morality.   Chapin, H.
New morn.   Carus, P.
New names for old.   Carey, A. V.
New Pandora.   Robinson, H. J.
New Parsival.   Trevelyan, R. C.
New planet; or, Harlequin out of place. Planché, J. R.
New poor.   Hamilton, C.
New poor.   Jennings, G. E.
New Portia.   Titheradge, D.
New race.   Wolfram, A.
New sin.   Hastings, B. M.
New spirit out of the dark.   Feuerlicht, E. M.
New system.   Bjørnson, B.
New way.   Meyer, A. N.
New woman.   Denison, T. S.
New word.   Barrie, J. M.
New world.   Read, H. F.
New Year's day.   Palmer, H. M.
New Year's day.   Payne, F. U.
New Year's day
Merington, M.   Father Time and his children
Olcott, V.   Cave of the fates
New York
Fawcett, E.   Buntling ball
New York idea.   Mitchell, L.
Newington Butts!   Morton, J. M.
Newly married couple.   Bjørnson, B.
Next door.   Crane, E. M.
Next door neighbors.   Inchbald, E. S.
Next of kin.   Klein, C.
Next religion.   Zangwill, I.
Next step on.   Butterfield, W.
Nice firm.   Taylor, T.
Nice people.   Crothers, R.
Nicholas Nickleby.   Stirling, J.
Nifwy the proud.   Richardson, P.
Nigel; or, The crown jewels.   Pocock, I.
Nigger.   Sheldon, E. B.
Night.   Asch, S.
Night.   Oppenheim, J.
Night asylum.   See Gorky, M.   Lower depths
Night at an inn.   Dunsany, E.
Night before Christmas.   Howells, W. D.
Night before Christmas.   Olcott, V.
Night brings a counselor.   Saunders, Lilian
Night in Avignon.   Rice, C. Y.
Night of "Mr. H."   Brighouse, H.
Night of peril.   See Coyne, J. S.   Old chateau; or, A night of peril
Night of the wedding.   Duffy, R.

Pride. Dillon, R. A.
Pride and prejudice.   MacKaye, M. K.
Pride of the market.   Planché, J. R.
Prima donna.   Boucicault, D.
Prince.   Davidson, J.
Prince.   John, G.
Prince chap. Peple, E. H.
Prince d'Aurec.   Lavedan, E.
Prince Dorus; or, The romance of the
   nose.   Taylor, T.
Prince for an hour.   Morton, J. M.
Prince Hagen.   Sinclair, U. B.
Prince Ivo of Bohemia.   Mann, A. S.
Prince of court painters.   Mackay, C. D'A.
Prince of Semberia.   Nooshich, B.
Prince of the Happy Land; or, The fawn in
   the forest.   Planché, J. R.
Prince of the moon.   Young, S.
Prince was a piper.   Brighouse, H.
Prince who learned everything out of
   books.   Benavente, J.
Princely bride.   Amalie of Saxony
Princess.   Gilbert, W. S.
Princess Aline play.   Smith, S. D.
Princess and a churn.   Olcott, V.
Princess and the butterfly.   Pinero, A. W.
Princess and the pea.   Jackson, M. B. S.
Princess and the pixies.   Mackay, C. D'A.
Princess Bebé.   Benavente, J.
Princess Elizabeth.   Williams, F. H.
Princess Far-Away.   See Rostand, E. Far-
   Away princess
Princess Ida; or, Castle Adamant.   Gilbert,
   W. S.
Princess in the fairy tale.   Wilcox, C. G.
Princess Maleine.   Maeterlinck, M.
Princess Moss Rose.   Merington, M.
Princess on the road.   Greene, K. C.
Princess of Hanover.   Woods, M. L.
Princess Pocahontas.   Mackay, C. D'A.
Princess Weaver of the skies.   Kaplan, Y.
   D.
La princesse Georges.   Dumas, A., *fils*
Princesses.   Joseph, H. H.
Princesses in the Tower; or, A match for
   Lucifer.   Talfourd, F.
Priscilla, Myles and John.   Merington, M.
Prison
   Heijermans, H. jr.   Jubilee
   Reed, J.   Freedom
Prisoner.   Ross, C.
Prisoner at large.   O'Keeffe, J.
Prisoner of war.   Jerrold, D. W.
Prisoners of war.   Akerley, J. R.
Private secretary.   Moser, G. von. Adapted
   by C. Hawtrey
Prize plays
   Drama League of American
   1921. Levinger, E. E. Jepthah's daughter
   Miscellaneous
   Brown, A. Children of earth. (Win-
      throp Ames prize play, 1915)
   Browne, P. Gloria mundi. (Second
      Samuel French prize play, 1925)
   Field, Rachel L. Rise up, Jennie Smith.
      (Drama League of America patriotic
      play competition)
   Flanagan, H. E. Curtain. (Des Moines
      Little Theatre contest, 1923)

   Harnwell, A. J. Star of the East. (Dra-
      ma League of America, 1921)
   Heidenstam, E. E. Soothsayer. (Nobel
      prize, 1916)
   Larkin, M. El Cristo. (Belasco cup
      prize play, 1926: *also* Samuel French
      prize, 1926)
   Sutton, G. W. Yellow triangle. (Second
      Samuel French prize play, 1925)
   Totheroh, D Wild birds. (California
      prize play)
   Pulitzer
   1918. Williams, J. L. Why marry?
   1919. No award.
   1920. O'Neill, E. Beyond the horizon
   1921. Gale, Z. Miss Lulu Bett
   1922. O'Neill, E. Anna Christie
   1923. Davis, O. Icebound
   1924. Hughes, H. Hell-bent fer heaven
   1925. Howard, S. They knew what they
      wanted.
Probationer.   Guthrie, A.
Probationer.   Rowley, A.
Problem *See also* Social
   Aldis, M. R.   Ten p.m.
   Bjørnson, B.   Beyond our power
   Brieux, E.   Maternity
   —— Three daughters of M. Dupont
   Cannan, G.   Same story
   Coward, N.   Vortex
   Crothers, R.   Man's world
   Dane, C.   Bill of divorcement
   Ferber, E. and Kaufman, G.   Old man
      Minick
   Goodman, J. E.   Chains
   Harcourt, C.   Intruder
   Hauptmann, G.   Gabriel Schilling's
      flight
   Hervieu, P.   Know thyself
   Hirschfeld, G.   Mothers
   Layton, F. G.   Philip's wife
   Lodovici, C.   Idiot
   Moore, G.   Esther Waters
   McLellan, C. M. S.   Leah Kleschna
   Manners, J. H.   Harp of life
   Mayo, M. and Gould, E.   Dancing
      mothers
   Paull, H. M.   Bolt from the blue
   Praga, M.   Closed door
   Roelvink, H. C. J.   Storm bird
   Scott-Maxwell, F.   Flashpoint
   Sutro, A.   Great well
   —— Man with a heart
   —— Salt of life
   Theis, G.   Crack in the bell
   Verhaeren, E.   Dawn
   Walter, E.   Easiest way
   Wolfram, A.   Living voice
   Young, S.   At the shrine
Proceed in the dance; or, Louise.   Ebin,
   A. B.
Processional.   Lawson, J. H.
Prodigal; or, A vice and virtue.   Osborn,
   L.
Prodigal doll.   Rusinol, S.
Prodigal son.   Kemp, H. H.
Professor Bernhardi.   Schnitzler, A.
Profligate.   Pinero, A. W.
Profligate.   Watson-Taylor, G.

Renegade. Reynolds, F.
Rent day. Jerrold, D. W.
Reparation. *See* Tolstoi, L. N. Man who was dead
Repertory. Rubinstein, H. F.
Reprobate. James, H.
Republicans of Brest. *See* Johnstone, J. B. Sailor of France; or, The republicans of Brest
Reputation. Planché, J. R.
Rescue. Smith, R.
Rescued by radio. Barbee, L.
Rescuing an angel. Kummer, C. B.
Resentment. Monkhouse, A. N.
Resources of Quinola. *See* Balzac, H. de. Quinola's resources
Respective virtues of Heloise and Maggie. Bartlett, R.
Rest cure. Jennings, G. E.
Restoration of Cain. Morland, H.
Restville auction sale. Smith, S. D.
Resurrection. Corkery, D.
Resurrection of Lazarus. Vojnovich, I.
Resurrection of Peter. Clinton, I. F.
Re-taming the shrew. Postgate, J. W.
Retired from business. Jerrold, D. W.
Retribution. O'Brien, S.
Retribution. Pellettiere, G. M.
Retribution. Taylor, T.
Return. Morgan, E. J.
Return of Alcestes. Housman, L.
Return of Buck Gavin. Wolfe, T. C.
Return of Christmas. Bangs, J. K.
Return of Harlequin. Clements, C. C.
Return of Letty. Thompson, A. C.
Return of Mr. Wiggleswick. Ratcliffe, D. U.
Return of Odysseus. Grant, P. S.
Return of Odysseus. Miller, M. M.
Return of Peter Grimm. Belasco, D.
Return of the druses. Browning, R.
Return of the "Mayflower". Harris, J. R.
Return of the prodigal. Hankin, St. J.
Return of the spring. Stevenson, A.
Return of Ulysses. Bridges, R. S.
Return to mutton. Rosenberg, J. N.
Returned "killed". Planché, J. R.
Revanche. Rubinstein, H. F.
Revellers. Housman, L.
Reverie. Wilde, P.
Review. Colman, C.
Revolt. Calderon, G.
Revolt. Villiers de L'Isle Adam, J. M.

Revolution, 1688
Lee, F. Historic change: The glorious revolution

Revolution, American
Allen, E. Washington; or, The revolution
Tayleure, C. W: Horseshoe Robinson
Revolutionary days. Wagstaff, B. J.
Revolutionist. MacSwiney, T. J.
Revueitis. Sargent, H. C.
Re-Ward. *See* Smith, Winchell and Cushing, T. Going crooked
Rib of the man. Kennedy, C. R.
Ribbemont; or, The feudal baron. Dunlap, W.
Rice pudding. Tiffany, E. B.

Rich citizens. Payne, F. U.
Rich young lady. Yates, E. H.
Rich young man. Kingsbury, S.
Richard II. Waight, J. F.
Richelieu. Payne, J. H.
Richelieu; or, The conspiracy. Bulwer-Lytton, E. G.
Rider of dreams. Torrence, F. R.
Riders to the sea. Synge, J. M.
Riding to Lithend. Bottomley, G.
Rienzi. Mitford, M. R.
Righ Seumas. Hyde, D.
Right you are! Pirandello, L.
Rightful heir. Bulwer-Lytton, E. G.
Rightful heir. Sapte, W.
Rights and wrongs of women. Morton, J. M.
Rights of the soul. *See* Giacosa, G. Sacred ground
Rigordans. Smith, E. P.
Rim of the world. Dell, F.
Rinaldo Rinaldini; or, The great banditti. Dunlap, W.
Rinaldo, the doctor of Florence. Lacy, E.
Ring. MacMillan, M. L.
Ring of magic power. Benton, R.
Rip Van Winkle (adapted). Burke, C.
Rip Van Winkle. Irving, W.
Rip Van Winkle. MacKaye, P. W.
Ripening wheat. Wolfram, A.
Riquet of the tuft. Brook, S. A.
Riquet with the tuft. Planché, J. R.
Rise up, Jennie Smith. Field, R. L.
Rising generation. Weaver, W. and Leycester, L.
Rising of the moon. Gregory, I. A.
Rival captains. *See* Kotzebue, A. F. F. von. How to die for love; or, The rival captains
Rival queens. Shaler, N. S.
Rivals. Sheridan, R. B.
Road agent. Ulrich, C.
Road to Connaught. Lord, D. A.
Road to yesterday. Sutherland, E. G. and Dix, B. M.
Road together. Middleton, G.
Roadhouse in Arden. Moeller, P.
Rob Roy Macgregor. Pocock, I.
Robbers. Schiller, F. von
Robber's wife. Pocock, I.
Robbery. Kummer, C. B.
Robbery under law; or, The battle of the millionaires. Challoner, J. A.
Robe of wood. Golden, J.
Robert Burns. Drinkwater, J.
Robert Burns. Gilliam, E. W.
Robert Burns. Lee, H. F.
Robert E. Lee. Drinkwater, J.
Robert E. Lee. Farris, C. S.
Robert Emmet. Tietzelieve, J. T.
Robert Macaire; or, The two murderers. Selby, C.
Robert the devil. Gilbert, W. S.
Robert the Devil, Duke of Normandy. Raymond, R. J.
Robin Hood and the pedlar. Drinkwater, J.
Robin Hood and the three kings. See Noyes, A. Sherwood; or, Robin Hood and the three kings

Spadassin! Major, M.
Spaniards in Denmark. Merimée, P.
Spaniards in Peru. *See* Kotzebue, A. F. F. von. Pizarro; or, The Spaniards in Peru
Spanish student. Longfellow, H. W.
Spark. Pailleron, E. J. H.
Spark neglected burns the house. Benton, R.
Spark of life. Brunner, E. B.
Sparkling cup. Denison, T. S.
Sparrow. Lopez, S.
Sparrows in the hat. Stevenson, A.
Spartan Dorothy and her fox. Teeple, L. R.
Speaking to father. Ade, G.
Special delivery. Sutphen, V. T.
Special pleading. Duffy, B.
Specimen. Rubinstein, H. F.
Spectre bridegroom; or, A ghost in spite of himself. Moncrieff, W. T.
Speed the plough. Morton, T.
Sphynx. Feuillet, O.
Spiced wine. Jones, W. K.
Spikenard. Lawrence, C. E.
Spinoza
  Greene, B. M. God-intoxicated man
Spirit of New England. Payne, F. U.
Spirit of the forest. Baldwin, S.
Spirits and spooks. Clements, G. L.
Splendid offer. King, G. E.
Spoilers. Beach, R. E. and MacArthur, J.
Spoiling the broth. Graham, B. M.
Sponge. Riley, A. C.
Spook sonata. Strindberg, A.
Spoop. Eckersley, A.
Sport of gods. Cournos, J.
Sport of kings. Beith, J. H.
Spot cash. Yates, E. H.
Spreading the news. Gregory, I. A.
Sprigs of laurel. O'Keeffe, J.
Spring. Clements, C. C.
Spring. Cook, G. C.
Spring. Murray, T. C.
Spring cleaning. Peattie, E. W.
Spring in Bloomsbury. Brighouse, H.
Spring recital. Dreiser, T.
Spring's awakening. *See* Wedekind, F. Awakening of spring
Spy. Besant, W. and Pollock, W.
Square peg. Beach, L.
Square pegs. Bax, C.
Squaring the circle. Murray, D.
Squaw man. Royle, E. M.
Squeaky. Vernon, H. M.
Squire. Pinero, A. W.
Stag and the fawn. Stevenson, A.
Stage-struck. Perkins, E. B.
Stage struck; or, The loves of Augustus Portarlington and Celestina Beverley. Dimond, W.
Staircase. Abercrombie, L.
Standing moving. Macmillan, M. L.
Standish of Standish. Marble, A. R.
Star. Creagh-Henry, M.
Star-child. Benton, R.
Star dust path. Clements, C. C.
Star in the east. Harnwell, A. J.
Star in the trees. Young, S.

Star of Bethlehem. Greene, C. M.
Star of Seville. Kemble, F. A.
Stars. Symonds, E. M.
Starveling. De Mille, W. C.
State forbids. Cowan, S.
Station Y Y Y Y. Tarkington, B.
Statue guest. Pushkin, A. S.
Statutory duel. Gilbert, W. S.
Steadfast princess. Meigs, C.
Steamer Tenacity. Vildrac, C.
Steed in the senate. Andreev, L.
Steeple-chase; or, In the pigskin. Morton, J. M.
Stella. Goethe, J. W.
Stephania. Field, M.
Stephania. Story, W. W.
Step-mother. Balzac, H. de
Stepmother. Bennett, A.
Stepmother. Milne, A. A.
Step-sister. Sapte, W.
Stick-up. Loving, P.
Stiggins entire. *See* Elwes, M. Temporary engagements; or, Stiggins entire
Still engaged. Owen, H.
Still waters run deep. Taylor, T.
Stoic. Titheradge, D.
Stoic's daughter. Baring, M.
Stolen horse. Forrest, C.
Stolen prince. Topelius, Z.
Stolen prince. Totheroh, D. W.
Stone Venus. Roof, K. M.
Stonefolds. Gibson, W. W.
Stop thief. Moore, C.
Storm. Drinkwater, J.
Storm. MacMillan, M. L.
Storm. Ostrovskiĭ, A. N.
Storm. *See* Strindberg, A. Thunderstorm
Storm in a tea cup. Bernard, W. B.
Storm; or, The battle of Tinderley Down. Munro, C. K.
Stormbird. Roelvink, H. C. J.
Stormy night. Kavanaugh, K.
Story brought by Brigit. Gregory, I. A.
Story of Ali Cogia. Stevenson, A.
Story of Eleusis. Ledoux, L. V.
Story-spinner. Fuller, H. B.
Strafford. Sterling, J.
Strange gentleman. Dickens, C.
Strange history. Lewes, G. H. and Mathews, C.
Stranger. Flamma, A.
Stranger. Gould, F.
Stranger. Hirschbein, P.
Stranger. Kotzebue, F. F. von
Stranger. Pinski, D.
Stranger within the gates. Fuller, H. B.
Strangers. Brunner, E. B.
Strathmore. Marston, J. W.
Straw. O'Neill, E. G.
Streaks of light. Sudermann, H.
Street singer. Echegaray, J.
Strenuous life. *See* John, G.
Stricklands. Monkhouse, A. N.
Strictly private. Applegarth, M. T.
Strife. Galsworthy, J.
Strike
  Galsworthy, J. Strife
  Tynan, B. Behold the man
  Wells, W. H. Brotherhood

Turandot. Vollmoeller, K.
Turandot, princess of China. Gozzi, C.
Turn of a hair. Hoffman, P.
Turn of the road. Waddell, S.
Turn-out. Campbell, J.
Turn to the right. Smith, W. and Hazzard, J. E.
Turning the tables. Poole, J.
Turtle dove. Oliver, M. S.
Tut-Ankh-Amen. *See* Brookman, K. B. Interpolated
'Twas I! Payne, J. H.
Tweedles. Tarkington, B. and Wilson, H. L.
$1200 a year. Ferber, E. and Levy, N.
Twelve labours of Hercules. Brough, R. B.
Twelve old maids. Hare, W. B.
Twelve pound look. Barrie, J. M.
24th of February. Werner, F. L. Z.
Twenty minutes under an umbrella. Dubourg, A. W.
Twenty per cent; or, My father. Dibdin, T. J.
Twice-told tale. Laws, A. C.
Twig of thorn. Warren, M. J.
Twilight. Bernstein, E.
Twilight of the gods. Bacon, J. D. D.
Twilight of the gods. Robertson, C. G.
Twilight saint. Young, S.
Twin brothers. Hugo, V.
Twisting of the rope. Hyde, D.
'Twixt axe and crown; or, The Lady Elizabeth. Taylor, T.
'Twixt eventide and dawn. Coppée, F.
Two black sheep. White, A. C.
Two blind beggars, and one less blind. Moeller, P.
Two blind men. Noguchi, Y.
Two blind men and a donkey. Dondo, M. M.
Two blocks away. Hoffman, A.
Two Bonnycastles. Morton, T. and J. M.
Two bumpkins. *See* Morton, J. M. Margery Daw; or, The two bumpkins
Two buzzards; or, Whitebait at Greenwich. Morton, J. M.
Two countrymen. Stevenson, A.
Two cowards. Labiche, E. M.
Two Cromwells. De Lesseline, L.
Two crooks and a lady. Pillot, E.
Two doctors of Akragas. Peterson, F.
Two dollars, please! Stevenson, M.
Two drams of brandy. McBride, H. E.
Two faces under a hood. Dibdin, T. J.
Two galley slaves. Payne, J. H.
Two gentlemen at Mivarts. Simpson, J. P.
Two ghosts in white. Denison, T. S.
Two Greens. Rede, W. L.
Two Gregories; or, Where did the money come from? Dibdin, T. J.
Two hearts. Fitzgerald, S. J. A.
Two holes. Stevenson, A.
Two husbands. Lavedan, H.
Two in a flat. Elwes, M.
Two in the morning. *See* Matthews, C. J. Bachelor's bedroom; or, Two in the morning

Two's company. Graham, M. S.
Two lamps. Goodman, K. S. and Hecht, B.
Two loves and a life. Taylor, T. and Reade, C.
Two men of Sandy Bar. Harte, B.
Two millers. Stevenson, A.
Two Mr. Wetherbys. Hankin, St. J.
Two murderers. *See* Selby, C. Married rake; or, The two murderers
Two negatives make an affirmative. Heermans, F.
Two of a kind. Sturgis, G. F.
Two passengers for Chelsea. Firkins, O. W.
Two philosophers. Chapman, J. J.
Two Polts. Courtney, J.
Two Puddifoots. Morton, J. M.
Two queens. Buckstone, J. B.
Two questions. Stevenson, A.
Two shepherds. Martínez Sierra, G.
Two slaps in the face. Molnár, F.
Two slatterns and a king. Millay, E. St. V.
Two sons. Boyce, N.
Two strings to her bow. Harrison, C. C.
Two talismans. Calderon, G.
2 × 2=5. Wied, G. J.
Two virtues. Sutro, A.
'Twould puzzle a conjuror!   Poole, J.
Tyndale. Hord, P.
Typhoon. Lengyel, M.
Tyranny of tears. Chambers, C. H.
Tyrant. Sabatini, R.
Uberto. Osborn, L.
Ugly duckling. Stevenson, A.
Ugo da Este. Osborn, L.
Ulster. Rosenfeld, S.
Ulstermen. Marsh, A.
Ulysses. Phillips, S.
Ulysses in Ithaca. Mather, F. J.
Unattainable. Maugham, W. S.
Unbidden guest. Firkins, O. W.
Unborn. Middleton, G.
Unchastened woman. Anspacher, L. K.
Under the gaslight. Daly, A.
Uncle. Amalie of Saxony
Uncle Crotchet. Phillips, Mrs. A.
Uncle Jimmy. Gale, Z.
Uncle Ned. Murray, D.
Uncle Pat. Moylan, T. K.
Uncle Rip. Peake, R. B.
Uncle Tom's cabin. Aiken, G. L.
Uncle Tom's cabin. Stowe, H. B.
Uncle Vanya. Chekhov, A. P.
Unconscious burglary. Francis, J. M.
Under a spell. Labiche, E. M. and Jolly, A.
Under conviction. Dorey, J. M.
Under cover. Megrue, R. C.
Under fire. Megrue, R. C.
Under the curse. McBride, H. E.
Under the eagle. Potter, D.
Under the flag. Bernard, F.
Under the gaslight; or, Life and love in these times. Daly, A.
Under the green flag. *See* Muldoon, J. and Muldoon, J. M. For Ireland's sake; or, Under the green flag

When the clock strikes.   Parrish, J.
When the clock strikes twelve.   Barbee, L.
When the clock struck twelve.   Fawcett, E.
When the devil was ill.   McEvoy, C.
When the dew falleth.   Hirschbein, P.
When the new wine blooms.   Bjørnson, B.
When the post has been.   Millward, F. M.
When the roses bloom again.   Marquina, E.
When the silver bell tree blooms.   Peattie, E. W.
When the toys awake.   Barbee, L.
When the whirlwind blows.   Dane, E.
When the willow nods.   Kreymborg, A.
When two's not company.   Macmillan, M. L.
When we dead awaken.   Ibsen, H.
When we were twenty-one.   Esmond, H. V.
When witches ride.   Lay, E. A.
Where but in America.   Wolff, O. M.
Where do we go from here?   Bates, W. O.
Where's my toothbrush?   Henderson, S.
Where it is thin, there it breaks.   Turgenev, I. S.
Where Julia rules.   Ford, N. and Duer, C.
Where love is, there God is also.   Benton, R.
Where saints have trod.   Baird, G. M. P.
Where shall we go?   Lavedan, H.
Where the cross is made.   O'Neill, E. G.
Where there is nothing.   Yeats, W. B.
Where there's a will there's a way.   Morton, T. and J. M.
Where war comes.   Dix, B. M.
Which is the greater man?   Ramspacher, A.
Which is witch? or, Mable and Maisie.   Rostetter, A.
Which of the two?   Morton, J. M.
While the mushrooms bubble.   Totheroh, D. W.
White canoe.   Stevenson, A.
White cargo.   Gordon, L.
White cat.   Planché, J. R.
White Christmas.   Hare, W. B.
White cockade.   Gregory, I. A.
White dresses.   Green, P.
White elephant.   Cameron, M. and Rector, J. L.
White elephants.   Nicholson, K.
White fan.   Hofmannsthal, H. von
White hawk.   Kemp, H.
White horse.   Moser, G. von
White horse.   Roberts, M.
White lies.   Koning, M. M.
Wild oats.   Noel, J.
White peacock.   Petrova, O.
White rose.   South, R.
White roses.   See Bowman, J. C.   Gift of white roses
White saviour.   Hauptmann, G.
White slave.   Chapin, H. L.
White stacks.   Hewlett, W.
White wings.   Barry, P.

Whitebait at Greenwich.   See Morton, J. M.   Two buzzards; or, Whitebait at Greenwich
Whiteheaded boy.   Robinson, L.
Whitewashing Julia.   Jones, H. A.
Whither.   Griffith, A. M. M.
Whitman, Walt
   Morley, C. D.   Walt
Who defeated Doogan?   Buchanan, F. R. and Wilson, C.
Who do they take me for.   Morton, J. M.
Who stole the pocketbook.   Morton, J. M.
Who told the lie?   Benedix, R.
Who wants a guinea?   Colman, G.
Whole town's talking.   Emerson, J. and Loos, A.
Whom the gods destroy.   Hilbert, J.
Who's my husband.   Morton, J. M.
Who's the composer?   Morton, J. M.
Who's who?   Gilbert, B.
Whose little bride are you?   Ellis, E.
Whose widow.   Clifford, H. C.
Whose wife?   Norton, F. P.
Why girls stay home.   Humphrey, M.
Why Jessica!   Knowlton, A. R.
Why marry?   Williams, J. L.
Why misery never dies.   See Brighouse, H.   Apple-tree; or, Why misery never dies
Why not?   Williams, J. L.
Why Smith left home.   Broadhurst, G. H.
Why the chimes rang.   McFadden, E. A.
Wicked man.   Gilbert, B.
Wicked wife.   Courtney, J.
Wicked world.   Gilbert, W. S.
Wicklow wedding.   See Boucicault, D.   Arrah-na-pogue; or, The Wicklow wedding
Widdy's mite.   Totheroh, D.
Widow.   Meilhac. H. and Halévy, L.
Widow and her wooers.   See Taylor, T.   Sir Roger de Coverley; or, The widow and her wooers
Widow and the riding horse.   Kotzebue, A. F. F. von
Widow of Wasdale Head.   Pinero, A. W.
Widow Sabrina.   Sturgis, G. F.
Widow's vow.   Inchbald, E. S.
Widower's houses.   Shaw, G. B.
Widowing of Mrs. Holroyd.   Lawrence, D. H.
Widow's cruise.   Temple, J.
Widow's marriage.   Boker, G. H.
Widow's veil.   Rostetter, A.
Wife.   Schnitzler, A.
Wife; a tale of Mantua.   Knowles, J. S.
Wife of Marobius.   Ehrmann, M.
Wife of two husbands.   Dunlap, W.
Wife of Usher's Well.   Martin, J. J.
Wife; or, Love and madness.   Brockhurst, J. S.
Wife to a famous man.   Martínez Sierra, G.
Wife without a smile.   Pinero, A. W.
Wife's confession.   Besant, W. and Pollock, W.
Wife's portrait.   Marston, J. W.
Wife's revenge.   See Buckstone, J. B.   Agnes De Vere; or, The wife's revenge

Wife's trial. *See* Augier, E. Good for evil; or, A wife's trial
Wild birds. Totheroh, D.
Wild duck. Ibsen, H.
Wild goose. Hunter, R.
Wild-goose chase. Kotzebue, A. F. F. von
Wild manners. Young, S.
Wild oats; or, The strolling gentleman. O'Keeffe, J.
Wild proxy. Clifford, L. L.
Wild swans. Stevenson, A.
Wild Westcotts. Morrison, A.
Wild youth. Kotzebue, A. F. F. von
Wilderness. Esmond, H. V.
Wilderness. Jenkins, F. and Darrow, R. P.
Wilderness rose. Cochran, E. O.
Wilfred the young. Chapman, J. J.
Wilhelm Tell. Schiller, F. von
Will. Barrie, J. M.
Will. Reynolds, F.
Will and the way. Calvert, G. H.
Will for the deed. Dibdin, T. J.
Will he come back? Grendon, F.
Will of song. MacKaye, P. W.
Will-o'-the-wisp. Halman, D. F.
Will o' the wisp. Kavanaugh, K.
Will o' the wisp. Kvapil, J.
Will-o'-wisp. Wolfram, A.
Will Shakespeare. Dane, C.
Will Shakespeare's ward. *See* Burrill, E. W. Master Skylark; or, Will Shakespeare's ward
Will Watch. Amherst, J. H.
William Penn. Bird, G. E. and Starling, M.
William II [Germany]
Barrie, J. M. "Der Tag"; or, The tragic man
William Rufus. Field, M.
William Shakespeare, pedagogue and poacher. Garnett, R.
William Tell. Knowles, J. S.
William Tell. Rees, A. D.
William Tell. Stevenson, A.
Willikind and his Dinah. Coyne, J. S.
Willow copse. Boucicault, D.
Willow-pattern plate
Talfourd, F. Mandarin's daughter
Willowdale. Tubbs, A. L.
Wilson, Woodrow
Housman, L. Instrument
Oppenheim, J. Shadow in the white house
Wind. Peterson, A. E.
Wind and sea. Mitchell, S. W.
Wind o' the moors. Peach, L. du G.
Wind over the water. Merivale, P.
Windmill man. Bowyer, F.
Window to the south. Reely, M. K.
Windows. Galsworthy, J.
Wings. Peabody, J. P.
Wings in the mesh. Levick, M.
Wings of Daedalus. Olcott, V.
Winner. Sargent, H. C.
Winning a husband. Sturgis, G. F.
Winning ways. Rice, W. F.
Winter, Asch, S.
Winter ballad. Hauptmann, G.

Winter dawn. Gibson, W. W.
Winterbloom. Hayes, B. T.
Winterbottoms; or, My aunt the dowager. Moncrieff, W. T.
Winterfeast. Kennedy, C. R.
Winter's stob. Gibson, W. W.
Wisconsin
Leonard, W. E. C. Red Bird
Wisdom of children. Tolstoi, L.
Wisdom of folly. Hamilton, C.
Wisdom of the wise. Craigie. P. M. T.
Wisdom teeth. Field, R. L.
Wisdom tooth. Connelly, M.
Wise crow. Stevenson, A.
Wise men of Gotham. Stevenson, A.
Wise man of Nineveh. Tupper, W. S.
Wise man of the east. Kotzebue, A. F. F. von
Wise man of the east. Inchbald, E. S.
Wish-bird. Stevenson, A.
Wishing man. Hare, W. B.
Wistful waiting. Joseph, L. E.
Witch. Macnamara, M.
Witch. *See* Wiers-Jenssen, H. Anne Pedersdotter
Witch, a miracle. Cawein, M. J.
Witch of Endor. Norwood, R. W.
Witchcraft. Baillie, J.
Witchcraft. Mathews, C.
Witchcraft
Benton, R. Margaret of Salem
Freeman, M. W. Giles Corey, yeoman
Lay, A. When witches ride
Wiers-Jenssen, H. Anne Pedersdotter
Witchcraft story. Wagstaff, B. S.
Witches' mountain. Gardel, J. S.
Witching hour. Thomas, A.
Witch's curse. *See* Gilbert, M. S. Ruddigore; or, The witch's curse
With chains of gold. Vasquez, J. A.
Within cloister gates. Draper, J. W.
Within and without. MacDonald, G.
Within the gates of Yildiz. Brodé, J. L.
Within the law. Veiller, B.
Without incumbrances. Simpson, J. P.
Without the walls. Trask, K.
Witness. Vrchlicky, J.
Witness for the defence. Mason, A. E. W.
Wittikind and his brothers; or, The seven swan princes and the fair Melusine. Taylor, T.
Wives as they were, and maids as they are. Inchbold, E. S.
Wives by advertisement. Jerrold, D. W.
Wizard of the sea. *See* Jones, J. S. Captain Kyd; or, The wizard of the sea
Wizard of woods. Bryce, C. T.
Wolf and the horse. Stevenson, A.
Wolf and the lamb. Stevenson, A.
Wolf-hunt. Verga, G.
Wolf of Gubbio. Peabody, J. P.
Wolfe, James. Bird, G. E. and Starling, M.
Wollstonecraft, Mary
Peabody, J. P. Portrait of Mrs. W.
Wolves. Bell, J. J.
Wolves. Rolland, R.
Wolves and sheep. Ostrovsky, A.
Wolves and the lamb. Thackeray, C. M.

Woman. Kosor, J.
Woman alone. Clifford, L. L.
Woman and superwoman. Neave, A.
Woman and the fiddler. Norrevang, A.
Woman hater. Benedix, R.
Woman I adore! Morton, T. and J. M.
Woman in red. Coyne, J. S.
Woman in the case. Fitch, C.
Woman intervenes. Manners, J. H.
Woman is a devil; or, The temptation of Saint Antony. Merimée, P.
Woman of no importance. Wilde, O.
Woman of no one. Lodovici, C.
Woman of Paris. Becque, H.
Woman of Samaria. Rostand, E.
Woman of seven sorrows. MacManus, S.
Woman of the world. Coyne, J. S.
Woman on her own. Brieux, E.
Woman the masterpiece. Greene, B. M.
Woman who could. Sutherland, H. V.
Woman who was acquitted. Lorde, A. de
Woman who wouldn't. Stokes, R. P.
Woman with the dagger. See Schnitzler, A. Lady with the dagger
Womankind. Gibson, W. W.
Woman's a woman for a' that. MacMillan, M. L.
Woman's choice. Dazey, L. H. and Dazey, C. T.
Woman's crowning glory. Swears, H.
Woman's heart. Phelps, A. L.
Woman's honor. Glaspell, S.
Woman's hour. Paulding, F.
Woman's influence. Jenkins, G. E.
Woman's love. Wilkes, T. E.
Woman's masquerade. Smith, N. D.
Woman's stratagem. Kavanaugh, K.
Woman's verdict. Moretté, E.
Woman's way. Buchanan. T.
Woman's way. Kavanaugh, K.
Woman's wit. Knowles, J. S.
Women as advocates. Litchfield, G. D
Women for votes. Hughes, E.
Women in war. Godshaw, E.
Women of Shakespeare. Bartholomew, J. H.
Women's town. Álvarez de Quintero, S. and J.
Won back. Tayleure, C. W.
Wonder hat. Goodman, K. S. and Hecht, B.
Wonder-hill. Olcott, V.
Wonderful woman. Wilde, P.
Wondership. Cunningham, L.
Wood demon. Chekhov, A. P.
Woodbarrow farm. Jerome, J. K.
Woodcock's little game. Morton, J. M.
Wooden bowl. Parson, M. C.
Wooden leg. Dane, E.
Woodland princess. Saunders, L.
Woodman's hut; a melodrama in three acts. London. Simpkin. 1818. 38p Attributed to S. J. and W. H. Arnold
Woodman's spell. Stirling, E.
Woods of Ida. Dargan, O. T.
Wooing of Eve. Manners, J. H.
Wooing one's wife. Morton, J. M.
Words and thoughts. Marquis, D.
Workers at the looms. Dane, E.

Workhouse ward. Gregory, I. A.
World and his wife. See Echegaray, J. Great Galeoto
World and his wife. Nirdlinger, C. F. Adapted from Echegaray, J.
World at auction. Field, M.
World beyond the mountain. Roof, K.
World discovered. See Morton, T. Columbus; or, A world discovered
World war. See also War
Anderson, M. and Stallings, L. What price glory?
Bagg, H. Behind the lines
Barclay, Sir T. Sands of fate
Barrie, J. M. Barbara's wedding
—— "Der Tag"
Beyerlein, F. A. Taps
Binyon, L. Bombastes in the shades
Brown, A. Hero
Brunner, E. B. Making a man
—— Over age
Cammaerts, É. Adoration of the soldiers
Clements, C. C. Four who were blind
Crocker, B. Pawns of war
Dix, B. M. Across the border
—— Moloch
Farrar, J. C. Nerves
Galsworthy, J. Defeat
Gordon, L. Gentleman ranker
Hagboldt. P. Test
Hankey, D. Passing in June 1915
Horne, E. Mushrooms
Leslie, N. For king and country
—— War fly
Lowe, L. Bitterly reviled
McKnight, R. W. Pigeon
Maeterlinck, M. Burgomaster of Stilemonde
Malleson, M. Black 'ell
—— 'D' company
Manners, J. H. God's outcast
—— Out there
Marsh, E. H. Kaiser's reasons
Megrue, R. C. Under fire
Miller, A. D. What are they fighting for?
Morette, E. In the swath
Pinero, A. W. Quick work
Pinski, D. Beautiful nun
—— Little heroes
Pollock, C. Enemy
Richardson, M. E. Of others weaving
Riley, A. C. Skim-milk
Rubinstein, H. F. Arms and the drama
Scott, M. Submarine shell
Shaw, G. B. O'Flaherty, V. C.
Sturgis, R. F. Our war babe
Theis, G. Numbers
Troubetzkoy, A. R. Out of the midst of hatred
Tull, M. C. Treason
Wentworth, M. C. War brides
Wilson, H. Stultilia
World we live in. See Capêk, K. and Capêk, J. "And so ad infinitum"
World's own. Howe, J. W.
World's triumph. Block, L. J.
Worship the Nativity. Farrar, J. C.
Worsted man. Bangs, J. K.

APPENDIX A

BOOKS BY ONE AUTHOR CONTAINING MORE THAN ONE PLAY

NOTE.—Single plays are not entered in this list. Full bibliographical information in regard to them may be found in the Author Index.

Abercrombie, Lascelles
Four short plays. London Secker 1922 12° 175p
Adams, Arthur Henry
Three plays for the Australian stage. Sydney. William Brooks & Co. 1914 12° 141p
Adams, Oscar Fay
Motley jest. Shakespearian diversions Boston Sherman 1909 12° 64p
Aitken, I. E. M.
Domestic experiments and other plays. London Lamley 1910 16° 133p
Akins, Zoe
Déclassée: Daddy's gone a-hunting: and Greatness—a comedy. N.Y. Boni 1923 12° 304p
Aldis, Mrs Mary (Reynolds)
Plays for small stages... N.Y. Duffield 1915 12° 105p $1.25
Amalie of Saxony, Princess
Six dramas illustrative of German life... London Parker 1848 12° 350p
Social life in Germany... London Saunders 1840 12° 20s
Anderson, Maxwell and Stallings, Lawrence
Three American plays. N.Y. Harcourt 1926 8° 263p $2.50
Andreev, Leonid
Plays: ... tr... by C. L. Meader and F. N. Scott. N.Y. Scribner 1915 12° 214p
Savva, The life of man, two plays. Tr.... by Thos. Seltzer N.Y. Kennerley 1914 12° 236p $1
Appelgarth, Margaret Tyson
More short missionary plays. N.Y. Doran [C1923] 12° 184p
Short missionary plays. N.Y. Doran [C1923] 12° 183p
Arnold, Matthew
Poetical works. N.Y. Macm 1923 12° (any complete edition)
Artsybashev, Mikhail P.
Jealousy; Enemies; The law of the savage. N.Y. Boni 1923 12° 320p
Augier, Émile
Four plays... N.Y. Knopf 1915 12° 234p
Baillie, Joanna
Dramas... London Longman 1836 8° 3vs 1762-1851
Dramatic and poetical works. London Longman 1853 8° 847p
Baldwin, Charles Crittenden
Airy nothings; or What you will. N.Y. Sturges 1917 12° 144p
Baldwin, Sidney
Five plays and five pantomines... Phila Penn Pub Co 1922 12° 128p
Balzac, Honoré de
Dramatic works... Chicago Laird 1901 12° 2v
Works (Croxley edition). N.Y. Society of English and French literature [C1900] 8° 36v in 18 Dramas: v 34-36
Bangs, John Kendrick
Bicyclers and three other farces. N.Y. Harper 1896 12° 176p
Real thing and three other farces. N.Y. Harper 1909 12° 135p
Barbee, Lindsey
Cinderella and five other fairy plays. Chicago Denison [C1922] 12° 146p
Let's pretend; a book of children's plays... Chicago Deninson [C1917] 12° 160p 75c
Baring, Maurice
Diminutive dramas. London Secker 1919 12° 200p
Grey stocking and other plays. London Constable 1911 12° 366p
His majesty's embassy and other plays... Boston Little Brown 1923 12° 222p $2.50

Barker, H. G.
Three plays. N.Y. Brentano 1909 12° 347p $1.50
Three short plays... Boston Little 1917 8° 86p
Barrie, Sir James M.
Admirable Crichton and other plays... N.Y. Scribner 1926 12°
Echoes of the war. London Hodder [C1918] 12° 168p
Half hours. N.Y. Scribner 1914 12° 207p
Old lady shows her medals. London Hodder [1921] 12° 168p (London edition of 1918 under title Echoes of the war)
Twelve pound look and other plays. London Hodder 1921 12° 180p (N.Y. edition 'Half hours')
Representative plays... N.Y. Scribner [C1926] 12° 439p
What every woman knows, and other plays... N.Y. Scribner 1926 12°
Bartlett, Archie Ernest
Dramas of camp and cloister. Boston Badger [C1907] 12° 252p
Bax, Clifford
Antique pageantry, a book of verse-plays. London Hendersons 1921 12° 138p
Polite satires... London Medici Society 1922 12° 51p
Beach, Lewis
Four one-act plays: The clod; A guest for dinner; Love among the lions; Brothers. New York Brentano's [C1921] 12° 96p
Becque, Henry
The vultures; The woman of Paris; The merry-go-round. Tr from the French... by F. Tilden N.Y. Kennerley 1913 12° 266p (Modern Dramas series)
Beddoes, Thomas Lovell
Poetical works. Edited... by Edmund Gosse London Dent 1890 8° 2vs
Beith, John Hay (pseud. Ian Hay)
Crimson cocoanut and other plays. Boston Baker 1913 12° 130p
Benavente y Martínez, Jacinto
Plays. Tr from the Spanish, with an introduction by John Garrett Underhill... N.Y. Scribner 1917 8° 267p $1.50
Plays. Second series Tr from the Spanish with an introduction by John Garrett Underhill... N.Y. Scribner 1919 8° 309p
Plays. Third series Tr from the Spanish with an introduction by John Garrett Underhill N.Y. Scribner 1923 8° 219p
Plays. Fourth series... Trans... by John Garrett Underhill N.Y. Scribner 1924 12° 224p
Bennett, Arnold
Polite farces for the drawing room. N.Y. Doran 1912 12° 97p
Benton, Rita
Bible plays... N.Y. Abingdon press [C1922] 8° 237p
Franklin, and other plays. N.Y. Writers pub co 1924 12° 229p
Shorter Bible plays. N.Y. Abingdon C1922 12° 135p
Star-child and other plays... N.Y. Writers' pub co [C1921] 12° 143p
Bergstrøm, Hjalmar
Karen Borneman, Lynggaard & co.; two plays; tr from the Danish... by E. Björkman. N.Y. Kennerley 1913 12° 255p $1.50
Besant, Sir Walter and Pollock, Walter
The charm, and other drawing room plays... N.Y. Stokes [1897] 12° 275p
Betts, Frank
Saga plays. Oxford Blackwell 1917 12° 101p

Bird, Grace Electa and Starling, Maude
Historical plays for children. N.Y. Macm 1912
12° 292p
Bjørnson, B.
Plays... tr from the Norwegian by Edwin
Bjorkman N.Y. Scribner 1913 12° 281p
Plays... 2nd series... tr from the Norwegian by
Edwin Bjorkman N.Y. Scribner 1914 12° 284p
Three comedies. N.Y. Dutton n.d. 198p 12°
Three dramas. N.Y. Dutton n.d. 12° 291p
(Everyman's library)
Blashfield, Mrs Evangeline (Wilbour)
Masques of Cupid... N.Y. Scribner 1901 8° 264p
Block, Louis J.
Capriccios. N.Y. Putnam 1898 12° 130p
Dramatic sketches and poems. Phila Lippincott
1891 12° 220p
Bodenheim, Maxwell and Hecht, Ben
Minna and myself. N.Y. Pagan Pub Co 1918 12°
91p
Boker, George Henry
Plays and poems... Boston Ticknor 1856 12°
2v Also Phila Lippincott 1883 2v
Bolton, G. and Middleton, G.
Polly with a past and Adam and Eva, two
comedies. N.Y. Holt 1923 12° 272p
Bottomley, Gordon
Gruach, and Britain's daughter; two plays. Lon-
don Constable 1921 8° 130p
King Lear's wife ₁and other plays₁. London Con-
stable 1921 12° 223p
Brace, Gladys
Rosamond and Simonetta; two poetic plays. N.Y.
Harold Vinal 1925 8° 69p
Brand, Alfred
The infernal masculine and other comedies. Bos-
ton Cornhill ₁c1918₁ 12° 106p
Brandane, John
The glen is mine and The lifting; two plays of
the Hebrides. London Constable 1925 12° 235p
Brieux, Eugène
Three plays... N.Y. Brentano's 1913 12° 333p
Woman on her own, False god and The red robe;
three plays... N.Y. Brentano's 1916 12° 33p
Blanchette, and The escape; two plays... Bos-
ton Luce 1913 12° 240p
Brighouse, Harold
Open-air plays; five one-act plays... N.Y. French
1927 8° $1.50
Plays for the meadow and plays for the lawn.
London French c1921 12° 112p
Brooks, Charles Stephen
Three Lancashire plays... N.Y. French c1920 12°
300p $2.50
Frightful plays!... N.Y. Harcourt ₁c1922₁ 8° 214p
Brown, Alice
One act plays. N.Y. Macm 1921 12° 235p
Browning, Robert
Complete poetical works. N.Y. Macm 1924 8ᵛ
1359p
Brunner, Mrs Emma B.
Bits of background in one act plays. N.Y. Knopf
1919 12° 120p $1
Bryce, Catherine Turner
Bound or free, and The wizard of words; plays.
Boston Atlantic monthly press c1922 32p
Bulwer-Lytton, Sir Edward G.
Bulwer's plays... N.Y. De Witt ₁c1875₁ 12° 396p
Bunner, Henry Cuyler
Three operettas... N.Y. Harper 1897 12° 163p
Burr, Amelia Josephine
Hearts awake; The pixy, a play. N.Y. Doran
₁c1919₁ 12° 155p
Plays in the market-place. Englewood, N.J. Hill-
side press 1910 12° 74p
Bynner, Witter
Book of plays. N.Y. Knopf 1922 12° 255p
Calderon, George
Eight one-act plays. London Richards 1922 12°
189p
Three plays and a pantomime. London Richards
1922 12° 352p
Calvert, George Henry
Comedies. Boston Phillips 1856 125p 8°
Cameron, Margaret
Comedies in miniature... N.Y. McClure 1903 12°
376p

Cannan, Gilbert
Four plays... London Sidgwick 1913 12° 84p
Seven plays. London Secker ₁1923₁ 12° 208p
Cannon, Charles James
Dramas. N.Y. Dunigan 1857 12° 355p
Carman, Bliss and King, Mary P.
Earth deities, and other rhythmic masques. N.Y.
Kennerley 1914 12° 85p
Cauldwell, Samuel Milbank
Chocolate cake and black sand, and two other
plays... N.Y. Putnam 1917 12° 150p $1.50
Caverly, Robert Boodey
Battle of the Bush. Dramas and historic
legends... Boston Russell 1886 12° 346p
Cawein, Madison Julius
Shadow garden and other plays. N.Y. Putnams
1910 12° 259p
Cayzer, Charles William
By the way of the gate: poems and dramas.
London K. Paul 1911 12° 2vs
Chapin, Harold
Comedies... London Chatto 1921 8° 241p
Three one-act plays... N.Y. French c1921 12°
75p
Chapin, Harry Lorenzo
Poems and plays. N.Y. Shakespeare press. ₁c1915₁
12° 259p
Chapman, John Jay
Cupid and Psyche. N.Y. Gomme 1916 12° 92p
Four plays for children. N.Y. Moffatt 1908 12°
156p
Homeric scenes... N.Y. Gomme 1914 12° 76p
Neptune's isle and other plays for children. N.Y.
Moffat 1911 12° 196p
Chekhov, A. P.
Cherry orchard and other plays. London Chatto
1923 12° 273p
Plays... N.Y. Scribner 1912 12° 233p
Plays by Anton Tchekoff. 2nd series... N.Y.
Scribner 1916 12° 277p
Three sisters and other plays... London Chatto
1923 12° 298p
Two plays by Tchekoff... London Richards 1912
12° 155p
Chenevix, Richard
Two plays... London Johnson 1812 8° 31p
Clements, Colin Campbell
Plays for a folding theatre. Cincinnati Stewart
Kidd ₁c1923₁ 12° 135p
Plays for pagans. N.Y. Appleton 1924 12° 162p
Clifford, Lucy Lane
Plays... N.Y. Kennerley 1910 12° 329p
Coleridge, Samuel Taylor
Poetical works... N.Y. Macm 1909 12° 667p
Colman, George (younger)
Dramatic works of George Colman the younger...
Paris Malepeyre 1823-24 12° 4v
Colum, Padraic
Fiddler's house; a play in three acts; and The
land, an agrarian comedy. Dublin Maunsel 1909
12° 113p
Three plays... Boston Little 1916 12° 223p
Same N.Y. Macm 1925
Conrad, Joseph
Laughing Anne, One more day; two plays... Gar-
den City Doubleday 1925 12° 124p
Converse, Florence
Garments of praise, a miracle cycle. N.Y. Dutton
₁c1921₁ 12° 208p
Cook, Winifred A.
Plays and poems. London Sherratt and Hughes
₁190?₁ 12° 135p
Corbin, John
Husband and The forbidden guests; two plays...
Boston Houghton 1910 12° 271p
Corkery, David
Yellow bittern and other plays. London Unwin
1920 12° 94p
Cowan, Sada
Pomp and other plays... N.Y. Brentano's
₁c1920₁ 12° 211p
Coward, Noel
Three plays: The rat trap, The vortex, Fallen
angels. London Benn 1925 8° 278p
Crocker, Bosworth, pseud.
Humble folk one-act plays. Cincinnati Stewart
Kidd ₁c1923₁ 12° 176p

Frank, Maude Morrison
Short plays about famous authors. . . N.Y. Holt 1915 12° 144p $1
Fuller, Henry Blake
Puppet-booth; twelve plays. N.Y. Century 1896 12° 212p
Galsworthy, J.
Works Manaton ed. London Heinemann 1923 Plays vol 18-21
Little man, and other satires. N.Y. Scribner 1915 12° 279p $1.30
Plays... N.Y. Putnam 1909 12° 263p
Plays. Second series... N.Y. Scribner 1913 12° 109p
Plays. Third series... N.Y. Scribner 1914 12° 77p
Plays. Fourth series... N.Y. Scribner 1920 12° 115p $2.50
Plays. Fifth series... N.Y. Scribner 1923 12° 108p, 110p, 91p
Plays. Sixth series; The forest, Old English, The show. N.Y. Scribner 1926 12° 115p, 112p, 97p $2.50
Representative plays... N.Y. Scribner ₁c1924₁ 12° 469p
Six short plays. N.Y. Scribner 1921 12° 142p
Galt, John
Tragedies of Maddalen, Agamemnon, Lady Macbeth, Antonia and Clytemnestra. London Cadell and Davis 1812 8° 262p
Garnett, Louise Ayers
Three to make ready: Hilltop, Muffins, The pig prince; three plays for young people. N.Y. Doran ₁c1923₁ 12° 194p
Gaskoin, Catherine Bellairs
Lumber room and other plays. London Paul ₁c1913₁ 12° 140p
Gerstenberg, Alice
Four plays for four women. N.Y. Brentano's 1924 12° 114p $1.50
Little world; a series of college plays for girls. Chicago Dramatic Pub Co ₁c1908₁ 8° 228p
Ten one-act plays. N.Y. Brentano's ₁c1921₁ 12° 256p
Giacosa, Guiseppe
Stronger; Like falling leaves; Sacred ground; three plays... N.Y. Kennerley 1913 12° 326p
Gibson, Wilfrid W.
Battle and other poems. N.Y. Macm 1916 12° 198p
Borderlands and thoroughfares. N.Y. Macm 1914 12° 195p
Daily bread. N.Y. Macm 1913 12° 189p
Daily bread. London Mathews 1913 12° 3vs Later edition complete in one vol.
Kestrel Edge and other plays. N.Y. Macm 1924 12° 150p $1.50
Poems. 1904-1917 N.Y. Macm 1917 12° 552p
Stonefolds ₁Cranleigh, nr. Guildford. Samurai press 1907₁ 12° 32p
Gilbert, Bernard
King Lear at Hurdle and other rural plays. London Collins ₁c1922₁ 12° 267p
Gilbert, Sir William Schwenck
H. M. S. Pinafore, and other plays. N.Y. Modern library ₁1925₁ 12° 218p
Iolanthe and other operas... London Bell 1910 12° 224p
Mikado, and other plays... N.Y. Boni 1917 12° 229p
Original comic operas... N.Y. Harper ₁1886₁ 12° 73p
Original plays. first series. London Chatto 1902 12° 287p
Original plays; second series. London Chatto 1920 12° 338p
Original plays; third series. London Chatto 1903 12° 453p
Original plays. fourth series. London Chatto 1911 12° 475p
Glaspell, Susan
People, and Close the book; two one act plays. N.Y. Shay 1918 12° 30p
Plays. Boston Small ₁c1920₁ 12° 315p
Three plays. London Benn 1924 12° 3v in 1
Glover, Halcott
Wat Tyler and other plays. London K. Paul, Trench 1925 12° 341p

Goethe, J. W.
Dramatic works... Trans by Anna Swanwick; and Goetz von Berlichingen, trans by Sir Walter Scott... London Boni 1851 12° 504p
Golden, John
Three John Golden plays. N.Y. French 1925 8° 126p
Goodman, Kenneth S.
More quick curtains. Chicago Stage Guild 1923 12° 159p
Quick curtains. Chicago Stage Guild 1915 12° 262p
Goodman, K. S. and Hecht, B.
Wonder hat and other one-act plays. N.Y. Appleton 1925 12° 188p $1.75
Goodman, K. S. and Stevens, T. W.
Daimio's head, and other masques. Chicago Stage Guild ₁c1912₁ 12° 61p
Masques of East and West. N.Y. Vaughan & Gomme 1914 12° 235p
Gordon, Leon
Gentleman banker, and other plays. Boston Four Seas 1919 12° 128p
Gould, Felix
Marsh maiden and other plays. Boston Four Seas 1918 12° 18p
Graham, Bertha M.
Spoiling the broth and other plays. London Chapman and Hall 1913 16° 202p
Gray, Terence
"And in the tomb was found;" plays and portraits of old Egypt. N.Y. Appleton 1923 12° 236p
Green, Paul
Field god and In Abraham's bosom. N.Y. McBride 1917 12° 317p
Lonesome road; six plays for the negro theatre. N.Y. McBride 12° 217p
Lord's will, and other Carolina plays... N.Y. Holb 1925 12° 264p
Greene, B. M.
Woman the masterpiece; ₁and₁ God-intoxicated man; two plays. Ryerson Toronto 1923 12° 148p $1.75
Greene, Clay Meredith
Dispensation and other plays. N.Y. Doran ₁c1914₁ 12° 96p
Greene, Henry Coply
Pontius Pilate; Saint Ronan of Brittany, Theophile; three plays in verse. N.Y. Scott—Thaw 1903 12° 90p
Greene, Kathleen Conyngham
Little boy out of the wood and other dream plays. London John Lane 1917 12° 105p
Gregory, Lady Isabella A.
Image and other plays. N.Y. Putnam 1922 12° 253p $2
Irish folk-history plays. N.Y. Putnam 1912 12° 2vs Ser 1 Tragedies Ser 2 Tragic-comedies
New comedies... N.Y. Putnam 1913 12° 166p
Poets and dreamers; studies and translations from the Irish. Dublin Hodges 1903 12° 254p
Seven short plays. Dublin Maunsel 1910 12° 211p
Three wonder plays... N.Y. Putnam 1922 12° 290p
Guild, Thacher H.
Power of a god, and other one-act plays... Urbana Univ of Ill 1919 12° 151p $1.25
Hagedorn, Hermann
Great maze and The heart of youth, a poem and a play. N.Y. Macm 1916 12° 171p
Halman, Doris F.
Set the stage for eight. Bost Little Brown 1923 12° 194p
Hamilton, Alexander
Dramas and poems... N.Y. Dick & Fitzgerald ₁1887₁ 12° 106p
Hamilton, Cosmo
Four plays... Boston, Little 1924 12° 350p
Hankin, St. John, Emile Clavering
Dramatic work of St. John Hankin... London Secker 1912 3vs 12°
Plays... London Secker 1923 2vs 8°
Three plays with happy endings. London French 1907 12° 134, 168, 160p
Hanning, S. C.
Caledonia. London J. & J. Bennett ₁1915₁ 12° 286p
Hardy, Thomas
Works in prose and verse... London Macm 1912-13 8° 20v

Norton, Franklin Pierce,
Foibles, a farcical comedy. N.Y. Schulte ₍c1920₎ 12° 36 + 6
Six dramas of American romance and history. N.Y. Schulte 1915 8° 209p

Noyes, Alfred
Collected poems. N.Y. Stokes v1913 12° 2vs

O'Brien, Seumas
Duty, and other Irish comedies. Boston Little 1916 12° 134p

O'Casey, Sean
Two plays: Juno and the paycock, The shadow of the gunman. N.Y. Macm 1925 12° 199p

O'Dea, Mark
Red bud women; four dramatic episodes... Cincinnati Stewart Kidd 1922 12° 123p $2

Ollcott, Virginia
Everyday plays for home, school and settlement... N.Y. Dodd Mead 1925 12° 167p (Published 1916 under title: Plays for home, school and settlement)
Holiday plays for home, school and settlement... N.Y. Moffatt 1917 12° 197p
International plays for young people. N.Y. Dodd Mead 1925 12° 245p
Patriotic plays for young people. Dodd N.Y. 1918 12° 174p

Oldershaw, Lucian
Cranford at home and other carpet dramas. London R. B. Johnson ₍1902₎ 24° [244p]

Oliver, Margaret Scott
Six one-act plays... Boston Badger 1916 12° 128p

O'Neill, Eugene G.
Collected plays. N.Y. Boni 1925-26 5vs 12° $2.50 ea
Complete works... N.Y. Boni 1924 8° 2vs
Emperor Jones, Diff'rent, The straw. N.Y. Boni ₍1921₎ 12° 285p
Great god Brown, The fountain, The moon of the Caribbees and other plays. N.Y. Boni 1926 8° 383p
Hairy ape, Anna Christie, The first man. N.Y. ₍1922₎ 12° 322p
Moon of the Caribbees and six other plays of the sea. N.Y. Boni 1919 12° 217p
Thirst, and other one-act plays. Boston Gorham c1914 12° 168p
Shakespeare's end and other Irish plays. London Swift 1912 12° 166p

Oppenheim, James
Book of self. N.Y. Knopf 1917 12° 273p

Orton, Jason Rockwood
Arnold and other poems. N.Y. Partridge 1854 12° 144p

Osborn, Laughton
Calvary, Virginia; tragedies. N.Y. Doolady 1867 12° 200p
Dramatic works. N.Y. Moorhead 1868-70 8° 4vs Imprint varies: v 1, N.Y. James Miller 1868; v 2 N.Y. American News Co. 1870; v 4 N.Y. James Miller 1868
Last Mandeville... tragedies... N.Y. American News Co. 1870 12° p 273-605
Magnetiser, The prodigal, comedies in prose. N.Y. Miller 1869 12° 321p
Meleagros; The new Calvary. N.Y. American News Co 1871 12° 164p
Montanini; The school for critics; comedies. Being in continuation and completion of the fourth volume of the dramatic series. N.Y. Miller 1868 12° p 265-517
Silver head; The double deceit; comedies. N.Y. Doolady 1867 12° 262p
Ugo da Este; Uberto; The Cid of Seville; tragedies. N.Y. Miller 1869 12° 269p

Ostrovsky, Aleksandr N.
Plays... N.Y. Scribner 1917 12° 305p

Ould, Herman
Plays of pioneers. N.Y. French c1925 45p
Three comedies. N.Y. French c1925 12° 57p

Pain, Mrs Amelia
More short plays for amateurs. London Chapman & Hall 1908 12° 123p
Nine of diamonds and other plays. London Chapman & Hall 1913 12° 142p

Pallen, Condé
Collected poems. N.Y. Kenedy 1915 12° 261p $1.25

Parsons, Margaret Colby (Getchell)
In the children's play-house. Boston Baker 1923 12° 83p
Red letter day plays. N.Y. Woman's press 1921 12° 224p

Paulding, James K. and Paulding, William I
American comedies... Phila Carey 1847 12° 295p

Payne, Fanny Ursula
Plays and pageants of citizenship. N.Y. Harper c1920 12° 222p
Plays and pageants of democracy. N.Y. Harper c1919 12° 128p
Plays for any child. N.Y. Harper ₍1918₎ 12° 144p

Peabody, Josephine P.
Fortune and men's eyes; new poems with a play... Boston Small 1900 111p

Peacock, Thomas L.
Plays of Thomas Love Peacock... London Nutt 1910 12° 157p

Pearse, Padraic H.
Collected works. N.Y. Stokes ₍c1917₎ 12° 341p $3.50
Singer, and other plays. Dublin Maunsel 1918 12° 123p

Peattie, Mrs Elia (Wilkinson)
Wander weed, and seven other little theatre plays. Chicago Sergel 1923 260p 8° $2.25

Pellettieri, Guiseppe, M.
Love enchained and other plays. Boston Stratford ₍c1924₎ 12° 171p

Phillips, David Graham
Worth of a woman; a play in four acts; followed by A point of law, a dramatic incident. N.Y. Appleton 1908 12° 128p

Phillips, Stephen
Collected plays... N.Y. Macm 1921 12° 894p $3
Lyrics and dramas. N.Y. Lane 1913 12° 179p $1.25

Phillpotts, Eden
Curtain raisers. London Duckworth 1912 12° 53p
Three plays: The shadow; The mother; The secret woman. London Duckworth 1913 12° 90p

Pinero, Sir A. W.
Social plays of Arthur Wing Pinero... N.Y. Dutton 1917-22 4vs 12°

Pinski, David
King David and his wives. N.Y. Huebsch 1923 12° 186p $2
Ten plays. N.Y. Huebsch 1920 12° 209p $2
Three plays; authorized translation from the Yiddish by Isaac Goldberg. N.Y. Huebsch 1918 12° 324p

Pirandello, Luigi
Each in his own way and two other plays. From the Italian by Arthur Livingston. N.Y. Dutton ₍c1923₎ 12° 258p $3
Three plays... N.Y. Dutton ₍c1922₎ 8° 223p $3.50

Planché, James Robinson
Extravagangas. 1825-1871... London French 8° 5v

Pollock, John
Twelve one-acters. Kensington. Cayme press 1926 8° 330p

Poole, Evan
Age of steel; plays and episodes. London Heath Cranton & Ouseley ₍1913₎ 12° 140p

Potter, Dorothy
Under the eagle; three plays with a prologue and epilogue. Boston Gorham 1916 12° 70p

Powell, Thomas
Dramatic poems. London Mitchell 1845 16° 290p
Marcian Colonna, an Italian tale with three dramatic scenes and other poems. London Warren 1820 8° 190p

Procter, Bryan Waller
Dramatic scenes. With other poems...N.Y. Appleton 1857 12° 404p

Quinton, Pauline Brooks
Locust flower and The celibate: two plays. Boston Sherman French 1916 12° 102p $1

Ramspacher, Anna
Lady of the Nile, and other plays. Boston Roxburgh Pub Co 1924 126p

Ratcliffe, Dorothy Una
Dale dramas; a book of little plays... London Lane ₍1923₎ 8° 125p

Sobel, Bernard
    Three plays. Boston, Poet Lore Co 1913 12° 79p $1

South, Robert
    Divine Aretino, and other plays. London Long 19— 8°

Stapp, Emilia Blackmore, and Cameron, Eleanor
    Happylands fairy grotto plays... Boston Houghton ₍c1922₎ 12° 149p $1.25

Steele, Wilbur Daniel
    Terrible woman, and other one-act plays... N.Y. Appleton 1925 12° 154p

Steiner, Rudolph
    Four mystery plays... N.Y. Putnam 1920 12° 2vs

Stevens, Henry Bailey
    Cry out of the dark; three plays... Boston Four Seas 1919 12° 88p $1.25

Stevens, Thomas Wood
    Drawing of the sword; together with the National Red Cross pageant. Boston Burchard ₍c1918₎ 12° 39p
    Nursery maid of Heaven, and other plays. N.Y. Appleton 1926 12° $1.75 177p

Stevenson, Augusta
    Children's classics in dramatic form. Boston Houghton ₍1908-10₎ 12° 4bks
    Plays for the home. Boston Houghton 1913 8° 181p (This book was first published as "Children's Classics in drama form." bk 3)

Stopes, Marie C. C.
    Gold in the wood; and The race; two new plays of life. London Fifield 1918 12° 101p

Strindberg, August
    Countess Julia, naturalistic tragedy. Phila Brown 1912 12° 101p
    Easter, a play in three acts... Cincinnati Stewart Kidd 1912 12° 269p
    Miss Julie and other plays. N.Y. Boni ₍1918₎ 167p
    Pariah; Simoon; two plays. London Hendersons 1914 12° 47p
    Plays: Comrades, Facing death, Pariah, Easter... Boston, Luce 1912 218p v 2
    Plays... Creditors, Pariah... N.Y. Scribner 1912 89p 75c
    Plays... The dream play, The link, The dance of death, Pt I The dance of death, Pt II... N.Y. Scribner 1912 268p
    Plays. Fourth series. The bridal crown, The spook sonata, The first warning, Gustavus Vasa... N.Y. Scribner 1916 283p $1.50
    Plays... Miss Julie... The stronger... N.Y. Scribner 1912 90p 75c
    Plays... Second series: There are crimes and crimes, Miss Julia, The stronger, Creditors, Pariah... N.Y. Scribner 1913 265p $1.50
    Plays: Swanwhite, Advent, The storm... Boston Luce 1914 $1.50 v 3
    Plays: The father, Countess Julie, The outlaw, The stronger... Boston Luce 1912 211p $1.50 v 1
    Plays... Third series: Swanwhite, Debit and Credit, Advent, The thunderstorm, After the fire... N.Y. Scribner 1913 276p $1.50

Strong, Austin
    Drums of Oude, and other one-act plays. N.Y. Appleton 1926 12° 90p $1.50

Sturgis, Granville Forbes
    Little plays for all occasions... Boston Cornhill 1923 12° 317p

Sturgis, Julian
    Little comedies. N.Y. Appleton 1880 12° 180p

Sudermann, H.
    Morituri; three one-act plays. Teja, Fritzchen, Eternal masculine... Scribner N.Y. 1910 12° 156p
    Roses, four one-act plays: Streaks of light; The last visit; Margot; The far-away princess... N.Y. Scribner 1909 12° 183p

Sutherland, Evelyn G.
    Po' white trash and other one-act dramas, certain of the plays being written in collaboration with Emma Sheridan-Fry and Percy W. MacKaye. N.Y. Duffield 1909 12° 232p

Sutro, Alfred
    Five little plays. N.Y. Brentano 1913 12° 131p

Swinburne, A. C.
    Poems. N.Y. Harper 1904 8° 6v
    Queen-mother, and Rosamond. Boston Ticknor & Fields 1866 12° 232p

Tragedies. N.Y. Harper 1906 12° 5vs
Works. Philadelphia McKay ₍1910₎ 8° 2v Poems and tragedies (Not volumed)

Symons, Arthur
    Cesare Borgia, Iseult of Brittany, The toy cart. N.Y. Brentano's 1920 12° 213p $1.75
    Collected works... London Secker 1924 8°
    Tragedies. London Heinemann 1916 8° 151p

Synge, John M.
    Four plays. Dublin Maunsel 1911 179p
    Plays. London Allen 1924 12° 377p
    Shadow of the glen, and Riders to the sea. London Mathews 1910 12° 63p
    Two plays. Dublin Maunsel 1911
    Works. Boston Luce 1912 12° 4vs
    Works. Dublin Maunsel 1910 4vs 1913 8vs

Taft, Grace E.
    Chimalman, and other poems. N.Y. Cameo press 1916 12° 96p $1.25

Tagore, Rabindranath
    Sacrifice, and other plays. N.Y. Macm 1917 12° 208p $1.75

Talfourd, T. N.
    Dramatic works. 11th ed London Moxon 1852 12° 369p
    Tragedies... Boston Crosby & Ainsworth 1865 12° 268p

Taylor, Sir Henry
    Works... London H. S. King 1877-78 12° 5v

Taylor, Tom
    Historical dramas. London Chatto & Windus 1877 12° 466p

Tennyson, Alfred
    Complete poems. Any edition

Theis, Grover
    Numbers, and other one-act plays. N.Y. Brown 1919 12°

Titheradge, Dion
    From the prompt corner. N.Y. French c1925 8° 75p
    Out of the box. N.Y. French c1925 8° 69p

Tolstoi, Lyof N.
    Complete works...Tr from the original Russian and ed by Leo Wiener. Boston Estes 1904-05 24v (v 18: dramas)
    Dramatic works... trans by Nathan Haskell Doyle. N.Y. Crowell c1923 12° 485p
    Father Sergius and other stories. N.Y. Dodd 1912 12° 318p Contains drama Wisdom of children *Also* Boston Estes
    Forged coupon, and other stories and dramas. N.Y. Nelson c1911 12° 429p
    Hadji Murad; trans by Aylmer Maude. The light that shines in the darkness, The man who was dead, The cause of it all; ed by Dr Hagberg Wright. N.Y. Willey ₍c1912₎ 8° 290 5-205, 9-190p *Also* Boston Estes
    Man who was dead; The cause of it all, dramas... ed by Dr Hagberg Wright. N.Y. Dodd 1912 12° 190p
    Novels and other works... N.Y. Scribner 1899 8° 22vs
    Plays... Complete edition including the posthumous plays. N.Y. Oxford Univ press ₍c1923₎ 12° 398p
    Plays: The power of darkness, The first distiller; Fruits of culture. N.Y. Funk and Wagnalls 1914 8° 413p
    Posthumous works, tr. by A. J. Wolfe. N.Y. Internat book Pub Co 1920 12° 8° 22vs
    Redemption, and two other plays... N.Y. Boni 1920 12° 2v ea $2
    Stories and dramas... London Dent c1926 12° 378p
    ₍Works₎ tr from the original Russian and ed by Professor Leo Wiener. N.Y. Willey ₍c1904₎ 8° 12v *Also* Boston Estes

Torrance, F. R.
    Granny Maumee, The rider of dreams, Simon the Cyrenian, plays for a negro theatre. N.Y. Macm 1917 111p $1.50

Townley, Morris MacDonald
    Two plays: Nothing else to do; Caught. Boston Graham press c1916 12° 90p

Trench, Herbert
    Collected works... London Cape 1924 8° 3vs

Troubetzkoy, Amelie R. C.
    Sea-woman's cloak and November eve; two plays. Cincinnati, Stewart Kidd 1923 12° 156p

Tupper, Wilbur S.
    Six short plays... Boston Four Seas Co 1922 12° 123p

APPENDIX B

COLLECTIONS OF PLAYS BY MORE THAN ONE AUTHOR

Armenian literature, comprising poetry, drama, folk-lore and classic tradition. With a special introduction by Robert Arnot. London Colonial press ₁c1901₁ 8° 142p

Baker, G. P., ed.
Modern American plays... N.Y. Harcourt 1920 12° 544p

Baker's anthology of one-act plays, selected and edited by Le Roy Phillips and Theodore Johnson. Boston Baker's International play bureau 1925 12° 186p

Bates, Alfred, ed.
Drama; its history, literature and influence on civilization... London Athenian Society 1903 8° 20v

Bechhofer, C. E., tr.
Five Russian plays, with some from the Ukrainian... N.Y. Dutton 1916 12° 173p
Russian anthology in English... N.Y. Dutton 1917 12° 288p

Bellevue dramatic club, Newport, R.I.
Plays for private acting; trans from the French and Italian... N.Y. U.S. Book Co c1878 12° 355p

Bierstadt, Edwin Hale, ed.
Three plays of the Argentine. N.Y. Duffield 1920 12° 147p

Block, Etta, tr.
One-act plays from the Yiddish; authorized trans. Cincinnati Stewart Kidd ₁c1923₁ 165p

Boston theatre guild
Plays, with an introduction by Frank Hersey. Boston Baker 1924 129p

British drama; a collection of the most esteemed tragedies, comedies, operas, and farces, in the English language. London Jones 1824 8v

Carolina folk-plays. See Koch, F. H., ed.

Clark, Barrett H., ed.
Four plays of the free theatre. . . Cincinnati Stewart Kidd 1915 12° 257p
Masterpieces of modern Spanish drama. . . Cincinnati Stewart Kidd ₁c1922₁ 8° 290p
Representative one-act plays by British and Irish authors... Boston Little 1921 8° 477p

Clarke, Amy Key, ed.
Three one-act plays: Persephone, Cloudbreak, by A. O. Roberts, Wind o' the morn by L. du Garde Peach... N.Y. French 1925 12° 10 11p

[Classic drama.] v. 2 In World's Great classics. Plays. (Julian Hawthorne, ed). N.Y. Colonial press c1900 8° 512p

Clements, Colin Campbell, ed.
Sea plays... Boston Small ₁c1925₁ 12° 241p

Coffman, George Raleigh, ed.
A book of modern plays... Chicago Scott ₁c1925₁ 12° 490p

Cohen, Helen Louise, ed. 1882-
Junior play book... N.Y. Harcourt ₁c1923₁ 12° 388p
Longer plays by modern authors (American). N.Y. Harcourt ₁c1922₁ 12° 357p
More one-act plays by modern authors... N.Y. Harcourt c1927 12° 369p
One-act plays by modern authors. N.Y. Harcourt 1921 8° 342p

Cumberland's British theatre... printed from acting copies as performed at the theatres royal. London J. Cumberland 1829 etc 37₁?₁vs

Dibdin, Thomas John, 1771-1841
London theatre. A collection of the most celebrated dramatic pieces... London Printed from Whittingham and Arliss 1815 12vs

Dickinson, Asa Don, ed.
Drama. Garden City. Doubleday 1924 292p

Dickinson, Thomas H., ed., 1877-
Chief contemporary dramatists; twenty plays from the recent drama... Boston Houghton c1915 8° 676p
Chief contemporary dramatists; the second series; eighteen plays... Boston Houghton c1921 8° 734p

Contemporary drama of England. Boston Little 1917 12° 303p
Contemporary plays; sixteen plays from the recent drama of England and America, selected and edited by Thomas N. Dickinson... and Jack R. Crawford... Boston Houghton ₁c1925₁ 12° 650p

Wisconsin plays... original one-act plays from the repertory of the Wisconsin dramatic society... N.Y. Huebsch 1914 12° 187p
Wisconsin plays. Second series; original one-act plays from the repertory of the Wisconsin dramatic society. Second series... N.Y. Huebsch 1918 12° 217p

Dillon, Robert Arthur
The drawing-room playlets for amateurs... London Greening ₁1914₁ 121p

Drawing-room plays. See Scott, Clement

Duran, Leo, tr., 1883-
Plays of old Japan, tr by Leo Duran. N.Y. Seltzer 1921 12° 127p

47 workshop plays. See Harvard plays

Four one-act plays... Oxford Blackwell 1923 127p

Franke, Kuno, ed.
German classics of the nineteenth and twentieth centuries; masterpieces of German literature... N.Y. German Pub Society ₁c1913-14₁ 8° 24v

Garnett, Richard, et al. eds.
Universal anthology. . . London. Clarke. 1899 8° 33vs

Giles, H. A.
History of Chinese literature. N.Y. Appleton 1901 8° 439p

Goldberg, Isaac, tr.
Plays of the Italian theatre ₁by₁ Verga, Morselli, Lopez, Pirandello; tr by Isaac Goldberg. Boston 1921 202p $2

Goldberg, Isaac, ed. & tr., 1887-
Six plays of the Yiddish theatre... Boston ₁c1916₁ 12° 210p
Six plays of the Yiddish theatre. Second series... Boston Luce ₁c1918₁ 12° 197p $1.50

Grove plays of the Bohemian club. San Francisco Privately printed at the press of H. S. Crocker 1918 3v

Harvard plays
Plays of the 47 workshop... N.Y. Brentano's 1918 12° 1918 First series
Plays of the 47 workshop... Second series... N.Y. Brentano's 1920 12° 139p
Plays of the 47 workshops. Third series... Brentano's 1922 12° 92p
Plays of the 47 workshop... Fourth series... N.Y. Brentano's ₁c1925₁ 12° 121p
Plays of the Harvard dramatic club. First series. N.Y. Brentano's
Plays of the Harvard dramatic club. Second series. N.Y. Brentano's

Herbert, Alan Patrick and others
Double demon, and other one-act plays by A. P. Herbert, Sladen Smith, Beatrice Mayer, Helen Simpson. N.Y. Appleton 1924 12° 204p
Four one-act plays... Oxford Blackwell 1923 12° 127p

Inchbald, Mrs Elizabeth [Simpson], ed., 1753-1821
British theatre; or, A collection of plays... printed under the authority of the managers from the prompt books... London 1808 16° 25vs
Collection of farces and other afterpieces... Printed under the authority of the managers from the prompt book... London 1809 12° 7vs
Modern theatre; a collection of successful modern plays as acted in the Theatres Royal, London... London 1811 10v

Indiana prize plays, as presented by the Little Theatre Society of Indiana during the season of 1922-23... Indianapolis Bobbs-Merrill 1924 12° 149p $1.50

Iwasaki, Yozan T., tr.
Three modern Japanese plays; authorized trans by Yozan T. Iwasawi and Glenn Hughes... Cincinnati ₍c1923₎ 8° 104p
Jagendorf, Moritz Adolf, ed.
One-act plays for young folks... N.Y. Brentano's c1924 12° 220p
Knickerbocker, Edwin Van Berglen, ed.,
Twelve plays... N.Y. Holt ₍c1924₎ 12° 336p
Koch, Frederick Henry, ed.
Carolina folk-plays... N.Y. Holt 1922 12° 160p
Carolina folk-plays; Second series. N.Y. Holt 1924 12° 173p
Ladies' Home Journal one-act plays.   Garden City. Doubleday 1925 12° 221p
Law, Frederick Houk, ed.
Modern plays, short and long... N.Y. Century 1924 12° 429p $1.50
Leonard, S. A. ed.
Atlantic book of modern plays... Boston Atlantic monthly press ₍c1921₎ 12° 324p
Lewis, Benjamin Roland, ed.
Contemporary one-act plays... N.Y. Scribner ₍c1922₎ 8° 410p $2
London stage; a collection of the most reputed tragedies, comedies, operas, melo-dramas, farces and interludes accurately printed from acting copies as performed at the theatres royal. London ₍1825-27₎ 8° 4vs
Loving, Pierre, ed.
Ten minute plays. N.Y. ₍c1923₎ 8° 215p
Mantle, Burns
Best plays of 1919-20... Boston Small 1920 12° 474p
Best plays of 1920-21. Boston Small 1921 12° 471p
Best plays of 1921-22. Boston Small 1922 12° 574p
Best plays of 1922-23... Boston Small c1923 12° 610p
Best plays of 1923-24 and the year book of the drama in America. Boston Small ₍c1924₎ 12° 471p
Best plays of 1924-25, and the year book of the drama in America... Boston Small 1925 635p $3
Best plays of 1925-26 and the year book of the drama in America. N.Y. Dodd 1926 12° 637p
Marriott, Joseph Weston
One-act plays of today... Boston-Small c1924 12° 270p
One-act plays of to-day; second series... Boston Small c1926 12° 280p Also Harrap, London 1924
Massey, Vincent, ed.
Canadian plays from Hart House theatre. Toronto Macm 1926 12° 213p v 1
Matthews, Brander, ed.
Comedies for amateur acting... N.Y. Appleton 1880 12° 245p
Matthews, James Brander, ed., 1852-
Chief European dramatists; twenty-one plays from the drama of Greece, Rome, Spain, France, Italy, Germany, Denmark and Norway from 500B.C. to 1879A.D... Boston Houghton 1916 786p
Matthews, James Brander, and Lieder, Paul Robert, eds.
Chief British dramatists excluding Shakespeare from the middle of the fifteenth century to the end of the nineteenth. Boston Houghton c1924 8° 1084p
Mayorga, Margaret G., ed.
Representative one-act plays by American authors. Boston Little 1919 8°
Morningside plays... N.Y. Shay 1917 106p 75c
Moses, Montrose J., ed.
Representative American dramas, national and local... Boston Little 1925 12° 681p
Representative British dramas, Victorian and modern. Boston Little 1918 8° 861p
Representative continental dramas, revolutionary and transitional... Boston Little 1924 12° 688p
Representative one-act plays by continental authors... Boston Little 1922 12° 463p
Representative plays by American dramatists from 1765 to the present day. v 2, 1815-1858. N.Y. Dutton 1925 8° 823p
Treasury of plays for children. . . Boston Little 1921 8° 550p

Nicholson, Kenyon, ed.
Appleton's book of short plays; actable short plays for amateurs... N.Y. Appleton 1926 12° 365p
One-act plays for stage and study; a collection of plays by well-known dramatists, American, English and Irish... N.Y. French 1924 8° 490p $3
One-act plays for stage and study; second series; twenty-one contemporary plays... preface by W. P. Eaton. N.Y. French 1925 12° 418p
One-act plays for stage and study; third series... N.Y. French 1927 12° $3.75
Oxberry, William, 1784-1824
New English drama... London Pub for the proprietors by W. Simpkin and R. Marshall 1818-25 12° 21v
Patriotic pageants of today... N.Y. Holt 1918 12° 82p
Pearse, Padraic H.
Collected works... plays, stories, poems. London Maunsel 1917 8° 341p
Phillips, Le Roy and Johnson, Theodore, eds.
See Baker's anthology of one-act plays
Pierce, John Alexander, and Matthews, Brander
Masterpieces of modern drama... abridged in narrative with dialogue of the great scenes... Garden City. Doubleday 1915 8° 2vs
Plays of to-day... London Sidgwick 1925 12° 2v
Scott, Clement
Drawing-room plays and parlour pantomines. Collected by Clement Scott... London Stanley Rivers 1870 12° 360p
Plays with a punch; a collection of one act plays and sketches serious and serio-comic. Boston Baker 1916 134p 25c
Provincetown plays, ed and selected by George Cram Cook and Frank Shay... Cincinnati Stewart ₍1921₎ 12° 272p
Provincetown plays; first series. N.Y. F. Shay 1916 8° 67p
Provincetown plays; second series. Second series. N.Y. F. Shay 1916 8° 70-144p
Provincetown plays; third series. Third series. N.Y. F. Shay 1916 8° 147-207p
Quinn, Arthur Hobson, ed., 1875-
Contemporary American plays, ed with an introduction upon recent American drama... N.Y. Scribner ₍c1923₎ 12° 382p
Representative American plays, 1767-1923... 1052p 8°
Sayler, Oliver Martin
Eleanora Duse series of plays...N.Y. Brentano's 1923 12° 475p
Moscow art theatre series of Russian plays... Second series. N.Y. Brentano's 1923 12° 498p
Schafer, Barbara Louise, comp.
A book of one-act plays... Indianapolis Bobbs-Merrill ₍c1922₎ 12° 216p
Selver, P., ed.
Anthology of modern Slavonic literature. London 1919 12°
Shay, Frank, ed
Contemporary one-act plays of 1921 (American)... Cincinnati Stewart Kidd 8° 630p (First impression of twenty contemporary one-act plays)
Plays for strolling mummers. N.Y. Appleton 1926 12° 174p
Treasury of plays for men. Boston 1923 8° 423p $3
Treasury of plays for women. Boston 1922 8° 443p
Twenty contemporary one-act plays (American). Cincinnati Stewart Kidd 1922 8° 630p. First impressions has title: Contemporary one-act plays of 1921
Twenty-five short plays, international... N.Y. Appleton 1925 8° 381p
Shay, Frank, and Loving, Pierre, ed.
Fifty contemporary one-act plays. Cincinnati Stewart Kidd 1922 12° 582p
Smith, Alice Mary, ed.
Short plays by representative authors. N.Y. Macm 1920 12° 318p $1.80
Smith, Milton Myers, ed.
Short plays fo various types... N.Y. Merrill ₍c1924₎ 12° 280p
Thomas, Charles Swain, ed. 1868-
Atlantic book of junior plays... Boston Atlantic monthly press ₍c1924₎ 12° 320p